Educational
Psychology

Windows on
Classrooms

Third Edition

Paul Eggen
University of North Florida

Don Kauchak
University of Utah

Merrill, an imprint of Prentice Hall
Upper Saddle River, New Jersey   Columbus, Ohio

Library of Congress Cataloging-in-Publication Data

Eggen, Paul D.
  Educational psychology : windows on classrooms / Paul
Eggen, Don Kauchak.—3rd ed.
    p.   cm.
  Includes bibliographical references and indexes.
  ISBN 0-13-374604-6
  1. Educational psychology—study and teaching
(Higher)—United States. 2. Learning, Psychology of—
Case studies.   I. Kauchak, Donald P.   II. Title.
LB1051.E463   1997
370.15—dc20   96-11912
                                              CIP

Cover photo: COMSTOCK, Inc.
Editor: Kevin M. Davis
Developmental Editor: Linda Kauffman Peterson
Production Editor: Sheryl Glicker Langner
Design Coordinator: Jill E. Bonar
Text Design: Proof Positive/Farrowlyne Assoc., Inc.
Cover Design: Proof Positive/Farrowlyne Assoc., Inc.
Production Manager: Patricia A. Tonneman
Marketing Manager: Kevin Flanagan
Electronic Text Management: Marilyn Wilson Phelps, Matthew
  Williams, Karen L. Bretz, Tracey Ward
Photo Researcher: Angela Jenkins
Illustrations: Jane Lopez

This book was set in Garamond by Prentice Hall and was
printed and bound by R.R. Donnelley and Sons Company. The
cover was printed by Phoenix Color Corp.

© 1997 by Prentice-Hall, Inc.
Simon & Schuster/A Viacom Company
Upper Saddle River, New Jersey 07458

Earlier edition, entitled *Educational Psychology: Classroom
Connections,* © 1994 by Merrill, an imprint of Prentice Hall.

Photo credits: pp. 2, 7, 10, 15, 26, 34, 51, 56, 123, 137, 152, 157,
180, 184, 186, 198, 218, 223, 234, 238, 244, 255, 269, 278, 284,
306, 338, 351, 358, 390, 434, 487, 506, 547 by Scott Cunning-
ham/Merrill/Prentice Hall; pp. 12, 17, 44, 82, 95, 168, 207, 211,
242, 248, 262, 270, 298, 366, 378, 407, 412, 422, 453, 463, 490,
519, 534 by Tom Watson/Merrill/Prentice Hall; pp. 19(top), 160,
172, 498, 537, 539 by Larry Hamill/Merrill/Prentice Hall; pp.
19(bottom), 63 by David Young-Wolff/Photo Edit; pp. 30, 131
by Anne Vega/Merrill/Prentice Hall; pp. 36, 81, 89, 110(right
and left), 113, 156, 199, 317, 323, 326, 477, 483 by Todd
Yarrington/Merrill/Prentice Hall; pp. 41, 67, 203, 400, 439, 444,
446 by Robert Finken; pp. 74, 194 by Cleo Freelance Photography; p. 76 by Gale Zucker; pp. 104, 568 by Bob
Daemmrich/The Image Works; pp. 119, 291, 344, 470, 516 by
KS Studios/Merrill/Prentice Hall; pp. 140, 395 by Paul
Conklin/Photo Edit; pp. 177, 252, by Susan Burger; pp. 212,
581 by Tony Freeman/Photo Edit; p. 216 by Lorraine Rorke/The
Image Works; p. 302 by Bill Bachmann/The Image Works; p.
356 by Blair Seitz; pp. 370, 416 by Michael Newman/Photo Edit;
p. 441 by David Napravnik/Merrill/Prentice Hall; p. 560 by C.
Pedrick/The Image Works; p. 564 by Mary Kate Denny/Photo
Edit.

Printed in the United States of America

10 9 8 7 6 5 4 3 2 1

ISBN: 0-13-374604-6

Prentice-Hall International (UK) Limited, *London*
Prentice-Hall of Australia Pty. Limited, *Sydney*
Prentice-Hall of Canada, Inc., *Toronto*
Prentice-Hall Hispanoamericana, S.A., *Mexico*
Prentice-Hall of India Private Limited, *New Delhi*
Prentice-Hall of Japan, Inc., *Tokyo*
Simon & Schuster Asia Pte. Ltd., *Singapore*
Editora Prentice-Hall do Brasil, Ltda., *Rio de Janeiro*

This book is dedicated to Clifton Eggen and
Martin Kauchak. They gave us their best.

Preface

As we considered our revisions for the third edition of this book, we spent many hours of discussion reflecting on the same issues that guided our thinking in preparing the first and second editions: to introduce the exciting field of educational psychology to you, our readers, and to show you how it applies to your personal and professional lives.

The students and professors who have used our book tell us that our connections to actual classrooms made the content more understandable, meaningful, relevant and consequently, more motivating for them. One of the strengths of the first and second editions was its focus on application—the link between the content of educational psychology and the "real world," and the implications it has for learning and teaching.

In the third edition we have attempted to expand on our original goals and have strengthened this link in three ways:

- We present case studies in a way that is unique to the field of educational psychology. Instead of "layering" case studies onto the content of the text, our case studies—both written and video—are truly *integrated* with topics that are introduced. As a topic is discussed, for example, frequent references to the cases are made, which help readers understand how the topics are applied in classrooms. Throughout the chapters actual dialogues from the case are frequently inserted into the discussion of a topic. This integration utilizes and capitalizes on recent research in important areas related to learning, such an ***anchored instruction*** and ***situated cognition.***
- We have broadened the learner-centered orientation of the text. This is a book that focuses on learners and learning, and each chapter examines influences on learning and ways that learning can be increased.
- We have presented prominent theories of learning, motivation, and development in detailed, yet succinct and applied, ways. The same approach was applied to the research on learner differences, instruction, and assessment.

We believe our emphasis—true integration in a learner-centered focus grounded in an accurate framework of theory and research—will result in a deeper understanding of educational psychology that you can apply both to your work as a teacher and to your personal life.

New To This Edition

We have attempted to further integrate the content of educational psychology with the "real world," increase the learner-centered focus, and present prominent theories and research in detailed and complete ways. Specifically, we have augmented our coverage of

Preface

Vygotsky's work, social cognitive theory, goal theory, and learner self-regulation. In addition, we have placed special emphasis on four critical areas. They are:

Constructivism

Clear and precise descriptions of constructivism *and* its connections to learning and teaching in classrooms can be found throughout the text. Expanded coverage of this progressively prominent view of learning occurs in Chapter 2 and is linked to cognitive development. In Chapters 7 and 8 we explain its relation to problem solving and other complex cognitive processes. The influences of constructivism are also explored in the chapters on learner-centered planning (Chapter 11); learner-centered approaches to instruction (Chapter 12); and authentic assessment (Chapter 13).

Assessing Classroom Learning

Our discussion of authentic assessment has been significantly extended with performance assessments, the design and use of portfolios, and involving learners in their own assessments (Chapter 13). In this chapter we include a comprehensive examination of assessment issues involved in accommodating the ever-increasing diversity of our students.

Diversity

In this edition, we have capitalized even more on our coverage of diversity with thorough discussions of different ways that learners communicate in school, school-related background knowledge, home-school continuities and discontinuities, different language development programs, and ethnic pride and self-esteem. Every chapter in this text has a section devoted to the diversity we will encounter in our learners, and Chapter 4, "Learner Differences," is devoted to an extended discussion of the various dimensions of diversity.

Video Case Studies

To truly *integrate* topics presented in the text with real-world applications, four of the end-of-chapter cases (*Windows on Classrooms*) exist in both written and video formats. These episodes, found in Chapters 2, 7, 8, and 12, illustrate actual classroom life—real learners and real teachers involved in the learning-teaching processes in authentic classroom contexts. This is the first text in the history of educational psychology to genuinely integrate video cases with the content of the book.

Features of This Text

This book focuses on learning and what teachers can do to promote learning in their students. We've included the following design features with this theme in mind:

Case Studies

Although learning is complex, research provides us with considerable insight into the process. Studies indicate that multiple and concrete representations of content are more effective for helping learners construct their understanding of the topics they study than are single and abstract representations. We have applied this knowledge with illustrations of the powerful concepts and principles of educational psychology through written and video case studies and the liberal use of classroom vignettes throughout the chapters.

Each chapter of the text begins with a case study taken directly from a teacher's classroom experience. The case study is then *integrated* throughout the chapter to illustrated the content as it is presented. In many instances, dialogue is taken directly from the case to illustrate the topic in a tangible and realistic way.

Each chapter also ends with a case. This feature, called *Windows on Classrooms*, shows how you might apply your understanding of the chapter content. The end-of-chapter case is followed by a series of "Questions for Discussion and Analysis" that encourage you to observe and assess the learning and teaching in the case and to reflect on your own knowledge and beliefs as your understanding of learning and teaching develops.

In addition to the cases at the end of Chapters 2, 7, 8, and 12 that exist in both written and video form, shorter case studies appear throughout the chapters to further illustrate the content and our theme of classroom application.

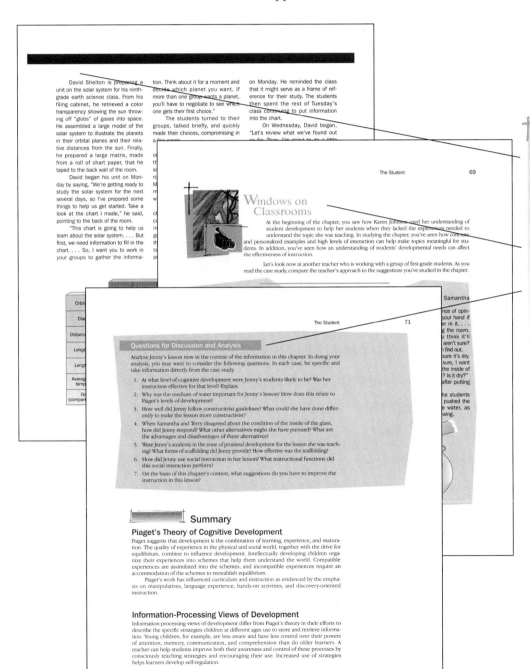

All chapters begin and end with a case study. **Chapter opening cases** are referred to throughout the chapter to bring concepts into sharper focus for the learner. Chapter ending cases, **Windows on Classrooms,** give learners a second look at chapter content in context. **Questions for Discussion and Analysis** that follow each case guide analysis and reflection.

Classroom Connections

As in the first and second editions, we have included sections throughout the chapters that offer suggestions for applying the content to learning and teaching situations. *Classroom Connections* describe and illustrate successful teaching practices in classrooms and include samples from all grade levels and content areas to show you a variety of appropriate applications.

Each chapter contains at least three **Classroom Connections**, that review practical strategies for improving the learning of diverse student populations. Designed to help you see the application of teaching in real classrooms, with real learners, they provide practical suggestions for implementing the content—by making connections to classroom learning.

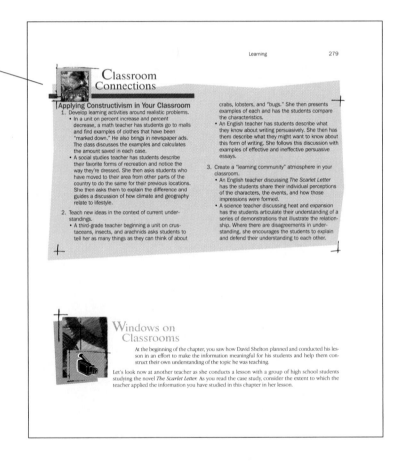

Learning   279

Classroom Connections

Applying Constructivism in Your Classroom

1. Develop learning activities around realistic problems.
   - In a unit on percent increase and percent decrease, a math teacher has students go to malls and find examples of clothes that have been "marked down." He also brings in newspaper ads. The class discusses the examples and calculates the amount saved in each case.
   - A social studies teacher has students describe their favorite forms of recreation and notice the way they're dressed. She then asks students who have moved to their area from other parts of the country to do the same for their previous locations. She then asks them to explain the difference and guides a discussion of how climate and geography relate to lifestyle.

2. Teach new ideas in the context of current understandings.
   - A third-grade teacher beginning a unit on crustaceans, insects, and arachnids asks students to tell her as many things as they can think of about

crabs, lobsters, and "bugs." She then presents examples of each and has the students compare the characteristics.
   - An English teacher has students describe what they know about writing persuasively. She then has them describe what they might want to know about this form of writing. She follows this discussion with examples of effective and ineffective persuasive essays.

3. Create a "learning community" atmosphere in your classroom.
   - An English teacher discussing *The Scarlet Letter* has the students share their individual perceptions of the characters, the events, and how those impressions were formed.
   - A science teacher discussing heat and expansion has the students articulate their understanding of a series of demonstrations that illustrate the relationship. Where there are disagreements in understanding, she encourages the students to explain and defend their understanding to each other.

Windows on Classrooms

At the beginning of the chapter, you saw how David Shelton planned and conducted his lesson in an effort to make the information meaningful for his students and help them construct their own understanding of the topic he was teaching.

Let's look now at another teacher as she conducts a lesson with a group of high school students studying the novel *The Scarlet Letter*. As you read the case study, consider the extent to which the teacher applied the information you have studied in this chapter in her lesson.

Learner Diversity

To respond to the increasingly diverse student populations that we, as teachers, will encounter, it is critical that we nurture and avail ourselves of the richness that this diversity can bring to the learning and teaching environment. Thus, learner diversity is an important theme for this text. Each chapter contains a section on diversity, with its own set of *Classroom Connections*, and Chapter 4 is devoted to this topic.

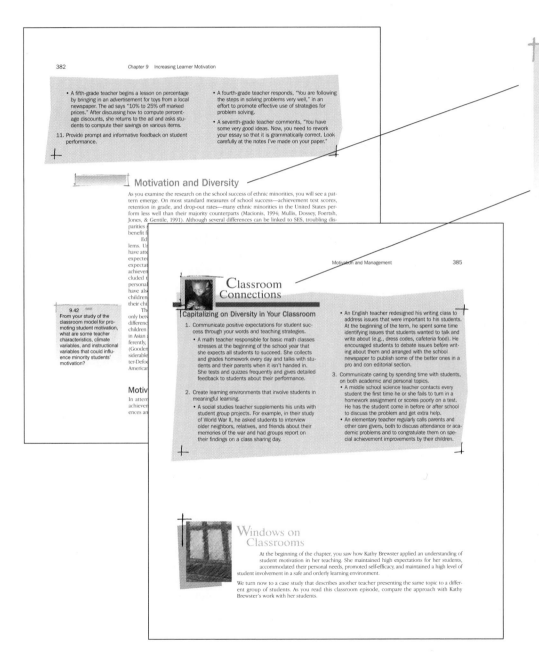

382   Chapter 9   Increasing Learner Motivation

• A fifth-grade teacher begins a lesson on percentage by bringing in an advertisement for toys from a local newspaper. The ad says "10% to 25% off marked prices." After discussing how to compute percentage discounts, she returns to the ad and asks students to compute their savings on various items.

11. Provide prompt and informative feedback on student performance.

• A fourth-grade teacher responds, "You are following the steps in solving problems very well," in an effort to promote effective use of strategies for problem solving.

• A seventh-grade teacher comments, "You have some very good ideas. Now, you need to rework your essay so that it is grammatically correct. Look carefully at the notes I've made on your paper."

Motivation and Diversity

As you examine the research on the school success of ethnic minorities, you will see a pattern emerge. On most standard measures of school success—achievement test scores, retention in grade, and drop-out rates—many ethnic minorities in the United States perform less well than their majority counterparts (Macionis, 1994; Mullis, Dossey, Foertsh, Jones, & Gentile, 1991). Although several differences can be linked to SES, troubling disparities

9.42
From your study of the classroom model for promoting student motivation, what are some teacher characteristics, climate variables, and instructional variables that could influence minority students' motivation?

Motivation and Management   385

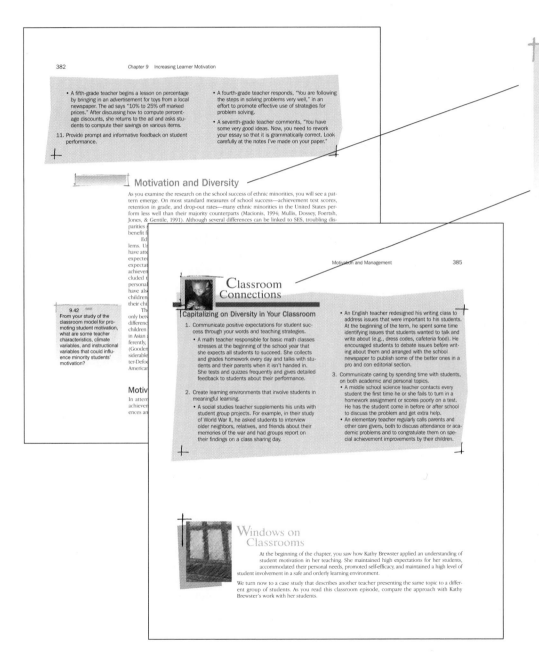

Classroom Connections

Capitalizing on Diversity in Your Classroom

1. Communicate positive expectations for student success through your words and teaching strategies.
   • A math teacher responsible for basic math classes stresses at the beginning of the school year that she expects all students to succeed. She collects and grades homework every day and talks with students and their parents when it isn't handed in. She tests and quizzes frequently and gives detailed feedback to students about their performance.

2. Create learning environments that involve students in meaningful learning.
   • A social studies teacher supplements his units with student group projects. For example, in their study of World War II, he asked students to interview older neighbors, relatives, and friends about their memories of the war and had groups report on their findings on a class sharing day.

• An English teacher redesigned his writing class to address issues that were important to his students. At the beginning of the term, he spent some time identifying issues that students wanted to talk and write about (e.g., dress codes, cafeteria food). He encouraged students to debate issues before writing about them and arranged with the school newspaper to publish some of the better ones in a pro and con editorial section.

3. Communicate caring by spending time with students, on both academic and personal topics.
   • A middle school science teacher contacts every student the first time he or she fails to turn in a homework assignment or scores poorly on a test. He has the student come in before or after school to discuss the problem and get extra help.
   • An elementary teacher regularly calls parents and other care givers, both to discuss attendance or academic problems and to congratulate them on special achievement improvements by their children.

Windows on Classrooms

At the beginning of the chapter, you saw how Kathy Brewster applied an understanding of student motivation in her teaching. She maintained high expectations for her students, accommodated their personal needs, promoted self-efficacy, and maintained a high level of student involvement in a safe and orderly learning environment.

We turn now to a case study that describes another teacher presenting the same topic to a different group of students. As you read this classroom episode, compare the approach with Kathy Brewster's work with her students.

Every chapter contains a section that examines issues relevant to diversity. And at least one **Classroom Connections** feature in every chapter offers learners practical suggestions and applications for implementing strategies that foster the learning of all students.

Margin Questions

Theory and research indicate that learning is increased when students are actively involved in the learning process. To put you in an active learning role, we have tried to make full use of margin questions that may ask you to do one or more of three things: explain a specific aspect of the content on the basis of theory and/or research, relate the immediate topic to one you've studied in an earlier chapter, or relate a topic to a common life experience. In this regard, the margin questions are intended to help you reflect on the content, further apply your understanding of educational psychology to classrooms, integrate topics, and make the content more personal by applying it to your everyday experiences.

The extensive use of concrete examples and margin questions that engage you in your own learning help you process and understand material more deeply.

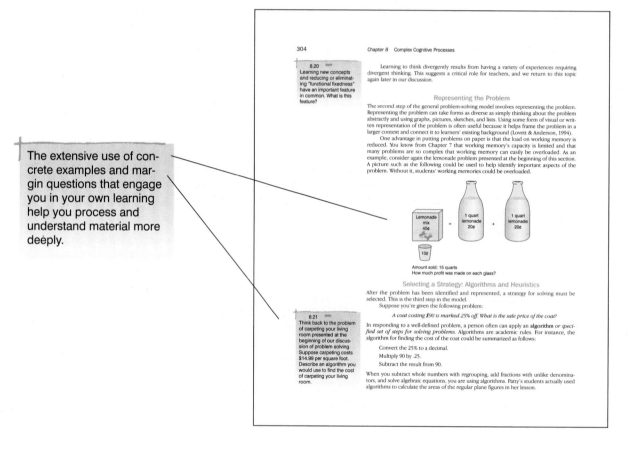

Important Concepts

As with the second edition, the important concepts in this book are identified in the body of the text with **bold-faced type** followed by an *italicized definition*. We believe this helps further contextualize the concepts without detracting from the overall thrust of the chapters. These important concepts also appear at the end of each chapter, identified by page number, and are listed and defined in the glossary as well.

Figures, Tables, and Outlines

Learning is more efficient when information is organized so that interconnections and relationships are apparent, rather than presented in isolated segments. Figures, tables, and outlines are used prominently to summarize important information and give you additional examples of each chapter's topics.

Chapter Endings

We know that learning is enhanced by summaries and reviews of important topics. For this reason, we close each chapter with a *Summary* that succinctly describes the significant ideas in the chapter. The summary for each chapter is organized using the major headings. This summary and synthesis of content is intended to further help you integrate the ideas you've studied in earlier chapters.

All chapter endings include a list of the *Important Concepts* with the page numbers on which they're defined.

End of Text

A *Glossary* at the end of the text defines all the important concepts listed at the ends of the chapters, and a *Reference* list provides bibliographic information for all the sources we cite. Detailed *Name* and *Subject Indexes* allow quick access to specific topics.

Text Supplements

To further aid your learning and development as a teacher, several supplements have been provided for you and your instructor's use. To maximize the opportunities for learning, the entire package—text, videocases, and supplements—should be thoroughly integrated. In our attempt to accommodate you and your instructor with the most complete educational psychology package that exists, we have written our own supplements, making every effort to ensure that all the components complement each other.

The supplements are:

Student Study Guide

The Student Study Guide is organized by chapters and each chapter includes an outline, objectives, a chapter overview, application exercises that put you in an active role and increase your understanding of the chapter content, and a self-help quiz using the same format as the items in the test bank that accompanies the text. The Study Guide provides feedback for the application exercises, answers to the self-help quiz, and suggested responses to the margin questions in the chapters.

In addition to the chapter-by-chapter materials, the Student Study Guide suggests the best use of each case study to help you make the text as meaningful as possible.

Transparencies

A transparency package will be available for your instructor's use. As with the figures and tables that appear throughout the text, the transparencies help organize the information you're studying to deepen and broaden your understanding. Other transparencies provide additional examples and relationships among the topics you are studying.

Transparency Masters

Additional applications, illustrations, and problems may be displayed by your instructor in the form of transparency masters that can be copied onto acetate. These transparency masters further supplement, integrate, and help you apply the information you're studying to "real world" classroom situations.

Video Tapes

In Chapter 1, we discuss the work of experts who suggest that teachers should think critically, practically, and artistically. They believe that teachers should carefully examine research, their own work, and the work of other teachers. To help you develop your critical thinking, you will have the opportunity to study videotaped segments that focus on cognitive development, classroom management, cooperative learning, metacognition, whole language, and diversity. Some episodes represent "slices of classroom life," that can serve as focal points for analysis and discussion. Questions such as "What are the major strengths and weaknesses of this lesson?" and "How could this have been taught more effectively?" are encouraged. This process of analysis will help cultivate your ability to critically examine your own work, and will complement the written and video *Windows on Classrooms* that we've already described.

Test Bank

Research consistently indicates that learning is enhanced when teachers have high expectations for their students and when they ask students to think critically and analytically about the content they are learning. In line with these findings, many of the test items you'll encounter on quizzes will be case studies that require you to analyze information taken from classrooms and to make decisions based on the evidence. Instead of memorizing strings of words, you'll apply what you have learned to new situations. This is a challenging and rewarding experience and, with practice, your ability to think critically and analytically will improve.

The self-help quizzes in the Student Study Guide will help you develop your analytical skills with practice items similar to those you'll encounter on quizzes and tests.

A print test bank and computerized versions in IBM and Macintosh are available to your professor.

Instructor's Manual

In addition to the supplements we've already described, your instructor will be offered suggestions for learning activities, groupwork, and out-of-class assignments. While you won't encounter the content of the Instructor's Manual directly, it is an integral part of this overall package.

All of the elements in this text and the supplements are designed to be consistent with what we know about learning and motivation. We believe that they reflect a realistic view of learning and teaching today and as we move toward the end of the millennium. We wish you the best of luck in your study. We hope that you find it both exciting and meaningful.

Acknowledgments

Every book reflects the work of a team that includes the authors, the staff of editors, and the reviewers. We appreciate the input we've received from professors and students who have used previous editions of the book, and gratefully acknowledge the contributions of the reviewers who offered us constructive feedback to guide us in this new edition: David Bergin, University of Toledo; Scott W. Brown, University of Connecticut; Kay S. Bull, Oklahoma State University; Barbara Collamer, Western Washington University; Betty M. Davenport, Campbell University; Charles W. Good, West Chester University; Hermine H. Marshall, San Francisco State University; Tes Mehring, Emporia State University; Evan Powell,

University of Georgia; Rozanne Sparks, Pittsburg State University; Robert J. Stevens, Pennsylvania State University; and Julianne C. Turner, Notre Dame University.

We also owe special thanks to Patricia Barbetta of Florida International University for her suggestions that helped shape and improve Chapter 5, "Learners with Exceptionalities." Additional, very special thanks go to Dale Schunk of Purdue University for his review of Chapter 7, "Cognitive Processes"; Chapter 8, "Complex Cognitive Processes"; and Chapter 9, "Increasing Learner Motivation." His expertise made an important contribution to our work.

In addition to the reviewers who guided our revisions, our team of editors gave us support in many ways. Kevin Davis, our editor, brought zeal and enthusiasm to our revision and meshed insight with knowledge of both content and market. Linda Peterson, our developmental editor, again fulfilled her role of helping us make the book more accessible to our readers. She is the champion of our student consumers, and she makes certain we give them the very best. A special thanks to Sheryl Langner for her conscientious work in producing the book. Through many phone conversations she was supportive, flexible, and positive in every way. We want to acknowledge the professional quality of her work and her commitment to excellence.

The visual appeal and superior design of our book can be attributed to the quality of our design team from Proof Positive and the Prentice Hall Electronic Text Management department—Connie Geldis, Marilyn Phelps, Matthew Williams, and Jill Bonar. They succeeded in creating a book that does something we thought not possible—surpass the visual appeal of our first two editions.

Our appreciation goes to all these fine people who have taken our words and given them shape. We hope that their efforts—together with ours—will result in enhanced learning for students and more meaningful and pleasurable teaching for the instructor.

Paul Eggen
Don Kauchak

Brief Contents

Contents

Part III: Motivation and Management

Chapter 9
Increasing Learner Motivation   338

Chapter 10
Managing the Learning Environment   390

▌ Chapter 14
Standardized Testing   560

Chapter Outline

Teaching 1
in the
Real World

"Good morning," Jan Davis, a sixth-grade math teacher greeted Keith Jackson, a 1st-year teacher and colleague at Lake Park Middle School. "How're you doing? You look beat. Never realized how tired you can get teaching, huh?" Jan continued with a wry smile.

After a short pause to see how Keith reacted, she went on, "Seriously, you look deep in thought. What's up?"

"Oh, not much really. I was just sitting here thinking about my last period math class. Sometimes I'm not sure what I'm doing. I think about it quite a bit, and then I get a little confused—well, not exactly confused—maybe uneasy, I think."

Reacting to the questioning look on Jan's face, Keith continued, "It's like this. The students are fine when we do the plain old mechanics. They do their work, seem to understand what they're doing, and even act like they sort of like it. Then, . . . we get to word problems. Ugh! It's the exact opposite. I know we're supposed to try to teach the students to solve problems. So, . . . I try it. They hate it. Then I ask myself what I'm doing. They drag their feet so badly. They act as if this is the first time they've ever had to solve word problems. . . . I understand why word problems are important, but I just hate cramming them down their throats. They always try to take the easiest way out. They memorize a formula and work like robots. If a problem is written even the teeniest bit differently, they can't do it, and they cry that they don't understand this material. See what I mean?

"Then," he continued, "some of them just blow the whole thing off.

They just sit like bumps on logs and barely try. . . . I thought I was going to be so great when I got out here. I have a really good math background, and I love math. I just knew the students would love it too. I'm not so sure anymore. No one prepared me for this.

"And then there's Kelly," Keith went on with a resigned shrug. "She disrupts everything I do. I can't get her to keep her mouth shut. I've tried everything. I've ignored her talking, given her referrals, put her in detention, tried to 'catch her being good.' I even bribed her. Nothing has worked. She's not really a bad student. . . . I even took her aside after school and simply leveled with her. I asked her straight out why she was giving me such a hard time. I said, 'Kelly, you're a good girl. Why are you acting like this?' Actually, I think she's a bit better lately.

"I know that I'm in my 1st year and that you've been here forever," Keith continued, "but don't you ever get frustrated? Maybe I'm just having a bad day."

"I'll just ignore that 'forever' remark," Jan replied, "but yes, I think about it. I think everybody does.

"You're actually in the process of becoming a real teacher," she continued. "You're looking at problems for which there are no easy answers, and for the most part, the solutions, to the extent they exist, must come from you. Very little in teaching is cut-and-dried . . . but then, that's also part of the fun of it," she added, smiling.

"Seriously, though, I do have a few reactions," she went on. "Think about Kelly. She's not actually a rotten kid. Stay with the personal approach. You said it seemed to help when you

took her aside. Make it a point to talk with her one-on-one every now and then. Talk with her about her behavior and continue to be straight with her. I don't think she has another adult she can talk to, and this may be her way of reaching out to someone. I know that sounds a little corny, but I actually think it's the case. She needs someone to be interested in her."

"I'll stay with it," Keith shrugged. "I've got nothing to lose."

"No, you don't—just like with your quiet ones in the back of the room. Every class has them. They just don't seem to care—and that can be discouraging. Let me tell you what works for me. First, I move them—right up to the front of the room. I tell them why: 'I want you to learn, and I want you up close where I can work with you.' Then I make it a point to call on all of them, and I do it randomly. At first, they complain that they didn't have their hands up, but after I explain that I'm trying to get everyone to participate, they actually like it. It really makes a difference."

"Hmm. Do you have any suggestions about the math part?" Keith asked, changing the subject. "I've tried explaining the stuff until I'm blue in the face. Or maybe I shouldn't worry about it. It's just that I keep thinking they don't really understand the material, and they resist all my efforts."

"As it happens, I'm taking a course to upgrade my certificate, and I wasn't too crazy about it at first, but I've really learned a lot. Anyway, the course is based on the NCTM standards . . . National Council of Teachers of Mathematics," Jan added, seeing the uncertain look on Keith's face, "and in a way they're talking about exactly the stuff you're struggling with, like problem solving and all that. . . . But the biggest thing was I actually thought I didn't have that much to learn. I've been around *forever* as you say, but this course and these new standards have opened my eyes. They're making a big deal of shifting emphasis, if that's the right way to say it. . . . What I mean is, they're trying to focus more on the student. We have to read these research articles for class, and then we're learning how to apply the research with our students. . . . Anyway, they talk about putting the student in the center of the process . . . take us out of simply telling them stuff. . . . I'm not sure I'm being clear. . . . Let me give you an example.

"By the way," she interjected, "I was really skeptical at first, but I said, 'what the heck; I'll give it my best shot,' and interestingly, the students really got into it.

"Anyway, here's what I did. We've been on percentages, and just as you're saying, the students don't get it and they don't like it all that well. So I went into class, and just as class started I began peeling a banana and started to eat it. Then I looked at it and asked matter of factly, 'I wonder how much I paid for the peel of this banana, because I don't get to eat it. Have you ever thought about that?' We talked about it a bit, and the students came up with the problem of how to find out how much of the banana is peel. I helped them rework it to the point where we were going to figure what percentage of the banana is edible. Then I asked the students to estimate. Some of them did fairly well, and from others I could

see that they didn't understand percentage, so I did a minilesson on fraction—percentage conversion, just enough to get by. Then I asked them to suggest ways we might figure out what percentage was edible. That's when the lesson got better. Frankly, I was surprised at their ideas. They were a lot better than I thought they would be. For example, they mostly agreed that we had to peel the banana and compare the weight with and without the peel, but they came up with 'What if different bananas have more peel that others?' so we decided to bring in several bananas, actually enough so that I could break the class into groups of three and each group had their own banana.

"It actually wasn't that difficult. I had to get some bananas and some balances from the science department, but that wasn't so bad, and the best part, good stuff came out of the lesson. We did estimating, and we did averaging. They wanted to know if there was a way to tell whether a banana had a thick peel so we could get more banana for the money, and we thought about the same thing with oranges, and they learned how to read a balance. And we made a data table, and we looked for errors in the table, and we talked about what would make us think there might be an error in the table. We worked on it for a week. The bottom line is that they have to see how math relates to them and their lives.

"Maybe even more important," she continued, "although I had to guide them, a lot of what we did came from them, and it gave me some things to think about. I'll do parts of it differently next time. At times I think I

jumped in too soon when they could have figured it out for themselves, and at other times I think I let them stumble around too long, and they wasted more time than necessary. But overall, I feel good about it, and I'm definitely going to do more of it."

"I hate to admit this," Keith responded almost sheepishly, "but some of my courses at the university suggested just what you did. It was fun, but I didn't think it was 'real' teaching. I thought it was all pie-in-the-sky stuff, and I didn't pay much attention to it. I guess I always thought that stuff wasn't quite real, and it didn't change my mind."

"Maybe you couldn't relate to it at that time," Jan returned. "You didn't have a real class with real students who 'didn't get it.'

"My compliments to you, and I mean that," she continued. "The fact that you're thinking about it means you really care about what you're doing. That's what we need in teaching. If you hadn't brought it up, we probably wouldn't have had this talk. For a rookie, you're okay," she added, bantering again.

Keith peered at Jan, impressed with her fervor. "Why aren't you burned out? I thought all 'old' teachers burned out."

"Watch it, kid," Jan returned in a mock threat. "But seriously," she went on, "I have my days. I get tired, and the students sometimes bother me, but I try to leave it here, go home, get a little exercise, let off some steam, and then everything is pretty good again.

"Uh-oh. There goes the bell. I'd better get moving, or my fourth-period class will be locked out."

Welcome! You are beginning what we hope will be an interesting and fascinating study: interesting because you'll be examining people, and fascinating because you'll be seeing yourself in many of the experiences described in the text. In some cases, you'll even find that the preconceived ideas you hold about people and teaching and learning aren't valid.

In this book, we focus particularly on school-age children—how they grow and develop, what makes them different, what motivates them (and what doesn't), how they learn, and particularly what teachers can do to improve these processes. This study makes up the content of "educational psychology," and this is where we're headed.

After you've completed your study of this chapter, you should be able to meet the following objectives:

- Identify the implications that studying educational psychology has for classroom practice.
- Explain how research in educational psychology is applied to classroom practice.
- Describe the relationships between research and theory.
- Explain how professional decision making affects teaching.
- Explain how reflective teaching uses educational psychology to improve professional decision making.

Educational Psychology: Teaching in the Real World

Although the focus in educational psychology is certainly on teaching and learning, it deals with much more than the study of school-age people. To illustrate, let's consider some questions:

- Have you ever listened to someone describe something to you, not quite follow their point, and said, "Give me an example"?
- Does a song, a picture, or even a smell sometimes conjure up a feeling or mood that you can't otherwise capture?
- Have you ever done one job to get it out of the way and saved a more enjoyable one for later?
- Have you ever been with someone who showered you with positive comments or flattery? Why did that person's attentions quickly lose their appeal?
- What kind of class are you most comfortable in—one in which the requirements are explicitly described, or one in which the requirements, schedule, and topics are somewhat loose?
- How do you feel when an instructor knows your name and seems to take a personal interest in you?
- For what kind of class do you usually study the most—one in which you're given weekly quizzes, or one in which you have only a midterm and final?
- Have you ever done a "double take" when something unusual or unexpected happened?
- Have you ever asked, "Why should I do that? There's nothing in it for me."

These questions and many others like them are all part of the real world. Educational psychology can help us explain your answers to these questions and even why people's answers vary. So although the primary focus in this text is on the teaching and learning of school-age people, it's also relevant to where you are at this point in your life.

Let's begin the study of educational psychology by examining the themes that guided us as we wrote the text.

Beginning Teachers and Learning to Teach

1.1

Research indicates that students enter teacher preparation programs with strong views about what is good teaching (Calderhead & Robson, 1991). On what basis are these views most likely formed?

As we wrote this book, several themes guided us, and many of those themes were evident in the case study at the beginning of the chapter. Keith Jackson, for instance, displayed characteristics typical of 1st-year teachers. Many are idealistic—some even unrealistically so; most believe that they will be better than teachers in the field. Many also believe that teaching is a process of transmitting knowledge, as Keith demonstrated with his comment, "I've tried explaining the stuff until I'm blue in the face" (Pajares, 1992). Further, his experience in his preservice program failed to change his beliefs, also typical of beginning teachers (Carter, 1990; D. Kagan, 1992b).

Misconceptions About Teaching and Learning to Teach

Evidence indicates that novices in different areas of study often have misconceptions about that area. Misconceptions are often embedded in complex networks of knowledge and are difficult to eliminate unless they are confronted directly (C. Anderson & Roth, 1989; Driver, Asoko, Leach, Mortimer, & Scott, 1994; Siegler, 1991). In introducing the text, we immediately confront three misconceptions about teaching and learning to teach: (a) Teaching is a process of transmitting knowledge to learners; (b) majoring in an academic subject provides all the knowledge needed to teach the subject; and (c) to learn to teach, experience in classrooms is all that is necessary.

Misconception: Teaching Is a Process of Transmitting Knowledge to Learners

1.2

What is the most likely reason that preservice and beginning teachers believe teaching is the process of transmitting knowledge to learners?

You saw in our example that "explaining until I'm blue in the face" often doesn't work. Simply "explaining" often fails to take into account students' motivation and the way they learn. Bransford (1993) describes this as "the 'wisdom can't be told' problem" (p. 6). Learners are not passive receptacles that simply receive information. Instead, they change what they receive into forms of understanding that make sense to them, while at the same time responding to their own beliefs and expectations. To be effective, teachers must consider these factors when they plan and teach.

Misconception: Majoring in an Academic Subject Provides All the Knowledge Needed to Teach the Subject

One of the most pervasive myths in teaching is that knowledge of subject matter is all that is necessary to teach effectively. By his own description, Keith's understanding of math was more than adequate. His problem was that he didn't know how to represent percentages in a way that was both understandable and engaging for his students.

1.3

What is the most likely reason that math majors were no more successful than nonmajors in effectively illustrating math topics?

This predicament is not uncommon. In a study of teacher candidates, math majors were no more able than nonmajors to effectively illustrate and represent math concepts in ways that learners could understand (National Center for Research on Teacher Learning, 1993). Both majors and nonmajors lacked **pedagogical content knowledge** (L. Shulman, 1986), which is *knowledge of effective ways to represent topics for learners plus an* *understanding of what makes topics difficult or easy to learn for students of different ages.* Acquiring pedagogical content knowledge takes time and effort. It doesn't automatically result from knowledge of content itself.

Knowledge of content is critical, of course, but it is not sufficient by itself. Teaching is a complex process that requires different kinds of knowledge—knowledge of content, understanding of the way people learn, information about learners' beliefs and expectations, and command of teaching techniques. This process is sophisticated, and it takes time to learn.

Misconception: To Learn to Teach, Experience in Classrooms Is All That Is Necessary

As with understanding subject matter, experience in classrooms is important in learning to teach. It is, however, another necessary, but not sufficient, condition. There are at least two problems with the "just watch and learn" approach. First, you won't always observe good teaching; second, you will see teachers who are good yet teach very differently. Which one or what part of their teaching provides the best modeling?

Studies of modeling and its impact on observers' behaviors indicate that unless observers are given specific guidance about which behaviors they're supposed to imitate, they're uncertain and often imitate inappropriate or irrelevant behaviors (Bandura, 1986, 1989). This especially applies to preservice teachers. Unless they know what to look for, experiences in classrooms can be quite confusing, in some cases increasing rather than eliminating misconceptions (Smylie, 1989). One way to combat this problem is to have a solid, conceptual base to guide your observations and your own teaching. Studying educational psychology can help provide that base.

> **1.4**
> What is the most likely reason that observers, if they don't know "what to look for" in classrooms, often imitate inappropriate or irrelevant behaviors?

Concepts learned in educational psychology help beginning teachers understand the complex events occurring in classrooms.

Goals for This Book

1.5

To what concept defined earlier does knowledge of "how ideas can be represented so that they're understandable" refer?

It is clear that one of the most important factors in learning to teach is knowledge—knowledge of content, of course, but also knowledge of learners, differences among them, the ways they learn and what motivates them, how ideas can be represented so that they're understandable, how classrooms can be organized to promote learning, and what teachers can do to assess learner understanding.

Our goal in writing this text is to provide some of this knowledge. You obviously won't learn everything you need to know about teaching from this book, but we believe that studying it can make an important contribution to your professional growth. In addition, you will draw from your past experience, learn from other teachers, some of whom, like Jan, are more experienced. You will also learn by doing, thinking, and reflecting on your successes and failures.

This book is based on the belief that a body of knowledge exists that *can* help beginners like Keith in their initial efforts as teachers and assist veterans like Jan in their efforts to become better teachers. This body of knowledge is the content of educational psychology, and our goal is to describe and illustrate its application in the real world of teaching.

Themes for This Book

In writing this book, we used four themes to organize our work. The first is the role of *research* in helping teachers understand students and classrooms. Educational psychology benefits from a growing body of research that studies the ways people learn and how teachers can help in this process. We share this research with you throughout the book. Our second theme is the *application* of this knowledge in the classroom. Without application, the research is of little use in the real world. In applying any research, teachers need to exercise sensitive and sound *decision making,* the third theme of the text. The findings of educational psychology don't exist as simple rules to be followed without critical examination. Although teaching would be easier if they did, it would also be less rewarding. As Jan commented in our opening case study, "Very little in teaching is cut-and-dried . . . but then, that's also part of the fun of it."

1.6

What kind of teaching method would be most common in instruction that is not learner focused?

Our final theme is related to each of the others and further contributes to the complexity of the process. This theme is *a focus on learners.* A focus on learners means that learners are at the center of the learning process. Much research emerged in the 1980s and 1990s suggesting that learners are active participants in the process of constructing their own understanding of the world around them (Alexander & Murphy, 1994; Brophy, 1992; Bruning, Shraw, & Ronning, 1995; Derry, 1992; Marshall, 1992; Resnick & Klopfer, 1989). Learners don't passively receive information from teachers, books, and other materials. Instead, they rework it in the context of what they already know until it makes sense to them, and the role of teachers is to assist them in this process.

These four themes are summarized in Figure 1.1. Let's look at them in a bit more detail.

Research on Learning and Teaching

In our opening case study, Jan offered Keith suggestions, and in making them she drew information from research. Her idea for helping students understand percentages by posing a concrete and practical problem was drawn from research she had read in journal articles. The research served as the conceptual foundation for what she did. Let's see how this works.

Figure 1.1

Organizing themes for this book

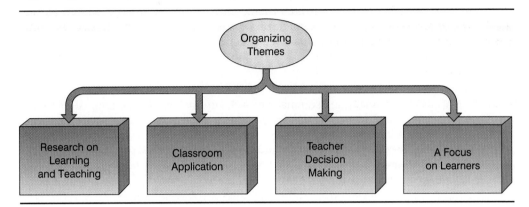

A Knowledge Base

Any academic pursuit has a **body of knowledge**, which is *the information on which content is built.* This is the case for physics, history, anthropology, political science, engineering, and every other field. Some professions—engineering and education, for example—rely heavily on other areas, such as physics or psychology, to develop their own base of knowledge. The primary process used for accumulating this body of knowledge is research.

Research often confirms common sense. For example, think about some of your own experiences. You study hard for a challenging test and do well. Because of the challenge and your success in meeting it, you feel a sense of near exhilaration (Schunk, 1994), and you are even more inclined to study hard for the next one. Both your achievement and motivation to succeed have increased. This is intuitively sensible, and these results are confirmed by systematic research; increased achievement and motivation go hand in hand (Stipek, 1993).

The link between intuition and research is not unique to education. For instance, a lifestyle that eliminates smoking and includes exercise and a proper diet as ways of maintaining health certainly makes sense. Also, it doesn't take a medical degree to recognize that excessive alcohol consumption is damaging to your health. Yet, much is made of medical research that confirms these notions. Similarly, educational research that confirms your intuitions is reassuring and thus allows you to proceed with renewed confidence.

Not all cases are common sense, however. For example, when teachers question their students, they typically call on the ones with hands raised or those they think will be able to answer much more often than they call on less aggressive or lower achieving students. Some even argue that a teacher shouldn't call on reluctant learners for fear of embarrassing them or "putting them on the spot." Research indicates, however, that this is not effective questioning practice. All students need to be drawn into lessons through questioning that invites, and even requires, participation (Good & Brophy, 1994; Kerman, 1979; Nystrand & Gamoran, 1989). When you are aware of these research findings, as Jan was, you can change your questioning patterns and call on all the students as frequently as possible. This change would be unlikely if you relied on intuition alone.

Other research results are even less intuitive. For instance, retaining students who underachieve in a particular grade with the idea of improving their achievement probably makes sense to many people, and on the basis of this "conventional wisdom," retention is

1.7
Which kind of research result—intuitive or non-intuitive—is more common? Why? What does this tell you about human nature?

1.8
When you learn to write, it makes sense intuitively to first learn the mechanics of grammar and spelling and then to apply these skills as you write. Does research confirm this intuitively sensible approach? Explain.

common. Research indicates, however, that the practice of retention not only fails to increase achievement but also detracts from motivation and damages self-esteem (R. Doyle, 1989).

These examples illustrate how intuition and common sense are often not sufficient for making professional decisions. Educational research supplements intuition by providing knowledge about learners, the learning process, and effective teaching strategies that allow professionals to improve and refine their practice.

Role of Theory in a Body of Knowledge

As research accumulates, results are summarized and patterns begin to emerge. After a number of related patterns are identified, general principles are formed; these in turn generate further research studies. As the knowledge accumulates, theories are gradually constructed.

A **theory** is *a set of related principles based on observations that in turn are used to explain additional observations.* Theories help organize research findings and can provide valuable guidance for teachers.

Let's look at a brief example. One research-based principle indicates that reinforced behaviors increase in frequency, and a related principle indicates that intermittently reinforced behaviors will persist longer than those that are continuously reinforced (Alberto & Troutman, 1995; Skinner, 1957). Too much reinforcement, however, can actually decrease behavior (satiation). A classroom application of these principles occurs in learning activities. If students are praised for their attempts to answer questions (reinforced), they are likely to increase their efforts, and they will persist longer if they are praised for some but not all of their attempts

---

1.9

Suppose the research base in teaching were complete. How would that influence controversies in education? Are the research bases in other areas, such as medicine and economics, more or less complete than the research base in education? How do you know?

1.10

In the opening case study, how did Keith use reinforcement theory (behaviors that are reinforced will increase in frequency) to explain and predict Kelly's behavior?

Theories help teachers understand the complex world of classrooms and the connections between teacher actions and student learning.

(intermittently reinforced). If they are praised too much or too effu-
sively, however, they might actually reduce their efforts.

These related principles are part of the theory of behaviorism,
which studies the effects of experience on observable behavior. Our
illustration, of course, is only a tiny portion of the complete theory.
(We examine behaviorism in depth in Chapter 6.) The key feature
of any theory is that a comprehensive body of information is
formed when a number of principles are related to each other.

Theories are useful in two primary ways. First, they allow us
to explain behaviors and events. For instance, look at the cartoon
to the right.

Because we understand theories of child development (which
we examine in Chapters 2 and 3), we're able to explain why the
child behaved the way he did. These theories suggest that young
children tend to be dominated by their perceptions: He could see
only the water and the faucet, so he concluded that all the water
was in it. Likewise, we explain why Las Vegas casino patrons persist
in playing slot machines, though coins only rarely fall into the trays,
by saying they are being intermittently reinforced. In that case, we
use the theory of behaviorism to explain the specific behavior.

Second, theories also allow us to predict behavior and events. For
instance, we predict that students who believe they are the ones who
control how good their grades will be try harder than those who believe
their grades are due primarily to luck or the whim of the teacher. Attribution theory, a topic we
present in Chapter 9, provides the basis for this prediction (Stipek, 1993; Weiner, 1990).

In all three instances—child development, behaviorism, and attribution theory—theories help us understand teaching and learning by allowing us to explain and predict people's behaviors. Whenever possible, we attempt to explain specific research results on the
basis of theory as we progress in this study.

FAMILY CIRCUS

Copyright 1988
Cowles Syndicate, Inc

"How do they fit so much water
in that little spigot?"

Classroom Application

This book focuses on **application**—*how the principles of educational psychology actually
work in classrooms.* Our study of the theories and research that make up the content of
educational psychology focuses on their implications for classroom practice. To assist you in
applying research findings, we build much of the content of this book around case studies.

Case studies are *segments or samples of students' and teachers' experiences in the
teaching-learning process and other professional events.* Some are specific classroom
scenarios illustrating students' experiences in learning activities; others, such as the one at
the beginning of this chapter, deal with larger issues, such as learning to teach and professional growth. All are designed to provide you with a window to the real world of teaching.

We have used case studies in our teaching, and the reactions of our students support
the claims of experts (W. Doyle, 1986; J. Shulman, 1992): Cases help students see how theories and abstract ideas relate to "real world" practice (Fernald, 1989), and they stimulate
the growth of professionals (Hmelo, 1995).

We use different types of cases in this book. Each chapter begins with a case study,
just as this one does. They are designed to illustrate many of the concepts and principles
in the chapters and provide a concrete reference point for the information you study.

Shorter cases are interspersed throughout the chapters to introduce problems and
to further illustrate ideas, and each chapter closes with a case that we ask you to analyze

Case studies provide opportunities for students to analyze and reflect on real-world classrooms.

on the basis of chapter content. The cases at the end of Chapters 2, 7, 8, and 12 exist in two forms. A written version appears at the end of the chapter. This version is based on an actual classroom lesson with real teachers and students. A videotaped version showing the lesson as it was actually taught exists as a companion to the text. Because it illustrates the teaching episode in context, it further integrates the text content with the classrooms you'll encounter. Research indicates that the use of video cases stimulates the development of expertise in teachers (Copeland & Decker, 1995).

Cases are also embedded in applied exercises in test items to provide you with opportunities to use the information in this text in solving classroom problems. Each type of case study is designed to help you apply the information in the text to the real world of teaching. Let's look at the following example:

> April Sumner teaches remedial English to a first-period class of inner-city high schoolers. Students need to pass the class to graduate from high school, but motivation and attendance are major problems.
>
> She likes the class, and because of its relatively small size, she knows all her students well. This closeness is rewarding, but the class is also frustrating: The students refuse to bring any materials to class. *Refuse* isn't exactly the right word. On students' lists of important things to do in the morning, finding a pencil and notebook paper doesn't rank high. Daily reminders don't seem to help, nor do threats of failure, especially because many students are repeating the class for the second or third time.
>
> April talks with other teachers. Some say, "Let them sit"; others respond, "Lend them your own," but warn of logistical nightmares and economic disaster when the pencils disappear and she runs out of paper.
>
> April has been hired to teach English, but first she has to solve the materials problem. What would you do?

1.11
Case studies are concrete examples of abstract ideas. What abstract ideas are the case studies intended to illustrate?

Case studies such as this can be powerful learning tools in classrooms, and that's why we share them with you. They're powerful because they're real; they stimulate your thinking and also illustrate how educational psychology can help you understand and solve real classroom problems.

The problem we just presented, like all our cases, was taken from a teacher's actual experiences in working with real students. In selecting the content to be included in this book, we carefully analyzed its applicability in the real world. We continually asked ourselves, "Is this real? Can it make a difference in the real world of teaching?"

As you study this text, ask yourself, "As a teacher, what do I do differently because I understand this theory or these research results, compared with what I would have done if I didn't know about them?" Because of the importance of classroom application, try to put yourself in the place of the teacher in each case study as you study this material. Looking at the content in the chapters in this way will make the information more meaningful by helping you relate to it personally.

Teacher Decision Making

In a previous section, we examined the role of research in guiding practice and pointed out that research in education and other professions is less than perfect. Just as medical research doesn't tell exactly how many times a week people can safely eat red meat or how much exercise is necessary to maintain a healthy lifestyle, educational research doesn't answer all questions about best classroom practice. For instance, research indicates that students should be taught to set personal learning goals, that the goals should be moderately difficult, and that students should monitor and assess the goals themselves (Schunk, 1994). It doesn't tell teachers, however, exactly how to approach the process as they introduce it, what "moderately difficult" means for a particular student, and how the goals students set are integrated with the goals for the class. Further, it doesn't tell teachers whom to call on at a particular time, how to assess students' verbal and nonverbal reactions, what examples will best illustrate a topic, or how to treat a shy and withdrawn student compared with an outgoing and assertive one. Research helps teachers understand patterns of student learning and effective teaching, but the specific decisions are left to them.

The process of teacher decision making is sometimes complicated by research results that appear contradictory. L. Shulman (1986) describes one such dilemma related to waiting after asking a question—a practice that gives students time to think and that results in increased learning:

> From Rowe's (1974) research on wait-time, for example, we learn the principle that longer wait-times produce higher levels of cognitive processing. Yet Kounin's (1970) research on classroom management warns the teacher against slowing the pace of the classroom too severely lest the frequency of discipline problems increase. How can the principle of longer wait-times and that of quicker pacing both be correct? (p. 13)

Should teachers wait longer to give students time to think through a question fully, or will long pauses result in choppy lessons that drag? Research doesn't provide a precise answer, so teachers must use their professional judgment and decide how much wait-time to give and how quickly the lesson should be moved along.

April Sumner's experience is another example of the need for teacher decision making. Providing students with pencils reinforces their coming to class unprepared. Allowing students to sit passively, however, runs counter to the research on both learning and motivation (Blumenfeld, 1992; Bruer, 1993; Good & Brophy, 1994).

It admittedly would be easier if teachers could simply call up a research result, apply it as a rule, and get consistent, predictable results. However, neither the world nor teaching and learning works this way. So, to be a successful teacher, your ability to cope with uncertainty and deal with ambiguity is critical. Decision making is an integral part of teaching.

1.12

Identify at least one decision that April Sumner had to make in working with her students.

Informed Decision Making

How should research be used in making decisions? Gage and Berliner (1989) suggest that teachers should think *critically, practically,* and *artistically* about the results of research.

If they're able to do so, they do more than simply apply research; they select, modify, and adapt the suggested applications to best meet the needs of their students.

Critical Decision Making: Impact of Classroom Context.   When using research results *critically*, teachers analyze their own situations and compare them with the settings that produced the results. For instance, one research study found that students called on in predictable patterns achieved more than students called on at random (L. Anderson, Evertson, & Brophy, 1979). Does this mean teachers should stop the intuitively sensible practice of calling on students at random? Certainly not. Examining the results critically, we find that the study was conducted with first graders in small reading groups, a context very different from whole-group instruction, in which calling on students at random is more effective.

Lesson context also helps teachers resolve the dilemma with wait-time that we mentioned earlier. For example, on the one hand, if a question is thought provoking, the lesson is proceeding smoothly, and the student "on the spot" is comfortable, the teacher should probably wait. On the other hand, if the lesson is dragging, the other students are fidgety, and the student appears uncomfortable, the teacher should probably reduce the amount of wait-time; the context in which the question is asked is different. Each situation requires a decision. Research helps in the process, but it does not substitute for sound teacher judgment.

Practical Decision Making: The Need for Efficiency.   *Practicality* is the second factor to consider in making informed decisions. To be useful, research must be applied efficiently, with a minimum of disruption to the class or extra work for the teacher. Classrooms are complex and busy places; researchers estimate that elementary teachers have more than 500 exchanges with individual students in a day (W. Doyle, 1986). Many, if not most, of these require a teacher decision. To be practical, research results must be applied efficiently.

For example, research indicating that all students should be called on equally is practical. On the one hand, it requires that teachers develop their questioning and monitoring skills, but it doesn't require reorganizing the curriculum or changing classroom routines and general patterns of instruction. On the other hand, students taught in a one-to-one, personalized mode of instruction will learn the most (B. Bloom, 1984a; Slavin, Madden, Karweit, Dolan, & Wasik, 1992). Unfortunately, this technique usually isn't economically or practically feasible.

April Sumner's dilemma was strongly influenced by practical considerations. On the one hand, allowing students to sit passively day after day can't be justified professionally. On the other hand, a teacher can spend a lot of money handing pencils to students who consider the whole process a game.

We know of two practical solutions to the problem. One teacher kept a box of short pencil stubs in his desk (L. Shulman, 1986). When a student forgot a pencil, the teacher would give the student the shortest stub he could find, require the student to complete the work with it, and return it after class. Another teacher required a personal article, such as an earring, bracelet, or belt, as collateral, which she exchanged for the pencil at the end of class. These were simple, practical solutions that worked.

Artistic Decision Making: Creativity in Teaching.   The *artistic* element, the third dimension of informed decision making, asks teachers to apply the results of research in original and creative ways. This aspect of teacher decision making requires effort and sound judgment. Let's look at an example of creativity in teaching.

> After three separate efforts to teach the principle of exposition, development and recapitulation in music—each of which failed—the teacher was at wit's end. Having repeatedly reminded her students that composers like Wagner depended on the listen-

1.13

Why might patterned turn-taking work with reading skills and first graders? Why might it not be as effective in other settings?

1.14

What specifically would you look for to determine whether students are uncomfortable when asked questions?

1.15

Why is a one-to-one teacher-to-student ratio most effective in promoting learning? What can teachers with classes of 25 students do to approximate these benefits?

Creative teachers design learning activities that motivate students to learn.

ers' remembering earlier themes, so as to recognize their later elaboration, she was determined to make her students understand musical form, no matter what it took.

The class had little trouble with simple variations and could easily identify themes that were repeated in a related key, but when it came to the development sections, the students' attention focused on the new detail to such an extent that they no longer "heard" the basic motif. For a week or two, the young teacher fretted over the problem. She discarded one idea after another as either too complicated or impractical. Older teachers advised her to go on with something else, suggesting that she was overly ambitious, and that such discrimination was impossible without formal music training. Still, the teacher searched in her mind for a solution.

One afternoon during the lunch hour, she noticed a group of students clustered in a corner of the yard. Several girls were swaying their bodies in a rhythmic cadence. Curious, she drew closer and found that the students were listening to a new rock hit. A slender boy in the center of the group held a tape recorder in his hand. A few moments later, as the teacher continued on her noon duty rounds, a sudden inspiration took hold.

The following day, when her music appreciation class arrived, she asked how many students had tape recorders. A dozen or so students immediately said, "I do." The teacher looked at her students pensively. "I have an idea," she said with sudden animation. "Maybe machines have better memories than people. What would you think," she said, "about trying an experiment? We could play Beethoven's 'Eroica' again, and one of you can record the theme of the second movement when it's first introduced. Then, later, when Beethoven gets into the development section, someone else can record that segment. Finally, when he comes to the recapitulation—the restatement—we'll have a third person record again. Of course," she added, "technically, it won't be a real recapitulation because we'll select passages in the same key. If," she finished triumphantly, "we can synchronize the timing, and start all three recorders at exactly the same instant, we'll play the three recordings together and see if they fit. What do you think?"

Her students looked at her in surprise. Suddenly, however, delight appeared on their faces.

"Neat," one boy exclaimed.

"We'll have to get three recorders with the same speed," another exclaimed. "I'll bring a timer."

And so it was arranged. They had difficulty starting the recorders simultaneously; there were slight variations in their pitch; and the tempo of the recorded passages was a bit uneven; but the sounds blended sufficiently for the students to recognize their commonality. (L. Rubin, *Artistry in Teaching,* 1985, McGraw-Hill, Inc., pp. 32–33, reproduced with permission of McGraw-Hill)

Research indicates that actively involving students and relating abstract ideas to their personal lives increases learning; artistic decision making, such as we presented above, applies these ideas to create meaningful lessons (Brophy, 1990; Maheady, Sacca, & Harper, 1987). The teacher's instruction was artistic, but it was informed by research.

Reflection and Decision Making

Teaching involves making an enormous number of decisions, most of which cannot be reduced to simple rules. How do teachers know whether their decisions are wise and valid? This is a tough question because teachers get little feedback about their performance. They are observed by administrators a few times a year at most, and they get only vague, sketchy, and uncertain feedback from students and parents. In addition, they get virtually no feedback from their colleagues unless the school has a peer coaching or mentoring program in place (Darling-Hammond, Wise, & Pease, 1983; Glickman & Bey, 1990). As a result, to improve, teachers must be able to assess their own classroom performance.

Can the ability to conduct this self-assessment be acquired? We think so. It requires that teachers develop a disposition to critically examine what they're doing. This is the essence of a simple, yet powerful notion called **reflective teaching** (Cruickshank, 1987; Schon, 1983), which simply means *think about what you're doing.* Reflective teachers are thoughtful, analytical, and even self-critical about their teaching. They plan lessons carefully and take the time to analyze and critique them afterward.

Educational psychology supports reflection by providing a knowledge base that teachers can use in critiquing their teaching. In Keith's case, the fact that he knew, for instance, that students should be actively involved in the learning process and that problem solving is important to understanding helped him in his reflection. Had he been less well informed, he wouldn't have reacted as strongly when some of his students wanted to sit like "bumps on logs" and were unable and unwilling to go beyond "the plain old mechanics." He also recognized that the problem Jan suggested could improve both student motivation and understanding. His uneasiness about his students' progress and his openness to new ideas indicated a tendency to be reflective, and his knowledge base made the process more effective.

Teachers can acquire the tendency to reflect by continually asking questions of themselves as they teach. Although they aren't exhaustive, some possibilities are listed in Figure 1.2.

More important than the questions themselves is the tendency to ask them. If teachers keep questions such as these at the forefront of their thinking, they can avoid the trap of teaching in a certain manner because they've always taught that way. Openness to change and the desire for improvement are two of the most important characteristics of professional growth, and careful reflection can have positive effects on the decisions teachers make about how best to plan for their students' learning.

1.16

How was the music teacher's problem similar to the one Keith faced in the opening case study when he attempted to teach problem solving to his students? How did they both apply an idea from educational psychology?

1.17

Identify a specific example in which Jan Davis demonstrated reflection in her teaching.

1.18

What evidence do you have that the music teacher practiced reflection in her teaching? How are reflection and artistry in teaching linked to each other?

A Focus on Learners

Now, we look again at Keith's experience with Kelly as a way of introducing our fourth theme. When his other efforts failed, a direct, personal appeal finally made an impact on her. Although this approach won't work in all cases, the experience is a convincing reminder that if teaching is to be effective, it must focus on learners. Effective teaching strategies don't exist for their own sake. They exist because they contribute to students' learning. Effective instruction is a means to that end.

A shift in emphasis away from the teacher and toward a focus on learners is a subtle but powerful turn in the direction of educational psychology. One indicator of that shift is the American Psychological Association's "Learner-Centered Psychological Principles" (Alexander & Murphy, 1994). These principles reflect the improved understanding of learning and factors that affect it. These factors include the following:

Reflective teachers analyze their teaching to ensure that learning activities meet the needs of students.

- The powerful impact of learners' prior knowledge on all new learning
- The importance of learners being able to reflect on and control their thoughts and behaviors in the learning process
- The role of learners' intrinsic motivation, explanations for their performances, and personal goals in the learning process
- The influence of stages of development, affected by both heredity and environment, on learning
- The importance of the context in which learning takes place

You can see some of these factors illustrated in Keith's and Jan's experiences. He noted that his students "act as if this is the first time they've ever had to solve word problems" and "memorize a formula and work like robots," suggesting that their prior knowledge may be limited, that their motivation to learn is less than desirable, and that they're exercising little control over their thoughts and behaviors in the process. You can also see

Figure 1.2.

Questions for reflective teaching

- Did I have a clear goal for the lesson? What specifically was the goal?
- Was the goal important? How do I know?
- Was my learning activity consistent with the goal?
- What examples or representations would have made the lesson clearer for students?
- What could I have done to make the lesson more interesting for students?
- How do I know whether students understand what I taught? What would be a better way of finding out?
- Overall, what will I do differently to improve the lesson the next time I teach it?

1.19 ■
Explain why "explaining
the stuff until I'm blue in
the face" is less than
desirable in promoting
learning.

that a teacher-centered or "teacher-focused" approach, such as "explaining the stuff until I'm blue in the face," isn't effective.

Guiding student learning is a complex process requiring sophisticated skills, much more so than simply presenting information. To guide students effectively, a teacher must take their backgrounds, needs, beliefs, expectations, and individual differences into account. Educational psychology provides some guidance in this task.

A Focus on Learners: Developing Self-Regulation

You also saw in the previous section that learners' personal goals and their control over their thoughts and behaviors are part of what is meant by "a focus on learners." Goals and control over thoughts and behaviors are part of **self-regulation,** or *the process of students using their own thoughts and actions to reach academic learning goals* (Bruning et al., 1995; Schunk, 1994). Jan's efforts helped her students begin to develop self-regulation, as reflected by her comments: "Although I had to guide them, a lot of what we did came from them" and "They wanted to know if there was a way to tell whether a banana had a thick peel so that we could get more banana for the money."

Acquiring self-regulation is a natural and valuable outgrowth of a focus on learners. It takes time and effort from both the teacher and the students, but its long-term benefits can be enormous.

Because of the importance of self-regulation, we reexamine it at several points in this book. Helping students take responsibility for their own learning is an essential element of learner-focused instruction.

1.20 ■
From the description so
far, are you self-regulated?
Do you do any things in
this class that suggest
self-regulation?

A Focus on Learners: Caring

A focus on learners also means that teaching is, at its heart, a *human* activity and that the relationships between teachers and students are another important part of the teaching-learning process. The decisions teachers make must always be made with their students in mind. Teachers don't teach algebra or reading or physical education—they teach people. To be effective, they must adopt a theme of **caring,** or *the ability to empathize with and invest in the protection and development of young people* (Chaskin & Rauner, 1995). Students know when teachers care, and it makes a difference in their learning; it makes them more willing to experiment with new ideas and to take personal and academic risks (W. Purkey & Novak, 1984). A focus on learners is virtually impossible without caring as a disposition.

1.21 ■
Describe specifically how
Keith, in the chapter's
opening case study,
demonstrated caring.

A Focus on Learners: Learner Diversity

Consider these statistics:

- Caucasians are now 75% of the U.S. population. By the year 2050, this figure will shrink to 51%, with the remainder consisting of 21% Hispanic, 16% African American, 11% Asian American, and 1.2% Native American.
- Living in the United States are more than 30 million people for whom English is not the primary language of the home.
- Minority enrollments now range from 70% to 96% in the nation's 15 largest school systems.
- Of today's immigrants, 83% come from South America and Asia and speak 300 languages and dialects. (Hakuta & Garcia, 1989; Oakes, 1990; U.S. Bureau of the Census, 1992)

These numbers paint a picture of diversity and challenge for today's teachers. Today's students are of different genders, they vary in ability and motivation, and they come from different cultural and economic backgrounds, bringing different experiences with them. In some cases, their backgrounds place them "at risk" of failing to complete their education with the skills needed to survive in a modern technological society (Slavin, Karweit, & Madden, 1989). To maintain a focus on learners, teachers must be aware of this diversity and make conscious plans to accommodate it.

Dimensions of Diversity.

Caring teachers create supportive learning environments that allow all students to reach their maximum potential.

> "What's wrong, Tanya? You look a little down," Clarice Hodgekins asked as she entered Tanya Redding's classroom during Friday's planning period. Tanya is a 1st-year teacher who has been paired with Clarice, a 6-year veteran, for mentoring and help.
>
> "I guess I am, a little. I spent the whole summer reading curriculum guides and material from the district and teachers' editions to plan for the year. I knew exactly what second graders were supposed to learn in each of the areas, and I was so excited. I was really ready. Hah, so I thought.
>
> "Look at these papers! Some of them can't add. A lot of them can't read. Some can't even speak English, much less learn reading and math."
>
> Clarice listened sympathetically and then sat down next to Tanya. She waited a moment until Tanya looked up, and then said with a smile, "I think I remember what it was like when I was starting out. Let's talk about it and see what we can do."

The diversity in students makes teaching both challenging and interesting. As Tanya discovered, student diversity includes a variety of student differences, as illustrated in Figure 1.3.

Two of the most important of these are student *intelligence* and *background*. Tanya encountered these when she found that some of her second graders couldn't add and that others couldn't read.

Culture is also an important dimension of diversity. Increasingly, students are coming from diverse and different cultures. Research indicates that the teaching force is overwhelmingly Caucasian (less than 10% of U.S. teachers are members of minority groups) and that many of these teachers work in schools with predominantly minority populations (Gollnick & Chinn, 1994). Understanding and capitalizing on cultural differences requires skill and sensitivity.

Socioeconomic status (SES)—the combination of parents' occupation, income, and level of schooling—is another dimension of diversity that has an important influence on learning. A growing percentage of students come from environments where poverty is a fact of life. Some students come to school tired, hungry, and emotionally ill-prepared for learning. Effective schools attempt to overcome these barriers with programs such as free

1.22
Describe specifically what made Jan Davis's problem-solving activity effective for working with students having diverse backgrounds.

Effective teachers respond to diversity by designing learning tasks that meet individual learning needs.

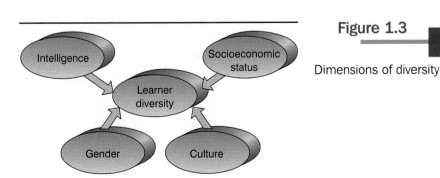

Figure 1.3

Dimensions of diversity

lunch, after-school activities, and parent involvement programs. However, nothing substitutes for caring and committed teachers who believe that all students can learn and accept responsibility for ensuring that they do.

Gender, a final dimension of diversity, also affects learning. Enter a kindergarten class and see how students' choices of toys are influenced by gender. Walk into a junior- or senior-level math class, and you're likely to see a disproportionately low number of females. Although awareness and sensitivity are changing some of these trends, some authorities believe that schools still shortchange girls (Sadker & Sadker, 1994).

What can teachers do to deal with the challenges raised by these different dimensions of diversity? Fortunately, research provides some answers.

Strategies for Dealing With Diversity.   Three general strategies have been found to be effective in dealing with all types of diversity:

1. A general attitude of acceptance and caring
2. Positive expectations for success
3. Valuing differences in learners

A general climate of acceptance and caring makes students feel safe and secure and forms a foundation for learning. Positive expectations communicate the belief that all students can learn and are expected to do so. Finally, an attitude that values diversity communicates that your classroom is a place for all students to live and grow.

Adapting Instruction to Meet Learners' Needs.   In addition to the general approaches, research has uncovered a number of specific strategies for working with diverse populations. These include providing experiences for students, providing language-embedded instruction, combining challenge and success, and use of peer tutoring, personalized examples, cooperative learning, individualization, and culturally responsive teaching. These strategies, described in Table 1.1, are discussed in later chapters and provide teachers with ways to adapt instruction to meet the needs of different learners.

> **1.23**
> To which of the four previous themes—*research, application, decision making,* and *a focus on learners*—do these three approaches most relate? Why?

Table 1.1

Strategies for accommodating diversity

Strategy	Goal	Chapters
Providing experiences	To help accommodate differences in learner backgrounds	2,5,7
Culturally responsive teaching	To match teaching strategies with student backgrounds and strengths	3,4,7,8,10,11,12,13
Language-embedded instruction	To aid the development of English as a second language	4
Combining challenge and success	To promote a sense of accomplishment	4,6,9
Peer tutoring	To increase involvement and interaction	5
Individualization	To adapt instruction to students' unique interests and needs	12
Cooperative learning	To increase achievement and improve relations among groups	12

Table 1.2

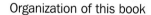

Organization of this book

Parts and Chapters	Goal
Part I: The Student	
Chapter 2: Development of Cognition and Language	To understand how learners' intellectual capacities and language abilities develop over time
Chapter 3: Personal, Social, and Emotional Development	To understand how learners' personal characteristics, moral reasoning, and socialization develop over time
Chapter 4: Learner Differences	To understand how intelligence, culture, socioeconomic status, and gender affect learning
Chapter 5: Learners with Exceptionalities	To understand how learner exceptionalities affect learning
Part II: Learning	
Chapter 6: Behaviorism and Social Cognitive Theory	To understand learning from a behaviorist and social cognitive perspective
Chapter 7: Cognitive Processes	To understand learning from a cognitive perspective
Chapter 8: Complex Cognitive Processes	To understand concept learning, problem solving, and the development of strategic learners
Part III: Motivation and Management	
Chapter 9: Increasing Learner Motivation	To understand factors that affect students' motivation to learn
Chapter 10: Managing the Learning Environment	To understand the role of orderly learning environments in promoting learning
Part IV: Instruction	
Chapter 11: Planning for Improved Learning	To understand the purpose and benefits of effective planning
Chapter 12: Teachers and Learners	To understand both teacher-centered and learner-centered approaches to instruction
Part V: Assessment	
Chapter 13: Assessing Classroom Learning	To understand different types of teacher-made assessments
Chapter 14: Standardized Testing	To understand the function and impact of standardized testing on learning and learners

Organization of This Book

Having discussed educational psychology in general terms, we now describe the specific content of this book. It is organized into five parts, which are summarized in Table 1.2.

Part I: The Student

Consistent with the theme of a focus on learners, the first part of the text examines the influence of student characteristics on learning. Chapter 2 provides an overview of cognitive development and language. It begins with a description of cognitive development based on the work of Jean Piaget, information-processing theorists, and Lev Vygotsky. Each describes the ways children's thinking changes over time. The chapter closes by presenting theories of language development and acquisition.

Chapter 3 begins with a discussion of Erik Erikson's description of personal and social development, followed in the second section by a discussion of self-concept and how it is formed. The chapter closes with an examination of Lawrence Kohlberg's explanations of the individual's developing conceptions of ethics and morals.

Chapter 4 examines questions such as, What is intelligence? How does student ability influence teaching? How do factors such as cultural and ethnic background, socioeconomic status, and gender influence learning? and What can be done to increase the learning of at-risk students?

The focus on learner differences continues in Chapter 5, where we discuss teaching students with exceptionalities. Who are these students, and what can and should teachers do to help them learn?

Part II: Learning

The focus changes in Part II to the process of learning. Two key questions are, What is learning? and What can teachers do to promote it?

Chapter 6 begins with a discussion of behaviorism, one of the oldest and most highly developed theories of learning. The second part of the chapter is devoted to social cognitive theory, which has its roots in behaviorism but goes beyond it to consider individual, internal factors such as learners' beliefs and expectations and how they influence learning.

Cognitive descriptions of learning are the focus of Chapter 7. The chapter begins with a discussion of information processing and follows with a description of factors that increase the meaningfulness of learning. The chapter closes with a discussion of constructivism, which is becoming increasingly influential in curriculum development, instruction, and assessment.

Chapter 8 continues the examination of cognitive descriptions of learning. Concept learning, problem solving, development of strategic learners, and transfer of learning are the major topics in the chapter.

Part III: Motivation and Management

Research indicates that the two biggest problems for beginning teachers are classroom management and learner motivation (Veenman, 1984), and we tackle them in the next two chapters of the book.

Chapter 9 begins with a discussion of motivation from behaviorist, cognitive, and humanistic perspectives and describes their implications for classroom practice. Personal factors in motivation, such as people's level of arousal and their beliefs and needs, are examined in the second part of the chapter. A classroom model for promoting learner motivation, which is synthesized from theory and research, makes up the third part of the chapter.

Chapter 10 analyzes the process of classroom management and describes the relationship between management and teaching. Procedures for preventing management problems are discussed in detail, and interventions for dealing with problems when they arise are examined.

Part IV: Instruction

Teaching begins with planning for effective instruction, but how do different planning processes influence teaching? Chapter 11 examines the research on teacher planning and discusses the influence of planning on teachers' behaviors.

Chapter 12 describes the expanding body of research on the role of teachers in promoting learning and discusses the application of these research findings in classrooms. The first section of the chapter is devoted to a discussion of the skills all teachers should possess, called essential teaching skills. The second section examines teacher-centered approaches to instruction, and the chapter's third part, influenced by constructivism and learner-centered psychological principles, discusses learner-centered approaches to instruction, such as guided discovery, discussions, individualization, and cooperative learning.

Part V: Assessment

One of the most critical teacher tasks is that of assessment. The process of gathering data and evaluating student progress is ongoing and has a powerful impact on instruction and learning. Chapter 13 discusses the assessment process, including both traditional and authentic teacher-designed assessments, preparing students for assessments, and grading and reporting. The role of assessment as an integral part of the teaching-learning process is analyzed.

Chapter 14 completes the book with a discussion of descriptive statistics, standardized testing, and issues involved in assessment.

Using This Book

We've tried to make the information in this text not only current and accurate but also accessible to you as learners. To assist you in your study, we have included the following features in each chapter.

- **Chapter Outlines** describe the major ideas in a chapter and how they're organized. Preview these before beginning a chapter to give you an overview of the chapter content.
- **Case Studies** open each chapter. The cases—all taken from actual classroom experiences—illustrate the content of the chapter, and frequent references to the case studies are made as the chapter's topics are discussed. The case studies reinforce our theme of application of educational psychology in the real world of classrooms.
- **Objectives** identify key concepts and ideas in each chapter. The objectives supplement the outlines and should provide you with a clear picture of the chapter's directions.
- **Important Concepts** identify the major ideas in each chapter. They appear in bold type and are all defined (in italics) in the body of the text. They are also listed at the end of each chapter to help you as you review the chapter.
- **Connections**, in the form of questions in the margins, appear throughout each chapter. They are intended to put you in the most active role possible as you study each chapter. We encourage you to think about and respond to them as you study.

  The **Connections** are designed to stimulate your thinking and to help you form links among (a) topics you study and your personal life, (b) topics from different chapters of the text with each other, and (c) topics you study and how they can be applied in classrooms. Answers to some of the questions can be found in the chapter itself; other questions require you to relate information from previous chapters. Some of the questions ask you to hypothesize, predict, explain, or apply. These processes are the foundation for your own analysis and reflection.

▌ **Classroom Connections** offer suggestions for applying each chapter's topics to classrooms. They exist in two types. The first helps you bridge the gap between theory and practice by offering classroom-tested suggestions for applying the chapter content to your own teaching. The second focuses specifically on ideas for adapting your teaching to the diverse learners in your classroom.

▌ **Windows on Classrooms** is the closing section of each chapter. The section is composed of a "slice of classroom life" in the form of a case study, together with questions to guide your analysis and reflection. In many cases, the teaching illustrated in the case study could be improved, and you will be asked to make specific suggestions for improving it on the basis of the chapter content. This view into classrooms is another way we make the content of the text applicable to your future role in classrooms. The case studies at the end of Chapters 2, 7, 8, and 12 are also available on videotape and further integrate the content of the book with teaching and learning in real classrooms.

▌ A **Summary** appears at the end of each chapter and attempts to capture the chapter's main ideas. You may wish to review it before reading a chapter a second time.

Again, we welcome you to your study of educational psychology. We sincerely hope this effort enhances both your personal and professional growth.

 **Important Concepts**

application (p. 11)

body of knowledge (p. 9)

caring (p. 18)

case studies (p. 11)

pedagogical content
knowledge (p. 6)

reflective teaching (p. 16)

self-regulation (p. 18)

theory (p. 10)

Chapter Outline

2

Development
of
Cognition
and Language

Karen Johnson, an eighth-grade physical science teacher, walked into the teachers' workroom with a clear plastic drinking cup filled with cotton balls.

"What are you up to?" asked Ken, one of her colleagues. "You drinking cotton these days?"

"I just had the most wonderful class," Karen exclaimed. "You know how I told you the other day that my third-period students didn't understand 'density.' They would memorize the formula and solve problems but didn't really get it. I also found out they were confused about basic concepts such as *mass, weight, size, volume,* everything. To them, mass and weight were the same, and if something is bigger it's heavier, so it has more mass and also is more dense. It was a mess."

"I thought you said they were your low class?" Ken responded. "You said they're a little slow."

"They're not that bad," Karen said, shaking her head. "Their backgrounds are weak, but then they've never really had this material other than to memorize some definitions, so what do you expect?

"Anyway," she continued, "I kept thinking they could do better, so I decided to try something a little different, even if it seemed sort of elementary. See," she went on, compressing the cotton in the cup. "Now the cotton is more dense. . . . And now it's less dense," she pointed out, releasing the cotton.

"Then yesterday I made some blocks out of wooden cubes, and we compared the densities of the large blocks with those of the small blocks. Some of them still wanted to say the density of a big block was greater, but after I went through the examples with them and we discussed each one, they started doing better.

"Now, this morning," she said with increasing animation, "I had them put water and vegetable oil in little bottles that were the same volume on our balances, and they saw that the mass of the water was greater, so water is more dense. I had asked them to predict which was more dense before we did the activity, and most of them said the oil was, so we talked about that and they concluded the reason they pre-dicted oil is the fact that it's 'thicker.'

"Here's the good part," she continued, gesturing and raising her voice, "Calvin—and he hates science—remembered that oil floats on water, so it made sense to him that oil is less dense. He actually got excited about what we were doing.

"So, we formed a principle that less dense materials float on more dense materials. Then, even better, Donelle wanted to know what would happen if the materials mixed together, you know, like water and alcohol. You could almost see the wheels turning. So, we discussed that and thought about more examples where that might be the case. We even got into population density, and a screen-door screen with the wires close together compared with one with the wires farther apart, and how that related to what we were studying. I loved it. It was genuinely exciting. I really felt as if I was teaching and the students were really into learning for a change, instead of poking each other. A day like that now and then keeps you going."

As you began your study of teaching and learning, one of the first principles you probably heard was "You must begin where the learner is." This nearly self-evident principle has important implications for teachers. If teachers are to be effective, they must have a clear understanding of their learners. One aspect of this understanding is knowing how students typically think, feel, and act at different ages and what factors influence their thoughts and actions.

In this chapter, we examine cognitive development—the ways students grow in thinking, reasoning, and problem solving. In this process, we cover five major topics. First, we look at the work of Jean Piaget, who described the ways children at different ages deal with information from their environments. Second, we turn to information processing, a view of development based on the specific strategies that children use to make sense of their worlds. Third, we discuss the work of Lev Vygotsky, a Russian psychologist; his work helps in understanding the role that activity, language, and social interaction play in development. Fourth, Piaget and Vygotsky have had a major impact on constructivism—an emerging perspective on development and learning. We introduce constructivism in this chapter and return to it throughout the text. Fifth, we examine language development and see how it relates to each of the other topics.

These theories help teachers understand students by describing their developmental differences in systematic patterns. They help teachers understand the ways children's minds grow and develop, and this understanding helps teachers respond more effectively to students' individual needs.

After you've completed your study of this chapter, you should be able to meet the following objectives:

- Explain how development is influenced by learning, experience, and maturation.
- Describe differences between an information-processing view and Piaget's descriptions of development.
- Explain the role of language, activity, and social interaction in Vygotsky's theory of development.
- Describe the implications of constructivism for teaching.
- Explain how language development reflects constructivist views of learning.

In the case study at the beginning of the chapter, Karen Johnson was describing an experience typical for many teachers. In working with her students, she found that they had only a superficial understanding of a basic concept. The students' behaviors were also typical; in their effort to cope, they memorized a formula, plugged in numbers, and cranked out answers that had little meaning for them.

Why are some concepts, such as *density,* so hard for students to understand? It would be easy to think of them as being a little slow, as Ken suggested, and let it go at that. This, however, leads nowhere. Even if these aren't the most able students, they're often capable of achieving much more than they demonstrate. Other, more useful explanations are needed.

Karen's experience and the search for explanations introduce the theme of this chapter. After we've finished, you'll see how differences in intellectual development influence students' ability to understand the content you try to teach, and we'll look at factors that affect that development.

Interestingly, it was a Swiss biologist named Jean Piaget (1896–1990), rather than an educator or a psychologist, who pioneered our current emphasis on development and developmental approaches to teaching and learning. Education in the United States has been strongly influenced by his work, and we begin our study of development with it.

Piaget's Theory of Intellectual Development

Piaget was an unlikely influence on American education. His initial work was in biology, rather than psychology or education, and his writing had to be translated from French into English. He wasn't even interested in education, instead being fascinated by *genetic episte-mology,* or the study of the growth of knowledge in people. He formed the beginnings of his theory by observing his own children. His research method—intensively observing small numbers of subjects—was very different from the behaviorist tradition so dominant in the United States at the time, and as a result it took time for his work to be accepted. As additional research has verified and expanded his findings, however, his work has had an increasingly important impact on our views of development and learning.

Development: A Definition

Mike began playing the trumpet as a sixth grader in his middle school band. Evenings were filled with odd sounds coming from his bedroom, and even Chews, his devoted dog, retreated to the relative sanctuary of the living room. As an eighth grader, however, practicing for his part in the piece that he and two friends were playing for a concert, he produced very different sounds. Now, after listening to his son play his last concert as a high school senior, Mike's dad is convinced that Mike could play in a professional orchestra.

Several factors influenced Mike's success. First, he practiced and worked and practiced some more. In the process, he learned much about playing the trumpet. In addition, he simply became stronger and was physically more capable as an eighth grader than he was as a sixth grader, and as a senior in high school, he was even more capable. In short, he matured. We use this example to illustrate the concept of **development**, *the orderly, durable changes in a learner resulting from a combination of learning, experience, and maturation.* Notice that the changes in Mike's ability were durable but not permanent. His development as an eighth grader was more advanced than it was as a sixth grader, but more change occurred as he matured further and gathered more experience. Development for all of us begins at birth and continues until we die, and this development results from the interaction of learning, maturation, and experience. Figure 2.1 illustrates this relationship.

The Drive for Equilibrium

A major idea that emerged from Piaget's studies was people's need for order (Piaget, 1952, 1959). To illustrate this need, think for a moment about some of the classes you've taken. Are you more comfortable when the instructor specifies the requirements, schedules the classes, and outlines the grading practices? Or, even consider a typical day. Do you tend to follow a routine when you get up in the morning? Does your life in general follow patterns more than random experiences? Most people's do.

People seem to have an innate need to find order, structure, and predictability in their existence, which Piaget calls the drive for **equilibrium**, *or a state of balance.* **Equilibration**, *the act of searching for order,* involves the testing of one's understanding against the real world. When people's understanding explains the events they observe, the world makes sense, and they have equilibrium. When they can't explain what they see on the basis of their understanding, disequilibrium occurs, and the search for new and better understanding begins.

Organization and Adaptation: The Creation of Schemes

The drive for equilibrium is a cornerstone of Piaget's theory. We are all motivated by a need to understand the world, and as we acquire experiences, we try to order them to fit what

---

2.1

A first grader tries to imitate her brother shooting baskets on the basketball court but has neither the strength nor the skill. She practices, receives tips from her brother, gets bigger and stronger, and by the fourth grade is making baskets consistently. Identify the experiential part of the development, the learning part of the development, and the maturation part of the development.

2.2

Before bedtime, a child requests a story her father has read to her many times. As he reads, she corrects each miscue. Why might she request such a familiar story, and why would she correct each mistake her father makes?

Figure 2.1

Factors influencing human intellectual development

we already know. Think about your experience when you first went off to college. When you began, you probably based your expectations on your high school experiences. When these experiences were similar, you remained at equilibrium. When your expectations weren't met, you needed to change your behavior accordingly. The same is true for interactions with other people. When someone else behaves in an unpredictable way, you're uneasy until you can resolve the inconsistency, and when you do, equilibrium returns.

In response to this need for equilibrium, people try to organize life's experiences into coherent patterns, which Piaget calls schemes. **Organization** *is the process of forming schemes;* **schemes** are *mental patterns or systems that describe the ways people think about the world.* Schemes are the building blocks of thinking. When a small child sitting on her father's lap says "Doggy" or points to a picture of a dog, she has formed a "dog" scheme. As you learned to operate a car, you developed a "driving" scheme to help you start the car, shift gears, maneuver in traffic, obey traffic signals and laws, make routine decisions about your speed, and respond to warning signs. (Although Piaget used the concept of *schemes* to refer to a narrow range of abstract operations, such as a "grasping" scheme in an infant or a "classification" scheme in young children, teachers and some researchers [e.g., Wadsworth, 1996] find it useful to extend his idea to include content-related schemes as they adapt their instruction to meet the developmental needs of their students. We use this extended conception in our description of Piaget's work.)

The formation of schemes abounds in school. A student seeing ¾ + ⅔ = ? as a math problem activates an "adding fractions with unlike denominators" scheme, which includes

2.3
Identify at least one or two "schemes" that you should have formed to this point in your study of this chapter.

Concrete experiences allow children to form schemes through the process of adaptation.

recognizing the problem's characteristics, using procedures for finding the lowest common denominator, and computing the answer. A language arts student seeing the exercise "Please come with Juanita and (I, me) to the mall" calls on an "object of preposition" scheme to select the correct pronoun, *me,* in the sentence. All the concepts, principles, rules, and procedures for their application that students learn in school are organized into schemes that allow them to make sense of the world.

Adapting Schemes

As all of us acquire experiences, our existing schemes often become inadequate, and we are forced to adapt to function effectively. **Adaptation** *is the process of adjusting our schemes and experiences to each other to maintain a state of equilibrium.* For example, if we have learned to drive a car with an automatic transmission and we buy one with a stick shift, we must adjust our "driving" scheme to accommodate driving with a standard shift.

Adaptation consists of two reciprocal processes: accommodation and assimilation. **Accommodation** *is a form of adaptation in which an existing scheme is modified in response to new experiences,* such as learning to drive with the stick shift. The "driving" scheme has been modified. It exists with its counterpart process called assimilation. **Assimilation** *is a form of adaptation in which an experience in the environment is incorporated into an existing scheme.* For instance, suppose the child who has formed a "doggy" scheme encounters a chihuahua and a German shepherd. Although the dogs are obviously very different from each other, she classifies them both as dogs. The child ignores characteristics such as size and color and focuses on the critical ones—those that make each a dog. This is adaptation through the process of assimilation. In contrast, suppose in response to seeing a bear, the child says, "Doggy," but hears her father say, "No, that's not a dog. That's a bear. Look how big it is." The child in this case has to modify her "doggy" scheme so that bears are not included and has to form a new "bear" scheme. Modifying her existing scheme and creating the new one is an example of accommodation. The relationship between assimilation and accommodation is illustrated in Figure 2.2.

Both assimilation and accommodation are required to maintain equilibrium. On the one hand, if new knowledge is only assimilated into existing schemes, they wouldn't change and

2.4 ▬
In this paragraph, we said that existing schemes become "inadequate." What does this mean?

2.5 ▬
Suppose a child sees a wolf and says, "Doggy." Does this illustrate assimilation, or does it illustrate accommodation?

Figure 2.2 ▬

Maintaining equilibrium through the process of adaptation

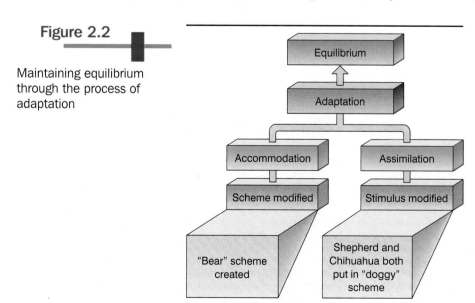

growth would not occur. "Flat-earthers," or people who still cling to the belief that Earth is flat, are an extreme example. On the other hand, if existing schemes never work, a person is in a constant state of disequilibrium. *Culture shock,* or the uneasy feelings people have when they visit a new country and must quickly adjust to different customs, food, and language, is an example. The amount of accommodation required is often overwhelming and disconcerting.

The processes of assimilation and accommodation, together with the drive for equilibrium, combine to promote cognitive development in the child. For instance, a math student modifies an "adding fractions" scheme that only works when the denominators are the same and creates one for when the denominators are different. The student's ability to cope with the mathematical world has expanded; development has occurred.

Factors That Influence Development

Piaget suggests that the drive for equilibrium is central to the process of development. In addition, three other factors combine to influence changes in thinking (Piaget, 1970): (a) maturation, (b) experience with the physical world, and (c) social experience.

Before we examine these factors, keep in mind an important principle: *All growth depends on existing schemes.* In other words, no information is ever added directly to memory, nor is any scheme formed in complete isolation. All new learning occurs in the context of existing understanding. For instance, the child formed a "bear" scheme in terms of her "doggy" scheme. The math student's ability to add fractions with unlike denominators developed from an understanding of adding fractions with like denominators, which was based on an understanding of fractions themselves, which began with an understanding of numbers and numerals. The language arts student's understanding of pronoun cases grew from an understanding of parts of speech, sentence structure, and grammar rules. This principle is one of the most important contributions of Piaget's developmental theory. Figure 2.3 illustrates this principle with an example from math.

This principle has important implications for designing and sequencing instruction. It suggests that topics should be presented that build on and extend learners' current understanding. Learning experiences should be designed to disrupt their equilibrium enough to be motivating but not overwhelming. On the one hand, if new information is presented at the same level as existing information, it is merely assimilated and no growth occurs. On the other hand, if it is too different from present understandings, learners will be incapable of linking it to what they already know. Teachers don't try to teach algebra to second graders because, among other things, these students lack the prerequisite schemes to cope with it. Let's look more closely at the factors that influence development.

2.6

A child believes that all mammals have four legs and that whales are fish. Then he learns that whales are mammals and are warm-blooded. Concluding that whales are fish illustrates what concept from Piaget's work? Learning that whales are mammals illustrates what concept?

2.7

Research consistently indicates that the best predictor of future academic achievement is past achievement. Use Piaget's ideas to explain this finding. Identify some subject matter areas in which this finding is more relevant than in others.

Figure 2.3

Illustration of growth in math depending on existing schemes

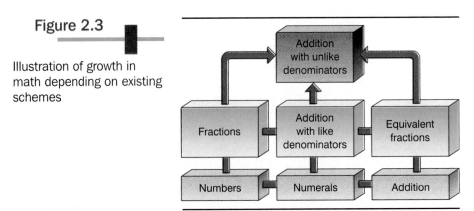

Maturation

Maturation refers to *the biological changes in individuals that result from the interaction of their genetic makeup with the environment.* A child's genes provide the blueprint for development; the environment interacts with these genes to influence the rate and direction of growth. In extreme cases, such as malnutrition or severe sensory deprivation, the environment can retard normal maturation. In most cases, however, genes and the environment interact to produce normal growth. Let's see how teachers can design environments to enhance that growth.

Experience With the Physical World

Carol Barnhart is a third-grade teacher working with her students on vocabulary development as part of their daily routine in reading. She wanted her students to understand the following words:

plain   boast   arrive   leap   verse

She began by saying, "Look at Gabriella's skirt and look at mine. Now, how are they different? . . . Peter?"

"Gabriella's has a bunch of flowers on it and yours doesn't."

Carol nodded. "Okay. And what does mine have on it? . . . Emilio?"

" . . . Just some lines," Emilio answered hesitantly.

"That's right," Carol responded, smiling. "The design on it is quite simple. How else might we describe it?"

She continued with the discussion, prompting the students until they came up with the word *plain.*

"Excellent!" she enthused. "We could call it a rather PLAIN skirt," she went on, extending and raising her voice as she said *plain.* Then she wrote *plain* and *simple* on the chalkboard.

"So, look at what I've written on the chalkboard. What do you suppose the word *plain* means? . . . Serafina?"

"Simple?"

"Yes. Good, Serafina. Now, find something else in the room that we would call plain. . . . Kim?"

" . . . The border on the bulletin board is plain. It's just white," Kim answered after thinking for a moment.

"Yes. Excellent, Kim!"

Carol then went on to illustrate each of the other words in a similar way.

Children form schemes through interaction with their environment. Carol was applying this principle by attempting to relate the words to something tangible and concrete that came from their own experience. This is how children develop the background knowledge necessary for further growth.

Piaget's emphasis on direct experience has provided the foundation for the current emphasis on "hands-on" activities in schools. Using sticks, blocks, and shapes helps children understand how abstract math concepts and operations relate to their everyday experience. In the introductory case study, Karen's eighth graders lacked background knowledge related to density, so rather than gaining a meaningful understanding of the concept, they memorized and mechanically applied the formula. Karen attempted to address this problem by providing concrete experiences that allowed students to develop more effective schemes. This strategy—providing opportunities to interact with concrete experiences—is one of Piaget's most lasting contributions to education.

The approach Carol used in helping her students build their vocabulary is another example. She could have merely written the words and definitions on the chalkboard and

2.8
A middle school science teacher starts discussing the principles behind sundials and realizes that most of the class is confused because they aren't familiar with how shadows are affected by the different positions of the sun. Describe what the teacher can do to help remedy the situation.

Hands-on science activities provide opportunities for students to test their schemes through active experimentation.

had the students memorize them; this would have taken less time and effort. However, we've all been in situations where we've memorized definitions that we promptly forget; without concrete references, Carol's third graders would fail to learn or would forget these abstract terms even more quickly.

Background Experience: A Source of Diversity

Celena Parker was beginning a social studies unit on the growth of cities with her sixth graders. She had taught the unit the previous year and was expecting similar results with basically the same materials. As an introduction to the first reading assignment, she was discussing concepts found in the text, such as *subway, mass transit, skyscraper, elevator,* and *escalator.* As she began discussing these terms, she could see blank looks on many faces.

"What's a subway?" Shareena finally asked.

"It's an underground train with funny writing on it," Leroy, who had recently moved here from New York, answered. "It's under the skyscrapers."

Celena was struck by the differences in the two students. Shareena had previously told Celena that she'd never been out of her neighborhood. She had never seen a subway or a skyscraper. In contrast, Leroy grew up in the canyons formed by New York's skyscrapers and had ridden on its graffiti-covered subways.

The next day, Celena brought in a series of color pictures. She showed the class a picture of a New York subway and another of a subway in Washington, D.C. She also showed them skyscrapers and had the students see how small cars and people looked in comparison. She explained what mass transit meant and asked the class to offer examples of different types of mass transit.

2.9 ▬
Use the concepts of *scheme, adaptation, assimilation,* and *accommodation* to explain Celena's attempts to make her topics meaningful.

Experiences make up the raw material that is the basis for development. Students construct their understanding (their schemes) of the world on the basis of these experiences. These schemes then determine how effectively new experiences can be assimilated and accommodated. If these experiences are lacking, the prerequisite schemes to which new learning can be attached won't exist. This was the case with Shareena, who had no schemes for *subway* and *skyscraper*. If Celena hadn't intervened with her pictures, the gap in Shareena's background would have become even wider.

Teachers often comment on how easily they can identify children whose parents have spent time and worked with them in activities that support schooling, compared with those whose backgrounds are less well matched to school-related activities. Children with a rich array of school-related background experiences find school meaningful because they are capable of assimilating and accommodating new knowledge. As a result, cognitive development is enhanced.

Dealing With Student Diversity.   What can teachers do when students come to them lacking the necessary experience to make the topics they're teaching meaningful? The answer is simple: *Provide it for them.* Although this can be a difficult task, it often isn't as difficult as it seems. For example, in the introductory case study, Karen's students lacked the experience needed to understand the concept of *density,* so she provided experience in the form of simple, easy-to-prepare examples that vividly illustrated the concept. *The examples became the experience* for the learners. Celena did the same for her students. The only thing better would have been a visit to a real mass transit system, allowing her students to experience firsthand the sights and sounds of a subway system. Because this was impossible, Celena's pictures were a reasonable compromise.

2.10
Parents are encouraged to read to their children, talk to them, and take them to places such as the zoo, the grocery store, concerts, and museums. Explain why parents are encouraged to do so.

2.11
A teacher wants her second graders to understand that the 2 in 21 is different from the 2 in 12. Describe specifically the experience the teacher might provide to help her students see this difference.

Classroom Connections

Capitalizing on Diversity in Your Classroom

1. To compensate for background differences, prepare concrete examples whenever possible.
   - A second-grade teacher writes the numeral 34 on the chalkboard. She then has the students make three groups of 10 interlocking cubes and place them alongside four unattached cubes. She then points out that the numeral 3 represents the three groups of 10 and that the numeral 4 represents those unattached.

2. Have students share their diverse experiences.
   - A geography teacher has a girl who grew up in Guatemala describe what life was like there. She brings in samples of clothing, food, and music to illustrate different aspects of the culture.
   - A fourth-grade teacher has her students write a detailed description of a single day in their lives, beginning with the time they get up and ending with the time they go to bed. Volunteers share their experiences with the class.

3. Encourage parents to become involved with the school.
   - A fifth-grade teacher writes a personal letter to each student's parents, describing his goals and encouraging them to contact him. He writes the letter to nonnative English speakers in their native language.
   - A middle school teacher invites parents to come in and talk about their jobs during a unit on career exploration. Parents talk about their jobs and explain how they prepared for them.

Social Experience

Piaget found that social experience is also an important factor in development. Without it, people would have to acquire their knowledge individually; this would severely limit their development. Social experience gives learners additional opportunities to test their schemes against those of others. When their schemes are comparable, equilibrium remains; when they aren't, equilibrium is disrupted, learners adapt their schemes, and development occurs.

As with experience in the physical world, recognizing the importance of social interaction has strongly influenced education and child-rearing practice. Parents, for example, organize play groups for their young children, cooperative learning is strongly endorsed in schools, and students are encouraged to get involved in service clubs and extracurricular activities. The positive influence of these activities attests to the power of social interaction.

Stages of Development

Perhaps the most widely known elements of Piaget's theory are his descriptions of stages of development. Piaget's stages describe the ways children at different ages use information and think about the world. Progress from one stage to another represents qualitative (different in kind, rather than amount) changes in children's thinking (Siegler, 1991). These stage changes are more analogous to the transformation of a caterpillar to a butterfly than to the slow and gradual accumulation of bricks to make a house. For example, preschool-

2.12

Child development experts consistently suggest that play is important in children's development. Explain this suggestion on the basis of Piaget's work. What implications does this have for the curriculum in a preschool or daycare environment?

Social interaction facilitates development by allowing students to test and compare their views of the world with those of other students.

ers' thinking is essentially limited to their perceptions, a conceptual "what you see is what you get." They typically don't reason logically. An elementary student, in comparison, can think logically but requires concrete objects as reference points, and more advanced students can think logically and hypothetically about abstract ideas. The differences in the ways students at different ages think have important implications for teaching.

As you study the characteristics of each stage, which are summarized in Table 2.1, keep three ideas in mind.

1. Development is continuous, rather than discrete. This means that a child develops steadily and gradually and that experiences in one stage form the foundation for movement to the next (Berk, 1994).
2. Although approximate chronological ages are attached to the stages, the rate at which specific children pass through them differs widely, depending on individual maturation rates and the culture (Papalia & Wendkos-Olds, 1992).
3. Although the rate varies, all children pass through each stage before progressing into a later one. No one skips any stage.

Sensorimotor Stage (0 to 2 Years)

In the **sensorimotor stage**, *children use their sensory and motor capacities to make sense of the world.* The schemes they develop are based on physical interactions, such as learning to make the jack-in-the-box pop out of its hole, as seen in Table 2.1.

> **2.13**
> Suppose you go up a set of steps to get to the door of a building; your friend walks up a ramp. Which of you corresponds to discrete movement, and which to continuous?
>
> *Sensorimotor Stage → Goal-directed Behavior*

Table 2.1

Piaget's stages and characteristics

Stage	Characteristics	Example
Sensorimotor (0–2)	Goal-directed behavior	Makes jack-in-the-box pop up
	Object permanence (Represents objects in memory)	Searches for object behind parent's back
Preoperational (2–7)	Rapid increase in language ability with overgeneralized language	"We goed to the store."
	Symbolic thought	Points out car window and says, "Truck!"
	Dominated by perception	Concludes that all the water in a sink came out of the faucet (our cartoon in chapter 1)
Concrete Operational (7–11)	Operates logically with concrete materials	Concludes that two objects on a "balanced" balance have the same mass even though one is larger than the other
	Classifies and serial orders	Orders containers according to decreasing volume
Formal Operational (11–Adult)	Solves abstract and hypothetical problems	Considers outcome of WW II if the Battle of Britain had been lost
	Thinks combinatorially	Systematically determines how many different sandwiches can be made from three different kinds of meat, cheese, and bread

2.14

Suppose that a small child has not acquired object permanence and that a mother takes a stuffed toy the child can see and puts it behind her back. What is the child likely to do? What will the child do after object permanence is acquired?

Initially, the sensorimotor child doesn't mentally represent objects; for these children, it is "out of sight, out of mind." Eventually, children acquire **object permanence,** *the ability to represent objects in memory,* during this stage. Sensorimotor children also develop the ability to imitate, an important skill that forms the basis for later observational learning.

Preoperational Stage (2 to 7 Years)

The **preoperational stage** *is characterized by perceptual dominance.* The name of this stage comes from the idea of *operation* or mental activity. A child who can classify animals as dogs, cats, and bears, for example, is performing a mental operation.

In one sense, use of the term *preoperational* is unfortunate because it suggests an incomplete stage of development. In fact, many dramatic changes occur in children as they pass through the preoperational stage, and a child at the end of the stage is very different from one at the beginning. For example, enormous progress in language development occurs during this stage. This development is rapid, reflecting growth in symbolic thought and conceptual ability. Children at this stage develop an understanding of many concepts. For example, a child riding with her parents in a car will look out the window, point animatedly, and say, "Truck," "Horse," and "Tree," delighting in exercising these newly formed ideas. These concepts are concrete, however; the horse, the truck, and the tree are physically present or associated with the current situation. Children at this age have limited notions of abstract concepts such as *fairness, truth, democracy,* and *energy.*

2.15

Children in kindergarten learn concepts such as *square, circle, triangle,* and many others. Given what is known about cognitive development, is this appropriate practice? Explain your answer.

Preoperational thinking is also characterized by five other aspects of development: egocentrism, centration, nontransformation, irreversibility, and lack of systematic reasoning.

Egocentrism.   Egocentrism *is the inability to interpret an event from someone else's point of view.* Consider the following example:

> Two 3-year-olds are playing in the same area. They are both talking enthusiastically but aren't the least bit concerned that each conversation is independent of the other. A toy truck is sitting between the children, and at the moment neither is playing with it. When Sean begins to play with the truck, however, Gail grabs it away from him, saying, "My truck!" Gail's mother reprimands her with an admonition to share. For Gail, however, the mother's reproof is incomprehensible, and she only reluctantly gives up the truck.

From the 3-year-old's perspective, the truck is hers: She saw it and wanted it. Later, through the process of accommodation, the child's thinking will expand to consider others' perspectives.

2.16

Which factor affecting development—experience with the physical world, social interaction, or maturation—is probably most important for reducing egocentrism? Why?

Centration.   Centration *is the tendency to focus on one perceptual aspect of an object or event to the exclusion of all others.* For instance, suppose 4- or 5-year-olds are shown two rows of nickels such as the following:

When asked whether the number of coins in each row is the same or which row of coins has more, they will say the number is the same. However, when one row is lengthened right in front of the children, like this,

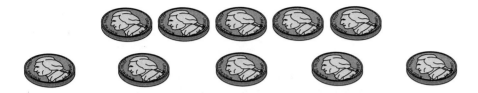

the children typically conclude that the bottom row has more coins. They are "centering" on the length of the bottom row, rather than considering the number.

Nontransformation.   Nontransformation *is the inability to mentally record the process of changing from one state to another.* Preoperational children, because of their preoccupation with the here and now of the physical world, have a difficult time thinking about the process of change. For instance, the children in the example with the coins are unable to mentally represent the process of change even though they directly observed one row being lengthened; they focused instead only on the beginning and ending state. They see it as a different row, rather than as the earlier one simply lengthened.

Irreversibility.   Irreversibility *is the inability to mentally trace a line of reasoning back to its beginning.* Again using the example with the coins, the children are mentally unable to "reverse" the lengthening process to determine that the two rows indeed have the same number of coins. Preoperational children don't mentally represent the process of lengthening the row, can't mentally reverse the operation, and focus on only one perceptual aspect of the event—the length—rather than on the number. So, it's easy to see why the children conclude that the bottom row is longer.

Lack of Systematic Reasoning.   Preoperational children also do not systematically use inductive or deductive reasoning. For instance, a child reasoning deductively—albeit unconsciously—would conclude that the number of coins in the two rows is initially the same, that no coin has been added or taken away and therefore the number must stay the same even though the bottom row is longer. A fourth grader given the problem would say simply, "You just made the row longer," or, "You just spread the coins apart," reflecting his or her reasoning about the event.

Conservation.

> As he's taking an order, the waiter at the pizza place asks, "Do you want that pizza cut into four or eight pieces?"
> The customer replies, "You'd better make it four; I couldn't eat eight all by myself!"

This joke illustrates an additional widely publicized feature of Piaget's work: his concept of conservation. **Conservation** *is the idea that the "amount" of some substance stays the same regardless of its shape or the number of pieces into which it is divided.* For instance, referring again to the example with the coins, preoperational children conclude that the number is somehow different even though only the length of the row is changed.

2.17
Suppose you are working with a child who is between the stages of pre-operational and concrete-operational thought. What might you do to help the child "decenter" in the case of the coin problem?

For them, the number can "magically" increase without disrupting their equilibrium; that number is not "conserved." Older thinkers realize that this is impossible.

The ability to conserve can be determined by a number of tasks. One was illustrated in the example with the coins. A second, measuring conservation of mass, is illustrated by the following:

A child is given two balls of clay, shown as follows:

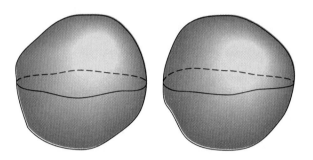

The child is asked which ball has more clay, and she concludes that they have the same amount. If she believes they are unequal, she is asked to remove clay from one and put it on the other until she says they have the same amount. The experimenter then rolls out one of the balls, as shown here:

The child is asked whether she now has the same amount of clay. The nonconserver concludes that the amounts are unequal; the conserver notes that the shape has changed but that the amount of clay is the same.

From this discussion, you can see that preoperational children don't think about the world in the same way adults do. Their thinking is dominated by perception, their mental representations are limited primarily to concrete objects, and they do not process abstract ideas of change.

Concrete Operational Stage (7 to 11 Years)

The concrete operational stage of development marks a significant advance in children's ability to think about the world around them. The **concrete operational stage** *is characterized by the ability to think logically about concrete objects.* Learners can form conclusions based on reason, rather than on perception alone.

Our fourth grader who concluded that the number of coins in the two rows was the same because all the experimenter did was "spread the coins apart" was performing a logical operation. As another example, consider the following:

2.18 ▬
Use the concepts of *egocentrism, centration, nontransformation,* and *irreversibility* to explain the nonconservation in the clay problem.

We have three sticks. We see 1 and 2 as shown:

1   2

2.19
Describe the "logic" in the
fourth grader's thinking.

Now we see 1 and 3 as follows (stick number 2 is no longer visible):

1   3

We're then asked, "What do we know about the relationship between sticks 2 and 3?"

A preoperational thinker would be incapable of dealing with the problem. A concrete operational thinker would conclude that 2 is longer than 3, reasoning that because 2 is longer than 1 and because 1 is longer than 3, 2 must be longer than 3. This is a logical operation.

Seriation and Classification.   Seriation and classification are two logical operations that develop during this stage (Piaget, 1977); both are critical to the understanding of number concepts (Gallagher & Reid, 1981). **Seriation** *is the ability to order objects according to increasing or decreasing length, weight, or volume.* Piaget's research indicates that this ability gradually evolves until it is finally acquired at age 7 or 8.

Classification *involves grouping objects on the basis of a common characteristic.* Prior to age 5, children can group along a single dimension, such as putting white circles in one group and black ones in another. When a black square is included, however, children simply add it to the black circles, rather than form subclasses of black circles and black squares. By age 7, they can form subclasses, but they still have problems with the idea of multiple class inclusion. For example, if children are shown 10 black circles and 3 white circles cut from cardboard, they agree that the circles are all made of cardboard with 10 black and 3 white. When asked whether there are more cardboard circles or more black circles, however, 6-year-olds typically respond that there are more black; this finding suggests that they center on the comparison between black and white, rather than on the larger class of cardboard circles and the subclass of black cardboard circles.

Although concrete operational thinkers have made important developmental strides, their thinking is still tied to available experiences; they need to solve problems such as the three sticks with concrete objects.

Teaching the Concrete Operational Student.   In working with concrete operational learners, the challenge for teachers is to structure learning activities that provide a concrete foundation for their thinking. Let's look at a third-grade teacher's efforts.

A nonconserver is influenced by appearances, believing that the flat pieces of clay have different amounts than the balls of clay even though they were initially the same size.

Lucy Amato introduced the concept of *graphing* to her third graders by having each student plant bean seeds in a pot. Each day after the seeds sprouted, the students measured them with a piece of paper and glued the actual length of paper on a graph. As the plants grew, the lines on the graph also got longer, and students could see the link between the actual plant growth and the graph.

Lucy Amato taught graphing by using concrete objects—the pieces of paper and actual plants. Her teaching demonstrates how teachers of elementary students can facilitate effective learning by using concrete materials that allow students to see abstract concepts and operations in action.

Use of manipulatives is common in elementary math, where concepts such as *place value, borrowing* in subtraction, and *carrying* in multiplication are illustrated with interlocking cubes that represent 100s, 10s, and units. As students perform these operations with the cubes, they begin to understand the abstract processes that lay the foundation for more advanced thinking. Examples with other topics can be found in Table 2.2.

Concrete Materials and Language.   Teachers often mistakenly believe that if their students are using manipulatives, then learning is taking place. This is not always the case, however (Ball, 1992). Unless links between the manipulatives and the symbols are carefully made, students are left uncertain about the connections and may even see the use of manipulatives and the use of symbols as two different lessons. Let's see how a second-grade teacher uses language to help students make these important connections.

Kristen Michler is teaching her students about place value. She begins by putting the students in pairs and has them make three groups of 10 interlocking cubes and then gather 4 separate cubes beside the groups.

2.20
Suppose you want to teach fourth graders about adverbs. Describe specifically what you might do to make the topic as concrete as possible.

Table 2.2

Use of concrete examples in teaching

Topic	Example
Geography: Longitude and latitude	A teacher draws longitude and latitude lines around a beach ball to illustrate that latitude lines are parallel and longitude lines intersect.
Elementary Science: Air takes up space	A first-grade teacher places an inverted cup into a fishbowl of water. To demonstrate that air keeps the water out of the cup, she tips it slightly to let some bubbles escape.
Chemistry: Charles's law	A teacher places one balloon into ice water, a second, equally inflated balloon, into room-temperature water, and a third into hot water. She asks the students to compare the final volumes of each.
History: Mercantilism	A teacher writes short case studies illustrating England and France trading raw materials from their colonies with manufactured products, forbidding trade with others, and requiring their ships for transport.

After the groups were finished, Kristen began, "Look at what you've made. What do we have there? . . . Jason?"

"Cubes."

"What have we done with the cubes? . . . Lonnie?"

"Put them together."

"All of them?"

" . . . No, not these" (pointing at the four separate ones).

"When we put them together, how many do we have in each group? . . . Jianna?"

" . . . 10."

"How many groups of 10?"

" . . . Three."

"Good," Kristen smiled. "What else do we have? . . . Trang?"

" . . . These" (pointing to the four separate ones).

"Good. So, we have three groups of 10 and 4 separate ones. Now, look up here." Kristen then wrote *34* on the chalkboard.

"Look at the number I've written. What do you suppose the 3 is?" she asked, pointing at the 3. . . . "Yolanda?"

" . . . "

"Look at your cubes. How many groups of 10 do you have?"

" . . . Three."

"Yes, good! So, what is this 3?"

" . . . It's . . . these."

"Yes," Kristen smiled encouragingly. "Go ahead and say it."

" . . . "

"It is the number of groups of . . . ," Kristen went on, " . . . 10."

"Okay, one more time. . . . Charlene?"

"It's the number . . . of . . . groups of 10."

"Yes, excellent. We have made three groups of 10, and this 3," again pointing at the 3 on the chalkboard, "is the number of groups of 10 that we have."

Kristen then continued by asking the students about the 4 on the chalkboard and then had the groups make two groups of 10 cubes and 6 separate ones, discussing the example as she had with the first one.

As you can see, students don't automatically form links between concrete materials and the abstract numerals. An essential part of Kristen's lesson was her questioning that led students to think about the relationship between the cubes and the numerals. This process is difficult for students, but it's critical if they are to understand the connection between abstractions and their experiences. If this link is missing, learning will be incomplete, with the manipulatives and numerals remaining unrelated in students' minds.

Formal Operational Stage (Adolescent to Adult)

Although concrete thinkers are capable of logic, their logical operations are tied to the real and tangible. Formal thinkers, in contrast, can think logically about the real, as well as the hypothetical, and even the impossible. The **formal operational stage** *is characterized by thinking in which the learner can examine abstract problems systematically and generalize about the results.* These abilities open a whole range of possibilities for formal thinkers that were unavailable to those at the concrete operational stage.

For instance, formal thinkers can also solve the problem with the three sticks but would do so by concluding that the problem was of a general type described as "If A is greater than B, and if B is greater than C, then A is greater than C." In generalizing this way, formal thinkers are thinking abstractly, an ability that allows them to use the solution in a variety of problems not tied directly to the three sticks.

2.21
Think again about Karen Johnson's work with her students. Describe a series of questions that she would need to ask to help her students link the abstract formula for density (density = mass/volume) to her demonstration with the cotton.

Formal operational learners can think logically about abstract and hypothetical ideas.

2.22 ▬

Adding and subtracting are considered to be concrete operations in math, whereas finding percentages is not. Using Piaget's ideas, explain the difference.

Formal thinkers also recognize the need to isolate and control variables in forming conclusions. For example, a girl hearing her father say, "I've got to stop drinking so much coffee. I've been sleeping terribly the last few nights," responds, "But, Daddy, maybe that's not it. You've also been bringing work home every night, and you didn't do that before." The girl recognizes that her father's sleeplessness may be caused by extra work, rather than by the coffee, and that they can't tell until they isolate each variable. This example illustrates formal thinking. Let's see what these characteristics look like in classrooms.

Characteristics of Formal Thought.   Flavell (1963, 1985) identified three characteristics of formal thinking:

1. Thinking abstractly
2. Thinking systematically
3. Thinking hypothetically and deductively

Differences between concrete and formal operational thinkers on these dimensions are illustrated in Figure 2.4.

As you can see in the figure, the formal operational learner is willing and able to consider the abstract and hypothetical, as in the question about laws. This ability makes the study of courses such as algebra, in which letters and symbols stand for numbers, meaningful on a different level. To the concrete operational child, $x + 2x = 9$ could be made meaningful only by representing it as a concrete problem:

> *Dave ate a certain number of cookies. His sister ate twice as many.*
> *Together they ate nine. How many did each one eat?*

The formal operational student, in contrast, can think about the equation as an abstract idea that can apply to a myriad of cases. In geometry, students are asked to consider different hypothetical arrangements—for example, "Are the interior angles of congruent triangles always identical?" The ability to use symbols to deal with abstract ideas—a characteristic of formal operational thinking—is central to thinking like a mathematician.

Because much of the content of middle, junior high, and high school curricula is abstract, the transition to formal thinking is very important. For instance, in American history, understanding that the Spanish, British, and French had primarily economic motives in their efforts to colonize the New World requires abstract thinking. Biology students are asked to consider the results of crossing different combinations of dominant and recessive genes. Art students must imagine multiple perspectives and light sources when they create drawings. In the study of literature, students are asked to consider the viewpoints of characters in the stories they read. Curricula are filled with experiences requiring formal operational thought.

The difficulty Karen Johnson's students had in understanding the concept of *density* further illustrates the need for formal thinking. When students are unable to think abstractly and to solve abstract problems, they revert to memorizing what they can or, in frustration, give up altogether.

Because of the direct link between development and learning, you can see how important it is to understand how this link will affect *how* you teach your students. Let's look further at how Piaget's work has influenced current conceptions of teaching and learning.

2.23 ▬
You saw earlier in our discussion that experience is critical for development. This factor has an important implication for teachers of junior high, high school, and even university students. Describe this implication.

Piaget's Theory: Classroom Applications

Influence on Instruction

The influence of Piaget's work on education is so pervasive that teachers take many of its contributions for granted, almost forgetting there was a time when curriculum and teach-

Figure 2.4

A comparison of concrete and formal operational thinking

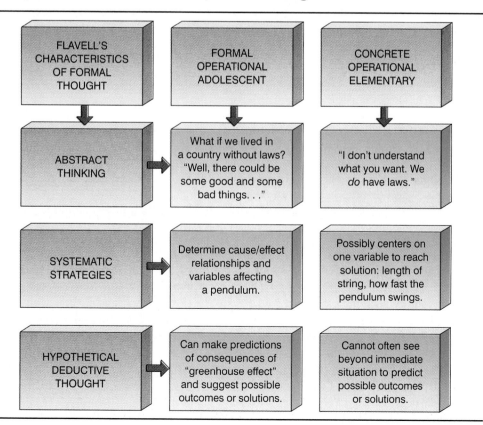

ing were different. Historically, educators emphasized the memorization of long passages for the purpose of training "mental faculties." More recently, students were encouraged to memorize rules and procedures, such as the algorithm for subtracting one two-digit number from another, in the hope that memorization would enable students to apply the rule. Research now suggests that the ability to transfer memorized rules is limited (Porter, 1989). If meaningful learning and transfer are to occur, students need to actively construct the concepts they are learning. Today, in part because of Piaget's work, learning is viewed as an active, constructive process in which students seek organization and meaning in their worlds (we discuss constructivism in more detail later in the chapter).

Influence on Curriculum Development

Because of Piaget's work, curriculum is designed differently than in the past. Lessons are organized with concrete experiences presented first, followed by more abstract and detailed ideas. Memorization is de-emphasized in favor of deeper understanding.

To help their students in the transition from concrete to abstract, we see elementary math teachers armed with beans glued to Popsicle sticks, boxes filled with cubes, and wooden geometric shapes. In reading and language arts, we see emphasis on "language experience" and "whole language" where reading and writing abilities are developed by building on children's experience and naturally developing language instead of memorized words and definitions (May, 1990). Carol Barnhart's vocabulary development activity (on p. 33) was a form of language experience. In social studies, the curriculum begins with a study of children's homes and families and then moves to their neighborhoods, cities, states, and finally to a study of theirs and other nations' cultures (Brophy, 1990; National Council for the Social Studies, 1984). Their neighborhood is concrete and personal, so it is the most appropriate point of departure. The emphasis on hands-on science is also designed to be developmentally appropriate.

Piaget's Theory: Research and Criticism

Research on Piaget's Theory

Research indicates that educators should use caution in applying Piaget's descriptions to any particular student or class; the ages attached to each stage are only approximations, and considerable variation exists within age-groups (Berk, 1994). Further, although his theory suggests that junior high and high school students should be formal thinkers, research indicates that this often is not the case.

Research examining the thinking of middle and junior high school students indicates that junior high students have difficulty isolating and controlling variables, as well as solving other problems that require formal thought (Karplus, Karplus, Formisano, & Paulsen, 1979; Lawson & Snitgren, 1982; Thornton & Fuller, 1981).

Additional research with junior high students reveals similar patterns. For example, consider the balance with the boxes on it shown in Figure 2.5.

Despite the fact that one box is bigger than the other, the balance is "balanced." Seventh graders were shown this demonstration and then were asked to judge the accuracy of the following propositions:

1. The volume of A is greater than the volume of B.
2. The mass of A is greater than the mass of B.
3. The density of A is greater than the density of B.

2.24 ■

Using Piaget's work as a basis, explain why junior high students have difficulty solving problems requiring formal thought.

Figure 2.5

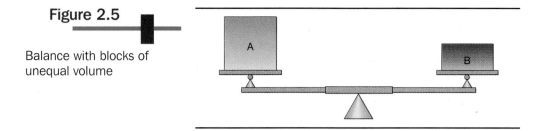

Balance with blocks of unequal volume

The reasoning involved can be described as follows:

> We can see that the volume of A is greater than B; the balance is level, so the masses are equal; because the masses are equal but A's volume is greater, its density is less than B's.

The problem occurs in the present and is tangible; thus, it requires a concrete operational level of thinking. This is confirmed by curriculum writers who commonly present these concepts at the fifth-grade level. The seventh graders, typically 12 or 13 years old, were chronologically at the formal operational stage; they should have been able to solve the problem. Researchers found, however, that the students were still dominated by perceptions, concluding that because A is larger, it must have more mass and also be more dense (Eggen & McDonald, 1987). This finding suggests that the students in the experimental sample were not even reasoning at the concrete operational level, let alone using formal operations.

These findings have important implications for teachers, particularly those in middle and junior high schools. Many students come to these grade levels without the concrete experiences needed to think at the level of abstraction often required. Wise teachers realize that these experiences are lacking and provide these experiences themselves, as Karen Johnson did with her eighth graders. Otherwise, the students will revert to whatever it takes for them to survive—in most cases, memorization without understanding.

2.25
What preoperational characteristic explains why the students would conclude that the bigger box was heavier even though the balance was balanced?

Criticisms of Piaget's Theory

As you've seen in our discussion to this point, Piaget has had an enormous impact on teaching and curriculum development. More recent research, however, has led to criticisms of his ideas:

1. Research indicates that Piaget may have underestimated the abilities of young children because overly abstract directions were used in his studies (Gelman, Meck, & Merkin, 1986).
2. A number of researchers are now questioning Piaget's idea of broad stages of development that affect all types of tasks. For example, research indicates that progression to concrete operational thinking doesn't occur all at once; instead, it begins with conservation of mass and ends with conservation of volume (Bee, 1989). Further, researchers argue that children's logical abilities strongly depend on past experiences and are more dependent on knowledge in a specific area than Piaget suggested (Byrnes, 1988; Overton, 1984; Resnick & Klopfer, 1989). For example, students who are provided appropriate experiences with proportional reasoning problems learn to master the problems, whereas students of the same age who are not provided the experiences may never learn to solve them.

3. Piaget's work is criticized on the grounds that it fails to take cultural differences into account. The role of culture is critical in development. Culture determines the kinds of experiences children have, the values they develop, the language they use, and the way they interact with each other. A description of development that doesn't consider culture is incomplete (P. Miller, 1983).

This concludes our discussion of Piaget's work. In the next section, we consider the contributions that information processing has made to the understanding of student development.

Classroom Connections

Applying an Understanding of Piaget's Views of Development in Your Classroom

1. Provide concrete and personalized examples, particularly when abstract concepts are first introduced.
   - A kindergarten teacher begins her unit on animals by taking her students to the zoo. She plans for most of the time to be spent at the hands-on activities in the petting zoo.
   - A social studies teacher involves his students in a simulated trial to help them understand the American court system. After the trial is over, he has participants discuss the process from their different perspectives.

2. Ask students questions and involve them in discussions to assess their present levels of development.
   - A kindergarten teacher is discussing geometric shapes with his students. Using a flannel board and shapes of different colors and sizes, he asks the students to group them in different ways. After each grouping, he asks the class, "Does that make sense?" At the conclusion of his lesson, he emphasizes that there are many ways to group objects.
   - A science teacher begins a unit on the moon by asking students to explain the phases of the moon by using a flashlight and balls of different sizes. As students explain the different phases, she asks, "Does that make sense?" and encourages other students to ask questions.

3. Expose non-formal-thinking students to the thought processes of more advanced students.
   - A high school math teacher talks about problems at the chalkboard, helping students see how he solves each one. He then encourages students who have solved problems to demonstrate solutions and asks questions that elicit their thinking in the process.
   - A junior high science teacher gives her students a brief pretest at the beginning of the year on formal operational tasks such as controlling variables and doing proportional thinking. She uses this information to group students for cooperative learning projects, placing some formal- and some non-formal-thinking students in the same groups. She encourages students to think aloud when they solve problems and does the same herself at the chalkboard.

4. In the upper elementary, middle, and junior high schools, provide practice in hypothetical reasoning.
   - An eighth-grade algebra teacher is working with factoring polynomials and has the students factor the expression

     $$m^2 + 2m + 1.$$

     She then asks, "What if no 2 appeared in the middle term? Would it still be factorable?"
   - A history class concludes that people often emigrate for economic reasons. The teacher asks, "Consider a family named Fishwiera, who are upper-class Lebanese. What is the likelihood of their immigrating to the United States?"

Information-Processing Views of Development

Piaget made a huge contribution to the understanding of children and their development in helping all of us realize that they aren't miniature adults and that young children and their older counterparts think about the world in different ways. In attempting to describe and explain these changes, researchers found that many of Piaget's concepts were valuable in a general sense but were less helpful in explaining specific, school-related changes in development.

Information-processing descriptions of development grew out of this need for more precise explanations. These descriptions share with Piaget a view of the mind as an active organizer of information; they differ from Piaget in that they attempt to map specific strategies and steps children use when faced with problems (Berk, 1994; Kail & Bisanz, 1992).

Information processing approaches to development *examine differences in children's abilities to acquire, store, and retrieve information for thinking and problem solving.* In addition, information-processing researchers examine the strategies children use to accomplish different learning tasks (Berk, 1994).

The Strategic Learner

At the heart of information-processing descriptions of development is the view of students as strategy users. **Strategies** *are plans for accomplishing learning goals,* such as rehearsing the spellings of a list of words. Remembering how to spell the words is the goal, and rehearsal is the strategy.

As children develop, they acquire an increasing number of strategies, the strategies become more efficient, and they are used more selectively. For example, young children view themselves as passive participants; they don't realize they can influence the learning process (Berk, 1994). Older children, in contrast, understand they have a great deal of control over their own learning. This strategic view of learning influences basic processes such as attention and memory, as you'll see in the next sections.

> **2.26**
> Identify two common strategies that you (and most other university students) use to help you learn.

Meta-Attention: Development of Attention Strategies

Meta-attention *is awareness and control of attention.* Meta-attention is involved when a student turns off a radio because it is interfering with learning or when a student starts taking notes to prevent drifting off during a lecture.

A simple experiment demonstrates students' developing ability to monitor and focus their attention (Lane & Pearson, 1982). Students of differing ages were given cards; some cards had circles on them, and others had triangles. The students were then directed to sort the cards into two piles, and the experimenters timed them to see how fast they could complete the sorting. To study children's ability to eliminate distractions (one important aspect of attention), the experimenters put differing amounts of irrelevant stimuli, such as stars and other shapes, on the cards in addition to the circles and triangles. Older children and adults had little trouble in screening out the irrelevant information; younger children (e.g., ages 6 to 9) took nearly 10 times longer to sort the cards. The younger children had not developed the ability to screen out distractions and to focus their attention on key aspects of the task.

Research on meta-attention reveals that older children differ from their younger, less-developed counterparts in at least three ways:

> **2.27**
> Suppose you are sitting toward the back of a large class. Because you find yourself frequently "drifting off," you move to the front row. Explain how this illustrates meta-attention.

1. They are more aware of the role of attention in learning.
2. They are better at ignoring distracting or irrelevant stimuli.
3. They are better at directing their attention toward important information (Berk, 1994).

Although meta-attention appears to develop naturally during the school years, direct effort by teachers can enhance it (P. Miller, 1985). Let's look at how this is done with first graders.

> Mrs. Meese began by saying, "We know how important it is to pay attention." She then modeled attention by focusing on a sample seatwork assignment, working carefully and keeping her eyes on the paper.
>
> Then she had Mrs. Morton, her parent volunteer, talk, and she listened intently to Mrs. Morton, maintaining eye contact and keeping her hands and body still. She next modeled inattention in both an interactive and a seatwork situation.
>
> She then asked, "Now, am I paying attention?" as she modeled inattention to seatwork by gazing out the window and playing with objects on her desk. She demonstrated several more examples, had the students classify them as attention or inattention, and then told the students, "I am going to click the 'cricket,' and if you're paying attention each time I click it, make an X in a box." She showed the students a sheet of paper with several boxes drawn on it and passed each student a sheet. She went on, "Each time you hear a click, put an X in the next box if you're paying attention."
>
> The next morning and for several consecutive mornings, Mrs. Meese demonstrated and had students demonstrate attentive and inattentive behaviors as part of the class routine. As time went on, the students' attention improved markedly. (based on Hallahan et al., 1983)

2.28

On which aspect of meta-attention was Mrs. Meese primarily focusing?

Young children often don't understand when they're inattentive, and this awareness needs to be developed. Over time and with the teacher's assistance, meta-attention increases, and students can begin the process of becoming self-regulated learners.

Metamemory: Development of Memory Strategies

An 8-year old is describing her strategy for remembering a telephone number:

> Say the number is 663–8854. Then what I'd do is say that my number is 663, so I won't have to remember that really. And then I would think now I've got to remember 88. Now I'm 8 years old, so I can remember, say, my age two times. Then I say how old my brother is, and how old he was last year. And that's how I'd usually remember that phone number. [Interviewer: Is that how you would most often remember a phone number?] Well, usually I write it down. (Kreutzer, Leonard, & Flavell, 1975, p. 11)

Information-processing researchers have also found that developmental differences exist in **metamemory,** *which is knowledge about and regulation of memory strategies.* The 8-year-old describing how she would remember a telephone number used a sophisticated memory strategy, linking the abstract numbers to information that was already encoded in her memory.

Research documents that older children and adults are much better than young children at using strategies for remembering information and that these strategies result in improved learning (E. Short, Schatschneider, & Friebert, 1993). In investigating these developmental patterns, researchers found, for example, that nursery school students didn't use rehearsal as a strategy when they were given a list of objects to memorize in order. Fourth graders, in contrast, not only rehearsed aloud but also anticipated succeeding items by naming them before they were shown by the experimenter (Flavell, Friedrichs, & Hoyt, 1970). Experiments in which categorical organization could be used to enhance recall indicate similar patterns. Preschool children don't categorize; fourth graders categorize and rearrange the lists. The same is true of imagery: Kindergartners can't use it effectively, but fourth graders can and do. In each case, differences in performance can be linked to specific use of strategies (Berk, 1994).

In addition to differences in strategy usage per se, older students are also more aware of the limitations of their memory. For example, when asked to predict how many objects, such as a shoe or ball, they could remember from a list, nursery school students predicted 7; when tested, they remembered fewer than 4 (Flavell et al., 1970). Adults given the same task predicted an average of 5.9 and actually remembered 5.5 (Yussen & Levy, 1975). These examples illustrate not only differences in memory capacities but also differences in students' awareness of them.

The development of metamemory in students is important because metamemory provides them with an arsenal of learning strategies that can be used in learning and remembering new information. As with meta-attention, teachers should help students become aware of their memory capacities and the importance of matching strategies to learning tasks. For simple tasks, such as remembering to tell a parent about a phone message, simple strategies, such as writing a note, are enough. For more complex classroom tasks, more sophisticated strategies are required.

2.29
Most college and university students take notes as a strategy. Does note taking better illustrate meta-attention or metamemory? Explain.

The development of metamemory allows learners to monitor their own learning and adjust learning strategies to the task at hand.

Information Processing: Instructional Implications

An information-processing view of development has a number of implications for class-room teachers. First, because of the precision of the approach, it has been able to specify a number of areas in which developmental differences exist. Attention and memory are two of these areas; others include metacomprehension and metacommunication, wherein students become aware of and learn to control their comprehension and communication processes. Because of its focus on strategy development, information processing identifies specific areas in which instructional efforts can be targeted. Perhaps most important, it makes educators aware of the fact that learners should be strategic; with this awareness, educators may be more likely to consciously teach strategies in their classrooms.

The goal for teachers at all levels should be the development of self-regulated, strategic learners who take responsibility for their own learning. Teachers can use this view of development to assess the strategies that students are currently using and to provide them with more efficient strategies. We examine ways of doing this in Chapters 7 and 8 when we continue our discussion of information processing and the strategic learner.

2.30
Suppose you're a third-grade teacher. Identify a strategy you might use to help your students better understand what they read. Describe specifically how you would teach the strategy.

A Sociocultural View of Development: The Work of Lev Vygotsky

An alternative to Piaget's theory and information-processing views of development comes from a Russian psychologist, Lev Vygotsky, who emphasized the critical role of culture and society in human development. As a boy, he was instructed by private tutors who used Socratic dialogue to transmit information and to clarify ideas (Kozulin, 1990). These sessions, combined with his study of literature and experience as a teacher, convinced him of the importance of two factors in human development: language and activity in social interactions (Vygotsky, 1978, 1986). These two ideas are his most powerful contributions to the field of human development.

Language: A Vehicle for Development and a Tool for Thinking

Language is central to Vygotsky's theory of development (Vygotsky, 1978). It allows people to learn from others and provides access to the knowledge that others already know. The ability to speak provides people with cognitive tools that allow them to think about the world and to solve problems. It is the key difference between humans and other living things.

> "Okay, here we go. Let's get dressed so we can go visit Grandma. First, we take off your pajamas and put on your underwear. Wow, these pajamas are tight. Next, we put on your shirt. There. Then your big boys, and now your pants. Look at those little doggies on the pants."
>
> "Doggy?"
>
> "Yes, those are doggies. Aren't they cute. Ruff, ruff! Grrr! Now we put on this sock. Then your shoe. Now you do the other one."
>
> "Shoe?"
>
> "Yes, that's a shoe. Wait a minute, though. What do we have to put on before the shoe? Look over here" (pointing to the sock). "That's right, first you put on your sock, then your shoe."

"Sock first?"

"Yeah, that's right. Put on your sock first, then your shoe. Atta boy!"

When people learn language, they aren't just learning words; they also are learning the ideas connected with those words, as in the exchange above. When a child learns the word *doggie,* he or she doesn't just learn how to pronounce it, but instead begins the process of learning a wealth of other ideas connected to doggie (e.g., doggies are warm, they lick your hand, pictures of doggies sometime appear on pants). In this sense, language becomes a "cultural tool kit" that children can carry around in their heads to help them make sense of the world. The acquisition of language facilitates cognitive development and provides children with a vehicle to produce, test, and refine their thoughts about the world. You saw this with the father teaching his son how to dress. Language provides opportunities for the sharing and refinement of ideas.

2.31
In mainstream American culture, the concept of *snow* is a relatively simple idea, whereas for Eskimos, there are many terms for the concept of *snow*. This difference illustrates what idea that was discussed in this section?

Language, Social Interaction, and Activity

Language serves another function in development. It allows a child to interact with other people and to begin the process of cultural exchange, or the trading of ideas between people. Vygotsky believed that culture plays an important role in people's development and that social interaction is the major way culture is shared and transmitted. You saw earlier how language provides children with a cultural tool kit; social interaction is the way the tool kit is filled. It is the way ideas are exchanged and refined.

Adults—particularly parents and other caregivers—and peers both play an important role in the process of cultural transmission. Adults explain, give directions, provide feedback, and facilitate the process of communication (Rogoff, 1990). Children use conversation to cooperatively solve problems both in play and in the classroom. This interaction allows the exchange of information and feedback about the validity of existing ideas.

The concept of *activity* is central to Vygotsky's theory. Children literally learn by doing—by becoming involved in meaningful activities with more knowledgeable people. Activity provides a framework in which dialogue can occur. The child says "Sock" after hearing his father say it, and this guides his actions as he gets dressed. Through dialogue driven by activity, ideas are naturally exchanged and development occurs.

2.32
Some educators believe that non-native English-speaking students should be immersed in "English only" programs as soon as possible. On the basis of the information in this section, how effective are those programs likely to be? Explain.

Language: A Tool for Self-Regulation and Reflection

In addition to helping people think about the world and communicate with others, language serves a third role in development: It provides people the means to reflect on and regulate their own thinking.

All of us talk to ourselves. For example, we grumble when we're frustrated or angry, "Now where did I put those x%#* keys? I'm going to be late to work." We also talk to ourselves when we're in an uncertain situation (e.g., "Oh no, a flat tire. Now what? Let's see. I hope the jack is in the trunk. Yeah. I'd better loosen the nuts before I jack up the car.") Children also talk to themselves; walk into a preschool or kindergarten during free play time and you'll hear muttering that appears to have no specific audience. Vygotsky believed that this free-floating external speech was the precursor of internalized, private speech.

Private speech *is self-talk that guides thinking and action.* Piaget (1926) observed it in young children and termed it "egocentric speech," reflecting his belief that it was a by-product of the preoperational child's inability to consider the perspectives of others. To Piaget, egocentric speech was an indication of cognitive immaturity, of not being aware of the need to target an audience.

2.33

Suppose you have assigned your second graders a series of word problems in math. As they work, you hear audible muttering about the problems. What might you infer on the basis of these mutterings? Would you expect similar mutterings if you were teaching sixth graders?

Vygotsky interpreted private speech differently. He believed that these seemingly targetless mutterings were the beginnings of private, inner speech and that this type of language played an important role in the development of self-regulation. Private speech, first muttered aloud and then internalized, forms the foundation for complex cognitive skills such as sustaining attention ("I better pay attention now. This is important."), memorizing new information ("If I repeat the number to myself, I'll be able to remember it."), and problem solving ("Hmm, what should I do first?").

Research supports Vygotsky's functional view of private speech. Children use more of it when tasks are difficult or when they are confused about how to proceed (Berk, 1994). In addition, children who use private speech during problem-solving tasks are more attentive and goal oriented and show more improvement in performance than their less talkative peers (Behrend, Rosengren, & Perlmutter, 1992). Finally, as Vygotsky predicted, private speech becomes internalized with age, converted from overt mutterings to whispers and lip movements.

Vygotsky's Work: Instructional Applications

Vygotsky's theory of development emphasizes the importance of language in learning that occurs in activity-oriented, social situations. By using language, more knowledgeable partners share their expertise about the world. Instructional strategies based on Vygotsky's theory place students in situations where the topics discussed are within the developmental grasp of the learner. This leads us to his concept called the *zone of proximal development.*

Zone of Proximal Development

The **zone of proximal development** *is the level of proficiency beyond what a child can do alone and represents the range of tasks that can be accomplished when assisted by a competent adult or peer.* Beyond the zone of proximal development, the child can accomplish tasks unaided; within the zone, additional assistance is necessary for successful accomplishment of tasks; below the zone, additional assistance still does not result in success. The zone represents a range of tasks in which a teacher can productively assist in learner development. Let's see what the zone of proximal development looks like in a classroom.

> Jeff Malone, a student intern, was working with a small group of students on percentage problems in math. He began by presenting the three students with a sample percentage problem and observing their work. Sandra zipped through the problem in no time; Javier struggled, muttering to himself; Stewart gave up and sat with his arms folded, a frown on his face.
>
> Instead of explaining the procedure to Javier and Stewart, as he had done in the past when students had difficulty, Jeff tried a different approach.
>
> "Let's see how we compute percentages in problems like this. Sandra, why don't you explain to us how you did the first problem," he said. "The rest of us will follow along, and then I'll ask someone else to do the next one."
>
> Sandra started, "Okay, the problem asks what percentage of the video games are on sale. Now, when I see a problem like this, I think, how can I make a fraction? After I make a fraction, then I make a decimal out of it and then make a percent. Yeah, that's what I'll do, so here's what I do first."
>
> As she continued to think aloud, Stewart and Javier followed along.
>
> On the next problem, Jeff actively involved the two who were having problems. "Javier and Stewart, follow along with me and help me solve this problem."
>
> *Joseph raised gerbils to sell to the pet store. He had 12 gerbils and sold 9 to the pet store. What percentage did he sell?*

Students differed in ability, but benefited from instruction

"The first thing," Jeff continued, "I need to find out is what fraction he sold. Now, why do I need to find a fraction? . . . Javier?"

"To . . . then . . . if . . . once we get a fraction, we can make a decimal and then a percent."

"Good," Jeff smiled. "What fraction did he sell?"

" . . . Nine . . . twelfths."

"Excellent, Javier. Now, Stewart, how might we make a decimal out of the fraction?"

" . . . "

"Look again at the fraction. What is it?"

" . . . Nine twelfths."

"Good. So, to find a decimal, we divide the twelve into what number? Go ahead and give it a try."

As Jeff watched, he saw that Javier quickly got .75. Stewart, however, began hesitantly, appearing confused by dividing a large number into a smaller one.

You can see how this episode relates to Vygotsky's theory. First, the students differed in their ability to benefit from instruction. Sandra was beyond the zone for percentage problems; she required no additional help. Stewart was below the lower limit; he was unable to perform the task even with Jeff's help. Javier was in the zone, as indicated by his ability to solve the problem with help from Jeff and Sandra. The zone represents a learning situation in which teachers, working with students, can promote development (Walsh, 1991).

Jeff also attempted to take advantage of inner speech as a tool for instruction by having Sandra think aloud. This task not only made her tacit problem-solving procedures observable but also provided a model the other students could follow.

Applying the Zone of Proximal Development to Teaching

Applying the zone of proximal development to teaching involves three tasks: assessing, selecting learning activities, and providing instructional support to help students move through the zone successfully. Let's look at these tasks.

The first task is to assess. As Jeff worked with the students, he *gauged their ability to understand a realistic problem,* a process called **dynamic assessment** (Spector, 1992). Reasoning ability, background knowledge, and interest and tolerance for ambiguity all influence a learner's zone of proximal development (Winn, 1992), and as Jeff worked with the students, he was able to assess each.

The second task is to fit the learning tasks to the developmental levels of the students. If the tasks are too easy, instruction is unnecessary; if they're too difficult, students become confused and frustrated. Jeff, for example, would need to simplify the task for Stewart and increase the challenge for Sandra in his next session.

In addition to selecting the tasks, the teacher must determine how they will be presented to students. The goal of this process is shared understanding. **Shared understanding** *occurs when the teacher and students have a common understanding of the task.* Shared understanding is important because it marks a beginning point for development through joint problem solving. The teacher can ensure this shared understanding in at least two ways. First, the task can be embedded in a meaningful context. Instead of presenting math problems in the abstract, for example, the teacher relates them to students' lives; rather than teaching writing as disengaged communication, a teacher has students write letters to friends and relatives and compose stories about their experiences. Second, shared understanding can be accomplished with dialogue that helps students analyze the problems they face. Jeff used questioning to help his students see how percentage problems could be solved by means of a fraction algorithm.

The third task is to provide instructional support. This is accomplished by applying the concept of *scaffolding,* which we discuss in the next section.

2.34 ▬

Suppose you are unsuccessfully trying to learn a new word-processing program on your computer. A friend comes over. You're fine with her help, but after she leaves, you again run into problems. Are you below, in, or beyond the zone of proximal development? In which of these three areas is your friend?

2.35 ▬

Identify the questions Jeff asked in his attempt to accomplish *shared understanding* with the students.

Scaffolding: Interactive Instructional Support.

A toddler is learning to walk. As she takes her first tentative steps, her father walks behind her, holding both hands above her head as she lurches forward with uncertain steps. As she gains confidence, the father holds only one hand, walking to the side, keeping an eye out for toys and other objects that could trip her. After a while, he lets go but continues at his daughter's side to catch her if she falls. When the child becomes tired or the terrain gets bumpy, Dad grabs her hand to make sure she doesn't fall and skin a knee. Eventually, his daughter will both walk and run on her own. (Adapted from Cazden, 1988)

This father has provided scaffolding for his daughter as she learns to walk. In an educational setting, **scaffolding** *is assistance that allows students to complete tasks they are not able to complete independently.* Scaffolding helps learners move through the zone of proximal development by enabling them to eventually complete tasks independently. Effective scaffolding is responsive to learners' needs; it adjusts the requirements to the learners's level of performance (Rosenshine & Meister, 1992). When learners need more help, the teacher steps in; when less help is required, the teacher steps back to allow learners to progress on their own.

Instructional scaffolding is a metaphor for the scaffolding that workers use as they construct a building. An instructional scaffold provides support to the learner. In the example of learning to walk, the father provided both literal and figurative support to his daughter. In classrooms, teachers provide scaffolding by breaking content into manageable pieces, modeling skills, providing practice with prompts, and letting go when the student is ready. The scaffold functions as a tool for students, helping them learn new skills, much as an actual scaffold supports workers as they complete construction work, painting, or plastering. The scaffold extends the range of learners, allowing them to accomplish tasks otherwise impossible. If children were faced with learning to walk with no intermedi-

Teachers provide individualized scaffolding for students through their numerous personal interactions during the day.

The Student 57

Table 2.3

Types of instructional scaffolds

Type of scaffolding	Example
Modeling	An art teacher demonstrates drawing with two-point perspective before asking students to try a new drawing on their own.
Think aloud	A physics teacher verbalizes her thinking as she solves momentum problems at the chalkboard.
Questions	After modeling and thinking aloud, the same physics teacher "walks" students through several problems, asking them questions at critical junctures.
Adapting instructional materials	An elementary physical education teacher lowers the basket while teaching shooting techniques and then raises it as students become proficient.
Prompts and cues	Preschoolers are taught "The bunny goes around the hole and then jumps into it" as they learn to tie their shoelaces.

ate props, such as a parent or even furniture to pull themselves up on, their development would be delayed because of a lack of scaffolding. Similarly, some classroom tasks are so formidable that they cannot be accomplished without a teacher's support along the way.

This is where skilled teachers are essential. They should provide *enough but no more* support than necessary to allow learners to complete tasks on their own. The scaffold supports the painter, but the painter does the painting. Similarly, the teacher provides instructional support, but the learner completes the task. If teachers provide too much support, learners fail to grow and move out on their own; if the challenge is too great, learners may fail and become discouraged. Effective scaffolding must be flexible and adapt to students' needs as they move through the zone of proximal development.

Types of Instructional Scaffolding. Teachers can provide instructional scaffolding in a number of ways. Some of these are listed in Table 2.3

One of the most common forms of scaffolding is teacher *modeling*. By demonstrating how to solve problems, teachers provide students with concrete examples of experts at work. Effective teachers also *think aloud* as they model the process. This technique provides students with access to their teacher's thinking as they wrestle with problems themselves. When students struggle to solve their own problems, teachers can use *questions* to provide assistance, focus attention, and suggest alternatives.

In addition to interactive forms of scaffolding, teachers can provide support through *adapting instructional materials.* One form of adaptation is to vary the demands of the task (Rosenshine & Meister, 1992). For example, when teaching students to ask questions about the material they are reading, the teacher can first focus on generating questions about a single sentence and then paragraphs and finally entire passages (Palincsar, 1987).

Instructional scaffolding can also occur through written or verbal *prompts and cues.* For example, Figure 2.6 provides a written set of cues—a scaffold—to help students organize their thoughts before beginning a writing assignment. The intent is that the scaffold will be removed when students internalize the process.

2.36
The distinction between *scaffolding* and simply *explaining* is subtle but important. What is the key characteristic of scaffolding that makes it different from simple explaining?

This concludes our discussion of Vygotsky's description of development. Having studied both Piaget and Vygotsky, we now move to an examination of constructivism, a view of learning and development embedded in their work.

Constructivism: A Developmentally Based View of Teaching and Learning

The study of development, learning, and teaching is going through something close to a revolution, and the learner is at the center of this change. Constructivism suggests that the

Figure 2.6

Cues to aid in a writing assignment

Planning to Write

Name _____   Date _____

TOPIC _____

Who: Whom am I writing for?

_____

_____

_____

Why: Why am I writing this?

_____

_____

What: What do I know? (Brainstorm)

1. _____
2. _____
3. _____
4. _____

How: How can I group my ideas?

_____   _____

_____   _____

_____   _____

How will I organize my ideas?

_____ Comparison/Contrast   _____ Problem/Solution

_____ Explanation   _____ Other

Source: Adapted from Englert, Raphael, and Anderson (1989).

learner's understanding of the way the world works is the result of his or her own active construction, rather than someone else's presentation. **Constructivism** *is a view of learning that says learners use their experiences to actively construct understandings that makes sense to them, rather than have understanding delivered to them in already organized form.*

> Constructivists believe that knowledge is the result of individual constructions of reality. From their perspective, learning occurs through the continual creation of rules and hypotheses to explain what is observed. The need to create new rules and formulate new hypotheses occurs when the student's present conceptions of reality are thrown out of balance by disparities between those conceptions and new observations. (J. Brooks, 1990, p. 68)

Constructivism emphasizes active learners, the linking of new knowledge to knowledge learners already possess, and the application of understanding to authentic situations (Good & Brophy, 1994). Direct experience and the interaction between teachers and students and students with each other are instructional tools for constructivists.

Piaget's and Vygotsky's Views of Knowledge Construction

Although they disagreed on some points, Piaget and Vygotsky were both constructivist in their orientation (Fowler, 1994). Some of these differences are outlined in Table 2.4.

As you can see in Table 2.4, Piaget more strongly emphasized each individual's creation of new knowledge, whereas Vygotsky focused on the transmission of the tools of knowledge—namely, culture and language (Fowler, 1994; Rogoff, 1990). Regardless of philosophical differences, however, all views of constructivism imply that teachers need to go beyond lecturing and "telling" as teaching methods and to move toward "structuring reflective discussions of the meanings and implications of content and providing opportunities for students to use the content as they engage in inquiry, problem solving, or decision making" (Good & Brophy, 1994, p. 415).

> **2.37**
> Which view provides for the more prominent role for teachers?

Table 2.4

A comparison of Piaget's and Vygotsky's views of knowledge construction

	Piaget	Vygotsky
Basic question	How is new knowledge created in all cultures?	How are the tools of knowledge transmitted in a specific culture?
Role of language	Aids in developing symbolic thought; It does not qualitatively raise the level of intellectual functioning. (The level of functioning is raised by action.)	Is an essential mechanism for thinking, cultural transmission, and self-regulation. Qualitatively raises the level of intellectual functioning.
Social interaction	Provides a way to test and validate schemes.	Provides an avenue for acquiring language and the cultural exchange of ideas.
View of learners	Active in manipulating objects and ideas.	Active in social contexts and interactions.
Instructional implications	Design experiences to disrupt equilibrium.	Provide scaffolding. Guide interaction.

Applying Constructivist Ideas in Teaching

To illustrate these ideas, let's look again at Karen Johnson as she worked with her students. First, she found that they had a limited, and in some cases inaccurate, understanding of the concept of *density*. For example, most of Karen's students believed, on the basis of their experience with the "thickness" of oil, that vegetable oil is more dense than water.

Then, Karen combined elements of constructivism in her teaching by having the students measure the densities of oil and water: They placed equal volumes on balances and discussed the results in detail. This approach provided the direct experience and the opportunity for individual constructions that Piaget would seem to suggest, as well as the use of language and social interaction that Vygotsky advocates. Constructing understanding that made sense to the students was illustrated in Calvin's connection between water being more dense than oil and the fact that oil floats on water. The evolving nature of constructed understanding was illustrated as students, on the basis of the experiences Karen provided for them, linked population density and the "density" of a screen to their understanding of the density of cotton, water and oil, and wood.

As you can see from our discussion, constructivism is a powerful idea. It helps teachers better understand Piaget's and Vygotsky's work and how it can be applied in classrooms. It has important implications for both development and learning. It suggests that teachers provide experiences, guide discussions, and assume a supportive role in the process of students' attempts at developing understanding.

Teaching based on constructivist principles is demanding and requires a great deal of expertise (A. Brown, 1994). For instance, Karen had to provide the experiences with the cotton, water and oil, and wood, and she had to be alert and flexible enough in her own thinking to capitalize on students' thoughts and insights when they surfaced in the discussions. A less alert teacher might have missed opportunities to help the students move through the zone of proximal development—as illustrated in Calvin's and Donelle's questions and comments. Worse yet, a less effective teacher might ignore or disapprove of their reactions. With effort and practice, however, teachers can learn to guide student learning and help develop both the thinking and the deep understanding of content you saw in Karen's classroom. We return to constructivism in later chapters to discuss specific implications for instruction, motivation, and even assessment.

2.38

Describe an approach to teaching that would be consistent and another approach that would be inconsistent with constructivism.

Classroom Connections

Applying an Understanding of Information-Processing Approaches to Development in Your Classroom

1. Teach students about the role of attention in learning.
   - A fourth-grade teacher plays an attention game with his students. During a lesson, he'll quietly say, "I want to see who's paying attention. Raise your hand if you are. Good, Billy is. Halima is. Now, next time let's see if all of us can do it."

   - A social studies teacher tries to teach attention-monitoring skills by saying, "Suppose you're reading and the book states that there are three important differences between capitalism and socialism. What should you do?"

2. Model metamemory for your students.
   - A ninth-grade economics teacher says, "Whenever I read something new, I always ask myself, 'How does this relate to what I've been studying?' For example, How is the liberal economic agenda different from the conservative economic agenda?"
   - A chemistry teacher, in trying to help his students remember the symbols for elements in the periodic table, asks students to volunteer mnemonic devices and images they use.

Applying Vygotsky's Descriptions of Development in Your Classroom

3. Use meaningful activity as an organizing theme for your curriculum.
   - A third-grade teacher structures a unit on weather around a daily recording of the weather conditions at her school. Each day, students observe the temperature, clouds, and precipitation; record the data on a calendar; graph it by using strips of paper; and compare it to the weather report in the paper.
   - A middle school social studies teacher tries to help his students understand political polls and the election process. Prior to a national election, he has students poll their parents and peers. Students then have a class election and compare their results with the national one.

4. Use scaffolding to help students progress through the zone of proximal development.
   - When her students are first learning to print, a primary teacher initially provides dotted outlines of letters for the students and half lines to help them gauge size. Gradually, these aids are removed.
   - A middle school teacher helps her students learn to prepare lab reports by doing a lab with the whole class and writing it up as a class activity. Later, she only provides an outline with the essential categories in it. Finally, she only reminds them to follow the proper format.

Applying an Understanding of Constructivism in Your Classroom

5. Provide concrete experiences that allow students to construct their own meaningful concepts.
   - An art teacher begins a unit on perspective by showing slides, displaying works from other students, and sharing her own work. As students turn in their products, she shares them with the class and asks the class to discuss how perspective contributed to each drawing.
   - To help his students understand the "process" of history, a history teacher asks them to write a "history" of some local event or phenomenon. He asks the students to find primary sources, interview people, and present their findings in writing.

6. Embed important concepts in authentic learning tasks.
   - A second-grade teacher teaches graphing by having the students graph class attendance. Information is recorded for both boys and girls, the figures are kept for several weeks, and patterns are discussed.
   - Students in a high school biology class adopt a local stream as a project for a study of ecology. They study stream conditions and identify local polluters. They share this information by writing to local newspapers and politicians.

7. Structure classroom tasks to encourage student interaction.
   - After students complete an experiment, their fourth-grade teacher has them verbally describe their observations and conclusions. When they disagree, she encourages detailed discussion of the differences and guides them to valid explanations.
   - An English teacher uses cooperative learning groups to discuss the literature the class is studying. The teacher asks each group to respond to a list of prepared questions and to share their conclusions with the class.

Language Development

A miracle occurs in the time from birth to 5 years of age. Born with a limited ability to communicate, the young child enters kindergarten with an impressive command of the language spoken at home. Kindergartners have vocabularies of thousands of words and can carry on conversations in complex sentences with adults and peers. How all this occurs is closely related to both Piaget's and Vygotsky's views of development. For Piaget, social interaction is a way of testing the validity of schemes, and social interaction can't occur without language. Language is at the core of Vygotsky's theory, essential to thought and action.

Theories of Language Acquisition

Psychologists who study the growth and development of human language have differing views of how language is acquired. The behaviorist position (Skinner, 1953, 1957) describes language learning as an increase in discrete behaviors resulting from reinforcement. Social cognitive theory (Bandura, 1977, 1986) places heavy emphasis on parent modeling and the child's imitation of adult speech. Psycholinguistic theories (Chomsky, 1972) assert that all humans are genetically "wired" to learn language and that exposure to language triggers this development. Let's take a look at these different theories.

Behaviorist Theories

Behaviorists explain language learning as the acquisition of specific behaviors that are reinforced by the environment. The child gurgles, parents ooh and aah, and the child figures out that the way to make his or her parents jump up and down and say strange things is to make funny sounds. Over time, certain sounds are reinforced whereas others are not, and language develops. For instance,

A 1½-year-old picks up a ball and says, "Baa."

Mom smiles broadly and says, "Good boy! Ball."

The little boy repeats, "Baa."

Mom responds, "Very good."

As you can see, interaction between child and parent is an essential component of behaviorist theories of learning.

Social Cognitive Theory

Social cognitive theory emphasizes the role of parent modeling, the child's imitation, and an adult's reinforcement and corrective feedback (Bandura, 1977, 1986).

"Give Daddy some cookie."

"Cookie, Dad."

"Good. Giselle gives Daddy some cookie."

Children learn language by hearing it spoken by others, by trying it out themselves, and by receiving praise or corrective feedback about their efforts. Social cognitive theory stresses the importance of observational learning in social interactions—thus the name. (We examine social cognitive theory in detail in Chapter 6.)

2.39
Children who grow up in bilingual families typically learn to speak both languages. Which approach—*behaviorism* or *social cognitive theory*—better explains this phenomenon? Why?

Through language embedded in meaningful activity, adults transmit important ideas in the culture to children.

Both behaviorism and social cognitive theory make intuitive sense. Children probably do learn certain aspects of language by observing and listening to others, trying it out themselves, and being reinforced. Scientists who have studied the development of languages in different cultures, however, believe something else is occurring.

Psycholinguistic Theories

Ms. Shin smiled as she watched the group of eager kindergartners wave their hands during show-and-tell.

"Antonio, do you want to tell us what your parents do?"

"He nurses at the hospital."

"He nurses at the hospital? Good. What does he do?"

"He fixes sick people."

"Oh, he's a nurse who fixes sick people. He helps the doctor make people feel better. That's a good job. Who else wants to tell us what their parents do?"

Virtually all humans learn to speak, and despite diversity, all languages share a basic form, such as subject-verb sentence structure, called *language universals* (Faw & Belkin, 1989). In addition, children pass through basically the same age-related stages when learning these diverse languages.

Noam Chomsky (1972), the father of psycholinguistic theories of language development, hypothesized that an innate, genetically driven language acquisition device (LAD) predisposes children to learn a new language. According to Chomsky, the **LAD** *is a genetic set of language-processing skills that enables children to understand the rules governing others' speech and to use these in their own speech.* When children are exposed to language, this program analyzes speech patterns for the rules of grammar—such as the subject after a verb when asking a question—that govern a language. The LAD explains why children are so good at producing sentences they have never heard before. For example,

2.40 ▬
Explain why behaviorists and social cognitive theorists have trouble explaining these original constructions.

Antonio said, "He nurses at the hospital" and "He fixes sick people." Both behaviorists and social cognitive theorists have trouble explaining these original constructions.

Chomsky's position is not without its critics, however. Most developmental psychologists believe that language is learned through a combination of factors that include both an inborn predisposition, as Chomsky proposed, and environmental factors that shape the specific form of the language. These environmental factors explain how different languages and dialects are learned, as well as why some home environments are better for language acquisition than others (D. Walker, Greenwood, Hart, & Corta, 1994). In addition, increased emphasis is being placed on the child as active participant in language learning (Genishi, 1992). This constructivist view of language learning emphasizes the importance of experience and interaction with others in a child's language development. Let's look at this view.

A Constructivist View of Language Development

As you saw earlier, language is central to Vygotsky's theory of cognitive development. It allows social interaction and provides a vehicle for both the transmission of culture and the internal regulation of cognitive processes. Vygotsky's theory also provides insights into the process of language development itself.

Activity is central to Vygotsky's theory of development. Children literally learn by doing, and language is no exception. Children learn language by using it in their interactions with adults and peers. As they interact with others, they use and practice language. Language development appears effortless because it is embedded in the everyday process of communication.

In helping young children learn to speak, adults adjust their speech to operate within the children's zone of proximal development (Bruner, 1985). Baby talk and "motherese" use simple words, short sentences, and voice inflections to simplify messages and to highlight important aspects of a message. These alterations in speech provide a form of linguistic scaffolding that facilitates communication.

Let's see why this linguistic scaffolding works. First, communication revolves around activities that are meaningful to participants. For example, the child wants a cookie or is unhappy about something, and language provides a medium for communication with the other. Both participants have a stake in the process. The more knowledgeable partner adapts language to fit the capabilities of the child, raising the ante by using bigger words and more complex sentences as the child becomes more capable. Children develop as they acquire more complex language skills. Teachers and other adults promote language development through interactions that encourage children's use of language and through feedback and expanding on children's use of language (Arnold, Lonigan, Whitehurst, & Epstein, 1994).

2.41 ■
Describe specifically how constructivist views of language development are different from each of the other three views that have been discussed. Which of the other three views is most closely related to constructivist views?

Stages of Language Acquisition

A parent listened one morning at breakfast while her 6-year-old and her 3-year-old were discussing the relative dangers of forgetting to feed the goldfish versus overfeeding the goldfish:

6-year-old:	"It's worse to forget to feed them."
3-year-old:	"No, it's badder to feed them too much."
6-year-old:	"You don't say badder, you say worser."

3-year-old:	"But it's baddest to give them too much food."
6-year-old:	"No it's not. It's worsest to forget to feed them."
	(Bee, 1989, p. 276)

Children pass through a series of stages as they learn to talk. In the process, they make errors, and their speech is an imperfect version of adult language. Most important, however, are the huge strides they make. Understanding this progress helps teachers make the best possible decisions as they interact with students to promote language growth.

Early Language: Building the Foundation

Learning to speak actually begins in the cradle when "Ooh" and "Aah" and "Such a smart baby!" are used to encourage the infant's gurgling and cooing. These interactions lay the foundation for future language development by teaching the child that communication is a reciprocal process between human beings.

The first words occur between ages 1 and 2 when the child uses holophrases to convey meaning. **Holophrases** *are one- and two-word utterances that carry as much meaning for the child as complete sentences.* For example,

"Momma car."	That's Momma's car.
"Banana."	I want a banana.
"No go!"	Don't leave me alone with this scary baby-sitter!

During this stage, the child also uses intonation to convey meaning. For example, the same word said differently has a very different message for the parent:

"Cookie."	That's a cookie.
"Cookie!"	I want a cookie.

This intonation is significant; it indicates that the child is beginning to use language as a functional tool.

Two patterns—overgeneralization and undergeneralization—creep into speech at this stage and stay with the child through the other stages. **Overgeneralization** *occurs when a child uses a word to refer to a broader class of objects than is appropriate* (Faw & Belkin, 1989). This occurs, for example, when *car* is used to refer not only to cars but also to buses and trains.

Undergeneralization is harder to detect. **Undergeneralization** *occurs when a child uses a word too narrowly,* such as *kitty* used only for a child's cat but not for cats in general. Both overgeneralization and undergeneralization are normal aspects of language development, and most instances are corrected through normal listening and talking. Sometimes a parent or teacher may intervene to clear up a misconception, such as, "No, spiders aren't really insects. See how they have eight legs instead of six?"

Notice here how closely language development relates to the development of schemes or mental structures in children. Overgeneralization occurs when children inappropriately assimilate new information into an already-existing structure; undergeneralization occurs when they overaccommodate. A variety of concrete experiences plus interaction with adults and peers helps young children fine-tune their language.

2.42　■
Have you ever noticed a child call all men "Daddy"? What is this an example of? How could it be remedied?

Fine-Tuning Language

During the "2s," children elaborate and fine-tune the choppy speech found earlier (Faw & Belkin, 1989). The present tense is elaborated to include the following verb forms:

Present progressive:	I eating.
Past regular:	He looked.
Past irregular:	Jimmy went.
Third person irregular:	She does it.

One problem that surfaces in this stage is overgeneralization of grammatical rules, for example, "badder," "worsest," and "He goed home." Piaget's work helps explain this tendency. "He goed home" uses an existing pattern, which allows the child to remain at equilibrium, whereas "He went home" requires accommodation.

Advancing Development

At about age 3, a child learns to use sentences more strategically. Subject and verb are reversed to form questions, and positive statements are modified to form negative statements. For instance, "He hit him" is changed to "He didn't hit him" and "Did he hit him?" The idea that the form of language is determined by its function begins to develop more fully in this stage.

Simple declarative sentences with subject-verb-object evolve into more complex forms during this stage. Two separate but related ideas that earlier appeared as distinct sentences now become one. For example, "The boy ran too fast" and "The boy fell down" can now be combined to produce "The boy ran too fast and fell down." Notice how the increasingly complex sentence structure also reflects more complex thinking.

The introduction of more complex sentence forms happens at around age 6 and relates to other aspects of cognitive development. For instance, "Jackie paid the bill" and "She had asked him out" become "Jackie paid the bill because she had asked him out." The ability to form and use more complex sentences relates to the child's developing understanding of cause-and-effect relationships.

Increasing Language Complexity

2.43 ■
What theory of language acquisition supports the fact that virtually all children reach school able to speak a language? What theory can explain the fact that some children have better language backgrounds than others?

The picture that emerges is one of a growing language that becomes increasingly complex and allows children to describe and think about their environment. The typical child brings to school a healthy and confident grasp of the powers of language and how it can be used to communicate with others and to think about the world. The importance of this language foundation for reading and writing instruction is becoming increasingly apparent to educators (R. Anderson, Hiebert, Scott, & Wilkinson, 1985; Hornberger, 1989), and in the next section, we examine implications of language development for classroom instruction.

Instructional Implications of Language Development

As we described in this chapter, language development is a natural process facilitated by opportunities to use language in everyday activities. Teachers can promote the process by encouraging students to express themselves verbally and in writing when they solve problems and work on other academic tasks. *Whole language* is a response to this view of language development. Let's see how this happens.

Whole Language

Samantha Taylor's third-grade classroom was a beehive of activity. One corner was decorated with a giant paper spiderweb with drawings and students' written descriptions

A whole language approach to literacy embeds reading and writing into social activities that are meaningful to students.

of spiders and insects. Students took turns reading the descriptions, matching them to the drawings, and checking their answers with a key on the back. Several students were at their desks, writing about and illustrating a recent trip to a fire station; the rest of the students would later read these. In a third corner, students were discussing word problems in math and using interlocking cubes and counters to illustrate the problems.

Samantha had the rest of the class in a half circle in front of her. She was reading a story about a dog who had run away from home. When she neared the end, she stopped and asked each student to create an ending for the story and to share it with the group.

The whole language approach to literacy development is designed to be a bridge between spoken and written language, especially at the lower elementary level (Stahl & Miller, 1989). Based on the idea "What I can think about I can talk about. What I can talk about I can write. What I can write I can read" (R. Allen, 1976, p. 51), whole language uses children's own language production as a bridge from oral to written language.

Whole language helps students develop language skills by using them. It has the following characteristics:

1. Using language to think about and describe experiences
2. Using language to communicate with others
3. Using language across the curriculum

Samantha capitalized on the first characteristic by having students write about things they had experienced—insects and the field trip.

The second characteristic of whole language instruction complements children's natural tendency to communicate with others. Through speaking, writing for others, and reading others' written work, students begin to see how speaking, reading, and writing are interrelated, and they also begin to understand the need for clear communication (Needels & Knapp, 1994).

2.44
Explain how *whole language* is based on Piaget's work. Explain how it's also based on Vygotsky's work.

Third, whole language instruction demonstrates how important language is in learning any content area. For example, instead of focusing exclusively on math or science during their scheduled times, teachers employing a whole language approach use content area instruction as an opportunity to practice the use of language in addition to the concepts themselves. One example is the students' discussion of their math problems in Samantha's class. Creative teachers seize opportunities to encourage students to develop their growing language skills across the curriculum.

Classroom Connections

Applying an Understanding of Language Development in Your Classroom

1. Begin language development and concept learning activities with concrete experiences.
   - A fourth-grade teacher begins a unit on cities by having her inner-city students describe their neighborhoods in as much detail as possible. She then illustrates a rural neighborhood with pictures and asks the students to compare their own neighborhoods with what they see in the pictures.
   - A third-grade teacher begins a unit on bones and muscles by having the students feel their own legs, arms, ribs, and heads.

2. Use open-ended questions to encourage the development of language.
   - The third-grade teacher doing the unit on bones and muscles begins her discussion by having the students simply describe what they feel when they squeeze their arms and legs and poke their ribs and heads. She writes these descriptions on the chalkboard and uses them to frame her discussion.
   - A fifth-grade teacher, in a unit on fractions, has the students first fold pieces of paper into halves, thirds, fourths, and eighths. She then has them shade different sections of the folded papers, describe what they've done, and compare the sections.

3. Focus on meaning, rather than on pronunciation and mechanics in reading comprehension activities. Model standard pronunciation for students.

- A first-grade teacher asks students to discuss stories, including what they think would happen in a different situation, why the characters behaved as they did, and what a good summary of the story would be. She accepts each response without correction and paraphrases the responses by using Standard English when necessary.

4. Use concrete objects for vocabulary development.
   - A second-grade teacher stops a passage reading or discussion whenever an unfamiliar word is used and asks for an example of it. He keeps a list of new words, writes them on cards, and displays them next to objects around the classroom. If the objects don't exist in the room, he gathers pictures and displays the words and pictures together.

5. Provide for differences in language proficiency in your classroom.
   - At the beginning of the school year, a junior high social studies teacher finds out which of his students has limited abilities in English. Asking for volunteers, he pairs these students with a student aide who sits next to the student, answers questions, and generally helps with the course. The teacher has discovered that the tutors not only enjoy their task but also benefit from it cognitively.
   - A second-grade teacher enlists the aid of older students to come into her classroom to tutor her students in reading. When possible, the tutors speak the same native language as her second graders and provide assistance in both English and the native tongue.

Windows on Classrooms

At the beginning of the chapter, you saw how Karen Johnson used her understanding of student development to help her students when they lacked the experiences needed to understand the topic she was teaching. In studying the chapter, you've seen how concrete and personalized examples and high levels of interaction can help make topics meaningful for students. In addition, you've seen how an understanding of students' developmental needs can affect the effectiveness of instruction.

Let's look now at another teacher who is working with a group of first-grade students. As you read the case study, compare the teacher's approach to the suggestions you've studied in the chapter.

Jenny Newhall gathered her first graders around her on the rug in front of a small table to begin her science lesson. After they were settled, she announced, "Today, we are going to be scientists. Scientists use their senses to find out about the world."

She then reviewed what the five senses were by asking students for examples as she proceeded, and then she asked, "How do you know if something is real? . . . Jessica?"

When Jessica failed to respond, Jenny continued by holding up a spoon and asking, "Jessica, is this real?"

Jessica nodded, and Jenny continued, "How do you know?"

" . . . "

"What is it?"

" . . . A tablespoon."

"How do you know it's a spoon?" Jenny prompted.

After some thought, students agreed they could touch it, see it, and even taste it. Jenny then asked, "Is air real? . . . Anthony?"

Anthony offered, "Yes, because you can breathe it."

Jenny probed further, "Can we see it?"

Her students thought for a moment and shook their heads, indicating no.

"Let's think about air for a while," Jenny said as she turned to a large fishbowl filled with water.

"What do you see?" she asked, pointing to the fishbowl.

"A tank with water in it," one student volunteered.

"Are you sure it's water?" Jenny continued. The students weren't sure how to answer.

"How do you know it's water?" Jenny continued.

"It's moving," Devon replied.

"How else can you tell?"

Receiving no answer, Jenny went on, "If you were to drink this, would you know it's water?"

After warning them about drinking things they don't know about, she assured them the liquid was safe to test. One student came up, put his finger in it, and said, "Yep, it's water."

"What is this?" Jenny continued, holding up an empty water glass.

After spending a few minutes asking them to use their sense of sight to describe various features of the glass, Jenny said, "I'm going to put this glass in the water upside down. What's going to happen? What do you think? . . . Michelle?"

" . . . Water will go in the glass."

"No, it'll stay dry," Samantha countered.

To address this difference of opinion, Jenny asked, "Raise your hand if you think it will get water in it. . . . Okay," she said, surveying the room. "Raise your hand if you think it'll remain dry. . . . How many aren't sure? . . . Well, let's see if we can find out.

"First, we have to be sure it's dry. Terry, because you're not sure, I want you to help me by feeling the inside of the glass. How does it feel? Is it dry?"

"Yeah," replied Terry after putting his hand into the glass.

Then, Jenny asked the students to watch carefully as she pushed the inverted glass under the water, as shown in the following drawing.

"Is the glass all the way under?" she asked, with her hand under the water.

The class agreed that it was.

Terry then offered, "There's water inside it. I can see the water inside."

"Then what will it feel like when I pull it out?" Jenny asked.

"Wet," Terry responded.

After pulling it carefully out of the water, she then asked Terry to check the inside of the glass.

"How does it feel?"

"Wet."

Jenny was momentarily taken aback. For the demonstration to work, the inside of the glass was supposed to be dry. After pausing a second, she said, "Samantha, come up here and tell us what you feel."

As Samantha placed her hand up the glass she said, "It's wet on the outside, but dry on the inside."

"It's wet!" Terry asserted.

With a look of concern, Jenny said, "Uh, oh! We have two differing opinions. We've got to find out how to solve this problem." After a short pause, she continued, "Let's dry this glass off and start again. Only this time, we're going to put a paper towel in the glass. Now if water goes in the glass, what is the paper towel going to look like?"

The class agreed it would be wet and soggy.

Then she held up the glass for the class to see. "Okay, it's dry. The paper towel is up in there. We're going to put it in the water again and see what happens."

The class watched carefully as Jenny put the glass into the water again, and after a few moments, she pulled it out.

"Okay, Marisse, come up here and check the paper towel and tell us whether it's wet or dry."

Marisse felt the towel, thought for a moment, and said, "Dry."

"Why did it stay dry? Raise your hand if you can tell us why it stayed dry. What do you think, Jessica?"

"'Cause it's inside and the rest is outside?"

"But why didn't the water go into the glass? What kept the water out? . . . Anthony?"

"A water seal."

"A water seal. Hmm, . . . There's all that water on the outside. How come it didn't go inside? How can the towel stay dry?"

A quiet voice volunteered, "Because there's air in there."

"*Air!* Is that what kept the water out?" Jenny asked with enthusiasm.

"Well, earlier Samantha said that when she was swimming in a pool and put a glass under some water, it stayed dry, but when she tipped it, it got wet inside. Now, what do you think will happen if I put the glass under the water and tip it? What do you think . . . Devon?"

"It'll get wet."

"Let's see. Now watch very carefully. What is happening?" Jenny asked as she slowly tipped the inverted glass partially over. " . . . Andrea?"

"There were bubbles."

"Andrea, what were those bubbles made of?"

"They're air bubbles."

"Now look at the glass. What do you see?" Jenny asked, pointing to the half empty glass upside down in the water. "In the bottom half is water. What's in the top half?"

"It's dry."

"What's up in there?"

"Air."

"*Air* is up there. Well, how can I get that air out?"

"Tip it over some more," several students responded. When Jenny did that, additional bubbles floated to the surface.

"Samantha, how does that work? When I tip it over, what's pushing the air out?"

" . . . The water," Samantha offered hesitantly.

"So, when I tip it this way (tipping it until more bubbles came out), what's pushing the air out?"

"Water," several of the class answered in unison.

Jenny then changed the direction of the lesson by saying, "Now, I have something else for you," as she showed the students a glass full of water. "What do you think will happen if I tip this glass over?"

"The water will spill," some of the students answered.

Jenny continued by suggesting that she cover the glass with a card, and she again asked what they thought would happen. This time there were some disagreements, some suggesting that the water would spill but others believing that the water would stay in the glass.

Jenny then held the card on the glass, tipped the glass over, and the students saw that the water didn't spill. Jenny asked for explanations, and one of the students suggested that the water acted like "super glue" to keep the card on the glass.

After some additional discussion, one of the children suggested that air kept the card next to the glass. They discussed this possibility a bit further, and Jenny then turned the lesson to small-group work.

She divided the class into groups of four or five and gave the students detailed directions about how to take turns. The students then used tubs of water, glasses, cards, and paper towels to experiment on their own.

After each student had a chance to try the activities, Jenny again called the children together and they reviewed and summarized what they had found.

Questions for Discussion and Analysis

Analyze Jenny's lesson now in the context of the information in this chapter. In doing your analysis, you may want to consider the following questions. In each case, be specific and take information directly from the case study.

1. At what level of cognitive development were Jenny's students likely to be? Was her instruction effective for that level? Explain.

2. Why was the medium of water important for Jenny's lesson? How does this relate to Piaget's levels of development?

3. How well did Jenny follow constructivist guidelines? What could she have done differently to make the lesson more constructivist?

4. When Samantha and Terry disagreed about the condition of the inside of the glass, how did Jenny respond? What other alternatives might she have pursued? What are the advantages and disadvantages of these alternatives?

5. Were Jenny's students in the zone of proximal development for the lesson she was teaching? What forms of scaffolding did Jenny provide? How effective was the scaffolding?

6. How did Jenny use social interaction in her lesson? What instructional functions did this social interaction perform?

7. On the basis of this chapter's content, what suggestions do you have to improve the instruction in this lesson?

 # Summary

Piaget's Theory of Cognitive Development

Piaget suggests that development is the combination of learning, experience, and maturation. The quality of experience in the physical and social world, together with the drive for equilibrium, combine to influence development. Intellectually developing children organize their experiences into schemes that help them understand the world. Compatible experiences are assimilated into the schemes, and incompatible experiences require an accommodation of the schemes to reestablish equilibrium.

Piaget's work has influenced curriculum and instruction as evidenced by the emphasis on manipulatives, language experience, hands-on activities, and discovery-oriented instruction.

Information-Processing Views of Development

Information-processing views of development differ from Piaget's theory in their efforts to describe the specific strategies children at different ages use to store and retrieve information. Young children, for example, are less aware and have less control over their powers of attention, memory, communication, and comprehension than do older learners. A teacher can help students improve both their awareness and control of these processes by consciously teaching strategies and encouraging their use. Increased use of strategies helps learners develop self-regulation.

Vygotsky's Description of Development

Lev Vygotsky offers a third view of development. His description focuses heavily on language and social interaction and the role they play in helping learners acquire an understanding of the culture in which they live. Language is the tool people use for cultural transmission, communication, and reflection on their own thinking.

Vygotsky's work has begun to exert influences in classrooms. Teachers are encouraged to engage students in meaningful learning tasks that involve language and social interaction. Those learners who are able to benefit from assistance are in what Vygotsky calls the zone of proximal development. Learners operating in this zone should be given instruction in the form of modeling, questions, prompts, and cues.

Constructivism

Constructivism suggests that learners form or develop their own understanding of the way the world works, rather than have that understanding delivered to them. Piaget and Vygotsky, both constructivists, agree that active learners and social interaction are important for development, but they differ in their reasons why: Piaget focuses on active manipulation of objects and ideas, together with the validation of schemes; Vygotsky emphasizes active participation in cultural exchange.

The implications of constructivism for teaching suggest that learners should be active participants in learning activities, that learning should be guided rather than presented by teachers, and that a great deal of language and discussion should be used in the learning process.

Language Development

All views of development are closely linked to language and its uses. Behaviorism, social cognitive theory, and psycholinguistic theories explain language development differently; each probably forms part of the explanation. Children progress from one- and two-word utterances to elaborated language that involves complex sentence structures by the time they reach school. Whole language approaches to instruction attempt to capitalize on children's naturally developing language.

 **Important Concepts**

nontransformation (p. 39)

object permanence (p. 38)

organization (p. 30)

overgeneralization (p. 65)

preoperational stage (p. 38)

private speech (p. 53)

scaffolding (p. 56)

schemes (p. 30)

sensorimotor stage (p. 37)

seriation (p. 41)

shared understanding
    (p. 55)

strategies (p. 49)

undergeneralization (p. 65)

zone of proximal develop-
    ment (p. 54)

Part **The** **S**tude **I**

In the classroom

Chapter Outline

Erikson's Theory of Personal and Social Development
Erikson's Stages of Psychosocial Development
• Erikson's Work: A Further Look

Self-Concept: Integrative Personal Development
Development of Self-Concept • Self-Concept: Instructional Implications • Ethnic Pride: Promoting Positive Self-Esteem and Ethnic Identity

Development of Morality, Social Responsibility, and Self-Control
Issues of Morality in School and Society • Growth of Internalization: Piaget's Description of Moral Development • Kohlberg's Theory of Moral Development • Moral Development and Classroom Structure

3

Personal, Social, and Emotional Development

"Ahh." Anne Dillard, an eighth-grade English teacher, sighed wearily as she slumped into a chair in the faculty lounge.

"Tough day?" her friend Beth asked.

"Yes. It's Sean again," Anne explained, straightening up. "I just can't seem to get through to him. He won't do his work, and he has a bad attitude about school in general. He can't get along with the other students, and when I try to talk with him about it, he always says they're picking on him for no reason. I don't know what's going to become of him. The funny thing is, I get the feeling that he knows he's out of line, but he just can't seem to change."

"I know what you mean," Beth responded. "I had him for English last year. He was a tough one—very distant. He lost his dad in a messy divorce; his mother got custody of him, and his father just split. Every once in a while, he'd open up to me, but then the wall would go up again."

"He's a bright boy, too," Anne continued, "but he seems to prefer avoiding work to doing it. If I could just help him get his act together, I think he'd do all right. If . . . "

In Chapter 2, we examined theories that described the cognitive, or intellectual, development of students. As a result of this study, you understand that younger students think, feel, and act in ways that are qualitatively different from those of adults. We now turn to an examination of the personal, social, and emotional development of students at different ages. Understanding differences in these areas helps teachers make informed decisions about ways to best meet students' emotional and interpersonal needs.

We begin the chapter with a discussion of Erikson's theory of personal and social development, followed by an analysis of research on self-concept. We then turn to the development of morality, social responsibility, and self-control by examining the contributions of Piaget and Kohlberg in these areas.

After you have completed your study of this chapter, you should be able to meet the following objectives:

▌ Explain the implications that Erikson's theory has for teaching.
▌ Explain the relationship between self-concept and academic achievement and what teachers can do to influence each.
▌ Describe similarities and differences between Piaget's and Kohlberg's theories of moral development.
▌ Identify different stages of moral reasoning and how they apply to classroom practice.

The world that students are now experiencing is the toughest in this country's history. The news is replete with stories about drug and sexual abuse, teen pregnancy, single-parent families, and an alarming school dropout rate. Teachers can no longer effectively teach without considering the personal, social, and emotional well-being of their students. If all of us as teachers understand our students' emerging senses of self, their search for identity, and how they relate to others, we are better prepared to help them function effectively in the classroom. Erik Erikson (1968) developed a theory linking these three elements, which we discuss in the next section.

Erikson's Theory of Personal and Social Development

Erik Erikson's background, like Piaget's and Vygotsky's, provides insights into his work. He dropped out of high school and spent time traveling and studying art. In the process, he met the famous Sigmund Freud and studied under Freud's daughter, Anna. As he studied young people in different cultures, Erikson became interested in how they acquire a personal identity and how they relate to society in general. *Because his theory integrates principles of personal, psychological, and cultural or social development,* it is often called a **psychosocial theory**.

Erikson's work is based on five important ideas:

1. People in general have the same basic needs.
2. The development of the ego or self occurs in response to these needs.
3. Development proceeds in stages.
4. Each stage is characterized by a psychosocial challenge, or *crisis,* that presents opportunities for development.
5. Different stages reflect differences in the motivation of an individual.

A **crisis** *is a time of particular vulnerability to a psychological challenge,* and the challenge is closely tied to social relationships. An acceptable resolution of a crisis means that a favorable ratio of positive to negative psychosocial traits emerges. Although a crisis is never permanently resolved, healthy resolution of the crisis at each stage leads to a positive view of oneself as a person, an accurate perception of oneself in the larger society, and an integration of the two. A negative resolution can retard development at later stages and leave the personality impaired.

3.1 ■
Erikson suggests that stages reflect differences in motivation for an individual. What differences are reflected in Piaget's stages?

3.2 ■
Is the statement "Motivation is an important part of Erikson's theory, but it isn't a part of Piaget's work" true or is it false? Explain your answer.

Erikson's Stages of Psychosocial Development

Erikson's descriptions of these developmental stages are outlined in Table 3.1. Notice how each stage involves a crisis that the person resolves through interaction with others.

Trust Versus Mistrust (Birth to 1 Year)

Developing a sense of **trust**, *or confidence in the honesty and justice of others,* is the first psychological challenge facing all people, and it is especially important to infants because of their dependence on others. An infant who receives consistent and predictably good care from parents develops a sense of trust; an infant who is left to cry and who receives inconsistent and unpredictable care can develop basic mistrust that leads to fear and suspicion of other people and the world in general. These ideas are consistent with studies of *bonding,* or the social attachment between babies and their primary care givers, usually parents (Isabella & Belsky, 1991). Although we are in no position to evaluate the care Sean received as an infant, his behavior suggests that he didn't fully resolve the trust-mistrust crisis. His perception that the other students are "picking on him for no reason" and his inability to communicate with his teachers are indicators of this problem.

Autonomy Versus Shame and Doubt (Ages 1 to 3)

Securely attached children next face the challenge of **autonomy**, *or doing things on their own.* They learn to feed and dress themselves, and toilet training begins. As you recall

Early childhood and elementary classrooms should provide opportunities for students to develop personal independence and initiative.

Table 3.1

Erikson's stages of psychosocial development

Stage	Approximate Age	Characteristics
Trust vs. Mistrust	Infancy (0–1 year)	Trust in the world is developed through consistent and continuous love and support.
Autonomy vs. Shame and Doubt	Toddler (1–3 years)	Independence is fostered by successful experiences formed by support and structure.
Initiative vs. Guilt	Early Childhood (3–6 years)	An exploratory and investigative attitude results from meeting and accepting challenges.
Industry vs. Inferiority	Middle Childhood (6–12 years)	Enjoyment of mastery and competence comes through success and recognition of accomplishment.
Identity vs. Confusion	Adolescence (12–18 years)	Personal, social, sexual, and occupational identity comes from success in school and experimentation with different roles.
Intimacy vs. Isolation	Young Adulthood	Openness to others and the development of intimate relationships result from interaction with others.
Generativity vs. Stagnation	Middle Adulthood	Productivity, creativity, and concern for the next generation are achieved through success on the job and a growing sense of social responsibilities.
Integrity vs. Despair	Old Age	Acceptance of one's life is achieved by an understanding of a person's place in the life cycle.

Source: Adapted from *Identity, Youth and Crisis* by Erik E. Erikson, by permission of W. W. Norton & Company, Inc. Copyright © 1968 by W. W. Norton & Company, Inc.

from studying cognitive development, they now demonstrate goal-directed behavior and begin to communicate verbally. They no longer want to depend totally on others. At this point, parents need to encourage children who try to put their shoes on, for example, and offer advice and reassurance while expressing confidence even though it would be easier to do the task for them. Overly restrictive parents or those who punish minor accidents, such as bed-wetting or spills while eating, lead children to doubt their own abilities or to have a sense of shame about their bodies. Ultimately, Erikson believes, this effect leads to a lasting lack of confidence in their power to deal with and control their world.

Initiative Versus Guilt (Ages 3 to 6)

Initiative *is characterized by an exploratory and investigative attitude that results from meeting and accepting challenges.* At the beginning of this stage, children are likely to be found upside down in the drawer with the pots and pans and indeed "into everything." Having developed a sense of autonomy, children are now ready to expand and respond to their curiosity. This is the stage at which children make enormous cognitive leaps, and those developing abilities provide the impetus for exploration in all areas of their lives. When a child offers to "help" his mother make cookies, for example, he needs the assurance that his contributions are welcome and valued. Parents who criticize or punish initiative cause children to feel guilty about their self-initiated activities. Sean's withdrawal and lack of personal initiative at school suggest problems at this stage.

> 3.3
>
> Suppose you're a preschool/kindergarten teacher. Identify at least two things you might do to encourage students' initiative.

School and the Development of Initiative.   As children enter preschool and kindergarten, they are moving forward, taking on more tasks, and searching eagerly for more experiences. "I can do it!" and "Let me try it" are signs of this initiative. They are interacting more with their peers, and their play is becoming more complex and interdependent. As children go through these changes, parents and teachers can do much to help them develop into happy and healthy children.

> "Good, Felipe. I see you've used a lot of colors to draw your bird. That's a very pretty bird."
>
> "Nice, Taeko. Those are really bright colors. They make me feel happy."
>
> "Look what Raymond did. He cut out his picture when he was done. That's a nice job of cutting."

Teachers play an important role in students' developing independence and initiative. Felipe and Taeko made their own decisions about coloring, and Raymond decided on his own to cut out the picture when he was finished. The kind of support they receive will influence their future sense of initiative and competence. Criticism of this initiative detracts from the feeling of independence and in extreme cases leads to guilt and dependency. Simple tasks such as buttoning clothes, putting away toys, and cutting paper with scissors form the concrete challenges that children use to estimate their own competence and self-worth. A child's performance on a task isn't as important as an adult's response to it. Children at this age are taking initiative and trying to be independent, but they still depend heavily on adult assessment. Supportive and encouraging teachers play a critical role in students' growing sense of initiative.

Industry Versus Inferiority (Ages 6 to 12)

The crisis at the industry versus inferiority stage also has enormous implications for teachers. The challenge is to develop a sense of **industry,** *or the enjoyment of mastery and competence through success and recognition of accomplishment.* Because children spend large amounts of time and energy at school, the influence of teachers and peers is very important. If challenges are too difficult and result in failure, the child may develop a sense of inferiority, or if accomplishments involve only trivial tasks, industry fails to develop.

In a longitudinal study of development, Vaillant and Vaillant (1981) found that of intelligence, family background, and industry, a healthy sense of industry was the most significant factor in later personal adjustment, economic success, and interpersonal relationships. This finding is encouraging because it suggests that if teachers can help students acquire a sense of challenge and success in developing a sense of industry, the students can overcome obstacles later in life.

As you study Erikson's work, it is important to keep in mind that children don't necessarily recognize the need to develop a sense of industry, competence, and success at the time they are going through the stage. For example, on the basis of observations of children in this stage, you might conclude that peer relationships are most important to them at this point in their lives. Erikson asserts, however, that during this period their main challenge is to develop a sense of competence. Although they don't realize it, if the development of that competence doesn't occur at this point, a fully functioning personality is less likely.

Identity Versus Confusion (Ages 12 to 18)

During adolescence, middle and junior high school youngsters experience major physical, intellectual, and emotional changes. Many go through growth spurts, and their coordina-

---

3.4
Given what you know about young children's socioemotional growth, is competition a generally healthy or generally unhealthy component of the early school curriculum? Explain.

3.5
Suppose students are consistently given schoolwork that is so easy they can complete it with little effort. Will this have a positive or a negative effect on their resolution of the industry/inferiority crisis? Explain. How would schoolwork that is too difficult influence development at this stage? Again explain.

3.6
Describe some specific items that you would expect to see on a report card designed to promote industry. What elements would be missing?

tion doesn't keep up with their bodies. The magnitude of physical change in early adolescence is surpassed only by those in infancy. Adolescents experience new sexual feelings, and not quite knowing how to respond, they're frequently confused. They are concerned with what others think of them; they are preoccupied with their looks. They are caught in the awkward position of wanting to assert their independence, yet longing for the stability of structure and discipline. They want to rebel, but they want something solid to rebel against. They write "Ms. Smith is a b_____" on the bathroom wall on Wednesday, but on Thursday they decide they really like her. Further, they would feel terrible if they thought she didn't like them.

During this period, youngsters are wrestling with the question *Who am I?* or **identity**. This, of course, doesn't mean that all teenagers are doomed to a period of distress and uncertainty. Most negotiate adolescence successfully, and most maintain positive relationships with their parents and other adults. Erikson, who coined the term **identity crisis**—*the feeling of uncertainty about who one is*—suggests that youngsters who have a basic sense of trust, can function on their own, aren't afraid to take initiative, and feel competent overcome the uncertainty of adolescence and develop a firm notion of who they are and what their role in society should be. Failure to resolve the crisis results in role confusion, which prolongs the behavioral traits characteristic of adolescence and inhibits successful functioning as adults. We've all heard remarks such as, "He never grew up," or, "She still behaves like an adolescent." These descriptions typify people who have failed to resolve the identity-confusion crisis. Teachers can help in the process by providing supportive but growth-enhancing classroom environments that encourage students to define themselves as developing young adults.

States of Identity Development.   Four seniors were talking about their after-high-school plans.

> "I'm not sure what I want to do," Sandy commented. "I've thought about veterinary medicine, and I've also thought about teaching. I've been working at the vet clinic, and I really like it, but I'm not sure about doing it forever. I guess I should take some kind of interest inventory or something. I don't know."
>
> "I wish I could do that," Ramon replied. "But I'm off to the university full-time in the fall. I'm going to be a lawyer. At least that's what my parents think. It's not a bad job, and they make good money."
>
> "How can you just do that, Ramon?" Nancy wondered aloud. "You don't really want to be a lawyer; you've said that before. Me, I'm not going to decide for a while. I'm only 18. I'm good in biology. I've thought about trying pre-med, and I'm going to take some more courses in biology-oriented stuff, but I'm not sure I'm ready for that many years of school. I'm going to think hard about it for a while. How about you, Taylor?"
>
> "I'm going into nursing," Taylor answered. "I've been working part-time at the hospital, and it feels really good. I thought I wanted to be a doctor at one time, but I don't think I can handle all the pressures. I've talked with the counselors, and I think I can do the chem and other science. I guess we'll see."

The process of identity formation isn't smooth and uniform; it takes different paths, like a railroad train (Marcia, 1980). Sometimes it's sitting on a holding spur beside the main track; at others it's chugging full speed ahead.

Researchers have studied identity resolution by interviewing adolescents and asking them about commitments they've made to occupational, religious, and political choices (Marcia, 1980). The researchers found that adolescents tended to cluster around one of four positions (Marcia, 1987). These are outlined in Table 3.2.

3.7

Which of the following contributes most to an adolescent's growing sense of identity: the formal school curriculum (e.g., math, English), extracurricular activities, friends, or family? Which contributes least? Explain.

3.8

Where would identity resolution be easier—in a rural community or in a large urban setting? Explain your choice.

3.9

Research indicates that, for American youngsters, identity resolution and formation are postponed until the post-high-school years. Why do these processes occur later for American youth than for youth in other countries?

Table 3.2

Positions in identity development

Position	Description and Example
Identity diffusion	Occurs when individuals fail to make clear choices. Confusion is common. Choices may be difficult, or individuals aren't developmentally ready to make choices. This state is illustrated by Sandy's comments.
Identity foreclosure	Occurs when individuals prematurely adopt ready-made positions of others, such as parents. This is an undesirable position, because decisions are based on the identities of others. Ramon's comments suggest this state.
Identity moratorium	Occurs when individuals pause and remain in a holding pattern. Long-range commitment is delayed. Nancy appears to be in this state.
Identity achievement	Occurs after individuals experience a period of crises and decision making. Identity achievement reflects a commitment to a goal or direction. Taylor's comments indicate that he has made this commitment.

From the descriptions in Table 3.2, you can see that identity moratorium and identity achievement are healthy positions on the path to identity formation. With identity diffusion and identity foreclosure—less healthy positions—adolescents fail to wrestle with choices that will have important consequences for them throughout life.

Research helps in understanding this process. In a synthesis of eight studies, Waterman (1985) found that identity achievement more often occurs in the post-high-school years than during high school, in contrast with what Erikson's theory suggests. This finding was especially true for college students, who had more time to consider what they wanted to do with their lives. These results suggest that the uncertainty of adolescence is more related to increasing independence than it is to career or gender identity resolution. Conflict with parents, teachers, and other adults peaks in early adolescence and then declines as teenagers accept responsibility and adults learn how to deal with the new relationship (J. Hill, Holmbeck, Marlow, Green, & Lynch, 1985; Steinberg, 1987). This finding helps explain why teaching junior high or middle school students is viewed as particularly challenging.

3.10

Erikson's work suggests three major tasks during the school years: the development of initiative, industry, and identity. With which of the three are schools most successful? As a classroom teacher, what can you do to help students resolve the crisis in each area?

Helping Adolescents Grow.   Understanding emotionally developing adolescents helps a teacher better respond to their capricious behavior. Fads and bizarre clothing and hairstyles, for example, reflect teenagers' urges to identify with groups while simultaneously searching for their individuality. If their behaviors don't interfere with learning or the rights and comfort of others, they shouldn't be major issues. A teacher can help by spending time discussing students' concerns and simply talking with them openly and honestly. This is the best advice we can give teachers struggling to reach a student like Sean.

Perhaps more significant is the sensitivity both Anne and Beth demonstrated in their efforts to reach Sean. Students, particularly at the middle and junior high levels, need firm, caring teachers—teachers who the students think "understand them" yet provide the security of setting limits for acceptable behavior. They don't need a teacher who is a

Conversations with caring adults provide opportunities for adolescents to think about and refine their developing personal identities.

"buddy." They need a solid adult who can guide their intellectual and emotional growth (Emmer, Evertson, Sanford, Clements, & Worsham, 1994). This is another illustration of the fact that there is much more to teaching than the simple delivery of content.

Intimacy Versus Isolation (Young Adulthood)

During Erikson's sixth stage, individuals wrestle with their relationships with other people. A person with a firm sense of identity is prepared for **intimacy**, *or giving the self over to another,* based on something other than a basic need. Giving for the sake of giving without expecting something in return characterizes a positive resolution of the crisis at this stage. In contrast, people who fail to resolve the crisis remain emotionally isolated, unable to give and receive love freely.

Generativity Versus Stagnation (Middle Adulthood)

The key characteristics of **generativity** are *creativity, productivity, and the concern for and commitment to guiding the next generation* (Erikson, 1980). Generative adults try in their own way to contribute to the betterment of society by working for principles such as a clean physical environment, a safe and drug-free social world, and adherence to the principles of freedom and dignity for individuals. Teachers who genuinely care about students and their learning typify a group having positively resolved the crisis at this stage. An unhealthy resolution leads to apathy, pseudointimacy, and self-absorption.

Integrity Versus Despair (Old Age)

Erikson describes people who *accept themselves, conclude that they have only one life to live, live it about as well as possible, and have few regrets* as having **integrity**. They accept responsibility for the way they've lived and face and accept the finality of death. A person filled with regret for things done or left undone, worried that there is no turning back and that time is running out, is filled with despair.

Erikson's Work: A Further Look

Having read the descriptions of Erikson's eight stages, you probably have some questions about his theory. A common one is "When a crisis at a particular stage isn't resolved, what happens later? Does the person not go on to the next stage?" Let's look at Sean and his development to begin answering these questions.

The evidence in our case study suggests that Sean didn't fully resolve the trust-mistrust crisis. However, this doesn't mean that it prevented him from wrestling with autonomy or initiative (although there is also some evidence that he lacked initiative). Rather, it

Teachers, in their commitment to helping young people, symbolize a positive resolution of the generativity versus stagnation stage of psychosocial development.

has left him with a personality "glitch" that keeps him from functioning as fully as he might and that results in his problems in school.

Sean's behavior also suggests that he is having problems resolving the identity-confusion crisis. His father's absence leaves him without an important male role model to help him in this process. This confusion, Erikson notes, can result in a negative identity, which rejects appropriate roles and substitutes negative ones. Sean may well grow up to be a successful adult, however, and the same is true for all of us.

No one knows for sure what the long-range ramifications of any personality imperfections might be. On the one hand, people who fail to resolve the autonomy-doubt crisis may be less successful than their ability would indicate, because they are afraid to move forward on their own. On the other hand, they may find satisfying careers in a support role.

Rather than being absolute causes of behavior, "glitches" are simply that—personality imperfections that we all have in some form. Erikson's theory doesn't give specific answers, such as precisely when a problem leaves a person dysfunctional, but neither do other theories.

Because of its descriptive nature, Erikson's theory is difficult to document with empirical research. This is typical of personality theories; few have an extensive body of experimental data supporting them (C. Hall & Lindzey, 1978). Erikson's work, however, is intuitively sensible and helpful in helping one understand people's developing personalities. We've all met people we admire because of their openness, drive, and enthusiasm. They seem to be comfortable around other people, have a good understanding of their own strengths and weaknesses, enjoy their work, and are committed to contributing to society. However, we all have also seen those who seem to believe that other people are always trying to take advantage of them or are somehow inherently "evil." We see good minds sliding into lethargy as the result of apathy or even substance abuse. We are frustrated, as well, by others who seem to be "paranoid" or to lack a zest for living. Erikson's work helps us understand these problems.

As teachers, we gain insight into the personalities of our students and how they can be nurtured and strengthened through Erikson's theory. Further, as we interpret his results, we see strong implications for our own behavior in working with students at all school levels. It also reminds us that we are there to do much more than help students learn to make subjects and verbs agree or to solve algebraic equations. We are also there to help them develop as individuals and relate productively with others.

> **3.11** ■
> Suppose you teach ninth graders and you have a student whom you can't "get going." He will do what is required of him and no more. He does a good job on his required work, however, and he seems to be quite happy. Explain his behavior on the basis of Erikson's work.

Classroom Connections

Applying Erikson's Work in Your Classroom

1. Help students achieve a high degree of success, especially in the elementary school.
   - In question-and-answer sessions, a fifth-grade teacher provides cues or prompting questions in response to incorrect answers.

- A sixth-grade teacher develops a grading system based partially on improvement so that each student can succeed by improving performance.
- A second-grade teacher carefully covers each topic and provides precise directions before making seatwork assignments. He conducts "monitored

practice" with the first few items to be sure all students get started correctly.

2. Be tolerant of honest mistakes when dealing with students at all levels.
   - A prealgebra teacher, working with a student on simplifying expressions involving signed numbers, sees a student repeat a mistake explained only moments before. The teacher patiently reminds the student of the rule and then models the solution to the problem.
   - A kindergarten student responsible for watering the classroom plants knocks one over and spills the water. The teacher says evenly, "It looks like we have a problem. What needs to be done?" She pauses and continues, "Sweep up the dirt and use the paper towels to wipe up the water."

3. In a middle and junior high school, provide the security of structure while allowing freedom of expression.
   - An eighth-grade history teacher consistently enforces her classroom rules and procedures. She also uses a few minutes of homeroom each day to discuss issues with students. They may say anything they wish other than criticizing people in the school by name.
   - A life science teacher jokes with her students as they enter the classroom. When the bell rings, however, the students are settled and ready to begin working.

4. Remember the emotional needs of young people and use it as an umbrella under which you conduct your instruction.

- A junior high earth science teacher pays little attention to the attire and slang of his students as long as offensive language isn't used, the rights of others are recognized, and learning occurs.
- After school, a seventh-grade geography teacher listens sympathetically as a girl talks about an incident in which her feelings were hurt as a result of an encounter with some of her friends.

5. Be a role model for students, both professionally and personally. With elementary-age students, particularly model industry; with older students, model the professionalism and individual dignity helpful in identity formation.
   - A third-grade teacher frequently comments on her own study in a master's program, how hard she has to work, how much she has learned during the previous year, and how good she feels about her new insights.
   - A fourth-grade teacher arranges his classroom procedures so that everyone—including himself—is given responsibilities, including homework. He encourages the students to check with him to see whether he has done his homework each night, and they all agree to do theirs.
   - A 10th-grade English teacher stresses that discourtesy and mistreatment of each other are the "mortal sins" in her class. She pledges her own courtesy and preservation of everyone's individual dignity.

Self-Concept: Integrative Personal Development

One child announced at the dinner table that she was an honest person. When asked how she knew she was honest, she replied, "Because my teacher asked me to help her grade papers!" (W. Purkey & Novak, 1984, p. 27)

"I'll never forget my seventh-grade teacher. At that time I was overweight and wore braces on my teeth. Our teacher asked us to turn in a paper of different types of sentences. To demonstrate an exaggeration, I wrote, 'I am the most beautiful girl in the world.' The teacher wrote back: 'This is an exaggeration?' He'll never know how good he made me feel." (W. Purkey & Novak, 1984, p. 28)

Children grow not only in size, knowledge, and skills but also in their awareness of themselves as persons. We call this awareness the development of self, or self-concept.

Self-concept *includes the total of people's perceptions about their physical, social, and academic competence* (Pintrich & Schunk, 1996).

Students enter school with positive views of themselves as learners, but unfortunately those views often become less positive over time (Frey & Ruble, 1987; Stipek, 1993). This is especially true for students who experience learning problems (Chapman, 1988).

A person's interactions with others affect that person's conclusions about who he or she is, and teachers are second only to parents in their influence on those evaluations (D. Phillips, 1990). Even young children sense whether adults have low or high expectations for them, and these expectations influence subsequent achievement. In this section, we trace the origins of self-concept and examine the ways students form estimates of their worth.

Development of Self-Concept

The first step in the development of self-concept is *self-recognition,* which occurs at about 18 months of age and is evidenced by young children's fascination with looking at themselves in the mirror—"Hey, I recognize you; you're me!" (Berk, 1994). With self-recognition, the process of self-definition begins, and these children also start differentiating between the ideal self and the real self. The *ideal self* is what a person would like to be—strong, brave, smart, attractive; the *real self* is a person's perception of what he or she actually is. People's developing **self-esteem** *is their evaluation of themselves derived by comparing their ideal and real selves* (Berk, 1994).

Sources of Self-Concept

As children develop, several factors influence their self-concepts. Young children (3- to 5-year-olds) place heavy emphasis on their interactions with the environment (Berk, 1994). This is consistent with Piaget's observation that young children's developing schemes depend heavily on direct experience with their environment.

As children grow older, interactions with others become increasingly important. Initially, parents are a powerful influence, and during early school years teachers are also important. Self-concept is already well-formed by the first grade, and students typically come to school expecting to succeed and do well (Stipek, 1993). As students progress through school, peers and friends become increasingly important (Berk, 1994).

Self-Concept and Achievement

The relationship between general self-concept and achievement is positive but weak (Walberg, 1984). In attempting to understand why, researchers have found that self-concept has at least three subcomponents—academic, social, and physical (Marsh, 1989)—with social and physical self-concepts being virtually unrelated to academic achievement (Byrne, 1984; Marsh & Shavelson, 1985). This makes sense; we've all known socially withdrawn students who are happy as academic isolates, and we've also known popular students who are only average in schoolwork.

Academic Self-Concept

The most important component of this general self-concept for a teacher is **academic self-concept,** *the part that deals with people's perception of their competence as students.* Self-concept and school performance strongly interact. Children enter school expecting to

3.12
Think about your own self-concept. For you, which is the most positive—physical, social, or academic self-concept? Why is that the case?

3.13
What is the primary way that social and physical self-concepts are developed in schools? What does this suggest about total school programs?

learn and do well (Stipek, 1993), but as they progress, this expectation is altered by their accomplishments (Harter & Connell, 1984). When learning experiences are positive, self-concept is enhanced; when they're negative, it suffers.

Subject Matter Specificity.   Although researchers find a moderate relationship between academic self-concept and achievement, the strongest correlations exist between specific academic self-concepts and their corresponding subject matter areas. For example, people with a positive self-concept of ability in math perform better on mathematical tests (and vice versa). Researchers also found that concepts of ability in different subjects, such as math and English, become more distinct over time and that students become better able to differentiate between their performances in the different areas (Marsh, 1992; Marsh & Shavelson, 1985). Unfortunately, we've all heard people make statements such as, "I'm okay in English, but I'm no good in math." Too often, comments such as these result, not from ability per se, but from perceived ability resulting from the lowered societal expectations of others (American Association of University Women, 1992).

The relationships between the components of self-concept and achievement are illustrated in Figure 3.1.

The connections among self-concept, academic performance, and students' attitudes toward school have prompted efforts to improve the way students view themselves. These efforts have used two distinct approaches:

1. Attempts to improve self-concept directly
2. Attempts to improve self-concept as a by-product of increased academic success

The first approach involves a variety of strategies, such as using multicultural learning materials with minority students, establishing residential summer camps, and focusing on the home, with attempts to improve parents' understanding of self-concept (Scheirer & Kraut, 1979). Alternative approaches focus on student success in meaningful learning tasks (Stipek, 1993). As students experience success, their confidence grows and self-concepts improve.

3.14
What specifically provides students with information on which their academic self-concepts are based? Describe what you as a teacher can do to help low achievers form positive self-concepts.

3.15
Does positive self-concept increase achievement, or does achievement improve self-concept? Explain your position.

Figure 3.1

The relationships among the dimensions of self-concept and achievement

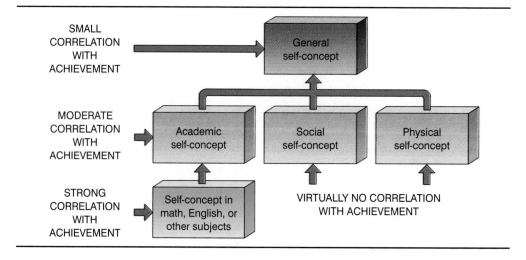

Both of these positions were tested in a federally funded compensatory education program in the primary grades (Scheirer & Kraut, 1979). The goal of the program was to supplement regular instruction with specially designed interventions for disadvantaged students. The approach to improve self-concept directly used open education programs that stressed a learning environment of support and trust, with students selecting from a variety of stimulating materials. Program components were designed specifically to enhance participants' self-concepts. The contrasting programs featured highly structured learning activities with immediate positive reinforcement; increases in self-concept, if they occurred, would be outcomes of academic success.

Comparisons of the two approaches indicated that students in the structured programs not only learned more but also had more positive self-concepts. This study, as well as others reviewed by researchers, indicates that efforts to improve academic achievement through self-concept intervention alone are misguided (Scheirer & Kraut, 1979). This conclusion is further supported by more recent research on the formation of academic self-concept (Marsh, 1992). In forming self-concepts in academic areas, students use both external (e.g., "How do my knowledge and skills in this area compare with those of other students?") and internal (e.g., "How do my knowledge and skills in this subject compare with those in other subjects?") comparisons. Attempting to change students' self-concepts without improving their performance ignores the critical role that information plays in forming and changing self-concepts.

Self-Concept: Instructional Implications

The implications for a teacher's role in the development of a student's self-concept are clear. Teachers must design learning activities so that students are successful; if they do, self-concept should improve as a result. The need for success and its impact on the developing self-concept are substantiated by classroom research. In addition to increasing achievement (Brophy, 1986), success also enhances learners' self-esteem. Berliner (1987) summarizes the research on success in this way:

> It is now thought likely that a high level of success in a learning environment causes students to develop an enhanced self-concept as a learner. Thus, to build a positive self-concept, a teacher needs to design environments and make assignments so that students can have experience in attaining high levels of success. (p. 100)

The process is more complex, however, than just ensuring success. For self-concepts to improve, students must perceive learning activities as substantive and worthwhile (Ames, 1990; Clifford, 1990). Teachers who challenge students with worthwhile tasks and help them meet these challenges enhance both achievement and self-concept.

In addition to influencing success on challenging tasks, classroom climate influences self-concept (Beane & Lipka, 1986). Positive teacher expectations communicate that all students can and will learn; these expectations affect both achievement and motivation. Democratic classrooms, in which students participate in the decision-making process, foster initiative and self-direction. The combination of these elements creates a learning environment in which students are not only successful but also feel valued as growing and developing people.

Classroom grading practices also influence the development of self-concept. Teachers who emphasize competition and encourage students to constantly make social comparisons create win-lose environments (Cohen, 1991). In contrast, teachers in multidimensional classrooms emphasize the many ways to succeed and that different students have different abilities. In these latter classrooms, the emphasis is on individual student growth

3.16
How powerful are grades in influencing self-concept? How can teachers use grades as a positive influence on self-concept?

and effort, rather than on ability. Teachers can enhance self-concept by rewarding effort and by recognizing genuine progress.

Ethnic Pride: Promoting Positive Self-Esteem and Ethnic Identity

Maria Robles squeezed her mother's hand tight as they entered through the busy doors of her new school. Her mother could tell she was nervous as she anxiously eyed the bigger boys and girls walking down the hallway.

As they stopped in front of the doorway marked Kindergarten, Room 3, Mrs. Avilla, a woman with a smiling face, came out to greet them.

"Hola. ¿Cómo te llamas, niña?" (Hello. What is your name, little one?)

Maria was still uneasy, but as she looked at her mother's face, she felt relieved.

"Dile tu nombre," (Tell her your name.) her mother prompted, squeezing her hand and smiling.

". . . Maria," she offered hesitantly.

Her mother added quickly, "Maria Robles. Yo soy su madre." (I am her mother.)

Mrs. Avilla looked on her list, found Maria's name, and checked it off. Then she invited them, in Spanish, to come into the room and meet the other boys and girls. Music could be heard in the background. Maria recognized some of her friends who were playing with toys in one corner of the room.

"Maria, ven aquí y juega con nosotros." (Maria, come here and play with us.)

Maria hesitated for a moment and looked up at her mother to see whether it was all right. When her mother smiled and nodded, Maria ran over to join her friends.

Self-Esteem and Ethnicity

We all wonder about our self-worth. Will others like us? Are we worthy of their love? Are we perceived by others as smart? Beautiful? Handsome? As you saw earlier, our interactions with others help shape our concepts, and schools play an important role in this process. The same applies with self-esteem.

Research suggests that culture plays an important role in the development of self-esteem in minority youth. Like self-concept, researchers have found that the self-esteem of minorities is multifaceted, composed of two major components: personal and collective (Wright & Taylor, 1995).

Collective self-esteem refers to *children's perceptions of the relative worth of the groups to which they belong.* For all of us, our membership in families, peer groups, and ethnic groups all contribute to our sense of self-worth. When we (and others) perceive these groups as valued and possessing status, our self-esteem is enhanced. The opposite is also true.

Children as young as Maria Robles know they are part of an ethnic group, and research dating back to the 1930s has documented that diverse groups of ethnic minority children such as African American (K. Clark & Clark, 1939), Mexican American (Weiland & Coughlin, 1979), and Chinese American (Aboud & Skerry, 1984) evaluate their own ethnic reference groups lower than the White majority. These results suggest that simply being part of a minority group can make students feel less confident and good about themselves; this is a disturbing problem for all teachers who want their students to develop healthy self-esteem.

What can teachers do to combat this problem? They can make every effort to communicate to students that their ethnic heritage and language are not only recognized but also valued. In a test of this idea, researchers taught elementary native Canadian children

3.17
What data do ethnic minority children use in forming these lower ethnic evaluations? How does this process compare with the process that occurs in forming personal self-esteem?

Teachers can help students develop ethnic pride and positive self-esteem by actively acknowledging and valuing the ethnic and cultural strengths different students bring to school.

in either their native (heritage) language or in a second language, such as French (Wright & Taylor, 1995). Children educated in their heritage language showed a substantial increase in their personal self-esteem, whereas children educated in the nonheritage second language did not. The researchers concluded that "early heritage language education can have a positive impact on the personal and collective self-esteem of minority language students" (p. 251).

Students who hear their home language used in the classroom learn that the language and the culture in which it is embedded is valued. Stories such as Maria Robles's are not atypical. Many students come to school wondering whether they will be welcomed and question whether they bring with them knowledge that will be valued. The way a teacher reacts to these students influences their views of their own self-worth.

Ethnic Pride and Identity Formation

Membership in an ethnic group also affects the process of identity formation. It affects who a person is and what he or she will become. For many minority youth, neighborhoods, family, and friends are important influences that shape their identities.

Sometimes the messages teenagers receive about their ethnic identities are mixed or even negative. An African American journalist reported, "If you were black, you didn't quite measure up. . . . You didn't see any black people doing certain things. . . . Well, it must mean that white people are better than we are" (Monroe, Goldman, & Smith, 1988, pp. 88–99). Similar problems with ethnic identity formation have also been documented with Mexican American (Matute-Bianchi, 1986) and Asian American (Wong-Fillmore, 1992) teenagers.

On a more positive note, research indicates that students who are encouraged and helped to explore their ethnic identities and who have adopted values from both the dominant culture and their own tend to have a clearer sense of their identity. They also have higher self-esteem and a more positive view of their ability to cope with their environment (Phinney, 1989; Phinney & Alipuria, 1990).

The research on both identity formation and influences on the self-esteem of minority children is clear. Minority students need to know that their cultures are valued and that the languages they bring to school are assets rather than obstacles or liabilities. Teachers play a crucial role in making every student feel wanted and loved by the overt and implicit messages they send through their teaching.

3.18

How might positive ethnic role models assist in the following identity resolution tasks: independence, career decision, sexual adjustment, and peer group relations?

Classroom Connections

Capitalizing on Diversity in Your Classroom

1. Build on students' cultures and ethnic background to develop positive self-esteem.
   - A first-grade teacher discovered that three different native languages were spoken in the homes of her students. With the help of other teachers and parent volunteers, she constructed a chart of common nouns and phrases (e.g., chair, table, mother, "Hello") in the different languages. She used the chart to explain to her students differences in the languages and to establish commonalities between them.
   - A social studies teacher teaching in an ethnically diverse school encourages her students to do their country reports on the country from which their ancestors came. She asks students to place the information they discover on a poster and to bring in things from home, such as clothes and food, to illustrate the culture of the ancestral country.
   - An elementary teacher emphasizes diversity in a unit on community. As the class discusses the community they live in, the teacher uses overlapping circles to show how different members of the community belonging to different groups contribute to the total community.

2. Use ethnic role models as a foundation for the development of students' personal identities.
   - A middle school teacher in a career exploration unit makes a special effort to bring in minorities in different occupations and professions. He encourages them to talk openly about the challenges and satisfactions they encountered in pursuing their careers.
   - A social studies teacher makes a special effort to emphasize the contributions of ethnic minorities and women to American society. As contemporary newspapers and magazines report the accomplishments of different ethnic groups, she brings these in to share with her students.

Development of Morality, Social Responsibility, and Self-Control

"Listen, everyone. . . . I need to go to the office for a moment," Mrs. Kellinger said as her students were completing a seatwork assignment. "You all have work to do, so work quietly on it until I get back."

The quiet shuffling of pencils and papers could be heard for a few moments, and then Gary whispered, "Psst, what math problems are we supposed to do?"

"Shh! No talking," Talitha said, pointing to the rules posted on the chalkboard.

"But he needs to know so he can do his homework," Krystal put in. "It's the evens on page 79."

"Who cares?" Dwain growled. "She's not here. She won't catch us."

What do students think about classroom rules? Perhaps more important, how do they think about the laws and conventions that make up the rules of society? What influences their interpretations of rules, and how do they learn to follow and modify them?

In this section, we expand our discussion of student development to include an examination of ethics, morals, and changes in children's thinking about issues of right, wrong, fairness, and justice.

Issues of Morality in School and Society

Dealing with moral issues is a very real part of life for individuals, groups, and even whole societies. During World War II, for instance, the United States was faced with the choice of dropping the atomic bomb or invading Japan at the cost of millions of lives. The U.S. intervention in Vietnam caused such a moral dilemma for the United States that only recently has it begun to clearly assess its involvement there. The United States went to war with Iraq, ostensibly to free Kuwait, but in reality to protect the flow of Mideast oil. And U.S. armed forces have also acted as "peacekeepers" in other volatile areas of the world, such as Haiti and Bosnia. All of these conflicts force us to consider the question: Should the United States use its military might to "police" the world?

At an individual level, what are the implications of laws requiring motorcyclists to wear helmets and car passengers to wear seat belts? How far should government go in regulating behavior to prevent injuries and save lives?

On a cultural level, what should be taught in the schools? Special interest groups, for example, have branded some of the classic literature of American culture, such as *Huckleberry Finn,* as racist or gender biased. Others have called for the study of creationism as a theory parallel with evolution. Again, where should the line be drawn? Society and schools created by society both wrestle with moral issues.

Some of the classic literature of this culture focuses on the issue of ethics. For example, Jean Valjean, the main character in Victor Hugo's *Les Miserable,* on which the popular Broadway musical was based, was faced with the choice of feeding his family by becoming a thief or allowing them to go hungry. Ethical issues have also been commonly used in literature designed for young people. For instance, Charlotte in *Charlotte's Web* was faced with the dilemma of saving Wilbur the pig at the loss of her own life. Old Yeller's master was faced with losing his dog or allowing the potential health menace of rabies. Students commonly study books such as *The Yearling* and *A Tale of Two Cities* not only because they are good literature but also because they introduce moral problems with no clear answers.

In the best-seller *The Closing of the American Mind,* Alan Bloom (1987) criticized higher education in the United States for its lack of courage in dealing with moral issues.

3.19
Some people argue that schools should be value-free and avoid ethical and moral issues. Others advocate the active teaching of ethical and moral values. Which position is more valid? Explain your choice.

Contemporary problems with drug abuse, teenage pregnancy, and teenage crime also present moral dilemmas. How should schools respond? A look at developmental theory can help in understanding these issues.

Growth of Internalization: Piaget's Description of Moral Development

Although most people think of Piaget primarily in the context of cognitive development, he examined the development of ethics and morals as well. He studied cognitive and moral development in much the same way: He presented children with problems or tasks, listened to their reactions, and asked questions to gain insight into their thinking.

He found that children's responses to moral problems could be divided into two broad stages of development on the basis of a principle he labeled "internalization" (Piaget, 1932/1965). **Internalization** *refers to the source of control for children's thoughts and actions.* In the first stage, which Piaget called *external morality,* children view rules as fixed and permanent and externally enforced by authority figures. External morality lasts to about age 10. In our introductory episode, Talitha, with her reference to the rules, demonstrated thinking at this stage. It didn't matter that Gary was only asking about the homework assignment; rules are rules. Dwain, who responded, "Who cares? She's not here. She won't catch us," was also responding at this level; he was focusing on the fact that no authority figure was there to enforce the rule. Piaget believed that parents and teachers who stressed unquestioning adherence to adult authority retarded moral development and thus encouraged students to remain at this level (DeVries & Zan, 1995).

At the second stage, called **autonomous morality,** *children develop rational ideas of fairness and see justice as a reciprocal process of treating others as they would want to be treated.* Children at this stage begin to rely on themselves instead of others to regulate moral behavior. Krystal, in saying, "But he needs to know so he can do his homework," viewed Gary's whispering as an honest request for assistance, rather than as a rule infraction. Her response is characteristic of thinking at this stage.

3.20

Use the concept of *egocentrism* (see Chapter 2) to explain the difference between external and autonomous morality. Describe what you as a teacher can do to help students progress from one stage to the next.

Kohlberg's Theory of Moral Development

Steve, a high school junior, is working at a night job to help support his mother, a single parent of three. Steve is a conscientious student who works hard in his classes, but he doesn't have enough time to study.

History isn't Steve's favorite course, and because of his night work, he has a marginal D average. If he fails the final exam, he will fail the course, won't receive credit, and will have to alter plans for working during his senior year. He arranged to be off work the night before the exam so that he could study extra hard, but early in the evening his boss called, desperate to have Steve come in and replace another employee who called in sick at the last moment. His boss pressured him heavily, so Steve went to work reluctantly at 8:00 p.m. and came home exhausted at 2:00 a.m. He tried to study but fell asleep on the couch, with his book in his lap. His mother woke him for school at 6:30 a.m.

Steve went to his history class, looked at the test, and went blank. Everything seemed like a jumble. Claribel, however, one of the best students in the class, happened to have her answer sheet positioned so that he could clearly see every answer by barely moving his eyes.

From what you've read here, is Steve justified in cheating on the test?

3.21

Describe two personal examples of moral dilemmas that you've faced. Describe a moral dilemma that schools face.

What you've just encountered is a moral or ethical dilemma. Steve was caught in a position in which a clear course of action wasn't apparent; circumstances were such that any decision had both positive and negative consequences. A **moral dilemma** *is an ambiguous situation that requires a person to make a moral decision.* The way people reason in responding to moral dilemmas provides some insight into their levels of moral development.

Influenced by the work of John Dewey and Jean Piaget, Lawrence Kohlberg, a Harvard educator and psychologist, used moral dilemmas to study ethical reasoning. While working with teenagers, he found a developmental progression in moral reasoning, and on the basis of research conducted in cities and villages in Great Britain, Malaysia, Mexico, Taiwan, and Turkey, he concluded that the development of moral reasoning is similar across cultures. Using responses to hypothetical moral dilemmas such as the one you just read, Kohlberg (1963, 1969, 1981, 1984) developed a theory of moral development closely related to the work of Piaget. Like Piaget, he concluded that morals develop in stages and that all people pass through all the stages in the same order but at different rates.

Kohlberg originally described moral development as existing in three levels consisting of two stages each. These levels represent different perspectives that people can take as they wrestle with moral dilemmas or problems. The levels and stages are outlined in Table 3.3.

As you read the descriptions of the levels and stages, keep in mind that the specific response to a moral dilemma is not the critical issue. Instead, the reasons a person gives for making the decision determine the stage or level. Let's see how this works.

Level I: Preconventional Ethics

The preconventional level is an egocentric orientation focusing on moral consequences for the self. As you would predict, on the basis of their egocentrism, young children reason at this level. The level consists of two stages: punishment-obedience and market exchange. Some research indicates that 15% to 20% of the U.S. teenage population still reason at this level (Turiel, 1973).

Stage 1: Punishment-Obedience. People reasoning at the **punishment-obedience stage** *make moral decisions based on their chances of getting caught and being punished.* Right or wrong is determined by the consequences of an action: If the child is punished, the act was wrong; if not, the act was right. A person encountering an unguarded wallet or purse and not taking it because of fear of getting caught is operating at this stage. The same principle applies in a classroom. A person who argues that Steve is justified in cheating because he could clearly see every answer on Claribel's paper by barely moving his eyes and so he probably won't get caught is reasoning at Stage 1.

Stage 2: Market Exchange. At the **market exchange stage**, *people focus on the consequences of an action for themselves, but reciprocity is involved.* "An eye for an eye and a tooth for a tooth" or "Don't bite the hand that feeds you" reflects morality at this stage, and "You do something for me and I'll do something for you" is a key characteristic. A naive hedonism is used to judge the rightness or wrongness of an action.

Aspects of the political system exist at this stage. Political patronage, or the tendency of successful office seekers to give their supporters "cushy" jobs regardless of qualifications, is an example of Stage 2 ethics. The general tendency of politicians to put "their people" into office because the people will be loyal to them illustrates reasoning at this stage.

Cheating is a common moral dilemma in classrooms. A person reasoning at Stage 2 might argue that Steve should go ahead and cheat because if he doesn't, he'll have to repeat the course and quit his job. From this perspective, "The right thing to do is what makes me the happiest." This reasoning again focuses on the self.

3.22
What teacher behaviors contribute to students continuing to reason at the preconventional level? What can teachers do to help students move to higher levels?

Table 3.3

Kohlberg's stages of moral development

Level I Preconventional Ethics	The ethics of egocentrism. Typical of children up to about age 10. Called preconventional because children typically don't fully understand rules set down by others.
Stage 1: Punishment-Obedience	Consequences of acts determine whether they're good or bad. Individuals make moral decisions without considering the needs or feelings of others.
Stage 2: Market Exchange	The ethics of "What's in it for me?" Obeying rules and exchanging favors are judged in terms of the benefit to the individual.
Level II Conventional Ethics	The ethics of others. Typical of 10- to 20-year-olds. The name comes from conformity to the rules and conventions of society.
Stage 3: Interpersonal Harmony	Ethical decisions are based on concern for or the opinions of others. What pleases, helps, or is approved of by others characterizes this stage.
Stage 4: Law and Order	The ethics of laws, rules, and societal order. Rules and laws are inflexible and are obeyed for their own sake.
Level III Postconventional Ethics	The ethics of principle. Rarely reached before age 20 and only by a small portion of the population. The focus is on the principles underlying society's rules.
Stage 5: Social Contract	Rules and laws represent agreements among people about behavior that benefits society. Rules can be changed when they no longer meet society's needs.
Stage 6: Universal Principles	Rarely encountered in life. Ethics are determined by abstract and general principles that transcend societal rules.

Level II: Conventional Ethics

As development progresses and egocentrism declines, people acquire the ability to see the world from others' points of view. Morality is no longer constrained by the immediate effects of punishment or reward, instead becoming linked to the perspectives and concerns of others. Values such as loyalty, others' approval, family expectations, obedience to the law, and social order become prominent. Stages 3 and 4 reflect this orientation, and it is how the bulk of the population reasons.

Stage 3: Interpersonal Harmony.   Individuals reasoning at Stage 3 do not manipulate people to reach their goals, as they might at Stage 2. Rather, the **interpersonal harmony**

stage *is characterized by conventions, loyalty, and living up to the expectations of others.* The Stage 3 person is oriented toward maintaining the affection and approval of friends and relatives by being a "good" person. This is sometimes called the "nice girl/good boy" stage. A teenager on a date who meets a curfew because she doesn't want to worry her parents is reasoning at this stage.

A person reasoning at Stage 3 might offer a variety of perspectives on Steve's dilemma. One could argue that he needed to work to help his family and that therefore he was justified in cheating. A contrasting view, still at Stage 3, would suggest that he should not cheat, because people would think badly of him if they knew about it.

Reasoning at Stage 3 includes the danger of being caught up in the majority opinion. Accepting that cheating on one's income taxes is okay because "everybody cheats" is an example. We might call Stage 3 the "ethics of adolescence" because of the influence peers have on young people's thinking at this age.

Stage 4: Law and Order.   A person reasoning at Stage 4 would argue that Steve should not cheat, because "It's against the rules to cheat." The focus at this stage is on adherence to laws and rules for their own sake, rather than on pleasing particular people, as in Stage 3. According to the ethics of the **law and order stage**, *laws and rules exist to guide behavior and should be followed uniformly.*

Concern for the orderliness of society is also characteristic of this stage, such as a person arguing that Steve should not cheat, because "What would our country be like if everybody cheated under those same conditions?" Concern for others is still the focus, but

3.23
Suppose heavy traffic is moving on an interstate highway at a speed limit of 65. A sign appears that says Speed Limit 55. The flow of traffic continues as before. How might a driver reasoning at Stage 3 behave, compared with a driver reasoning at Stage 4?

Cheating is a persistent problem in classrooms. How students think about this problem and how teachers should respond to it depend on students' levels of moral development.

rules and order are the key criteria at this stage. People reasoning at Stage 4 don't take the tag off the pillow because it says not to, and if checkout time is noon, they check out at noon. They don't care whether the rest of the world cheats on their income taxes; they pay theirs because the law says to pay them.

Level III: Postconventional Ethics

A person reasoning at Level III has transcended both the individual and societal levels and makes moral decisions based on principles. People operating at this level, also called *principled morality,* follow rules but also see that, at times, rules need to be changed or ignored. Only a small portion of the population attains this level, and most don't reach it until their mid- to late 20s.

Historically, some of the great figures in history have sacrificed their lives in the name of principle. Sir Thomas More, who knew that he was ultimately ending his own life by refusing to acknowledge King Henry VIII as the head of the Church of England, nevertheless stood on a principle. Mahatma Gandhi chose jail rather than adhere to England's laws as he applied the principle of nonviolent noncooperation. Benigno Aquino knew in 1983 that he faced certain death on returning to the Philippines, but his commitment to his country and its social order made him return anyway.

Stage 5: Social Contract.   The person reasoning according to **social contract** *understands that a society of rational people needs socially agreed-on laws in order to function.* The laws are not accepted blindly or for their own sake, however; rather, they are based on the principle of utility, or "the greatest good for the greatest number," and are followed because they adhere to rights such as life, liberty, and the dignity of the individual.

Stage 5 is the official ethic of the United States. The constitutional Bill of Rights is an example of a cultural social contract; for example, Americans agree on principle that people have the right to free speech, and the legal profession is conceptually committed to interpreting the laws in this light. In addition, the American system has provisions for changing or amending laws in the light of new values or conditions. A person reasoning at Stage 5 would say that Steve's cheating is inappropriate because earning grades amounts to an agreement among teachers and learners that the grade will reflect individual effort. Cheating violates the agreement.

Stage 6: Universal Principles.   **Universal principles** *is the stage at which moral reasoning is based on abstract and general principles above society's rules.* People at this stage define rightness in terms of internalized universal standards that go beyond concrete laws. Examples such as "Render unto Caesar" and "The Golden Rule" are commonly cited. Research indicates that very few people operate at this stage (Kohlberg, 1984). Because of this, Kohlberg de-emphasized this stage in his later writings.

Kohlberg's Theory: Research and Criticism

Research on Kohlberg's Work.   Kohlberg's work has been widely researched, and this research supports the following conclusions (Berk, 1994; R. Taylor, 1987):

- Every person's moral reasoning develops through the same stages in the same order.
- People pass through the stages at different rates.

3.24
How would a person at Stage 5 respond to the problem of people cheating on their income tax?

▌ Development is gradual and continuous, rather than sudden and discrete.

▌ Once a stage is attained, a person continues to reason at that stage and rarely regresses to a lower stage.

▌ Training usually results in achieving only the next higher stage of moral reasoning.

Despite this support for Kohlberg's theory, there have also been criticisms.

Criticisms of Kohlberg's Work. Kohlberg's original work has been criticized because of a lack of cross-cultural validations, a lack of people reasoning at the postconventional level, and the sometimes loose connection between moral thought and moral behavior. Cross-cultural research indicates that the stages exist for people in other cultures and that children pass through these stages in the same sequence as they do in Western cultures. The rate and end point of moral development may vary, however, with the extent to which different societies encourage moral problem solving (Berk, 1994). In addition, postconventional reasoning appears biased in favor of Western cultures. In describing Stage 5, for example, we used the phrase "rights such as life, liberty, and the dignity of the individual." The dignity of the individual certainly reflects Western values. Other cultures, such as the Amish and Native Americans, de-emphasize individuality, instead placing greater value on cooperation and collaboration. A person from a more group-oriented culture, for example, might respond to the cheating dilemma by saying, "He shouldn't have been placed in a situation like that. Other people—his mother, his teacher, and other students—should be helping him so that he wouldn't be forced into such a dilemma." Teachers should be sensitive to the different interpretations of morality that people from different cultures may carry with them.

Kohlberg's focus on moral reasoning rather than moral behavior has also been criticized. People may reason at one stage but behave at another. Reasoning and behavior are correlated, however. Kohlberg (1975) found that only 15% of students reasoning at the postconventional level cheated when given the opportunity to do so, that 55% of those reasoning at the conventional level cheated, and that 70% of those reasoning at the preconventional level cheated. The tendency is for students reasoning at higher levels to act in accordance with their beliefs. Other research has linked moral development to a variety of behaviors as diverse as altruism, defending victims of injustice, and defending free speech and the rights of minorities (Berk, 1994).

Gender Differences: The Morality of Caring. Early research examining Kohlberg's theory identified differences in the ways men and women responded to moral dilemmas (Gilligan, 1982; Gilligan & Attanucci, 1988). Men were more likely to base their judgments on abstract concepts, such as justice, individual rights, and obligations. Women, in contrast, were more likely to base their moral decisions on personal relationships and interpersonal connections.

These findings resulted in females' responses being scored lower, thus suggesting a lower stage of moral development (Haan, Smith, & Block, 1968; Holstein, 1976). Gilligan (1982) argued that the findings instead indicate an "ethic of care" in women, which is not inferior; rather, Kohlberg's stage descriptions don't adequately represent female thinking. Caring appears to be more central to females' sense of identity, and when asked to identify moral dilemmas, they are more likely than males to choose them from the interpersonal problems of real life rather than those more abstract and impersonal (Skoe & Dressner, 1994). As with cross-cultural studies, Gilligan's research provides a more complete picture of moral development.

3.25 ■
Identify elements of Kohlberg's work that are similar to Piaget's.

3.26 ■
On the basis of Gilligan's work, how might a woman respond to the problem of the student not knowing his assignment, presented in the case study at the beginning of this section? How might her response be different from that of a man?

Moral Development and Classroom Structure

Understanding moral development is valuable for all of us as teachers because it helps us understand that the way we structure our classrooms and interact with our students influences their moral growth. If our goal is self-regulation, with students who understand and appreciate the need for orderly classrooms, we must explain the reasons for rules and involve them in the rule-setting process (McCaslin & Good, 1992). This emphasis on explanation and involvement changes the classroom culture from an adherence to rules because punishment is threatened—an external form of regulation—to one in which rules are followed because students realize they're necessary—self-regulation.

Research indicates that moral development is enhanced in an atmosphere where adults are verbal, rational, and affectionate and where a cooperative spirit exists (Berk, 1994). Teachers who reason at higher stages of development promote this spirit to a greater extent than do those reasoning at lower levels (S. Strom, 1989). The opposite is also true. Students working in an environment where punishment or the threat of punishment is emphasized will obey rules, but growth in self-control and regulation suffers. (We discuss these ideas further in Chapter 10 when we focus specifically on classroom management.)

3.27

Explain why teachers reasoning at higher levels would likely be more democratic and involve students more in classroom discussions than would teachers reasoning at lower levels.

Moral Development Through Peer Interaction

Teachers can also promote moral development by consciously creating opportunities for students to share and analyze their views. Let's look at an example.

"We've been reading an interesting story, and now I'd like to focus on a particular incident in it. Let's talk a bit about the boy in the story who found the wallet. Would it be wrong for him to keep the money? . . . Okay, I see a lot of heads nodding. . . . Why? . . . Jolene?"

"Because it didn't belong to him."

"Helena?"

"Because it was a lot of money, and his parents would probably make him give it back anyway."

"Todd?"

"Why not keep it? It wasn't his fault that the person lost it."

"Juan?"

"But what if the person who lost the money really needed it?"

"Okay. Those are all good reasons. We'll return to them in a moment, but there are a lot of other interesting questions to consider. First, put yourself in his shoes. Would you keep the money? What else might the boy have done, rather than keep the money? If he gives the wallet back, does he have the right to expect a reward? What do you think?"

Research on Kohlberg's work indicates that moral development can be enhanced through classroom discussions that allow students to examine their own moral thinking and to compare it with that of others (Oser, 1986). Interaction among peers is particularly effective because it encourages active listening and analysis of different moral positions (Kruger, 1992). Exposure to higher or more complex ways of thinking about moral dilemmas helps students reevaluate their own thinking by examining it in relation to others. These comparisons can disrupt a person's equilibrium and thus increase the chance for development.

Some guidelines for effective discussions about moral dilemmas are as follows:

3.28

Predict, on the basis of Piaget's theory, what stage of cognitive development would be necessary in order for a learner to reason at the conventional level. What stage of cognitive development would be required for postconventional reasoning?

▌ Focus on concrete moral conflicts and different ways of resolving them.

▌ Encourage students to consider the perspectives of others.

▌ Ask students to make personal choices in responding to dilemmas and to justify the choices.

▌ Analyze different courses of action by discussing the advantages and disadvantages of each.

Moral Framework of Schools

Kohlberg's work also reminds us that much of what teachers do in schools is grounded in moral decisions. When teachers emphasize student responsibility, make rules that prevent students from ridiculing each other, emphasize industry, and advocate honesty, they are teaching ethics. Laws that apply to schools also promote these values. For example, Public Law 94–142, which requires that students with learning exceptionalities be placed in the least restrictive environment possible, is based on an ethical issue. It says that it is not fair to deny a student with a learning exceptionality, for example, access to the mainstream learning environment. (We examine PL 94–142 in detail in Chapter 5.)

Arguments that schools shouldn't teach morals are naive. Values are involved every time a teacher emphasizes one topic instead of another, and morals reflect the values of individuals as well as cultural groups. A more realistic approach is to become as well informed as possible, and this allows you as a teacher to make sensitive and considered decisions based on your understanding.

This concludes our discussion of moral development. The next section, "Windows on Classrooms," provides you with an opportunity to apply the knowledge you've learned in this chapter.

> **3.29**
> Write a specific statement describing how you would respond to parents who strongly express the opinion that the teaching of morals should exist in the home and that teachers should not deal with the subject.

Classroom Connections

Developing Positive Self-Concepts in Your Classroom

1. Make students feel wanted and valued in your class.
   - A fourth-grade teacher starts the school year by having students write autobiographical sketches and bring in pictures of themselves taken when they were preschoolers. They list their strengths and weaknesses and describe what they want to be when they grow up.
   - A sixth-grade teacher begins each school year by announcing that everyone is important in her class and that she expects everyone to learn. She stays in her room every day after school and invites any students who are having problems to come by for help.

2. Provide learning experiences that promote success.
   - A fifth-grade teacher allows students to drop their lowest quiz grade, and he gives bonus points if students show consistent improvement.
   - A sixth-grade teacher has students keep portfolios of products they create in art, music, science, and social studies. She shares the portfolios with par-

ents and encourages parents to take the portfolios home and discuss them with their children.

Applying Moral Principles in Your Classroom

3. Openly discuss ethical dilemmas when they arise.
   - A high school teacher's students view cheating as a game, seeing what they can get away with. The teacher addresses the issue by saying, "Because you feel this way about cheating, I'm going to decide who gets what grade without a test. I'll grade you on how smart I think you are." This statement forms the basis for a discussion on fairness and cheating.
   - The day before a new student joins the class, a first-grade teacher discusses with the class how they would feel if they were new, how new students should be treated, and how they should treat each other in general.

4. Make and enforce rules requiring ethical treatment of each other.

- A seventh-grade teacher has a classroom rule that students may not laugh, snicker, or make remarks of any kind when one of their classmates is trying to answer a question. In introducing the rule, she has the students discuss the reasons for it.
- A second-grade teacher is explaining classroom rules at the beginning of the school year. One of them is "Respect other students' property." In the discussion, the teacher encourages students to think about the importance of the rule from other students' perspectives.

5. Model ethical behavior for students.

- A science teacher makes a commitment to students to have all their tests and quizzes graded by the following day. One day, he is asked, "Do you have our tests ready?" "Of course," he responds. "I made an agreement, and people can't go back on their agreements."

- A group of 10th graders finishes a field trip sooner than expected. "If we just hang around a little longer, we don't have to go back to school," someone comments. "Yes, but that would be a lie, wouldn't it?" the teacher counters. "We said we'd be back as soon as we finished."

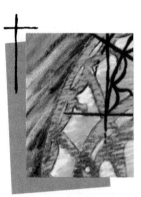

Windows on Classrooms

As you've studied this chapter, you've seen how the characteristics of preschool and primary-age learners, elementary students, and adolescents affect the ways they feel about themselves and the way they learn. You've seen how (a) an environment that combines structure with opportunities for autonomy and decision making and (b) teachers who are sensitive to their students promote personal, social, and emotional development.

Let's look now at another teacher working with a group of middle-school students. As you read the case study, compare the teacher's approach to the suggestions you've studied in the chapter.

Gee, this is frustrating," Helen Sharman, a seventh-grade teacher, mumbled as she was scoring a set of quizzes in the teachers' workroom after school.

"What's up?" her friend Natasha asked.

"Look," Helen directed, pointing to Item 6 on the quiz that read:

Theirs were the first items to be loaded.

"These students just won't think at all," Helen continued. "Three quarters

of them put an apostrophe between the *r* and the *s* on this one. The quiz was on using apostrophes in possessives. I warned them I was going to put some questions on the quiz that would make them think and that some of them would have trouble if they weren't on their toes. I should have saved my breath. . . . Not only that, but I had given them practice ones to work that were just like those on the quiz. We had one almost exactly like number 6, and they still missed it. . . .

And I explained it so carefully," she mumbled, shaking her head.

Helen returned to scoring her papers.

Hearing Helen mumble some more, Natasha asked, "Not getting any better?"

"No," Helen said firmly. "Maybe worse."

"What are you going to do?"

"What's really discouraging is that some of the students won't even try. Look at this one. Half of the quiz is blank. This isn't the first time Kim has done this either. When I confronted him about it last time, he said, "But I'm no good at English." I replied, "But you're doing fine in science and math." He thought about that for a while and said, 'But, that's different.' I wish I knew how to motivate him. You should see him on the basketball floor—all poetry in motion—but when he gets in here, nothing."

"That can be discouraging. I've got a few like that myself," Natasha replied empathically.

"What's worse, is that I'm almost sure some of the students cheated. I left the room to go to the office, and when I returned, several of them were talking and had guilt written all over their faces."

"Why do you suppose they did it?" Natasha returned.

"I'm not sure; part of it might be grade pressure. I grade on the curve, and they complain like crazy, but how else am I going to motivate them? Some just don't see any problem with cheating. If they don't get caught, fine. I really am discouraged."

"Well," Natasha shrugged, "hang in there."

The next morning, Helen returned the quizzes.

"We need to review the rules again," she commented as she fin-ished. "You did so poorly on the quiz, and I explained everything so carefully. You must not have studied very hard.

"Let's take another look," she went on. "What's the rule for singular possessives?"

" . . . Apostrophe s," Felice volun-teered.

"That's right, Felice. Good. Now, how about plurals?"

"S apostrophe," Scott answered.

"All right. But what if the noun doesn't end in s? . . . Russell?"

"Then it's like singular. . . . It's apostrophe s."

"Good. And how about pro-nouns?"

"You don't do anything," Connie put in.

"Yes, that's all correct," Helen nodded. "Why didn't you do that on the quiz?"

" . . . "

"Okay, look at number 3 on the quiz."

It appeared as follows:

The books belonging to the lady were lost.

"It should be written like this," Helen explained, and she wrote "The lady's books were lost" on the chalkboard.

"Ms. Sharman," Nathan called from the back of the room. "Why is it apostrophe s?"

"Nathan," Helen said evenly. "Remember my first rule?"

"Yes, Ma'am," Nathan said quietly.

"Good. That's the second one today. If you speak without permission again, it's a half hour after school.

"Now, to answer your question, it's singular. So that's why it's apostrophe s.

"Now look at number 6." Helen waited a few seconds and then contin-ued, "You were supposed to correctly punctuate it. But it's correct already because theirs is already possessive. Now, that one was a little tricky, but you know I'm going to put a few on each quiz to make you think. You'd have got-ten it if you were on your toes."

Helen identified three more items that were commonly missed. She then gave the students a review sheet for some additional practice.

"Now, these are just like the quiz," she said. "Practice hard on them now, and we'll have another quiz on Thursday. Let's all do better. Please don't let me down again.

"And one more thing. I believe there was some cheating on this test. If I catch anyone cheating on Thurs-day, I'll tear up your quiz and give you a failing grade. Now, go to work."

The students then worked on the practice exercises as Helen walked among them, offering periodic sug-gestions.

Questions for Discussion and Analysis

Analyze Helen's lesson now in the context of the information in this chapter. In doing your analysis, you may want to consider the following questions. In each case, be specific and take information directly from the case study in answering these questions.

1. How might Erikson explain Kim's behavior in Helen's class?

2. Using research findings from the research on self-concept, explain Kim's behavior.

3. Using concepts from Kohlberg's theory, analyze Helen's cheating problem. From Kohlberg's perspective, how well did she handle this problem?

4. If you think Helen's teaching could have been improved on the basis of the informa-tion in Chapter 3, what suggestions would you make? Again, be specific.

 **Summary**

Erikson's Theory of Personal and Social Development

Erikson's psychosocial theory, an effort to integrate personal and social development, is based on the assumption that people's development of self is a response to needs. He suggests further that development is in stages, each marked by a psychosocial challenge, which he called a *crisis.* As people develop, their motivations change.

According to Erikson, positive resolution of the crisis in each stage results in an inclination to be trusting, feelings of autonomy, willingness to take initiative, and a sense of industry, from the period of birth through approximately the elementary school years. Continued resolution of crises leaves people with a firm identity, the ability to achieve intimacy, desire for generativity, and finally a sense of integrity as life's end nears. As teachers work with students, they should keep these developmental challenges in mind and structure their classrooms and interactions with students to facilitate growth in these areas.

Self-Concept: Integrative Personal Development

Self-concept, based largely on experience, describes people's perceptions of their physical, social, and academic competence. Academic self-concept, particularly in specific content areas, is correlated with achievement, but physical and social self-concept and achievement are essentially unrelated.

Attempts to improve students' self-concepts by direct intervention have been largely unsuccessful. In contrast, attempts to improve self-concept as an outcome of increased success and achievement have been quite successful. This finding suggests that teachers should direct their efforts toward improving students' effort and achievement, and then self-concept will improve as well.

Development of Morality, Social Responsibility, and Self-Control

Piaget is identified with cognitive development, but he studied the development of morals as well. He suggests that individuals progress from external morality, in which rules are enforced by authority figures, to autonomous morality, in which they see morality as rational and reciprocal.

Lawrence Kohlberg, in developing his theory of moral development, was influenced by Piaget's work. Kohlberg presented people with moral dilemmas—ambiguous problems requiring moral decisions—and, on the basis of their responses to the dilemmas, developed a classification system for moral reasoning. At the first level, called *preconventional ethics,* people make egocentric moral decisions focused on consequences for themselves. At the *conventional ethics* level, people's moral reasoning focuses on the consequences for others, and at the *postconventional ethics* level, moral reasoning is based on principle. Kohlberg suggested that conventional reasoning required concrete operational thinking and that postconventional reasoning required formal operational thinking.

Teachers can promote moral development in their classrooms in several ways. As they explain and implement their management systems, they should emphasize individual responsibility and the functional nature of rules designed to protect the rights of others. Students should be encouraged to think about topics such as honesty and respect for others in terms of consequences for others and basic principles of human respect. As teachers interact with students, they should recognize the powerful influence they have as role models in encouraging the moral development of their students.

 **Important Concepts**

academic self-concept (p. 85)

autonomous morality (p. 92)

autonomy (p. 76)

collective self-esteem (p. 88)

crisis (p. 76)

generativity (p. 81)

identity (p. 79)

identity crisis (p. 79)

industry (p. 78)

initiative (p. 77)

integrity (p. 82)

internalization (p. 92)

interpersonal harmony stage (pp. 94–95)

intimacy (p. 81)

law and order stage (p. 95)

market exchange stage (p. 93)

moral dilemma (p. 93)

psychosocial theory (p. 76)

punishment-obedience stage (p. 93)

self-concept (p. 85)

self-esteem (p. 85)

social contract (p. 96)

trust (p. 76)

universal principles (p. 96)

Chapter Outline

Learner 4
Differences

Tim Wilkinson is a fifth-grade teacher in a large urban elementary school. He has 29 students—16 girls and 13 boys. His group includes 10 African Americans, 3 students of Hispanic descent, and 2 Asian Americans. Most of his students come from low-income families.

He smiled slightly as he watched the students, bent over their desks, busy with seatwork. He enjoyed working with the students, fascinated by the differences in their backgrounds. As Tim walked among his students, he glanced at Selena's work. As usual, it was nearly perfect. Everything was easy for her, and she seemed to be a happy, well-adjusted child.

He smiled slightly as he walked by Helen's desk. She was his "special project," and she had begun to blossom in response to his attention and effort. The quality of her work had improved dramatically since the beginning of the year.

As he stepped past Juan, Tim's warm glow turned to concern. Juan had been quiet from the first day of school, and he was easily offended by perceived slights from his classmates. Because his parents were migrant workers, the family moved constantly, and he had repeated the fourth grade. Now, his parents were separated, and his mother had settled in this area so that the children could stay in the same school.

Juan had to struggle to keep up with the rest of the class. Spanish was his first language, and Tim wasn't sure how much of his instruction Juan understood. What seemed certain, however, was that Juan was falling farther and farther behind, and Tim didn't know what to do. Not knowing where else to turn, he consulted the school psychologist.

When all of us as teachers enter our classrooms for the first time, a sea of faces appears before us. At one level, these students seem very much alike; they are nearly the same age, they have similar interests, and they study common subjects and topics. A closer look, however, reveals many differences. Almost certainly, we have both males and females in our classes. We know from our study of Chapters 2 and 3 that students develop at different rates. Learning is nearly effortless for some; others struggle with even basic ideas. A few students have affluent parents; other students' families barely eke out a living. Depending on location, we have students with different ethnic and cultural backgrounds—African American, Hispanic, Asian, European, Native American and others—in our classes.

Suddenly, our sea of faces turns into 30 individuals! Unfortunately, some demographic combinations may place our students at risk of not being able to fully benefit from the educational system. In this chapter, we examine these differences among students and the implications they have for teachers.

After completing your study of this chapter, you should be able to meet the following objectives:

▌ Explain how different views of intelligence influence your teaching.
▌ Define socioeconomic status and explain how it may affect school performance.
▌ Explain the role that culture and language play in learning.
▌ Describe the influence of gender on different aspects of school success.
▌ Describe ways that schools and classrooms can be adapted to meet the needs of at-risk students.

As we saw in the opening case, Tim's concerns for Juan are important. In a perfect world, all learning would be as easy as it is for Selena, and teaching would be a nearly effortless pleasure. All teachers know, however, that students vary greatly in ability and in many other ways. They truly are individuals, and teachers must make professional decisions with this fact in mind. Figure 4.1 illustrates some of these sources of individuality.

Figure 4.1 illustrates sources of learner differences. Beginning at the top is *intelligence,* or aptitude. It determines how quickly and easily a person might learn and, in some instances, whether the learning is even possible.

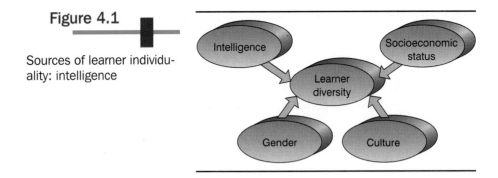

Figure 4.1

Sources of learner individuality: intelligence

Socioeconomic status (SES) refers to parents' income, occupation, and level of education, all of which influence student learning. Children of high-SES parents are likely to have a wealth of school-related experiences, and they are usually well nurtured physically. Children of low-SES parents, in contrast, often come from homes where parents spend much of their time and energy trying to meet essential needs. Some children even lack nutrition and a home, and they may come to school emotionally ill-prepared for the demands of school.

Culture and *ethnicity* also influence school success. Cultural background and values can be strong foundations on which learning is based, or they can be obstacles to both achievement and motivation. Teachers who value students' differing cultural backgrounds and build on them help make all students feel accepted and capable of learning.

Gender is also a source of individuality. In the United States, males and females are perceived and treated differently. Unfortunately, these perceptions and treatments can result in different expectations and achievement for boys and girls.

The focus of this chapter is the individual differences of students and how these differences affect students' learning. Let's begin with a discussion of intelligence.

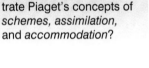

4.1

How does the practice of building on students' cultural backgrounds illustrate Piaget's concepts of *schemes, assimilation, and accommodation?*

Intelligence

Intelligence: What Does It Mean?

Everyone has a commonsense notion of intelligence; it's how "sharp" people are, or how much they know, how quickly they learn, and how perceptive and sensitive they are. Teachers have an intuitive sense of intelligence and use quizzes, assignments, and students' comments to gauge abilities. Used properly, this intuition can help teachers design learning activities that best match students' abilities; but misused, intuition can lead to lowered expectations and false stereotypes (Good & Brophy, 1994). Tim's sensitivity and concern guided him as he considered seeking additional help for Juan. A teacher less alert than Tim might miss the fact that Juan is struggling or, worse yet, write him off on the grounds that he is too far behind the others.

Experts define **intelligence** as three dimensional: *(a) the capacity to acquire knowledge, (b) the ability to think and reason in the abstract, and (c) the capability for solving problems* (Snyderman & Rothman, 1987; Sternberg, 1986). The capacity to acquire knowledge has also been called *aptitude,* and some learning theorists equate it with the time and quality of instruction needed to master a subject (B. Bloom, 1981; J. Carrol, 1963). According to this model, learners with high aptitude need less time and instruction than those whose aptitude is lower. In seeing Juan falling farther and farther behind, Tim was intuitively reacting to this dimension.

From another perspective, intelligence is simply defined as the attributes that intelligence tests measure. Let's examine some of them.

Measuring Intelligence

Following are some items commonly found on intelligence tests:

1. Cave: Hole; Bag:____ (Cave is to hole as bag is to ____.)
    a. paper   b. container   c. box   d. brown
2. Sharon had X amount of money, and this could buy eight apples. How much money would it take to buy four apples?
    a. $8X$ b. $2X$ c. $X/2$ d. $4X$
3. Inspect the following list of numbers for 5 seconds.
    9   7   4   6   2   1   8   3   9

Now cover them and name the digits in order from memory.

Each of these items has been used on standardized intelligence tests, and an individual's intelligence is inferred from her or his performance on such a test.

Examination of these items makes one aspect of the tests strikingly clear: Experience is an important factor in test performance (Perkins, 1995). For instance, the first item requires both vocabulary and an understanding of analogies, and experience with analogies would certainly improve performance. The second item is based on background in math. Even the third item, a seemingly simple memory task, can be improved with experience and training (A. Brown, Bransford, Ferrara, & Campione, 1983).

The impact of experience on intelligence test performance corroborates Piaget's work. In Chapter 2, you saw that experience is one factor affecting cognitive development and that children who have the advantage of rich experiences consistently perform better than their less-experienced peers. Clearly, intelligence tests measure something more than raw, or innate, ability.

Intelligence: One Trait or Many?

Because scores on different measures of intelligence, such as verbal and numerical ability and abstract reasoning, were all highly correlated, early researchers believed intelligence to be a single trait. Spearman (1927), one of the major early figures, described it as "g" or general intelligence. Raymond Cattell (1963, 1971), one of Spearman's students, later expanded the description to include *fluid intelligence,* which reflects general ability and adaptability to novel tasks (Lohman, 1995), measured by tests such as matrices and block designs, and *crystallized intelligence,* which reflects people's experience—measured by school tasks, such as vocabulary and math problems. As the field developed, other kinds of intelligence, such as verbal, mathematical, spatial, and perceptual, were proposed (Jensen, 1987).

Contemporary researchers have further extended the idea that intelligence is composed of several abilities (Woodcock, 1995). We describe three of these models in the following sections: (a) Guilford's structure of intellect (SOI), (b) Gardner's theory of multiple intelligences, and (c) Sternberg's triarchic theory of intelligence.

Guilford's Structure of Intellect (SOI)

J. P. Guilford (1967), one of the multiple-trait pioneers, believed that intelligence depends on what people are thinking about (*content*), their mental *operations,* and the *products*

4.2

Which of the three dimensions of intelligence is most important? Least? How is your answer influenced by the culture you live in, such as 20th-century America, compared with a primitive, nomadic culture?

4.3

How does experience influence a person's "capacity to acquire knowledge"? Explain your answer with a specific example.

4.4

Refer to researchers' definition of intelligence again. Does it suggest one intelligence or several? How similar are the elements?

Figure 4.2

Guilford's structure of intellect model

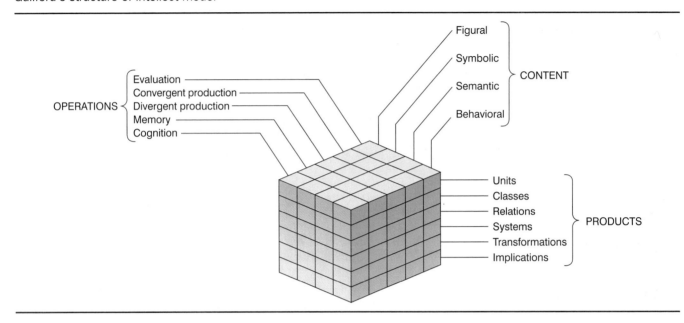

of these operations. He developed a *structure of intellect* (SOI) model that describes intelligence as the intersection of four content areas, five cognitive operations, and six products. For example, remembering a telephone number requires a memory operation in a symbolic content area to produce a single product—the number (Perkins, 1995).

Spatially, Guilford's model can be visualized as shown in Figure 4.2. In a last article before his death at age 90, Guilford (1988) speculated that even this 120-celled conceptualization of intelligence may be oversimplified.

When compared with the Guilford model, school curricula focus a disproportionate amount of time and resources addressing certain aspects of intelligence, such as memorizing facts and definitions, while virtually ignoring others, such as evaluation and the search for relationships (Gall, 1984; Goodlad, 1984). Changes in both the math and science curricula are attempting to address this imbalance by increasing the emphasis on problem solving and processes such as hypothesizing, analyzing, and evaluating (American Association for the Advancement of Science [AAAS], 1993; National Council of Teachers of Mathematics [NCTM], 1991).

Guilford's pioneering work is valuable because it encouraged researchers and educators to broaden their concept of ability, but the complexity of the model makes it difficult to apply in classrooms.

4.5

What implications would Guilford's model have for intelligence testing? For reporting test scores?

Gardner's Theory of Multiple Intelligences

Influenced by Guilford's original work, Howard Gardner (1983) concluded that most conceptions of intelligence were too narrow and should be broadened beyond the confines of traditional academic subjects. He describes seven major and relatively independent dimensions of intelligence and makes a persuasive argument for the idea of multiple talents. Table 4.1 outlines these dimensions.

Gardner's argument for multiple intelligences derives from two sources. One source is research on people with brain damage that indicates the neural functioning is localized and specific to a single domain, such as speech or aesthetic ability. The second source is the variety of skills found in modern society. Many people are not high in verbal or logical dimensions but excel in others, such as spatial ability (artists and architects) and interpersonal skills (effective counselors and empathic teachers).

Gardner's ideas make intuitive sense. For example, we all know people who don't seem terribly "sharp" analytically but who have excellent instincts for getting along with others. This ability serves them well, and in some instances they're more successful than their "brighter" counterparts. Others seem very self-aware and have the ability to capitalize on their strengths and to minimize their weaknesses. Gardner would simply explain these examples as interpersonal and intrapersonal intelligence, respectively.

Gardner's Theory: Educational Applications.   Attempts to apply Gardner's ideas to school settings have focused on both curriculum and instruction. Curriculum developers have attempted to prepare materials in underrepresented areas of the curriculum; modules to develop skills in areas such as imaginative writing, visual arts, and music notation are being pilot-tested in both elementary and secondary schools (H. Gardner & Hatch, 1989).

Table 4.1

Gardner's theory of multiple intelligences

Dimension	Example
Linguistic intelligence: Sensitivity to the meaning and order of words and the varied uses of language	Poet, journalist
Logical-mathematical intelligence: The ability to handle long chains of reasoning and to recognize patterns and order in the world	Scientist, mathematician
Musical intelligence: Sensitivity to pitch, melody, and tone	Composer, violinist
Spatial intelligence: The ability to perceive the visual world accurately, and to re-create, transform, or modify aspects of the world on the basis of one's perceptions	Sculptor, navigator
Bodily-kinesthetic intelligence: A fine-tuned ability to use the body and to handle objects	Dancer, athlete
Interpersonal intelligence: The ability to notice and make distinctions among others	Therapist, salesperson
Intrapersonal intelligence: Access to one's own "feeling life"	Self-aware individual

Source: Adapted from H. Gardner and Hatch (1989).

Spatial intelligence includes the ability to perceive and re-create physical relations in the world.

Bodily-kinesthetic intelligence allows dancers and athletes to use their bodies in effective and creative ways.

4.6
On which of Gardner's seven intelligences does the typical school curriculum focus most strongly? On which report card—an elementary or a secondary—are more of the intelligences evaluated? Why is this the case?

In planning instruction for students, teachers are encouraged to introduce and foster knowledge based on the different intelligences (Armstrong, 1994). Table 4.2 presents some applications of how Gardner's theory translates into classroom practice. Gardner emphasizes, however, that not all ideas or subjects can be approached by using all the intelligences: "There is no point in assuming that every topic can be effectively approached in at least seven ways, and it is a waste of effort and time to attempt to do this" (H. Gardner, 1995, p. 206).

Sternberg's Triarchic Theory of Intelligence

Robert Sternberg (1988, 1990), like Gardner, approaches intelligence from a multi-ability perspective. Sternberg proposes a triarchic theory of intelligence composed of three parts: (a) processing components—skills used in problem solving, (b) contextual components—links between intelligence and the environment, and (c) experiential components—mechanisms for modifying intelligence through experience.

At the core of Sternberg's theory is the idea that intelligence can be separated into component processes that influence the way people think about the world and solve problems. These processes and their features are illustrated in Figure 4.3.

Processing Components.   The most basic parts of Sternberg's model are the processing components people use to solve problems: a *knowledge acquisition component,* a *performance component,* and a *metacomponent.* Sternberg describes these components as analogous to trainees, labor, and management in a corporation. Knowledge-acquisition components (trainees) allow people to learn new information, performance components (labor) actually work with problems to produce solutions, and metacomponents (management) organize and manage the other aspects of intelligence. Intelligent behavior includes selecting effective problem-solving strategies, monitoring progress, and changing the approach if it doesn't work.

Table 4.2

Instructional applications of Gardner's multiple intelligences

Dimension	Application
Linguistic	How can I get students to talk or write about the idea?
Logical/Mathematical	How can I bring in number, logic, and classification to encourage students to quantify or clarify the idea?
Spatial	What can I do to help students visualize, draw, or conceptualize the idea spatially?
Musical	How can I help students use environmental sounds, or set ideas into rhythm or melody?
Bodily Kinesthetic	What can I do to help students involve the whole body or to use hands-on experience?
Interpersonal	How can peer, cross-age, or cooperative learning be used to help students develop their interactive skills?
Intrapersonal	How can I get students to think about their capacities and feelings to make them more aware of themselves as persons and learners?

The components interact when people apply intelligence to a complex task such as writing a term paper (Sternberg, 1988). Metacomponents decide on a topic, plan the paper, and monitor progress as the paper is written. Knowledge-acquisition components research the topic and combine facts into integrated ideas. Performance components do the actual writing. All three work together to produce a final product.

4.7 Illustrate the three processing components with an example such as buying a car.

Contextual Components: Intelligence and the Environment.   The second part of Sternberg's triarchic theory attempts to explain how intelligence relates to operating in the everyday environment. Intelligent people adapt to the environment to accomplish goals, changing it or selecting out of it when necessary. For example, in an attempt to get a good grade in a college course, a student adjusts her note taking and studying on the basis of a professor's explanation of testing procedures (adapts to the environment). She can't clearly hear the presentation, so she moves up front (changes the environment). Despite these efforts, she just isn't learning enough, so she drops the class (selects out of the environment). In each instance, the student is sensitive to the effect that environment is having on performance. Sternberg considers this an important part of intelligence.

4.8 Consider Sternberg's strategies for dealing with the environment—adapting to it, changing it, and selecting out of it. Which do schools emphasize the most? Which *should* they emphasize most? Least?

Experiential Components: Modifying Intelligence Through Experience.   The third aspect of Sternberg's theory describes how intelligence is modified by experience. In Sternberg's view, intelligent behavior has two important characteristics: (a) the ability to cope effectively with novel experiences and (b) the ability to solve problems efficiently and automatically. An intelligent person learns from experience by relating new experiences to old and converting this information into patterns that can be used automatically and efficiently. Consider this example:

A beginning reader encounters the word *she*. The teacher says, "Shheee."
Then the reader encounters the word *show*. The teacher says, "This word sounds like 'Shho.'"

Figure 4.3

Sternberg's triarchic model of intelligence

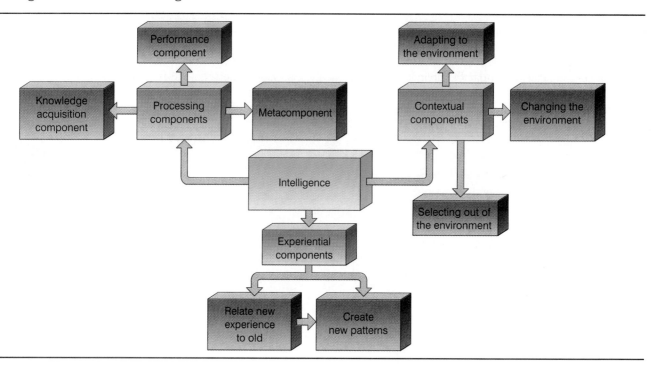

4.9

Identify at least two ways in which Sternberg's and Piaget's theories are similar. What implications do these similarities have for schools?

4.10

Of the three legs of Sternberg's triarchic theory, which is most clearly related to Spearman's notion of "g" or general intelligence? What do the other two legs attempt to explain about intelligence?

Next, the student sees the word *ship.* He tries pronouncing it himself: "Shhip." He now has a rule to decode future words. When *s* and *h* are together, they go "shh."

According to Sternberg, an intelligent child recognizes patterns quickly and is able to use rules automatically. The ability to analyze data and find patterns increases with age and makes older children more efficient problem solvers. This ability to process information efficiently is one cornerstone of increased intellectual functioning (Sternberg, 1988).

Educational Implications of Sternberg's Work.   Sternberg's view of intelligence suggests that learners should be given extensive experience with novel situations in which they're required to relate new experiences to old, rather than focus on the drill and practice of basic skills. Sternberg also views intelligence as alterable, capable of being improved. This view has implications for teaching. According to Sternberg, intelligence is a complex process that can be divided into subcomponents to be trained and improved on in school. For example, if solving analogies is an important part of intelligence (and intelligence tests), then it should be possible to improve intelligence and intelligence test performance by giving students experience with analogies. This issue—the extent to which intelligence can be altered—is the topic of the next section.

Intelligence: Nature Versus Nurture

No aspect of intelligence has been debated more hotly than the issue of heredity versus environment. The extreme **nature view of intelligence** *asserts that intelligence is solely* *determined by genetics;* the **nurture view of intelligence** *emphasizes the influence of the environment.* Most experts take a position somewhere in the middle, believing that a person's intelligence is influenced by both (Snyderman & Rothman, 1987; Weinberg, 1989).

The relationship between the two can be viewed quite simply. A person's genes provide the potential, and stimulating environments make the most of the raw material, whereas stultifying environments hamper intellectual growth (MacKenzie, 1984). In one study, for example, researchers tracked children born of low-income parents but adopted as infants into high-income families. The experiences the children were provided produced an average IQ 14 points higher than that of comparable siblings (Schiff, Duyme, Dumaret, & Tomkiewicz, 1982).

Intelligence also changes over time. One review found IQ changes of 28 points over a period of 2½ to 17 years; one seventh of the students had changes of more than 40 points (McCall, Appelbaum, & Hogarty, 1973)! Although some testing error is likely, intelligence itself was probably altered in many cases because of changes in an individual's social setting, level of intellectual challenge, or others' expectations (Perkins, 1995).

Efforts to improve intelligence have also been fruitful. Attempts to directly teach the cognitive skills tapped by intelligence tests have been successful with preschool and elementary students (Consortium for Longitudinal Studies, 1983; Sprigle & Schoefer, 1985), adults (Whimbey, 1980), and students with learning disabilities (A. Brown & Campione, 1986). A longitudinal study of disadvantaged, inner-city children also indicated that early stimulation can have lasting effects on IQ (Garber, 1988).

> **4.11**
>
> If environments to promote an increase in intelligence were designed, what in the typical American environments would need to be changed?

Ability Grouping

Although other adaptations exist (we discuss them in detail in Chapter 5), the most common way that schools have responded to differences in learner ability is by **ability group-**

Intelligence can be enhanced by learning activities that emphasize abstract reasoning and problem solving.

ing, which places students together on the basis of ability and attempts to match instruction to the needs of different groups. Because ability grouping is so common, yet controversial and politically charged, we devote this section to its examination.

Types of Ability Grouping

Ability grouping in elementary schools is very popular (B. Clements & Evertson, 1982), and it typically exists in three forms. They are described and illustrated in Table 4.3. Most teachers of elementary students endorse ability grouping, particularly in reading and math.

In the junior high and high schools, ability grouping goes further, with high-ability students studying college preparatory courses and their low-ability counterparts receiving vocational or work-related instruction. In some cases, students are grouped only in certain areas, such as English or math; in other cases, it exists across all content areas—a practice called *tracking.* **Tracking** *is the practice of placing students in different classes or curricula on the basis of ability.* Some form of tracking exists in most middle, junior high, and high schools (Braddock, 1990).

4.12 ▬

If forced to choose between between-class ability grouping and within-class ability grouping, which would Guilford and Gardner prefer? Why?

4.13 ▬

Why is within-class grouping so uncommon in secondary schools?

Ability Grouping: Research Results

Why is ability grouping so pervasive? Advocates, on the one hand, argue that it enhances instruction by allowing teachers to adjust the rate, methods, and materials to better meet students' needs. Because pace and assessment are similar for a particular group, instruction is easier for the teacher (Cotton & Savard, 1981).

Critics, on the other hand, identify a number of problems with all forms of ability grouping. Some of their criticisms are listed at the top of the next page:

Table 4.3 ▮

Types of ability grouping in elementary schools

Type	Description	Example
Between-class grouping	Divides students at a certain grade into levels, such as high, average, and low	A school with 75 third graders divides them into one class of high achievers, one of average, and one of low.
Within-class grouping	Divides students in a class into subgroups based on reading or math scores	A fourth-grade teacher has three reading groups based on reading ability.
Joplin plan	Regroups across grade levels	Teachers from different grade levels place students in the same reading class.

▌ Within-class grouping creates logistical problems because different lessons and assignments are required and monitoring seatwork is difficult (Good & Brophy, 1994; Oakes, 1992).

▌ Improper placements exist, and placement tends to become permanent. Cultural minorities are underrepresented in high-ability classes (Good & Marshall, 1984; Grant & Rothenberg, 1986; Oakes, 1992).

▌ Low groups are stigmatized. The self-esteem and motivation of low groups suffer (Cotton & Savard, 1981; Good & Marshall, 1984; Hallinan, 1984).

▌ Homogeneously grouped low-ability students achieve less than heterogeneously grouped students of similar ability (Good & Brophy, 1994).

4.14
Explain how ability grouping could affect students' self-esteem and motivation.

Negative Effects of Grouping: Possible Explanations

Negative effects of grouping are related, in part, to instructional effectiveness. Research indicates that presentations to low groups are more fragmented and vague than those to high groups; they focus more on memorizing instead of understanding, problem solving, and "active learning"; and students in low-ability classes are often taught by teachers who lack enthusiasm and stress conformity versus autonomy (Good & Brophy, 1994; Oakes, 1992; S. Ross, Smith, Loks, & McNelie, 1994).

Grouping also affects the students themselves. In addition to the lowered self-esteem and motivation to learn discussed above, absentee rates tend to increase. One study found that absenteeism increased from 8% to 26% after transition to a tracked junior high (Slavin & Karweit, 1982), with most of the truants being students in the low-level classes. Tracking can also result in the racial or cultural segregation of students and make social development and the ability to form friendships across cultural groups difficult (Oakes, 1992).

Grouping: Implications for Teachers

Suggestions for dealing with the problems of grouping vary. At one extreme, critics argue that the negative effects of grouping are so pernicious that the practice should be abolished completely. Grant and Rothenberg (1986) summarize this position:

> We suggest . . . that there is a fundamental conflict between the practice of ability grouping and public schools' avowed goal of providing equal opportunity to all students. More equitable alternatives must be sought, even if they involve major changes in classroom organization. (p. 47)

A more moderate position suggests that grouping may be appropriate in some areas, such as reading and math (Good & Brophy, 1994), but that every effort should be made to de-emphasize groups in other content areas. Researchers have found that use of the Joplin plan in reading, combined with heterogeneous grouping in other areas, can have positive effects on reading achievement without negative side effects (Slavin, 1987). At the junior and senior high levels, between-class grouping should be limited to the basic academic areas, with heterogeneous grouping used in others.

When grouping is necessary, specific measures to reduce the negative effects should be taken. Summaries of some suggestions are presented in Table 4.4.

The suggestions in Table 4.4 are demanding. Teachers must constantly monitor both the cognitive and affective progress of their students and make careful decisions about group placements. The need to maintain flexibility in this process cannot be overemphasized.

4.15
Suppose an enthusiastic second-grade teacher will be teaching science to all three classes at her grade level and is considering ability grouping. What advice would you give her? Provide a specific rationale for your advice. Would your advice change if the grade level were sixth instead of second?

Table 4.4

Suggestions for reducing
the negative effects of
grouping

1. Keep group composition flexible and reassign students to other groups when their rate of learning warrants it.
2. Make every effort to ensure that the quality of instruction is as high for low-ability students as it is for high-ability students.
3. Treat student characteristics as dynamic rather than static; teach low-ability students appropriate learning strategies and behaviors.
4. Avoid assigning negative labels to lower groups.
5. Constantly be aware of the possible negative consequences of ability grouping.

Classroom Connections

Applying an Understanding of Ability Differences in Your Classroom

1. Remember that intelligence test scores are just one indicator of school ability.
   - In deciding whether to place a student in a special education class, a team of teachers and the guidance counselor consider grades, work samples, and teacher observations, in addition to the intelligence test score.

2. Be cautious when using intelligence test scores to make educational decisions about cultural minorities.
   - A first-grade teacher working in an inner-city school consults with the school psychologist in interpreting intelligence test scores. She reminds herself of the effect that language and experience can have on test performance.

3. Use instructional strategies that minimize narrow definitions of aptitude and that maximize student interest and effort.
   - A math teacher allows students two opportunities to pass his quizzes. When they need extra help, he uses peer tutoring and special small-group work as additional aids.
   - An English teacher makes two types of assignments: required and optional. Seventy percent of the

assignments are required for everyone; the other 30% provide students with choices, and they negotiate with the teacher on the specific assignments.

4. Consider the implications of multiple intelligences for teaching and learning.
   - In a unit on the Revolutionary War, a teacher has all students take a test on basic information but bases 25% of the unit grade on special projects. Groups of students research topics such as the music and art of the times and present their information to the class on poster boards, in tape recordings, or in replicas of battle sites.

Using Grouping Appropriately in Classrooms

5. View group composition as flexible and reassign students to other groups when warranted by their learning progress.
   - A team of four first-grade teachers meets at the end of each grading period to reexamine groups and to move students when appropriate.

6. Use heterogeneous grouping whenever possible.
   - A second-grade teacher uses different ability groups in his reading instruction but uses whole-

class instruction when he does units on poetry and American folktales.

7. When using ability groups, make every effort to ensure that the quality of instruction is the same for each ability level.

• A teacher has a colleague observe and monitor her questioning behavior during a series of language arts lessons. She asks the colleague to record all her questions to ensure that each ability group receives the same amount of active teaching and appropriate mix of high- and low-level questions.

Socioeconomic Status (SES)

One of the most powerful factors influencing school performance is **socioeconomic status (SES)**, *the combination of parents' incomes, occupations, and levels of education.* SES consistently predicts intelligence and achievement test scores, grades, truancy, and dropout and suspension rates (Ballantine, 1989; Macionis, 1994). School dropout rates for students from poor families are twice those of the general population; for students from the poorest families, they exceed 50% (Catterall & Cota-Robles, 1988). Figure 4.4 identifies SES as an important source of learner individuality.

Influence of SES on Learning

Never before have schools attempted to teach so many students who are physically and mentally ill-prepared to learn. A combination of economic and social forces threatens the ability of many students to profit from their educational opportunities. Consider these statistics:

- One fourth of U.S. children currently live below the poverty level, the highest percentage in 20 years. Fifteen million children are being raised by single mothers whose family income averaged $11,400 in 1988 dollars.
- Forty-four percent of African American children and 36% of Latino children live in poverty.
- Between one fourth and one third of today's children have no adult at home when they return home from school.
- Twenty percent of America's preschoolers have not been vaccinated against polio (Hodgkinson, 1991; Kellog, 1988; U.S. Department of Education, 1993).

Physical Needs and Experience

How does SES influence learning? One way is through basic needs. Many families lack adequate medical care, and an increasing number of children are coming to school without proper nourishment. In addition, homelessness is becoming a major problem; experts estimate that families now account for one third of the homeless, that more than 500,000 children were homeless in 1989, and that 43% of school-age homeless children do not attend school at all (Lawler-Prince & Holloway, 1992).

Poverty also influences the quality of home life. Unstable work conditions increase economic problems that lead to parental frustration, anger, and depression. These pressures can lead to family problems and marital conflicts and result in less stable and nurtu-

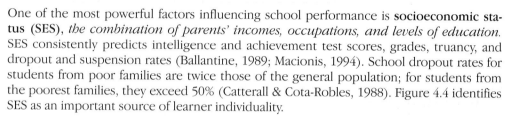

4.16 ■
Look ahead in your text to page 353, where Maslow's hierarchy of needs is described. Then explain, on the basis of Maslow's work, why children of poverty might be ill-equipped for learning.

Figure 4.4

Sources of learner individuality: socioeconomic status (SES)

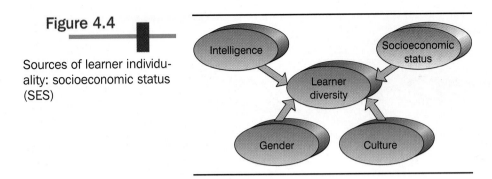

rant homes (Conger et al., 1992). Children of poverty often come to school without a sense of safety and security, and so they are less well equipped to tackle school-related tasks.

SES also influences children's background experiences. High-SES parents are more likely than low-SES parents to provide their children with experiences and materials such as:

- Educational activities outside school (e.g., visits to art, science, and history museums; attendance at concerts; borrowing books from the library)
- Learning materials at home (e.g., newspapers, encyclopedias, dictionaries, pocket calculators, computers)
- Lessons outside school (e.g., art, music, religion, dance, computer)

> **4.17**
> The term *cultural capital* uses an analogy to compare cultural experiences to money in the bank. How are early experiences like money in the bank? How are they different?

These activities complement and reinforce classroom learning by providing an experiential base for school activities (Peng & Lee, 1992). Some researchers view these experiences as "cultural capital" that forms a foundation for the concepts young children bring to school (Ballantine, 1989). In studying Piaget's work in Chapter 2, you found that these early experiences are crucial to intellectual development. B. Bloom (1981) estimated that 80% of human potential intelligence is developed by age 8; this point underscores the importance of early, family-based experiences.

Interaction Patterns in the Home

SES also influences learning through the interaction patterns of parents and their children (Hess & McDevitt, 1984). Low-SES parents are more likely to "tell," rather than explain. Their language is less elaborate, their directions are less clear, and they are less likely to encourage problem solving. High-SES parents, in contrast, talk more with their children, explain ideas and the causes of events, and encourage independent thinking. In addition, high-SES parents are more likely to ask "wh" questions (*who, when, where,* and *why*), promoting language development and preparing their children for the kind of verbal interaction found in the schools. Sometimes called "the curriculum of the home," these rich interaction patterns, together with the experiences described in the previous section, provide a strong foundation for reading and vocabulary development (Walberg, 1991).

Attitudes and Values

The impact of SES is also transmitted through parental attitudes and values. Reading is a classic example. Adults who have books, newspapers, and magazines around the home and read themselves have children who are more likely to read, and students who read at home show larger gains in reading achievement than those who don't (R. Anderson et al., 1985). When involved in school activities, these children are familiar with the power of the printed word and are eager to read.

Parents promote both cognitive and language development by discussing ideas and experiences with their children.

The educational aspirations parents have for their children are probably the most powerful variables affecting achievement; parents who expect their children to graduate from high school and to attend college have children who achieve more than the children of parents with lower aspirations. These expectations are communicated through dialogues between parents and children. High-achieving students talk frequently with their parents about school activities, topics they're studying, and their high school programs (Peng & Lee, 1992). Again, you can see how links between home and school contribute to student success. (In Chapter 10, we talk about strategies to involve parents in the educational process.)

Compared with low-SES parents, middle-class parents play the "schooling game" better, being much more likely to monitor their children's learning progress and to contact schools for information (Rothman, 1990). In a study of eighth graders, researchers documented how middle-class parents "managed" the system, "steering" their sons and daughters into college-prep high school courses (D. Baker & Stevenson, 1986). Low-SES parents, in contrast, allowed their children to "drift" into classes, relying on the decisions of others. The low-SES students often got lost in the shuffle, ending up in inappropriate or less challenging classes and tracks.

Differences between low- and high-SES families also reflect the emphasis placed on student autonomy and responsibility. High-SES parents emphasize self-direction, self-control, and individual responsibility; low-SES parents, in contrast, place greater emphasis on conformity and obedience (Ballantine, 1989).

To succeed in schools, low-SES students need more structure and motivational support than do their high-SES peers. In addition, they need help in seeing connections between learning tasks and the outside world, as well as in understanding that effort leads to accomplishment.

> **4.18**
> Of the three major factors influencing SES—occupation, income, and level of education—researchers have found that the last is most influential in school performance. Explain why this is the case.

SES: Some Cautions

As with all sources of diversity, teachers should exercise caution in applying information about SES to individual students or families. These are general patterns that may not apply to each individual. Keeping this fact in mind can help prevent inappropriately lowered expectations for students from low-income families. Many low-income families provide not only a rich learning environment but also a strong system of parental support. Tapping into and using this system is one effective way of promoting learning for these children.

Culture

Think about the way you dress, the music you like, the kinds of things you eat, how you spend time with your friends, and the kinds of recreation you enjoy. These and other factors, such as religion, family structure, and values, are all part of your culture.

Culture *refers to the attitudes, values, customs, and behavior patterns that characterize a social group.* The enormous impact it has on even the most basic aspects of human lives is illustrated in the following quote:

> Culture not only helps to determine what foods we eat, but it also influences when we eat (for example, one, three, or five meals and at what time of the day); with whom we eat (that is, only with the same sex, with children or with the extended family); how we eat (for example, at a table or on the floor; with chopsticks, silverware, or the fingers); and the ritual of eating (for example, in which hand the fork is held, asking for or being offered seconds, and belching to show appreciation of a good meal). These eating patterns are habits of the culture. (Gollnick & Chin, 1986, pp. 6–7)

Like SES, culture influences school success through the attitudes, values, and ways of viewing the world that are held and transmitted by it (see Figure 4.5).

4.19 ▬
Explain the influence of culture on learning from a constructivist perspective. Which theorist—Piaget or Vygotsky—places more emphasis on culture? Explain.

Ethnicity

An important part of culture is a person's ethnic background. **Ethnicity** *refers to a person's ancestry or membership in a group in which members continue to identify themselves with the nation from which they or their ancestors came* (Gollnick & Chinn, 1994). Members of an ethnic group have a common:

▌ history
▌ language (although sometimes not spoken)
▌ value system
▌ set of customs and traditions

More than 100 ethnic groups and 170 Native American groups live in the United States. The largest ethnic group in the school-age population is African American, about

Figure 4.5 ▬

Sources of learner individuality: culture and language

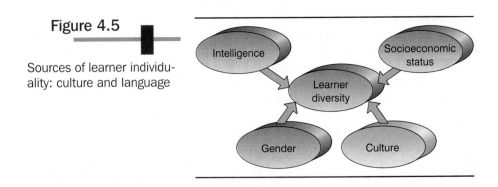

15% of the total. Hispanic groups—Mexican Americans, Puerto Ricans, Cubans, Central Americans, and South Americans—make up 10% of the school-age population, and Asian American students—Chinese, Japanese, Filipino, Korean, and Vietnamese—total about 3% (U.S. Department of Education, 1994).

More than 7 million people immigrated to the United States during the 1970s, and another 7 million came during the 1980s. Between 1980 and 1990, the minority population increased by over 9%. The fastest-growing minority groups were Asian American (up almost 100%) and Hispanic (up 53%). Experts estimate that the number of ethnic minorities in the school-age population will increase to 40% by the year 2000 (Villegas, 1991). Each of these groups brings a distinct set of values and traditions that influences student learning.

> **4.20**
> How do the foods Americans commonly eat in their day-to-day living suggest increasing ethnic diversity in the U.S. culture? Is this diversity greater or less than in the past?

Culture and Schooling

A second-grade class in Albuquerque, New Mexico, was reading *The Box Car Children* and was about to start a new chapter. The teacher said, "Look at the illustration at the beginning of the chapter and tell me what you think is going to happen." A few students raised their hands. The teacher called on a boy in the back row.

He said, "I think the boy is going to meet his grandfather."

The teacher asked, "Based on what you know, how does the boy feel about meeting his grandfather?"

Trying to involve the whole class, the teacher called on another student—one of four Native Americans in the group—even though she had not raised her hand. When she didn't answer, the teacher tried rephrasing the question, but again the student sat in silence.

Feeling exasperated, the teacher wondered if there was something in the way the lesson was being conducted that made it difficult for the students to respond. She sensed that the student she had called on understood the story and was enjoying it. Why, then, wouldn't she answer what appeared to be a simple question?

The teacher recalled that this was not the first time this had happened, and that, in fact, the other Native American students in the class rarely answered questions in class discussions. She wanted to involve them, wanted them to participate in class, but could not think of ways to get them to talk. (Villegas, 1991, p. 3)

Why do students respond differently to instruction? How does culture influence school-related attitudes and values? How do communication patterns vary from culture to culture? Is classroom structure a factor? What can teachers do to build on the culturally influenced behavior patterns their students bring to school? In this section, we examine these questions together with the relationships between culture and (a) attitudes and values, (b) adult-child interactions, (c) classroom organization, and (d) school communication.

Attitudes and Values

Our students come to us with a long learning history. In their homes, they have learned to talk, dress, care for themselves, and function as family members. On their streets and playgrounds, they have learned to interact with their peers, make friends, and solve interpersonal problems. When they enter our classrooms, they bring attitudes and values with them that can either complement school learning or work against their motivation to learn. Research on different minority populations provides insights into how these attitudes and values influence learning.

Ogbu (1992) divides minority cultures in the United States into two broad categories: voluntary and involuntary. Members of *voluntary minorities,* such as recent Chinese, Vietnamese, and Indian immigrants, come to the United States seeking a better life; schooling, hard work, and integration are seen as vehicles to accomplishing it. In contrast, some *involuntary minorities,* such as African Americans, were brought into the United States against their will, and others, such as Native Americans, were conquered.

Ogbu (1992) suggests that the two groups approach assimilation and integration into U.S. culture (and schooling) in different ways. Voluntary minorities see school as an opportunity for quick assimilation and integration into the economic and social mainstream. Involuntary minorities, because of a long history of separatism and low status, defend themselves through isolation, or "cultural inversion." **Cultural inversion** *is "the tendency for involuntary minorities to regard certain forms of behavior, events, symbols, and meanings as inappropriate for them because these are characteristic of white Americans"* (Ogbu, 1992, p. 8). To adopt these attitudes, values, and ways of behaving is to reject their own culture, to become different from their peers and family.

Language is an example. Students are hesitant to drop the use of non-Standard English dialects in favor of "school English" because it would alienate their peers and distance their families. The same problem occurs in second-language learning. Research indicates that immersion programs that encourage students to drop their native language in favor of English cause distancing problems with their parents, many of whom cannot speak English (Wong-Fillmore, 1992).

School success is often interpreted as rejecting a native culture; to become a good student is to become "White"—adopting White cultural values and rejecting their own. Students who study and become actively involved in school risk losing the friendship and respect of their peers. Ogbu believes that, in many schools, peer values either don't support school learning or actually oppose it; students form what he calls "resistance cultures" (Ogbu, 1987). Low grades, management and motivation problems, truancy, and high dropout rates are symptoms of this cultural conflict.

Ogbu (1987) advocates that teachers help minority students accommodate to the dominant culture (including schools) without losing their cultural identity by becoming completely assimilated, a process he calls "accommodation without assimilation." The challenge for teachers is to help students learn about the "culture of schooling"—the norms, procedures, and expectations necessary for success in school—while honoring the value and integrity of the students' home culture. (We discuss what teachers can do to aid "accommodation without assimilation" later in the chapter in the section "Culturally Responsive Teaching.")

Cultural Differences in Adult-Child Interactions

Children from different cultures also learn to interact with adults in different ways; sometimes it complements communication in schools, and sometimes it doesn't. This phenomenon can be illustrated with one of your author's personal experiences.

> I was a Chicago-raised person living in the South for the first time. I soon developed a warm relationship with a family having three children, ages 3, 7, and 10. I reacted when the children would always call me "Dr. Kauchak" and my fiancée "Miss Lake," rather than "Don" and "Kathy," as we preferred. We thought these addresses were formal, but quaint. The parents also referred to us in this way, so we didn't press the issue. As we worked in schools, we noticed that middle-class children said, "Yes, ma'am," and, "No, ma'am," when talking with teachers. We came to realize that these formal (to us) ways of addressing adults were expected by both middle-class families and the teachers who came from these families. To encourage these children to call us by our first names would have been inappropriate in social situations and in conflict with accepted behavior in the schools.

Although the previous case reflects a minor (and positive) cultural difference, others can result in misunderstanding or even conflict. An experience described by a principal

---

4.21

Identify another example of a voluntary and an involuntary minority. Identify an example that is not clearly one or the other.

4.22

Why are positive minority role models important for the concept of *accommodation without assimilation*? Is the concept consistent or inconsistent with the idea of America as a "melting pot"?

Minority role models help minority youth understand how they can succeed without losing their ethnic or cultural heritage.

working with Pacific Island students is an example. The principal had been invited to a community awards ceremony at a local church that was to honor a number of the students from her school. She gladly accepted, arrived a few minutes early, and was ushered to a seat of honor on the stage. After an uncomfortable (to her) wait of over an hour, the ceremony began late and the students proudly filed to the stage to receive their awards. Each student was acknowledged, given an award, and applauded. After this part of the ceremony, she had an eye-opening experience.

> The children all went back and sat down in the audience again, and the meeting continued on to several more items on the agenda. Well, the kids were fine for a while, but as you might imagine, they got bored fast and started to fidget. Fidgeting and whispering turned into poking, prodding, and open chatting. I became a little anxious at the disruption, but none of the other adults appeared to even notice, so I ignored it, too. Pretty soon several of the children were up and out of their seats, strolling about the back and sides of the auditorium. All adult faces continued looking serenely up at the speaker on the stage. Then the kids started playing tag, running circles around the seating area and yelling gleefully. No adult response—I was amazed, and struggled to resist the urge to quiet the children. Then some of the kids got up onto the stage, running around the speaker, flicking the lights on and off, and opening and closing the curtain! Still nothing from the Islander parents! It was not my place, and I shouldn't have done it, but I was so beyond my comfort zone that with eye contact and a pantomimed shush, I got the kids to settle down.
>
> I suddenly realized then that when these children, say, come to school late, it doesn't mean that they or their parents don't care about learning . . . that's just how all the adults in their world operate. When they squirm under desks and run around the classroom, they aren't trying to be disrespectful or defiant, they're just doing what they do everywhere else. (Winitzky, 1991, pp. 137–138)

4.23

Ogbu's concept of *accommodation without assimilation* requires considerable teacher judgment and tact to implement. Explain specifically how you, if you were a teacher working with the Pacific Island children in this anecdote, would deal with their conception of time and their spirited behavior in your classroom.

This experience gave the principal insights into the ways (and reasons) her students often acted as they did. All students bring with them ways of acting and interacting with adults that may differ from the traditional teacher-as-authority-figure role. (We discuss the difficult question of what to do about these differences later in the chapter.)

Classroom Organization: Working With and Against Students' Cultures

In most classrooms, emphasis is placed on individual responsibility, which is often reinforced by grades and competition. Competition demands successes and failures, and the success of one student is often tied to the failure of another (Cushner, McClelland, & Safford, 1992).

Contrast this orientation with the learning styles of the Hmong, a mountain tribe from Laos that immigrated to the United States after the Vietnam War. The Hmong culture emphasizes cooperation, and Hmong students constantly monitor the learning progress of their peers, offering help and assistance. Individual achievement is de-emphasized in favor of group success. A researcher working with the Hmong described her classroom in this way:

> When Mee Hang has difficulty with an alphabetization lesson, Pang Lor explains, in Hmong, how to proceed. Chia Ying listens in to Pang's explanation and nods her head. Pang goes back to work on her own paper, keeping an eye on Mee Hang. When she sees Mee looking confused, Pang leaves her seat and leans over Mee's shoulder. She writes the first letter of each word on the line, indicating to Mee that these letters are in alphabetical order and that Mee should fill in the rest of each word. This gives Mee the help she needs and she is able to finish on her own. Mee, in turn, writes the first letter of each word on the line for Chia Ying, passing on Pang Lor's explanation.
>
> Classroom achievement is never personal but always considered to be the result of cooperative effort. Not only is there no competition in the classroom, there is constant denial of individual ability. When individuals are praised by the teacher, they generally shake their heads and appear hesitant to be singled out as being more able than their peers. (Hvitfeldt, 1986, p. 70)

Consider how well these students would learn if instruction were competitive and teacher centered, with few opportunities for student help and collaboration.

4.24

How do Native Americans' views of competition and cooperation illustrate Ogbu's concept of *cultural inversion*?

Native Americans experience similar difficulties with competitive classrooms. They are also taught that cooperation is important; they view competition as silly, if not distasteful. When the children enter school and are asked to compete in the classroom, they experience cultural conflict (S. Phillips, 1983). Getting good grades at the expense of their fellow students is not only strange but also offensive. Raising hands and jousting for the right to provide the correct answer isn't congruent with the ways they interact at home. The result is that Native American students are often forced to choose between two cultures, and too often they conclude that schools are not for them. (We examine competitive classroom structures and their impact on motivation in Chapter 9.)

School Communication Patterns: Cultural Matches and Mismatches

Cultural conflict can occur in communication. A study of differences in language patterns between White and African American students illustrates this possibility (Heath, 1982). For example, teachers would say, "Let's put the scissors away now." White students, accustomed to this indirect way of speaking, interpreted this as a command; African Americans did not. Failure to obey was then viewed as either a management or motivation problem—a result of the mismatch between home and school cultures.

Similar disparities caused problems during instruction. From their home experience, White children were accustomed to language used to explore abstract relationships and were asked questions requiring specific answers, such as "Where's the puppy?" and "What's this story about?" African American children were accustomed to questions that were more "open-ended, story-starter" types that did not have a single answer. African American children "were not viewed as information-givers in their interactions with adults, nor were they considered appropriate conversation partners and thus they did not learn to act as such" (Heath, 1982, p. 119). When these children went to school, they were unprepared for the verbal give-and-take of fast-paced, convergent questioning. Made aware of these differences, teachers incorporated more open-ended questions in their lessons, and they worded commands more directly, such as "Put your scissors away now." They also helped African American students become more comfortable with answering factual questions. In this way, effective bridges were built between African American students' natural learning styles and the schools.

Cultural Matches With School Learning

Culture can also complement school learning. In a cross-cultural study comparing Chinese, Japanese, and American child-raising practices, researchers found significant differences in parental support for schooling (Stevenson, Lee, & Stigler, 1986). Over 95% of native Chinese and Japanese fifth graders had desks at home on which to do their homework; only 63% of the American sample did. Also, 57% of the Chinese and Japanese parents supplemented their fifth graders' schoolwork with additional math workbooks, as compared with only 28% of the American parents. Finally, 51% of the Chinese parents and 29% of the Japanese parents supplemented their children's science curriculum with additional work, compared with only 1% of the American parents.

A study attempting to understand the phenomenal successes of Indochinese children in U.S. classrooms further documents the effects of home values on learning (Caplan, Choy, & Whitmore, 1992). In examining the school experiences of Vietnamese and Laotian refugees who had been in the United States for a relatively short time (an average of 3½ years), the researchers found amazing progress. The Indochinese children received better than a B average in school, and scores on standardized achievement tests corroborated the grades as reflecting true achievement, not grade inflation.

In attempting to explain this encouraging pattern of school acculturation and progress, the researchers looked to the families. They found heavy emphasis on the importance of education, hard work, autonomy, perseverance, and pride. These values were reinforced with a nightly ritual of family homework in which both parents and older siblings helped younger members of the family. Indochinese high schoolers spent an average of 3 hours a day on homework; junior high and elementary students spent an average of 2½ hours and 2 hours, respectively. These times are greater than the 1½ hours a day U.S. junior high and senior high students spend on homework.

Culture and Learning: Deficit or Difference?

In the previous sections, you've seen how cultural differences can affect school success. Efforts have been made to synthesize this information into coherent theories or models that can then be used to further explain the relationship between school learning and culture.

Cultural deficit models suggest that *"the linguistic, social or cultural backgrounds of minority children prevent them from doing well academically"* (Villegas, 1991, p. 5). They have at least three weaknesses. First, they don't account for the many successes of

4.25
On the basis of Stevenson et al.'s (1986) study, what would you infer about the attitudes, beliefs, and values of Japanese, Chinese, and American parents? Does this inference apply to all members of these groups? What does this tell you about the process of inferring cultural attributes?

different cultural groups. Second, because of their negative orientation, they result in lowered expectations for minority students. Third, they can't explain why the longer some minorities are in school the farther behind they fall. If deficit models were valid, the gap should be greatest when students first enter school and should gradually narrow over time (Villegas, 1991).

4.26
Using Ogbu's concept of *cultural inversion*, explain why some minorities might fall farther and farther behind.

Cultural difference models *emphasize the strengths of different cultures and look for ways that instructional practice can recognize and build on those strengths* (Tharp, 1989; Villegas, 1991). They begin with the premise that different cultural groups have unique ways of learning and that no single way of teaching is most effective for all. They then attempt to understand different cultural groups and to adapt instruction to best meet these groups' learning needs. Evidence supports their premise, and we discuss implications for teaching cultural minorities on the basis of this conception.

Culturally Responsive Teaching

Culturally responsive teaching *acknowledges cultural diversity in classrooms and accommodates this diversity in instruction.* It does this in three important ways, which are illustrated in Figure 4.6. Let's look at them.

Accepting and Valuing Differences

By recognizing and accepting student diversity, teachers communicate that all students are welcome and valued. This notion is important for every learner, but particularly so for cultural and ethnic minorities, who may feel alienated from school. Teachers need to develop healthy communication channels with minority students and to help them understand that school success and belonging to their minority culture are not antagonistic.

Genuine *caring* is the critical element in the process; students quickly see through artificial attempts to communicate caring, and lip service to minorities will be seen as superficial. This dilemma can be difficult, of course, because teachers can never be certain that their intentions are being accurately perceived. Teachers can, however, take the following actions, which are rarely misperceived:

Figure 4.6

Characteristics of culturally responsive teaching

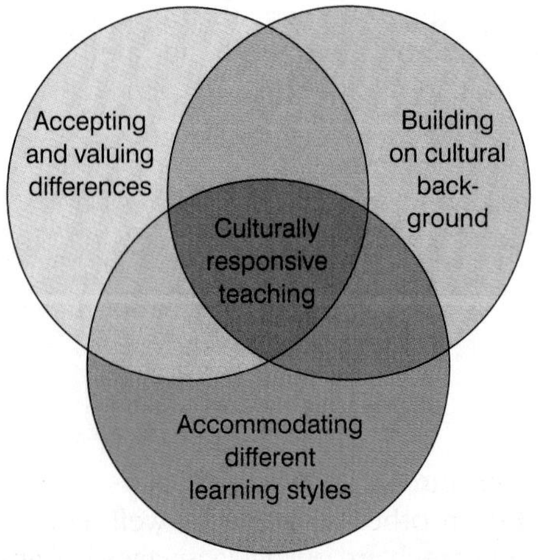

❚ Time: Giving your time is one of the most effective ways to communicate caring.
❚ Personal Interest: All people react positively to someone taking an interest in their personal lives.
❚ Involvement: Teachers who try to involve all students equally in classroom activities communicate that everyone is important and that his or her contributions to learning activities are valued.

Accommodating Different Learning Styles

Teachers who are sensitive to possible differences between home and school patterns are in a position to adapt their instruction to best meet their students' needs. For example, you saw earlier that the values of Native Americans often clash with typical classroom practice. Recognizing that these students learn more effectively when cooperation rather than competition is emphasized, teachers can incorporate peer tutoring and the various kinds of cooperative learning to complement teacher-centered approaches (we describe cooperative learning in detail in Chapter 12). This adaptation can result in increased learning for all students (Phillips, 1983).

Another example illustrates how sensitive and creative teachers can accommodate different learning styles. When one teacher learned that Asian American students are often overwhelmed by the hustle and bustle of American schools, she tried to keep her classroom quiet and orderly. She also found that Asian Americans are often shy and sometimes reluctant to speak in class, so she made a special effort to promote their participation by using open-ended questioning and by encouraging them to speak loudly and clearly (Shields & Shaver, 1990).

Building on Students' Cultural Backgrounds

Effective teachers also learn about their students' cultures and use these to develop personal pride and motivation in their students, as the following illustration demonstrates:

> In one third-grade classroom with a predominately Central American student population, youngsters are greeted most mornings with the sound of salsa music in the background, instruction takes place in both English and Spanish, magazines and games in both languages are available throughout the classroom, maps of both the United States and Latin America line one wall with pins noting each student's origin, and every afternoon there is a Spanish reading lesson to ensure that students learn to read and write in Spanish as well as English. Here the teacher argues very clearly that a positive instructional environment for these students must be tailored to the home cultures. (Shields & Shaver, 1990, p. 9)

The benefits of this approach are felt in both the classroom and the home. In addition to increases in student achievement, parents are more positive about school, which in turn enhances student motivation, and a positive learning cycle is created. Students bring with them a wealth of experiences embedded in their home culture. Sensitive teachers build on these experiences to help all students reach their full potential.

4.27
To work effectively with students from different cultures, teachers must understand those cultures. Explain the advantages of learning about students' cultures from both a cognitive and an affective perspective.

Culture and Language: English Dialects

Language is a powerful and important aspect of culture and ethnicity, not only in the United States but in other countries as well. For instance, because of political pressure, both English and French are official languages in Canada, and labels, signs, and other information are printed in both languages. Because language is such an important aspect of culture, we devote these sections to a discussion of its influence on learning.

Anyone who has traveled can confirm the fact that the United States has many regional and ethnic dialects. A **dialect** *is a variation of Standard English that is distinct in vocabulary, grammar, or pronunciation.* Everyone in the United States speaks a dialect; people merely react to those different from their own (Wolfram, 1991). An important question is, How should teachers deal with dialects in classrooms?

English Dialects: Research Findings

Research indicates that use of non-Standard English results in lowered teacher expectations for student performance (Bowie & Bond, 1994), lowered assessments of students' work and the students themselves (J. Taylor, 1983). Teachers often confuse non-Standard English with mistakes during oral reading (Washington & Miller-Jones, 1989), and some critics argue that dialects, such as Black English, are substandard, lacking in structure and complexity. Linguists, however, argue that these variations are just as rich and semantically complex as Standard English (Labov, 1972). The primary reason for teaching Standard English is that it allows access to other educational and economic opportunities. Students often become aware of this when they interview for their first job or when they plan for post-high-school education.

Dialects in the Classroom: Implications for Teachers

You saw in the previous section that culturally responsive teaching begins with accepting and valuing differences, and this is particularly important when responding to learners with nonstandard dialects. Keep in mind that dialects are both functional and valued in the culture of students' neighborhoods. Requiring that they be eliminated communicates that differences are neither accepted nor valued.

So, what should a teacher do when a student says, "I ain't got no pencil," bringing a nonstandard dialect into the classroom? Opinions vary from "rejection and correction" to complete acceptance. The approach most consistent with culturally responsive teaching is to accept the dialect and build on it (Speidel, 1987). For example, when the student says, "I ain't got no pencil," the teacher (or adult) might say, "Oh, you don't have a pencil. What should you do, then?" Although results won't be apparent immediately, the long-range benefits make the effort worth it.

Language differences don't have to form barriers between home and school. **Bidialecticism,** *the ability to switch back and forth between a dialect and Standard English,* provides the best of both worlds, allowing access to both (Gollnick & Chinn, 1994). As another example of culturally responsive teaching, a teacher explicitly taught differences between Standard and Black English, analyzing the strengths of each and respective places for their use (Shields & Shaver, 1990). The teacher read a series of poems by the African American poet Langston Hughes, focusing on the ability of Black English to create vivid images. The class discussed the contrast with Standard English and ways in which differences between the two languages could be used strategically to accomplish different communication goals.

Culture and Language: English as a Second Language

In an urban fourth-grade class composed of 11 Asian and 17 Black children, Sokhom, age 10, has recently been promoted to the on-grade-level reading group and is

4.28 ▬
How would behaviorism explain the development of dialects? How would social cognitive theory explain them?

4.29 ▬
State one disadvantage and one advantage of the "rejection and correction" approach. Identify an advantage and a disadvantage of the complete acceptance approach.

doing well. Instead of being "pulled out" of her regular classroom for special instruction in English, she now spends her whole day in the mainstream classroom. At home, she pulls out a well-worn English-Khmer dictionary that she says her father bought at great expense in the refugee camp in the Philippines. She recounts that when she first came to the United States and was in second grade, she used to look up English words there and ask her father or her brother to read the Cambodian word to her; then she would know what the English word was. Today, in addition to her intense motivation to know English ("I like to talk in English. I like to read in English, and I like to write in English."), Sokhom wants to learn to read and write in Khmer, and in fact has taught herself a little via English.

In another urban public school across the city, Maria, a fifth grader who has been in a two-way maintenance bilingual education program since prekindergarten, has both Spanish and English reading every morning for 1¼ hours each, with Ms. Torres and Mrs. Dittmar, respectively. Today, Mrs. Dittmar is reviewing the vocabulary for the story the students are reading about Charles Drew, a Black American doctor. She explains that "influenza" is what Charles's little sister died of. Maria comments that "you say it [influenza] in Spanish the same way you write it [in English]."

In the same Puerto Rican community, in a new bilingual middle school a few blocks away, Elizabeth, a graduate of the two-way maintenance bilingual program mentioned above, hears a Career Day speaker from the community tell her that of two people applying for a job, one bilingual and one not, the bilingual has an advantage. Yet Elizabeth's daily program of classes provides little opportunity for her to continue to develop literacy in Spanish; the bilingual program at this school is primarily transitional. (Hornberger, 1989, pp. 271–272)

As a result of rapidly increasing immigration (more than 7 million people a decade during the 1970s and 1980s), increasing numbers of students with limited backgrounds in English are entering classrooms across the United States. Coming with their families from places such as Southeast Asia, the Middle East, Haiti, and Mexico in search of better lives, the number of non-English-speaking and limited-English-proficient (LEP) students is growing at about 4% a year—about twice the population growth rate for the nation (Catterall & Cota-Robles, 1988).

The diversity is staggering. Currently, 2.3 million LEP students in U.S. schools (U.S. Department of Education, 1993) and about 50% of all California students speak a language other than English as their primary or only language (Fitzgerald, 1995). In the Los Angeles School District, more than 81 languages are represented, with as many as 20 found in some classrooms. Nationwide, the number of students whose primary language is not English is expected to triple during the next 30 years (Pallas, Natriello, & McDill, 1989).

This linguistic diversity presents challenges to both the students and the schools. A study in California found that 45% of Hispanic students do not complete high school, with 40% of that group leaving school before 10th grade (Cortes, 1986). In response to these trends, in 1988 the U.S. Department of Education listed as its first research priority "the teaching and learning of reading, writing and language skills, particularly by non- or limited-English speaking students" (U.S. Department of Education, 1988, p. 192). This language diversity poses a challenge to teachers because most instruction is verbal. How should schools respond to this linguistic challenge? Bilingual programs offer one solution.

Types of Bilingual Programs

True bilingual programs offer instruction to non-native English speakers in two languages: English and their primary language. They attempt to maintain and enhance the native language while building on it to teach English. The term *bilingual,* however, has been expanded to refer to a range of second-language programs (V. Allen, 1992; Stowe, 1992).

We look at three of them: maintenance programs, transitional programs, and English as a second language (ESL) programs.

4.30

Using Piaget's concepts of *equilibrium, assimilation,* and *accommodation,* describe the process of second-language learning in maintenance programs.

Maintenance Bilingual Programs.   **Maintenance bilingual programs** *teach in both the native language and English, maintaining and building on the students' native language* (Gollnick & Chinn, 1994). Found primarily at the elementary level, these programs have the goal of developing students who are truly bilingual. Maria, the fifth grader in the episode above, had both a Spanish-speaking and an English-only-speaking teacher to help her develop proficiency in both languages. Maintenance programs have the advantage of maintaining students' heritage, language, and culture. They can be difficult to implement, however, because they require groups of students with the same native language and bilingual teachers or teacher teams in which one member speaks the heritage language.

4.31

Identify at least one similarity and one difference between maintenance and transitional programs. From an economic perspective, with the current emphasis on a move to a global economy, which approach would be preferable?

Transitional Bilingual Programs.   **Transitional bilingual programs** *use the native language as an instructional aid until English is proficient.* Transitional programs begin with the first language and gradually develop learners' English proficiency. The transition period is often too short, however, and leaves the students inadequately prepared for learning in English (Gersten & Woodward, 1995; Spencer, 1988). In addition, loss of the first language and lack of emphasis on the home culture can result in communication gaps between children who no longer speak the first language and parents who don't speak English.

English as a Second Language (ESL) Programs.   Although, technically, all bilingual programs fit this category because mastery of English is a goal, **English as a second language (ESL) programs** *focus explicitly on the mastery of English.* Unlike the other programs, they emphasize teaching students English and mainstreaming them into the regular classroom. Sokhom, the Cambodian student in the episode above, was initially in a pull-out ESL program until she could function in an English-only environment. Pulling students out of the regular classroom, however, disrupts the continuity of their instruction, and cultural discontinuities similar to those associated with transitional programs can result. ESL programs are common when classes contain students who speak a variety of languages and thus make maintenance or transitional programs difficult to implement.

4.32

Describe an ESL program based on behaviorist principles. Describe one based on social cognitive theory.

Evaluating Bilingual Programs

In comparing bilingual with English-only programs, researchers have found that students in bilingual programs achieve higher in math and reading and have more positive attitudes toward school and themselves (Arias & Casanova, 1993; Díaz, 1983). Also, because of their exposure to two languages, they better understand the role of language in communication (Díaz, 1990).

These findings make sense. Programs that use a student's native language not only build on an existing foundation but also say to the student, "To do well in school, you don't have to forget the culture of your home and neighborhood."

Teaching Bilingual Students

Teachers are crucial to the success of bilingual programs. Let's see why.

Tina Wharton had read about diversity in her education classes, but she wasn't expecting what she encountered when she took a job in a suburb of Los Angeles. Her first-grade class of 29 students had 9 who spoke Spanish as their first language. In working with them, she knew that building strong communication skills would need to be a top priority in her class.

Effective bilingual programs teach English while building on and enriching students' native language.

At the suggestion of other teachers, she wrote to each of the parents—in Spanish—and asked for their help during the year. With the help of Spanish-speaking teachers, she labeled all the objects in the room with both Spanish and English names and encouraged students to learn to read both. Her class made frequent field trips to local parks, a nearby food-processing plant, and the airport. After they returned, they talked about their trips, and students drew pictures and wrote about their visits. She enlisted the aid of several parents and had these stories transcribed into both Spanish and English.

Six blocks down the street, Jim Harrison taught the brothers and sisters of Tina's students in his middle school science class. He had attended a workshop on the problems that LEP (limited-English-proficient) students might encounter in different content areas and adjusted his classes accordingly. He taught science with hands-on experiments, de-emphasized reading, and paired LEP students with other students to discuss, analyze, and write about the experiments. At the beginning of each unit, he used demonstrations, concrete examples, pictures, and diagrams to introduce new vocabulary and abstract ideas.

It is likely that you will teach students whose first language is not English, and you can use a number of strategies to help LEP students learn both English and academic content. These begin with awareness and move to language and concept-development strategies.

Awareness.   Research indicates that a surprising number of teachers are unaware of the home languages that students bring to school; one study found that teachers recognized only 27% of the non-native English speakers in one sample of Asian students (Schmidt, 1992). Teachers can't adjust their teaching to meet the needs of LEP students if they aren't aware that these students exist. Talking with counselors, administrators, and other teachers, especially minority ones, as well as with the students and their parents, can help teachers learn about the backgrounds of their students. Then teachers can communicate with actions and words that they respect and value this diversity.

Facilitating Language and Concept Development.   Students learn English by using it in their day-to-day lives. At least in part, language is a skill, and students in general, and LEP students in particular, need to spend as much time as possible literally "practicing the language" (Fitzgerald, 1995; Ravetta & Brunn, 1995). Teacher-centered instruction, in which the teacher talks most of the time and students listen passively, should be avoided (Adamson, 1993). Instead, students should be provided with concrete experiences and opportunities to talk, write, and read about them. Also, open-ended questions that allow students to respond without the pressure of giving specific answers are valuable tools for eliciting student responses (Langer, Bartolme, Vasquez, & Lucas, 1990). Let's look at an example.

Felyce Marquez has a group of 8 non-native English speakers in her second-grade class of 24 students. She has been reading a story to her class from a book liberally illustrated with pictures depicting the events in the story. As she read, she showed the pictures and had the students identify the object or event being illustrated, such as a cave in the woods that the boy and girl in the story decided to explore.

After she finished reading the story, she continued by discussing the events in it.

"Please tell us something you remember about the story. . . . Carmela?" she began.

" . . . A boy and a girl," Carmela responded hesitantly.

"Yes, good, Carmela," Felyce smiled. "The story is about a boy and a girl," and she pointed again to the picture of the boy and girl.

"Tell us something about the boy and girl. . . . Segundo."

" . . . Lost . . . cave."

"Yes," Felyce nodded encouragingly. "The boy and girl were exploring a cave and they got lost," again pointing to the pictures in the book. "What do you think exploring means? . . . Anyone?"

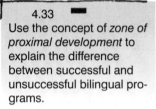

4.33

Use the concept of *zone of proximal development* to explain the difference between successful and unsuccessful bilingual programs.

Felyce employed at least three simple strategies to promote language and concept development in her students. First, she used the pictures to provide concrete reference points for the vocabulary she was developing. Second, she used open-ended questions to allow Carmela and Segundo to "practice" using English without the pressure of providing a specific answer. Third, she modeled elaborated descriptions such as, "The boy and girl were exploring a cave and they got lost," in response to Segundo's " . . . Lost . . . cave." The strategies took little preparation; all she needed was the book with pictures. These same strategies can be used in the content areas as well. When consistently used, they can do much to help students develop their language while simultaneously learning concepts.

Classroom Connections

Using Socioeconomic Status and Culture as Tools to Understand Your Students

1. Use concrete examples and open-ended questions to help learners acquire experiences and reference points for language.
   - A first-grade teacher working in a low-SES classroom begins each science lesson with a demonstration, concrete example, or hands-on experience. She begins discussions by asking individual students to describe what they see in the examples. On the basis of their observations, she guides them to an understanding of the topic.

2. Communicate with students about who they are and who you are.
   - On the first day of class, a sixth-grade teacher has students write essays about themselves. He has them include a description of their favorite activities, the kind of music they like, and any information they want to include about parents or other close relatives. He asks them to include, if they would like, anything about school that scares them or makes them worry. He writes an essay of his own and shares it with the students.
   - A math teacher makes an effort to get to know each of his students. He tries to learn something personal about each and refers to it in one-on-one conversations.

3. Make an attempt to learn about the cultures of the students you are teaching.
   - A third-grade teacher asks the students about their after-school activities and their holiday customs. She designs classroom "festivals" that focus on different cultures and invites parents and other care givers to help celebrate and contribute to enriching them.

- A high school teacher in an inner-city school makes himself available before and after school. Although the focus in these sessions is on academics, the conversation often turns to students' lives and the problems they encounter in school.

4. Accept and value the language diversity in your classroom.
   - As they use variations of Standard English in his classroom, a fifth-grade teacher asks his students to describe the meanings of vocabulary and phrases and where they originated. He describes the explanations as interesting and paraphrases them in different ways in Standard English.

5. Use instructional strategies that accommodate diversity.
   - A physical education teacher uses the "buddy system" to help students with limited English skills participate in class. She asks bilingual students with well-developed English skills to pair with less-proficient students to explain rules and concepts during instruction and games.
   - A second-grade teacher uses seating patterns to foster class cohesion and intergroup friendships.

She puts the desks in groups of four and places students from different ethnic groups and ability levels in the same group.

6. Make students aware of the values and accomplishments of ethnic minorities.
   - A second-grade teacher emphasizes values, such as courtesy and respect, that cross all cultures. He has students discuss the ways these values are displayed differently in various cultures.
   - An art teacher decorates the room with pictures of Native American art and discusses its quality and contributions to the general field of art.
   - An inner-city American history teacher displays pictures of prominent African Americans and discusses the contributions they have made to the American way of life. She emphasizes that many history books often underrepresent the contributions of minorities and females.
   - A teacher with many Hispanic students in her classroom points out the accomplishments of Americans of Latin heritage, such as the Cuban population in Miami and the prominent Hispanic politicians around the country.

Gender

What Marti Banes saw on her first day of teaching advanced-placement chemistry was both surprising and disturbing. Of the 26 students watching her, only 2 were female, and they were sitting quietly in the back of the room. One reason that Marti had gone into teaching was to share her interest in science with other females but this situation gave her little chance to do so.

The fact that some of our students are boys and others are girls is so obvious that we sometimes miss this important difference. When we're reminded, we of course notice that boys and girls look different and often act and think differently from each other. In this section, we examine gender-related student differences and explore their implications for teaching (see Figure 4.7).

Differences exist in boys' and girls' developmental rates; girls develop faster, with differences in verbal and motor skills appearing at an early age. Boys and girls are different in other areas as well, and these differences appear as early as the preschool years. Girls tend to play with dolls and other girls and to gravitate toward activities such as make-believe and dress-up. Boys play with blocks, cars, dinosaurs, and other boys. Why? As with the nature-nurture argument regarding intelligence, this is a controversial question, but much of the evidence points to the way boys and girls are treated (Clark-Stewart & Friedman, 1987; M. Linn & Hyde, 1989).

Figure 4.7

Sources of learner individuality: gender

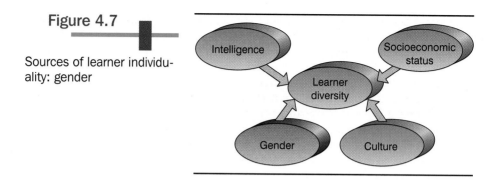

Unfortunately, differences in societal support often result in differences in achievement between males and females. Consider these findings.

- In the early grades, girls are ahead of or equal to boys on almost every standardized measure of achievement and psychological well-being. By the time they graduate from high school or college, they have fallen back. Girls enter school even or ahead, but leave behind.
- In high school, girls score lower on the SAT and ACT, which are critical for college admission. The greatest gender gaps are in science and math.
- Boys are much more likely to be awarded state and national college scholarships.
- Women score lower on all sections of the Graduate Record Exam, which is necessary to score high on to enter many graduate programs (Sadker & Sadker, 1994, p. 13).

Let's examine some possible explanations for these findings.

Different Treatment of Boys and Girls

Societal and Family Influences

In 1993, Mattel attempted to market a new "Teen Talk Barbie," which said the following things when you pressed her tummy:

"I like shopping."

"I like boys."

"Math class is tough."

Mattel withdrew this recording under a storm of protest, yet this is an example of how U.S. society perpetuates differences between males and females.

From the day they are born, male and female babies are treated differently. Girls are given pink blankets, are called cute and pretty, and are handled delicately. Boys are dressed in blue, are regarded as handsome, and are seen as tougher, better coordinated, and hardier. Fathers are rougher with their young sons and engage them in more physical stimulation and gross motor play; they tend to be gentler with their daughters and offer more sex-stereotyped toys, such as dolls and stuffed animals (Ruble, 1988). Differences in treatment continue in later years. In high school, girls become cheerleaders for the boys, who become football or basketball players.

Unfortunately, these differences include expectations for school success. Parents—probably unconsciously—often communicate different expectations for their sons and

4.34
Mattell presumably thought the phrases uttered by the Teen Talk Barbie were unoffensive, or else they wouldn't have been included. What does this mentality suggest about the values of different groups in the United States? What implications do these values have for you as a teacher?

daughters. Researchers have found that parents' gender-stereotyped attitudes toward girls' ability in math adversely influenced their daughters' achievement in math and their attitudes toward it (Nagy-Jacklin, 1989). A longitudinal study indicated that girls who thought they were good at math declined from 64% in 3rd grade to 57% in 7th and 48% in 11th grade; boys' attitudes only dropped from 66% in 3rd grade to 60% in 11th.

Given this differential treatment, it's not surprising that early research on gender effects found differences between boys and girls in different academic areas. Boys did better in math and on visual and spatial tasks (e.g., those required in geometry); girls did better on verbal skills (Maccoby & Jacklin, 1974). In addition, researchers found small differences favoring boys in science, both in achievement and participation (Fennema, 1987). These differences were small, and within any population, we expect to find boys and girls who don't follow this pattern.

A more recent review offers more encouraging results. Researchers concluded that current gender differences in verbal ability are "negligible," that differences in quantitative ability and science are "declining," and that small differences in visual and spatial tasks are probably due to uneven opportunities to practice these skills (M. Linn & Hyde, 1989). These researchers further concluded that gender "differences were always small, that they have declined in the last 2 decades . . . and that educational programs can influence when differences arise" (p. 17). How do school programs contribute to any differences that do exist, and what can teachers do to ensure that boys and girls are provided equal opportunities for success in their classroom?

Different Treatment in Schools

Unfortunately, societal influences sometimes carry over into schools and result in different treatment for boys and girls. According to persistent sexual stereotypes, teachers view boys as more independent thinkers and more likely to do better in math and science because these are "male" subjects. Girls, in contrast, are viewed as more submissive and conforming (Fennema & Peterson 1987; Grant, 1984).

Both male and female teachers treat boys and girls differently. They interact with boys more often (Sadker & Sadker, 1985) and ask them more questions, and those questions are more conceptual and abstract (Sadker, Sadker, & Klein, 1991). Boys receive more approval, are taught more directly and listened to more, and are rewarded more for creativity (Torrance, 1983).

Researchers also found that boys are more likely to ask questions and make comments about ideas being discussed in class (Sadker et al., 1991). The differences increase as students move through school, with an especially noticeable drop at the junior high level. In the seventh grade, girls initiated 41% of the student-to-teacher interactions (compared with 59% for boys); by eighth grade, this number had dropped to 30%. This drop appears at the time when adolescent girls are often wrestling with their sex role identities. In a society that often views female roles as submissive and conforming, junior high girls may feel uncomfortable asserting themselves as independent learners.

This decline of female-initiated contacts might also be a result of different treatment. Boys were eight times more likely than girls to call out in class, and the teacher's most frequent response was to accept the call-out and continue. When girls did the same, the teachers were more likely to reprimand or correct the student. The effect is to reinforce boys for aggressive intellectual behaviors and to punish girls for those same behaviors.

Interestingly, when teachers were asked to analyze videotapes of classroom interactions containing differential treatment of boys and girls, they failed to see these patterns. In fact, despite the fact that boys participated more than girls by a ratio of 3:1, the teachers concluded that girls received more teacher attention than boys (Sadker & Sadker, 1985).

4.35 How would an extreme "nature" position describe gender differences? How about an extreme "nurture" position? How would an interactionist position describe these differences?

4.36 Explain the decline in gender-related differences in achievement. Predict what will happen in the future in this area.

4.37 Explain why an increase in male-initiated contacts during junior high years might occur.

4.38 Explain why teachers might have difficulty recognizing different treatment of boys and girls.

Experiences in Science and Math.   Girls also have different experiences in science and math classes. When teachers organized science demonstrations, 79% were carried out by boys (Sadker et al., 1991). At the third-grade level, 51% of boys reported experience with microscopes compared to 37% of girls. In an 11th-grade sample, 49% of males, but only 17% of females, reported experience with electrical equipment. Coincidentally, girls' attitudes toward science, science courses, and science careers all declined as they grew older (American Association of University Women, 1992).

The slight advantage for males in math can also be explained by different treatment and teacher expectations. In Sweden, where sex role differences are less emphasized, differences in math achievement tend to be smaller (Svenson, 1971). In the United States, girls attending all-female schools take more math and science and have higher achievement in these areas (Finn, Dulberg, & Reis, 1979). In regular public schools, girls are much less likely to take nonrequired math and science courses (Pallas & Alexander, 1983). When they do take math, they are less confident than boys and more likely to attribute success to luck rather than ability (Stipek & Gralinski, 1991). Achievement differences in math between boys and girls decrease when girls take more math courses (American Association of University Women, 1992). Instruction also appears to make a difference: Girls do better in math when it is taught in noncompetitive, cooperative small groups (Fennema & Peterson, 1987).

Gender Stereotyping Influences Career Decisions.   Differences in students' views of gender-appropriate careers appear as early as kindergarten (Kochenberger-Stroeher, 1994). Significantly, when the children chose nontraditional roles for males or females, their choice was based on personal experience (e.g., "One of my friends' dad is a nurse").

These gender-stereotypic views influence career decisions. In 1980, 30% of college-bound high school women, compared with 50% of comparable men, planned to study science and engineering in college. At the doctoral level, the differences were even greater: Only 25% of the doctoral degrees in science and engineering were awarded to women (National Research Council, 1980). More recent research shows that this trend continues: Girls were less than half as likely as boys to pursue careers in engineering and physical and computer sciences.

Gender Differences: Implications for Teachers

Significantly, girls who go into science-related fields reported that the encouragement received from teachers was a critical factor in their career decisions (American Association of University Women, 1992). Further, intervention studies designed to increase female participation in math resulted in girls having more positive attitudes about math and taking more math courses (Fennema & Koehler, 1983). Similar results were achieved in science (Mason & Kahle, 1989).

Teachers can help reverse the negative impact of gender stereotyping in education. As with many aspects of individual differences, the first step is awareness. Teachers who know they may unconsciously treat boys and girls differently are more sensitive to their own behavior. The next step is to make every effort to treat boys and girls as equally as possible and to encourage the same academic behaviors in both. "Academic" behavior is a key idea. You're not saying that boys and girls are the same in every way, and you're not asking them to be. You are, however, suggesting that, academically, they will be given the same opportunities and encouragement.

Open communication is critical. Simply telling the students that teachers often treat boys and girls differently and that you're going to try to treat them equally is a positive step. Then make your best effort to be true to your commitment.

4.39 ▬
Explain female achievement in math and science. Use Erikson's stage of identity versus confusion as the basis for your explanation.

4.40 ▬
How are gender-related differences in math and science influenced by SES? What implications does this have for teachers of low-SES students?

Science activities that actively involve female students in designing and carrying out science experiments help combat gender stereotypes that the sciences are a male domain.

At-Risk Students

I was told that "the class was all right, but some children were pretty hopeless." I was also told that the children were used to working through their arithmetic book and were tested at the end of each week. After receiving the first test papers in long division, most of which were disastrous, I did not know what to do. Nothing in my training had prepared me for a class where some children failed because they did not understand the meaning of zero, some because they had not learned how to carry over numbers from one stage to another; others seemed to have very little understanding of division and would try to divide the smaller number by the larger one, while some children seemed confused and unable to make any sense of the set number work.

I subsequently divided the papers into small groups according to the main errors they revealed and spent my next lunch breaks working with the children on their own specific difficulties. I soon realized that some of the "hopeless" children were pretty bright, but for different reasons had lost confidence in their ability to cope with their schoolwork. However, I found out that when each child was helped to understand the specific problem in arithmetic that had been holding him back, his progress was not only remarkable, but also quite out of proportion to the effort I invested. (Butler-Por, 1987, p. 3)

Many teachers face their first teaching assignment in classrooms where students don't fit the desired pattern of being motivated and eager to learn. A very real trend in U.S. schools today is the changing composition of the student population. Students won't be coming from two-parent households in which the father works and the mother stays home. Instead, both parents will probably work, and the likelihood of a single-parent family is high (Maciones, 1994).

Who are the students of tomorrow? The class of 2001, which started kindergarten in 1988, has this profile:

- Minority enrollment levels now range from 70% to 96% in the nation's 15 largest school systems.
- Twenty-five percent of U.S. children currently live below the poverty level, the highest proportion in more than 20 years.
- Fifteen percent of U.S. schoolchildren today have a physical or mental disability.
- Fourteen percent are children of teenage mothers.
- Fourteen percent are children of unmarried parents.
- Ten percent have poorly educated, sometimes illiterate, parents.
- Between one fourth and one third of today's schoolchildren have no adult at home when they return from school.
- Twenty-five percent (or more) will not finish high school (Kellogg, 1988).

These figures have critical implications for schools and teachers. Educating these children will be more difficult; the students of tomorrow will be more diverse, less cared for, and less ready to profit from schools. To meet the challenge, teachers will have to adapt their instruction to meet the needs of these students.

At-Risk Students: A Definition

Let's look again at Juan in our case study at the beginning of the chapter. He is from a low-SES background and is a cultural minority, he missed a great deal of school, and he was retained in the fourth grade. His tendency to be easily offended suggests low self-esteem. Juan exhibits many of the characteristics of an at-risk student (see Table 4.5).

At-risk students *are those in danger of failing to complete their education with the skills necessary to survive in a modern technological society* (Slavin et al., 1989). The term came into wide use soon after the National Commission on Excellence in Education proclaimed the United States a "nation at risk" (National Commission on Excellence in Education, 1983). The report emphasized the critical link between education and economic well-being in the modern technological society. Since that time, much attention has been given to problems and issues relating to at-risk students, not only out of concern for the students themselves but also in recognition of the national need for well-educated citizens (Vito & Connell, 1988). It is a virtual certainty that you will have at least some of these students in your classes.

At-risk students have learning problems and adjustment difficulties, and they often fail even though they have the capacity to succeed (Scott, 1988; Vito & Connell, 1988). These students used to be called *underachievers,* but the term *at-risk* more clearly signals the long-term consequences of school failure. A male high school dropout, for example, will earn a quarter of a million dollars less over a lifetime than a high school graduate. Families whose primary breadwinners lack high school diplomas earned 30% less in 1987 than they did in 1973 (adjusted for inflation) (Mishel & Frankel, 1991). These statistics reflect some of the consequences at-risk students face.

4.41 ▬
Using our discussion of the influences of SES and home culture on learning, explain why at-risk students are more difficult to teach. What instructional adjustments need to be made?

4.42 ▬
Why are at-risk students increasingly seen as both educational and economic problems? Will this trend increase or decrease? Why?

Table 4.5

Characteristics of at-risk students

Background Factors	
Low SES	Minority
Inner city	Non-native English speaker
Male	Divorced families
Transient	
Educational Problems	
High dropout rate	High rates of drug use
Low grades	Management problems
Retention in grade	Low self-esteem
Low achievement	High criminal activity rates
Low involvement in extracurricular activities	Low test scores
Low motivation	Dissatisfaction with and lack of interest in school
Poor attendance	High suspension rates

As you can see from Table 4.5, at-risk students suffer from a myriad of academic, social, and emotional problems. The presence of "Male" as a background variable needs clarification. Research shows that males are more likely to experience difficulties in school and to drop out. However, many low-SES female students who either leave school before graduation or graduate with inadequate survival skills still live in poverty. Girls who drop out commonly do so for school-related reasons and are more likely to end up in poverty than male dropouts (American Association of University Women, 1992). In addition, many girls who drop out are pregnant and are left with the burden of single parenting on an income below the poverty level. Being at risk is a problem facing both male and female students.

Before continuing, let's consider a note of caution. Some educators worry that use of the term *at-risk* is ill-advised because it blames students for the problem and doesn't hold schools accountable for their education (Benard, 1994). Critics contend that using the term results in low expectations for success and low achievement. Teachers need to guard against negative stereotyping as they work with these students and continually to ask themselves, "Am I providing every opportunity for success for all students?" The following sections describe some practices to help ensure that this occurs.

At-Risk Students: Promoting Resilience

Recent research on at-risk students has focused on the development of resilience. **Resilience** *results in a heightened likelihood of success in school and in other aspects of life despite environmental adversities* (Wang, Haertel, & Walberg, 1995). Researchers have become

Resilient children come from homes and classrooms that are supportive but demanding and where caring adults provide nurturant challenge.

interested in the concept of *resilience* for both theoretical and practical reasons. Theoretically, the study of resilience helps in the understanding of the larger process of development, especially as it occurs in at-risk youth. Practically, the study of resilient youth provides promise of practices that might result in healthier, more academically successful learners.

The study of resilience focuses on youth who have survived and even prospered despite obstacles of poverty, poor health care, and fragmented services. Resilient children have well-developed "self systems," including high self-esteem and feelings that they are in control of their destinies. They are good at setting personal goals, and they have positive expectations for success and good interpersonal skills (Benard, 1993; Wang et al., 1995).

How do these adaptive skills develop? Resilient children come from families that are nurturant and caring. The families provide structure and hold high moral and academic expectations for their children (Masten, Morison, Pelligrini, & Tellegen, 1990). Resilient youth also come from schools that are both demanding and supportive; in many instances, schools served as a home away from home (Haynes & Comer, 1995). Let's examine more closely these connections between school experiences and the development of resiliency.

4.43

Identify two of Gardner's multiple intelligences that are particularly important for resilient children.

Effective Schools for At-Risk Students

4.44

Why are these characteristics of effective schools especially important for at-risk students?

Important research has been conducted on schools that are effective in developing student resilience (Good & Brophy, 1986; Wang et al., 1995). In these schools, students and teachers treat each other with respect, and personal responsibility and cooperation are stressed (Kim, Solomon, & Roberts, 1995; Roberts, Horn, & Battistich, 1995). The meaning and purpose of rules are emphasized, and mastery of content rather than passive attendance is required. The characteristics of these schools are summarized in Table 4.6.

Effective Teachers for At-Risk Students

What makes an effective teacher for at-risk students? How do teachers help students develop resilience and make connections between their lives and the classroom? Let's have the students tell you:

> Ninth grader: Well it's like you're family, you know. Like regular days like at home, we argue sometimes, and then it's like we're all brothers and sisters and the teachers are like our guardians or something.
>
> And the teachers really get on you until they try to make you think of what's in the future and all that. It's good. I mean it makes you think, you know, if every school was like that I don't think there would be a lot of people that would drop out. (Greenleaf, 1995, p. 2)

Melinda: I act differently in his [Appleby's] class—I guess because of the type of teacher he is. He cuts up and stuff. . . . He is hisself—he acts natural—not tryin' to be what somebody wants him to be . . . he makes sure that nobody makes fun of anybody if they mess up when they read out loud.

Bernard: [I like him] just by the way he' talk, he were good to you . . . he don't be afraid to tell you how he feels—he don't talk mean to you, he just speak right to you . . . some teachers only likes the smart people—and Coach Appleby don't do that.

LaVonne: Appleby's fun, he helps you when you feel bad, he'll talk to you. Appleby's got his own style, he makes his own self . . . he's not a brag . . . he get(s) into it—what they [the students] like. Appleby always has this funny grin. . . . He's funny, he tells jokes, laughs with the class. He makes me want to work, he makes me want to give and do something. . . . He show me that I can do it. (Dillon, 1989, pp. 241–242)

Alienation from school is a pattern that emerges from the research on at-risk students (Dillon, 1989; Goodenow, 1992a). Boredom, lack of involvement, and feelings of not belonging keep them on the fringe, prevent them from participating in school experiences, and inhibit motivation. When bright spots appear, they are often the result of teachers who care about these students as people and who communicate this caring through their actions.

A study of at-risk students at an urban junior high found that teachers differed in their ability to help these students and that the terms *high impact* and *low impact* were used to describe the differences (Kramer-Schlosser, 1992). High-impact teachers attempted to cre-

Table 4.6

Characteristics of effective schools

- Safe, orderly school climate
- Concentration on academic objectives
- Positive teacher attitudes and high expectations for all students
- Continuous monitoring of student performance
- Emphasis on the development of cooperation, a sense of community, and prosocial values
- Emphasis on student responsibility and self-regulation; decreased emphasis on external controls
- Strong parental involvement

ate caring, personal learning environments and assumed responsibility for their students' progress. They talked with students, found out about their families, and shared their own lives. They maintained high expectations, used a variety of teaching strategies, and emphasized success and mastery of content. They motivated students through personal contacts, instructional support, and attempts to link school to students' lives.

Low-impact teachers, in contrast, were more authoritarian. They distanced themselves from students and placed primary responsibility for learning on them. They viewed instructional help as "babying the student" or "holding the student's hand." Instruction was teacher directed and lecture oriented. The primary responsibility for motivation was the student's.

In the light of these differences, the effects are not surprising. At-risk students thought of low-impact teachers as adversaries, to be avoided if possible, tolerated if not. In contrast, they sought out the high-impact teachers, both in class and out. The researchers highlighted the human elements of caring and communication in concluding that "relationships with teachers were related to marginal students' behaviors and attitudes. Marginal students reported losing interest in learning when teachers distanced themselves" (Kramer-Schlosser, 1992, p. 138).

Personalized learning environments are important for all students; for at-risk students, they may be essential. But beyond the human element, what else can teachers do?

Effective Instruction for At-Risk Students: Structure and Support

When the students entered the classroom, they saw a review assignment written on the chalkboard. As Mrs. Higby took roll and prepared for the lesson, they routinely started on the assignment.

At exactly 9:05, Mrs. Higby began with a brief review of the previous day's lesson. Both the pace and accuracy of the answers convinced her that the class knew the content and was ready to move on.

As she introduced two-column subtraction, she explained the new idea, guided the students through the steps by using manipulatives, and used questioning to link the manipulatives to the written numerals. Then she had the students solve problems on their own "mini" chalkboards and then hold them up to allow her to check their solutions. Whenever mistakes occurred, she stopped, analyzed the errors, and helped students correct them.

When 90% of the class was correctly solving the problems, the teacher started the students on seatwork, which they checked in pairs when they were done. As they worked, she gave some extra help to those still having difficulty, periodically getting up to respond to pairs who disagreed with each other or had questions.

How should regular classroom teachers adapt their instruction to meet the needs of at-risk students? The overall suggestion is to offer more structure and support, yet retain the best effective teaching strategies that work with other students (Corno & Snow, 1986). In a review of the research in this area, Brophy (1986) concluded that "research has turned up very little evidence suggesting the need for qualitatively different forms of instruction for students who differ in aptitude, achievement level, socioeconomic status, ethnicity or learning style" (pp. IV–122).

In short, teachers of at-risk students don't need to teach in fundamentally different ways; they need to provide enough instructional support to ensure student success while at the same time teaching students strategies that allow them to take control of their own learning. Effective strategies for at-risk students are outlined in Table 4.7 (Brophy, 1986; Peterson, 1986; Wang et al., 1995). These are characteristic of good instruction in general; their importance with at-risk students is even more crucial.

4.45

How are the characteristics of high-impact teachers similar to those of effective schools for at-risk students? What additional characteristics are added?

4.46

Earlier, at-risk students were described as having poorer motivation than their peers not at risk. How do *greater structure and support, more frequent feedback, higher success rates,* and *high expectations* address this problem?

Table 4.7

Effective instruction for at-risk students

Characteristic	Description
Greater structure and support	Course expectations need to be clearly laid out, and assignments and grades need to be designed to encourage achievement.
Active teaching	The teacher needs to carry the content to students personally through interactive teaching rather than depend on curricular materials, such as the text or workbooks.
Instruction emphasizing student engagement	Interactive teaching with high questioning levels invites students to participate in lessons. Open-ended questions allow successful responses and give students a chance to explain their thinking.
More frequent feedback	Student progress should be monitored frequently through classroom questions, quizzes, and assignments.
Higher success rates	Classroom questions, assignments, and quizzes should be designed to maximize opportunities for success.
High expectations	Teachers should assume that all students can learn and emphasize higher order thinking in all classes.
Emphasis on learning strategies	Teachers teach and model learning strategies, emphasizing how they contribute to effective learning.
Emphasis on student motivation and self-regulation	Teachers stress the importance of student control over their own learning; teachers demonstrate and model how learning tasks can be accomplished through proactive planning, monitoring and self-assessment.

Effective Instruction for At-Risk Students: The Need for Challenge

Increased structure and support may not be enough, however. A study of at-risk high school students in a blue-collar community found that many characteristics of effective practices were being implemented (S. Miller, Leinhardt, & Zigmond, 1988). The schools were adapting at every level, from school policies to classroom instruction, and this adaptation kept students in school. However, researchers also found the following:

- Lowered expectations for students
- Lack of emphasis on higher level thinking and problem solving, with a concomitant increase in low-level work sheets
- Student apathy and boredom

In essence, the increased structure and support had resulted in a remedial program that lacked intellectual rigor and excitement.

Several programs have been developed to provide challenge for at-risk students. The *Accelerated Schools Program* builds on student strengths by combining high expectations with an enriched curriculum focusing on a language-based approach in all academic areas (Levin, 1988; Rothman, 1991). The *Higher Order Thinking Skills Program* (HOTS) focuses on teaching students skills such as inferencing and generalizing to help at-risk students understand the process of understanding and how it contributes to learning (Pogrow, 1990).

Results from both programs have been encouraging. One Accelerated Schools site in San Francisco registered the highest achievement gains on standardized test scores in the city, and spring-to-spring comparisons of achievement gains in one program showed HOTS students were 67% above the national average in reading and 123% higher in math (Rothman, 1991).

Common to both programs are high expectations, emphasis on enrichment versus remediation, and the teaching of higher order thinking skills and cognitive strategies. Recent research in this area indicates that these strategies should be integrated into the regular curriculum so that students can see their usefulness in practice (Means & Knapp, 1991).

The dilemma in working with at-risk students is how to be structured and responsive while still presenting a challenging intellectual menu. It isn't an easy task, but many teachers do it. The most famous example is Jaime Escalante, a math teacher in an inner-city section of Los Angeles (Escalante & Dirmann, 1990). He combined an extremely challenging curriculum with enormous personal support to produce a stunning success rate with at-risk students in advanced-placement calculus. The movie *Stand and Deliver,* released in the late 1980s, was based on his experience. Although he paid a high personal price in energy and emotion, the accomplishments of his students demonstrate what can be achieved.

> **4.47** ▬
> Think about classes you've attended in which the content is trivial or the standards are low. How satisfied were you after you finished the classes? Why did you feel this way?

Classroom Connections

Eliminating Gender Bias in Your Classroom

1. Be sensitive to the possibilities of unconscious gender bias.
   - A junior high teacher checks her interaction with her students by periodically videotaping one of her classes. She checks the tape to ensure that boys and girls are called on equally, are asked the same number of high-level questions, and receive the same quality of feedback.
   - A first-grade teacher consciously de-emphasizes sex roles and differences in her classroom. She has boys and girls share equally in chores, and she eliminates gender-related activities such as competition between boys and girls and forming lines by gender.

2. Actively attack gender bias in your teaching.
   - At the beginning of the school year, a social studies teacher explains how gender bias hurts both sexes, and he forbids sexist comments in his classes. As classes study historical topics, he emphasizes the contributions of women and how they have been ignored by historians and points out the changes in views of gender over time.
   - A second-grade teacher selects stories and clippings from newspapers and magazines that portray women in nontraditional roles. She matter-of-factly talks about nontraditional careers with the students in reference to "when you grow up."

Using Effective Teaching Practices for At-Risk Students in Your Classroom

3. Communicate positive expectations by carefully specifying the procedures and requirements for your class.
   - A fourth-grade teacher spends the first 2 weeks of school teaching her students her classroom procedures. She makes short assignments, carefully monitors students to be certain the assignments are turned in, and immediately calls parents if an assignment is missing. This positive beginning lays the foundation for the rest of the year.
   - A junior high math teacher takes extra time explaining his course procedures to his basic math classes. He explains how homework and quizzes contribute to the overall grade. He emphasizes the importance of attendance and effort and expects all to pass his course. He makes himself available before and after school for help sessions.

4. Make active attempts to involve parents or guardians in your classroom.

- An English teacher sends home a description of his class expectations at the beginning of the school year. He makes this letter upbeat and positive and carefully explains student work requirements and grading practices. He also invites questions and comments from parents or other care givers.
- An inner-city elementary teacher makes a special effort to make parents welcome at parent-teacher conferences. She mails a letter of invitation a week before the conference and sends an additional reminder home with students. So that parents feel comfortable, she puts a welcome sign on the door and provides light refreshments in the waiting area.

5. Maintain high levels of student involvement in your teaching.
   - In language arts activities, a teacher builds her teaching around questioning and examples. She comments, "My goal is to call on each student in the class at least twice during the course of a lesson. I also use a lot of repetition and reinforcement as we cover the examples."

6. Give frequent quizzes and return them the following day to provide feedback.
   - An earth science teacher gives students a short quiz of one or two questions every day. It is discussed at the beginning of the following day, and students calculate their own averages each day during the grading period.

7. Use grading practices that promote success and encourage effort and achievement.
   - An eighth-grade general math teacher computes students' averages after the 3rd week of the grading period, shares them with the students, and from that point on awards bonus points for improvement on tests and quizzes. She writes a brief note on the paper every time students improve, praising them for their effort and achievement.

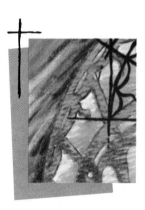

Windows on Classrooms

Throughout this chapter, you've seen how sources of individuality—intelligence, socioeconomic status, culture, and gender—can all influence learning. You also saw how some unfortunate combinations of these factors can place students at risk. Further, you've examined the implications these factors have for teachers: sensitivity to differences, building on students' backgrounds, structure and support, active teaching, frequent feedback, small steps, and high success rates with appropriate challenge.

Now, please read the following case study and assess the teacher's effectiveness in the context of the information you've studied.

Diane Smith is a fifth-grade teacher at Oneida Elementary, a school in a lower-middle-class section of the city. The school is crowded, and Diane has 33 students, 14 of whom are ethnic minorities, in a classroom built for 25. The students sit facing each other across an aisle as shown in the outline of her classroom below. Her desk, with a filing cabinet behind it, is on one side of the screen—the chalkboard is behind the screen—with an area for the students to file papers on the opposite side of the screen, next to the door. A worktable is at the back of the room, and the pencil sharpener (ps) is near the door.

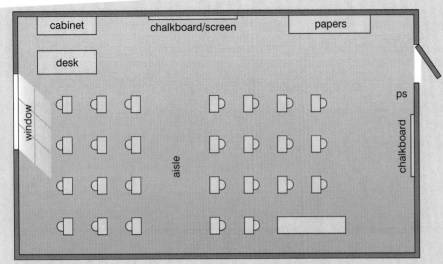

Diane has her day scheduled as follows:

8:55-9:00	Roll; announcements
9:00-10:00	Reading
10:00-11:00	Math
11:00-11:30	Science
11:30-11:45	Silent reading
11:45-11:55	Prepare for lunch
11:55-12:30	Lunch
12:30-12:35	Bathroom break
12:35-1:45	Language Arts
1:45- 2:15	Social Studies
2:15- 2:45	P.E.
2:45- 3:00	Evaluate day; give homework; prepare for dismissal
3:00- 3:15	Dismissal

In language arts, Diane has already covered adjectives with her students and now wants to cover the comparative and superlative forms of adjectives.

We join her class at 12:33 as the students are filing into the room from their lunch break. As they come into the room, they look at the screen and see a series of 10 sentences on the overhead with directions stating, "Number your paper from 1 to 10, write down the adjective in each of the sentences, and also write the noun that it modifies."

The students move to their desks, take out paper, and begin working on the exercises.

At 12:35, all the students are seated and busy. As the students are working, Diane surveys the room, identifying students who have pencils of different lengths and students whose hair colors vary. She decides that she will use these as examples for her lesson, rather than the pencils and colored pieces of paper she brought with her. She puts the pencils and paper back into her filing cabinet.

"I can't see," Rick, the shortest boy in the class, announces as he bobs up and down in his desk next to the table at the back of the room.

"Rick and David (the student next to Rick in the last row near the table), move your desks into the aisle so that you will be able to see the screen," Diane directs.

Diane then walks among the students to see how they are doing. As she surveys their work, she sees that Eric and Amado have missed Item 3 but that all the students have gotten all the other exercises correct.

The students finish at 12:50, and Diane begins, "It looks like we're in good shape on these exercises, but let's go over them just to be sure."

Diane goes over each exercise, identifying both the adjective and the noun in each case.

At 1:10, they finish, and Diane announces, "Okay, very good, everyone. Now put your materials away, and we'll move on to today's lesson."

At 1:11, the students have their papers in their desks and Diane begins, "Caleasha and Daniel, hold your pencils up high so that everyone can see. What do you notice about the pencils? . . . Naitia?"

" . . . Caleasha's is red and Daniel's is blue."

"Okay. What else?" Diane smiles. . . . "Sheila?"

"You write with them."

"Indeed you do!" Diane nods and smiles again. "What else, Kelvin?" she asks quickly.

"Caleasha's is longer."

"That's true," Diane confirms. "Does everyone see that? Hold them up again," she directs energetically.

Caleasha and Daniel hold their pencils up again, and Diane moves to the chalkboard and writes:

Caleasha has a long pencil.

Caleasha has a longer pencil than does Daniel.

"Now, let's look at Matt and Leroy. What do you notice about their hair? . . . Judy?" Diane asks as she walks down the aisle.

As she walks back to the front of the room, Diane takes a note Elaine has been writing to Hanna, folds it so that Elaine sees she doesn't read it, and says quietly, "Please pay attention. You can have this back after school."

"Leroy's is black, and Matt's is brown," Randy responds.

"Okay. Good, Randy. So who has darker hair?"

"LEROY!" the class blurts out.

"Okay, everyone. I understand your eagerness, and I think it's good,"

Diane waves at the class. "Just as a reminder, what is one of our most important rules in here? . . . Todd?"

"We wait until you call on us before we answer."

"Okay. Excellent, everyone. You've all done very well with this. We just need a little reminder now and then."

"Now, let's see where we are. What did we say about Leroy's and Matt's hair? . . . Vicki?"

"Leroy's was darker."

"Good!" and Diane then writes three more sentences on the chalkboard, and they appeared as follows:

Caleasha has a long pencil.

Calesha has a longer pencil than does Daniel.

Leroy has black hair.

Matt has brown hair.

Leroy has darker hair than does Matt.

"Now, let's look at the adjectives in the sentences and compare them with each other. How do they compare? . . . Heather?"

" . . . The adjectives in the bottom sentences have an -*er* on the end of them," Kim Soo responds hesitantly.

"Yes, good," Diane smiles reassuringly.

"So, what are we doing in each of the sentences? . . . Jason?" Diane continues.

"We're comparing two things to each other."

"Very good, Jason! And what are we comparing in the first sentence? . . . Lawsikia?"

"The length of the pencils."

"And how about the second sentence? . . . Jana?"

"The color of Leroy's and Matt's hair."

"Good! Now, Caleasha and Daniel, hold your pencils up again, and Kerri and David, you hold yours up too. Now, what do you notice? . . . Tom?"

"Kerri's pencil is longer than any of the others."

"Good, Tom. We can see that it is. Now, look at Theresa's hair. What do you notice about it? . . . Angie?"

"It's blonde."

"Yes, it is," Diane nods, and she then writes three more sentences on the chalkboard, so they appeared as follows:

Caleasha has a long pencil.

Caleasha has a longer pencil than does Daniel.

Kerri has the longest pencil.

Leroy has black hair.

Matt has brown hair.

Teresa has blonde hair.

Leroy has darker hair than does Matt.

Leroy has the darkest hair.

"Now, what do you notice about the adjectives in the third set of sentences? . . . Sean?"

Sean suddenly looks up at the sound of his name. " . . . Could you repeat the question?"

"What do you notice about the adjectives in the third set of sentences?" Diane repeats.

" . . . They have -*est* on the end of them," Sean says hesitantly.

"Okay. Good, Sean. And what did we do in each of those cases? . . . Spence?"

"We compared the pencils and the hair."

"How many pencils? . . . Steve?"

"Four."

"And how many people's hair? . . . Debbie?"

"Three."

"So, how do we write adjectives if we compare two things? . . . Todd?"

"We put an -*er* on the end of them."

"And suppose we have three or more things. Then what? . . . Sara?"

"We put an -*est* on them."

"Very good, everyone. In describing nouns, if we're comparing two, we use the comparative form of the adjective, which has an -*er* on the end, and if we have three or more, we have an -*est* on the end of the adjective.

"Now, look," Diane continues, and she reaches back and takes a tennis ball and a golf ball from her desk. "Write a sentence that tells us about the size of the two balls."

The students then take out paper and begin writing their sentences. As they work, Diane walks up and down the rows, looking at each student's work.

"Now, let's look at some sentences," Diane begins after a few minutes. "Someone volunteer a sentence, and I'll write it on the chalkboard. . . . Okay, Rashad?"

"The tennis ball is bigger than the golf ball," Rashad volunteers.

"Very good, Rashad. And why did you write *bigger* in your sentence?"

"We're comparing the size of two balls."

"That's excellent. Now, I want you to write a paragraph that has in it at least two examples of using the comparative form of adjectives and at least two other examples that use the superlative form of the adjectives. Underline the adjectives in each case."

The students then begin writing their paragraphs. As they work, Diane circulates among them, periodically stopping for a few seconds to comment on a student's work and to offer suggestions.

At 1:40, Diane announces, "All right, everyone. Please turn in your paragraphs, and we're going to get ready for social studies."

The students then pass the papers forward. By 1:45, the students have turned in their papers and have their social studies books out and waiting.

Questions for Discussion and Analysis

Analyze Diane's teaching. In conducting your analysis, consider the following questions. In each case, be specific and take information directly from the case study to defend your assessment.

1. Describe the structure and support in Diane's teaching. How effective was this structure and support?
2. Did Diane demonstrate active teaching? Cite specific examples to support your answer.
3. To what extent was Diane's teaching designed to emphasize active engagement of the students? Again, cite specific examples.
4. How did Diane attempt to ensure success in her teaching?
5. Most of Diane's students are from relatively low SES backgrounds. Overall, how effective was her teaching for these students?
6. To what extent did Diane display culturally responsive teaching in her lesson?
7. To what extent did Diane's teaching reflect sensitivity to gender issues?
8. How effective was Diane's teaching for at-risk students?

 **Summary**

Students differ in intelligence, socioeconomic status (SES), culture, and gender, each of which influences learning. Some combinations of these factors place students at risk of not being able to take full advantage of their educational experience.

Intelligence

Intelligence is the ability to think and reason abstractly, to solve problems, and to acquire new knowledge. Some theories suggest that intelligence is a single entity; others describe intelligence as existing in several forms.

Experts disagree about the contributions of heredity and environment on the development of intelligence. *Nature* advocates argue that intelligence is genetically determined; *nurture* proponents contend that it is influenced primarily by a child's cumulative experiences. Most theorists believe that intelligence is determined by a combination of the two.

The most common response to differences in ability has been to group students according to those differences. Within- and between-class ability grouping is common in elementary schools; tracking is prevalent in middle and secondary schools. Ability grouping can lower performance and stigmatize students in low-ability classes.

Socioeconomic Status

Socioeconomic status (SES) includes parents' income, occupation, and level of education. SES strongly influences student attitudes, values, background experiences, and school success.

Culture

Culture helps determine the attitudes, values, customs, and behavior patterns a child brings to school. The match between a child's culture and the school has a powerful influence on school success. Culturally responsive teaching creates links between a student's culture and classroom instruction.

Language

Language is a crucial aspect of culture and ethnicity. An increasing number of students are coming to U.S. classrooms with limited expertise in English. Bilingual programs are designed to teach English while maintaining the first language. ESL programs attempt to teach English as quickly as possible.

Gender

Gender differences in aptitude or intelligence are minor and are caused primarily by different treatment of boys and girls. Teachers can minimize the negative effects of gender differences by treating boys and girls equally and by actively combating negative stereotypes in their teaching.

At-Risk Students

At-risk students are more likely to exit school with subminimal learning skills. Effective schools for at-risk students stress high expectations, an academic focus, continuous monitoring of progress, and strong parent involvement. Effective programs for at-risk students prevent rather than remediate learning problems by being flexible and adaptive to student needs. Effective teachers for at-risk students hold high expectations for academic success, use a variety of instructional and motivational strategies, and demonstrate caring through sincere interest in students' lives. Effective instruction for at-risk students provides greater structure and support, more active teaching, greater student engagement, and more feedback with higher success rates. Research also documents the need for challenge in classes for at-risk students; effective teachers balance support with challenge to create lessons that are both stimulating and successful. The study of resilient youth provides teachers with an overall goal for their work with at-risk students, as well as concrete suggestions for developing healthy students.

 ## Important Concepts

ability grouping (p. 113)

at-risk students (p. 138)

bidialecticism (p. 128)

cultural deficit models (p. 125)

cultural difference models (p. 126)

cultural inversion (p. 122)

culturally responsive teaching (p. 126)

culture (p. 120)

dialect (p. 128)

English as a second language (ESL) programs (p. 130)

Chapter Outline

5

Learners
with
Exceptionalities

Sabrina Curtis is a beginning first-grade teacher in a large inner-city school district. She survived the hectic first weeks of school and was beginning to feel comfortable as she worked her way into the routines of teaching. At the same time, something bothered her.

"It's kind of frustrating," she admitted, sandwich in hand as she shared her half-hour lunch break with Clarisse, a "veteran" of 3 years who had become her friend and confidant. "I'm teaching most of the students, but some of them just don't seem to 'get it.'"

"Maybe you're being too hard on yourself," Clarisse responded. "Students are different. Remember some of the stuff you studied in college? One thing they emphasized was that it just takes some students a little longer to mature."

"Well, . . . yes, . . . I understand that, but that seems almost too easy. I still have this feeling. For instance, there's Rodney. You've seen him on the playground. He's a cute boy, but his engine is stuck on fast," she smiled wryly, rolling her eyes up. "I can barely get him to sit in his seat, much less work.

"When he sits down to do an assignment, he's all over his desk, squirming and wiggling. It takes just the smallest distraction to set him off. He can usually do the work when he sticks to it, but that's a major challenge for him. I've spoken with his mother, and he's the same way at home. I wonder if he has some type of learning disability.

"Then there's Amelia; she's so sweet, but she simply doesn't get it. I've tried everything under the sun with her. I explain it, and the next time, it's as if it's all brand new again. I feel sorry for her, because I know she gets frustrated because she can't keep up with the other students. What she seems to lack are basic learning strategies such as paying attention and keeping track of her assignments. When I work with her individually, it seems to help, but I just wish I had more time to spend with her. I just see her falling farther and farther behind."

"Maybe it's not your fault. You're supposed to be bright and energetic and do your best, but you're going to burn yourself out if you keep this up," Clarisse encouraged. "Check with the Teacher Assistance Team. Maybe these students need some extra help."

As you saw in Chapter 4, students differ in a number of ways, and effective teachers consider these differences when they plan and teach. In some cases, the *differences are such that special help and resources are needed to help students reach their full potential*. In these cases, the students are said to have **exceptionalities**. These exceptionalities range from mild learning disabilities and physical impairments to gifted and talented. Special help and resources include special schools, self-contained classrooms, resource rooms, and inclusion in regular classrooms with the support of specially trained professionals.

Special education *refers to instruction designed to meet the unique needs of students with exceptionalities.* Teachers in regular classrooms are being asked to play an ever-increasing role in identifying and teaching students who need special help. This chapter is designed to help you prepare for that role.

After you have completed your study of this chapter, you should be able to meet the following objectives:

▮ Explain the role of classroom teachers in working with students with exceptionalities.
▮ Explain how different exceptionalities—mental retardation, learning disabilities, behavior disorders, communication disorders, and visual and hearing impairments—affect student learning.
▮ Describe different methods of identifying and teaching students who are gifted and talented.
▮ Explain how instructional strategies can be adapted to meet the needs of students with exceptionalities.

Incidents like the ones in the opening case study are not uncommon in today's schools. Although we can't be certain from the brief descriptions, Rodney and Amelia may have problems that prevent them from taking full advantage of their educational opportunities. As teachers, we all work with students who, despite our best efforts, fail to learn as their classmates do. They include students with learning disabilities, behavior disorders, impaired speech or hearing, communication problems, and physical impairments that interfere with learning and living in regular classrooms.

How common are these problems? On any given day, about 5 million students are enrolled in special programs, two thirds of them for relatively minor problems (Heward, 1996). Approximately 1 of 10 students in a typical school receives special education services (Hallahan & Kauffman, 1994).

Changing Views of Special Education

In the past, many students with exceptionalities were separated from their peers and placed into segregated classrooms or schools. Instruction in these classrooms, however, was often inferior, achievement was no better than in regular classrooms, and students didn't learn the life skills needed to live in the real world. Educators looked for other ways to help these students.

Federal Laws Redefine Special Education

In 1975, the U.S. Congress passed Public Law 94–142, the *Individuals With Disabilities in Education Act* (IDEA), a law that ensures a free and public education for all students with exceptionalities. IDEA, combined with more recent amendments, provides for the following guidelines in working with students having exceptionalities:

▌ Identify the needs of students with exceptionalities by nondiscriminatory assessment.
▌ Involve parents in developing each child's educational program.
▌ Create an environment that is minimally restrictive.
▌ Develop an individualized education program (IEP) of study for each student.

IDEA has affected every school in the United States and has changed the roles of regular and special educators.

The Evolution Toward Inclusion

As educators realized that segregated classes and services were not meeting the needs of students with exceptionalities, they wrestled with alternatives. One of the first was **mainstreaming,** *the practice of moving students with exceptionalities from segregated settings into regular classrooms.* Popular in the 1970s, mainstreaming had advantages and disadvantages (Hardman, Drew, & Egan, 1996). It began the move away from segregated services. On the one hand, it allowed students with exceptionalities and other students to interact, but on the other hand, students with exceptionalities were often placed into classrooms without the necessary support and services.

As educators grappled with these problems, they developed the concept of the **least restrictive environment (LRE),** *one that places students in as normal an educational set-*

5.1 ▬
Imagine drawing two circles, one inside the other. Which would be an LRE, and which would be mainstreaming?

ting as possible while still meeting their special academic, social, and physical needs. Broader than the concept of *mainstreaming,* the LRE can consist of a continuum of services ranging from mainstreaming to placement in separate facilities. Mainstreaming to a regular classroom occurs only if parents and educators decide it best meets the child's needs.

Central to the LRE is the concept of **adaptive fit**, *which is the degree to which a student is able to cope with the requirements of a school setting and the extent to which the school accommodates the student's special needs* (Hardman et al., 1996). Adaptive fit implies an individualized approach to dealing with students having exceptionalities; it can only be determined after an analysis of a student's specific learning needs. As educators considered mainstreaming, the LRE, and adaptive fit, they gradually developed the concept of *inclusion.*

Inclusion *is a comprehensive approach to educating students with exceptionalities that advocates a total, systematic, and coordinated web of services.* The inclusion movement has three components:

1. Placing students with special needs in a regular school campus
2. Creating appropriate support and services to guarantee an adaptive fit
3. Coordinating general and special education services

Inclusion is both proactive and comprehensive; it makes all educators responsible for creating supportive learning environments and leaves open the possibility of services being delivered in places other than the regular classroom. Its basic thrust is to include students with exceptionalities in regular classrooms whenever possible, but it also allows for delivering services in other places.

> **5.2**
> Identify at least two advantages of inclusion. Identify at least one potential problem with inclusion.

A Legal Framework for Working With Students Who Have Exceptionalities

Kevin had mild retardation and had been going to a resource program for an hour a day during his elementary school years. The resource teacher worked closely with the regular teacher to ensure that Kevin's work in each classroom was consistent. Through their combined efforts, they were able to help him learn in the regular classroom even though his achievement test scores were well below his grade level.

The move to junior high posed new challenges for Kevin. He would have five teachers instead of one, and the prospect of moving from one class to the next was frightening. Before school started, Mr. Endo, Kevin's resource teacher in the junior high, called a meeting of Kevin's parents and teachers. They discussed Kevin's strengths and weaknesses and what kinds of teaching strategies had worked at his old school. He liked science and art, and a special effort was made to provide him with some additional science materials. Out of this meeting came an *individualized education program* (IEP) that provided short- and long-term goals and additional teaching strategies to use with him. The IEP would take effect with the start of his next semester and would guide teachers during the next year, after which it would be reviewed and revised. The group shared the IEP with Kevin, and knowing that he was being looked after made him feel more at ease.

As you saw earlier, IDEA fundamentally changed the way schools educate students with exceptionalities. One way this change occurs is through specific provisions that require (a) due process through parental involvement, (b) protection against discrimination in testing, (c) least restrictive environment (LRE), and (d) an individualized education program (IEP).

Inclusion creates a web of services to integrate students with exceptionalities into the educational system.

5.3

You saw that Kevin's parents were involved in the development of his IEP. What law required that they be involved?

Due Process Through Parental Involvement

Due process guarantees parents' involvement in identifying and placing their children in special programs, access to school records, and the opportunity for an independent evaluation if they're not satisfied with the initial one. Legal safeguards are also in place if the parents don't speak English; they have the right to an interpreter, and their rights must be read to them in their native language. Involving Kevin's parents in developing his IEP is one facet of due process.

5.4

Suppose you suspect that a Hispanic student in your class, who speaks halting but understandable English, has a learning disability in math. Because he speaks understandable English, can he be given a placement test written in English? Explain.

Protection Against Discrimination in Testing

One aspect of the law guarantees that any testing used in the placement process will be conducted by qualified personnel and in the student's native language and that no single instrument, such as an intelligence test, will be used as the sole basis for placement. In response to a court decision (*Larry P. v. Riles,* 1979), California severely restricted the use of standardized intelligence tests in identifying minority children with disabilities. In recent years, assessment has placed increased emphasis on a student's classroom performance and general adaptive behavior, rather than on narrow, isolated tests (Heward, 1996).

5.5

How could integration into the regular classroom help a student with special needs improve academic performance? Self-concept? Peer acceptance?

Least Restrictive Environment (LRE)

You saw earlier that the intent of an LRE is that all students have the right to learn in an environment that best promotes their academic and social growth. They are taken out of the regular classroom only when an exceptionality is such that regular classes with the use of supplementary help cannot meet their needs.

The LRE provision means that *you will have students with exceptionalities in your classroom* and that you will be asked to work with special educators to design and implement programs for these students. The thrust of the LRE is that students with exceptionalities should participate as much as possible in the regular school agenda, including academics, recess, lunch in the cafeteria, regular school assemblies, and extracurricular activities. The exact form of these programs varies with the nature of the problem and the capabilities of the students.

Figure 5.1 presents a continuum of services for implementing the LRE, starting with the least confining at the top and moving to the most confining at the bottom.

These placement options represent a continuum from greater to lesser involvement in the regular classroom. A primary goal of inclusion is to identify the point on the continuum that is the LRE that best meets the student's needs.

Individualized Education Program (IEP)

An individualized education program ensures that inclusion works and that the special education student doesn't get lost in the regular classroom. An **individualized education program (IEP)** is *an individually prescribed instructional plan devised by special education and classroom teachers, other resource professionals, and parents to meet the specific needs of a student.* It must be developed cooperatively with parents, and it specifies the following:

- An assessment of the student's current level of performance
- Long- and short-term objectives
- Services or strategies to be used
- Schedules for implementing the plan
- Criteria to be used in evaluating the plan's success

When completed, the IEP must be approved and signed by the student's parents or legal guardians; this signals their involvement in the process and their approval of the product.

Figure 5.2 presents a sample IEP. It has three important features. First, the initials of all participants indicate that its development was a cooperative effort involving both school pro-

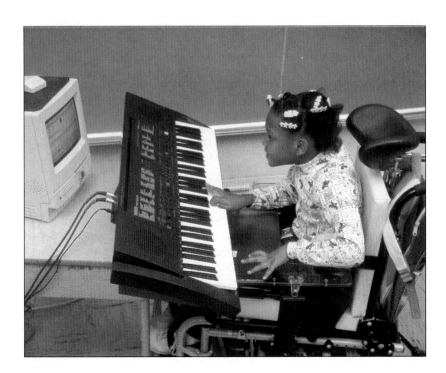

The least restrictive environment provides students with opportunities to develop to their fullest potential.

5.6

Which of the options in Figure 5.1 will serve the greatest number of students having exceptionalities? The smallest number? What implications does this have for you as a regular classroom teacher?

5.7

Explain specifically how an IEP accommodates the previously discussed concepts of *due process, parental involvement,* and *least restrictive environment.*

Figure 5.1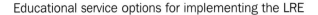

Educational service options for implementing the LRE

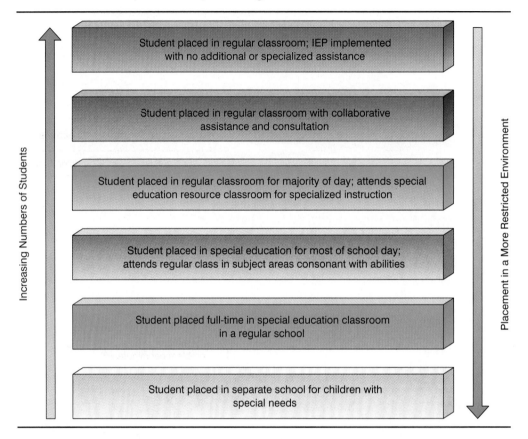

fessionals, the student, and his or her parents. Second, the specific information in columns 3, 4, 5, and 6 and in section 7 helps guide the classroom teacher and special education personnel when they implement the IEP. Third, the parent's signature at the bottom of the plan indicates that the parent was involved in developing the plan and agrees with its details.

Functions of the IEP

The IEP performs at least four functions: First, it provides support for the classroom teacher, who is often uncertain about dealing with special needs students. Second, it creates a tangible link between the regular classroom and the resource team. Third, it helps give parents some peace of mind about their child's progress. Fourth and most important, it provides an instructional program designed to meet the individual needs of the student.

IEPs often provide for work in alternative settings, such as a resource room, as well as the regular classroom; at other times, they focus exclusively on regular classroom adaptations. They are most effective when the two are coordinated, such as when a classroom teacher working on word problems in math asks the resource teacher to focus on the same type of problems.

Figure 5.2

Individualized education program (IEP)

INDIVIDUAL EDUCATION PROGRAM

Date _____ 3-1-96 _____

(1) Student

Name: Joe S.
School: Adams
Grade: 5
Current Placement: Regular Class/Resource Room

Date of Birth: 10-1-84   **Age:** 11-5

(2) Committee

		Initial
Mrs. Wrens	Principal	D.a.W.
Mrs. Snow	Regular Teacher	A.S.
Mr. LaJoie	Counselor	SLJ
Mr. Thomas	Resource Teacher	M.T.
Mr. Ryan	School Psychologist	H.R.R.
Mrs. S.	Parent	J.S.
Joe S.	Student	Joe S.

EP from _3-15-96_ to _3-15-97_

(3) Present Level of Educational Functioning	(4) Annual Goal Statements	(5) Instructional Objectives	(6) Objective Criteria and Evaluation
<u>MATH</u> <u>Strengths</u> 1. Can successfuly compute addition and subtraction problems to two places with regrouping and zeros. 2. Knows 100 basic multiplication facts. <u>Weaknesses</u> 1. Frequently makes computational errors on problems with which he has had experience. 2. Does not complete seatwork. Key Math total score of 2.1 Grade Equivalent.	Joe will apply knowledge of regrouping in addition and renaming in subtraction to four-digit numbers.	1. When presented with 20 addition problems of 3-digit numbers requiring two renamings, the student will compute answers at a rate of one problem per minute and an accuracy of 90%. 2. When presented with 20 subtraction problems of 3-digit numbers requiring two renamings, the student will compute answers at a rate of one problem per minute with 90% accuracy. 3. When presented with 20 addition problems of 4-digit numbers requiring three renamings, the student will compute answers at a rate of one problem per minute and an accuracy of 90%. 4. When presented with 20 subtraction problems of 4-digit numbers requiring three renamings, the student will compute answers at a rate of one problem per minute with 90% accuracy.	Teacher-made tests (weekly) Teacher-made tests (weekly) Teacher-made tests (weekly)

(7) Educational Services to be Provided

Services Required	Date initiated	Duration of Service	Individual Responsible for the Service
Regular Reading-Adapted	3-15-96	3-15-97	Reading Improvement Specialist and Special Education Teacher
Resource Room	3-15-96	3-15-97	Special Education Teacher
Counselor Consultant	3-15-96	3-15-97	Counselor
Monitoring diet and general health	3-15-96	3-15-97	School Health Nurse

Extent of time in the regular education program: 60% increasing to 80%
Justification of the educational placement:

It is felt that the structure of the resource room can best meet the goals stated for Joe; especially when coordinated with the regular classroom.

It is also felt that Joe could profit enormously from talking with a counselor. He needs someone with whom to talk and with whom he can share his feelings.

(8) I have had the opportunity to participate in the development of the Individual Education Program.
   I agree with Individual Education Program   (✓)
   I disagree with the Individual Education Program   ( )

Parent's Signature _____ Mrs S. _____

Source: From *Developing and Implementing Individualized Education Programs* (3rd ed.) (pp. 308, 316) by B. B. Strickland and A. P. Turnbull, 1990, New York: Macmillan. Reprinted by permission.

Teachers and other professionals meet with parents to design an IEP that meets a student's individual learning needs.

5.8
Describe a curriculum-based measurement designed to measure a student's ability to find "main ideas." Be specific in your description.

Curriculum-Based Measurement

To assist both the classroom teacher and the special education teacher in designing IEPs, educators are placing increased emphasis on **curriculum-based measurement,** *which assesses learners' performance in specific areas of the regular classroom curriculum* (Shinn & Hubbard, 1992). As opposed to broader measures, such as standardized achievement tests, curriculum-based measurement attempts to identify specific areas in which students need help, such as finding the main idea in reading or knowing multiplication facts. Identifying these areas helps the team design IEPs that can best meet a student's specific needs.

Students With Learning Problems

The terms *children with exceptionalities, special education students, children with handicaps, students with special needs,* and *individuals with disabilities* have all been used to describe students needing additional help to reach their full potential. Currently, the term *students with disabilities* is often preferred because it emphasizes that disabilities can be altered and that they don't necessarily result in handicapped performance (Hallahan & Kauffman, 1994). About 10% of the school-age population is in this group, and the kinds of disabilities range from mild learning disabilities to physical impairments such as deafness and blindness (U.S. Department of Education, 1994). Federal legislation has created categories to identify specific learning problems, and educators use these categories in developing programs to meet the needs of each type of student.

Use of categories and the labeling that results is controversial. Advocates argue that categories provide a common language for professionals and encourage specialized instruction that meets the specific needs of all students (Heward, 1996). Opponents claim that categories are somewhat arbitrary, that many differences exist within the categories themselves, and that categorizing encourages educators to treat students as labels rather than as people. Despite the controversy, however, these categories are widely used, so teachers need to be familiar with the terms and the implications they have for working with students.

Figure 5.3 represents the percentage of students in each of the categories commonly used in education (U.S. Department of Education, 1994). The figure shows that three categories—mental retardation, learning disabilities, and behavior disorders—make up a large majority of the total population (about 70%) of students with disabilities, and they are ones you will most likely encounter in your classroom.

Mental Retardation

Gail Toomey watched her first-grade class as they worked on their reading assignment. Most of the class was working quietly, with occasional whispers and giggles. Stacy, in contrast, was wandering around the classroom for the third time, supposedly sharpening her pencil. Gail had reminded her once to sit down and this time went over to see what the problem was.

"I can't do this! I don't get it!" Stacy responded in frustration when Gail asked her why she hadn't started her work.

After helping her calm down, Gail worked with Stacy for a few moments but could tell by her responses and her facial expression that she truly didn't "get" the seatwork assignment. Gail made a note to herself to talk with a member of the school's Teacher Assistance Team about Stacy.

All first-grade teachers have had experiences similar to Gail's. Stacy, as with Amelia in our opening case study, seems to be slower than others and may be frustrated because she can't keep up with her peers. Unfortunately, this problem is often not identified until students are well into their school experience—sometimes several years. Many of these students have mild mental retardation. (You may also encounter the terms *educationally* or *intellectually handicapped,* which a few educators prefer.)

5.9
Explain why some educators might prefer the term *intellectually handicapped.*

Figure 5.3

The exceptional student population

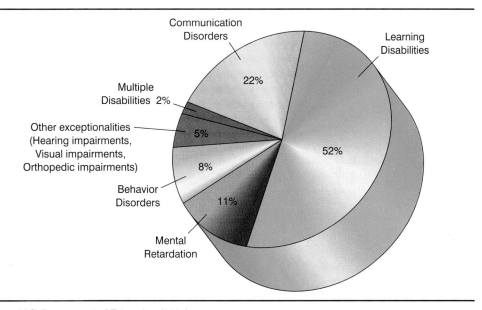

Source: U.S. Department of Education (1994).

The American Association on Mental Retardation (AAMR) defines **mental retardation** as follows:

> Mental retardation refers to substantial limitations in present functioning. It is characterized by significantly subaverage intellectual functioning, existing concurrently with related limitations in two or more of the following applicable adaptive skill areas: communication, self-care, home living, social skills, community use, self-direction, health and safety, functional academics, leisure, and work. Mental retardation manifests before age 18. (AAMR Ad Hoc Committee on Terminology and Classification, 1992, p. 5)

Two important characteristics are embedded in this definition (Turnbull, Turnbull, Shank, & Leal, 1995). The first identifies limitations in intellectual functioning, as indicated by difficulties in learning; the second focuses on adaptive skills, such as communication, self-care, and social ability. The characteristics suggest the need for a system of support that shifts the focus from limitations of the person to designing an array of services to meet the person's needs.

Prior to the 1960s, definitions of mental retardation were based on below-average scores on IQ tests (typically, two standard deviations below the mean or an IQ of about 70), but this approach had several problems. The first was the tests themselves; as you will see in Chapter 14, any test has built-in error, and this imprecision requires caution when making decisions about people. Second, disproportionate numbers of minorities and non-English-speaking students were identified as having mental retardation and placed in inappropriate educational settings (Hallahan & Kauffman, 1994; Hardman et al., 1996). Third, the tests could not reliably predict success in the real world (Heward, 1996). Educators found that people with the same IQ scores varied widely in their ability to cope with life. Some functioned quite well, both in classrooms and in the outside world, whereas others needed a great deal of training and support to survive in either setting. As a result, the definition was broadened to include behavioral and adaptive functioning, as well as test data. This is where the classroom teacher's input is essential.

Levels of Mental Retardation

There are four levels of mental retardation, and each relates to the level of needed support (Luckasson et al., 1992):

1. Intermittent: Support on an "as-needed" basis
2. Limited: Support consistently needed over time
3. Extensive: Regular (e.g., daily) support required
4. Pervasive: High-intensity, potentially life-sustaining support required

This system replaces one that was linked to IQ scores and categorized people as having either mild (50 to 70 IQ), moderate (35 to 50 IQ), or severe and profound (IQ below 35) mental retardation. The transition from the old, IQ-anchored system to the new one is not complete, so you will probably encounter both in your work.

Programs for Students With Mental Retardation

Programs for students who have intermittent or mild mental retardation focus on creating support systems to augment existing instructional programs. Inclusion often places these students in regular classrooms and adapts instruction to the special needs of these students. Attempts are made to help students fit in both socially and academically.

Research indicates that many of these students fail to acquire basic learning strategies that regular students pick up naturally, such as maintaining attention, organizing and mem-

5.10 ▬
In Chapter 4, *intelligence* was defined as "the capacity to acquire knowledge, the ability to think and reason in the abstract, and the capability for solving problems." To which of these is adaptive behavior most closely related? Least related?

5.11 ▬
Again consider the definition of intelligence from Chapter 4 and referred to in Note 5.10. To which of these dimensions is strategy training most directly targeted? Explain.

orizing new material, and studying for tests (Macmillan, Keogh, & Jones, 1986). Amelia, in our opening case study, was an example of a student who needed additional instructional support to help her cope in the classroom. Like many students who have mental retardation, she lacked basic learning strategies to help her attend to and benefit from instruction. Sabrina Curtis, her teacher, recognized this need and attempted to provide greater structure and support to maximize success and to minimize failure and frustration.

Learning Disabilities

Tammy Fuller, a junior high social studies teacher, was surprised as she scored Adam's test. He seemed to be doing so well. He was rarely absent, paid attention, and participated willingly and intelligently. Why was his test score so low? Tammy made a mental note to watch him, because his classroom behavior and his test performance were inconsistent.

In her second unit, Tammy emphasized both independent and collaborative work, so she prepared study guide questions and had students work in groups to study the material. As she circulated around the room, she noticed that Adam's sheet was empty; when she asked him about it, he mumbled something about not having time the night before. Because the success of the unit depended on students coming to class prepared, Tammy asked Adam to come in after school to complete his work.

Adam arrived promptly at 3:10 and opened his book to the chapter. When Tammy stopped to check on his progress 15 minutes later, his page was virtually empty; in another 15 minutes, it was still blank.

As she sat down to talk with him, he appeared embarrassed and evasive. When they started to work on the questions together, she discovered that he couldn't read the text.

Some students, such as Adam, are average or even above average in intelligence but, despite teachers' best efforts, have a difficult time learning. They score within the "normal" range on intelligence tests, they don't have mental retardation, typically they don't have other physical disabilities, and they don't necessarily come from troubled homes. These are students with **learning disabilities (LDs),** *disorders that hamper learning within a specific domain or context,* usually reading, writing, and listening. Students with this problem have "normal" intelligence; in fact, a discrepancy between IQ and below-average classroom performance is one of its defining characteristics.

The National Joint Committee on Learning Disabilities (1994) describes learning disabilities as significant difficulties in acquiring and using listening, speaking, reading, writing, reasoning, or mathematical abilities. Learning disabilities are presumed to be due to central nervous system dysfunction, and they may exist along with, but are not caused by, other handicapping conditions such as sensory impairment or cultural differences. Experts also agree that there is considerable heterogeneity among students with learning disabilities (Hallahan & Kauffman, 1994).

Students with learning disabilities comprise the largest group of students with exceptionalities—approximately 4% of the school-age population. Cases were first identified in the early 1960s, and the number of school-age children diagnosed as LD has continually increased so that they comprise over half of all children with disabilities (U.S. Department of Education, 1994).

5.12
Identify at least one similarity and one difference between learning disabilities and intellectual disabilities or mental retardation.

Characteristics of Students With Learning Disabilities

What are the characteristics of students with learning disabilities? They look like other students, but their problems manifest themselves in patterns such as those outlined in Table 5.1. Keep in mind that each student with a learning disability is unique and that the specific problem and educational adaptation will need to be addressed by the IEP.

Table 5.1

Characteristics of students with learning disabilities

General Patterns
Hyperactivity and fidgeting
Lack of coordination and balance
Attention deficits
Disorganization and tendency toward distraction
Lack of follow-through and completion of assignments
Uneven performance (e.g., capable in one area, extremely weak in others)

Academic Performance	
Reading	Lacks reading fluency
	Reverses words (e.g., *saw* for *was*)
	Frequently loses place
Writing	Makes jerky and poorly formed letters
	Has difficulty staying on line
	Is slow in completing work
	Has difficulty in copying from chalkboard
Math	Has difficulty remembering math facts
	Mixes columns (e.g., 10s and 1s) in computing
	Has trouble with story problems

Many of these characteristics are typical of general learning problems or immaturity. Unlike developmental lags, however, learning disabilities don't go away. In fact, problems associated with learning disabilities often increase over time. A pattern develops in which students fall farther behind in achievement, with concomitant increases in management problems and decreases in self-esteem (Hardman et al., 1996; Heward, 1996). A cycle develops in which lowered achievement and lowered self-concept amplify each other and result in major learning problems.

Rodney, in the case study at the beginning of this chapter, had a learning disability. He was hyperactive and easily distracted and had difficulties focusing his attention on instructionally related tasks. Sabrina Curtis was correct in seeking additional professional help with Rodney. The characteristics he displayed suggested either a learning disability or attention deficit/hyperactivity disorder.

Attention Deficit/Hyperactivity Disorder

Attention deficit/hyperactivity disorder (AD/HD) *is a learning problem characterized by students' inability to focus their attention on the learning task at hand.* Attention problems and hyperactivity are often connected with a learning disability; estimates indicate that at least 33% of students with learning disabilities also have attention problems (Halla-han & Kauffman, 1994).

The American Psychiatric Association has identified three categories of AD/HD: (a) *predominantly inattentive,* which describes students who are forgetful, easily distracted, and have problems focusing their attention; (b) *predominantly hyperactive-impulsive,* which describes students who fidget and talk excessively, and (c) a third that includes characteristics of the other two.

Observable characteristics of AD/HD include:

- Difficulty in concentrating and failure to finish tasks
- Failure to listen and easy distractibility
- Inordinate need for supervision
- Impulsiveness (e.g., acting before thinking, shifting from one activity to another)
- Frequent calling out in class and difficulty awaiting turns

From these characteristics, it's easy to see why students with AD/HD have difficulties adjusting to the "sit-down" pace of school life in which most activities are done quietly at a desk (Nahmias, 1995). They also experience problems interacting with their peers. AD/HD usually appears early (at 2 or 3 years of age), and three to nine times as many boys as girls, depending on the research cited, are identified (Gelfand, Jenson, & Drew, 1988). Treatments are as diverse as medication (e.g., the highly controversial drug Ritalin), reinforcement programs, and structured teaching programs (described later in this section). Diagnosis and treatment of AD/HD are usually done in consultation with medical experts.

> **5.13** ▬
> Explain the high ratio of boys to girls with AD/HD from a genetic or nature position. Explain from an environmental or nurture position. From an interactionist position.

Identifying and Working With Students Who Have Learning Disabilities

As with all exceptionalities, identification is the first step in helping students with learning disabilities, and it must be done early to prevent the damaging effects from accumulating. Although early identification is essential, at least two factors complicate the process. First, uneven rates of development can easily be mistaken for learning disabilities. Developmental lags are typically outgrown, however, and need only a sensitive teacher who is able to adjust instruction to slower development. Second, classroom management issues can complicate identification. On the one hand, students with learning disabilities frequently display inappropriate classroom behavior, and misbehaving students are referred as LD at a much higher rate than those who behave. On the other hand, LD students who comply with rules and complete assignments on time are often passed over for referral (Meyer & Foster, 1988). These patterns can be connected to gender differences; more boys are identified because of acting out, and fewer girls are identified because they tend to be quiet.

Using Classroom-Based Information for Identification.   The teacher plays an important role in identifying and working with a learning disability. Information taken from teachers' assessments of behavior, anecdotal records, direct observation, and curriculum-based measurements are combined with test scores. Often, a discrepancy model, which looks for differences in three areas, will be used to diagnose the problem (Salvia & Ysseldyke, 1988). The areas are:

1. Differences between IQ and achievement test performance
2. Differences between IQ and school achievement
3. Large differences between subtests on either an IQ or achievement test

5.14   ▬

Why wouldn't the discrepancy model be useful in identifying students who have an intellectual disability or mental retardation?

The rationale for the discrepancy model is that performance in one area, such as an IQ test, should predict performance in others; when the two are not comparable, a learning disability may be the cause.

Adaptive Instruction.   Once a student is identified as having a learning disability, a plan is prepared by a team in cooperation with the parents and the student. The student is usually kept in the regular classroom, and the following modifications are made: (a) A resource teacher working in a pull-out program provides supplementary instruction, (b) the classroom teacher modifies instruction to meet the special needs of the student, and (c) the resource teacher teams with the classroom teacher to provide additional assistance within the classroom.

Students with learning disabilities are similar to other students in that their success often requires modified instruction and support from the teacher. Because learning disabilities have different causes, the most effective strategies are tailored to meet each student's unique needs. One study of the coping behaviors of 25 college students having learning disabilities illustrates some modifications that are used to increase success (Cowan, 1988). These students budgeted their time carefully, attended class regularly, and completed all work on time. To compensate for reading deficits, they always read in a quiet environment, subvocalized (read aloud to themselves), and even purchased previously highlighted books. In writing, they used a dictionary, frequently substituted an easier word if they had trouble spelling one, and asked other people to proofread their papers. Other strategies included using taped textbooks, tape-recording lectures to compensate for poor note taking, and asking for extra time on tests or for someone to help them read through the test questions.

Common to all of these strategies is personal awareness of the problem and adapting to it. Some students with learning disabilities learn this naturally and adapt well enough on their own to be able to succeed in college. Others don't. That's when a skilled and understanding teacher is essential.

5.15   ▬

Which of these adaptations could be easily taught and incorporated into the regular classroom? What role might the teacher play?

Behavior Disorders

Kyle came in from recess sweaty and disheveled, crossed his arms, and looked at the teacher defiantly. The playground monitor had reported another scuffle. Kyle had a history of these disturbances and was a hard student to work with. He struggled at his studies but could handle them if provided with structure and support. When he became frustrated, he would sometimes act out, often ignoring the feelings and rights of others.

Ben, who sat next to Kyle, was so quiet that the teacher almost forgot he was there. He never caused problems. In fact, he seldom participated in class. He had few friends and walked around at recess by himself, seeming to consciously avoid other children.

Although their behaviors were very different, these two students both have a *behavior disorder, emotional disturbance,* or *emotional disability,* and you may encounter all three in your work. These terms are often used interchangeably by special educators, and "behaviorally disordered" is sometimes preferred because it focuses on overt behavior, rather than on internal causes.

Students with **behavior disorder (BD)** *display serious and persistent age-inappropriate behaviors that result in social conflict, personal unhappiness, and school failure* (Kirk & Gallagher, 1989). In this definition, two features—serious and persistent—are important. Many children periodically fight with their peers, and all children go through periods when they want to be alone. When these patterns are chronic and consistent, however, and they interfere with normal development and school performance, a behavior disorder may exist.

Prevalence of Behavior Disorders

What is normal development, and when is an exception serious enough to warrant special help? Estimates of the frequency of behavior disorders vary (Hardman et al., 1996). The percentage of school-age students identified with this problem is about 1% of the total school population and about 8% of the special education population (U.S. Department of Education, 1994). Experts estimate that the prevalence of the problem is closer to 6% to 10% of the total population (Hallahan & Kauffman, 1994). Identification is a problem because the characteristics are elusive. In a study of teachers' assessments of 1,586 kindergarten through sixth-grade students, 60% of the students were classified as having a behavior problem at least once, but only 7% were identified as having problems serious enough to require special help (Rubin & Balow, 1978).

Kinds of Behavior Disorders

Behavior disorders fall into two major categories: internalizing and externalizing (Hallahan & Kauffman, 1994). Characteristics of students, such as Kyle, who fall into the externalizing category include hyperactivity, uncooperativeness, defiance, hostility, cruelty, and sometimes even maliciousness. Children with this disorder often don't respond to typical rules and consequences. Males are three times more likely to be labeled as having a behavior disorder than are females, and a higher incidence of this category exists in low-SES and minority students, especially African American. Evidence suggests that some forms of aggressive behavior are learned from aggressive parents and peers (Hallahan & Kauffman, 1994). In addition, students with behavior disorders often have academic problems, some of which are connected with learning disabilities (Gelfand et al., 1988). The combination of these problems results in a dropout rate of 40%, the highest of any group of students with special needs (U.S. Department of Education, 1994).

Internalized behavior disorders are characterized by social withdrawal, guilt, depression, or anxiety. Like Ben, in our example, these children lack self-confidence and are often shy, timid, and depressed—sometimes suicidal. Peer relations are a problem; they have few friends and are isolated and withdrawn (Walker & Bullis, 1991). Because they don't have the high profile of the acting-out student, they may go unnoticed, so a teacher's sensitivity and awareness is crucial in identifying these students.

> **5.16**
> Offer another explanation for the disproportionate number of boys who are referred for special help because of behavior disorders (think about our discussion of gender and cultural differences in Chapter 4).

> **5.17**
> Identify at least two similarities and two differences between students with learning disabilities and those with behavior disorders.

Teaching Students With Behavior Disorders

Behavior Management Strategies.   Students with behavior disorders often have problems monitoring and controlling their own behaviors. Regular classroom teachers can help by providing an environment that invites participation and success while at the same time clearly stating and uniformly enforcing rules and expectations.

Behavioral management strategies can be used to bring about changes in specific behaviors. These include the following:

- Positive reinforcement: Identifying and rewarding positive behaviors (e.g., negotiating for a wanted toy)
- Extinction: Ignoring disruptive behaviors

▌ Actively teaching "replacement" behaviors that substitute for inappropriate ones (e.g., expressing personal feelings vs. verbal aggression toward another student)

⇥ Time out: Removing the child from opportunities for reward for brief periods of time

▌ Overcorrection: Requiring restitution beyond the damaging effects of the immediate behavior (e.g., requiring a child to return one of his own cookies in addition to the one he took from another student)

In implementing behavioral approaches, it is important to focus on positive behaviors by actively teaching and reinforcing alternatives to unwanted ones.

Self-Management Skills.   Teaching self-management skills can also be effective in working with students having behavior disorders (Heward, 1996). Through self-management, students are helped to identify specific behaviors they want to either increase, such as making eye contact with the teacher, or decrease, such as finger-snapping or playing with a pencil.

Students are taught to evaluate their own behavior when a timer goes off at their desks. By counting and graphing the results, the students monitor their own behavior over the course of the day. The teacher also meets with them—frequently at first—to reinforce progress and to set new goals. This strategy has been successful in encouraging and controlling diverse behaviors, including paying attention and responding in class, decreasing talking out, and leaving seats without permission (Alberto & Troutman, 1995).

Teacher Flexibility and Sensitivity.   Students with behavior disorders can be difficult to teach, and frustrated teachers sometimes forget that these students have unique needs. An encounter with one such student by a school psychologist illustrates this point:

> The psychologist was testing a 4-year-old who had been referred to her for aggressive behaviors and acting "out of control in the classroom." The psychologist found the young boy to be friendly, polite, and cooperative, and the session went smoothly until the child announced he was done. When the psychologist tried to get him to continue, a behavioral outburst followed with screaming, kicking, and shoving and the boy running out of the room.
>
> I assumed the testing phase of the evaluation was over and started writing a few notes. . . . A few minutes later, however, the little boy returned . . . and said that he was

5.18 ▬
Which behavioral management strategy would be least effective in working with Kyle, the student at the beginning of this section? Explain.

Encouraging positive behavior and self-management skills requires conscientious effort and continuous communication between teachers and students.

ready to continue. After another 10 minutes or so . . . the child again said, "I'm done now," to which I replied, "That's fine." The child calmly got out of his chair, walked around the room for a minute, and then sat down to resume testing. This pattern was repeated. . . .

It was easy to see in a one-to-one testing situation that this child recognized the limits of his concentration and coped with increasing frustration by briefly removing himself. . . . It is equally easy to see, however, how this behavior created problems in the classroom. By wandering around, he would be disrupting the learning of other children. When the teacher tried to make him sit back down, she was increasing his frustration by removing from him the one method he had developed for coping. (Griffith, 1992, p. 34)

But, how do teachers deal with this behavior in the regular classroom? The psychologist suggested marking an area in the back of the room where the child could go when he became frustrated. With this safety valve in place, the teacher could return to her teaching and work with the boy on other, long-term coping strategies. By attempting to understand the acting-out child as an individual, the teacher was able to continue with her instructional agenda while meeting the needs of the student.

Classroom Connections

Teaching Students With Exceptionalities in Your Classroom

1. Identify resources that are available for working with students having exceptionalities.
   - A 1st-year teacher talked with the principal about programs and personnel available in the building and the school district. She made an effort to introduce herself to the special education team in the building and found out how the referral process works.
   - A beginning teacher talked with other teachers about their past experiences in working with students having exceptionalities: What approaches worked for them? Who was especially helpful in working with these students? Who would they turn to when they needed help?

2. Use a variety of data sources for help in identifying and understanding the students with exceptionalities in your classroom.
   - A third-grade teacher started the school year by giving her students diagnostic work sheets in all the subject matter areas. The work within each assignment was arranged in order of difficulty. After the teacher had a complete battery from each student, she spent a weekend reviewing the work sheets and identifying each student's strengths and weaknesses.
   - A junior high teacher was having trouble with one student. After talking with the student's other teachers, he looked over her previous record and discussed the problem with the guidance counselor. Then he called the student in and talked with her about the problem directly.

3. Work to create a positive classroom learning environment for students who are mainstreamed in your classroom.
   - At the beginning of the school year, a first-grade teacher explains to the class where resource students go and why. He explains that all people are different and that some people learn in different ways.
   - A sixth-grade teacher sits with his pull-out students in one-to-one sessions to voice his support for the program and to explain that any assignments they miss will be written on assignment sheets for them. He also sends a letter home to parents, explaining these procedures and inviting their questions or comments.

Communication, Visual, and Hearing Impairments

In the previous section, we discussed mild mental retardation, learning disabilities, and behavior disorders, three types of disabilities that can interfere with learning in the regular classroom. In this section, we examine communication, visual, and hearing impairments, and other disabilities that influence learning.

Communication Disorders

That communication is essential for learning is obvious. Students must be able to both receive and understand information from others and express their own ideas and questions. Communication disorders interfere with these abilities and exist in two forms. **Speech, or expressive, disorders** *involve problems in forming and sequencing sounds.* Examples are stuttering and mispronouncing words, such as "I taw it" for "I saw it." **Language, or receptive, disorders** *include problems with understanding language or in using language to express ideas.* Language disorders are often connected to other problems, such as a hearing impairment, learning disability, or mental retardation.

When considering the possibility of a communication disorder, teachers should also keep cultural diversity in mind. As you saw in Chapter 4, English is not the primary language for many students. The difficulties involved in learning both school content and a second language should not be confused with communication disorders.

As Table 5.2 indicates, there are three kinds of speech, or expressive, disorders. If they are chronic, a therapist is usually required, but sensitive teachers can help students cope with the psychological and social problems that can result from these problems.

5.19
Should teachers' interaction patterns, such as calling on students and waiting for them to answer, be different for students with speech disorders? Why or why not?

Language Disorders

Language disorders are more serious than speech disorders and go beyond the mere production of sounds. As you saw in Chapter 2, the vast majority of students learn to communicate quite well by the time they start school. A small percentage (less than 1%), however, do have trouble expressing themselves verbally.

Table 5.2

Kinds of speech disorders

Disorder	Description	Example
Articulation disorders	Difficulty in producing certain sounds, including substituting, distorting, and omitting	'Wabbit' for rabbit 'Thit' for sit 'Only' for lonely
Fluency disorders	Repetition of the first sound of a word (stuttering)	'Y, Y, Y, Yes'
Voice disorders	Problems with the larynx or air passageways in the nose or throat	High-pitched or nasal voice

Symptoms of a language disorder include the following:

▌ Seldom speaking, even during play
▌ Using few words or very short sentences
▌ Overrelying on gestures to communicate

The causes of language disorders include hearing loss, brain damage, learning disabilities, mental retardation, severe emotional problems, and inadequate experiences in a child's early developmental years. As we said earlier, language disorders can be confused with problems caused by disadvantaged backgrounds or English as a second language; these students will respond to an enriched language environment and teacher patience and understanding. Students with language disorders require the help of a language specialist.

Helping Students With Communication Disorders

Primary tasks for the teacher working with students who have communication disorders are identification, acceptance, and follow-through on classroom instruction. As with other exceptionalities, teachers play an important role in identification because they are in the best position to observe and assess students' performance in classroom settings. Modeling and encouraging acceptance are crucial because teasing and social rejection can cause lasting psychological damage. It is not easy being a student who talks differently. In communicating with these students, a teacher should be patient and refrain from finishing sentences and correcting speech problems in class; this calls attention to the problem. In addition, cooperative and small-group activities provide opportunities for students to practice their language skills in more informal and less threatening settings.

Helping other students understand the problem is important. The teacher should ensure that the classroom environment is supportive of all students and that they understand the harm that results from teasing and laughing at others.

Visual Impairments

One in 10 students enters school with some type of visual impairment (Kirk & Gallagher, 1989). Fortunately, most of these impairments can be corrected with glasses, surgery, or therapy. In some situations, though, the impairment cannot be corrected. People with this type of condition possess a visual disability.

Approximately 1 child in 1,000 has a **visual disability**, which is *an uncorrectable impairment that interferes with learning in the regular classroom.* Most (64%) visual impairments of school-age children exist at birth, and most children are screened for visual problems at the time they enter elementary school. Some impairments, however, do appear during the school years as a result of growth spurts, and teachers should remain alert to the possibility of an unscreened visual impairment in students. Some symptoms of potential vision problems are outlined in Table 5.3.

Identifying the problem, notifying parents, and referring the student to the school nurse are the first steps in correcting a typical vision problem. After a student gets glasses, a teacher may also have to follow through to ensure the student wears them during class. For those students whose impairments are not corrected by glasses, additional learning requirements exist.

Research on people with visual impairments reveals little or no lag in intellectual development (Kirk & Gallagher, 1989), but word meanings in language development may not be as rich or elaborated because of the students' lack of visual experience with the world. As a result, hands-on experiences are even more important for students with visual impairments than they are for other learners.

5.20 ▬
How would Piaget and Vygotsky each react to instructional modifications emphasizing hands-on experience for visually impaired students?

Table 5.3

Symptoms of potential visual problems

1. Holding the head in an awkward position when reading, or holding the book too close or too far away.
2. Squinting and frequently rubbing the eyes.
3. Tuning out when information is presented on the chalkboard.
4. Constantly asking about classroom procedures, especially when information is on the board
5. Complaining of headaches, dizziness, or nausea.
6. Having redness, crusting, or swelling of the eyes.
7. Losing place on the line or page and confusing letters.
8. Using poor spacing in writing or having difficulty in staying on the line.

Source: Hallahan and Kaufman (1994).

Working With Students Who Have Visual Impairment

Suggestions for working with students with visual impairment include seating them at the front of the room near chalkboards and overheads, verbalizing while writing on the chalkboard, and ensuring that duplicated handouts are dark and clear (Heward, 1996). Large-print books and magnifying aids also help adapt instructional materials. Peer tutors can also provide valuable assistance in explaining and clarifying classroom assignments and procedures.

Two potential side effects of a visual impairment are lowered self-concept and *learned helplessness.* Learned helplessness results from teachers and other students overreacting to the disability by doing everything for the student. The result is an unhealthy dependence on others to do what the student, with training, can do alone. This dependence can cause negative self-concept, as well as the now-decreasing practice of institutionalization (Hallahan & Kauffman, 1994).

Adaptive instructional devices, such as machines and books with large print, allow students with visual impairments to integrate into the regular classroom.

Hearing Impairments

Because much of classroom teaching and learning is auditory, students with hearing impairments are at a serious disadvantage. Hearing impairments can be divided into two categories. A student who has a **partial hearing impairment** *uses a hearing aid and hears well enough to be taught through auditory channels.* A student who is **deaf** *has hearing that is impaired enough so that other channels or senses, usually sight, are used to communicate.* Only about 1 student in 1,000 is deaf; 3 to 4 in 1,000 are severely hard of hearing (Kirk & Gallagher, 1989).

Hearing impairments result from rubella, or German measles, during pregnancy; heredity; complications during birth or pregnancy; meningitis; and other childhood diseases (Kirk & Gallagher, 1989). Unfortunately, in almost 40% of cases involving hearing loss, the cause is unknown; this makes prevention and remediation more difficult.

A specially trained audiologist working in a school screening program is the best method of identifying students with hearing problems, but these programs don't exist everywhere, and students can be overlooked because of transfers or absences. When such an omission happens, the classroom teacher's awareness of the signs of hearing difficulties is essential. These are described in Table 5.4.

Working With Students Who Have Hearing Impairment

Learning problems associated with hearing impairments usually involve lack of proficiency in speech and language. These problems then affect other content areas that use reading, writing, and listening as major learning tools. Teachers should remember that these language deficits do not mean a deficit in intellectual functioning; students with hearing impairment can learn if appropriately helped.

Programs for students with hearing impairment combine mainstreaming with supplementary special education classes; 92% of students who are deaf are in full- or part-time special education classes, and about half of these are mainstreamed in regular classes (Kirk & Gallagher, 1989). Supplementary programs for students who are deaf are as diverse as oral techniques focusing on lipreading and using whatever hearing there is, and manual approaches using sign language and finger spelling. Total communication, which uses the simultaneous presentation of manual approaches (signing and finger spelling) and speech (through speech reading and residual hearing), is becoming more popular because of the additive benefit of its component processes (Heward, 1996).

> **5.21**
> What can teachers do to make their classrooms instructionally friendly for students who have hearing impairment?

Students Who Are Gifted and Talented

What is it like to be gifted in a regular classroom? Listen to one 9-year-old gifted student:

> Oh what a bore to sit and listen,
> To stuff we already know.
> Do everything we've done and done again,
> But we still must sit and listen.
> Over and over read one more page
> Oh bore, oh bore, oh bore.
> Sometimes I feel if we do one more page
> My head will explode with boreness rage
> I wish I could get up right there and march right out the door.
> (Delisle, 1984, p. 72)

Table 5.4

Indicators of hearing impairment

1. Favoring one ear by cocking the head toward the speaker or cupping a hand behind the ear.
2. Misunderstanding or not following directions, and exhibiting nonverbal cues (e.g., frowns or puzzled looks) when directions are given.
3. Being distracted or seeming disoriented at times.
4. Asking people to repeat what they have just said.
5. Poorly articulating words, especially consonants.
6. Turning the volume up loud when listening to cassette recorders, radio, or television.
7. Showing reluctance to participate in oral activities.
8. Having frequent earaches or complaining of discomfort or buzzing in the ears.

Source: Adapted from Kirk and Gallagher (1989).

We don't often think of gifted and talented students as having an exceptionality, but they do when our definition of exceptional includes those students who can't reach their full potential in the regular classroom. **Gifted and talented** students are *those at the upper end of the ability continuum who need supplemental help to realize their full potential.* At one time, the term *gifted* was used to identify these students, but over time, this category has been enlarged to include both students who do well on IQ tests (typically 130 and above) and those who demonstrate above-average talents in such diverse areas as math, creative writing, and music.

The modern-day history of gifted and talented education in the United States began with a longitudinal study of gifted students by Louis Terman (Terman, Baldwin, & Bronson, 1925; Terman & Oden, 1947, 1959). He used teacher recommendations and IQ test scores to identify 1,500 gifted individuals to track over a lifetime of development (the study is projected to run until 2010). In addition to finding that these students did better academically, Terman also found that they:

▌ Were better adjusted as children and adults
▌ Were better achievers and learned more easily
▌ Had more hobbies
▌ Read more books
▌ Were healthier

This research did much to dispel the stereotype of gifted students as maladjusted and narrow "brains."

Present views of gifted and talented students see them as possessing diverse abilities and needs. The current definition used by the federal government identifies them as possessing demonstrated or potential abilities that give evidence of high performance capability in areas such as intellectual, creative, specific academic or leadership ability or in the performing and visual arts, and who by reason thereof require services or activities not ordinarily provided by the school. (U.S. Congress, Educational Amendment of 1978 [PL 95–561, IX(A)])

Another popular definition uses three criteria (Renzulli, 1986):

1. Above-average ability
2. High levels of motivation and task commitment
3. High levels of creativity

5.22 ▬
The definition of gifted and talented has changed over time. What similarities exist between this trend and trends with respect to other types of exceptionalities?

According to this definition, not only are gifted people "smart," but they also use this ability in focused and creative ways.

Creativity: What Is It?

Creativity *is the ability to identify or prepare original and divergent solutions to problems.* Creativity is related to IQ but is not identical to it (Sternberg, 1989; Torrance, 1984); intellectual ability that is at least average can be thought of as a necessary, but not sufficient, component of creativity. People who score low on IQ tests typically don't score high on measures of creativity; people who score high on IQ tests may or may not score high on measures of creativity.

Research on creativity suggests that it requires three kinds of intelligence (Sternberg & Lubart, 1995). *Synthetic intelligence* allows a creative person to redefine or see a problem in a new way. *Analytic intelligence* allows a person to recognize which new ideas are productive and to effectively allocate resources to solve the problem. *Practical intelligence* allows a person to promote an idea by using feedback from others. In all three, the emphasis is on problem solving in real-world settings.

J. P. Guilford (1967, 1988), whose work we examined in Chapter 4, was one of the most influential researchers in the area of creativity. He divided mental operations into five classes, one of which is divergent thinking, or the ability to generate a variety of original answers to questions. It has three dimensions: fluency, flexibility, and originality. *Fluency* is the ability to produce many ideas relevant to a problem; being able to break from an established set to generate new perspectives is *flexibility*; and *originality* is the facility for generating new and different ideas. To illustrate each, let's look at a social studies class discussing the problem of world hunger. Fluency would result in multiple solutions to the problem, such as growing food in domes in deserts, altering humans' genetic makeup so that they require less food, and growing food in space or on the moon; flexibility would cast the problem in a new light (e.g., from economic or political rather than traditional perspectives); and originality would produce new and creative solutions to the problem (e.g., superpower cooperation).

More recently, Howard Gardner, who we also studied in Chapter 4, defined the creative person as "a person who regularly solves problems, fashions products or defines new questions in a domain in a way that is initially considered novel but that ultimately becomes accepted" (1993, p. 35). Notice here that creativity is viewed as a recurring trait, rather than as a one-time event. Also, creativity typically occurs within, rather than across, domains, such as within art or within music but probably not both. As with most aspects of learning, creativity requires background knowledge (Sternberg & Lubart, 1995). Knowledge makes a person aware of what has gone before—prevents "reinventing the wheel"—and also allows a person to concentrate on new ideas, rather than expend energy on basic ones.

5.23
Suppose a science class is discussing the problem of pollution and the environment. Explain how the creative elements of fluency, flexibility, and originality might be evident in a class discussion.

5.24
Identify at least one similarity between research findings on creativity and research findings on problem solving.

Measuring Creativity

Creativity is usually measured by giving students a verbal or pictorial stimulus and asking them to generate as many responses as they can, such as listing as many uses as possible for a brick (e.g., doorstop, bookshelf, paperweight, weapon, building block) or suggesting ways to improve a common object such as a chair (Davis, 1989). Pictorial tasks involve turning an ambiguous partial sketch into an interesting picture. Responses are then evaluated on the criteria of fluency, flexibility, and originality.

Current ways of measuring creativity are controversial, with critics charging that existing tests are too narrow and fail to capture the different aspects of creativity (Sternberg, 1989; Ward, Ward, Landrum, & Patton, 1992). Research indicates that creativity can be taught but that some people are more creative than others (Torrance, 1986). Like intelligence, creativity is probably influenced by both genetics and the environment.

Identifying Students Who Are Gifted and Talented

Meeting the needs of gifted and talented students requires early identification. Failure to do so results in gifted underachievers with social and emotional problems linked to boredom and unmotivating school experiences (Clinkenbeard, 1992). A study of 1,172 school districts across the United States found that they use the following identification methods:

Identification Method	Percentage of Districts Using
Teacher nomination	91%
Achievement test	90%
Intelligence test	89%
Grades	50%
Peer and self-nomination	6% (Wilkie, 1985)

Experts question relying so heavily on achievement and intelligence tests and recommend more flexible and less culturally dependent measures. These include creativity measures, peer and parent nomination, and classroom-based efforts by teachers to identify gifted minorities (Davis & Rimm, 1993).

As with all exceptionalities, teachers are critical in the identification process because they constantly work with students and can identify behaviors that tests may miss. Unfortunately, some research indicates that teachers often confuse conformity, neatness, and good behavior with being gifted and talented (Davis & Rimm, 1993). In addition, minorities appear to be underrepresented in gifted programs in which identification depends so heavily on tests (B. Strom, 1990; VanTassel-Baska, Patton, & Prillaman, 1989).

What should teachers look for? Experts (Davis & Rimm, 1993) have identified the following characteristics of the gifted and talented:

- Likes to work alone
- Is imaginative, enjoys pretending
- Is highly verbal and flexible in thinking
- Is persistent, stays with a task
- Goes beyond assignments
- Is often bored with routine tasks
- Is sometimes impulsive, with little interest in details

As you might expect, working with these students can be challenging. Their giftedness places unique demands on teachers, and the flexibility of teachers' responses can make school a happy or an unhappy experience for these students.

Programs for the Gifted: More and Faster or Deeper and Different?

Programs for the gifted and talented are based on one of two ideas: acceleration and enrichment. **Acceleration** *provides the same academic menu as the regular students have but allows students to move through the curriculum at a faster rate.* **Enrichment** *provides richer and more varied content through strategies that supplement usual grade-level work.* Table 5.5 offers examples of each.

Time for acceleration or enrichment can be generated with a process called curriculum compacting. **Curriculum compacting** *is an approach to individualization that identifies mastered content, concentrates teaching on content not yet mastered, and uses the time saved for acceleration or enrichment* (Reis, 1992). For example, a primary teacher might pretest math skills at the beginning of a new unit and then focus on unmet objectives, freeing students to pursue additional math topics or content in other areas. The practice evolved from research indicating that gifted students were often asked to spend time on content they had already learned (Renzulli, Smith, & Reis, 1982).

Curriculum areas most easily compacted are math, spelling, and language arts. One study of curriculum compacting in these areas found that gifted students had already mastered from 25% to 75% of the curriculum before it was taught (Reis & Purcell, 1992).

Which is better—acceleration or enrichment? Critics of enrichment call it busywork and irrelevant, contending that students should be provided a healthy menu of regular academic fare. Critics of acceleration point to the narrowness of the regular curriculum, the dangers of pushing students too fast, and possible social mismatches in relating to older students. A review of research found that accelerated students surpassed by nearly one grade level the achievement of nonaccelerated students of equal age and intelligence

5.25
On the basis of the criteria *above-average ability, high levels of motivation and task commitment,* and *creativity,* which method of identifying gifted students is probably most effective?

5.26
Why could curriculum compacting be most easily adopted in such areas as math and reading?

Enrichment activities provide opportunities for gifted students to explore alternative areas of the curriculum.

(Kulik & Kulik, 1984). These students were also equivalent in achievement to older, talented, but nonaccelerated students. No affective differences, such as attitudes toward school or self-concept, were found. A 10-year longitudinal study also found no negative effects resulting from acceleration (Swialth & Benbow, 1991).

Supporters point to these studies as evidence for the superiority of acceleration (Feldhusen, 1989). Critics counter that the comparison is unfair because the outcomes of enrichment, such as creativity and problem solving, are not easily measured on standardized achievement tests. Which is better? There is obviously no easy answer, and the debate is likely to continue.

5.27
How are the ideas of enrichment and acceleration similar to mainstreaming and LRE, discussed earlier in the chapter?

Table 5.5

Options in enrichment and acceleration programs

Enrichment Options	Acceleration Options
1. Independent study and independent projects	1. Early admission to kindergarten and first grade
2. Learning centers	2. Grade skipping
3. Field trips	3. Subject skipping
4. Saturday programs	4. Credit by exam
5. Summer programs	5. College courses in high school
6. Mentors and mentorships	6. Correspondence courses
7. Simulations and games	7. Early admission to college
8. Small-group investigations	
9. Academic competitions	

Classroom Connections

Teaching Students With Disabilities in Your Classroom

1. Work closely with parents and other professionals to understand the special needs of students with physical disabilities in your classroom.

   • A second-grade teacher, knowing a student with hearing impairment would be in her class, talked with the student's previous teacher and discussed strategies that had worked for him. She also met with the special education teacher, who gave her materials on working with those who have hearing impairment. At the IEP meeting, she made a special effort to communicate with the student's parents about the student's strengths and needs.

   • A high school math teacher works with parents and the special education specialist in his school to adapt his instruction for a student with partial vision. He seats her at the front of the room, consciously uses the front chalkboard, and makes a special effort to write clearly, using large numbers and letters. He also repeats written information aloud. If the print on quizzes and assignments is too small, he enlists the aid of other students in recopying problems.

2. Help other students understand the disability and enlist their aid in helping the student.

   • Before a blind student was transferred into a sixth-grade teacher's class, the teacher held a class meeting at which she discussed the new student's disability and asked the other students to think of ways to make the classroom a positive learning environment.

   • A junior high teacher noticed nervous shuffling and muffled laughter when a quiet boy stuttered during the first week of class. The next day, the teacher sent the student to the office on an assignment and discussed the problem with the rest of the class. She explained how everyone stutters when he or she is nervous and how important it is to give each student a chance to participate. In the next few days, she made a special effort to call on the student, especially when she thought he knew the answer. When the student responded, she was careful to make eye contact and not interrupt or complete sentences for the boy.

Teaching Gifted and Talented Students in Your Classroom

3. Prevent boredom in the classroom by providing supplementary activities.

   • A sixth-grade teacher confers with her students who are gifted and talented at the beginning of each grading period to identify areas of interest and to outline projects. After students have finished their regular work, they are free to read books and work on their projects.

   • A junior high math teacher pretests students at the beginning of each unit. Whenever a student has mastered the concepts and objectives of the unit, he or she receives an honor pass to work on an alternative activity in the school media center. The activities may be extensions or applications of the concepts taught in the unit, or they may involve learning about mathematical principles or math history not usually taught in the regular classroom.

4. Integrate activities that require creativity and critical thinking in the classroom.

   • A high school social studies teacher caps off every unit with a hypothetical problem (e.g., What would the United States be like today if Great Britain had won the Revolutionary War?). Students work in groups to address the question.

   • A junior high science teacher begins every unit with a problem or question (e.g., How are birds and airplanes similar?). She leaves the question unanswered and returns to it for discussion at the end of the unit.

Working With Exceptional Students in the Regular Classroom

In earlier sections, you learned about different kinds of disabilities and how these disabilities affect the students you teach. In this section, we shift our focus to strategies teachers can use to help these students reach their full potential. In this process, teachers have three roles: (a) helping identify students with exceptionalities, (b) teaching students with exceptionalities in the regular classroom, and (c) fostering the acceptance of students with exceptionalities by other students. Let's take a look at them.

Identifying Students With Exceptionalities

Because classroom teachers work with these students every day, they are in the best position to help identify students with exceptionalities. Identification often begins by simply monitoring a student's learning progress on regular classroom tasks. When involved in the process, teachers should remember that there tends to be a disproportionate number of males and cultural minorities in the special education population (Hardman et al., 1996). This imbalance suggests that you should ask yourself, for example, whether a difficulty truly indicates a learning problem or whether some other factor might be operating. This is the dilemma that Sabrina Curtis faced in our opening case study as she worked with Rodney and Amelia.

Prereferral Strategies: Gathering Data for Instructional Problem Solving

Current approaches to working with students having exceptionalities encourage the use of a team-based problem-solving model with the teacher as a central team member. The process begins when a learning problem is identified; the teacher's first step should be to analyze the problem and try alternative instructional strategies. If this fails, other educators are called in to help understand the problem and work toward a solution. Data are gathered from several sources, including standardized tests, classroom performance, and interviews with parents and other teachers.

If the data warrant additional help, a "prereferral team" is formed, often consisting of the school psychologist, a special educator, and the classroom teacher. The team further evaluates the problem, suggests ways that existing classroom procedures could be modified to create a better adaptive fit, and assists the classroom teacher in adapting instruction.

Before a referral is made, the classroom teacher should check the student's records to see whether the student has had a previous psychological evaluation, has any physical problems, is qualified for special services, or has been included in other special programs (Hallahan & Kauffman, 1994). Other teachers may also be consulted to determine the student's strengths and weaknesses and to identify any teaching strategies that have been successful.

Before making a referral, the teacher will be expected to document the strategies attempted in solving the problem (Hallahan & Kauffman, 1994). Specifically, the teacher should describe:

- The nature of the problem
- How it affects classroom performance
- Dates, places, and time the problem has occurred
- Strategies the teacher has tried
- Evidence of their success

5.28 ■
Why are tests, quizzes, papers, and other work samples important in the referral process? How is using them similar to the concept of *curriculum-based measurement,* discussed earlier?

Technology can be used to provide students with opportunities for practice with frequent and specific feedback.

It is also essential that teachers communicate with parents *prior* to initiating a process. Parents need to be informed and involved for at least three reasons:

1. They can provide valuable information about the student's past history.
2. Due process legally requires their involvement.
3. Involving parents is a professional courtesy.

When considering a referral, the teacher should check with school administrators or the school psychologist to learn about the school's policy. If the referral results in a recommendation for special services, a remediation plan is developed by the IEP we discussed earlier in the chapter.

Teaching Students With Exceptionalities

Students with exceptionalities will be included in your classroom, and you will be expected to teach them as effectively as possible. Fortunately, the changes will be more in how than in what you teach (Ysseldyke, O'Sullivan, Thurlow, & Christenson, 1989), and you will have help in making these modifications. Also, special educators will be available to you—in the form of *resource teachers,* specially trained educators who are expert at modifying instruction for students with exceptionalities; the *prereferral teacher assistance teams* we discussed in the previous section; and *site-based teams* or *collaborative consultation teams*—as resources.

Effective Teaching for Inclusive Classrooms

Most modifications that work with students having exceptionalities are based on principles of effective teaching that work with all students, such as managing a classroom effectively, matching learning tasks to student abilities, and providing frequent and specific practice and feedback (C. Mercer & A. Mercer, 1993). This is encouraging because it means the knowledge and effective strategies that teachers use with regular students only need to be adapted, not fundamentally changed. Table 5.6 outlines these teaching practices.

You can see five areas in Table 5.6. Teachers need to use their time well so that students are kept on-task and have sufficient opportunity to learn. The classroom should be emotionally warm and supportive, and students must believe that they can and will learn. Management reinforces instruction, and disruptions should be minimized. Tasks should be designed so that students have high rates of success on classwork, seatwork, and homework. Finally, effective feedback reinforces instruction and provides learning correctives. These teaching behaviors are effective for students in general and are particularly important for students with exceptionalities.

Of the five areas, the most difficult will be adapting instruction to ensure high success rates. This often means spending more time with individual learners and providing more opportunities for practice and feedback. For example, teachers may need to shorten assignments, giving 10 instead of 20 problems, or a teacher might break an assignment of 20 problems into four groups of 5, with opportunities for teacher, peer, or self-checking after each group.

Adapting Instruction.   To help students overcome a history of failure and frustration and to convince them that renewed effort will work, the teacher often has to change instructional methods. Peer tutoring has been used effectively, and much of the benefit comes from doing the actual tutoring (D. Miller, Barbetta, & Heron, 1994). Home-based tutoring

5.29
Examine the teaching strategies in Table 5.6. Which of these focus on achievement-oriented goals? Which focus on affective or motivational goals? What do your answers imply about working effectively with students having exceptionalities?

Table 5.6

Effective teaching practices for inclusion

Practice	Description
Effective use of time	• High rates of on-task behavior • Minimal losses of instructional time to transitions and disruptions
Warm academic climate	• Supportive responses to *all* students—particularly those mainstreamed • Supportive responses when problems occur (e.g., "I know we can learn this if we try.")
Effective classroom management	• Structured and orderly classroom • Minimal use of punishment • Minimal loss of instructional time to manage misbehavior
High success rates	• Correct answers to most teacher questions • Success rate of 80%–90% on seatwork and homework assignments
Effective feedback	• Feedback that is immediate • Feedback that provides information (e.g., "Good, Sarah. You remembered to borrow from the tens column.") • Feedback that includes no criticism

programs that actively involve parents also have proved effective in providing additional support (Barbetta & Heron, 1991). You can set up a home-based tutoring program by contacting parents and explaining simply and specifically what they can do in working with their youngster. Additional adaptations are outlined in Table 5.7.

A Successful Homework Program.   An essential characteristic of successful adaptive instruction is increased structure and support. Students with learning problems need to be taught in small steps, with success ensured along the way. Inappropriate assignments or homework that is too difficult can be frustrating for the regular student; for students with learning disabilities, it can be devastating.

One successful homework program made a concerted effort to guarantee student success (Rosenberg, 1989). To ensure an appropriate level of difficulty, the homework was an extension of seatwork successfully completed in class. To provide support at home, the assistance of parents was solicited. They orally administered a quiz each night on material being studied and confirmed the completion of the homework and quiz with their signatures. A signature was both concrete and symbolic; concretely, it required parents to participate in their child's homework, and symbolically, it provided a cooperative link between home and school. To reinforce students, tokens or points were used; students

5.30
Earlier, we said that most modifications for mainstreamed students were more of degree than of kind. Explain this statement; use Rosenberg's (1989) homework study as an example.

Table 5.7

Instructional adaptations for students with exceptionalities

Skill Area	Adaptations
Math	• Model correct solutions on the chalkboard.
	• Use peer tutors to explain problems.
	• Break long assignments into several shorter ones.
	• Encourage the use of calculators and other manipulative aids.
Reading	• Use old textbooks and other alternative reading materials at the appropriate level.
	• Use study guides that identify key concepts.
	• Preteach difficult concept before presenting a reading passage.
	• Encourage group assignments in which students assist each other.
Spelling	• Avoid spelling as a grading criterion.
	• Focus on spelling words used in science, social studies, and other areas.
	• Stress mastery of several short spelling lists, rather than one long list.
	• Encourage students to proofread papers, circling words of which they're uncertain.
Writing	• Increase time allotted for writing assignments.
	• Allow assignments to be typed, rather than handwritten.
	• Allow reports to be taped or dictated to others.
	• Encourage daily writing through the use of short, creative assignments.

Source: Dolgins, Myers, Flynn, and Moore (1984).

received some points for doing homework and additional ones for doing both homework and the quiz. The program was demanding, but the time and energy were well spent.

Adapting Reading Materials.   Reading poses particular problems for teachers because the special texts their students need are usually unavailable. However, teachers can supplement the materials they have by:

- Setting goals at the beginning of an assignment
- Using advance organizers that structure or summarize passages
- Introducing key concepts and terms before students read the text
- Creating study guides with questions that focus attention on important information
- Asking students to summarize information in the text (Graham & Johnson, 1989)

These strategies increase reading comprehension with regular learners (Dole, Duffy, Roehler, & Pearson, 1991), and using them with mainstreamed students provides an additional level of support.

Strategy Training: Learning How to Learn

One of the most promising approaches to helping students with learning problems is strategy training. In Chapter 2 we defined a strategy as a plan for accomplishing a learning goal. Let's see how a strategy might be applied when encountering a task such as learning a list of 10 spelling words. For example, a student might say to himself,

> "Okay, . . . 10 words for the quiz on Friday. That shouldn't be too hard. I have 2 days to learn them.
>
> "Let's see. These are all about airports. Which of these do I already know—*airplane, taxi, apron,* and *jet.* No problem. Hmmm. . . . Some of these aren't so easy, like *causeway* and *tarmac.* I don't even know what a 'tarmac' is. I'll look it up. . . . Oh, that makes sense. It's the runway. I'd better spend more time on these words. I'll cover them up and try to write them down and then check 'em. Tonight, I can get Mom to give me a quiz, and then I'll know which ones to study extra tomorrow."

This student's actions were strategic in several ways. First, separating the words he already knew from those he didn't, spending extra time on the difficult ones, and looking up *tarmac* in the dictionary indicate the presence of clear learning goals. Second, he took a deliberate approach to the task; the student assessed the difficulty of the problem and matched his effort to it. He allocated more time to the words he didn't know and skipped the ones he did. In addition, he monitored his progress through quiz-like exercises (Palincsar & Brown, 1987).

In contrast, research on the way students with learning difficulties approach learning tasks indicates they are often "strategically inactive," either approaching a learning task passively or using the same strategy for all learning goals (Montague, 1990). For example, learners often approach a spelling task, such as the one above, by merely reading the words, rather than by trying to actually spell them—a passive approach. They might also spend an equal amount of time on the words they already know and make little effort to test themselves and receive feedback.

In contrast with most students who learn strategies naturally as they progress through school, students with learning problems often have to be explicitly taught strategies. Teacher modeling and explanation are essential, together with opportunities for practice and feedback (G. Miller, 1990). For example, in one study, junior high students with learning disabilities were taught self-monitoring. After each study session, they charted

5.31

Describe specifically how a teacher might instruct students to more strategically attack the spelling list in the example.

their learning by counting the number of exercises they completed correctly and recording the results on bar graphs. Posttest results showed greater on-task behaviors and increased inclination to practice (R. Reed, 1992). The benefits probably resulted from students seeing the link between studying and performance.

Collaborative Consultation: Help for the Classroom Teacher

Collaboration between regular and special educators is essential if inclusion is to work. In the *consulting teacher model,* a special education expert assists the classroom teacher in meeting the needs of students requiring special help (Hardman et al., 1996). The consulting teacher has training in instructional strategies and in building trusting relationships among team members working with students who have exceptionalities. In working with the classroom teacher, the consulting teacher can perform a number of valuable functions:

- Assist in collecting appropriate assessment information
- Compile, organize, and maintain students' records
- Propose alternative instructional strategies and help the classroom teacher implement these
- Develop special curriculum materials
- Coordinate the efforts of team members in implementing the IEP
- Work with parents

Obviously, the consulting teacher can be an invaluable resource in helping classroom teachers work with mainstreamed students. Perhaps most important is helping teachers implement instructional strategies that increase academic achievement and affective and social development. One way that consulting teachers assist in adapting instruction is through collaborative team teaching, which includes collaboration on planning, instruction, and evaluation.

Advantages of collaborative team teaching include eliminating the fragmentation of pull-out programs, reducing the stigmatization of pull-out programs, and using special education resources more efficiently. Research on collaborative team teaching is encouraging. One study found that this arrangement resulted in an improved learning environ-

Creative teachers design learning activities that allow students of differing abilities to interact and learn about each other.

ment; the special education teacher brought additional resources and alternative instructional strategies that benefitted all students (Pugach & Wesson, 1995).

Strategies for Social Integration and Growth

Perhaps the most difficult obstacles that students with exceptionalities face are the negative attitudes of others and the impact of these attitudes on their own confidence and self-esteem (Chapman, 1988; Gresham, Evans, & Elliott, 1988). Often, having a disability and being labeled as different is neither well understood nor accepted by other students.

In addition, these students are often behind in their academic work, frequently act out in class, and sometimes lack social skills. Being pulled out for extra help calls attention to their differences (Hallahan & Kauffman, 1994). Special efforts are needed to promote their acceptance in regular classrooms.

Attempts to foster acceptance have focused on three approaches: (a) helping regular students understand and accept students with exceptionalities, (b) helping students with exceptionalities behave acceptably, and (c) using instructional strategies that encourage social interaction and cooperation.

5.32
How does mainstreaming help foster acceptance of students with exceptionalities? In addition to mainstreaming, what else is necessary?

Helping Regular Students Understand and Accept Students With Exceptionalities

Regular students often have negative attitudes toward students with exceptionalities because they don't understand the disabilities. The first approach is to change that. Providing information about disabilities and creating opportunities for interacting with students having exceptionalities have proved successful (Heward, 1996). One program, for example, presented films and discussions of disabilities, taught students the manual alphabet, had students perform routine activities when blindfolded, and used wheelchairs and crutches. These experiences improved regular students' attitudes toward students with exceptionalities (T. Jones, Sowell, Jones, & Butler, 1981).

In addition, teachers can promote acceptance by making a special effort to integrate students with special needs into the regular classroom flow by calling on them regularly, including them in classroom activities, identifying areas of interest or strength (e.g., art or science), and highlighting accomplishments in those areas. Above all, teachers communicate through their language and actions that they value these students as individuals, expect these students to learn, and want to have these students in their classrooms.

Helping Students With Exceptionalities Behave Acceptably

A second approach attempts to improve the social skills of students with exceptionalities. These students often misbehave, acting out because of frustration or learned inappropriate behaviors (Zens, Curtis, Graden, & Ponti, 1988). Ways of changing these behaviors include reward systems in which individuals receive tokens or points for appropriate behavior, group rewards in which the whole class is reinforced for desired behavior, and contracts that specify appropriate behavior in advance. These programs, as with behavioral programs in general, are controversial: Critics charge that students shouldn't be rewarded for merely displaying acceptable behavior. (We discuss this issue further when we present other applications of behavioral approaches in Chapters 6, 9, and 10.)

Students with disabilities often avoid contact with regular students because they lack the social skills to make friends. Teachers can help by modeling and coaching. For example, a

5.33
Describe at least two ways in which teaching students with exceptionalities social skills and teaching them cognitive strategies are similar.

teacher says, "Barnell's over there on the playground. I think I'll say, 'Hi, Barnell! Want to play ball with me?' Now you try it, and I'll watch." Another effective strategy is to teach social problem solving; for instance, a teacher comments, "Hmm. Mary has a toy that I want to play with. What could I do to make her want to share that toy?" Direct approaches have proved successful in teaching social skills such as empathy, perspective taking, negotiation, and assertiveness (M. Anderson, Nelson, Fox, & Gruber, 1988; Vaughn, McIntosh, Spencer, & Rowe, 1990).

Using Instructional Strategies That Encourage Social Interaction and Cooperation

One obstacle to social integration is the classroom itself. Teachers often use strategies in which students work alone and in which grades are based on competition rather than cooperation. Peer tutoring and cooperative learning can help break down these barriers.

Peer Tutoring.   Peer tutoring places students in groups of two or three and provides them with structured learning activities, including practice and feedback. For example, after introducing a new concept in math, the teacher assigns students in pairs to work on practice exercises. Students take turns as tutor and being tutored, one doing the sample problems and the other checking the answers and providing feedback. Various combinations have been used: high and low ability, students with and without exceptionalities, and students with exceptionalities tutoring each other. All have proved successful in teaching content while also fostering social interaction and improved attitudes toward those with exceptionalities (D. Miller et al., 1994). For both cognitive and affective gains to be maximized, it is important that students with exceptionalities have opportunities to tutor and

Cooperative learning activities encourage students to interact as they learn content and depend on each other for mutual help and support.

be tutored (D. Cole, Vandercook, & Rynders, 1988). In addition, training for the tutors is essential; research shows that the quality of the instruction during peer tutoring can be improved markedly by teaching students to be more interactive and structured in their feedback (Fuchs, Fuchs, Bentz, Phillips, & Hamlett, 1994).

Cross-age tutoring, in which older students tutor younger ones, appears to be an especially promising practice for students with disabilities. In one study, upper elementary students categorized as having either learning disability or behavior disorder served as tutors for first graders (Top & Osgthorpe, 1987). After 12 weeks of tutoring, both the tutors and those tutored showed significant gains on both criterion and standardized tests. In addition, tutors increased in their perceptions of their general academic ability and their reading/spelling ability. Anyone who has taught something successfully knows how personally fulfilling it can be. Successful tutoring appears to provide these same feelings of competence and satisfaction that spill over to and positively influence general self-concept.

Cooperative Learning. Cooperative learning strategies place students in teams and encourage them to work together toward common goals. In essence, students are rewarded for helping and encouraging other students to learn. Cooperative learning strategies have been used effectively at all grade levels and in all content areas. In addition to increasing achievement, the strategies have helped improve attitudes toward minorities and those with disabilities and increased their inclusion in mainstream classroom activities (Slavin, 1995). (We discuss cooperative learning in more detail in Chapter 12.)

Classroom Connections

Teaching Students With Exceptionalities in the Regular Classroom

1. Adapt regular instruction to meet the unique needs of students with exceptionalities.
   - A third-grade teacher circulates around the room after an assignment is given, making sure his mainstreamed students understand the directions. If necessary, he gathers them together in a small group or works with them one-on-one to go over the directions again.
   - A junior high math teacher has organized a buddy system in which his abler students are paired with mainstreamed students. A short training program teaches students how to assist with homework assignments and helps them understand the difference between educational and noneducational help.

2. Teach students with exceptionalities learning strategies they can use in the classroom.

- An English teacher teaches and models strategies step-by-step. A unit on writing one-paragraph essays taught students to use four steps:
  a. Write a topic sentence.
  b. Add two reasons they believe it is the topic sentence.
  c. Add a summary sentence.
  d. Reread and edit it.
- An elementary math teacher teaches problem-solving strategies by thinking aloud at the chalkboard while she's working through a problem. She breaks word problems into the following steps:
  a. Read: What is the question?
  b. Reread: What information do I need?
  c. Stop and think: What do I need to do—add, subtract, multiply, or divide?
  d. Compute: Put the numbers in and solve.
  e. Label and check: What answer did I get? Does it make sense?

Fostering Acceptance of All Students in Your Classroom

3. Emphasize the value of diversity in the classroom.

   • A first-grade teacher began a unit on diversity with a discussion on how all students in the class were similar. The next day, he focused on diversity, both physical and cultural. Students drew pictures of themselves, and the teacher helped each student point out on the pictures, "I'm me because . . . "

   • A junior high homeroom teacher begins the school year by asking students to fill out an autobiographical fact sheet that asks them to think about their favorites (e.g., food, hobby, movie), as well as their strengths and weaknesses. The teacher also fills out a fact sheet and puts them all up on the bulletin board. The teacher discusses these in the first few weeks to get to know students and to introduce the idea "Different is great."

4. Deal with the subject of exceptionalities in an open and straightforward manner.

   • An elementary teacher attacks the problem in the first week of class when she discusses classroom rules and procedures. One of these is "Respect the rights of others." She uses role playing and modeling to discuss problems such as teasing and laughing at others, and she specifically brings up the topic of students who look or act differently.

   • A junior high school English teacher uses literature, such as *Summer of the Swans,* by Betsy Byars, as a springboard for talking about individual differences. Students are encouraged to reflect on their own individuality and how important this is to them.

Windows on Classrooms

As you've studied this chapter, you've examined characteristics of students with different kinds of learning exceptionalities. As a teacher, you will have all types of students in your classrooms. You know they all can learn if you adapt your instruction to meet their needs. Efficient use of time, a supportive academic climate, effective classroom management, high success rates, and frequent and informative feedback are important in helping students with exceptionalities achieve to their maximum potential.

Read the following case study and assess the teacher's effectiveness in the context of the information you've been studying.

Mike Sheppard is a math teacher at Landrom Junior High School. He teaches three sections of seventh-grade prealgebra and two sections of eighth-grade algebra.

We join him in his second-period prealgebra class on Thursday morning. The day before, Mike introduced his class to a procedure for solving word problems, and he modeled the solution of some examples by using the procedure. He then assigned five problems for homework.

Mike has 28 students in his second-period class, which includes 5 students with exceptionalities: Herchel, Marcus, and Gwenn, who have learning disabilities, and Todd and Horace, who have a behavior disorder. Herchel, Marcus, and Gwenn each have problems with decoding words, reading comprehension, and writing. Todd has been described by other teachers as verbally abusive, aggressive, and lacking in self-discipline. He is extremely active and has a difficult time sitting through a class period. Horace is just the opposite, a very shy, timid, and withdrawn boy.

It is 10:07, and Herchel, Marcus, and Gwenn are among the first of Mike's students to file into class. As the students come in, they look in anticipation at the screen in the front of the room. Mike typically displays one or more problems on the overhead for the students as "warm-up" exercises, which they are directed to complete while he takes roll and completes other beginning-of-class routines.

Mike watches, and as soon as Herchel, Marcus, and Gwenn are in their seats, he slowly reads the displayed problem: "On Saturday, the Trebek family drove 17 miles from Henderson to Newton, stopped for 10 minutes to get gas, and then drove 22.5 miles from Newton through Council Rock to Gildford. The trip took 1 hour and 5 minutes, including the stop. On the way back, they took the same route but stopped in Council Rock for lunch. Council Rock is 9.5 miles from Gildford. How much farther will they have to drive to get back to Henderson?"

As Mike reads, he points to each displayed word. "Okay," he smiles after he finishes reading. "Do you know what the problem is asking you?"

"Could you read the last part again, Mr. Sheppard?" Gwenn asks.

"Sure," Mike nods, and repeats the part of the problem that describes the return trip, again pointing to the words as he reads.

"All right, jump on it. Be ready because I'm calling on one of you first today," he again smiles and touches each of them on the shoulder.

The students are in their seats, and most are studying the screen as the bell rings at 10:10. Mike quickly takes roll and then moves back to Todd's desk.

"Let's take a look at your chart," he says. "You've improved a lot, haven't you."

"Yeah, look," Todd responds, proudly displaying the following chart.

	2/8–2/12	2/15–2/19	2/22–2/26
Talking out	⊪⊪ ⊪⊪ ⊪⊪ ⊪⊪	⊪⊪ IIII ⊪⊪	⊪⊪ II
Swearing	⊪⊪ ⊪⊪	⊪⊪ II	IIII
Hitting/ touching	⊪⊪ III	⊪⊪ IIII	III
Out of seat	⊪⊪ ⊪⊪ ⊪⊪ III	⊪⊪ ⊪⊪ ⊪⊪ IIII	⊪⊪ ⊪⊪ ⊪⊪ III
Being friendly	II	IIII	⊪⊪ II

"That's terrific," Mike whispers to Todd as he leans over the boy's desk. "You're doing much better. We need some more work on 'out-of-seat,' don't we? I don't like getting after you about it, and I know you don't like it either," he went on. "Stop by after class. I have an idea for you. I think it will help. Don't forget to stop. I'll give you a pass to your next class if you're late. . . . Okay. Get to work on the problem." Mike then gives Todd a light thump on the back and returns to the front of the room.

Mike monitors the students, and seeing that most of them have either finished the problem or have stopped working, he begins at 10:15, "Okay, everyone. How did you do on the problem?"

Amid a mix of "Okay," "Terrible," "Fine," "Too hard," some nods, and a few nonresponses, Mike begins, "Let's review for a minute. . . . What's the first thing we do whenever we have a word problem like this?"

He then looks knowingly at Marcus, remembering his pledge to call on one of them first. . . . "Marcus?"

"Read it over at least twice."

"Good. . . . That's what our problem-solving plan says," Mike contin-

ues, pointing to a chart hanging from the top of the chalkboard that has the following information on it.

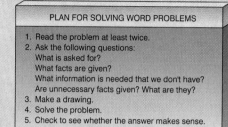

PLAN FOR SOLVING WORD PROBLEMS

1. Read the problem at least twice.
2. Ask the following questions:
   What is asked for?
   What facts are given?
   What information is needed that we don't have?
   Are unnecessary facts given? What are they?
3. Make a drawing.
4. Solve the problem.
5. Check to see whether the answer makes sense.

"Then, what do we do? . . . Melissa?"

"See what the problem asks for."

"Very good. What is the problem asking for? . . . Rachel?"

" . . . How much farther they will have to drive?"

"Excellent. Now, think about this. Suppose I solved the problem and decided that they had 39½ miles left to drive. Would that make sense? Why or why not? Everybody think about it for a moment."

Mike hesitates for several seconds and then says, "Okay. What do you think? . . . Herchel?"

" . . . I . . . I . . . don't know."

"Oh, yes you do," Mike encourages. "Let's look. . . . How far from Henderson to Gildford altogether?"

"Thir . . . " Rico begins until Mike puts his hand up, stopping him in mid-word. He then waits a few seconds as Herchel studies the sketch on his paper that appears as follows:

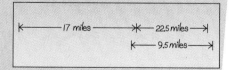

" . . . 39 and ½ miles," Herchel says uncertainly. "Oh! . . . The whole trip was only that far, so they couldn't still have that far to go."

"Excellent thinking, Herchel. See, I told you that you knew. That's very good.

"Now, go ahead, Rico. How far do they still have to go?"

"Thirty miles," Rico, one of the higher achievers in the class, responds quickly.

"Good," Mike nods. "Someone explain carefully how Rico might have gotten that. . . . Go ahead, Brenda."

" . . . The total distance is 39½ miles over, . . . and they came back 9½, . . . so, 39½ minus 9½ is 30."

"Good, Brenda, that's a good, clear description.

"Now," Mike goes on, "is there any unnecessary information in the problem?"

"Yes!" several students respond at once.

"Okay. Like what? . . . "Horace?" Mike asks, lowering his tone of voice slightly and moving toward Horace's desk.

" . . . "

"Look at the problem," Mike encourages softly.

" . . . "

"How long did the trip take?"

" . . . An hour and 5 minutes."

"And again, what does the problem ask us for?" Mike continues, nodding to Horace.

" . . . How much farther they had to drive."

"Excellent, so the amount of time they took is irrelevant," Mike shrugs, raising his tone of voice and turning back to the front of the room.

"What does *irrelevant* mean?" he asks, suddenly turning back to the class.

"Not necessary," Sherry volunteers quickly.

"Heck," Mike snaps his fingers. "I thought I had you on that one. You're on your toes today," he grinned at the class.

Mike proceeds to guide the class into identifying other items of unnecessary information in the problem, and then he asks students to raise their hands, holding up three fingers if they had solved it correctly, two fingers if they had solved it but got an incorrect answer, and one finger if they had gotten no solution. Seeing about a third of the class holding up three fingers, he thinks wryly, "We're going to need some work on this material.

"Okay. Not too bad for the first time through," he continues cheerfully. "Let's take a look at your homework."

Mike then goes through each homework problem as he had done with the first one, asking students to relate the problems' parts to each of the steps in the problem-solving plan, drawing a sketch on the chalkboard, and calling on a variety of students to supply specific answers and describe their thinking as they worked their way to the solutions.

With 20 minutes left to go in the period, he assigns 10 more problems for seatwork/homework, and the students begin working.

Once the class is working quietly, Mike nods to Herchel, Marcus, and Gwenn, and the three of them quietly get up from their desks and move to a table at the back of the room. The four of them sit at the table, with Gwenn and Marcus on one side of Mike and Herchel on the other.

"How'd you do on the homework when we went over it?" Mike asks. "Do you think you get it?"

"Sort of," Gwenn responds, and the other two nod.

"Good," Mike smiles. "Now, let's see what we've got, but before we start," he continues, "I noticed your drawing on our practice problem," he says to Herchel. "Let's take another look at it. . . . Go ahead and get it out."

Herchel then gets out his sketch.

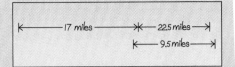

"Take a good look at it," Mike directs. "What looks funny? . . . Gwenn, you and Marcus look too."

"The 9½ miles is longer than the 22½ miles," Gwenn answers after looking at the sketch for a few seconds.

"Exactly," Mike nods. "Now remember, this has to make sense. We know that 22½ is longer than 9½, and also we know that 22½ is longer than 17. So, when you make your sketches, be sure they make sense. Now, you all can do this work. So, I want to see good work from each of you. Okay? Good," he finishes, nodding encouragingly.

"Okay. Go ahead and read the first problem, Gwenn."

"Ramon b . . . b . . . "

"Bought," Mike interjects.

"Bought," Gwenn continues, " . . . bought a CD for $13.95." She finishes reading the problem, haltingly, and with Mike's help.

"Okay. What are we trying to find in this problem?"

"How much more the first CD cost than the cassette?" Marcus answers.

"Good. You all understand the problem?"

The three nod.

"Okay. Let's look at the next one. . . . Go ahead and read it, Marcus."

Mike goes through each of the problems with the three students to be sure they are able to read the problems and comprehend the information in each. As they work, individual students periodically come back to the table and briefly ask questions. Mike then momentarily stops his work with Marcus, Herchel, and Gwenn to answer the question and then returns to working with them. He also stops briefly to go over and speak to Connie and Pamela, who are whispering.

After he returns, he says, "There are about 5 minutes left in the period. Run back to your desks now and see whether you can get one or two of them done before the bell rings."

Mike then watches as the students work until the bell rings.

As the students file out of the room, Mike catches Todd's eye, Todd stops, and Mike then leads him to a small area in the back of the room, partially enclosed but facing the front of the class.

"Look here," Mike directs. "Here's what we'll do. When you have the urge to get out of your seat, you quietly get up and move back here for a few minutes. Stay as long as you want, but be sure you pay attention

to what we're doing. When you think you're ready to move back to your seat, go ahead. All I'm asking is that you move back and forth quietly. . . . Okay? . . . What do you think?"

Todd nods, and Mike then puts his arm around him and says, "You're doing so well on everything else, this will help, I think. You're a good student. You hang in there. . . . Now, get out of here," Mike smiles, giving Todd a little push. "Here's a pass into Mrs. Miller's class."

Questions for Discussion and Analysis

Now analyze Mike's teaching. In conducting your analysis, you may want to consider the following questions. In each case, be specific and take information directly from the case study to defend your assessment.

1. Describe Mike's use of time. How efficiently did he use his time?
2. Did he create a warm academic climate for his students? Cite specific evidence from the case study.
3. How effective was Mike's classroom management? Again cite specific evidence.
4. How did Mike attempt to ensure success in his teaching?
5. What did Mike do to alter instruction for his students with learning disabilities? How effective were these modifications?
6. What did Mike do to meet the needs of his students with behavior disorders? How effective were these interventions?
7. Give Mike's teaching an overall assessment; use the information in this chapter as a basis for your conclusions. You may also want to consider your answers to items 1 through 6 in making your analysis.

Summary

Changes in the Way Teachers Help Students With Exceptionalities

A series of federal laws has changed the way teachers work with students having exceptionalities. These laws require that students with exceptionalities be taught in an LRE, guarantee due process through parental involvement, protect against discrimination in testing, and provide for IEPs.

The concept of *inclusion* has been developed to create a comprehensive web of services to meet the needs of students with exceptionalities. Inclusion is more comprehensive than mainstreaming, whose primary focus was placement in regular classroom settings. Inclusion means that teachers will be an integral part of a schoolwide system for helping students with exceptionalities and will have access to resources to assist in this process.

Students With Learning Problems

Many students with exceptionalities have mild learning problems that interfere with classroom performance but do not require separate instructional settings. Students who have mental retardation have below average intellectual functioning and impairment in adaptive behavior. Students with learning disabilities have normal levels of intellectual capability but below-average academic performance. And students with AD/HD have difficulties focusing their attention on the learning task at hand. Teachers will need to modify their classroom instruction for students with mild learning problems and will have various forms of support to assist them in doing this.

Behavior disorders involve serious, persistent, and age-inappropriate behaviors that interfere with classroom learning and social development. Externalizing behavior disorders are characterized by behaviors such as hyperactivity, uncooperativeness, and defiance. Students with internalizing disorders are withdrawn, depressed, or anxious. Both types of behavior disorders respond to teaching strategies that provide structured support and teach prosocial behaviors.

Communication, Visual, and Hearing Disorders

Communication disorders include speech or expressive disorders, which involve problems in forming and sequencing sounds. Language or receptive disorders are more global and involve problems with the ability to understand or use language to express ideas. Care should be taken to differentiate language disorders from culturally influenced difficulties encountered in learning English as a second language.

Other disabilities include visual and hearing disorders. Although less common than other disabilities, these disorders can be serious because of their potentially adverse influence on communication channels that affect learning. In both instances, teachers can take adaptive steps to modify instruction to meet the special needs of these students.

Students Who Are Gifted and Talented

Students who are gifted and talented constitute a sometimes overlooked category of students with exceptionalities. These students are at the upper end of the ability continuum and display unique talents in specific domains. Acceleration moves these students through the regular curriculum faster; enrichment provides alternative instruction to encourage student exploration.

Adapting Instruction for Students With Exceptionalities

Effective teaching for students with exceptionalities uses basic principles of effective teaching, such as effective management and high success rates as a foundation. In addition, strategy instruction teaches students to approach learning tasks by setting and monitoring progress toward goals.

Social acceptance for students with exceptionalities can be promoted in two ways. Socials skills can be directly taught through modeling, practice, and feedback. Attitudes of other students can be improved though instructional approaches focusing on increased understanding and through strategies such as peer tutoring and cooperative learning, which provide students with opportunities to interact in productive ways.

 **Important Concepts**

acceleration (p. 176)

adaptive fit (p. 155)

attention deficit/hyperactivity disorder (AD/HD) (p. 164)

behavior disorder (BD) (p. 166)

creativity (p. 174)

curriculum-based measurement (p. 160)

curriculum compacting (p. 176)

deaf (p. 172)

enrichment (p. 176)

exceptionalities (p. 153)

gifted and talented students (p. 174)

inclusion (p. 155)

individualized education program (IEP) (p. 157)

language disorders (p. 170)

learning disabilities (LD) (p. 163)

least restrictive environment (LRE) (p. 154)

mainstreaming (p. 154)

mental retardation (p. 162)

partial hearing impairment (p. 172)

special education (p. 153)

speech disorders (p. 170)

visual disability (p. 171)

The Classroom Learner Part II

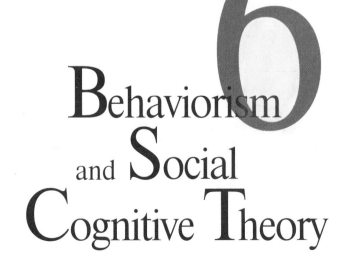

Chapter Outline

6

Behaviorism and Social Cognitive Theory

Tim, a 10th grader, was taking Algebra II and had been doing fairly well, getting a few C's but mostly B's on the weekly tests. In fact, he had become fairly confident about his ability to do algebra until the last test, when something inexplicably went wrong. For some reason, he became confused, got solutions mixed up, seemed to "blank out," panicked, and badly failed the test. Even with his parents' sympathy and support, he was devastated. On the next test, he was so anxious and nervous that when he started, the first few answers he circled on his problems had wiggly lines around them from his shaking hand.

"What if I fail again? I still don't understand this material. What am I doing in here?" he thought as he struggled with the problems. Although he did better than he had on the previous test, he still barely passed it.

"I'm not sure I can do this," he concluded.

After making only a halfhearted effort on the next test and again barely passing it, he thought, "Maybe I should drop algebra."

He was also more nervous when he took chemistry tests than he had been previously even though he hadn't done poorly on any chemistry exam. Fortunately, he still did fine in his English and world history classes.

Mrs. Lovisolo, his Algebra II teacher, talked with him, exhorting him to remember that he had only failed one test and hadn't been making his usual effort as he studied.

"Thanks, Mrs. Lovisolo," Tim said, on the brink of tears, "but math has always been hard for me. I'm not sure. Maybe geometry is as far as I can go."

"I don't want to hear those words," she said with a supportive smile. "Now, I want you to relax. You can do this work. I'm going to keep an eye on you in class, and if you're having trouble, just let me know and we'll work together after school. Okay?"

"Okay," Tim said, and although he remained unconvinced, he vowed to redouble his efforts.

Tim's friend Susan sat directly in front of him in Algebra II; another friend, Karen, sat behind him, and he talked with them about his uneasiness. They always did so well on the tests.

Karen was sympathetic, but shrugged. "I pay careful attention in class and always do the problems," she commented, "and the tests are usually pretty easy."

"I think the tests are tough," Susan retorted, "so I really study for them. How about if we get together and study?" Susan added. "Maybe it would help, and it could be kinda fun. . . . You want to?"

"Sure," Tim responded uncertainly. Then after thinking about it some more, it sounded like a really good idea. "Yeah, . . . yeah, that would be great!"

Anticipating working with Susan, he thought to himself determinedly, "She has to study hard, and she can do it. I ought to be able to do better."

On Thursday, the night before the next test, Tim went to Susan's home to study with her. In the process, he saw how she selected problems from the book and solved them completely in writing, rather than just reading over the sample problems and explanations. As she began working on her third problem, he asked her why she was doing another one.

"I try to do as many different kinds as I can, to be sure I don't get fooled on the test," she explained "That way, I'm more confident when I go into the test.

"See, this one is a little different," she continued. "The first thing I look for is how it is different from the others. Then, I attack it. . . . See, on this one I think we need to find c in terms of $b,$ and then we have it down to two equations. . . . Now it's simpler.

"I sometimes even make a little chart. I try to do at least three problems of each type we study, and then I check them off as I do them. It's fun to see the progress I'm making. If I get all of them right, I treat myself with a bowl of ice cream."

"That's a good idea," Tim said. "I usually do one, maybe two, and if I'm okay on them, I quit."

Tim now has a goal to do three problems of each type, selecting the odd problems so that he can check the correct answers in the back of the book. Also, when Mrs. Lovisolo uses a term in class that he doesn't understand, he writes it down, together with the definition, and then studies it so that he immediately understands what she means when she uses it in her explanations.

Tim did much better on the next test. "Whew, what a relief," he said to himself.

He was still somewhat nervous for the following week's test, but his effort had paid off, and he did very well; in fact, his score was the highest for the year. "Maybe I can do this material after all," he concluded with an inward smile.

His new strategy seems to be working; he's less nervous, and his test scores are steadily improving. With each success, he's more comfortable, and he has brought his average back up to nearly a B since his bad experience.

A major theme of this text is learning, and the focus is on what teachers can do to promote learning in all students. This chapter is the first of three devoted to theoretical descriptions of the topic. We begin this chapter by describing learning from a behaviorist perspective. This is followed by a discussion of social cognitive theory, a view of learning that includes elements of behaviorism but that goes beyond it to examine processes, such as beliefs and expectations, that behaviorists don't consider. In Chapters 7 and 8, we extend this discussion to examine cognitive learning in greater detail.

After you've completed your study of this chapter, you should be able to meet the following objectives:

- Identify examples of classical conditioning in classroom situations.
- Explain cases of student behavior by using concepts such as *reinforcement, punishment, generalization, discrimination, satiation,* and *extinction.*
- Explain the influence of different reinforcement schedules on student behavior.
- Identify examples of modeling and vicarious learning in classroom situations.
- Describe the characteristics of self-regulated behavior in people.

Behavioral Views of Learning

Tim's experience in the opening case illustrates a major theme of this section. The incident involves learning, and in this section of the chapter we examine learning from a behaviorist point of view. From a behaviorist perspective, **learning** *is a relatively enduring change in observable behavior that occurs as a result of experience* (Mazur, 1994). Notice that this definition specifies only observable behavior. Behaviorism gets its name from this focus on behaviors that people can see. It doesn't consider any internal structures, insights, processes, or needs.

Consider our definition again. Notice that it says a change in behavior is relatively enduring. We all have seen or experienced temporary changes in behavior resulting from illness, injury, or emotional distress. These changes would not be classified as learning.

Changes in behavior as a result of maturation would also not be called learning. For example, a 15-year-old can carry a large bag of groceries that his 6-year-old brother cannot even lift. He is bigger and stronger as a result of maturation. Parents say with excitement that their small child has "learned" to walk, but although some experience with crawling is certainly a factor, walking depends more on maturation than on learning.

Let's look again at Tim's situation. He makes wiggly lines around his problems. This behavior is observable, and as you saw in the example, it was relatively enduring. His making wiggly lines was a result of his experience on the earlier test. We would say that these wiggly lines are "learned" behaviors. Other learned behaviors are illustrated in the case study as well, and we discuss each later in the chapter.

In this section, we examine three different types of learning. They are outlined in Figure 6.1.

Contiguity

Think back to the first paragraph of the previous section. Suppose you say to yourself, "Learning—enduring change in observable behavior—a result of experience," and then you repeat it to yourself several times until you think you have the definition memorized.

6.1 ■
Identify two other types of enduring behaviors that would not be called learning. Give an example of each type.

6.2 ■
A teacher asks students, "When was the Magna Carta signed?" They are unable to answer. Explain their inability to answer; use the principle of contiguity as the basis for your explanation.

Figure 6.1

Types of learning in behaviorism

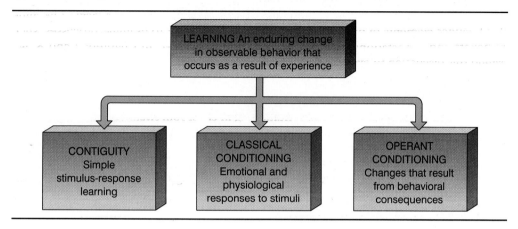

This is a form of learning that occurs through **contiguity**, *the simple pairing of stimuli (S) and responses (R)*. Contiguity is based on the principle that if two sensations occur together often enough, they become associated (Leahey & Harris, 1993). **Stimuli** *are all the sights, sounds, smells, and other influences the senses receive from the environment;* **responses** *are the behaviors that result from the association.* When Tim wrote new terms and definitions and practiced them, he was applying the principle of contiguity. If you pair 7 × 8 with 56 often enough, you respond "56" when you see 7 × 8 or hear "What is 7 times 8?" Seeing or hearing the 7 × 8 is the stimulus, and 56 is the response. Contiguity occurs in classrooms when stimuli and responses are paired and repeated, such as drill-and-practice activities with flash cards.

Classical Conditioning

Although S-R pairings can be used to explain fact learning and other simple behaviors, most learning is more complex. For example, Tim had been reasonably confident about his abilities in Algebra II until he got confused and failed the test. As a result of his failure, he was nervous on later tests, as evidenced by the wiggly lines around his problems. Somehow, math tests, which had previously not bothered him, became associated with his failure and caused his nervousness, an emotion related to the feeling of panic that resulted from failing the test. You can see that stimuli and responses are involved, but simple S-R pairings cannot adequately explain Tim's behavior. Something more complex is taking place.

Classical Conditioning: Pavlov's Work

Historically, interest in this type of learning was generated by Ivan Pavlov, a Russian physiologist who won a Nobel Prize in 1904 for his work on digestion. As a part of his research, he attempted to measure dogs' rates of salivation under different conditions. Initially, he had his assistants feed the dogs meat powder to induce the salivation, but as the research continued, the dogs began to salivate at the sight of the assistants even when they didn't

Flash cards and drill and practice help students learn facts through contiguity.

carry the meat with them (Pavlov, 1928). This startling phenomenon resulted in a turn in Pavlov's work and opened a new field of study called **classical conditioning**, or *respondent learning*, because the learner is *responding* to the environment.

Let's see how our example relates to classical conditioning. When Tim failed the test, he was devastated. He didn't choose to feel that way. The feeling was involuntary and emotional; it was an **unconditioned response**, *a reflexive involuntary response* induced by failure on the test. The failure was an **unconditioned stimulus**, *the initial stimulus that produces the unconditioned response*. In Pavlov's experiments, the unconditioned stimulus was the meat powder, which induced salivation as the involuntary physiological response.

Now the process becomes a bit more complex. Initially, Tim didn't react to tests one way or another, just as Pavlov's dogs had no initial reaction to the laboratory assistants. At first, the tests and the assistants were **neutral stimuli**, *which are stimuli that don't elicit any response*. Subsequent math tests became *associated* with failure, however, and they elicited a response similar to the response Tim experienced when he failed the first test. The tests became **conditioned stimuli**, *which are stimuli that become associated with unconditioned stimuli* and produce **conditioned responses**, *which are responses similar to the unconditioned responses*. In Pavlov's experiments, the assistants became conditioned stimuli for the dogs and resulted in salivating as conditioned responses.

Characteristics of Classical Conditioning

Our examples illustrate the essential characteristics of classical conditioning. First, learning took place. Tim's behavior underwent an enduring change as a result of his experience. Second, the classically conditioned responses were *emotional* or *physiological* and *involuntary* (Mazur, 1994), meaning they were out of the conscious control of the learner. Third, the conditioned and unconditioned stimuli, which *initially may not be related in any way*, became associated. Pavlov's assistants became associated with the meat powder, and Tim's tests became associated with failure. Finally, the conditioned and unconditioned responses were either *identical* or *similar*. In Pavlov's experiments, they were identical. In Tim's case, panic and anxiety are related emotions.

Classical Conditioning in the Classroom

Classroom examples of classical conditioning are actually quite common. For example, many students experience test anxiety (Covington & Omelich, 1987); it's not uncommon for some young children to become physically ill in anticipation of school, and some parents are reluctant to attend school functions or respond to teacher requests. Classical conditioning can help us explain these examples.

It can also explain more positive feelings. Does a song, a picture, or even an odor sometimes conjure up a feeling or mood you can't otherwise capture? Many people have had this experience. A song, for example, which was initially neutral, became associated with a positive incident that left you with the feeling. The song has become a conditioned stimulus, eliciting the feeling or mood as the conditioned response.

Understanding classical conditioning can help sensitize teachers to the importance of classroom climate and the associations their students form. For example, imagine students—often uneasy about a new school or class—who are treated with warmth and caring by their teacher. It is sensible to suggest that learners respond instinctively and positively to displays of genuine warmth. If the teacher is consistent in his or her manner, students begin to associate school with the teacher's warmth, and the school then elicits comfortable and safe feelings in the students. The teacher's displays of warmth operate as

---

6.3 ▬

Using concepts from classical conditioning, explain a child becoming ill in anticipation of school, and explain why a parent might be reluctant to attend school functions.

6.4 ▬

Teachers are discouraged from giving students writing assignments as a form of punishment for misbehavior. Using classical conditioning as a basis, explain why using writing assignments as punishment is unwise practice.

Classical conditioning helps teachers understand how supportive classroom environments and warm and caring teachers result in positive feelings toward schools and learning.

unconditioned stimuli; the school or class become conditioned stimuli when they are associated with the warmth of the teacher. They then elicit positive emotional responses (conditioned responses) similar to the responses (unconditioned responses) elicited by the teacher's initial displays of warmth.

Generalization and Discrimination

Let's look once more at our opening case study. Tim was nervous when he took his Algebra II tests; this was a learned behavior as a result of classical conditioning (demonstrated by his wiggly lines). He also became nervous when he took chemistry tests, however, even though he hadn't done poorly on any of them. His fears had generalized to chemistry. **Generalization** *occurs when a stimulus related to the conditioned stimulus elicits the conditioned response all by itself.* The physical sciences are somewhat related to algebra, so chemistry tests are stimuli related to the algebra tests, and they elicited the conditioned response—nervousness. The process can work the other way as well. The student who has come to associate school with the caring of one teacher may have similar reactions to other classes, club activities, and school-related functions. The other classes and club events are related to the teacher's classroom, which is the conditioned stimulus, and through generalization they elicit the conditioned response by themselves.

The opposite of generalization is discrimination. **Discrimination** *is the ability to give different responses to related but not identical stimuli.* For example, Tim is nervous during his chemistry tests, but not during those in English and history. He discriminates between English and algebra, for example, and his response differs.

Extinction

In our case study, Tim has been doing better since he started working with Susan and changed his study habits. In time, if he continues to succeed, his nervousness will disappear, or the conditioned response will become extinct. **Extinction** *occurs when the conditioned stimulus occurs repeatedly in the absence of the unconditioned stimulus.* Eventually, the conditioned stimulus no longer elicits the conditioned response. In Tim's case, repeated test taking (the conditioned stimulus) occurring without failure (the unconditioned stimulus) will, in time, no longer result in anxiety (the conditioned response).

6.5 ▬
One of this text's authors gets a funny feeling when he enters a dentist's office. This doesn't happen when he goes to see a medical doctor. Using the concepts of *generalization* and *discrimination,* explain the feeling.

6.6 ▬
Suppose you repeatedly hear a song that elicits a warm feeling, but you don't have another positive experience similar to the original one that caused the warm feeling. What will eventually happen to the feeling? Explain.

Classroom Connections

Applying Contiguity in Your Classroom

1. Carefully consider the forms of fact learning for which students will be responsible. Provide frequent review and drill to cement the contiguous links in the facts.
   - An elementary teacher takes a few minutes each morning to review difficult multiplication facts in a simple drill-and-practice activity.
   - A history teacher wants students to remember several crucial dates. She identifies the dates and their significance on a handout and tells students they're responsible for knowing the information. She reviews the material with them periodically before they are tested.

Applying Classical Conditioning in Your Classroom

2. Provide a safe and warm environment so that the classroom will be associated with positive emotions.
   - A first-grade teacher greets each of her students with a smile when they come into the room in the morning. She makes an attempt to periodically ask each of them about a pet, a relative, or some other personal part of their lives.
   - A junior high teacher makes a point of establishing and enforcing rules that forbid students to ridicule each other in any way, particularly when they're involved in class discussions or responding to teacher questions. He makes respect for each other a high priority in his classroom.

3. When questioning students, put them in safe situations and arrange the results to ensure a positive outcome.
   - A fourth-grade inner-city teacher tries to get all his students to participate by doing the following:
     a. When calling on reluctant responders or low-achieving students, he begins with questions such as, "What do you notice about the problem?" and "How would you compare the two examples?" These are questions for which virtually any answer is appropriate.
     b. When students are unable or unwilling to respond, he prompts them until they give an acceptable answer. (Effective prompting techniques are discussed in Chapter 12.)
     c. He calls on all students in his class so that being in his class becomes associated with responding and making an effort.

4. Provide students with practice in potentially anxiety-inducing situations.
   - A senior high math teacher deals with test anxiety by specifying precisely what information students are accountable for on tests. He gives them sample items to practice on and provides ample opportunity to go over problem areas before the test.
   - When a middle school social studies teacher encounters students who are anxious about making a presentation to the whole class, she has them come in and make their presentations to her alone so that they can practice and she can provide reassurance and support.

Operant Conditioning

So far, our discussion has progressed from simple S-R pairings, which we can apply to fact learning (contiguity), to more complex S-R relationships (classical conditioning), and we've used these relationships in explaining emotional and physiological reactions to classroom activities and other events. These explanations are still inadequate, however, because people often generate or initiate behaviors, rather than merely respond to stimuli. In other words, people "operate" on their environments, which is the source of the term *operant conditioning*.

This explanation leads us to work popularized by B. F. Skinner (1904–1990), a behavioral psychologist whose influence in the mid-1960s was so great that heads of psychology departments late in the 1960s identified him as the most influential psychologist of the 20th century (Myers, 1970). Skinner believed that responses to specific stimuli accounted for only a small proportion of all behaviors. He suggested instead that behavior is more controlled by the consequences of actions than by events preceding the actions. **A conse-quence** *is an outcome (stimulus) occurring after the behavior that influences future behaviors.* For example, a teacher's praise after a student answers is a consequence. Being stopped by the highway patrol and fined for speeding is also a consequence. Test results and grades are consequences, as are recognition for outstanding work and reprimands for inappropriate behavior.

Operant and classical conditioning are often confused. To help clarify the differences, a comparison of the two is presented in Table 6.1. From the table, you can see that learning occurs as a result of experience for both classical and operant conditioning but that the type of behavior is different and the behavior and stimulus occur in the opposite order for the two.

Let's turn to a detailed discussion of operant conditioning and the different consequences of behavior as they are presented in Figure 6.2.

Reinforcement

Reinforcement *is an increase in the frequency or duration of behaviors.* Reinforcement commonly occurs in the classroom when students are given compliments, pats on the back, or 5 extra minutes of recess. Reinforcement is of two types: positive and negative.

Positive Reinforcement.   **Positive reinforcement (PR)** *is an increase in behavior as the result of presenting the learner with a stimulus.* When working with humans, we commonly view what is presented as desired or valued, but an increase in student horseplay following a reprimand, for example, is also PR. The consequence is called a *reinforcer,* and something acts as a reinforcer when the behavior it follows increases in frequency or duration. For example, Sergio is writing a story and the teacher comments, "I really like your writing, Sergio. Your grammar and punctuation are accurate, and your descriptions are clear." If Sergio's

6.7
Suppose a child approaches a dog and is bitten. From that point on, the child is filled with fear whenever a dog approaches, and the child runs away. Describe the classically conditioned aspect of this example, and also describe the operantly conditioned aspect of this example.

6.8
Under what conditions might praise not be a positive reinforcer? How would you know that it wasn't?

Table 6.1

A comparison of classical and operant conditioning

	Classical Conditioning	Operant Conditioning
Behavior	Involuntary (Person does not have control of behavior) Emotional Physiological	Voluntary (Person has control of behavior)
Order	Behavior follows stimulus	Behavior precedes stimulus (consequence)
How learning occurs	Neutral stimuli become associated with unconditioned stimuli	Consequences of behaviors influence subsequent behaviors
Example	Learners associate classrooms (initially neutral) with the warmth of teachers, so classrooms elicit positive emotions.	Learners attempt to answer questions and are praised, so their attempts to answer increase.
Key researcher	Pavlov	Skinner

Figure 6.2

Consequences of behavior

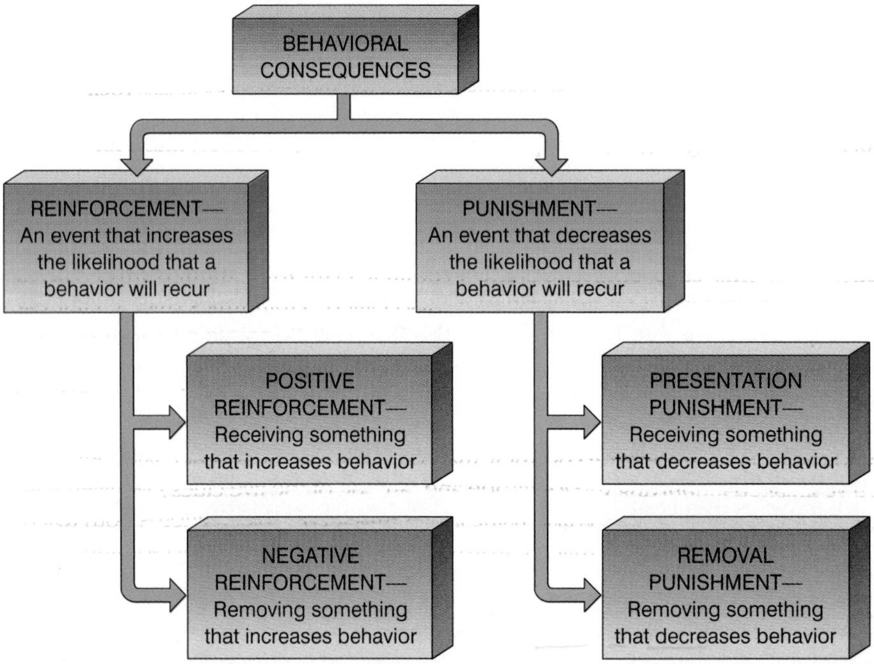

writing continues to improve, the teacher's comments acted as positive reinforcers. Teacher praise in all its forms is perhaps the most common reinforcer in classrooms. Good grades, high test scores, "happy faces" for young children, tokens that can be cashed in for privileges, stars on the bulletin board, and compliments are all used as positive reinforcers for students. Likewise, attentive looks from students, student questions, high student test scores, and compliments from students or parents are positive reinforcers for teachers.

Negative Reinforcement.   Not all reinforcement exists in the form of a consequence given after a behavior. **Negative reinforcement (NR)** *is an increase in behavior that results from avoiding or removing a stimulus* (Skinner, 1953). A classroom example is, "Okay, everyone. You've done such a good job of turning in your homework this week that you don't have to do your assignment for the weekend. We'll do it Monday instead." The teacher's intent is to *increase* the students' doing homework in the future by removing the weekend assignment. Notice that although the term *negative* appears in the label, NR results in an *increase* in the frequency of a behavior, rather than a decrease.

A teacher is also using NR when he says, "If everyone is sitting quietly in his or her seat when the bell rings, we'll go to lunch. If not, we'll miss some of our lunch period." By demonstrating the desired behavior (orderliness), the students can *avoid* the consequence (missing a portion of the lunch period).

Notice that when NR is used, one of two situations exists:

1. The learners *are in* the situation before they demonstrate the desired behavior.
2. The learners can avoid a consequence.

6.9
People often take aspirin or some other painkiller for a headache. Explain the taking of painkillers as an example of NR.

In the homework example, students were in a routine of having assignments over the weekends. Had they not been in this situation prior to their conscientious effort, there would be nothing for the teacher to remove. In the lunch example, students quickly become quiet—exhibit the desired behavior—thereby avoiding the consequence (missing some of their lunch period). Both situations are examples of NR.

The Premack Principle.

> Don Zentz's jazz band students love playing some of the modern, upbeat jazz-rock compositions but are less enthusiastic about some of the standards.
>
> "No, not 'Mood Indigo' again," they protest when he holds up the sheet music for the Duke Ellington classic.
>
> "A good job one time through it, and we'll do 'Watermelon Man,'" he counters.
>
> "All right! Let's do it!" they shout.

The teacher in this case employed the Premack Principle, named after David Premack (1965), the person who first described it. Also called "Grandma's rule" ("First eat your vegetables, and then you can have dessert"), the **Premack Principle** *says that a more frequent or more preferred activity can be used as a reinforcer for a less frequent or less preferred activity.* Mr. Zentz's students preferred playing "Watermelon Man" to "Mood Indigo," so he used it as a reinforcer for playing the less preferred piece.

When geography students want to do their map projects and the teacher says, "All right, as soon as you've finished identifying the longitude and latitude of the five cities I've given you, you may begin your map projects," she is also using the Premack Principle. It affords both teachers and students a variety of reinforcers that are instructionally related and easy to administer.

6.10

Suppose that, in an effort to increase car pooling, a city allowed cars with three or more people to pass through toll booths without paying. Using the information in this section, explain the city's efforts.

6.11

In Chapter 1 we asked, "Have you ever done one job to get it out of the way and saved a more enjoyable one for later?" Assuming the answer is yes, use the information in this section to explain that behavior.

Positive reinforcers, such as grades, can be powerful motivators for students.

Punishment

Positive and negative reinforcers are consequences that strengthen behavior. Some consequences, however, weaken behaviors or decrease their frequency. *Consequences that result in a decrease in behavior are called* **punishment**.

Presentation Punishment.   From Figure 6.2, you can see that **presentation punishment (PP)** *occurs when a learner's behavior decreases as a result of being presented with a consequence.* Presentation punishment is intended when students have to pick up the trash in the lunchroom because of excessive rowdiness or when teachers verbally reprimand students for misbehavior. Picking up the trash and the reprimand are punishers.

Removal Punishment.   Figure 6.2 illustrates two kinds of punishment. Whereas presentation punishment is the weakening of a behavior by presenting a consequence, *the decreasing of behavior by removing a stimulus or the inability to get positive reinforcement (PR) is* **removal punishment (RP)**. As with negative reinforcement, the learner is in the situation prior to the consequence; but unlike with negative reinforcement, removal punishment reduces rather than increases behavior.

A fairly common and somewhat controversial application of RP is called *time-out*. A misbehaving student is removed from the class and physically isolated behind filing cabinets or some other barrier. The rationale is that removal from the class eliminates the student's chances to gain positive reinforcement, so the isolation is a form of removal punishment. In other cases, students are sent to another teacher's classroom or kept in detention after school. In the case of detention, the student's opportunity to play and interact with classmates is taken away. When not used excessively, time-out can be an effective management technique (Skiba & Raison, 1990; A. White & Bailey, 1990).

Let's consider another teacher's management application of removal punishment.

> Bette Ponce has been having management problems with her second-grade class. To try to solve these problems, she hands each of her second graders a small packet containing three slips of paper every morning when they come into the room. Each time a student breaks one of her classroom rules, a slip of paper is taken from that student's packet. Bette then calls the parents of any students who lose all three slips during the course of the day. Losing all three slips for a second day results in half an hour of detention.
>
> Bette also combines PR with the program. Any student who has 10 or more slips left in his or her packet by the end of the week can trade the slips for free time and other rewards.

Bette's technique is sometimes called **response cost**, *the application of removal punishment by taking away reinforcers already given*. Bette's students are given the slips of paper, which they lose for infractions of the rules. Traffic fines, revoked drivers' licenses, 10-yard holding penalties in a football game, and loss of free classroom time previously earned are all additional examples of response cost.

Reinforcement and Punishment: Research Results.   What long-range impact does the use of reinforcement or punishment have on learners? Is punishment justified? Should it ever be used? Does it work?

Work done in the 1950s indicated that punishment would only temporarily weaken undesirable behaviors (Sears, Maccoby, & Levin, 1957), but these findings were later refuted (J. Johnson, 1972). If the punishment is severe enough, behavior can be suppressed, and such punishment may be justified in extreme cases. Chronically and severely disruptive students do not have the right to destroy the classroom environment for students who want to learn, and if the only choice is removing the disrupters, this action is

---

6.12 ■
Corporal (physical) punishment is an example of PP and is still used in some U.S. schools. Using classical conditioning as a basis, describe some possible undesirable outcomes of corporal punishment.

6.13 ■
Explain how allowing students to talk with each other during detention or even allowing them to finish their homework might defeat its purpose.

appropriate. Remember, however, that punishment doesn't teach desired behaviors; it only suppresses undesirable ones. Students must still be taught appropriate behaviors.

6.14
According to behaviorists, how are desirable behaviors taught?

Sensitivity and professional judgment are required in using punishment. For instance, if punishments are routinely administered, students may become desensitized to punishment, the teacher may become aversive, and punished students may generalize their aversion to the class, other teachers, and the school (Jenson, Sloan, & Young, 1988). A classroom management system based on punishment is flawed and should be reexamined.

Many educational leaders emphasize positive reinforcement; for example, everyone's heard the maxim "Catch 'em being good." The researcher who conducted one survey of successful management approaches concluded that systems focusing on positive behaviors were vastly superior to those emphasizing a decrease in inappropriate behaviors (R. Williams, 1987).

Focusing exclusively on positive behaviors isn't a panacea, however. After all aversive consequences are eliminated, some students actually become more disruptive (Pfiffer, Rosen, & O'Leary, 1985; Rosen, O'Leary, Joyce, Conway, & Pfiffer, 1984). A probable solution is a combination of classroom rules with clear consequences. We discuss these issues further in Chapter 10.

Positive reinforcement should also be used cautiously as a form of motivation. Research indicates that, if administered indiscriminately, it can detract from intrinsic motivation and adversely affect students' views of classroom tasks (Harter, 1978; Morgan, 1984). We examine these issues in detail in Chapter 9.

Operant Conditioning: Applications

In the previous section, we introduced important concepts involved in operant conditioning and began to examine some classroom applications. We turn now to a more systematic look at those applications.

Generalization and Discrimination. We examined generalization and discrimination when we discussed classical conditioning, and now we consider them from an operant perspective. For instance, when kindergarten students see shapes such as those in Figure 6.3a, they learn to say "square." Similarly, after dissecting a shark, a frog, and a fetal pig, biology students recognize the heart in each case. The hearts are similar but not identical: The shark's

Figure 6.3

Squares and a rectangle

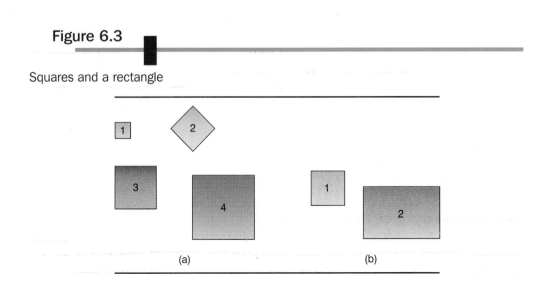

(a)   (b)

is two-chambered, the frog's three-chambered, and the pig's four-chambered. Nevertheless, students learn that they are all hearts despite these differences. They have generalized.

As with classical conditioning, **generalization** *is giving the same response to similar but not identical stimuli.* The responses are voluntary, however, rather than involuntary—as they are in the case of classical conditioning—and are the result of reinforcement. For example, the child is reinforced for saying the first shape in Figure 6.3b is a square but is told, "No, it's a rectangle," when he says the second shape is a square. Such feedback help him learn to discriminate between the two shapes. Likewise, the biology student who recognizes the difference between the frog's heart and its liver is also discriminating.

Discrimination *is the ability to give different responses to similar but not identical stimuli.* A common example of the importance of discrimination occurs in reading readiness tasks in which young children learn to respond differently to *p* and *q* or *b* and *d* and other related letters. They learn these discriminations through reinforcement and feedback.

Generalization and Discrimination: The Role of Feedback.   The need to generalize and discriminate is obvious. On the one hand, it would be impossible, for example, for children to learn each individual shape they encounter; to help them, shapes are categorized into concepts such as *square, circle,* and *rectangle.* On the other hand, if they couldn't discriminate between concepts, the world would be incredibly complex and confusing. The role of teachers in this process is to provide feedback. **Feedback** *is information about the accuracy or appropriateness of a response,* and it has been consistently linked to student learning (Brophy & Good, 1986; Rosenshine & Stevens, 1986).

Effective feedback has four essential characteristics:

1. It is immediate.
2. It is specific.
3. It provides corrective information for the learner.
4. It has a positive emotional tone. (Brophy & Good, 1986; J. Murphy, Weil, & McGreal, 1986)

To illustrate these ideas, let's examine three examples.

Mr. Dennis:	What kind of figure is shown on the overhead, Jo?
Jo:	A square.
Mr. Dennis:	Not quite. Help her out, . . . Steve?
Ms. West:	What kind of figure is shown on the overhead, Jo?
Jo:	A square.
Ms. West:	No, it's a rectangle. What is the next figure, . . . Albert?
Ms. Baker:	What kind of figure is shown on the overhead, Jo?
Jo:	A square.
Ms. Baker:	No, remember we said that all sides have the same length in a square. What do you notice about the lengths of the sides in this figure?

In comparing the three examples, you can see that the feedback is *immediate* in each case but that Mr. Dennis's feedback gave Jo no information about her answer other than it was incorrect; it was not *specific* and provided no *corrective information.* Ms. West's feedback was specific, but it gave Jo no corrective information. Ms. Baker, in contrast, provided specific, corrective information in her feedback.

The examples provide no information about the emotional tone of the feedback. Positive emotional tone means that the teachers are supportive in their responses to student answers. Harsh, critical, or sarcastic feedback detracts from both learning and student motivation.

6.15
Identify two differences between generalization and discrimination in the context of operant conditioning, compared with generalization and discrimination in the context of classical conditioning.

6.16
A language arts teacher displays the sentence "The car sped quickly away from the scene of the crime" on the overhead and then asks, "Can anyone find an adverb in this sentence?" Bryan answers, "Sped." On the basis of the principles of effective feedback, what should the teacher do?

Genuine and effective praise that matches the student's accomplishment provides positive reinforcement in the classroom.

Praise.   Perhaps the most common form of teacher feedback, praise is adaptable to a variety of teaching situations. For this reason and because research reveals some interesting features related to praise, we examine it in this section.

First, praise is used less often than most teachers believe. Brophy (1981) found that praise for good answers occurs less than five times per class period and that praise for good behavior is actually quite rare, once every 2 or more hours in the elementary grades and even less as students get older. Second, praise tends to depend as much on the type of student—high achieving, well behaved, attentive—as on the quality of the student's answer. Teachers praise students on the basis of the answers they expect to receive as much as on what they actually hear.

Third, effective praise includes each characteristic of effective feedback but goes beyond them (see Figure 6.4; Brophy, 1981). For example, as with everything else in life, if praise is perceived as insincere, it loses its credibility. Praise for effort and incidental answers communicates that effort and original thinking are valued; it is an indicator of a positive classroom climate.

Finally, as with everything else in teaching, careful judgment is required. For example, if every desired answer is praised specifically, the praise begins to sound stilted and artificial, and the flow of a lesson can be disrupted. As a teacher, you must judge the appropriate mix of specific and general praise.

Rosenshine (1987) offers a solution to this dilemma. He suggests that praise for student answers that are delivered with confidence should be simple and general. In contrast, praise for student answers that are correct but tentative should be specific and provide information. Let's see how this works in the classroom.

Mrs. Barnhart: How does the direction of the ocean current off the coast of Chile affect the rainfall in the Chilean Desert?

Figure 6.4

Characteristics of effective praise

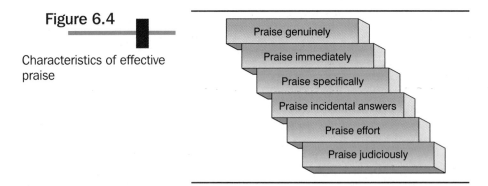

Praise genuinely
Praise immediately
Praise specifically
Praise incidental answers
Praise effort
Praise judiciously

> *Tanya:* (confidently) The current comes from the south, so the water is cold. The air over the water is more dense than the air over the land, so the air that goes over the land is warmed up, and it doesn't rain.
>
> *Mrs. Barnhart:* Yes, good description, Tanya.

In contrast, if Tanya had said essentially the same thing but had sounded tentative and uncertain, Mrs. Barnhart might have responded with a statement such as the following:

> *Mrs. Barnhart:* Very good, Tanya. You recognized that the air would be warmed as it moved over the land. This was because the air above the water was cold, caused by the cold water itself flowing from the south. Good analysis.

Specific praise in the first case wasn't necessary because the student gave a clear, confident answer. If Tanya's answer were tentative, however, specific praise would emphasize important information and help eliminate uncertainty.

Flexibility in praise is also necessary. Young children bask in praise given openly in front of a class, and they tend to take praise at face value regardless of its validity (Stipek, 1984). High-anxiety students and those from low-SES backgrounds tend to react more positively to praise than do their more confident and advantaged counterparts. In their effort to achieve independence, however, junior high students often react better to praise given quietly and individually.

Praise must match the accomplishment. Effusive praise given after every answer loses its credibility even if the teacher is sincere. This is particularly true with older students. They ignore praise they perceive as invalid and interpret praise given for easy tasks as indicating that the teacher has low expectations for them (Emmer, 1988; Good, 1987a).

Let's turn now to some additional applications of positive reinforcement.

Shaping.

> "I start out praising every answer even if it's only partially right," Ms. Brugera commented. "I also praise them for trying even if they can't give me an answer. Then as they improve, I praise them only for better, more complete answers, until finally they have to give well thought-out explanations before I'll say anything."
>
> "I don't," Mr. Jordan responded. "I like to give a lot of praise, but I think praising every answer takes too much time. I also think if you do too much, you lose your credibility, so I start right off praising them only when they give me a really good answer."

According to Ms. Brugera, her students weren't always able to give her the answers she was after, so she praised partial answers and even effort. Gradually, they had to give more complete responses to earn her praise. She was applying the concept of **shaping**, *the process of*

6.17 ▬

Using Piaget's work discussed in Chapter 2 and Erikson's work discussed in Chapter 3 as a basis, explain why young and older students might respond differently to praise. Why might older students interpret praise for easy tasks negatively?

6.18 ▬

When given a math assignment, Felicia puts her pencil down and says, "I can't do these!" Describe specifically how the teacher could use shaping to help Felicia.

reinforcing successive approximations of a desired behavior. Although Ms. Brugera was obviously after the correct answer, student effort was a beginning step, and a partially correct response was a close approximation of the desired behavior. By reinforcing each step, she hoped to eventually get complete and thoughtful answers from her students.

Reinforcement Schedules.   Reinforcement schedules describe patterns in the frequency and predictability of reinforcers. They can be classified into two basic types. **Continuous reinforcement** *occurs when every desired response is reinforced,* and this is what Ms. Brugera did in the beginning of her shaping process when she praised every student answer. In contrast, *reinforcing a behavior only periodically is called* **intermittent reinforcement**, which was what Mr. Jordan used.

Intermittent reinforcement schedules can be classified as two types. **Interval schedules** *are used when the schedule depends on time;* **ratio schedules** *are used when reinforcement is based on the number of responses.* Teachers use a **fixed-interval schedule** *when the learner is reinforced with an interval that is predictable,* such as every 3 minutes or every day. *When the amount of time between reinforcers is allowed to change unpredictably,* a **variable-interval schedule** is used.

Mr. Jordan praised students on the basis of responses, rather than time, and he praised on the basis of his judgment of the answer's quality, rather than every fifth answer, for example. He was using a **variable-ratio schedule,** *which is a schedule that reinforces students in an unpredictable way based on the number of responses.* If he had chosen to praise every third or fifth or some other numbered answer, he would have been using a **fixed-ratio schedule,** *which is a schedule that reinforces students in a predictable way based on the number of responses.* Slot machines at gambling casinos use variable-ratio reinforcement; gamblers never know which pull of the lever will pay off. The power of this schedule in maintaining behaviors is demonstrated by the large number of people who play the machines for hours.

Continuous and intermittent reinforcement schedules have important places in learning. Some of their uses are outlined in Table 6.2.

Each schedule has advantages and disadvantages. On the one hand, a continuous schedule yields the fastest rates of initial learning, so it is effective when students are learn-

> **6.19** ▬
> To encourage on-task behaviors, a teacher has a classroom beeper that makes a noise at unexpected moments. If students are on-task when the beeper goes off, the class gets points toward a party. What reinforcement schedule is the teacher using? Explain.

Table 6.2 ▬

Reinforcement schedules and examples

Schedule	Example
Continuous	A teacher "walks students through" the steps for solving simultaneous equations. They are liberally praised at each step as they first learn the solution.
Fixed-ratio	The algebra teacher announces, "As soon as you've done two problems in a row correctly, you may start on your homework assignment so that you'll be able to finish by the end of class."
Variable-ratio	Students volunteer to answer questions by raising their hands and are called on at random.
Fixed-interval	Students are given a quiz every Friday.
Variable-interval	Students are given unannounced quizzes.

ing new behaviors, such as the algebra students learning to solve equations. On the other hand, the behaviors are less persistent after the reinforcers are removed, so to maintain the behavior, students should be shifted to an intermittent schedule as soon as possible.

Fixed schedules also have disadvantages: Behavior increases rapidly just before the reinforcer is given and then decreases rapidly and remains low until just before the next reinforcer is given. For instance, in the case of a quiz every Friday—a fixed-interval schedule—students study diligently on Thursday and then don't study again until the following Thursday.

This behavior might suggest that a variable-interval schedule be used, such as giving "pop" quizzes. Such a prospect, however, might cause high anxiety levels in students, so careful judgment is needed if it is to be implemented. The best compromise is probably brief, frequent, announced quizzes once a week or even more often (Kika, McLaughlin, & Dixon, 1992; Mazur, 1994).

Potency and Satiation.   As you would expect, reinforcers vary in their effectiveness. Behaviorists use the term **potency**, *which refers to a reinforcer's ability to strengthen behaviors,* to describe this effectiveness. Reinforcement potency depends on at least three factors. First, differences among learners are important. For example, high grades and test scores are effective reinforcers for some students but not for others. For many, recognition and attention are often potent reinforcers, and the students will sometimes engage in inappropriate classroom activity to gain them.

Second, the source of a reinforcer influences its potency. Compliments are more potent reinforcers when they come from respected teachers than from those less respected. Just as a compliment from a coach is likely to be a more potent reinforcer for an athlete, a compliment from an orchestra leader is likely to be more potent for a student interested in music, or from the English teacher if the student is interested in writing.

Third, the frequency of a reinforcer influences its potency. A simple "Excellent!" written beside a response on a test paper can be a potent reinforcer, but if it appears too often or is written on every student's paper, it may lose its potency. When *a reinforcer occurs so frequently that it loses its potency,* **satiation** is the result. Mr. Jordan demonstrated that he was aware of the possibility of satiation when he chose to be judicious in his use of praise.

Satiation can be used to eliminate the power of a reinforcer. We've all heard the tale of the father who catches his son smoking behind the barn and then forces the boy to smoke the rest of the pack of cigarettes. This is an attempt to use satiation to eliminate a behavior.

Although we wouldn't recommend that father's technique, other classroom applications have been used successfully. Let's look at an example.

> Ms. Ortega was having a problem with chronic note passing in her seventh-grade English class, so she developed the following plan. After identifying the culprits, she required them to write a long note to a friend near the end of class while the other students began their homework. The note could not be a theme, nor could it be copied, and she required it to be a full handwritten page. She didn't read any of the notes but did inspect them to be certain they were of proper length. If they weren't, she demanded that the students continue writing until the page was full or until the period ended.
>
> By the end of the second day, several of the students asked whether they could stop writing notes and work on their homework, and by the end of the third day, Ms. Ortega stopped the process. She has not had problems with note writing in her class since that time.

This example also illustrates the importance of teacher sensitivity and professional judgment. For instance, Ms. Ortega made a point of not reading any of the notes, so she didn't embarrass the students or violate their privacy. She required that the topic be some form of personal note so that note writing became the aversive behavior. Had she allowed them to write about a class topic, the topic or writing itself could have become aversive instead.

6.20   ■
Explain how pop quizzes might increase test anxiety; use classical conditioning as a basis for your explanation.

6.21   ■
With what kind of a reinforcement schedule—continuous or intermittent—would satiation occur first? What implication does this have for the classroom?

6.22   ■
Using concepts from classical conditioning, explain how writing might become aversive if it is used as a form of punishment.

Praise that comes from a respected teacher can be a powerful reinforcer for students of all ages.

Ms. Ortega was also respected by the students as a teacher who was strict but fair. Her classroom was orderly, and she was clearly in charge of her environment. Had these factors not existed, her application of satiation might not have succeeded.

Extinction.   You saw in our opening case study that Tim's nervousness was reduced with each test and that, in time, it could be eliminated completely. This was an example of extinction in the case of classical conditioning.

Operantly conditioned behaviors can also become extinct, as illustrated in the following example.

> Renita, a 10th grader, enjoyed school and liked to respond in her classes. She was attentive and raised her hand, eager to answer most teachers' questions. She said she could "stay awake better when the teacher asks questions."
> Mr. Frank, her world history teacher, asked a few questions but usually lectured. Renita raised her hand when he did ask a question, but someone would usually blurt out the answer before she could respond.
> Renita rarely raises her hand now and often catches herself daydreaming in world history.

This situation demonstrates how operantly conditioned behaviors can become extinct and, further, how important instructional strategies are in promoting student attention and learning. For Renita, being called on by the teacher apparently reinforced two behaviors: attempting to respond and paying attention. Because she wasn't called on or allowed to respond, she wasn't reinforced, and her behaviors were disappearing; they were becoming extinct. **Extinction,** *from an operant perspective, is the elimination of a response as a result of nonreinforcement,* and Renita's case is an example.

Often, teachers are not sufficiently interactive; this is unfortunate because research documents a link between interactive classrooms and learning (Good & Brophy, 1994; Nystrand & Gamoran, 1989). Renita's experience illustrates this link, and the study of behaviorism helps in understanding why. (We discuss the role of teaching technique in promoting learning in detail in Chapter 12.)

Cues: Antecedents to Behavior.   In our discussion of operant conditioning, we have focused on the consequences of behavior. What do we do, however, when we have identified student behaviors that we want to reinforce, but we can't because students don't demonstrate the behavior? One example is to try to get students to respond to teacher questions. When we ask questions, we want to reinforce our students' responses but often can't because they don't give us any answers, or they give wrong ones. Unfortunately, this situation often occurs with the very kind of student—low achieving or poorly motivated—we're trying to involve in the first place. We can't reinforce the behavior because it doesn't occur. We can, however, provide **cues,** *which are antecedent stimuli that prompt the learner to display the desired behavior.* Consider the following exchange.

> Mrs. Wendt was working with her fourth graders on adverbs. She wrote this sentence on the chalkboard: "John quickly jerked his head when he heard his name called." Then she asked, "What is the adverb in the sentence? . . . Wendy?"
> " . . . "
> "Look at the sentence. What did John do?"
> " . . . Jerked his head."
> "How did he jerk it?"
> " . . . Quickly."
> "So what is the adverb?"
> " . . . Quickly."
> Mrs. Wendt smiled, "Yes! Well done, Wendy."

6.23   ▬
Describe the difference between extinction in the context of operant conditioning and extinction in the context of classical conditioning. What key feature is similar in both?

6.24   ▬
Identify one characteristic that satiation, extinction, and punishment have in common. Describe the differences in each.

Teacher questions act as effective cues to elicit responses from a number of students.

6.25

Look again at the example with Mrs. Wendt. What specific cues did she use to help Wendy respond?

Mrs. Wendt provided cues that allowed Wendy to produce the desired behavior, which Mrs. Wendt then reinforced. Combining cues with shaping can be very powerful in promoting desired behaviors.

Cues, come in other forms as well. The teacher moving to the front of the class is a cue for students to turn their attention toward her. The light switch being turned off is a cue for students to become quiet, and a teacher's walking among students as they do seatwork is a cue to remain on-task. In each case, the cue signals appropriate behavior, which can then be reinforced. Expert teachers use cues such as these to develop routines that result in smoothly running classrooms (Cazden, 1986; W. Doyle, 1986).

Implications of Behaviorism for Instruction.   What do the applications you've studied in this section suggest for instruction? Think, for a moment, about how you learned many of the grammar rules you use in your writing. Most of us have completed many exercises similar to "Juanita and (I, me) went to the football game." The tacit assumption is that being able to complete exercises such as this one will ultimately result in us becoming skilled writers. This type of exercise is so common that we may not realize it is based on principles of behaviorism. According to behaviorism, information must be broken down into small, specific, decontextualized pieces. This destructuring allows learners to display observable behaviors; teachers can *see* whether the learner identifies the "I" or the "we" in the sentence above, for example. Then, if learners demonstrate the behaviors, they're reinforced; if not, they receive corrective feedback until they do. This tactic promotes generalization and discrimination.

The teacher's role is to organize and present information in highly organized and tightly sequenced segments that promote learners' demonstrating the desired behaviors.

Learners are viewed as passive recipients of the information, and learning is described as hierarchical, with prerequisite skills to be mastered before more advanced ones are tackled.

Historically, programmed learning, teaching machines, and some of the early instructional computer programs were also based on behaviorist principles. Criticisms of this approach have increased in recent years, and we discuss these criticisms in the chapters that follow.

Classroom Connections

Applying Operant Conditioning in Your Classroom

1. When applying behavioral methods in your classroom, use reinforcement rather than punishment whenever possible. When punishment is necessary, use removal punishment rather than presentation punishment.
   - After giving an assignment, a first-grade teacher circulates around the room and gives tickets to students who are working quietly. The tickets may be exchanged for opportunities to play games and work at learning centers. Initially, he rewards all on-task behaviors; later, he requires an extended period of time-on-task.
   - A fifth-grade teacher gives students "behavior points" at the beginning of the week. If they break a rule, they lose a point. At the end of the week, a specified number of remaining points may be traded for free time.

2. Carefully select reinforcers for their potency.
   - A seventh-grade teacher asks students what they would like as rewards. (They typically suggest watching videos or being given free time to visit.) Then she's careful to use their suggestions to give them the feeling that they have some control over their environment.
   - A math teacher increases the potency of grades as reinforcers by awarding bonus points for improvement. After an average for each student is determined, she offers them incentive points for scoring higher than their average.

3. Promote generalization and discrimination by encouraging students to make comparisons among examples and other information.
   - A life science teacher, in a unit on deciduous and coniferous trees, asks students to compare a pine and an oak tree. Through questioning, he focuses their comparisons of essential differences between the trees.
   - A teacher praises a third grader who, on her own, notices that frogs and toads are not the same and that frogs climb trees but toads don't.

4. Use appropriate schedules of reinforcement.
   - At the beginning of the school year, a first-grade teacher plans activities that all students can do. She praises liberally and rewards frequently. As students get used to first-grade work, she pushes them harder by requiring more effort.
   - A second-grade teacher is careful to provide compliments on an intermittent basis for consistent work and effort. She knows that students who do steady, average to above-average work and are not disruptive tend to be taken for granted and are often "lost in the shuffle."
   - An algebra teacher gives frequent announced quizzes to prevent the decline in effort that often occurs after reinforcement with a fixed-interval schedule.

5. Provide clear, informative feedback on student work.
   - A sixth-grade teacher has students do sample math problems that are similar to their homework, the class goes over the problems, and the teacher

answers any questions they have before having them work independently.

- A high school history teacher uses essay items to teach, not just to assess. With each essay question, she provides written feedback to each student, giving a concrete explanation for the grade. If this is too time-consuming, she prepares an "ideal" response to the item and shares it with the class.

6. Shape desired behaviors.
- A language arts teacher begins a unit on paragraph writing by assigning a written paragraph from each student. As she scores them, she is initially generous with positive comments, but she becomes more critical as time goes on and the students' work improves.

- A second-grade teacher openly praises a student whose behavior is improving. With continued improvement, she requires longer periods of acceptable behavior to earn the praise.

7. Provide cues for appropriate behavior.
- After completing a lesson and assigning seatwork, a seventh-grade English teacher circulates around the room, reminding students both verbally and nonverbally that they are to begin working.
- Before the students line up for lunch, a first-grade teacher reminds them to stand quietly while waiting to be dismissed. When they're standing quietly, she compliments them on their good behavior and lets them go to lunch.

Social Cognitive Theory

"What are you doing?" Jason asked Kelly as he came around the corner and caught her in the act of swinging her arms back and forth.

"I was sort of practicing my batting swing," Kelly responded with a red face. "I was watching a game on TV last night, and the way those guys swing. It always looks so easy, but they hit it so hard. It just seems like I should be able to do that. It was running through my head, so I just had to try it."

Three-year-old Jimmy crawled up on his dad's lap with a book. "I read too, Dad," he said as his father put down his own book to help Jimmy up on his lap.

"Wait a minute," Mrs. Edwards said as she saw Joanne struggling with the microscope. "Let me show you once more. . . . Now, watch closely as I adjust the microscope. This is important because these slides crack easily and are expensive. The first thing I think about is getting the slide in place. Otherwise, I might not be able to find what I'm looking for in the microscope. Then I want to be sure I don't crack the slide while I lower the objective lens, so I watch from the side. Finally, I slowly raise the objective lens until I have the object in focus. You were trying to focus as you lowered it. It's easier and safer if you try to focus as you raise it. Now, go ahead. Try it again."

What do these events have in common? Although they are three distinct situations—a girl practicing her softball swing, a child wanting to be like his father, and a girl learning a laboratory technique—they all involve learning by observing the behavior of others.

Researchers have become interested in what happens as people learn by watching others and have found that the process is more complex than the simple imitation of others' behaviors. This line of inquiry, pioneered by Albert Bandura (1925–) and originally called *observational learning,* has evolved into what is known as *social cognitive theory* (Bandura, 1986).

Social cognitive theory *examines the processes involved as people learn from observing others and gradually acquire control over their own behavior.* Social cognitive theory has its historical roots in behaviorism but goes well beyond it. Let's look at some differences between the two.

Differences Between Behaviorism and Social Cognitive Theory

Social cognitive theory differs from behaviorism in at least three ways: (a) the way learning is defined, (b) the way interactions among behavior, the environment, and personal factors are described, and (c) the way reinforcement and punishment are viewed. Let's look at them.

Definitions of Learning

You saw in our section on behaviorism that learning was defined as a relatively enduring change in behavior that occurred as a result of experience. For social cognitive theorists, this exclusive focus on behavior is too limited. They instead view **learning** *as an internal mental process that may or may not be reflected in immediate behavioral change* (Bandura, 1986). Social cognitive theory considers, in addition to behavior and the environment, the storing of information in learners' memories as well as personal factors, such as beliefs and expectations. Kelly, for example, didn't try to imitate the baseball swing until the next day; her observations of the players on television had to be stored in her memory. Also, her comment, "It just seems like I should be able to do that," suggests a belief about her ability, and this belief influenced her behavior.

Interactions Among Behavior, the Environment, and Personal Factors

Second, whereas behaviorism focuses exclusively on the influence of the environment on behavior, social cognitive theory suggests that behavior, the environment, and personal factors all influence each other. For instance, Tim's low score on his algebra test (an environmental factor) influenced his belief (a personal factor) about his ability to do algebra. His belief, in turn, influenced his behavior—he adapted his study habits—and his behavior influenced the environment—he went to Susan's home to study. Social cognitive theorists call these mutual influences *reciprocal causation.*

Views of Reinforcement and Punishment

Third, behaviorists and social cognitive theorists describe the influence of reinforcement and punishment differently. For behaviorists, they're direct causes of behavior; in contrast, for social cognitive theorists, they cause people to form *expectations* about consequences that are likely to result from various behaviors. For example, if you study hard and do well on a test, you expect to do well on a second test with a similar amount of study. If you see someone being reinforced for a certain behavior, you expect to be reinforced for a similar behavior.

The fact that people form expectations about consequences means they're aware of the behaviors that will be reinforced. This mechanism is important because, according to social cognitive theory, reinforcement only changes behavior when learners know what behaviors are being reinforced (Bandura, 1986). Tim believed that his changed study habits were the cause of his improved scores, so he maintained those habits. If he had believed that some other strategy was more effective, he would have changed his behavior accordingly.

These factors have two implications for teachers. First, they suggest that teachers should specify what behaviors will be reinforced so that students can adapt their behavior accordingly; second, learners need feedback so that they know what behaviors have resulted in desired consequences. For instance, if a student gets full credit on an essay item on a test but doesn't know why full credit was given, she may not know how to respond correctly the next time.

6.26 ▄▄

Greg concludes, "I seem to have a feel for French," as he begins his homework. His teacher often compliments him on the high quality of his written work, and his effort has continually increased. Explain these incidents; use reciprocal causation as a basis for your explanation.

6.27 ▄▄

Look again at the incident with Greg in Note 6.26. Behaviorists would describe Greg's increased effort as the result of being positively reinforced by the teacher's compliments. How would social cognitive theorists explain Greg's increased effort?

6.28
A student knowingly breaks a classroom rule, but the teacher doesn't notice. Regarding the rule, what is the student likely to do in the future? Explain on the basis of the information in this section.

6.29
Consider the statement "Modeling doesn't work unless the observer sees the model being reinforced." Is that a true or a false statement? Explain.

6.30
A teacher shows her students Dr. Martin Luther King Jr.'s famous "I Have a Dream" speech. What form of modeling is illustrated in the speech?

Social cognitive theory also helps us explain behavior when expectations aren't met. For example, suppose your instructor gives you a homework assignment, you work hard on it, but she doesn't collect it. The non-occurrence of the expected reinforcer (credit for the assignment) can act as a punisher. You will probably be less likely to work hard for the next assignment. Just as the non-occurrence of an expected reinforcer can act as a punisher, the non-occurrence of an expected punisher can act as a reinforcer (Bandura, 1986).

Modeling

Central to social cognitive theory is the idea that people learn through interacting with and observing each other. The primary mechanism in this process is modeling. **Modeling** *refers to changes in people that result from observing the actions of others.* For example, consider Tim's situation again. He observed that Susan was successful in her approach to studying for exams. As a result, he imitated her behavior; imitation is one form of modeling.

The importance of modeling in everyday lives is difficult to overstate. Modeling helps explain the powerful influence of culture on student learning described in Chapter 4. Young fathers and mothers are urged to use correct grammar and pronunciation in talking to their infants, rather than gurgle back at them. Studies of disadvantaged youth indicate that a lack of appropriate adult role models is an important factor in how they handle the problems they encounter.

In addition to direct modeling, as illustrated by Tim's imitation of Susan's behavior or children imitating their parents, at least two other forms of modeling exist (Bandura, 1986). These are outlined in Table 6.3. Common to each form of modeling is the fact that people learn by observing the actions of others.

Cognitive Modeling

An important application of modeling that is increasingly emphasized in instruction is called cognitive modeling. **Cognitive modeling** *involves modeled demonstrations,*

Students are able to learn a wide range of complex behaviors through modeling.

Table 6.3

Different forms of modeling

Type	Description	Example
Direct modeling	Simply attempting to imitate the model's behavior	Tim imitates Susan in studying for exams. A first grader forms letters in the same way a teacher forms them.
Symbolic modeling	Imitating behaviors displayed by characters in books, plays, movies, or television	Teenagers begin to dress like characters on a popular television show oriented toward teens.
Synthesized modeling	Developing behaviors by combining portions of observed acts	A child uses a chair to get up and open the cupboard door after seeing her brother use a chair to get a book from a shelf and seeing her mother open the cupboard door.

together with verbal descriptions of the model's thoughts and actions (Pintrich & Schunk, 1996). Think back, for example, to Mrs. Edwards showing Joanne how to use the microscope. As she demonstrated the procedure, she also described her thinking, " . . . The first thing I think about is getting the slide in place. Otherwise, I might not be able to find what I'm looking for in the microscope. Then I want to be sure I don't crack the slide while I lower the objective lens, so I watch from the side." Cognitive modeling provides access to the thinking of experts and thus allows the teacher to share the thought processes involved in analyzing and solving problems.

As another example, let's look at how a teacher models his thinking about cause-and-effect relationships.

> Have you noticed how the roses in the park bloomed early this year? I'm asking myself why. What factors caused these early blooms? I recall it was a warm winter. That was probably an important factor. But certainly there are other factors involved—probably some hidden ones—and I know it is important to search for them. In fact, now that I have stopped to think, I remember that we had very heavy rains in March. This may be a factor too. (Perkins, Jay, & Tishman, 1993, p. 80)

When teachers think aloud about the information their students are studying, they provide students with specific, concrete examples of how to process information and solve problems.

Vicarious Learning

Although merely observing the actions of other people can affect a learner, the effects are amplified if the learner also observes the consequences of those actions. This is called **vicarious learning**, *and it occurs when people observe the consequences of another person's behavior and adjust their own behavior accordingly*. For example, Tim saw how well Susan did on tests with her approach to studying, so he was *vicariously reinforced* through her success. When students hear a teacher say, "I really like the way Jimmy is working so quietly," they are also being vicariously reinforced.

If a student receives a verbal reprimand for leaving his seat without permission, however, other students are *vicariously punished* by observing the consequences of this action. Research demonstrates that vicarious reinforcement and punishment can have powerful effects on student behavior. Modeling and vicarious learning work together to affect behavior in several ways. Let's look at them.

6.31 ▬
Identify an example of cognitive modeling in our opening case study in which Tim and Susan were working together.

6.32 ▬
Explain how vicarious reinforcement and punishment can change a person's behavior; base your explanation on the concept of *expectations*.

Effects of Modeling on Behavior

Modeling can affect behavior in at least four ways: (a) learning new behaviors, (b) facilitating existing behaviors, (c) changing inhibitions, and (d) arousing emotions.

Learning New Behaviors

Through modeling, people can learn behaviors they didn't have prior to observing the model. Examples include watching a tennis instructor properly demonstrate a forehand, a student seeing—for the first time—an algebra teacher factor a trinomial, and teenagers dressing like popular peers.

Facilitating Existing Behaviors

Modeling can also strengthen existing behaviors. Tim already practiced solving problems prior to tests, but by his own admission, "I usually do one, maybe two, and if I'm okay on them, I quit." After observing Susan's behavior, he increased his efforts. Susan's behavior facilitated a behavior that Tim had already learned.

Another example includes behavior seen in concerts, plays, and other performances. After a speaker gives a particularly rousing finish to a speech, someone in the audience stands and begins to applaud. This is followed by others and results in a "standing ovation." Obviously, people already know how to stand and applaud. Their behavior is "facilitated" by the first person.

Vicarious learning occurs in classrooms when students observe the consequences of other students' actions.

Changing Inhibitions

An **inhibition** *is a self-imposed restriction on one's behavior,* and modeling can either strengthen or weaken the inhibition. Unlike facilitating an existing behavior, inhibitions involve socially unacceptable behaviors, such as breaking classroom rules (Pintrich & Schunk, 1996).

Pedestrians stopped at a red light are more likely to obey or disregard that red light if they see others doing the same, for example. On the one hand, if a teacher has a classroom rule requiring students to raise their hands before speaking, students are less likely to break the rule if they see one of their peers reprimanded for doing so. The inhibition against speaking without permission is strengthened. On the other hand, if a student speaks without permission and isn't reprimanded, other students are more likely to do the same. The inhibition is weakened.

Arousing Emotions

Finally, a person's emotional level can be changed by observing a model's expressed emotions. For example, observing the uneasiness of a diver on a high board may cause an observer to become more fearful of the board as well. As another example, if you see a couple having a heated argument at a party, you find yourself feeling awkward and embarrassed. Notice here that the emotions modeled aren't necessarily the same ones aroused in others. You see anger modeled, but your emotions are more likely to be embarrassment or uneasiness.

On the positive side, the emotional arousal effect of modeling is a strong endorsement for teacher enthusiasm. Observing teachers genuinely enjoying themselves as they talk about a topic helps generate excitement in students.

From these examples, you can see that modeling can result in behavioral, cognitive, and even affective outcomes. Behavioral outcomes occur when behaviors are learned or facilitated; cognitive outcomes result from observing the consequences of others' actions, such as the example in which a student broke a classroom rule, and affective outcomes are the result of modeling emotions.

Learning From Models: The Processes Involved

In the previous section, we described some effects of modeling: learning and facilitating behaviors, changing inhibitions, and arousing emotions. How do these effects occur, and what mechanisms are involved?

Learning from models involves four processes, which are illustrated in Figure 6.5 (Bandura, 1986): attention, retention, reproduction, and motivation.

Attention

Learning begins when the observer attends to the behavior of the model. Merely attracting the learner's attention isn't enough to make learning effective, however. The learner's attention must be drawn to the critical aspects of the modeled behavior (Bandura, 1986). For example, when Tim worked with Susan, he was able to directly observe her study strategies, and he identified the important aspects of her behavior that he intended to imitate. As another example, if an English teacher is trying to teach students to write clear expository paragraphs, merely sharing well-written paragraphs probably won't be enough; the teacher will have to direct students' attention to specific elements that made the paragraphs well written.

6.33 ▬
A second-grade teacher and several members of the class see Shelley throw a pencil at Kim. The teacher can't decide whether to reprimand Shelley publicly or privately. What would social cognitive theory suggest? Identify at least two other factors the teacher should consider in making the decision.

6.34 ▬
Research indicates that teachers who model persistence in problem-solving tasks have students who persist longer than teachers who do not model these behaviors (Zimmerman & Blotner, 1979). Which modeling effect is best illustrated in this research finding? Explain.

Figure 6.5

Processes involved in learning from models

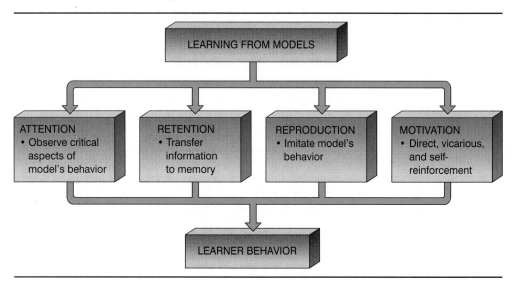

Retention

6.35 ▬
Using the information in this section, explain why the label "social *cognitive* theory" is appropriate.

Once students have attended to the critical aspects of the modeled behavior, it must be transferred to memory before it can be reproduced. This transfer involves mentally verbalizing the steps or visually representing the processes in some way. (We discuss the processes involved in transferring information to memory in Chapter 7.)

Reproduction

Ideally, learners are now ready to reproduce modeled behaviors on their own. The information in memory should now guide the learners' performance. In classrooms, however, this often doesn't happen. Although teachers have modeled the desired behaviors, students often can't reproduce them. To help these students, teachers often walk them through the process, providing feedback along the way. To illustrate, let's look at a teacher who has modeled the procedure for solving simultaneous algebraic equations but whose students are having difficulty solving them on their own.

> "Let's look up here," Sally Hernandez commented after seeing that her students were struggling with the assigned problems. "I see you're still having a little difficulty, so let's look at another example.
> "Try this one," she said, writing on the chalkboard:

$$4a + 6b = 24$$
$$5a - 6b = 3$$

6.36 ▬
As Sally questions, she first asks the question, pauses briefly, and then calls on a student. By pausing in this way, Sally is implementing what concept from behaviorism that was discussed earlier in the chapter?

> "What's one way of solving this problem? . . . Alfino?"
> " . . . By addition."
> Sally nodded. "How do we know that will work?"
> "There's a 6*b* in the first equation and a negative 6*b* in the second equation," Kim volunteered.

"Yes. Good, Kim. That's the key that determines whether you can use addition. Let's go on. What do we do first? . . . Lakesha?"

". . . We add the two equations together."

"And we get? . . . Hue?"

". . . Nine *a* plus zero *b* equals 27."

"Okay," Sally smiled. "And what is the value of *a*? . . . Chris?"

". . . Three."

"Good! That's right. Now let's look for the value of *b*. What should we do first? . . . Mitchell?"

Through questions and feedback, Sally helped her students put into action previously modeled behaviors. The value of Sally's interactive guidance has been confirmed by classroom research (Rosenshine, 1983). Not all students pay close attention when teachers teach, and the connections between the modeled behaviors and their representations in learners' memories often aren't ideal. As a result, the retention phase provides a shaky foundation for subsequent action. Sally helped overcome those problems by guiding students' initial reproductions as a group process. This tactic allowed her to provide immediate feedback in the case of incorrect answers, and cues when students were unable to answer. Sally's strategy is sometimes described as *controlled practice* (J. Murphy et al., 1986).

Motivation

The motivation component of learning from models illustrates an important difference in the way social cognitive theorists and behaviorists view reinforcement. Behaviorists suggest that reinforcers are direct causes of behavior; in contrast, social cognitive theorists describe both direct and vicarious reinforcers as sources of motivation.

According to social cognitive theorists, people will imitate others' behaviors if it is reinforcing to do so. If Sally's students are able to solve sets of equations, for example, they will be reinforced with high test scores and good grades, and Tim's improved test scores reinforced him for reproducing Susan's behavior.

Vicarious learning operates as well. When a teacher praises Timmy, one of her first graders, for working quietly, the other students are likely to imitate Timmy's diligent behavior because they are vicariously reinforced; the reinforcer increases their motivation. Likewise, when an English teacher recognizes a student for bringing in a review of a new biography of Ernest Hemingway, the class is vicariously reinforced, and similar behaviors are more likely to occur in the future.

Finally, as learners see themselves making genuine progress as a result of imitating a model's behavior, they may experience forms of self-reinforcement. In many ways, this feeling of accomplishment is the most motivating reinforcer of all.

6.37
Social cognitive theorists suggest that reinforcement motivates learners. How does behaviorism view reinforcement?

Effectiveness of Models

As you might expect, not all models are equally effective, and learners are more affected by some models than by others. A model's effectiveness depends on at least three factors: (a) perceived similarity, (b) perceived competence, and (c) perceived status.

6.38
One group of students watched teachers successfully solve math problems, a second group watched peers do the same, and a third group saw no models. Which group successfully solved the most math problems, and which group solved the fewest? Explain the results on the basis of the information in this section.

Perceived Similarity

Observers who perceive models to be similar to themselves are more effective than those who perceive models to be different (Schunk, 1987). In addition, several models are more effective than a single model or even a few; the likelihood of finding a model perceived to be similar to the observer increases as the number of models increases. Further, although students can learn academic skills from either gender, they are more likely to imitate behaviors from same-sex models, probably because of perceived similarity. This is one reason it is important to present a balanced curriculum that accurately portrays the contributions of women and minorities, and it highlights the importance of nontraditional career models (e.g., female engineers) in helping students develop nonsexist views of possible occupations.

Perceived Competence

Perception of a model's competence interacts with perceptions of similarity to influence a model's effectiveness. Students are more likely to imitate those perceived as competent models than those perceived as less competent, regardless of similarity. In Tim's case, although Susan was his classmate, had she not been a successful student, it is unlikely he would have imitated her behaviors.

Perceived Status

Individuals acquire high social status by distinguishing themselves from others in their fields, and people tend to imitate these individuals more often than others. Professional athletes, popular rock stars, and world leaders are all high-status models. At the local level, high school athletes, cheerleaders, and in some cases even gang leaders may have high status for other students.

Teachers are also influential models. Despite concerns expressed by educational reformers and teachers themselves, they remain and will continue as powerful influences on students.

Status has an additional effect. High-status models often get tacit credit for competence outside their own areas of expertise. This is the reason you see professional basketball players (instead of nutritionists) endorsing breakfast cereal, and actors (instead of petroleum engineers) endorsing motor oil.

Self-Regulation

Earlier, you saw that social cognitive theory emphasizes the importance of the learner influencing both behavior and the environment. Through the process of self-regulation, students attain increasing control over their thoughts and actions. **Self-regulation** *is the process of students using their own thoughts and actions to reach academic learning goals.* Self-regulated learners identify goals and adopt and maintain their own strategies for reaching the goals.

To illustrate the process of self-regulation, let's look at Tim's case once more. He chose to go to Susan's home to study. He didn't go because he had been reinforced for doing so in the past, and he wasn't immediately reinforced when he did go. Not until after he had developed a pattern of changed study strategies, which he monitored himself, was he reinforced with higher test scores.

Self-regulation is critical to understanding social cognitive theory because much of human behavior occurs without immediate reinforcement; the consequences exist too far in the future to affect behavior in the present (Bandura, 1986). Without self-regulation, people wouldn't maintain the behavior until it could be reinforced.

Self-regulation has four aspects: goal setting, self-observation, self-assessment, and self-reinforcement. Let's look at each in turn.

6.39 ▬
Susan and Karen, Tim's classmates, were both successful, but Tim chose to imitate Susan's rather than Karen's behavior. Why might this have been the case?

6.40 ▬
Consider the effect of a model's status on the behavior of observers. Does this effect illustrate the concept of *reinforcement potency*? Explain why or why not.

A teacher can help students develop self-regulation by providing them with complex learning activities that require goal setting and monitoring of learning progress.

Goal Setting

Goal setting is a critical component of self-regulation. Goals not only establish purposes for a person's action but also provide ways of measuring progress. Susan, in our opening case study, set the goal of working at least three of each type of problem, and Tim imitated her behavior by setting goals of his own.

Also, challenging but realistic goals and goals set by students themselves are often more effective than those imposed by the teacher (Schunk, 1994; Spaulding, 1992). An important role for teachers is to help students learn how to set appropriate goals. (We examine goal setting again in Chapter 9 when we consider the relationship between goals and learner motivation.)

6.41
Think about your work in this class. Identify at least two goals that you could use to increase your learning.

Self-Observation

Once goals have been set, self-regulated learners monitor themselves to determine the progress they're making. Susan, for example, pointed out, "I sometimes even make a little chart. I try to do at least three problems of each type we study, and then I check them off as I do them." Self-observation allowed Susan to monitor her own progress.

Students can be taught to monitor a variety of behaviors. For example, they can keep a chart and make a check every time they catch themselves "drifting off" during an hour of study, the number of times they go off-task during seatwork, the number of times they blurt out answers in class, or on the positive side, the number of times they use a desired social skill (Jenson et al., 1988).

Self-observation combined with appropriate goals can change student behavior, sometimes dramatically (Mace, Belfiore, & Shea, 1989; Mace & Kratochwill, 1988). With effort and teacher monitoring, study habits and concentration can be improved and social interactions can be made more positive and supportive.

6.42
Think about one of the goals you identified in Note 6.41. Now describe a simple form of self-observation that you could use to monitor your progress toward the goal.

Self-Assessment

Schools historically have been places where a person's performance is judged by someone else. Although teachers provide valuable feedback in assessing student performance, they don't have to be the sole judges; students can learn to assess their own work (Stiggins, 1994). For example, students can assess the quality of their solutions to word problems by learning to ask themselves whether their answers make sense and to compare their answers with estimates. Tim was involved in a form of self-assessment when he checked his answers against those given at the back of the book.

Developing self-assessment skills takes time, and students won't automatically be good at it. The best way to help students develop these skills is to be sure their goals are specific and quantitative, as Susan's and Tim's were. Helping students make valid self-assessments based on accurate self-observations is one of the most important instructional tasks teachers face.

6.43 ▬

Again consider one of the goals you identified in Note 6.41. Describe a form of self-assessment that you could use to measure your success in reaching the goal.

Self-Reinforcement

We all feel good when we accomplish a goal, and we often feel regretful or even guilty when we don't, vowing to do better in the future (Bandura, 1989). As learners become self-regulated, they learn to reinforce and punish themselves for meeting or failing to meet their goals.

Self-reinforcers and self-punishers can be a person's feelings, or they can be something more tangible, such as Susan's, "If I get all of them right, I treat myself with a bowl of ice cream." A powerful form of self-reinforcement is the feeling of accomplishment that can result from setting and meeting challenging goals.

Self-reinforcement is controversial. Some researchers argue that it is unnecessary, that goals, self-observation, and self-assessment are sufficient in themselves (S. Hayes et al., 1985). Others argue that self-reinforcement can be a powerful strategy, particularly for low achievers. In one study, low achievers were taught to award themselves points, which they could use to buy privileges, when they did well on their assignments. Within a few weeks, the low achievers were achieving as well as their classmates (Stevenson & Fantuzzo, 1986). Bandura (1986) argues that rewarding oneself for good work can lead to higher performance than goals and self-monitoring alone.

Classroom Connections

Applying Social Cognitive Theory in Your Classroom

1. Act as a role model for your students.
   - A school committee charged with improving the quality of instruction in their school developed the following guidelines to encourage teachers to be good role models.

   a. Treat students with respect and courtesy. Avoid criticism and any form of sarcasm.
   b. Require that students respect you and each other. Enforce this rule consistently.
   c. Communicate your interest in reading and studying.
   d. Approach the topics you teach with enthusiasm, energy, and effort.

2. As you model the skills you teach, verbally describe your thinking.
   - A kindergarten teacher helping students form letters says, "I start with my pencil here and make a straight line down," as she begins to form a *b*.
   - A physics teacher solving acceleration problems involving friction writes $F = ma$ on the chalkboard and says, "First, I think about finding the net force on the object. Let's see what the problem tells me."

3. As students are beginning to reproduce skills, provide group practice by "walking" them through examples before having them practice on their own.
   - A sixth-grade teacher has his class adding fractions with unlike denominators. He displays the problem $\frac{1}{4} + \frac{2}{3} = ?$ and then begins, "What do we need to do first? . . . Karen?" He continues until the class finds the answer and then does a second example in the same way.

4. Use vicarious reinforcement to increase the effectiveness of modeling.
   - As one reading group moves back to their desks, a first-grade teacher comments loud enough for the class to hear, "I like the way this group is returning to their desks. Karen, Vicki, Ali, and David each get a star because they have gone so quickly and quietly."
   - An American history teacher hands back an exam. She then displays an answer to an essay question on the overhead projector and comments, "Look at this answer, everyone. It's an excellent answer. Let's see why. . . . "

   The history teacher accomplished three things in this example. First, the student whose answer was displayed was directly reinforced, but he wasn't "put on the spot" because the teacher didn't identify him. Second, the class was vicariously reinforced. Third, the teacher gave the class feedback and provided a model response for future imitation.

5. Promote self-regulation in your students.
   - A geography teacher helps her students set individual goals for studying the content of each unit.
   - A fifth-grade teacher has students design a checklist for monitoring desired social skills in cooperative learning groups. They mark the checklist whenever they use one of the skills.

Dealing With Diversity: Behaviorism and Social Cognitive Theory

As Carlos entered his second-grade classroom early Tuesday morning, he heard salsa music in the background. Donna Evans sometimes played it as she prepared her classroom for the day. The walls were decorated with colorful prints from Mexico and Central America, and vocabulary cards in both Spanish and English were hung near the blinds, chalkboard, clock, file cabinet, and other areas in the room.

"Buenos días, Carlos. How are you today?" Donna asked. "You're here very early."

"Buenos días. I'm fine," Carlos responded, smiling as he went to his desk to take out his homework from the night before.

Donna watched Carlos for a few moments as he worked in the empty room. Then she walked over to him, put her hand on his shoulder, and asked, "What are we working on today, Carlos? . . . Math?"

"I can't do it! I do not understand," Carlos replied in his halting English, frustration in his voice.

As Donna looked over his shoulder at the 12 problems she had assigned for homework, she noticed that he had done the first 2 correctly but then had forgotten to borrow on the next 3 and had left the last 5 undone.

"Carlos, look," she said, kneeling down so that she was at eye level with him. "You did the first two just fine. Then you forgot an important step. Look here. . . . How is this problem different from this one?" she asked, pointing to the two following problems.

$$
\begin{array}{cc}
36 & 45 \\
-14 & -19 \\
\hline
\end{array}
$$

" . . . The numbers are different."

"Okay," she smiled. "What else?"

"This number is bigger," he said, comparing the 45 with the 36.

"How about the 9 and the 5? . . . Which is bigger?"

"The 9."

"Good, and how about the 6 and the 4?"

"The 6."

"And where is the bigger one in each case?"

"Up there," Carlos said, pointing to the first problem, "and down there," pointing to the second.

"Very good, Carlos. This is very important," she continued. "Now, let's work this one together. . . . Watch what I do."

Donna solved the next two problems, carefully describing her thinking and what she was doing as she went along and comparing problems that require regrouping to those that don't.

"Now, try the next three," she said, "and I'll be back in a few minutes to see how you're doing. Remember what Juanita's father said about becoming a scientist when he came and visited our class. You have to study very hard and do your math. I know you can do it, especially because you already did it on the first two. . . . Now, go ahead."

Carlos nodded and then bent over his work and was finishing the last of the three problems as the other students were coming into the classroom. Donna went to him, checked his work, and commented, "Very good, Carlos. You got two of them right. Now, check this one. You have just enough time before we start."

In another elementary school in the same city, Roberto shuffled into class and hid behind the big girl in front of him. If he was lucky, his teacher wouldn't discover that he hadn't done his homework—12 problems! How could he ever do that many? Besides, he wasn't good at math.

Roberto hated school. He was very uncomfortable. It seemed so strange and foreign. His teacher would sometimes frown when he spoke, because his English wasn't as good as most of the other students'. Sometimes when the teacher talked, he couldn't understand what she was saying.

Even lunch wasn't much fun. If his friend Raul wasn't there, he would eat alone. One time when he sat with some other students, they started laughing at the way he talked, and they asked what he was eating when he had tortillas for lunch. He couldn't wait to go home.

As you saw in Chapter 4, students from different cultures sometimes feel that they aren't welcome and don't belong in some classes. Schools seem strange and cold, and classrooms are threatening. School tasks are difficult, and failure is common. Behaviorism and social cognitive theory can help teachers understand why schools aren't friendlier places for these students.

Classical Conditioning: Learning to Like and Dislike School

You learned earlier in the chapter that classically conditioned learning takes place when neutral stimuli become associated with stimuli that elicit unconditioned responses.

Although you may have heard about schools from your parents or siblings, schools are essentially neutral stimuli when you first enter them, and these early experiences often determine your emotional reactions to them.

When these experiences are positive, as they were for Carlos, people develop positive feelings about school and learning. We all respond instinctively to warmth and support, as Carlos did to Donna's manner. In time, school becomes associated with a teacher like Donna, and the school and class elicit positive emotions similar to those Donna elicited with her behavior. Had Donna been of Hispanic background, Carlos's experience might have been still more positive. However, teachers can create warm and supportive environments for all their students, regardless of ethnic origin.

Unfortunately, the opposite can also be true, as it was in Roberto's case. School was not associated with positive feelings for him, and he didn't feel wanted, safe, or comfortable.

6.44 ▬
Using the terms *unconditioned stimulus, unconditioned response, conditioned stimulus,* and *conditioned response,* explain how Donna Evans's room made Carlos feel good about being there.

Reinforcement: Motivating Hesitant Learners

When students learn new things, what kind of reinforcement matches their efforts? The answer to this question not only determines initial learning but also can affect lifelong views of competence.

Donna Evans was sensitive to this fact when she used behaviorism and social cognitive theory to help Carlos with his subtraction problems. She did this in several ways:

⏐ She reinforced Carlos for the problems he had done correctly.
⏐ She provided corrective information in her feedback to help him understand where he had made mistakes.
⏐ She reduced the task to three problems to ensure that the reinforcement schedule would be motivating.
⏐ She provided immediate feedback to ensure he was doing the problems correctly.
⏐ She used both direct and cognitive modeling to show him the correct procedures for solving the problems.
⏐ She helped Carlos increase his sense of accomplishment by encouraging him and by providing only enough assistance so that he could do the problems on his own.

Through the structure and support provided by behaviorism and social cognitive theory, teachers can minimize the risk of failure and maximize opportunities for success.

6.45 ▬
If Donna Evans checked and reinforced Carlos for every three problems that he completed, what schedule of reinforcement would she be using?

Roberto: A Study in Contrasts

Compare Carlos's experience with Roberto's. The classroom to Roberto was a strange and unfriendly place. No teacher greeted him, and nothing in the classroom invited him in and made him feel wanted. When faced with the same number of problems as Carlos, he viewed the task as impossible. Previous experiences with math had taught him that he wasn't "good" at it.

In Chapter 4, we examined the ways students from different backgrounds and cultures respond to schooling. In this chapter, behaviorism and social cognitive theory show how factors such as warmth, affection, positive reinforcement, and feedback can be used to help all students learn successfully.

Classroom Connections

Capitalizing on Diversity in Your Classroom

1. Make your classroom a warm and friendly place that welcomes all students.
   - A sixth-grade teacher invites students to bring in posters and pictures to decorate their room. On Friday afternoons during earned free time, she allows them to bring in music to play.
   - An inner-city high school social studies teacher displays on her bulletin board some pictures of historical figures who are minorities. When she begins the school year, she talks about these people and emphasizes that American history is the story of all people.

2. Provide instructional support to ensure high success rates.

- A junior high English teacher assigns a research paper at the beginning of the term. He breaks the assignment into parts, such as doing a literature search, making an outline, and writing a first draft before the final paper is finished. He meets with students each week to check their progress and give them feedback.

- A fifth-grade teacher uses student graders to provide immediate feedback on math assignments. Two students are chosen each week and are provided with answers for each day's assignment. After students have completed their work, they have it checked immediately; if their scores are below 80%, they see the teacher for help.

Windows on Classrooms

From reading the chapter's opening case study and the content of each section, you've seen how contiguity, classical and operant conditioning, modeling, vicarious learning, and self-regulation can be used to explain the behavior of students.

Let's look now at a case study describing a teacher working with his students. As you read the case study, analyze the teacher's effectiveness in applying the behavioral and social cognitive principles described in the chapter.

Warren Rose is a seventh-grade math teacher working on a unit on decimals and percents. He's beginning class on Thursday of the third week of the grading period.

"Here are your tests from last Thursday," Warren said as he handed the students their papers. "The ones you missed have a check by them. Your grades are at the top of your paper."

Warren paused briefly and then said, "Be sure you write your grade in your notebook."

He paused for a few minutes as the students looked over their tests.

He then said, "Okay. Pass the tests back in. Remember now, the next test is at the end of next week, so you need to work hard to be ready for it."

The students passed their test papers forward, and as he picked up the last one, he redirected their attention by saying, "All right, everyone, let's look up here at the problems on the chalkboard. . . . I realize that percents and decimals aren't your favorite topic, and I'm not wild about them either, but we have no choice, so we might as well buckle down and learn them.

"Let me show you a few more examples." He then displayed the following problem on the overhead: "You have gone to the mall, shopping for a jacket. You see one that looks great, originally priced for $84, marked 25% off. You recently got a check for $65 from the fast-food restaurant where you work. Can you afford the jacket?"

"Now," he continued. "The first thing I think about when I see a problem like this one is, 'What does the jacket cost now?' So, I have to figure out the price, and to do that I will take 25% of the $84. That means I first convert the 25% to a decimal. I know when I see 25% that the decimal is understood to be just to the right of the 5, so I move it two places to the left. Then I can take .25 times 84."

Warren demonstrated the process as he spoke, working the problem through to completion. He then had the students work one at their desks and discussed their solution. He then said, "Okay, do you all understand?"

Hearing no response, Warren then said, "Okay, for homework, do the odd problems on page 113. The answers are at the back of the book."

"Do we have to do all six of the word problems?" Robbie asked.

"Why not?" Warren answered after looking at the problems he had assigned.

"Aww, gee, Mr. Rose," Will put in, "they're always so hard."

"Yeah," Ginny added. "I can't do them."

"Do you know how long they take?" Mark added. "All I ever do is math homework."

Several other students chimed in, arguing that six word problems were too many.

"Wait, people, please," Warren held up his hands. "All right. You only have to do the first four word problems . . . but! . . . you have to promise not to complain if I give you homework over the weekend."

"Yeah!" the class shouted.

"No problem, Mr. Rose," Matt nodded. "You've got a deal."

"Sheesh, Friday," Helen commented to Jenny as they walked into Warren's room Friday morning. "I just blanked out last week. I get really nervous when he calls us up to the chalkboard and we have to work a problem with everybody staring at us. If he calls me up today, I'll die."

Warren had the students exchange their papers, score the homework, and pass their papers forward. He then turned to the day's work by saying, "Let's look at this problem on the chalkboard": "A bicycle selling for $145 was marked down 15%. What is the new selling price?"

"First. Let's estimate so that we can see whether our answer makes sense. About what should the new selling price be? . . . Helen?"

" . . . I . . . You . . . I'm not sure," Helen stammered.

"Callie, what do you think?"

" . . . I . . . think it would be about $120."

"Good thinking. Describe for everyone how you arrived at that."

" . . . I . . . Well, 10% of the cost would be $14.50, so 15% would be about another $7, which would be about $21, and $21 off would be a little over $120."

"Good," Warren nodded. "Now, let's go ahead and solve it. What do we do first? . . . David?"

"We make the 15% into a decimal."

"Good, David. Now, what next? . . . Leslie?"

"Take the .15 times the 145."

"Okay. Do that everybody. . . . What did you get? . . . Someone?"

"$200.17," Cris volunteered. "Whoops, that can't be right. . . . That's more than the bicycle cost to start with. . . . Wait, I've got it. . . . $21.75."

"Good," Warren smiled. "That's what we're trying to do. We are all going to make mistakes, but if we catch ourselves, we're making progress. Keep it up. You can do these problems. Now what do we do?" he continued.

"Subtract," Matt volunteered.

"All right, go ahead," Warren directed.

"$142.83," Molly answered.

"Now, think about that for a second. What was our estimate?"

"Oh . . . yeah, . . . I see . . . It's $123.25."

"What did you do the first time?" Warren queried.

"Had my decimal point in the wrong spot."

"Okay, good work. Now, let's look at another one," Warren responded, and then he displayed the following problem: "Christy has a job working at a novelty store, making $5.25 an hour. After 4 months on the job, her boss gave her an 8% raise. What does she make now?"

"Let's see who can solve this one. Go ahead, Helen."

" . . . I . . . I don't know," Helen said after looking at the problem briefly.

"Shannon?"

"Make a decimal out of the 8% and take it times the $5.25," Shannon responded.

"Good, Shannon. Let's do it, everybody." Warren then watched as the students solved the problem, and the class worked two more examples together. Then he said, "For home-work, do the problems on page 116, and look, only four word problems."

The class began the problems, and Warren circulated around the room as they worked. Seeing Kevin had the wrong answer on the second word problem, he commented, "Look at this one again, Kevin. I know you can figure it out. Try it again. I'll be around to check on you in a few minutes."

As he continued his monitoring, he saw that Helen was just staring at her paper. "How are you doing?" he smiled.

"I'm lost. I don't have a clue on this one," she shrugged in frustration, pointing at the second word problem.

"Here, let me show you," Warren said encouragingly. "I know that math is a little tough for you. Watch what I do."

Warren then solved the problem while Helen watched.

"There, you see. Not so bad. Now, you try the next one."

Warren again circulated among the students, making occasional comments and suggestions. "How're you coming?" he said as he walked by Kevin. "Very good, I see you figured it out. That's super.

"Let's look at the next one," he said to Helen, seeing that she had gotten the third one wrong. "First, remember that you have to change the percent to a decimal, and then the problem says that the value *increased* by 30%. You subtracted, and you didn't change the percent to a decimal. Here, let me show you." He then carefully solved the problem and left the solution with Helen.

Warren continued monitoring the students until there were 2 minutes left in the period. "All right, everyone, the bell is going to ring in 2 minutes. Get everything cleaned up around your desks and get ready to go."

Questions for Discussion and Analysis

Analyze Warren's teaching in the context of the information in this chapter. In conducting your analysis, you may want to consider the following questions. In each case, be specific and take information directly from the case study in conducting your analysis.

1. How well did Warren apply an understanding of classical conditioning in working with his students? Provide a specific example that illustrates classical conditioning.

2. Describe specifically how operant conditioning affected the behavior of both Warren and the students. What might Warren have done to change the effect?

3. Identify at least two examples in the case study where Warren (perhaps inadvertently) negatively reinforced student behaviors that detracted from the student's learning.

4. How well did Warren apply an understanding of reinforcement schedules in his teaching (and particularly in his testing)? Provide a specific explanation based on your understanding of reinforcement schedules and information taken from the case study.

5. Assess Warren's use of feedback and praise in the lesson. Describe specifically what he might have done to improve it. Be sure to refer directly to the case study in making your assessment.

6. How effectively did Warren provide cues to elicit behaviors that he could then reinforce?

7. Assess Warren's modeling in his lesson. Identify at least one positive and one negative example.

8. What could Warren have done to increase his students' self-regulation? Be specific in your response.

9. Identify any other ways in which Warren could have more effectively applied principles from behaviorism and social cognitive theory. Be specific in your suggestions.

 **Summary**

Contiguity and Classical Conditioning

Contiguity helps in explaining the learning of simple memorized information through the pairing of stimuli and responses. Classical conditioning occurs when a formerly neutral stimulus becomes associated with a naturally occurring (unconditioned) stimulus to produce a response similar to an instinctive or reflexive response. Classical conditioning helps teachers understand emotional reactions such as test anxiety and how students learn to be comfortable in school environments.

Operant Conditioning

Operant conditioning focuses on overt, voluntary responses that are influenced by consequences. Praise, high test scores, and good grades are consequences that increase behavior and are called reinforcers, whereas reprimands are consequences that decrease behavior and are called punishers. The schedule of reinforcers influences both the rate of initial learning and the persistence of the behavior.

Social Cognitive Theory

Social cognitive theory extends behaviorism and focuses on the influence that observing others has on behavior. It considers, in addition to behavior and the environment, learners' beliefs and expectations. Social cognitive theory suggests that reinforcement and punishment affect learners' motivation, rather than directly cause behavior.

Modeling lies at the core of social cognitive theory. Modeling can be direct (from live models), symbolic (from books, movies, and television), or synthesized (combining the acts of different models). It can cause new behaviors, facilitate existing behaviors, change inhibitions, and arouse emotions. In learning from models, observers go through the processes of attention (observation), retention in memory, reproduction of the observed behavior, and motivation to produce the behavior in the future.

Learners become self-regulated when they set learning goals on their own, monitor their progress toward the goals, and assess the effectiveness of their efforts.

 **Important Concepts**

classical conditioning (p. 198)

cognitive modeling (p. 216)

conditioned responses (p. 198)

conditioned stimuli (p. 198)

consequence (p. 201)

contiguity (p. 197)

continuous reinforcement (p. 209)

cues (p. 211)

discrimination (pp. 199, 206)

extinction (pp. 199, 211)

feedback (p. 206)

fixed-interval schedule (p. 209)

fixed-ratio schedule (p. 209)

generalization (pp. 199, 206)

inhibition (p. 219)

intermittent reinforcement (p. 209)

interval schedules (p. 209)

learning (pp. 196, 215)

modeling (p. 216)

negative reinforcement
  (NR) (p. 202)

neutral stimuli (p. 198)

positive reinforcement
  (PR) (p. 201)

potency (p. 210)

Premack Principle (p. 203)

presentation punishment
  (PP) (p. 204)

punishment (p. 204)

ratio schedules (p. 209)

reinforcement (p. 201)

removal punishment (RP)
  (p. 204)

response cost (p. 204)

responses (p. 197)

satiation (p. 210)

self-regulation (p. 222)

shaping (p. 208)

social cognitive theory
  (p. 214)

stimuli (p. 197)

unconditioned response
  (p. 198)

unconditioned stimulus
  (p. 198)

variable-interval schedule
  (p. 209)

variable-ratio schedule
  (p. 209)

vicarious learning (p. 217)

The Classroom

Learn

Chapter Outline

7

Cognitive
Processes

David Shelton is preparing a unit on the solar system for his ninth-grade earth science class. From his filing cabinet, he retrieved a color transparency showing the sun throwing off "globs" of gases into space. He assembled a large model of the solar system to illustrate the planets in their orbital planes and their relative distances from the sun. Finally, he prepared a large matrix, made from a roll of chart paper, that he taped to the back wall of the room.

David began his unit on Monday by saying, "We're getting ready to study the solar system for the next several days, so I've prepared some things to help us get started. Take a look at the chart I made," he said, pointing to the back of the room.

"This chart is going to help us learn about the solar system. . . . But first, we need information to fill in the chart. . . . So, I want you to work in your groups to gather the informa-tion. Think about it for a moment and decide which planet you want. If more than one group wants a planet, you'll have to negotiate to see which one gets their first choice."

The students turned to their groups, talked briefly, and quickly made their choices, compromising in a few cases.

David listed the groups' choices on the chalkboard and then directed the students to books, computer software, and other resources in the room. The students spent the rest of Monday's class gathering their information and putting it on the chart with marking pens.

At the beginning of Tuesday's class, David displayed and briefly discussed the color transparency showing the sun throwing off globs of gases into space. He also referred them to the model of the solar system he had assembled and suspended from the ceiling after school on Monday. He reminded the class that it might serve as a frame of reference for their study. The students then spent the rest of Tuesday's class continuing to put information into the chart.

On Wednesday, David began, "Let's review what we've found out so far. Then, I'm going to do a little demonstration, and I want you to think about how it relates to what you've been doing."

After completing his review, David tied a pair of athletic socks to a 3-foot piece of string, another pair to a 5-foot piece of string, and whirled the two around his head simultaneously to demonstrate that the planets revolve around the sun on the same plane and in the same direction.

After having the students make a number of observations about what they saw, he continued, "Now the task gets a bit more challenging. Each group should identify a piece of

	Mercury	Venus	Earth	Mars	Jupiter	Saturn	Uranus	Neptune	Pluto
Orbital plane									
Diameter									
Distance from sun									
Length of year									
Length of day									
Average surface temperature									
Gravity (compared to earth)									

information from the chart that might explain or provide evidence about how the solar system was formed. . . . Let me give you an example. . . . For instance, when we look at Pluto, we see that the plane of its orbit is different from the plane of all the other planets. What Tanya, Juan, and Randy, who are studying Pluto, must do is figure out why it's different," he said pointing to the orbital plane cell for Pluto on the chart, "and be able to explain to the rest of the class why you think that's the case. Use any of the information you have—the demonstration I just did, the transparency, the model we have hanging from the ceiling—and anything else.

"Let me give you one more example," he went on. "Here," referring to the diameter and gravity cells for Saturn. "Saturn is much bigger than Earth, but its gravity is about the same as Earth's. Now, why might that be the case? . . . Karen, Jack, and Karl will have to explain that to the rest of us. . . . Okay, see what I mean? . . . If you get totally stuck, let me know, and I'll come around and help you. Any questions? . . . Go ahead."

The room was again quickly filled with the buzz of voices as the students prepared for the discussion to follow. As they worked, David moved from group to group, offering periodic comments, suggestions, and compliments to groups that were working hard.

"Pluto wasn't part of the solar system to begin with," Juan commented to Randy and Tanya as they started their work.

"What do you mean?" Randy responded.

"I was watching *Nova* with my mom, and the narrator said that scientists think Pluto was floating around and the sun kinda grabbed it. . . . See, when Mr. Shelton did that thing with the socks, the socks stayed sorta level," he continued, moving his hand back and forth to demonstrate a flat plane.

"What's that got to do with it?" Randy asked, still confused.

"Oh, I get it! Pluto isn't level with the rest of them," Tanya interrupted.

"Gee, I didn't even notice that," lamented Randy.

"Yeah, and look there," Tanya added, pointing to the chart. "See how little Pluto is? It's the littlest one, so it would be sorta easy to capture."

"And it's the last one," Randy added, beginning to warm to the task. "I better write some of this stuff down, or I'll never remember it."

David listened as the students in this group talked, and then he suggested, "I think you're doing a super job, but you might be forgetting something. Take another look at the transparency and see how it relates to what you're talking about. . . . Look at how the globs are coming off the sun, and look at the title of the transparency."

The students studied the transparency for a moment, and Juan finally said, "Look, all those globs are even too, you know, level, like the socks. . . . And it says, 'One Theory of the Formation of the Solar System.' So, that's how the planets were made."

"Now, what was that again about Pluto being the littlest?" Randy

wondered. "What's that got to do with anything?"

"If it was really big and floating around out there, the sun's gravity might not be strong enough to grab it," Juan offered.

"But it's easier to grab if it's little," Tanya added.

The students continued their work for a few more minutes, and then David called the class together. "Now, let's see what we've got. Are you all ready? . . . Which group wants to go first? . . . "

"We will," Tanya offered after several seconds.

"Go ahead."

"We can explain why Pluto isn't on the same plane with the other planets," she continued, pleased with her group's accomplishments. "It wasn't part of the solar system when it was first made."

"Now, the rest of you should be asking for what . . . what else do you need to know?" David probed.

" . . . "

"You should be asking for evidence," David continued after hearing no response. "Each group needs to provide evidence that makes sense to the rest of us. . . . Go ahead, Tanya or Juan or Randy."

Juan and Randy motioned for Tanya to continue. "It's the littlest one, and it's way out there," motioning to the end of the model.

"Does that support or contradict what the group said?" David queried.

"Supports," Lori volunteered.

"How?" David nodded, gesturing for her to continue.

"If it were captured from somewhere else, it makes sense that it would be the last one."

"Wait, Mr. Shelton, you're going too fast. I'm getting lost. What is this about supporting the theory?" Alfredo asked.

"That's a good question, Alfredo. Let's think about that one, everyone. What do you think?"

" . . . If the rest of the solar system were already in place, and if Pluto came by and was snagged by the sun's gravity, then it would be the farthest one out," Dena offered.

"I see that, but what if Pluto was snagged first? Then how could it be the farthest out?" Alfredo continued.

" . . . Yes, but we found out that the planets weren't snagged; they spun off as molten stuff . . . globs, so Pluto, if it was caught by the sun, would be the last one," Dena returned.

"What do you think, Alfredo?" David gestured.

" . . . Yeh, I see what she means. . . . I guess it makes sense."

"And, it isn't in line with the others," Juan added, motioning with his hand to indicate that its orbital plane was different from the others, "And its path is funny too. Sometimes it's actually inside Neptune's."

"And what did we call the paths?" David probed.

"Orbits," several of the students responded in unison.

"Excellent, everyone. See how this relates to what Dena said a minute ago? When I think of location and orbit, the first thing that pops in my mind is 'origin.' I relate the location and orbit to their origins," David continued, thinking aloud for the students.

David continued with the process of having groups present their information and explanations until he saw that the period was nearing an end. He then said, "Okay, everyone. We'll continue tomorrow. You've done an excellent job of gathering and relating items of informa-tion about the solar system. Now, to check on us, I have a short assign-ment. For tonight's homework, I want you to write a paragraph summarizing how Earth became a member of the solar system and compare that with how Pluto became a member. Use all the information we have and today's discussion to help you. This should take less than a page."

"Just a reminder in passing," he added as he pointed to the over-head. "This is just one theory of how the solar system was formed. There are others, but we're focusing on this one for now. Also remember," David emphasized, "the information must be in a paragraph. You cannot merely write down isolated sentences."

As the students began their summaries, David circulated around the room, answering questions and offering suggestions.

We began Chapter 6 by examining behavior and its emphasis on experience and observable behavior. We then turned to social cognitive theory and said that although it has behavioral roots, it marked a transition from behaviorism to more cognitively oriented learning theories. We continue our discussion of cognitive learning theories in this chapter and in Chapter 8, expanding our discussion of internal processes to include attention, per-ception, imagery, encoding, and retrieval, as well as strategies, such as elaboration and organization, that help make information meaningful.

We begin this chapter with a discussion of information processing, one of the most thoroughly studied cognitive learning theories. From there, we examine the process peo-ple use in finding meaning in the topics they study, and we complete the chapter with a discussion of constructivism, a view of learning receiving increasing emphasis in both psy-chology and education.

After you've completed your study of this chapter, you should be able to meet the following objectives:

- Understand the components of information processing, including sensory mem-ory, working memory, and long-term memory.
- Explain the role of cognitive processes in learning.
- Explain how teachers can help students develop metacognitive abilities.

▌ Identify the essential elements of constructivist views of learning.
▌ Describe the implications that constructivism has for teaching.

Cognitive Views of Learning

As you saw in Chapter 6, behaviorists explain learning as a change in observable behavior that occurs as a result of experience. In contrast, **cognitive learning theories** *explain learning by focusing on changes in internal mental processes that people use in their efforts to make sense of the world.* These processes are used for tasks as simple as remembering a phone number and as complex as solving detailed mathematical problems. The influence of cognitive learning theories on education has increased steadily during the last 40 years (Brophy, 1992; Bruer, 1993; Resnick & Klopfer, 1989).

From a cognitive perspective, **learning** *is a change in a person's mental structures that provides the capacity to demonstrate changes in behavior.* These "mental structures" include knowledge, beliefs, skills, expectations, and other mechanisms "in the learner's head." The focus for cognitive theorists is on the potential for behavior, as well as observable behavior itself. In David Shelton's lesson, for example, Randy consciously thought about his need to take notes, and Tanya, Randy, and Juan all used *higher order reasoning* to help them relate the information from the chart, transparency, model, and demonstration. Cognitive learning theory stresses the importance of mental processes, such as reasoning, and focuses on what is happening in the learner. These processes allow learners to actively interpret and organize information, an underlying principle of all cognitive theories.

Cognitive psychology is an eclectic theoretical orientation. There isn't *one* cognitive theory of learning, but rather a cluster of cognitive theories. We begin by examining infor-

7.1 ▬
In our study of behaviorism, we didn't discuss any of these internal mental processes. Why not?

Models allow students to visualize abstract relationships that are often difficult to understand.

mation processing, one of the first and most influential of the cognitive views of learning. **Information processing** *is a cognitive theory that examines the way knowledge enters and is stored and retrieved from memory.* It has important implications for teaching.

Information Processing

Models: Aids to Understanding

Think back for a moment to courses you've taken during your schooling. Among others, you probably studied geography, perhaps chemistry, and now you're taking educational psychology. In geography, you examined the face and makeup of the earth, and in chemistry, you studied the structure of the atom. Because you can only directly experience a small portion of the earth, you doubtless made frequent use of maps and globes. The globe is a miniature representation of the earth, faithful in shape and proportion—a *model.* Likewise, in chemistry, you cannot directly observe the atom with all its individual parts, so scientists created a representation, such as the one in Figure 7.1, to help people visualize it. This is also a model, but different from the globe. Rather than a miniature representation of the atom, this **model** *is a representation that helps people describe and visualize what is impossible to observe directly.*

People encounter a similar situation when they try to visualize what occurs during information processing. They cannot directly observe the structures and mechanisms that operate when they process information, so they create a model to help them represent this process. The model in Figure 7.2 contains a current view of how cognitive psychologists think the mind processes information (E. Gagne, Yekovich, & Yekovich, 1993; Leahey & Harris, 1993).

The model has three major components:

1. Information stores
2. Cognitive processes
3. Metacognition

The first component is **information stores**, *which are repositories for data, used to hold information.* They are analogous to filing cabinets, address books, or computer disks where people store information. The information stores in the information-processing model are *sensory memory, working memory,* and *long-term memory.*

The second component consists of **cognitive processes**, *which are internal, intellectual actions that transfer information from one store to another.* We have already

7.2
There is an important difference between the model of the atom and the model of Earth. What is this difference? The information-processing model is more like which of the two? Explain.

7.3
In the model in Figure 7.2, fewer lines connect "attention" and "perception" than connect "sensory memory" and "attention." Why is this the case?

Figure 7.1

Model of an oxygen atom

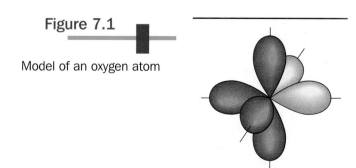

Figure 7.2

An information-processing model

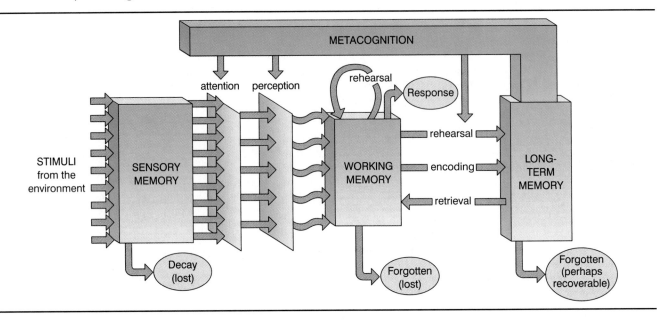

mentioned *attention* as one cognitive process. Others include *perception, rehearsal, encoding,* and *retrieval.* Cognitive processes are analogous to the programs that direct and transform information in computers.

The third component of the model is **metacognition,** *which consists of knowledge about and control of cognitive processes.* (In Chapter 2, you studied meta-attention and metamemory, which are two specific types of metacognition.) When Randy decided to take notes because he realized that note taking would help him pay attention better, he was demonstrating knowledge and control over his attention. Metacognition controls and coordinates the processes that move information from one store to another.

First, let's focus on the information stores. Then, to help you understand the model in operation, we discuss the processes that move information from one store to another. Finally, we analyze the metacognitive abilities that regulate those processes.

Sensory Memory

People are constantly bombarded with stimuli from their environment. The sound of a lawn mower, the acrid smell of car exhaust, a teacher's voice, words on a book page, and other students shuffling in their seats are all stimuli. These stimuli are what people "process" when they learn and remember, and this processing begins with the senses.

Hold your finger in front of you and rapidly wiggle it. Do you notice a faint "shadow" that trails behind your finger as it moves? Or, suppose someone says, "That's an oxymoron," and you respond, "Ox see what?" as you repeat part of the word without any understanding. The "shadow" and the fact that you're able to repeat the word even though it's meaningless are both representations of stimuli that are retained in your sensory memory. **Sen-**

7.4

In this section, we said information in sensory memory is unprocessed. What does *unprocessed* mean? In which memory store does processing take place?

sory memory *is the information store that briefly holds stimuli from the environment until they can be attended to and further processed* (Neisser, 1967). The material in sensory memory is "unprocessed." It is held in sensory memory in the same form as it exists in the outside world (Leahey & Harris, 1993). Sensory memory is nearly unlimited in capacity, but if processing doesn't begin almost immediately, the memory trace quickly fades away (in about a second for vision and a second or 2 for hearing; J. Walker, 1996).

The existence of sensory memory is critical to further processing. In trying to read, for example, if the words at the beginning of a sentence were lost from your sensory memory before you got to the end, it would be impossible to get any meaning from the sentence. The same is true for spoken language. Sensory memory allows you to hold information long enough to transfer it to working memory, the next store. (We discuss this transfer in the chapter section "Cognitive Processes.")

Working Memory

Working memory *is the information store that retains information as the person consciously works with it.* It is where deliberate thinking takes place and is a "workbench" of memory that temporarily holds information as it is being used or worked on (Best, 1992). For example, consider students working on "comparison shopping" problems who are to determine whether 32 ounces of rice for $1.97 is a better buy than 48 ounces of rice at $2.79. These figures, the mental arithmetic, and the answers are all temporarily stored in working memory. After the computations are completed, a decision is made and some information is moved to long-term memory. The remaining details are "swept off the workbench and forgotten." Because these details are no longer useful, retaining them would clog people's memories with useless information.

Working memory has two important characteristics: (a) It screens information that comes into it, and (b) it is limited in capacity and duration; without rehearsal, it can hold about five to nine items for about 10 to 20 seconds in adults (E. Gagne et al., 1993).

Working Memory as a Screen

We said earlier that people are constantly bombarded by stimuli. Working memory screens and decides what to do with these stimuli. There are three choices:

1. Disregard the information (purge from memory).
2. Retain the information in working memory by repeating it over and over (rehearsal).
3. Transfer the information into long-term memory through rehearsal or by connecting it with information already there (encoding). (We discuss this transfer in the section on cognitive processes.)

To illustrate these choices, let's look again at Randy's experience. Tanya said that Pluto was the smallest planet and so it was easy to capture, and this information entered Randy's working memory. Later, however, he had to ask Tanya and Juan what Pluto being small had to do with anything. Because he had not rehearsed the information sufficiently and was unable to connect it to information already in long-term memory, it was lost; he had disregarded it. In contrast, Juan connected the information by linking Pluto's size to the sun's gravity and the orbit of the other planets; he encoded it into long-term memory.

Why was some of the information lost from Randy's working memory? Why don't people retain significant parts of the information they hear or read? The characteristics of working memory, which are summarized in Figure 7.3, help us answer these questions.

7.5

Research indicates that multiple questioning—asking a second question before a student has a chance to respond to the first one—detracts from learning. On the basis of what you know about sensory memory, explain why multiple questioning is ineffective.

7.6

Suppose the next day you remember some of the information from the comparison shopping problem, such as $1.97 for the rice. Was this information retained in your working memory, or had it been moved to long-term memory? How do you know? As you think about these questions, where is your thinking taking place?

7.7

In Figure 7.3 there is a rehearsal "loop" above "working memory" and a response arrow coming out of "working memory." What is each intended to help you understand?

Working memory is the "work-bench" where students think about and solve problems.

Limitations of Working Memory

Working memory's most salient characteristic is the fact that it is limited in capacity (G. Miller, 1956); it can hold only small amounts of information for limited periods of time. As a result, it is often a "processing bottleneck" (E. Gagne et al., 1993). Randy probably lost the relationship between size and origin because his working memory was "overloaded"; it never made it through the bottleneck.

As you saw in Chapter 2, the capacity of working memory is influenced by development. Three-year-olds, on average, can hold only about three items in working memory; the capacity increases to about five by age 7, and by the teenage years, learners acquire adult capacities, about seven bits of information (Bruer, 1993). These limitations of working memory can be partially overcome, however, through the processes of *chunking* and *automaticity*.

Increasing Processing Efficiency: Chunking.   **Chunking** *is the process of combining separate items into large, meaningful units* (G. Miller, 1956). To illustrate, try this simple exercise. Look at the following row of letters for 5 seconds.

A E E E G G I I I I L N N N N R R S S T T

Now, cover them up and try to write down all 21 letters (in any order). How did you do? Most people are unable to remember the list even though the letters are presented in

Figure 7.3

Characteristics of working memory

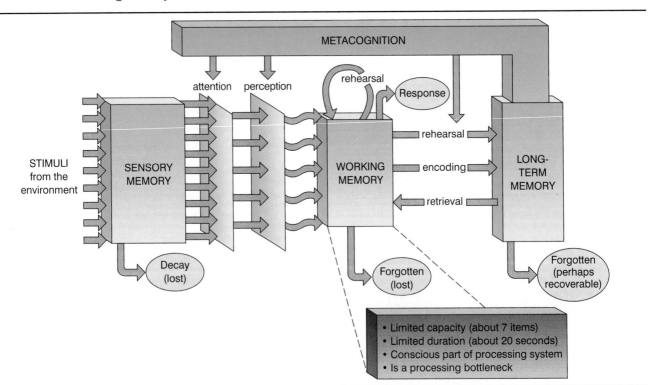

Table 7.1

Saving working memory space through chunking

Information "Unchunked"	Information "Chunked"
u, n, r	run
2492520	24 9 25 20
jump jumping hit hitting fight fighting run running	When adding a suffix, double the final consonant when the consonant is preceded by a vowel.
	Less dense materials float on more dense materials (if they don't mix).

Cooking
oil

Water

alphabetical order, all but two are repeated and grouped together, and you're told that there are 21 letters in all. The capacities of their working memories has been exceeded.

Now, look at the same letters presented as follows:

LEARNING IS INTERESTING

Here, you have no trouble remembering the letters because they have been "chunked" into three meaningful words (three units) and into a meaningful sentence (one unit).

Table 7.1 presents other examples of chunking. In each case, you can see that remembering the chunk requires less working memory space than the individual items of information because you remember the chunked information as a single unit.

Increasing Processing Efficiency: Automaticity.   A second way of increasing the efficiency of working memory is to make some of the mental processes involved in a task virtually automatic. **Automaticity** (sometimes described as "automatic processes") *refers to those mental operations that can be performed with little awareness or conscious effort* (Schneider & Shiffrin, 1977). Driving a car is a simple example. Once overlearned, people can drive and do other things, such as talk and listen, at the same time.

As automaticity develops, the time and effort to perform tasks is dramatically reduced (LaBerge & Samuels, 1974). For example, decoding words in reading, and grammar and punctuation in writing, must be largely automatic so that working memory space is left for comprehension and composition (Samuels, 1988). The same applies in math, where basic operations, such as addition and multiplication, ideally become automatic and thus allow working memory to be used for problem solving. When learners must consciously focus on basic operations, not enough working memory space remains to perform complex operations such as reading comprehension, writing, and problem solving.

7.8
Why would a health club prefer to advertise its telephone number as 2HEALTH rather than 243-2584?

7.9
Suppose two students are about equal in general ability but one is a better algebra student than the other. Using the information in this section, explain why the better algebra student would likely be more successful in physics than the other student.

As teachers interact with students, processes developed to the point of automaticity allow them to think on their feet while still maintaining the flow of the lesson and monitoring the classroom.

Limitations of Working Memory: Implications for Instruction.   One solution to the problem of working memory limitations is to practice basic skills to the point of automaticity. A second solution to overcoming this bottleneck is to use teaching aids that present information both orally and in printed form (Mousavi, Low, & Sweller, 1995), together with high levels of interaction in learning activities. In combining the model and chart with his verbal presentation, David Shelton helped both visual and verbal learners overcome the limitations of working memory. Also, his questioning gave him immediate feedback on whether his students' working memories were overloaded. Had they been, he would have known immediately because the students would have been unable to answer his questions correctly.

The opposite is true in a teacher lecture, in which the pace and amount of information can easily exceed learners' working memory capacities. When this happens, students grasp what they can, take notes so that they can rehearse the information later, or out of frustration, tune out altogether.

The limitations of working memory also have implications for teachers as they teach. They must monitor students' attention, respond to students as individuals, ask questions, make decisions about what to cover next, and guide student groupwork, sometimes all simultaneously. Unless several aspects of the teaching process, such as knowledge of content and the ability to form questions, are automatic, teachers' working memories can also quickly become overloaded. This prospect might help in explaining why teachers commonly revert to lectures. Lecturing is simpler than questioning and guiding student learning, so it is less likely to overload teachers' working memories.

7.10
Figure 7.3 identifies working memory as a "processing bottleneck." What does this phrase mean? What can teachers do about this bottleneck?

Long-Term Memory

Long-term memory *is the permanent information store.* In a sense, it's like a library with millions of entries and a network that allows them to be retrieved for reference and use. It differs from working memory in both capacity and duration. Whereas working memory is limited to approximately seven chunks of information for a matter of seconds, long-term memory's capacity is vast (some argue nearly unlimited) and durable. Some experts suggest that information in it remains virtually forever (Ashcraft, 1989). These traits are evidenced, for example, in situations in which people report returning to a place from their youth and then some environmental cue triggers memory of a series of events they haven't remembered in years. Although they hadn't recalled the information in a very long time, it was still stored in their long-term memories.

Representing Knowledge in Long-Term Memory

Let's look now into this vast information repository. What is it like? Does it have different compartments? In what form is the information stored?

Declarative and Procedural Knowledge

One of the most widely accepted descriptions of the way knowledge is stored in long-term memory is based on the concepts of *declarative and procedural knowledge* (J. Anderson, 1990; E. Gagne et al., 1993; Leahey & Harris, 1993). **Declarative knowledge** *is knowledge of facts, definitions, generalizations, and rules,* whereas **procedural knowledge** *is knowledge of how to perform activities.* For example, a learner who says, "To add fractions, you must first have like denominators," knows the rule for adding fractions but might not be able to actually perform the operation. Being able to state the rule is a form of declarative knowledge, whereas being able to actually add the fractions involves procedural knowledge. Declarative knowledge can be determined directly from a person's comments, whereas procedural knowledge is inferred from the person's performance. Similarly, information about the planets in our opening case study is declarative knowledge; procedural knowledge was required to write the summary David assigned.

Representing Declarative Knowledge. Declarative knowledge is represented in a variety of forms. They are outlined below and described in Table 7.2. They include the following:

- Propositional networks
- Linear orderings
- Images
- Schemas (E. Gagne et al., 1993)

Propositional networks combine **propositions,** *the smallest bits of information a person can judge to be true or false,* such as "Pluto is a planet," into interrelated knowledge structures. Linear orderings organize information such as the alphabet or days of the month into stable and coherent patterns. In contrast with both propositional networks and linear orderings, visual images store the physical characteristics of information in memory in the form of mental pictures.

Combining Propositions, Images, and Linear Orderings: Schemas. Propositions, images, and linear orderings "represent information at the level of a single idea, image, or relation" (E. Gagne et al., 1993, p. 81). We know, however, that combining single bits of information into more general patterns is a more efficient way of processing information, and this leads us to the concept of *schemas.*

Theorists don't agree on a single definition, but most think of **schemas** (also called *schemata*) as *complex knowledge structures that represent one's understanding of*

7.11

Suppose that, in a class, you state, "When using adjectives in writing, the adjective always precedes the noun it describes." Does your statement represent declarative or procedural knowledge? Explain.

7.12

Suppose you have a thorough understanding of cognitive development, whereas one of your friends' understanding is much less thorough. In what two ways do your schemas differ? Explain.

Table 7.2

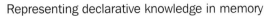

Representing declarative knowledge in memory

Type of Representation	Description	Example
Propositional Networks	Sets of interconnected items of declarative knowledge	Combining propositions such as "Pluto is a planet" and "It is the smallest," into a network
Linear Orderings	Ranking or ordering items of declarative knowledge according to some dimension	Representing the days of the week in order in memory
Images	Mental pictures	An image of a map of Canada and the United States representing the land area of each
Schemas	Combinations of propositions, images, and linear orderings	Randy's and Juan's schemas for parts of the solar system

events and objects. As a way of understanding schemas, look at Figure 7.4, which will help you in visualizing Randy's schema for the solar system.

This illustration, though it doesn't capture any imagery that Randy may have used, helps you see how his ideas were connected to each other. It suggests that he has linked Pluto and the solar system to the sun and that globs and the orbital plane are loosely linked to the sun as well. His understanding of the relationship between the sun, the globs, and the orbital plane is uncertain, however, as indicated by the dotted lines, and none of the information is linked to the origins of the solar system, as illustrated by the "origins" label sitting alone.

In contrast, examine Figure 7.5, which will help you in visualizing the way Juan related the ideas in the lesson. Juan understood how the origins of the solar system, the orbital plane, the location of Earth, and Pluto's size and distance from the sun were all related. This is indicated by the links in Figure 7.5.

Both Randy's and Juan's schemas illustrate the idea that individual items of information are related in long-term memory; they rarely exist in isolation. The interrelationship of ideas has important implications for both learning and memory, as you'll see later.

7.13 ▬
How would Juan's schema look if he simply memorized the information about the planets' names, their order from the sun, and their orbital planes?

Figure 7.4

Schema illustrating Randy's understanding

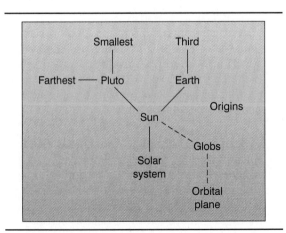

Schemas as Scripts.   Schemas can also guide a person's actions. For example, when you first go into a university class, you may ask yourself some questions:

Figure 7.5

Schema for Juan's under-standing

- What are the instructor's expectations?
- What are the course requirements?
- How should I prepare for quizzes and other assessments?
- How will I interact with my peers?

Your answers come from your schema, which represents your understanding of the proper way to operate in university classes. One kind of schema is a **script**, which is *"an organized plan of action in a particular situation"* (J. Walker, 1996, p. 231). The script guides your behavior as you prepare for and attend class. Your schema may include propositions about proper interpersonal behavior, images of past classes, and linear orderings about what tasks to complete first.

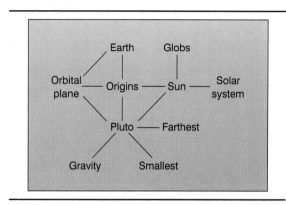

Schemas: Implications for Teaching.   Schema theory is important because it helps teachers in understanding why background knowledge is so important in learning. Learners' schemas interact with new information and influence the way they interpret it. To illustrate, let's look again at a portion of David Shelton's lesson.

Juan: Pluto wasn't part of the solar system to begin with.

Randy: What do you mean?

Juan: I was watching *Nova* with my mom, and the narrator said that scientists think Pluto was floating around and the sun kinda grabbed it. . . . See, when Mr. Shelton did that thing with the socks, the socks stayed sorta level.

Randy: What's that got to do with it?

Juan: Well, look. (pointing to the model)

Tanya: Oh, I get it! Pluto isn't level with the rest of them.

Randy: Gee, I didn't even notice that.

Because his schema was more complex and interrelated, Juan was able to relate David's demonstration to both a television documentary and information in the unit. In contrast, Randy initially didn't even notice one of the relationships. The concept of *schemas* and how they affect learning helps in understanding why Juan's and Randy's experiences were different.

Well-developed schemas, such as Juan's, are **generative knowledge**; they contain *"knowledge that can be used to interpret new situations"* (Resnick & Klopfer, 1989, p. 5), instead of *knowledge in memory that exists in isolated pieces,* which is **inert knowledge.** Inert knowledge is a common problem in classrooms.

The way topics are presented is critical in the development of generative knowledge. To learn effectively, students must encounter information represented in different ways and discuss and interpret it. The matrix and the information the students gathered, David's transparency, model, and demonstration, together with the discussion that followed, were all attempts to help students develop generative knowledge. The role of schemas and generative knowledge again demonstrates an underlying principle in all cognitive learning theories: *Learners are not passive recipients of information, but rather are active organizers of their own understanding.*

7.14
Research indicates that high-SES students are generally more successful in school than low-SES students. Using the information in this section, explain this research result.

A teacher can help students develop generative knowledge by encouraging them to connect ideas and share these connections with each other.

Representing Procedural Knowledge in Memory: Conditions and Actions.   As you saw earlier, procedural knowledge is knowledge of "how to do things." In implementing procedural knowledge, learners need to adapt their behavior to changing *conditions* and then *act* according to these conditions. For example, in adding fractions, if the denominators are the same, you merely add the numerators. If they are different, you must find a common denominator and then add the numerators. The conditions for adding fractions are different, depending on the denominators, and the ability to add them correctly depends on recognizing these conditions and responding appropriately. Procedural knowledge also depends on declarative knowledge; you must first *know the rule* to adapt to the different conditions and correctly perform the addition.

Acquiring Procedural Knowledge.   Acquiring procedural knowledge typically exists in three stages (J. Anderson, 1990; E. Gagne et al., 1993). In the *declarative stage,* learners acquire declarative knowledge about the procedure, such as being able to describe how to shift gears when driving or state rules for adding fractions. Performing the action is painstaking at this stage and occupies most of the learners' working memory spaces.

As the learners practice and receive feedback, they must still think about the steps, but they're able to combine them and perform the action smoothly. This is the *associative stage* (J. Anderson, 1990).

With additional practice, learners finally move to the *automatic stage,* during which they're able to perform the process with little conscious thought or effort. A person's ability to shift gears smoothly, maneuver through traffic, and simultaneously carry on a conversation, for example, or solve word problems with little thought to adding fractions, illustrates this stage.

Importance of Context in Acquiring Procedural Knowledge.   You saw earlier that applying procedural knowledge first requires that learners identify conditions in a problem or

---

7.15

Suppose you are given a problem that asks, "How much pizza have you eaten if you eat a piece from a pizza cut into six pieces and another piece from an identical pizza cut into eight pieces?" What are the conditions and what are the actions required in this problem? What declarative knowledge is required in solving the problem?

7.16

Suppose you're a math teacher. Describe specifically what you might do to give your students practice in identifying appropriate conditions for adding fractions.

exercise before they can appropriately apply procedures. To get this practice in identifying conditions, students should practice procedural knowledge in **context**, which *involves embedding problems and exercises in realistic settings.* This means, for example, that students should be learning mathematical operations by solving realistic word problems as soon as possible and that they should be practicing grammar and punctuation rules in the context of their own writing, not in isolated sentences. Having students complete decontextualized exercises, such as finding common denominators in abstract problems, doesn't provide them with opportunities to identify conditions and apply the appropriate actions. (We examine the role of context again later in this chapter and in Chapter 8.)

As a review, take a moment now to examine Figure 7.6, which presents a summary of the characteristics of long-term memory.

Classroom Connections

Applying an Understanding of Sensory Memory in Your Classroom

1. As information is presented, give students time to process it before changing the stimulus.
   - A second-grade teacher displays problems on the overhead projector and waits until the students have copied the problems before she starts talking.
   - In a social studies lesson, a teacher puts a map on the overhead and says, "Look at the map of the neighborhood where our school is located. I'll stop for a second to give you an opportunity to examine it. Then we'll go on."

2. Ask only one question at a time. Otherwise, the memory trace for succeeding questions may be lost before students can attend to them.
   - A first-grade teacher gives students directions for seatwork by presenting them slowly and one at a time. She asks different students to repeat the directions before she has them begin.

Applying an Understanding of Working Memory in Your Classroom

3. Keep descriptions short and slow enough to prevent overloading students' working memories. Proceed more slowly with younger and less capable students.
   - A teacher in woodworking class begins by saying, "The hardness and density of wood from the same tree varies, depending on the amount of rainfall the tree has received." He waits a moment, holds up two pieces of wood, and says, "Look at these wood pieces. What do you notice about the rings on them?"

4. To develop automaticity, provide frequent practice and review in basic skills as part of your classroom routine.
   - A first-grade teacher begins language arts each morning by having the students write one or two sentences about some event of the night before. She selects samples to review the basic structure of sentences.

5. Encourage organization by identifying and highlighting key points in your presentation and writing them on the chalkboard or overhead.
   - A history teacher prepares an outline of the events that lead up to the Revolutionary War. As he presents the information, he refers to the outline for each important point and encourages students to use the outline to organize their note taking.

Applying an Understanding of Long-Term Memory in Your Classroom

6. Encourage students to explore relationships among ideas to help in developing complex networks and schemas.
   - During story time, a first-grade teacher asks the students to explain how the events in a story contribute to the conclusion.

Figure 7.6

Characteristics of long-term memory

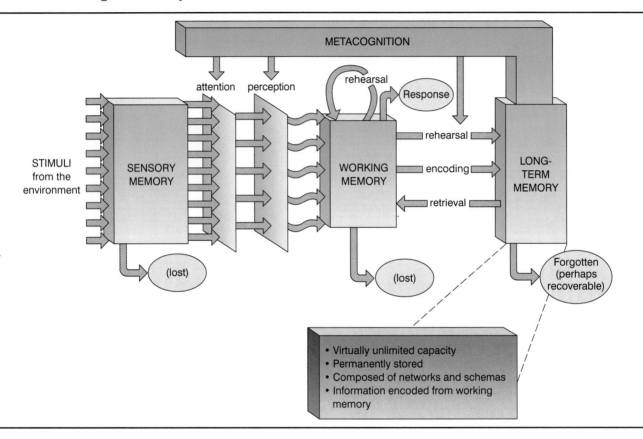

- A third-grade teacher presents examples of writing in which facts, inference, and opinions are embedded and asks students to explain how fact, inference, and opinion are each similar to and different from each other.

7. Connect new ideas to previous learning.
   - In developing the rules for multiplying fractions, a math teacher asks the class, "How does this process compare to what we did when we added fractions? What do we do differently? Why?"

8. Encourage meaningful learning by presenting topics in context.
   - An English teacher presents the rules for singular and plural possessives in the context of a passage about the school. She guides students into an understanding of the rules by using the passage.
   - A geography teacher introduces the topics of longitude and latitude by asking students to explain how they would direct a friend of theirs to a remote location in the middle of the Atlantic Ocean.

Cognitive Processes

To help in understanding cognitive processes, let's return to our model. We've just described the information stores—sensory memory, working memory, and long-term memory—and you now have a better understanding of the characteristics of each and how information is represented in long-term memory. Now, let's shift attention to the processes that move information from one store to another: *attention, perception, rehearsal, encoding,* and *retrieval.* These are also highlighted in Figure 7.7.

Attention: Processing Information From a Learner Perspective

Consider the room you're in right now. A myriad of stimuli exist—pictures, furniture, other people moving and talking, the whisper of an air conditioner—even though you're not conscious of some of them. Others, however, attract your **attention**, which is *the process of consciously focusing on a stimulus or stimuli.*

Reexamine the model in Figure 7.7. "Attention" appears next to "sensory memory," so this is where processing begins. All additional processing depends on how well learners attend to appropriate stimuli in the learning environment.

Attracting and Maintaining Student Attention. Attracting and maintaining student attention is a critical first step in teaching. It can be difficult because people's attention wanders, and as you saw in the study of development in Chapter 2, this is especially true for young students. Teachers should consciously plan their lessons so that students attend to what is being taught and ignore outside noises and other stimuli irrelevant to the learn-

> 7.17
> Suppose you are at a party and suddenly jerk your head when you hear someone in another group say your name. What does your reaction imply about your information-processing system and the stimuli around it?

Figure 7.7

Cognitive processes in the information-processing model

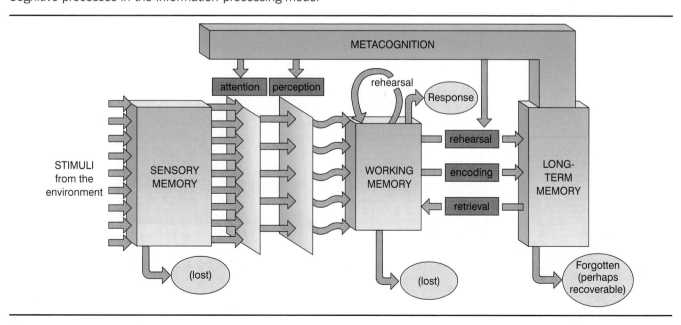

Effective teachers use a variety of visual aids to attract and maintain students' attention.

ing experience (Brophy & Good, 1986; Rosenshine & Stevens, 1986). If a teacher pulls a live, dripping, wriggling crab out of a cooler to begin a lesson on crustaceans, for example, even the most apathetic student is likely to pay attention.

Attention getters exist in a variety of forms. Demonstrations, displays on transparencies, pictures, maps, graphs, thought-provoking questions, and even the chalkboard can attract students' attention. Enthusiastic teachers move around the classroom; change their rate, pitch, and intensity of speech; and use gestures and other energetic movements to maintain attention. Despite these efforts, however, students can become "satiated." Relying on one form of attention getter can lose its effect, so variety is necessary. Additional examples of attention-focusing events are presented in Table 7.3.

David Shelton used several different attention getters in his lesson. Perhaps most significant was his demonstration with the strings and socks, which he used to begin Wednesday's lesson. His model, the transparency, and the matrix were also attention getters.

The use of students' names is also a powerful attention getter. Effective teachers direct their questions to individual students, and when this becomes a pattern, attention and achievement increase (Kauchak & Eggen, 1993; Kerman, 1979).

Perception: Finding Meaning in Stimuli

Perception *is the process by which people attach meaning to their experiences*. After attending to certain stimuli in their sensory memories, processing continues with perception. Perception is critical because the information that enters working memory is determined by the learner's perception. Information in working memory is in the form of "perceived reality," not "true reality." If students misinterpret the teacher's examples, the information that enters working memory will be invalid, and the information they transfer to long-term memory will also be invalid.

Background Knowledge Affects Perception.   You saw earlier that background knowledge in the form of schemas affects learning, and you also saw that Randy didn't even

7.18
Research indicates that teacher enthusiasm improves student learning and motivation. Explain why this would be the case; base your answer on the information-processing model. How would social cognitive theorists explain the positive effects of enthusiasm?

7.19
One teacher asks, "John, why do you think people are fascinated by the legends of King Arthur?" Another asks, "Why do you think people are fascinated by the legends of King Arthur? . . . John?" How will these two questioning patterns influence John's attention and that of the rest of the class?

"notice" that Pluto's plane was different from that of the other planets. His *perception* of the model and demonstration was affected by his background knowledge.

As another example, suppose science students are studying the formation of calcium deposits from hard water and see the following on the chalkboard:

$$CaCO_3 + CO_2 + H_2O \rightarrow Ca + 2HCO_3$$

For learning to be effective, students must accurately perceive several aspects of this equation:

- A symbol without a subscript implies one atom of the element in the compound.
- Some elements have two letters in their symbols; others have only one.
- The subscript indicates the number of atoms of the element.

Accurate perceptions of these features depend on students' background knowledge with respect to chemical equations.

An excellent way of checking students' perceptions is to review by asking open-ended questions (Kauchak & Eggen, 1993). For example, after writing the equation on the chalkboard, the science teacher might ask, "Look at the equation. What do you notice about it?" If students can't identify the appropriate information, such as the elements involved, the numbers of each in the compounds, and what the arrow means, the teacher would know that their perceptions are inaccurate or incomplete, and she could then adjust her review to cover these features.

Expectations Affect Perception.   The meaning people attach to an object or event is also affected by what they "expect" to experience. For example, if you've been told, "Oh, you'll really like Lisa. She's outgoing and has a great sense of humor," you're likely to have

> **7.20**
> We said that perception depends on background knowledge. How is background knowledge organized in learners' memories?

Table 7.3

Examples of attention getters

Type	Example
Demonstrations	A physical science teacher pulls a student in a chair across the room to demonstrate force and work in a physical science class.
Discrepant events	A world history teacher who usually dresses conservatively comes to class in a sheet, makeshift sandals, and a crown to begin a discussion of ancient Greece.
Visual displays	A health teacher displays a chart showing the high fat content of some popular foods.
Thought-provoking questions	A history teacher begins a discussion of World War II with the question, "Suppose Germany had won the war. How might the world be different now?"
Emphasis	A teacher says, "Pay careful attention now. The next two items are very important."
Student names	In her question and answer session, a teacher always asks her question, pauses briefly, and then calls on a student *by name* to answer.

a much different reaction when initially meeting her than if you've been told, "She's a little spacey and kind of out of it, but you'll get used to her."

Expectations also have a strong impact on learning. If students expect information to be challenging yet interesting, their perceptions of the activity will be much different than if they expect the lesson to be boring or the topic to be impossibly difficult.

Rehearsal: Retaining Information Through Practice

You have your students' attention; you've checked to make sure their perceptions are accurate; and the information is now in working memory. Knowing that it will remain there for only a short time, what can you do to move important parts into long-term memory? Rehearsal is one of the most commonly used strategies, and there are two types: maintenance rehearsal and elaborative rehearsal (Craik & Lockhart, 1972).

Maintenance rehearsal *is the process of repeating information over and over, either aloud or mentally, without altering its form.* It is analogous to rehearsing a piece of music. When people do so, they play the music as written; they don't alter it or change its form.

As an example, suppose you're adding a series of numbers on a calculator. Rather than read a number and punch it in, to speed up the process you might read four numbers, repeat them once or twice, and punch in all four in the same action. This is a form of rehearsal, and it is used to retain information in working memory until the learner chooses to do something with it.

If information is rehearsed enough, it can sometimes be transferred to long-term memory (R. Atkinson & Shiffrin, 1968). This is an inefficient method of transferring information, however, and not surprisingly, it's one of the first memory strategies that develops in young children (Berk, 1994).

Rehearsal can be made more effective by capitalizing on the fact that memory tends to be associative. **Elaborative rehearsal** *is the process of associating information the person wants to remember with information already stored in long-term memory.* For instance, if you know that the Civil War was fought during the years 1861 to 1865, you can remember the approximate dates of the Lincoln presidency because you associate his presidency with the Civil War. Let's see how this happens in a learning activity.

T: What year did we say the Civil War began? . . . Jane?
S: . . . 1859?
T: Let's back up a minute. What year did we say Lincoln was elected?
S: 1860.
T: Good, and how were his election and the start of the Civil War connected?
S: The South thought Lincoln as president would take a strong abolitionist position, so they thought secession was the only viable alternative.
T: So, would the start of the Civil War be before or after the election of 1860?
S: . . . Now I remember. It was 1861.

(Kauchak & Eggen, 1993, p. 190)

Encoding: Making Connections in Long-Term Memory

Encoding is perhaps the most critical cognitive process in the information-processing model. **Encoding** *occurs when a person forms mental representations of information and stores them in memory* (Siegler, 1991). Encoding involves organizing and connecting

---

7.21

According to social cognitive theory, what is one thing that causes people to form the expectations they have?

7.22

Look again at the information-processing model in Figure 7.7. What in the model is intended to help you understand that some information can be transferred to long-term memory through rehearsal?

7.23

What is the difference between elaborative rehearsal and encoding? Why is understanding the difference important?

information to information that already exists in long-term memory. For example, Juan formed a mental representation of the solar system's formation by connecting the globs thrown off from the sun—stored in long-term memory—to the formation of the planets. He also encoded the information about Pluto's different origin by associating it with the fact that its orbital plane was different from that of the other planets.

Organizing and attaching new information to old is a critical element of learning, and this is the reason that background knowledge and an understanding of schemas is important. The more "old" information that exists, the more locations a learner has to attach the new information and the more likely it is to be encoded. This was the point we made earlier in the chapter when we discussed networks and schemas in long-term memory.

To avoid transferring information to long-term memory through rehearsal alone, student learning should be meaningful. **Meaningfulness** *describes the number of connections, or associations, between one idea and other ideas in long-term memory* (E. Gagne et al., 1993). On this basis, we would infer that the information in David's lesson was more meaningful for Juan than it was for Randy because there were more connections or "links" in Juan's network than in Randy's. Although some information may enter long-term memory through rehearsal alone, most must be meaningfully encoded to be retained; it must be connected to information that already exists in long-term memory. (Later in the chapter, we discuss ways of making information meaningful.)

> **7.24**
> Describe the relationship between encoding and perception. Illustrate your description with a specific example.

Meaningfulness is enhanced when students are encouraged to find connections in the new material they are learning.

Levels of Processing: Encouraging Meaningful Encoding.   Think again about David Shelton and the matrix he used to organize information about the solar system. To guide his students as they processed the information, he could have used several statements or questions, such as:

> "Which planet is the fourth one from the sun?"

> "What patterns can you find in the information in the chart?"

> "Why do you suppose Mercury is so hot on one side and so cold on the other?"

Which of these would result in the most learning?

7.25

Identify three kinds of questions that would promote deep levels of processing. Identify one kind of question that would promote shallow processing.

Levels of processing *is a view of learning that suggests the more deeply information is processed, the more meaningful it becomes.* Although originally proposed as an alternative to the three-store information-processing model (Craik & Lockhart, 1972), more recent views describe it as a way of processing information into long-term memory (Cermak & Craik, 1979). The more deeply information is processed, the more connections are made and the more meaningful the information becomes. For instance, merely asking students to identify the fourth planet from the sun is a "shallow" form of processing, whereas asking students to find patterns in the chart or to explain why the temperature on Mercury varies so much requires much deeper processing. To find patterns, students must identify relationships in items of information, such as visualizing the four inner planets as small and relatively close to the sun, compared with the outer planets, which (except for Pluto) are much larger and more distant. Explaining the temperature differences on Mercury also requires a deeper level of processing because it requires identifying cause-and-effect relationships among temperatures, Mercury's period of rotation, its gravity, and atmosphere. This point suggests that teachers should be constantly looking for ways of encouraging students to process information as deeply as possible by looking for relationships in the information they're learning.

Forgetting

No discussion of memory would be complete without a consideration of **forgetting**, which is *the loss of, or inability to retrieve, information from memory.* Forgetting is both a very real part of people's everyday lives ("Now, where did I put those car keys?") and a very important factor in school learning.

Let's look again at the information-processing model first presented in Figure 7.2. There you can see that information can be lost from the memory stores in different ways. If a person doesn't quickly attend to the information in sensory memory, it is lost and cannot be retrieved. Information can be retained in working memory if it is rehearsed; otherwise, it is also disregarded or purged and cannot be recovered. In the case of long-term memory, the information has been rehearsed enough to be transferred to long-term memory or has been encoded in some way. Why can't the learner find it or use it?

Forgetting as Interference.   One view of forgetting uses the concept of **interference**, *which is the loss of information because something else learned either before or after detracts from the learning* (Postman & Underwood, 1973; Schunk, 1991). Many people have had the experience of understanding an idea, even being quite confident and comfortable with it, but later, however, after learning a related idea, being uncertain about the original one. The idea of interference helps in explaining this experience.

When you examine topics commonly taught in school curricula, you can see how interference occurs. For example, students learn that possessives are formed by adding an apostrophe *s* to singular nouns. They also study plurals as well as contractions, and they find that the apostrophe is used differently: It comes after the *s* in some cases, it appears before the *s* in the case of plural nouns, such as *women* and *children,* and it comes between letters in the case of contractions. Students' understanding of plural possessives and contractions can interfere with their understanding of singular possessives and vice versa.

One classroom solution to the problem of interference is review and comparison. After a new topic is discussed, teachers should compare it with closely related information already studied and identify easily confused similarities. Doing so elaborates on the original schema, and interference is reduced.

A second solution is to teach closely related ideas together—for example, adjective and adverb phrases, longitude and latitude, and adding and subtracting fractions with similar and different denominators. As teachers present related ideas together, they need to highlight the relationships for students, emphasize differences, and identify areas that are easily confused.

Forgetting as Retrieval Failure.

Phew, this test is a bear. Maybe I should have studied more last night. Oh, well, almost done.

Now for the fill-in-the-blanks section. First question: Landing site for the Allied invasion of France? I know that. I remember reading it in the text and seeing it in my notes.

Paris? No, that's inland. We talked about Calais. No, that was a diversion to trick the Nazis. Darn! I know that I know it. . . . Why can't I think of the name?

Encoding is important because, without it, information won't be meaningfully stored in long-term memory. However, unless the learner can **retrieve** the information—*pull it into working memory again for further processing*—it's useless. It's like putting some information into a file folder and then trying to figure out where the folder is stored; the information is there but can't be found. Many researchers now believe that learners don't literally "lose" information when they forget, but rather that they can't retrieve it (Ashcraft, 1989).

In attempting to retrieve information, people are often aware they've stored something in long-term memory, but they can't put their "mental" finger on it. Researchers call this event the "tip-of-the-tongue" phenomenon (R. Brown & McNeill, 1966), and it occurs when, for example, a person sees a face and says, "I know that person, but I can't place her," or in classrooms when students think, "I saw that in the book. Now, what did it say?" The student trying to remember Normandy knew the information was there; the problem was finding it. This brings us to the role of context.

Improving Retrieval Through Effective Encoding: The Role of Context.
You saw earlier that context is important in acquiring procedural knowledge and that it is also important for encoding and retrieval. For instance, you know a person at work or school but you can't remember her name when you see her at a party. The party is a different context from the one in which the information was encoded. Similarly, if classroom contexts are changed by noise or other factors, retrieval can be more difficult.

Context extends beyond factors such as the general environment, however. Researchers have found that learners encode both the desired information and the context in which the information is presented. As an illustration, do this simple exercise. Quickly name the months of the year. You doubtless named them effortlessly. Now, quickly name them in alphabetical order. This time, you probably named them quite slowly. The first task is easy because most people encode the months chronologically. Alphabetical order is a different context, and because the months haven't been encoded alphabetically, stating them that way is a more difficult task. Practicing the lines of a play on the stage where it will be performed is another example. This context will facilitate retrieval better than practicing the lines at home and then trying to retrieve them on stage. This contextual influence on retrieval is sometimes called the *encoding specificity hypothesis* (Tulving, 1979).

David Shelton capitalized on the impact of context when he presented his information about Pluto in different ways. He didn't merely *say* that the first eight planets had one

7.26
In which case would interference be most likely to occur—when studying similes and metaphors, or when studying figures of speech and parts of speech? Explain.

7.27
How would meaningfulness affect the tip-of-the-tongue phenomenon?

7.28
Explain why encoding specificity might be harmful in classroom learning. What can teachers do to help learners cope with its effects?

origin and that Pluto had another. Instead, he presented the information in the context of the planets' orbital planes, their direction of revolution, and the origin of the solar system. He also asked questions such as, "Does that support or contradict what the group said?" By encouraging his students to learn new information in a variety of ways, he increased the likelihood of later retrieval.

Problems as Contexts.   Problems can be used as meaningful contexts to help students see how abstract ideas relate to the real world (Sherwood, Kinzer, Bransford, & Franks, 1987). On the one hand, for example, the concept of *density* is often reduced to the formula $D = m/v$ (density equals mass divided by volume) and students memorize it, plugging in numbers and getting a meaningless answer (that sometimes isn't even sensible). On the other hand, a teacher might begin a lesson with a description such as the following:

> *You want to buy a gold necklace, and at a jewelry store you find one that seems surprisingly inexpensive. The jeweler claims it's 18-carat gold, but you're skeptical. The jeweler won't let you take the chain out of the store without buying it, and you wouldn't know whom to ask anyway. What could you do to determine the authenticity of the necklace?*

7.29
Consider David Shelton's lesson again. Prepare an introduction to his lesson that would put the lesson in the context of a problem as suggested in this section.

Studying density in this context provides much greater opportunity for meaningful encoding than merely presenting the formula (because a "fake" will have a density different from that of the genuine article). Karen Johnson, the teacher in the case study at the beginning of Chapter 2, demonstrated a beginning point for enriching the topic of density by varying the density of cotton in a cup. In each case, a concrete problem provides a meaningful context for both encoding and retrieval.

Metacognition: Knowledge and Control of Cognitive Processes

We have now examined the first two parts of the information-processing model. Our study has included an examination of the memory stores—sensory memory, working memory, and long-term memory—as well as the cognitive processes—attention, perception, rehearsal, encoding, and retrieval—that move information from one store to the next.

Cognitive processes are not simple mechanisms that merely turn on or off, however. To be useful, these components must be integrated so that they can be used strategically. Metacognition serves this function.

Metacognition includes (a) *people's knowledge or awareness of their cognitive processes and* (b) *the ability to use self-regulatory mechanisms to control these processes.* As you saw in Chapter 2, types of metacognition, such as meta-attention and metamemory, develop with age and experience. The metacognitive components of the information-processing model are illustrated in Figure 7.8.

Metacognition operates from the beginning of the learning process, starting with attention. It gives the learner's attention a purpose, focusing it on the important features of the learning activity. If you choose to sit near the front of the class because you "drift off," for example, you are demonstrating meta-attention.

Metacognition can play a role in perception as well. Being aware of the possibility of misperceiving something and consciously reserving judgment until you have additional information demonstrates awareness of and control over your perception.

Metacognition also helps regulate the flow of information through working memory. We've all been in situations where we've had to remember a phone number or address. If we're going to dial the number or write down the address immediately, we simply

rehearse; if we're going to call or write later, we'll probably write down the number or address. Each decision is strategic, influenced by our goal and the awareness and control over our memories—metamemory. Alfredo, in David Shelton's lesson, demonstrated metamemory when he said, "Wait, Mr. Shelton, you're going too fast. I'm getting lost. What is this about supporting the theory?" He was aware that he was missing some of the information, and he demonstrated control over his memory by asking David to slow down and explain the information about Pluto. The ability to monitor the processing of information in working memory is critical because of this memory store's limited capacity.

Finally, metacognition involves awareness and control of long-term memory and encoding. For example, knowing that you tend to associate items of information in long-term memory rather than store them in isolation can help you consciously look for relationships in the topics you study. Being *aware* of the way you store information and *making a conscious effort* to look for relationships is a form of metacognition.

7.30:
What are some indicators for teachers that metacognition is operating in students? What can teachers do to encourage metacognitive growth?

Classroom Connections

Applying an Understanding of Attention in Your Classroom

1. Use examples in your teaching that attract students' attention.
   - A teacher introducing the concept of *pressure* to her science students has them stand by their desks, first on both feet and then on one foot.

They then discuss the force and pressure on the floor in both cases.

- An economics teacher introduces the concept of *opportunity cost* by saying, "You could spend your after-school time at a job, or you could socialize with your friends. If you work, what happens?" She then guides them to the idea that the opportunity

Figure 7.8

Metacognition in the information-processing model

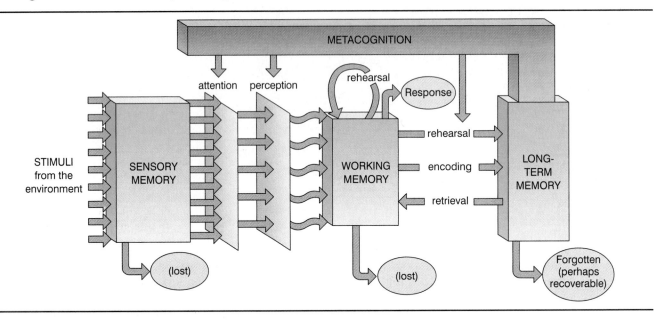

cost for the job is the amount of time they don't get to spend with their friends.

2. Call on all students equally and by name to capitalize on the attention-arousing element.
   - A first-grade teacher calls on all students, including those who don't have their hands up. He tells them in advance what he is going to do and explains why it is important.
   - A third-grade teacher mentally keeps track of whom she has called on. She periodically asks, "Whom have I not called on lately?" to be sure students are treated as equally as possible.

3. Use emphasis to ensure that students attend to important information in the lesson.
   - An earth science teacher emphasizes, "Class, listen carefully now because the idea of volcanism is important in the way landforms are created."

Applying an Understanding of Perception in Your Classroom

4. Check to be certain that students are perceiving your examples accurately.
   - A kindergarten teacher begins every lesson by asking students to describe what they see in the examples she uses.
   - A geography teacher, when teaching about landforms, shows her class a series of colored slides. After displaying each one, she asks the students to describe the slide before she moves on to the next.

Applying an Understanding of Interference in Your Classroom

5. Teach closely related ideas together, stressing similarities and differences.

- A life science teacher combines the topics of reptiles and amphibians in the same lesson, stressing the features that make them different.

6. Carefully review and compare closely related topics after they're covered.
   - A teacher presenting a unit on verbals states, "We've finished our discussion of participles now. Yesterday, we covered gerunds. Tell me the key difference between the two and give us an example of each."

Applying an Understanding of Retrieval in Your Classroom

7. Present information in enriched contexts.
   - A life science teacher begins a unit on arteries and veins by saying, "We've all heard of hardening of the arteries, but we haven't heard of 'hardening of the veins.' Why not? Are we using the term *artery* to mean both, or is there a difference? Why is hardening of the arteries bad for people? I'm going to write these questions down so that we keep them in mind as we study arteries, veins, and capillaries."

Applying an Understanding of Metacognition in Your Classroom

8. Consciously teach students about the role of attention in learning.

- A fourth-grade teacher plays an attention game with his students. During a lesson, he'll hold up a card with the sentence "If you're paying attention, raise your hand." He'll then acknowledge those who are and encourage them to share their strategies for maintaining attention during class.

9. Teach students the importance of listening carefully.
   - To encourage students to listen to each other, a middle school teacher periodically has the class write down what a student has just said in answering a question. She has them monitor their listening and try to continually improve.

10. Model metacognitive abilities for your students.
    - A ninth-grade economics teacher says, "Whenever I read something new, I always ask myself, 'How does this relate to what I've been studying? For example, how is the liberal economic agenda different from the conservative economic agenda?'"
    - In a health lesson, a third-grade teacher says, "If I understand what Dana meant by her comment, she is suggesting that we should stay away from smoky places because of the danger of second-hand smoke." The teacher then asks the students why they think Dana would make such a statement and leads them to conclude that she was aware of possibly misperceiving Dana's comment.

Impact of Diversity on Information Processing

As a "warmup" activity for his world geography class, Mike Havland asked his students to turn to page 267 of their text, on which was a "modern" map of Europe.

As Carl looked at the map, he thought it looked familiar. "Yeah," he thought, "there's England, France, Germany, and Russia. Hey, there's Yugoslavia. That's where Goran's grandparents came from."

Next to him, Celeena, whose father was a career military man with whom she had traveled all over Europe, was also looking at the map, but with a look of disbelief. "How old *is* this book?" she thought. "Look at Yugoslavia. It doesn't exist anymore. It's been torn apart. Hmm, where's Barcelona? . . . Oh yeah. Down there on the coast of Spain. We saw it when we went to the Olympics."

After a few minutes, Mike began. "Okay, everyone. It's important to have some idea of the geography of Europe because the geography reflects an important idea that we'll return to again and again." With that, he wrote on the chalkboard: "The history of Europe reflects the tension between nationalism and intercountry cooperation."

He continued by saying, "As you've already noticed, the face of Europe is continually changing, reflecting the ebbs and flows of nationalistic fervor and efforts to reduce cultural and trade barriers."

As he was talking, he noticed a few nods but more blank looks. Celeena sat knowingly, while Carl thought, "What's he talking about? Nationalism? Cultural and trade barriers? What is this?"

Not knowing what to do about the blank looks, Mike continued with his planned lecture.

Teachers know that background knowledge is a powerful influence on perception and encoding. Students come to class with widely varying experiences, and dealing with this diversity is one of the biggest challenges facing all teachers (Veenman, 1984).

Diversity and Perception

Experience is one of the two most important influences on perception. As you saw in Mike Havland's lesson, what students perceive from something complex, such as a map, largely depends on their background knowledge. This notion has been verified in areas as varied as chess, reading, math, and physics (Glover, Ronning, & Bruning, 1990).

Experience affects both *what* and *how much* students learn. For example, one student seeing a movie on the Vietnam conflict interprets the war as an effort to stop the spread of communism, whereas another perceives it as the imposing of American values on a distant country. When Carl viewed the map of Europe, he perceived an accurate representation; when Celeena viewed it, she perceived it as an antiquated document. People's schemas influence the way they perceive information.

Diversity, Encoding, and Retrieval

Just as people's background knowledge influences their perceptions, it also influences how effectively people encode new information. Celeena, for example, has a richer geography background than does Carl. As a result, the statement "The history of Europe reflects the tension between nationalism and intercountry cooperation," was meaningful to her, whereas it meant little to Carl: He had little in his background to which ideas such as "nationalism" and "intercountry cooperation" could be linked.

7.31
Consider the following two statements: "Many students have less well developed schemas than do other students" and "Many students have different schemas than do other students." On the basis of the information in this section, which is the more accurate statement?

The diverse experiential backgrounds of students can be used to enrich the learning experiences of all students.

We've all been in situations in which a presentation or passage in a book doesn't "make sense," and we've all been in conversations in which we're not "connecting" with the other person. In each case, we may lack the background to which new information can be linked, and so meaningful encoding doesn't occur.

Instructional Adaptations for Background Diversity

What can you as a teacher do when this lack of encoding happens in your classroom? Research suggests several strategies (Glover et al., 1990):

▌ Begin lessons by asking students what they know about the topic you're planning to teach.

▌ Provide background experiences with rich examples and representations of the content you're teaching.

▌ Use open-ended questions to assess student perceptions of your examples and representations.

▌ Use the experiences of students in the class to augment the backgrounds of those lacking the experiences.

For example, it would have been easy for Mike to say, "Celeena, you lived in Europe. What do people in Europe say about the conflict in the former Yugoslavia?" Also, because *nationalism* was an organizing idea for much of what followed, Mike could have asked, "What does *nationalism* mean? Give two examples that compare strong and weak nationalism." If students are unable to respond, he must alter his plans to focus on the concept, laying the groundwork for subsequent learning. For example, he could have used the school as context for his discussion of nationalism by describing school spirit, pride in the school, and the school's traditions as analogies for the feelings of nationalism in European countries. The analogies would make the notion of nationalism more meaningful for students, and subsequent encoding and retrieval would be improved. The ability to adapt lessons in this way is one characteristic of teaching expertise.

> **7.32**
> We recommended in this section, "provide background experiences with rich examples and representations of the content you're teaching." Describe specifically what is meant by "rich examples and representations."

Classroom Connections

Capitalizing on Diversity in Your Classroom

1. Assess students' backgrounds prior to lessons.
   - A second-grade teacher begins a unit on communities by requesting, "Tell us what you know about the community we live in." He encourages a number of students to respond so that he can get an accurate idea of what students know.
   - An art teacher begins a unit on perspective by asking students to sketch a three-dimensional scene. He has students put their names on the back of

the sketches and then discusses the sketches during the following class period.

2. Use open-ended questioning to assess students' perceptions.
   - A fourth-grade teacher begins a unit on the North and South prior to the Civil War by preparing a matrix comparing the economy, geography, and climate of the North and South. He displays the matrix and says, "Now, tell us what you see in the

first column on the chart. . . . Anything you notice or observe there?"
- An English teacher puts a sonnet on the overhead and says, "Someone describes what's on the overhead." In the discussion that follows, he tries to relate characteristics of sonnets to the students' observations.

3. Have students with different backgrounds share their experiences and ideas.
- A sixth-grade teacher beginning a study of plants says to a student whose parents are farmers, "Selinda, you've had some interesting experiences working with plants and crops. Tell us about the kinds of plants your parents grow, what they're

used for, and anything else about plants you think might be interesting."

4. Provide concrete experiences to develop students' background experiences.
- Prior to a unit on chemical change, a science teacher burns paper, mixes vinegar and baking soda, and puts bleach on a piece of colored cloth to illustrate chemical changes.
- Before beginning a unit on geometric shapes, a kindergarten teacher has his students draw, color, and cut out squares, triangles, rectangles, and circles. He then has the students identify examples of the shapes around the classroom.

Making Information Meaningful

In the previous section, we analyzed information processing, one cognitive theory that describes learning in terms of stores and processes. In this section, we broaden our focus to examine some principles of cognitive learning that extend beyond information processing and that describe how learners acquire and organize information.

Central to these principles is the concept of *meaningfulness*. We said earlier that **meaningfulness** *describes the number of connections or associations between one idea and others in memory* (E. Gagne et al., 1993). Cognitive views of learning emphasize the central role that students play in making information meaningful. Teachers can help in this process by applying three principles in their instruction:

1. Organization increases learning by imposing order and connections on new information.
2. Elaboration increases learning by linking new information to existing schemas.
3. The greater the level of activity in meaningful experiences, the more students learn.

These principles are illustrated in Figure 7.9 and are discussed in the sections that follow.

Organization

7.33
We've said that complex and interrelated schemas organize information more meaningfully than do less complex schemas. Why don't these complex schemas overload learners' working memories?

In our discussion of information processing, you saw that learners store knowledge in the form of schemas that combine propositions, images, and linear orderings. One of the most important features of schemas is that they *organize* information. They remind teachers that learners don't ingest information in unrelated pieces, that learners associate items of information with each other and organize it in ways that make sense to them. Because the tendency of learners to organize information is at the heart of cognitive theories of learning, we begin this section with it.

Figure 7.9

Making information meaningful

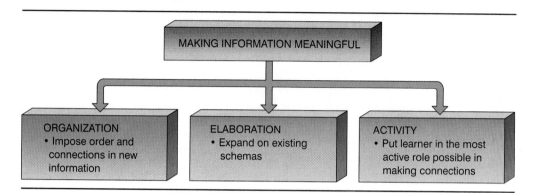

Let's consider David Shelton's model of the solar system once more. It displayed the sun, the relative distances of the planets, and the orbital plane. He also provided a matrix in which students recorded information about the planets. Each was a form of organization.

Organization *is the process of clustering related information into categories or patterns.* The matrix David's students used helped in forming categories and patterns, and all the planets, except Pluto, being on the same plane was another pattern. When teachers present information in charts, graphs, and diagrams, as David did, relationships between ideas become apparent, and these relationships make information meaningful. Research in reading (Eggen, Kauchak, & Kirk, 1978), memory (Bower, Clark, Lesgold, & Winzenz, 1969), and classroom interaction (Cruickshank, 1985) confirms the value of organization in promoting learning.

Charts and Matrices

Charts and matrices are useful for organizing large amounts of information into meaningful patterns. You saw how David Shelton used a matrix in his lesson. As another example, look at the chart in Table 7.4, used to help students understand immigration patterns in an American history class.

From the chart, you see patterns in the two immigrant groups' reasons for coming, characteristics, and rates of assimilation. These patterns reflect similarities, providing links between the different items of information. The teacher can then guide the students in their efforts to make these connections that result in more meaningful learning.

Hierarchies as Organizers

Hierarchies are another common type of organization, useful where new information can be subsumed under existing ideas. An English teacher, for example, might organize information as shown in Figure 7.10. In this case, the definition is linked to the part of speech it represents in a sentence—noun, adjective, or adverb—which in turn is linked to the specific type of verbal. Each of these links promotes meaningfulness.

The hierarchy we used in our discussion of operant conditioning in Chapter 6 was an attempt to capitalize on this form of organization, and you will encounter hierarchies in other chapters as you progress through the text.

7.34
Look again at the chart organizing information about immigrants (Table 7.4). Identify at least three patterns in the chart that would help make the information meaningful to learners.

7.35
Suppose you're an English teacher and you use the hierarchy displayed in Figure 7.10. What, in addition to displaying the hierarchy, would you have to do to ensure that your students find the information about verbals meaningful? Describe specifically what you would do.

Table 7.4

Chart used to organize information in American history

	Italians	Chinese
Reasons for coming	Small farms that couldn't support families Population increase Poor land, poor equipment Few factories and plants in which to work Heavy taxes Stories of wealth in America	Overpopulation Fixed status Inefficient warlords High taxes Crop failures and famine Active recruitment—promise of high wages
Characteristics	Lower socioeconomic class Large families Tight family structure Low literacy rate in English Quick to learn English	Originally coolie laborers Tight family structure Low literacy rate in English Laborers' jobs Slow to learn English
Assimilation	First generation: very religious, little outside contact Second generation: increased intermarriage Third generation: "Americanized"	Settlement in Western U.S. Togetherness Establishment of "Chinatowns" Preservation of Chinese customs

Source: Strategies for Teachers: Teaching Content and Thinking Skills, 3rd ed., by P. Eggen and D. Kauchak, 1996, Needham Heights, MA: Allyn & Bacon. Copyright 1996 by Allyn & Bacon. Adapted with permission.

Figure 7.10

Organizational hierarchy in English

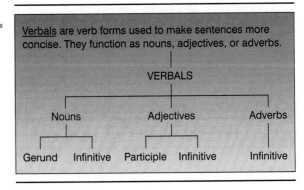

Other Types of Organization

Other forms of organization include graphs, tables, outlines, models, flowcharts, and maps. The outlines at the beginning of each chapter, together with the figures, tables, and models we've included in this text, are additional attempts to make the information you're reading meaningful through the process of organization. Additional types of organization are summarized in Table 7.5.

Teacher Organization and Learner Understanding

For organization to be effective, students must understand the organizing principles and connections and use them to form valid schemas. If the information doesn't make sense to them, they may "reorganize" it in a way that isn't valid. The most carefully organized content presented in a lecture will be useless if students can't use this structure to encode and retrieve information.

David Shelton not only organized the information for his students by using the model, demonstration, and matrix but also went a step farther. Through questioning and class discussion, he helped guide the students to ensure that the understanding they developed was valid and organized. Both organization and interaction are important.

Enhancing Imagery With Organization

Think again about models, matrices, charts, graphs, and hierarchies. They both organize information conceptually and represent it visually. As such, they assist students in their efforts to use imagery, or mental pictures, as a strategy to promote meaningfulness. A teacher can encourage students' use of imagery by suggesting that they "picture" the organizer, such as a hierarchy, as they think about the content. Imagery (the visual code) complements the verbal code and provides an additional avenue for storage and retrieval. Research indicates that the combination of the two promotes the retention of information (J. Clark & Paivio, 1991).

Elaboration

To begin this section, let's look again at David Shelton's lesson. He began his Wednesday's class by saying, "Let's review what we've found out so far. Then, I'm going to do a little demonstration, and I want you to think about how it relates to what you've been doing."

By having students review their current understanding and then expanding on it with his demonstration, David was capitalizing on the process of elaboration, one of the strategies most widely applicable in making information meaningful. **Elaboration** *is the process of increasing the number of associations in information (it makes information more meaningful) either by forming additional links in existing knowledge or by adding new knowledge* (Willoughby, Wood, & Khan, 1994). It is a naturally occurring process in which each person adds details to information by linking new information to information in long-term memory. It occurs in a noisy party, for example; when you miss some of a conversation, you fill in details, trying to make sense of the message. You do the same as you read or listen to a lecture. You expand on and sometimes distort information to make it fit your expectations and current understanding.

Elaboration can enhance meaningfulness in one or both of two ways. For example, when Tanya said, "Oh, I get it! Pluto isn't level with the rest of them," her conclusion about

7.36 ▬
Think about the use of charts, matrices, and outlines from the perspective of information processing. What function would they serve for beginning lessons? What function would they serve later in lessons?

7.37 ▬
Research indicates that students commonly think green plants get their food from the environment, as animals do, rather than make their own. Does this research finding imply that the information is *not* organized for these students? Explain.

7.38 ▬
Look again at Figures 7.4 and 7.5. How do these figures illustrate the information in this section?

Table 7.5

Types of organization and examples

Type	Example
Chronological	History: Which occurred first, the Dred Scott decision or the Missouri Compromise? How are they related?
Cause and effect: One variable causes the other	Home economics: The yeast in the dough gives off CO_2, which causes bread to rise. What are some factors that affect the metabolism of yeast?
Part/whole or subcomponents	Life science: The digestive system can be divided into subsystems: mouth, esophagus, stomach, small intestine, and large intestine. What are the structure and function of each?
Narrative: Stories have a setting, theme, plot, and resolution	Literature: What is *Romeo and Juliet* about, and what message was Shakespeare trying to deliver in this play?

7.39
Suppose you're a language arts teacher and have covered direct objects. Describe specifically how you would begin a lesson on indirect objects to capitalize on elaboration.

Earth's orbit was a form of elaboration. She formed an additional link in her schema without adding any new information.

David's review provided a way of capitalizing on a second type of elaboration. It reactivated his students' schemas, to which the information from Wednesday's lesson would be attached. Research indicates that teacher questioning, such as David's, can be a powerful tool to encourage student elaboration (Seifert, 1993; J. Simpson, Olejnik, Tam, & Supratthathum, 1994).

Promoting Elaboration: Analogies

An **analogy** *is a comparison in which similarities are created between otherwise dissimilar ideas* (Glynn, Duit, & Thiele, in press). For example:

> *Our circulatory system is like a pumping system that carries the blood around our bodies. The veins and vessels are the pipes, and the heart is the pump.*

In this example, the circulatory system (the new information) is linked to pipes and a pump (familiar ideas). As a result, links and alternative pathways between the new information and information that is already stored in long-term memory are provided that might not otherwise be available.

Promoting Elaboration: Mnemonic Devices

Quickly, name the Great Lakes. Or, what are the names of the notes on the staff of the treble clef? If you remembered the acronym HOMES (Huron, Ontario, Michigan, Erie, and Superior) or said, "Every good boy does fine," for E, G, B, D, and F, you were using a mnemonic device. Mnemonics are widely and successfully used in classrooms to help students remember vocabulary, names, rules, and other kinds of factual knowledge.

Mnemonic devices *are strategies that promote meaningfulness by forming associations between items or ideas that don't exist naturally in the content.* Because they create links between new and existing ideas, mnemonic devices are forms of elaboration.

Teachers help students encode information in effective ways by organizing content and sharing this organization with students.

Other mnemonics use acronyms, such as NASA (National Aeronautics and Space Administration) and SCUBA (self-contained underwater breathing apparatus), or place information to be remembered into statements or phrases that are meaningful to learners. As these devices are used to recall information, learners remember the mnemonic and then link it to the items it represents. Examples are shown in Table 7.6.

7.40
What is an important limitation in the classroom use of mnemonics?

Activity

Because the notion of learners being active participants in learning is at the heart of cognitive learning theories, we use this idea as a capstone for this section. You first saw "activity" emphasized in our study of Piaget and Vygotsky in Chapter 2, and you also saw in our discussion of information processing that learners attend to, perceive, rehearse, and make conscious efforts to represent information in their memories. Further, as they become aware of strategies for improving their understanding, their metacognitive abilities improve and they take steps toward self-regulation. These are all active processes.

Effective and Ineffective Activity

Activity can be deceiving, however, and not all kinds of activity promote learning equally (Robins & Mayer, 1993). As an example, consider two chemistry students who use the worked examples in their text to help them understand the material in the chapter.

> Selena reads the sample problem and then carefully reads through the solution provided by the text's authors. Gretchen covers up the solution, first trying to work the problem on her own and then comparing the solution in the book to hers.

7.41
One student highlights entire paragraphs of her text, whereas another highlights only sentences and small sections. Which of the two is likely to be the more "active" in her study? Explain.

At a casual glance, both girls appear to be studying effectively. However, Gretchen is in a more mentally "active" mode than is Selena. She prepares a solution that she can compare to the one provided; this procedure makes her studying more meaningful.

As another example, how do you use the margin notes in each chapter? Do you read them and then read the feedback provided in the supplement, or do you read them, write

Table 7.6

Examples of mnemonic devices

Biology	
Kingdom, Phylum, Class, Order, Family, Genus, Species	King Phillip came over from Greece singing.
Astronomy	
Mercury, Venus, Earth, Mars Jupiter, Saturn, Uranus, Neptune, Pluto	My very educated mother just served us nine pizzas.
Grammar	
Spelling rules	"I" before "e" except after "c."
The Calendar	
Days of the months	Thirty days hath September, April, June, and November . . .

an answer, and then compare your answer with the feedback. The latter more "actively" involves you in making the content meaningful.

Putting students in the most active role possible is powerful in promoting meaningfulness and learning, but this activity must be clear and purposeful. It is somewhat analogous to hands-on learning that is so strongly emphasized in science. Hands-on activities are effective only if they are directed to a clear goal and encourage students to think about connections between the new information and information already in long-term memory. Hands-on merely for the sake of hands-on is little more effective than traditional instruction. Similar arguments could be made for manipulatives in math (Ball, 1992) or cooperative learning—in any content area—that doesn't require the meaningful processing of information.

Active learning encourages students to encode information in meaningful ways.

A number of teaching and learning strategies encourage activity:

▌ Putting content in the form of problems to solve, rather than information to be memorized

▌ Questioning that requires students to analyze, rather than recall, information

▌ Requiring students to provide evidence for conclusions, rather than merely form conclusions

▌ Developing lessons with examples and applications, instead of definitions

▌ Testing and quizzing that requires application, rather than rote memory

The critical features of each are that students are put in as active a role as possible, the activity is purposeful, and it requires making connections and deep processing.

Classroom Connections

Applying an Understanding of Organization in Your Classroom

1. Carefully organize the information you present to your students.
   - A biology teacher displays an outline of the topics covered to that point in the unit and then highlights the topics to be covered in the current day's lesson.
   - A math teacher presents to students a flowchart with a series of questions they're encouraged to ask themselves as they solve word problems. She then models the process, using the flowchart as a guide.

Applying an Understanding of Imagery in Your Classroom

2. Whenever possible, encourage students to form images of the topics they study.
   - A geography teacher encourages her students to visualize, as they think about longitude and latitude, flat parallel lines on the globe and to picture vertical lines coming together at the North and South Poles.
   - A language arts teacher asks students to imagine how the characters would look in the books they read. She asks them to describe the characters in detail, including their facial features, the way they wear their hair, how they're dressed, and any other details.

Applying an Understanding of Elaboration in Your Classroom

3. Relate new information to previously learned material.
   - A fourth-grade teacher states, "We've been studying the digestive system. We're turning now to the circulatory system. As we study the circulatory system, think about aspects of it that are similar to or different from the digestive system."
   - An art teacher begins, "Color is one way to give pictures depth. Another way that we'll study is perspective. As we study perspective, keep in mind how both it and color interact to give the perception of depth."

4. Ask questions requiring students to make comparisons, find relationships, and search for patterns.
   - A science teacher states, "We've just examined physical changes. How does this compare with chemical changes? Can you give me an example of each?"
   - A class studying Shakespeare is asked, "How are the plot and the setting related in *Macbeth*?"
   - A math teacher asks, "Why are the units for volume cubic centimeters, whereas the units for area are square centimeters?"

5. Review at the beginning and end of each class period.
   - A class studying American literature is asked, "We started our discussion of Hemingway's *The Sun*

Also Rises yesterday. What were the key ideas we discussed yesterday?"

- A math teacher states, "Our class period is nearly over, so let's review what we've learned today. We know some new formulas. Who can tell me how we would find the volume of this box?"

6. Ask for and use examples to illustrate abstract ideas.
   - A third-grade science teacher demonstrates that heat causes expansion by placing a balloon-covered soft drink bottle in a pot of hot water. He supplements the demonstration with a drawing simulating the spacing and motion of the air molecules.
   - An English teacher dealing with the concept of *internal conflict* in literature displays the following on the overhead: "Joanne didn't know what to do.

She was looking forward to the class trip, but if she went, she wouldn't be able to take the scholarship qualifying test."

Applying an Understanding of Activity in Your Classroom

7. Actively involve students in the learning process.
   - In discussing word problems, a math teacher asks individual students to explain how they arrived at their solutions and why they chose a particular process.
   - A history teacher begins new topics with a description of a historical event and asks students why they think the event occurred. The unit is then developed around the students' search for an explanation.

 # Constructivism

To begin this section, let's look in on a teacher working with a class of 29 fourth graders in a science lesson.

Tracey Stoddart began her unit on heat by innocently asking, "What is heat?" Her students, confident of their 9 years of experience with the world, were more than willing to share their knowledge of the sun, fires, radiators, and other sources of heat.

Everything was going smoothly until Nick shared his belief that heat came from clothes such as sweaters and coats. The rest of the class nodded in agreement. Tracey was momentarily at a loss for words. How should she deal with this situation? We have all had the experience of being "cold," putting on a sweater, and "warming up."

After thinking for a few moments, she set aside her plans for the day and continued by asking, "Which do you think produces more heat, a sweater or a coat?"

"A coat!" the class unanimously agreed.

"What about a sweater and a jacket? Which one makes more heat?"

Students weren't so sure about this one. Some of them had heavy wool sweaters that they said kept them warmer than jackets; others thought they felt warmer in jackets because they blocked the wind.

"How could we find out for sure?" Tracey wondered aloud.

"How about we put a thermometer in a coat," Brad suggested.

"Yeah, and we can put another one in a sweater, and see which one gets hotter," Sonja added.

"Very good ideas," Tracey smiled. After more discussion, the class divided into seven groups of three and two groups of four. Three groups dug out thermometers from the file cabinet, read and recorded the temperature, and carefully wrapped them in coats. Three other groups did the same with sweaters, and the final three with jackets. They then went out for recess.

They returned, again read the temperatures, and recorded them on the chalkboard.

		Before	After
Coat	1:	72	72
	2:	73	72
	3:	72	73
Sweater	1:	74	73
	2:	74	74
	3:	73	73
Jacket	1:	71	72
	2:	72	71
	3:	72	73

As they looked at the information, the students began mumbling and commenting that the numbers didn't seem to make sense.

"None of them got hot," Brad said with uncertainty in his voice.

"About three of them got colder," Anne added in bewilderment.

"Yeah, but the sweaters and coats weren't the same," Anthony countered.

"That doesn't matter," Greta responded. "They shoulda still got hot."

"Maybe we didn't do it long enough," Gary suggested.

"When I was up in the attic with my mom, it was terrible hot 'cause air couldn't get in there," Suzanne added. "I think we should put plastic around them."

Several additional suggestions were made, and the groups went back to work on additional experiments. To the students' amazement, the results were the same, and finally, most of the students were willing to consider the possibility that coats and sweaters don't actually generate heat.

"If that's the case, how do they keep us warm?" Tracey wondered aloud. After additional discussion, Tracey asked what the class would expect if they wrapped a book with a sweater. Would the book warm up? How about a piece of metal? A pencil?

Opinions varied. The class did additional experiments to check and confirm their ideas. Finally, Tracey asked the students for some important differences between them and the book, pencil, and piece of metal.

"We're big, and they're little."

"The book is square, sort of."

"The pencil is skinny."

"We're alive; they aren't."

After several additional comments, Sonja noted, "The iron is cold."

"Do you think that's important?" Tracey queried.

". . . Maybe. We're not cold."

". . . Maybe if we're warm, a coat just keeps us warm," Andrew added after several seconds.

They then considered and discussed the idea that clothing merely traps heat rather than generates it. As the discussion came to a close, most of the students suggested that this was probably a more sensible idea.

The process had taken more time, but the time was well spent.[1]

As we said earlier, all cognitive theories emphasize that learners are active in developing their own understanding of the topics they study. Some researchers argue, however,

---

[1]*Source:* "Teaching for Conceptual Change: Confronting Children's Experience" by B. Watson and R. Konicek, 1990. *Phi Delta Kappan, 71,* 680–685. Copyright 1990 by *Phi Delta Kappan,* Adapted by permission.

that certain theoretical approaches, such as information processing, don't stress the process of *knowledge construction* as much as they should (Derry, 1992).

You first encountered the idea of knowledge construction in Chapter 2, when we said that learners "construct" their own understanding of the topics they study, rather than have understanding delivered to them by other people or materials. You also saw that Piaget and Vygotsky were pioneers in the constructivist movement.

Emerging Role of Constructivism in Education

The influence of constructivism in teaching and learning is increasing. The shift toward literature-based approaches to reading, for example, and process approaches to writing are both grounded in constructivism (S. McCarthy, 1994). The *Curriculum and Evaluation Standards for School Mathematics* (NCTM, 1989) and the *Benchmarks for Science Literacy* (AAAS, 1993) both have a constructivist foundation, and modern school textbooks also describe themselves as based on constructivist views of learning (Thompson, McLaughlin, & Smith 1995). The increasing influence of constructivism can be seen across the school curriculum.

Different Views of Constructivism

We said at the beginning of this chapter that there isn't *a* cognitive theory of learning, and the same is true of constructivism. Constructivists disagree on the nature of knowledge and the importance of different elements of the process. We describe two positions in this section.

The first position, based largely on Piaget's work, is called *cognitive constructivism* by some researchers (Cobb, 1994). It focuses on internal, individual constructions of knowledge (Fowler, 1994; Moshman, 1982). Knowledge does not exist as such in the social environment; rather, social interaction is important primarily as a stimulus or catalyst for individual, internal cognitive conflict. When one child suggests an idea that causes disequilibrium in another, for example, the second child might resolve the disequilibrium by individually constructing, or reconstructing, mental structures. For instance, if two children are playing and one jumps up and yells, "Look out," at the sight of an approaching dog, the second child may change the way he thinks about dogs, even if he hasn't had a bad experience with dogs.

Cognitive constructivism emphasizes learning activities that are child determined and discovery oriented. For instance, math educators taking this position would argue that children will learn math facts more effectively if they discover these facts on the basis of what they already know, rather than have them presented by a teacher or other expert (Pressley, Harris, & Marks, 1992).

Cognitive constructivism poses a dilemma for educators. Direct applications of Piaget's work, with emphasis on "pure" discovery, "fundamentally distrusted all attempts to instruct directly" (Resnick & Klopfer, 1989, p. 3). So, other than providing materials and a supportive learning environment, what is the teacher's role in this process? The question has never been fully or satisfactorily answered for classroom teachers.

A second position, strongly influenced by Vygotsky's (1978) work, is called *social constructivism* (Bruning et al., 1995; Turner, 1995). Although social constructivists vary in what they emphasize (e.g., Rogoff, 1990), they agree that knowledge exists in a social context and is, at least initially, shared with others rather than represented solely in the mind of an individual (M. Cole, 1991). As people interact, the process of sharing results in learn-

---

7.42 ▬
On the basis of the information in this section, on what fundamental principle is constructivism based?

ers refining their own ideas and helping shape the ideas of others. Social constructivism acknowledges the contributions of others in learning, whereas cognitive views of learning, with their individual, "in-the-head" view of knowledge construction, have historically ignored them.

Social constructivism helps resolve the Piagetian constructivists' dilemma. It "does not suggest that educators get out of the way so children can do their natural work, as Piagetian theory often seemed to imply" (Resnick & Klopfer, 1989, p. 4). Unlike the Piagetian-based downplaying of the role of the social environment, social constructivism highlights that role and suggests that teachers consider all the traditional questions of teaching: how to organize and implement learning activities, how to motivate students, and how to assess learning. It answers these questions, however, with a focus on learners' own constructions of understanding, rather than on the mere presenting of information. It has become a dominant influence in education.

> **7.43**
> Both cognitive and social constructivism emphasize the importance of social interaction. They differ, however, in the function it performs. Describe this difference.

Characteristics of Constructivism

Despite their differences, most constructivists agree on four characteristics that permeate all learning (Bruning et al., 1995; Good & Brophy, 1994; S. McCarthy, 1994). These characteristics are outlined in Figure 7.11.

Learners Construct Understanding

The core idea of constructivism—knowledge construction—emphasizes that learners develop their own understanding that makes sense to them; they don't receive understanding from an outside source. Brophy (1992) observes,

> Current research, while building on the findings indicating the vital role teachers play in stimulating student learning, also focuses on the role of the student. It recognizes that students do not passively receive or copy input from teachers, but instead actively mediate it by trying to make sense of it and to relate it to what they already know (or think they know) about the topic. Thus, students develop new knowledge through the process of *active construction.* (p. 5)

You can see the process of "knowledge construction" in Tracey Stoddard's students. They believed that heat was generated not only by the sun and other common heat sources but also by coats, jackets, and sweaters. As the lesson developed, their understanding gradually evolved to the point where they believed heat was simply trapped by garments.

You can also see from the students' comments that they didn't "receive understanding" from Tracey. Rather, they were faced with the problem of understanding an abstract idea, and in their efforts to understand, they conducted experiments and constructed their own meaning. This process of students developing their own meaning is the core of constructivism.

Figure 7.11

Characteristics of constructivism

- Learners construct their own understanding.
- New learning depends on current understanding.
- Learning is facilitated by social interaction.
- Meaningful learning occurs within authentic learning tasks.

7.44

Identify two similarities between information processing and constructivism. Identify one important difference.

7.45

Identify at least four ways in which background knowledge can be organized. What implications do they have for instruction?

7.46

Using Piaget's work as a basis, explain why people are reluctant to modify their existing understanding of the way the world works.

7.47

Constructivists might have one criticism of the social interaction illustrated in David Shelton's teaching. What might this criticism be?

7.48

On the basis of the information in this section, does constructivism have more implications for curriculum development or for instruction? Explain.

Tracey played an important role in the process. She could have simply explained the idea that coats and sweaters trap rather than generate heat, and this is what teachers commonly do. But abstract explanations don't do much to help ideas "make sense." In contrast, Tracey demonstrated a great deal of expertise as she guided students to a more mature understanding of heat, and most important, the ideas made sense to them.

In addition to Tracey's lesson, you can see elements of instruction based on constructivism in David Shelton's lesson. They both illustrate an important implication for instruction based on constructivism: *The way the information is presented is critical.* Instead of lecturing, Tracey and David *guided* their students to an understanding of the content in the lessons. In the extreme, lecturing and explaining are based on behaviorist views of learning, treating learners as passive recipients of understanding.

New Learning Depends on Current Understanding

We emphasized the role of background knowledge and current understanding in our discussion of information processing and again when we discussed making information meaningful. Constructivists also emphasize the importance of students' current understanding; they see new learning interpreted in the immediate *context* of current understanding, not first as isolated information that is later related to existing knowledge.

This principle was explicitly illustrated in Tracey's lesson. At the beginning of her lesson, her students' understood clothing to be a source of heat. This understanding guided the design of their experiments, caused their confusion and uncertainty about the results, and directed new experiments. Different understandings would have directed different experiments and caused different interpretations. During the lesson, Tracey's students, with her guidance, gradually developed a more mature understanding of heat and clothing. This is the essence of knowledge construction.

Tracey's students were also reluctant to give up their ideas about heat. This reluctance to "give up" current understandings helps in explaining why merely telling or explaining to students—such as Tracey explaining that coats and sweaters only trap heat—aren't effective. Students must be provided with experiences that make sense to them, or else current understandings are unlikely to mature or change.

Learning Is Facilitated by Social Interaction

Tracey's lesson also underscores the importance of social interaction in learning. Nick's suggestion that heat comes from coats and sweaters originated in a discussion of the nature of heat. Designs for the experiments, their results, and interpretations of their findings all resulted from shared thinking and decision making.

Tracey played a critical role in this process. She provided only enough guidance to keep them on track, and she encouraged their interactions with each other as well as with her. She also provided sufficient guidance and support to help the students make progress, but not so much that she reduced their active role in the learning process. This is a sophisticated form of instruction and requires a great deal of teacher expertise (A. Brown, 1994).

To emphasize the importance of social interaction, researchers have called for the creation of "communities of learners" within classrooms (A. Brown & Campione, 1994). Learning communities encourage students to take responsibility for their own learning through cooperative ventures. Both Tracey Stoddart and David Shelton attempted to create learning communities by forming groups that were responsible for problem solving. As students worked on problems, both teachers facilitated the process by offering only enough guidance to ensure that they were making progress.

Importance of Dialogue in Learning.   You've seen how important social interaction is in the learning process. The way that "more knowledgeable members of the culture"—the teachers, in these cases—assist in learning is by encouraging dialogue, both teacher-student and student-student. Let's look again at a brief example.

Sonja:	The iron is cold.
Tracey:	Do you think that's important?
Sonja:	Maybe. We're not cold.
Andrew:	Maybe if we're warm, a coat just keeps us warm.

This dialogue was primarily teacher-student. Let's look at an example of student-student dialogue from David's lesson.

Juan:	Pluto wasn't part of the solar system to begin with.
Randy:	What do you mean?
Juan:	I was watching *Nova* with my mom, and the narrator said that scientists think Pluto was floating around and the sun kinda grabbed it. . . . See, when Mr. Shelton did that thing with the socks, the socks stayed sorta level.
Randy:	What's that got to do with it?
Juan:	Well, look. (pointing to the model)
Tanya:	Oh, I get it! Pluto isn't level with the rest of them.
Randy:	Gee, I didn't even notice that.
Tanya:	Yeah, and look there. (pointing to the chart) See how little Pluto is. It's the littlest one, so it would be sorta easy to capture.
Randy:	And it's the last one.

Both forms of dialogue allow learning to move from the external, socially shared level, to the individual, internalized level (S. McCarthy, 1994). Socially shared ideas provide opportunities for students to rethink and reconstruct their internal ideas about the world.

As you look again at the progress of Tracey's lesson, you can see that the final outcome was her students' individual understanding of heat and clothing. At the end of her lesson, most students thought that clothing trapping heat was a more sensible idea than clothing generating heat. Their understanding originated in social experiences but was individually internalized at the end.

Meaningful Learning Occurs Within Authentic Learning Tasks

Think about Tracey's lesson once more. In it, she seized on the opportunity to help students advance their current understanding of heat and how they're kept warm. The lesson uses an **authentic task,** *which is a classroom learning activity that requires understanding similar to understanding that would be used in the world outside the classroom.* The students were dealing with a "real" problem—how do coats and sweaters keep people warm?

Authentic tasks simulate real-world problem situations and provide students with practice in thinking in realistic, lifelike situations (Needels & Knapp, 1994). Teachers provide this practice by posing problems that are embedded in realistic situations. Such authentic situations can also increase students' motivation to learn, which in turn can further increase learning. Other examples include actually going to a supermarket to do com-

7.49
Identify at least two types of authentic learning tasks that we have included in this text.

parison shopping problems, writing a persuasive essay for a school or class newspaper, and conducting an ecological study of a tract of land near a school.

Epilogue: The Teacher's Role Revisited

Throughout this section, you've seen illustrated the important role that constructivism suggests for knowledgeable members of the classroom—most notably the teacher. Through her guidance, Tracey encouraged students to share their ideas and to compare them with ideas of others. Through the process of shared inquiry, her students were helped to analyze their own and others' ideas. Left on their own, they wouldn't have keyed on the idea that their bodies were warm and the book, pencil, and metal were cool. Constructivism offers a conceptual framework for providing this guidance through group activities in which students cooperatively construct new knowledge.

This guidance role is extremely sophisticated. Teachers must have a clear picture of the desired goals of the overall lesson, and sometimes they must form this picture very quickly, as Tracey did. They must also decide how the content will be represented, how the learning activities will be organized, and how students will interact and work together. These decisions require the well-developed "pedagogical content knowledge" that we discussed in Chapter 1. Tracey accomplished these tasks "on the spot"; David had more time to plan his lesson carefully.

Once the lesson is under way, teachers again have demanding roles. As they guide learners, they must make instant decisions about whether to intervene, and if so, when. If students are struggling with an important principle, for example, a quick intervention is probably necessary; if it is only a trivial error, teachers may let it pass (A. Brown & Campione, 1994). They may even scrap their initial plans and allow the lesson to take a distinct turn, as Tracey did.

All this may seem a bit overwhelming to a beginning teacher. With effort and practice, however, these abilities can be acquired, and you've seen them illustrated in several of the case studies you've already studied in this book. In time, the ability to adapt, to "go with the flow" and capitalize on learning opportunities as Tracey did, will become essentially automatic. When it does, the rewards, both in student learning and in personal satisfaction, can be enormous. This is the essence of instruction based on constructivism.

Teaching strategies based on constructivism require teachers who are responsive to the learning needs of students.

Classroom Connections

Applying Constructivism in Your Classroom

1. Develop learning activities around realistic problems.
   - In a unit on percent increase and percent decrease, a math teacher has students go to malls and find examples of clothes that have been "marked down." He also brings in newspaper ads. The class discusses the examples and calculates the amount saved in each case.
   - A social studies teacher has students describe their favorite forms of recreation and notice the way they're dressed. She then asks students who have moved to their area from other parts of the country to do the same for their previous locations. She then asks them to explain the difference and guides a discussion of how climate and geography relate to lifestyle.

2. Teach new ideas in the context of current understandings.
   - A third-grade teacher beginning a unit on crustaceans, insects, and arachnids asks students to tell her as many things as they can think of about crabs, lobsters, and "bugs." She then presents examples of each and has the students compare the characteristics.
   - An English teacher has students describe what they know about writing persuasively. She then has them describe what they might want to know about this form of writing. She follows this discussion with examples of effective and ineffective persuasive essays.

3. Create a "learning community" atmosphere in your classroom.
   - An English teacher discussing *The Scarlet Letter* has the students share their individual perceptions of the characters, the events, and how those impressions were formed.
   - A science teacher discussing heat and expansion has the students articulate their understanding of a series of demonstrations that illustrate the relationship. Where there are disagreements in understanding, she encourages the students to explain and defend their understanding to each other.

Windows on Classrooms

At the beginning of the chapter, you saw how David Shelton planned and conducted his lesson in an effort to make the information meaningful for his students and help them construct their own understanding of the topic he was teaching.

Let's look now at another teacher as she conducts a lesson with a group of high school students studying the novel *The Scarlet Letter.* As you read the case study, consider the extent to which the teacher applied the information you have studied in this chapter in her lesson.

Sue Southam, an English teacher at Highland High School, is discussing Nathaniel Hawthorne's *The Scarlet Letter.* This novel, set in Boston in the 1600s, describes a tragic and illicit love affair between the heroine (Hester Prynne) and a minister (Arthur Dimmesdale). The novel gets its title from the letter *A,* meaning "adulterer," that the Puritan community makes Hester wear as punishment for her adultery with—to the community—an unknown sinner. The class has been discussing the book for several days, and the focus for this lesson is on Reverend Dimmesdale's character.

After the class enters the room and quickly settles down, Sue begins by briefly reviewing the novel's plot to date.

She then asks about Hester's illicit lover. After the class identifies Dimmesdale as the baby's father, Sue challenges them by asking, "How do you know it's Dimmesdale's? What are the clues in the text in Chapter 3? . . . Nicole?"

"He acts very withdrawn. He doesn't want to look her in the face and doesn't want to be involved in the situation."

"Okay, anything else, any other clues?"

"The baby . . . it points at Reverend Dimmesdale."

"Good observation. That is a good clue and one of my favorite scenes from the novel," Sue adds.

After several more comments, Sue pauses and says, "Class, I'd like to read a passage to you from the text describing Dimmesdale. Listen carefully, and then I'd like you to do something with it."

After reading the paragraph, Sue continues, "In your logs, jot down some of the important characteristics in that description. If you were going to draw a portrait of him, what would he look like? Try to be as specific as possible. Try that now."

Sue gives the students a few minutes to write in their logs and then, with a questioning look, continues by asking, "If you were directing a film of *The Scarlet Letter,* what would Dimmesdale look like? . . . Mike?"

" . . . Thin, 5 feet 10, nervous, trembling lips," Mike offers.

"Yeah, and he's always mopping his brow with a handkerchief," Todd adds, gesturing with his hands as if he's mopping his brow.

"What else?" Sue encourages.

"Wire-framed glasses," Tamara contributes.

"With brown, melancholy eyes," Jeremy adds.

After the class discusses additional characteristics, Sue shifts gears by asking, "What do these characteristics tell us about Dimmesdale as a person? . . . Anyone? . . . Sonya?"

"I think he's worried about getting caught."

" . . . Kasha?"

"I think he feels bad about what has happened to Hester. He feels guilty," Kasha adds.

After a few additional comments, Sue says, "Let's see whether we can find out more about the Dimmesdale character through his actions. I'd like you to listen carefully while I read the speech by Reverend Dimmesdale in which he confronts Hester Prynne in front of the congregation and exhorts her to identify her secret lover and partner in sin. Think about both Dimmesdale's and Hester's thoughts while I'm reading."

She reads Dimmesdale's speech, and after she's finished, she divides the class into Dimmesdales and Hesters by counting "One, two" in front of different rows around the room.

Then she says, "Now I'd like you to role-play; pretend you're either Hester or Dimmesdale during the speech. All the 'ones' are Dimmesdales, and all the 'twos' are Hesters. Dimmesdales, in your logs I want you to tell me what Dimmesdale is really thinking during this speech. Hesters, I want you to tell me what Hester is thinking while she listens to Dimmesdale's speech. Write in your logs in your own words what the private thoughts of your character are. Do that right now, and then we'll come back together in a few minutes."

As students write in their logs, Sue circulates around the room, clarifying the task and encouraging students to be creative in their perspective taking.

After giving them a few minutes to write in their logs, she sorts them into groups of four, with each group composed of two Hesters and two Dimmesdales. Once students are settled, she says, "In each group, I want you to start off by having Dimmesdale tell what he is thinking during the first line of the speech. Then I'd like a Hester to respond. Then continue on with Dimmesdale's next line, and then Hester's reaction. Go ahead and share your thoughts in your groups."

After giving students about 5 minutes to share their perspectives, she reconvenes the class with, "Okay, let's hear it. A Dimmesdale, first. Just what was he thinking during his speech? . . . Mike?"

"The only thing I could think of was, 'Oh God, help me. I hope she doesn't say anything. If they find out it's me, I'll be ruined. . . . And then here comes Hester with her powerful speech," Mike concludes, turning to his partner in the group, Nicole.

With a nod, Sue acknowledges Mike's reply and gestures to Nicole. "Nicole, what do you think Hester is thinking during this speech?"

"I wrote, 'Good man, huh. So why don't you confess then? You know you're guilty. I've admitted my love, but you haven't. Why don't you just come out and say it?'"

"Interesting. . . . What else? How about another Hester? . . . Sarah?"

"I just put, 'No, I'll never tell. I still love you, and I'll keep your secret forever,'" Sarah offers.

Sue pauses for a moment, looks around the room, and comments, "Notice how different the two views of Hester are. Nicole paints her as very angry, whereas Sarah views her as still loving him." Sue again pauses to look for reactions. Karen raises her hand, and Sue nods to her.

"I think the reason Hester doesn't say anything is that people won't believe her because he's a minister," Karen suggests. "She's getting her revenge just by being there reminding him of his guilt."

"But if she accuses him, won't people expect him to deny it?" Brad adds, responding to Karen.

"Maybe he knows she won't accuse him because she still loves him," Julie offers.

"Wait a minute," Jeff interrupts, gesturing with his hands. "I don't think he's such a bad guy. I think he feels guilty about it all, but he just doesn't have the courage to admit it in front of all of those people."

"I think he's really admitting it in his speech but is asking her secretly not to tell," Caroline puts in. "Maybe he's really talking to Hester and doesn't want the rest of the people to know."

The class continues, with students debating the hidden meaning in the speech and trying to decide whether Reverend Dimmesdale is really a villain or a tragic figure.

As the end of class nears, Sue says, "Interesting ideas . . . And who haven't we talked about yet? . . . Sherry?"

"Hester Prynne's husband . . . ?"

" . . . Who's been missing for several years," Sue adds.

"Tomorrow, I'd like you to read Chapter 4, in which we meet Hester's husband. That's all for today. Please put the desks back. . . . Thank you."

Questions for Discussion and Analysis

Analyze Sue's lesson now in the context of the information in this chapter. In doing your analysis, you may want to consider the following questions. In each case, be specific and take information directly from the case study.

1. To what extent did Sue apply the information-processing model in her teaching? Explain, using the concepts of *attention, perception, working memory, encoding,* and *long-term memory,* together with information taken directly from the case study.

2. To what extent did Sue help make the information meaningful for the students? Explain, using the concepts of *elaboration, organization,* and *activity,* together with information taken from the case study.

3. To what extent did Sue apply constructivist principles of learning in her lesson? Explain, using information taken directly from the case study.

4. Provide an overall assessment of the lesson. Provide evidence taken from the case study in making your assessment. What could Sue have done to make the lesson more effective? Be specific in your suggestions.

 # Summary

Cognitive Views of Learning

Behaviorism and cognitive learning theories differ fundamentally in that behaviorism treats learners as passive respondents to the environment, whereas cognitive theories assume that learners are mentally active and construct their own understanding of the topics they study.

Cognitive theories acknowledge the role of environmental influence but emphasize internal, mental processes in attempting to understand learning. Behavioral theories contend that mental processes are not necessary to explain learning; rather, one looks to stimuli and reinforcers in the environment. Cognitive theories were developed, in part, because behaviorism was unable to adequately explain both research results and everyday events, especially complex phenomena such as language learning and problem solving.

Information Processing

Information processing is a cognitive view of learning that compares human thinking to the way computers process information. Information stores—sensory memory, working memory, and long-term memory—hold information; cognitive processes, such as attention, perception, rehearsal, and encoding, move the information from one store to another.

Information received by sensory memory is moved to working memory through the processes of attention and perception. Working memory, with its limited capacity, can easily be overloaded and become a bottleneck to subsequent processing. The capacity of working memory can, in effect, be increased, however, through chunking and making aspects of processing automatic.

Information-processing theory assumes that knowledge is encoded in long-term memory in complex interrelationships (schemas) of declarative knowledge, which includes knowledge of facts, concepts, and other ideas, and procedural knowledge, which is knowledge of how to perform operations, such as writing an essay. Information processing is governed by metacognition—an awareness of and control over the processes that move information from one store to another. As metacognitive knowledge and skills improve, learners develop the capacity for self-regulation.

Making Information Meaningful

Information that is meaningful is interconnected with other information in memory, and an important goal in teaching is to help learners increase the number of connections between individual items of information. A teacher can help learners make information meaningful by putting them in the most active role possible, encouraging visual imagery, organizing content in various ways, and encouraging learners to elaborate on their own understanding. Mnemonic devices help create connections in information where no natural connection exists.

Constructivism

Although all cognitive views of learning focus on learners being active, constructivism places more emphasis on learners constructing their own understanding than do other cognitive theories. Constructivists disagree on the nature of knowledge, but they generally agree that learners construct their own understanding, that new learning exists in the context of prior understanding, that learning is enhanced by social activity, and that authentic tasks promote learning. Many constructivists suggest that teachers should create a "learning community," where teachers and students work together to solve problems.

 **Important Concepts**

The Classroom

Part II

*C*hapter Outline

8

*C*omplex
*C*ognitive
*P*rocesses

Patty Kramer, a 2nd-year seventh-grade teacher, was reading her notes as she planned for the following week's instruction. She kept a journal in which she wrote comments about units and lessons and referred to them when she planned to teach the topics the next time.

She reacted with a nod when she read a note from the previous year—"Can't find areas—don't know how to begin. Memorize instead of understand"—referring to a section on finding the area of irregularly shaped plane figures. Reflecting on her experience, Patty decided, "I'm going to try to make it more real for them this year. I need some real problems instead of that stuff in the book, something they can relate to."

After considering a series of possibilities, she thought, "Why not use the school grounds? They have irregular shapes." She thought about it some more and then decided, "What the heck, I'll give it a try. It can't be any worse than last year. All we need to do is measure the grounds and take it from there. I bet they'll like it."

After her beginning-of-class routines were completed on Monday, she began by saying, "I just read an article that says the cost of educating people like all of you is skyrocketing. What do you think are some of the things that contribute to that cost?"

After thinking for a few seconds, Jerome offered, "We have a nice school. I suppose schools are one thing."

"No question about it," Patty nodded. "The school itself and the land it sits on all cost a lot of money."

"How much?" Eddy wondered.

"The school cost about $5 million, but I don't know about the land. That's a good question. How might we find out?"

In the course of discussing the question, Segundo, whose father is a surveyor, offered, "Don't we have to know how much land we have before we can do anything else? Then, once we know how many acres we have, all we have to find out is how much an acre is worth, and we can figure it out."

The class agreed that Segundo's plan was a good one, and they then began discussing ways to find out how many acres made up the campus.

"What's an acre?" Pamela wondered aloud.

"Good question," Patty smiled. She then drew the following rectangles on the chalkboard.

| FB field | 48,000 sq. ft |

| Acre | 43,560 sq. ft |

"As it turns out," Patty explained, "an acre is 43,560 square feet—a bit smaller than a football field, which is 48,000 square feet. It's what we use to describe the size of farms and ranches. I drew a rectangle on the chalkboard, but obviously, any shape that has this area is an acre."

During their continuing discussion of the problem, the class decided they needed to measure the school grounds and that they would "pace" off the lengths.

"Won't we be off if we do that?" Deanna wondered. "People don't walk the same way."

" . . . What if we do it a few times, and then we can see if they're the same," Tanya responded after thinking for a few seconds.

"What if they aren't?"

" . . . We could average them," Mike offered. Others agreed, so it was decided that they would pace off the grounds at least twice and average them to get a more accurate figure.

Patty then directed, "Beginning tomorrow, you'll get into your groups at the beginning of the period and go to work."

The students took most of Tuesday's class period to gather their measurements. Some teams decided to pace the grounds three times to check on their own consistency. As the groups returned to the room and reported their dimensions, Patty wrote them on the chalkboard. Most of the dimensions were similar, but a few were way off.

"What do you suppose happened here?" Patty wondered aloud.

"We musta measured wrong," Anthony shrugged.

"That's all part of the game," Patty smiled. "The important thing is what we do about it."

After a brief discussion, Anthony's group agreed to take their measurements again after school. "Now, we know what we're doing. It won't take long," they agreed.

"Wonderful," Patty said with a broad smile. "That's terrific. Bring them in tomorrow."

On Wednesday morning, Patty began class by referring to the table of numbers again, reviewed with the students the process for averaging, and had the students calculate the averages. She then had them compare the averages to the array of numbers so that they could see concretely what "average" meant. She also asked the students what they thought the height of the "average" boy and the "average" girl in the class might be and how they arrived at that figure. She then drew a sketch on the chalkboard that appeared as follows:

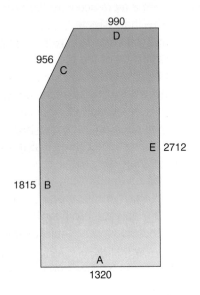

Patty labeled each side of the shape with a letter for easy reference, and she then began, "Now, what do we need to do? . . . Kara?"

" . . . Find the area, I guess."

"Yes, good. That's what we decided. Now, keep that in mind, and we'll get started tomorrow."

On Thursday, Patty began reviewing by asking, "Okay, everybody, what is it we're after?"

"The area of the school grounds," Cassy offered.

"And why do we want that?"

"So we can get the number of acres, so we can find out how much the land is worth."

"All right, good. . . . Go ahead and get back into your groups and attack our problem. See what you can do about finding the area. Remember, the way you go about finding the area is also important. We're interested in the area, that's true, but we're also interested in your strategies and your thinking as you find it."

The groups then went to work, and the classroom was soon filled with a hum of voices as students began working on the problem. As they worked, Patty moved among the groups to check on their progress, answering questions and making periodic suggestions.

"What do we do about this?" Eddy asked, pointing to the irregular shape as he, Carol, and Aniva started their work.

After thinking about it for several seconds, Aniva suggested, "We have this graph paper. . . . We could draw the thing on it. Then we could figure out the area for each square, and we could get the area."

"Okay, let's try it," Eddy nodded. "I'll get some paper."

As they started drawing the figure on the paper, Carol wondered aloud, "What about the line that goes partly through some squares? That's no good. We'll have to guess."

"Well, how close do we have to come?"

"I don't know, but this doesn't seem too good to me."

"How about if we try this?" Aniva responded after studying the figure some more. "If we draw lines through it like this, we have two rectangles and a triangle. That doesn't seem so hard," and she drew lines through the figure so that it appeared as follows:

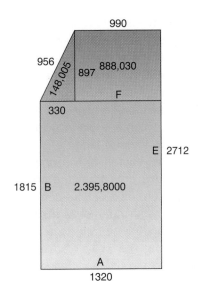

"Hey, good idea!" Carol nodded.

"All right," Eddy agreed.

"So, the area of this piece is 1,320 times 2,712," Aniva said, beginning to punch the numbers on her calculator.

"Are you sure?" Eddy wondered, looking over her shoulder. "That 2,712 is the whole length."

" . . . Oh yeah, . . . it's 1,320 times 1,815," and she put the new numbers into her calculator. They did the same thing with the smaller rectangle, and then they turned to the triangle.

"What's the formula for the area of a triangle?" Eddy wondered. "I forget."

"It's . . . it's . . . yeah, if I draw it like that, . . . that's it," Carol said more to herself than to Eddy and Aniva. "Its 330 times 897 times ½."

"What were you mumbling?" Eddy wondered.

"To remember it, I just make a rectangle. . . . See?" she said, extending the lines to make a 330 x 897 rectangle on the drawing. "Then I can see that it's half that. That way I don't have to memorize some formula."

"Neat," Eddy responded.

"Yeah," Aniva added.

Seeing that Patty was standing, waiting to reassemble the class, the students finished their calculations and turned to the front of the room.

"Let's see what we have," she said. "Does some group want to explain how they found the area? . . . Carol, Aniva, and Eddy? Go ahead."

Carol, speaking for the group, then explained how they had done the problem.

"Excellent strategy," Patty smiled. "Did any other group do it differently?"

"We did," Sandra volunteered.

"Go ahead," Patty nodded.

" . . . You do it," Sandra said to Salvado.

"We drew a line across the top and up the side so we had a rectangle. . . . Like this," he motioned with his hands, pointing to the chalkboard.

"Come up and show us," Patty encouraged.

Salvado went to the chalkboard and added to Patty's sketch so that it appeared as follows:

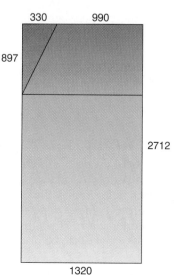

"Then, we found the area of the whole thing and the area of this," he continued, pointing to the triangle, "and we subtracted it from the whole thing, and we got it. . . . We got the same thing they did," referring to Carol's group.

The class continued discussing possible strategies for solving the problem. Jim, Aaron, and Trish used the fact that the top portion was a trapezoid, found the area of it, and added that area to the area of the rectangle.

Several members of the class didn't know what a trapezoid was, so Patty drew three quick sketches of trapezoids on the chalkboard; they appeared as follows:

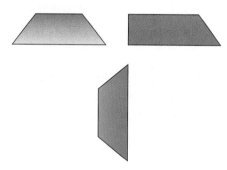

She then asked, "What do these figures have in common?"

" . . . Two of the lines are parallel," Karen volunteered after studying the figures for several seconds.

"Good," Patty smiled.

"They have four sides," Jeff added.

"Okay, good."

"That one has three 90° angles," Megan added, pointing to the figure in the middle.

" . . . None of the others do," Brad countered.

"Oh, yeah, right," Megan nodded.

"That's good, everyone," Patty smiled again, seeing that the students seemed to be satisfied. "Trape-

zoids are four-sided figures with two of the sides parallel. That's their essential feature."

Patty then had the group explain again how they got the area of the trapezoid, and she said finally, "Now, let's look back at our problem. We've found the area. What else do we need?"

After a short discussion, the class concluded that they needed to divide the area by 43,560 to get the number of acres. They found that the campus was just under 79 acres.

"Gee, 79 football fields. That's a lot," Greg commented.

Patty smiled, nodded, and then went on, "Now, we found the area of a plane figure—our school grounds—that doesn't have a regular shape; let's review some of the strategies the groups used."

The class reviewed the strategies that had been discussed, and then Patty said, "Suppose the school grounds had been shaped like this instead," and she drew the following figure on the chalkboard.

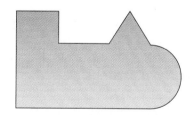

"Now, because we've shared our thinking on the school grounds problem, you have more strategies available to you than you did before. . . . So, get back in your groups for a few more minutes, and let's attack this problem."

Several of the groups struggled with the problem because they didn't know how to cope with the circular portion of the figure. So Patty provided some extra guidance for those groups in finding the area. Then, they again discussed their strategies as a large group.

She then gave the students a sheet with three more irregular figures on it and, for homework, assigned the students the task of finding those areas.

She reminded the class, "I want you to solve these problems alone. Then, once you have a solution, check with your teammates to see whether you agree and to compare your strategies. If you can't resolve your disagreements or just get stuck, raise your hands, and I'll help you. . . . Okay, go to work." The students then worked on the problems, and Patty provided periodic assistance for those needing help.

In this chapter, we extend our study of cognitive learning by discussing learners' knowledge and metacognition in terms of the content and strategies they learn in school. We begin by examining concepts, one of the most common forms of school content. We continue with an analysis of problem solving, which is being increasingly emphasized in both school curricula and research. We then move to a discussion of the strategic learner and how learners can use self-regulation to take responsibility for and increase their own learning. We complete the chapter with a discussion of transfer—the ways learning and understanding in one setting can be applied in others.

After you've completed your study of this chapter, you should be able to meet the following objectives:

▌ Explain the application of concept learning to classroom activities.
▌ Apply problem-solving strategies to well-defined and ill-defined problems.
▌ Explain how thinking skills can be used in classroom learning activities.
▌ Describe how study skills can be used to increase student learning.
▌ Discuss ways of increasing transfer of learning.

Teachers often encounter challenges similar to those of Patty Kramer in the opening case study. Their students struggle with certain topics, and the teachers are often frustrated in their efforts to help. As a result, they approach a topic reluctantly the next time they teach it, or they even skip it completely. Patty took a positive approach instead. Knowing that her students had tried to "memorize their way through" the unit the year before, she increased her efforts to make the information meaningful to them. She also recognized that the unit involved different types of learning, and she consciously directed her teaching to each. We examine these aspects of learning in this chapter, beginning with concepts.

Concept Learning

Concepts: Categories That Simplify the World

8.1

Think about this book and the class that's using it. Identify at least five concepts that you've learned in your study to this point.

Concepts, or *mental abstractions that categorize sets of objects, events, or ideas,* represent a major portion of the school curriculum, and much of teachers' efforts are directed at teaching them. The categories, based on rules or prototypes, help simplify the world for learners. For example, if learners saw the polygons in Figure 8.1, they would describe them all as triangles even though the shapes vary in size and orientation. "Triangle" represents a mental category into which all instances or examples of triangles can be placed.

People think in terms of concepts because this allows them to simplify the world. The concept of *triangle* allows people to think and talk about the objects in Figure 8.1 as a group, rather than as specific, discrete objects. Having to remember each separately would make learning impossibly complex and unwieldy.

Although not the central focus, concept learning was an important part of Patty's lesson. For example, her students were uncertain about the concepts of *acre, average,* and *trapezoid,* and some time in the lesson was devoted to each. In addition, the students used concepts such as *triangle, rectangle,* and *area* in their problem solving. Significantly, the concepts were developed in the context of the lesson, rather than in isolation, and each time the students used them, their understanding evolved as the concepts were cast in new and richer contexts (J. Brown, Collins, & Duguid, 1989).

Examples of concepts in language arts, social studies, math, and science are presented in Table 8.1. This is only a brief list, and you can probably think of many more for each area. Concepts are taught in music, art, physical education, and other areas as well, and in addition, students learn abstract or defined concepts such as *honesty* and *justice* as they go through school and life.

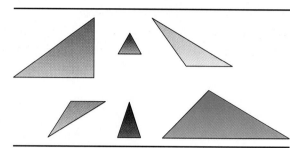

Figure 8.1

Triangles

Characteristics: The Defining Features of Concepts

Some concepts, such as those Patty taught, have clear and precise **characteristics** (sometimes called "attributes" or "features"), *which are a concept's defining elements.* Triangles, for example, have four essential characteristics: plane, closed, straight lines, and three sides. Other characteristics, such as color, size, and length of lines, are not essential, so learners can put red, green, large, small, equilateral, isosceles, and scalene triangles all into the category *triangle.* These additional, or nonessential, characteristics don't alter the concept of *triangle.*

Factors Influencing the Ease of Learning Concepts

The ease of learning a concept is directly related to the *number* of characteristics and how tangible and *concrete* they are (Tennyson & Cocchiarella, 1986). When a concept's characteristics are clear, concrete, and observable, concept learning is simplified. You saw this with *triangle,* and the same is true for other concrete concepts, such as *adjective, latitude,* and *mammal.*

8.2
Identify at least two concepts each in music, art, and physical education.

8.3
Think about the concepts of *adjective* and *conifer* in Table 8.1. What are the characteristics of each of these concepts?

8.4
Consider the concepts of *noun* and *culture.* On the basis of the information in this section, which of the two should be easier to learn? Explain your answer.

Table 8.1

Concepts in different content areas

Language Arts	Social Studies	Science	Math
Adjective	Culture	Acid	Prime number
Verb	Longitude	Conifer	Equivalent fraction
Plot	Federalist	Element	Set
Simile	Democracy	Force	Addition
Infinitive	Immigrant	Inertia	Parabola

8.5

Identify two additional concepts that have fuzzy boundaries and are therefore better described with a prototype than with characteristics.

Others are much more difficult. Could you, for example, describe with precision what makes a democracy a democracy? Most people can't because its characteristics are abstract and not precisely defined; it has "fuzzy boundaries" (Schwartz & Reisberg, 1991). Concepts such as *democracy* are often effectively learned with a **prototype**, *which is the best representative of its category* (Busmeyer & Myung, 1988; Nosofsky, 1988; Schwartz & Reisberg, 1991). When we teach concepts, we try to present a prototype as one of our first illustrations to provide a clear example for students.

Examples: The Key to Teaching and Learning Concepts

Regardless of the complexity of a concept, the key to effective concept teaching is a carefully selected set of **examples**, or *prototypes that tell the learner what the concept is,* and nonexamples, which illustrate what the concept is not (Tennyson & Cocchiarella, 1986). A valuable question to keep in mind as you prepare to teach concepts is, What can I show the students or what can I have the students do that will clearly illustrate the concept? The best examples are ones in which characteristics of the concept are clearly observable or the example is the best prototype available. To illustrate this idea, look at the following examples of the concept of *snurf.* Can you identify it's characteristics?

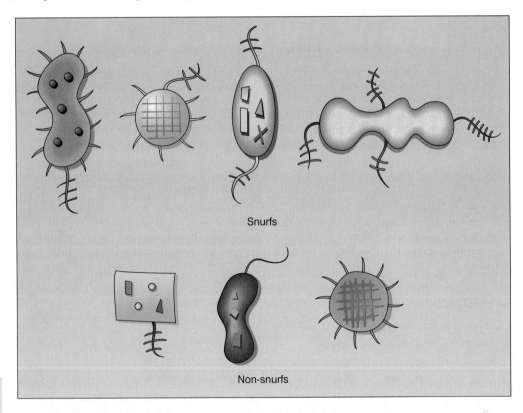

Snurfs

Non-snurfs

8.6

In teaching a concept, should you first present an example, or should you first present a nonexample? Why? Would there ever be exceptions to this order?

You can see that snurfs are curved shapes with cross-hatched tails. All other characteristics are irrelevant. You can also see that the grouping included nonexamples—cases that were not snurfs. In situations such as this, in which a concept can easily be confused with a closely related concept, nonexamples are particularly important (Tennyson & Cocchiarella, 1986). For example, if a teacher wants her students to understand the concept of *reptile,* she would include a frog—an amphibian—as a nonexample to be certain that stu-

Effective teachers use concrete examples to help students learn concepts and relate them to the real world.

dents don't confuse reptiles and amphibians. The strategies discussed in the next sections capitalize on these ideas.

Strategies for Teaching Concepts

Concept learning includes two goals: (a) acquiring the concept itself and (b) relating the concept to other concepts in a complex schema. Let's look at two strategies that attempt to reach these goals.

Rule-Example: A Concept-Teaching Strategy

The *rule-example* strategy is a tried and tested method of teaching concepts that includes four steps (Tennyson & Cocchiarella, 1986):

1. Define the concept, linking it to a superordinate concept and identifying essential characteristics.
2. Clarify terms in the definition, making sure the essential characteristics are understood.
3. Provide positive and negative examples to illustrate the essential characteristics.
4. Provide additional unlabeled positive and negative examples, asking students to categorize and explain the basis for their categorization, or have students provide their own examples.

In the rule-example strategy, a **definition**, *which is a statement that includes the concept name, a superordinate concept, and the concept's characteristics,* is presented first.

8.7
What is a superordinate concept to the concept of *adjective*? What is the difference between the *concept* of adjective and the *name* adjective?

A definition of the concept of *metaphor* might be, "Metaphor is a form of figurative language that compares one object to another as if it were the other and avoids terms such as *like* or *as.*" A **superordinate concept** *is a larger class into which the concept fits. Figurative language* is the superordinate concept to the concept of *metaphor.* In this definition, " . . . compares one object to another as if it were the other and avoids terms such as *like* or *as*" describes the characteristics of the concept. The definition and superordinate concept help embed the concept into a meaningful schema (G. Murphy & Allopena, 1994).

In the second step, the teacher helps students clarify the terms and ideas in the definition, such as knowing what " . . . compares one object to another as if it were the other . . . " means.

The third step is critical. In this step, students use *examples,* such as, "John's Camaro is a lemon," "My grandmother's hat was a garden of daisies," and "Autumn leaves are hands wrinkled with age," together with *nonexamples,* such as "Hurricane Andrew hit the Florida coast like a truck" and "I had a million pages of homework last night," to identify essential characteristics of the concept. Students discuss and analyze the examples and nonexamples as they're presented, identifying similarities and differences in them and explaining why the examples are metaphors and the others are not.

Finally, the teacher presents additional examples and nonexamples and has the students classify them, or the students produce their own. When the examples illustrate the concept's characteristics and when students are actively involved in analyzing them, the strategy can be very effective.

Concept Mapping: Embedding Concepts in Complex Schemas

Concept mapping, *a teaching strategy in which the relationships among concepts are represented visually,* focuses explicitly on the goal of helping learners relate a concept to other concepts in complex schemas (Novak & Gowin, 1984; Novak & Musonda, 1991). Concept mapping is a form of organization, which you saw in Chapter 7 is one way information can be made meaningful. The visual aspects of concept mapping also allow learn-

---

8.8

Think again about teaching the concept of *adjective.* Would a noun, a verb, or an adverb be the best nonexample? Why? To which cognitive process in the information-processing model in Chapter 7 does the use of examples and nonexamples most closely relate?

Figure 8.2

Concept map for closed plane figures

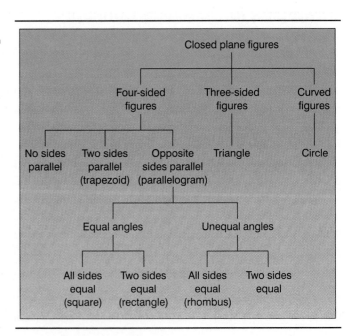

ers to use imagery as another way of representing information. Concept maps can be presented initially by teachers as they model the strategy; later, students can then develop their own. Figure 8.2 illustrates a concept map for closed plane figures.

The concepts in Figure 8.2 are organized hierarchically. Not all concepts fit into this hierarchical representation, however, so other types of maps are more appropriate. Figure 8.3 illustrates a network, which is similar to a hierarchy, except the arrows illustrate different types of relationships among the concepts.

The point in concept mapping is that students use the map to construct relationships that embed the concept into an organized framework and thus increase its meaningfulness. The form students use should be the one that best illustrates the associations. Hierarchies often work best in math and science; in other areas, such as reading, social studies, and literature, a network may be better.

Concept Learning: Misconceptions and Conceptual Change

The importance of background knowledge was one theme emphasized in Chapter 7, and it is important in concept learning as well. Although we have emphasized the importance of examples and nonexamples, you must remember that students process these examples in the context of their background knowledge and that if misconceptions exist, they can be hard to eliminate (Brandes, 1995).

An example from educational psychology is the concept of *negative reinforcement.* We repeatedly emphasized that negative reinforcement is an *increase* in behavior resulting

8.9
Create a network, based on our study of behaviorism in Chapter 6, for the concept of *operant conditioning.*

8.10
Suppose you find that your social studies students tend to view communism and fascism as synonymous. Describe specifically what you would do to eliminate this misconception.

Figure 8.3

Network for parts of a novel

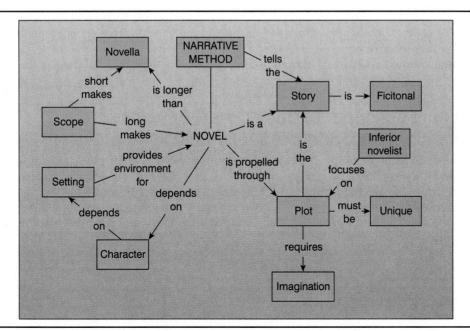

from the removal of a consequence. We carefully illustrated it with several examples because learners commonly confuse negative reinforcement with punishment, believing that negative reinforcement results in a decrease in behavior. Similar examples can be found in many areas. For instance, in science, students often confuse the concepts of *reptiles* and *amphibians* and of *spiders* and *insects.* Students give up misconceptions reluctantly and only when the misconceptions are directly confronted (Chinn & Brewer, 1993). For example,

Elaine Madison has been working with her students on basic concepts in science and has defined *force* as any push or pull and *work* as the combination of force and movement. She knows that students often incorrectly think that work is done if effort is expended, regardless of whether movement occurs.

To try to eliminate these misconceptions, she suggested, "Kari, stand up and hold up the chair."

Kari stood, lifted the chair that was at the side of the room, and remained standing motionless.

"Now," Elaine continued. "Is Kari doing any work?"

"Yes," Jared volunteered.

"What did we say the definition of work is?" Elaine probed.

"The combination of force and movement," Natalie offered.

"Okay, is Kari doing any work?" Elaine went on.

"If she stands there for a while, she'll get tired, and you get tired when you work," Jared persisted.

"But she's not moving," Kathy added. "For work to be done, there has to be movement."

"That doesn't make sense," Jared continued. "That means you can get tired without doing any work."

"What actually makes you tired?" Elaine queried.

"Holding up the chair."

"Sure. So, the effort of holding up the chair would make any of us tired. Effort is the force we're exerting, and exerting a force can make us tired."

The class continued to discuss the example, noting that Kari actually did do work when she first lifted the chair. They then discussed additional examples, noting that because of their day-to-day experience, they tend to relate effort, work, and being tired. Finally, Jared accepted the idea that work requires movement.

As we see from this example, misconceptions are difficult to change. They are formed because they make sense to us, and changing them requires restructuring our schemas. You saw this illustrated in Chapter 7, and you see it again here in the context of concept learning.

8.11
Which of the concepts from Piaget's work discussed in Chapter 2 best helps you understand why students are reluctant to give up their misconceptions?

Relating Concepts to Each Other: Principles, Generalizations, and Academic Rules

People simplify the world by forming categories that they call concepts. They can further simplify their experience by relating concepts to each other in broad patterns, which can be powerful as a basis for forming explanations and making predictions.

Principles *are relationships between concepts that are accepted as valid for all known cases.* The terms *principles* and *laws* are often used interchangeably. The following are examples:

▌ Like magnetic poles repel and unlike poles attract.
▌ The greater the force on an object, the greater its acceleration.

Principles are an important part of the school curriculum, particularly in the sciences. They are valuable because they connect concepts and help in summarizing large amounts of information. Principles also play a vital role in problem solving, as you'll see later in the chapter.

Generalizations *also are relationships between concepts, but they are more probabilistic and less certain than principles.* The following are examples of generalization:

- People immigrate for economic reasons.
- Thunderstorms occur during the afternoon hours.
- People who consume large quantities of fat have a higher incidence of heart disease than those who don't.

Although each statement describes a relationship, they have obvious exceptions. For example, many people immigrate for religious or political reasons, some thunderstorms occur during other parts of the day, and some people who consume large quantities of fat have no evidence of heart disease.

Most of the health-related information people receive from the medical profession is in the form of generalizations, and the patterns described in this text are also generalizations. Intermittent reinforcement leads to slower extinction than does continuous reinforcement. Teachers need to remember that many students don't fit this pattern; this is why careful judgment and reflection are needed when teachers make decisions based on generalizations.

Academic rules, a third type of statement linking concepts, *describe relationships between concepts that have been arbitrarily derived by people.* For example:

- A pronoun must agree with its antecedent in number and gender.
- When making nouns ending in *-y* plural, drop the *-y* and add *-ies* if the *-y* is preceded by a consonant, but add *-s* if the *-y* is preceded by a vowel.
- To round off a number, if the last digit is 5 or above, round up, and if the last digit is 4 or below, round down.

Whereas principles and generalizations describe patterns observed in the natural world, rules are conventions derived arbitrarily by people. Academic rules are important, however, because they simplify the world and provide for consistency. If there were no rules for forming plurals, for example, writing would be chaotic and communication would suffer. One part of Patty's lesson involved rules. Using formulas for finding the areas of rectangles, triangles, and circles was an application of a rule in each case.

> **8.12** ▬
> Would the statement "When students are praised for desirable behavior, the behavior increases" be more accurately called a principle or a generalization? Explain your answer with a specific example.

> **8.13** ▬
> Principles, generalizations, and academic rules have an important feature in common. What is this feature? What is the primary difference between a generalization and an academic rule?

Classroom Connections

Applying Concept Learning in Your Classroom

1. Use concrete examples to illustrate abstract or hard-to-teach concepts.

   - A physical education teacher was helping her students learn to serve a tennis ball. She videotaped several people, some with good serves and others with poor ones. During the next class period, she showed the class the videotapes and discussed the differences before having them practice their own serves.
   - A fourth-grade teacher's students were having difficulty understanding the concept of *ecosystem.* She went into her stack of *National Geographic*'s and cut out several pictures of different ecosystems—the jungle, the desert, and northern tundra. As she presented the pictures, she discussed them with

her students and helped them identify the characteristics of ecosystems in each.

2. Link essential characteristics to examples.
   • A kindergarten teacher wanted her class to understand the concept of *living thing*. She displayed and discussed examples, such as themselves, their pets, grass near the school grounds, and plants in their classroom. They identified "the ability to grow and change," and "the need for food and water" as two characteristics that the examples had in common.
   • A language arts teacher, working with her class on summary sentences, displayed paragraphs on the overhead. With her guidance, the class analyzed the summary sentences in each paragraph, determining which were good and poor and explaining why in each case.

3. Link new concepts to related concepts.
   • The term *cultural revolution* came up in a social studies lesson. The teacher asked the students to compare cultural revolutions to other revolutions they had studied, such as the Industrial Revolution and the American Revolution, pointing out similarities and differences in each case.
   • An earth science class was learning about "old" and "new" geologic formations. The teacher showed slides of the two kinds of formations, with examples of young mountains and young rivers serving as the nonexamples for the old mountains and old rivers. The class then related "old" and

"new" mountains and rivers to climate, weathering, and erosion, which had been discussed in earlier lessons.

Teaching Principles, Generalizations, and Academic Rules in Your Classroom

4. Provide examples that illustrate the relationship you're teaching.
   • A science teacher, wanting his students to understand the principle "The longer the vibrating column, the lower the pitch," had students lay rulers on their desks, extend different lengths of the rulers over the edge, and snap the rulers to hear differences in pitch.
   • A first-grade teacher wants her students to understand the rules for basic punctuation. She has the students write several sentences, and she also writes some. As the students share, and as she shares hers, she helps the class recognize that each sentence begins with a capital letter and ends with a punctuation mark.

5. Have students apply relationships to new situations.
   • The science teacher working with length and pitch put different amounts of water into three identical soft-drink bottles and asked students to predict how the amount of water would affect pitch. He then had students blow across the bottle openings to make sounds and asked them to explain the different pitches in each case.

Adaptive Instruction: Dealing With Diversity in Students' Thinking

Jody Curtis is a third-grade teacher in an ethnically diverse school. Of her 27 students, over a third are non-native English speakers. They come from a variety of backgrounds and have widely varying experiences.

Jody is beginning a unit on reptiles. She prepared by gathering colored pictures from magazines and other sources. She knew that her class had studied amphibians in the second grade, and she planned to build on their knowledge by comparing reptiles to amphibians.

As she showed each picture, she called on different students to describe and discuss what they observed. Disagreements began to emerge almost immediately.

"They're sort of worms, except they have eyes," Sarina suggested. "They wiggle when they move."

"No, they got bones," Miguel countered.

"Yeah, I saw a skeleton once," Bryan added. "It looked funny, but it had bones."

When the discussion turned to reproduction, there was more disagreement.

"They lay eggs in a nest like birds," Monica said.

"Uh huh," Jamille agreed. "In the water."

"No, they have babies born like dogs and cats," Horace retorted, arguing that the young were born alive.

They even disagreed about basic features.

"They're yucky and slimy," Sanra asserted.

"Gross," Lucia added. "All slippery and gross."

"What makes you say that?" Jody wondered aloud.

" . . . Uhh."

"No," Muhammed interjected. "My brother has a snake, and I felt it. It was dry, not slimy. It was smooth and clean," he added, reacting to the skeptical looks on his classmates' faces.

"What's your reaction to what Muhammed said?" Jody turned to Lucia, trying to reinvolve her in the discussion.

"I . . . I . . . What do you mean, reaction?"

"I mean, how does Muhammed's experience compare to what you said?"

" . . . I . . . don't know."

"Tell us about your experience with snakes," Jody encouraged.

" . . . My brother caught one in a pond, and he was holding it up by its head, . . . and I was so scared, and finally I touched it, . . . and it was all wet and slimy."

Jody and the students continued the discussion for the remainder of the science period.

In reflecting on the lesson later in the day, Jody was struck by two aspects of it. First, individual students' experiences with reptiles varied widely, and as a result, they had strong and varying preconceptions about reptiles.

Second, the way the students responded to the social interaction in the lesson also varied. Some were comfortable and confident, whereas others were less comfortable, perhaps even confused. For example, when Jody asked Lucia, a non-native English speaker of Hispanic background, "What makes you say that?" Lucia was uncertain about how to respond. Jody was asking her to provide evidence for her conclusion that snakes are slippery and gross, but Lucia didn't realize that this is what the question called for. A similar thing happened when Jody asked her, "What's your reaction to what Muhammed said?" and her effort to clarify the question by asking, "I mean, how does Muhammed's experience compare to what you said?" still didn't help. Until she simply asked Lucia to describe her experience with snakes, Jody had little insight into Lucia's understanding.

Differences in background experiences and patterns of interaction require two forms of accommodation. Let's look at them.

Accommodating Differences in Background Experiences

To begin this section, let's look at what Jody did to follow up with her students:

> To deal with the differences in the students' experiences, Jody arranged to have several reptiles brought to class. She had Muhammed bring his brother's snake, and she went to a pet store and talked the owners into letting her borrow a turtle and a lizard.
>
> The next day, as the students observed and handled the animals, they realized that snakes do have bones and that reptiles have dry, clean skin. Using additional photos, Jody showed how some reptiles laid their eggs in the ground, whereas others are born alive. On the basis of their new experiences, even Sanra and Lucia reluctantly agreed that reptiles are usually dry and clean.

> **8.14** ▬
>
> What factor in Piaget's descriptions of development best explains why the students came to the lesson with strong preconceptions about reptiles? What other factor from Piaget's work is critical in helping a student change preconceptions if they're invalid? Explain.

Because Jody was able to provide concrete experiences for the students, their concept of *reptile* was clarified and enriched. Providing these experiences can be demanding for teachers—Jody had to go to a pet store to get a live turtle and lizard, for example—but the results are worth the effort. Merely explaining that snakes are usually dry and clean would have been unconvincing for students such as Sanra and Lucia.

Although Jody's was a science lesson, similar approaches can be used in other content areas. If students are consistently misspelling the same types of words, for example, teaching rules that directly address the errors allows students to restructure their understanding (R. Hall, Gerber, & Stricker, 1989). When adapting their instruction, teachers design their lessons to build on students' current understandings. This is congruent with both cognitive and constructivist approaches to instruction.

Accommodating Differences in Patterns of Interaction

Although accommodating differences in background is demanding, dealing with differences in patterns of interaction are, in some ways, even more difficult because these differences are easy to miss. A teacher less sensitive than Jody, for example, might not have persisted with Lucia, concluding instead that the girl didn't understand the topic or was a generally weak student.

In Chapter 4, we addressed the issue of discontinuities between the home and the school, and this could have been the case with Lucia. As it turns out, her problem was not that her reasoning was faulty or that she had misconceptions about the topic. On the basis of her experience with snakes, they *are* slippery and "gross." Instead, it's likely that her home experience didn't prepare her for questions such as "What makes you say that?" "What's your reaction to what Muhammed said?" and " . . . how does Muhammed's experience compare to what you said?" When Jody persisted and asked her about her experience

8.15 ◼
What concept from Chapter 7 best helps you understand why the way students respond to your questioning and other aspects of instruction vary so much?

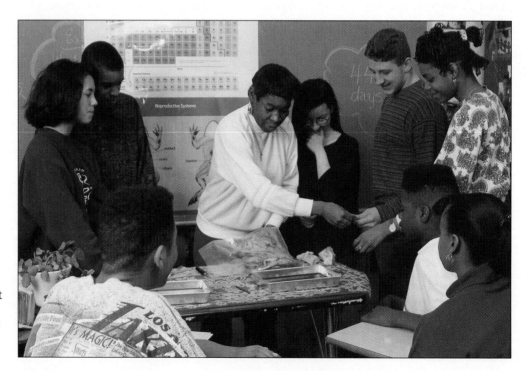

By designing activities that encourage student involvement and group problem solving, teachers help students acquire and understand classroom-effective ways of interacting.

with snakes, the basis for Lucia's comment was revealed. Had Lucia been familiar with the questioning patterns in the class, she would have responded to Jody's first question by simply saying something such as, "I felt a snake once and it was slippery and gross."

One task of teachers is to help students learn to function effectively in school. "The key challenge for schools is to introduce and enculturate students into these school-based discourses, without denigrating their culturally specific values and ways of using language" (Michaels & O'Connor, 1990, p. 18).

Teachers can help students acquire these "school affective" ways of interacting in at least three ways (Michaels & O'Connor, 1990). First, they can provide and lead discussions that build on common experiences, such as having the students observe, describe, and discuss the reptiles Jody brought to class.

Second, during the discussions, they can introduce "new kinds of talk," such as Jody's questions that asked for evidence. Because the "new talk" was related to concrete and familiar experiences—snakes and Muhammed's comments in Jody's lesson—the questions gradually become meaningful.

Third, teachers can discuss the "new talk" explicitly. For instance, Jody could discuss the intent of questions such as "What makes you say that?" with the students and model responses to them. Gradually, as students become familiar with the patterns of classroom questioning and discussion through teachers' explicit efforts to involve students, they learn that their contributions are valued.

In doing this procedure, teachers must be careful to monitor their own communication and be sensitive to the possibility that students' inability to respond may indicate miscommunication rather than lack of understanding, as was illustrated in the example with Lucia. Asking open-ended questions, as Jody did when she asked Lucia to describe her experience with snakes, is an excellent way to informally assess learners' current understanding.

Classroom Connections

Capitalizing on Diversity in Your Classroom

1. Assess students' background knowledge related to the topics you plan to teach.
   - A health teacher beginning a study of nutrition and eating habits asks her students to describe what they believe to be a good meal.
   - A math teacher beginning a unit on percentage increase and percentage decrease preassesses students by giving them several problems that require changing fractions to decimals and decimals to percentages.

2. Adapt instruction to students' different backgrounds.
   - A middle school English teacher finds that several of his students don't use Standard English in speaking and writing. He regularly assigns them short essays and encourages them to express themselves in whatever way they're comfortable. He then builds on the students' thinking and helps them learn to rephrase their writing to conform to standard practice.
   - A fourth-grade teacher beginning a unit on Central America asks his students to describe their lives in their neighborhoods. He reminds them that this is their local "culture" and to use it as a comparison when they study the different cultures in Central America.

3. Provide examples that contain all the information needed to understand the concept.

- To illustrate the concept of *adverb,* a sixth-grade teacher has a student walk quickly across the front of the room, asks the students to describe how the student walked, and writes on the chalkboard: "Brenda walked quickly across the front of the room." As the students discuss the sentence, the teacher leads them to conclude that *quickly* tells how Brenda walked, so it describes the verb in the sentence.

- A third-grade teacher demonstrates the process of multiplication by having the students make four groups of seven interlocking cubes, then three groups of eight interlocking cubes, and six groups of eight interlocking cubes. She then writes on the chalkboard 4 x 7 = 28, 3 x 8 = 24, 6 x 8 = 48 and leads the class in a discussion of what the numeral means in each case, carefully linking each numeral to the sets of cubes.

Problem Solving

As an introduction to this section, think about the following.

- You want to write a greeting card to a friend who has moved to New York, but you don't know her address.
- You're planning to buy a new carpet for your rectangular living room. To determine the cost, you need to tell the retailer the area of the room.
- You're a teacher, and your seventh graders resist thinking on their own. They expect to find the answer to every question laid bare by the textbook.

What do the three incidents have in common? Although they look different, each can be described as a *problem.* A **problem** *exists when you're in a state that differs from a desired goal or end state and there is some uncertainty about reaching the goal state* (Bransford & Stein, 1984). To solve a problem, you must figure out how to move from the "initial state" to the "goal state" (Bruer, 1993). In our cases above, for example, the present states are not knowing the address, not knowing the area of the room, and the students not wanting to think on their own. The desired states are knowing the address, knowing the area of the room, and the students thinking for themselves.

You can see from our examples that we're thinking of problems more broadly than has historically been the case. In the past, we might have focused on problems such as wanting to know the cost of carpeting the room, but we probably wouldn't have thought of wanting to know an address as a problem.

Thinking of problems more broadly is beneficial in at least two ways. First, it recognizes the pervasiveness of problem solving in people's everyday lives; and second, it allows people to apply general strategies to solve virtually all problems (Bruning et al., 1995).

8.16 ▬
Suppose you don't know the meaning of a word, so you look it up in a dictionary. Is not knowing the meaning of the word a problem under these conditions? Explain.

Well-Defined and Ill-Defined Problems

Problem-solving theorists have found it useful to distinguish between well-defined and ill-defined problems (Eysenck & Keane, 1990; Simon, 1978). A **well-defined problem** *is one in which the goal is clear and the potential solution paths to the goal are known or can be easily accessed,* whereas an **ill-defined problem** *has an ambiguous desired state and no generally agreed-on strategy for solving it* (Dunkle, Schraw, & Bendixon, 1995; Ormrod, 1995). Our first two examples are well-defined; wanting to know the address and the area of the room are unambiguous, and straightforward strategies for finding each exist. Many problems in math, physics, and chemistry are well-defined, such as this example:

> *Roger and Diana are selling lemonade. The lemonade mix was $.40 for a package that made 2 quarts. They sold the lemonade at $.10 for an 8-ounce glass and sold a total of 15 quarts. How much money did they make on each glass they sold?*

Although students often have difficulty solving this type of problem, its desired end state is clear, and specific strategies exist for solving it. Most of students' experiences in school focus on well-defined problems.

In contrast to these well-defined problems, students not wanting to think for themselves is an ill-defined problem. The desired state isn't clear; teachers are often not even sure what "thinking" means, and a readily agreed-on strategy for getting students to "think" doesn't exist. The problem can be effectively solved with several strategies, and several "right" answers can be found.

A General Problem-Solving Model

Since the 1950s, computer scientists and cognitive psychologists have worked to develop approaches to problem solving that can be applied across a variety of domains. This work has led to the development of the five-step problem-solving model that is illustrated in Figure 8.4 and discussed below (based on work by Bransford & Stein, 1984).

Identifying the Problem

Question: There are 26 sheep and 10 goats on a ship. How old is the captain?

Amazingly, in one study, 75% of the second graders who were asked this question answered 36 (cited in Prawat, 1989)! Obviously, these students had difficulty understanding what the problem was asking.

At first glance, it appears that identifying a problem, the first step in the five-step problem-solving model, is simple and straightforward. In fact, it is one of the most challenging aspects of problem solving because it requires creativity, persistence, and a willingness to avoid committing to a solution too soon (Hayes, 1988).

Four obstacles to effective problem finding are (a) lack of experience in defining problems, (b) lack of domain-specific knowledge, (c) the tendency to rush toward a solution before the problem has been clearly identified, and (d) the tendency to think convergently (Bruning et al., 1995).

8.17 Suppose you're involved in a relationship with a member of the opposite sex but the relationship isn't as satisfying as you would hope. Is this a well-defined or an ill-defined problem? Explain.

Figure 8.4

A general problem-solving strategy

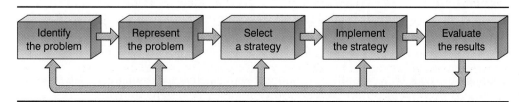

A teacher can help students learn general problem-solving strategies by focusing their attention on specific strategies, such as identifying and representing the problem during their problem-solving efforts.

8.18 ▬
What did Patty Kramer do to help her students acquire experience in defining problems? Identify specific information in the case study to defend your answer.

Lack of Experience in Defining Problems.   If you reflect back for a moment to your own experience, how much formal training have you had in searching for and defining problems? Most problem-solving experiences in schools are in math at the lower grades and in math, chemistry, and physics in the upper grades. These problems are usually well defined and presented by the teacher or textbook. Students can go through 13 or more years of formal schooling and have virtually no experience in framing and defining problems.

Lack of Domain-Specific Knowledge.   In Chapter 7, you saw that background knowledge is important in forming schemas, making information meaningful, and constructing understanding. It is important in problem solving as well; in fact, it is one of the most important factors in problem solving in general and problem defining in particular. For instance, Patty started out by posing a question about the increasing cost of education, which led to wondering about the cost of school buildings and land. Patty was adept in guiding the students, but they wouldn't have been able to specify their problem without some understanding of concepts such as *area* and *acre* and the fact that land in cities is expensive. Teachers can help students access background knowledge by encouraging them to analyze and discuss problems before they attempt to identify solutions (Bernardo, 1994; M. Lawson & Chinnappan, 1994).

8.19 ▬
What is the most effective thing a teacher can do to prevent students from rushing toward a solution before they fully understand the problem?

Tendency to Rush Toward a Solution.   One characteristic of novice problem solvers of all ages is their tendency to "jump" into a solution before they've clearly identified the problem (Moore, 1990; Shoenfeld, 1989; Van Leuvan, Wang, & Hildebrandt, 1990). The second graders who added sheep and goats to get the age of the captain illustrate this tendency. Even university students will quickly select and then persist with a strategy despite the fact that it isn't working or making sense (Schoenfeld, 1989).

Tendency to Think Convergently.   In contrast with **convergent thinking**, *which is thinking that tends to focus on one solution to a problem,* **divergent thinking** *occurs when* *problem solvers consider solutions that are novel or even seemingly inconsistent with what appears to be the original problem.*

For example:

> Paula Waites, a 2nd-year teacher, is having classroom management problems. Her students are inattentive and disruptive, and despite clearly stated rules and an effort to enforce them consistently, the behaviors persist.
>
> "I'm not sure what to do," Paula confided to her friend, Linda, an 8-year veteran. "I know I'm supposed to be consistent, and I'm trying. I told them I mean business, and I've written several referrals during the past week, but it isn't helping that much. I guess I'll just have to get tougher, but I hate coming down on them all the time. I've thought and thought about it, and that's all I can come up with."
>
> "I'm not sure," Linda responded, "but maybe you ought to try something a little different."
>
> "I don't know what you mean."
>
> "Maybe try working up a few really nifty activities, even if it takes some extra work. If the students like them, maybe they'll behave better. . . . Whenever my students are acting up, the first thing I ask myself is whether I'm doing a good job of motivating and involving them in my lessons. I mean, that isn't always the case, but it's often a factor in their behavior."
>
> "Gee, I guess I never actually thought about approaching it that way. I admit that most of what I do is lead discussions about what they've read or were supposed to read in the book."
>
> A week later, Paula reported that she had been working very hard and that her students were behaving much better.

In this case, Linda prompted Paula to look at her problem in a different way. What on the surface appeared to be a management problem was actually a problem with student motivation caused by unimaginative instruction. Paula was so focused on management that she was unable to see the problem in another way until Linda prompted her.

Patty Kramer also demonstrated the ability to think divergently as she planned her instruction. Her students of the year before weren't able to find the areas of irregular plane figures, but instead of attempting to solve the problem by giving them more drill and practice with abstract figures, Patty introduced the topic by focusing on the school grounds, something the students could relate to personally. She dealt with the problem in a creative way.

One barrier to thinking divergently is a concept called **functional fixedness** (Duncker, 1945), *which is the tendency to think of objects as having only one function.* To illustrate this phenomenon, let's try the famous "nine-dot" problem as a simple exercise. Look at the nine dots below. Your task is to connect all nine dots with four straight lines without lifting your pencil from the paper and without retracing any lines.

$$\begin{matrix} \bullet & \bullet & \bullet \\ \\ \bullet & \bullet & \bullet \\ \\ \bullet & \bullet & \bullet \end{matrix}$$

If you haven't had experience with this problem, you may find it difficult. Your tendency may be to "fixate" by seeing the problem in only one way (Mayer, 1992). Let's give you a hint: Think about extending the lines beyond the "boundary" formed by the nine dots. Notice that the directions don't say anything about any restriction on the lengths of the lines. Now, were you able to solve the problem?

8.20 ▬

Learning new concepts and reducing or eliminating "functional fixedness" have an important feature in common. What is this feature?

Learning to think divergently results from having a variety of experiences requiring divergent thinking. This suggests a critical role for teachers, and we return to this topic again later in our discussion.

Representing the Problem

The second step of the general problem-solving model involves representing the problem. Representing the problem can take forms as diverse as simply thinking about the problem abstractly and using graphs, pictures, sketches, and lists. Using some form of visual or written representation of the problem is often useful because it helps frame the problem in a larger context and connect it to learners' existing background (Lovett & Anderson, 1994).

One advantage in putting problems on paper is that the load on working memory is reduced. You know from Chapter 7 that working memory's capacity is limited and that many problems are so complex that working memory can easily be overloaded. As an example, consider again the lemonade problem presented at the beginning of this section. A picture such as the following could be used to help identify important aspects of the problem. Without it, students' working memories could be overloaded.

Amount sold: 15 quarts
How much profit was made on each glass?

Selecting a Strategy: Algorithms and Heuristics

After the problem has been identified and represented, a strategy for solving must be selected. This is the third step in the model.

Suppose you're given the following problem:

A coat costing $90 is marked 25% off. What is the sale price of the coat?

8.21 ▬

Think back to the problem of carpeting your living room presented at the beginning of our discussion of problem solving. Suppose carpeting costs $14.99 per square foot. Describe an algorithm you would use to find the cost of carpeting your living room.

In responding to a well-defined problem, a person often can apply an **algorithm** *or specified set of steps for solving problems.* Algorithms are academic rules. For instance, the algorithm for finding the cost of the coat could be summarized as follows:

Convert the 25% to a decimal.

Multiply 90 by .25.

Subtract the result from 90.

When you subtract whole numbers with regrouping, add fractions with unlike denominators, and solve algebraic equations, you are using algorithms. Patty's students actually used algorithms to calculate the areas of the regular plane figures in her lesson.

Many problems can't be solved with algorithms, however. Algorithms don't exist for ill-defined problems, and many well-defined problems also lack algorithms. In those cases, problem solvers use **heuristics**, *which are general, widely applicable problem-solving strategies* (Mayer, 1992). Some common heuristics that illustrate the range from unstructured strategies to specific plans of action include (a) trial and error, (b) means-ends analysis, (c) working backward, and (d) drawing analogies.

Trial and Error.   When inexperienced problem solvers encounter a new problem, they often pick a solution and see how it works. Trial and error is obviously an inefficient strategy, but it is one that problem solvers often try first when faced with unfamiliar problems. Trial and error can be valuable, however, because it allows learners to gain experience with new problems, and experience is one of the most important factors in acquiring expertise (J. Hayes, 1988; Wagner & Sternberg, 1985). As learners gain experience, they often switch to a more efficient strategy.

Means-Ends Analysis.   **Means-ends analysis** *is a heuristic in which the problem solver attempts to break down the problem into subgoals and works successively on each.* Patty Kramer's students used means-ends analysis in solving their problem. The problem was to determine the value of the school grounds. They first broke it into the following subgoals: (a) Find the area of the land, (b) convert the area to acres, (c) determine the "going price" per acre, and (d) calculate the value.

They actually had to break down their problem even further because they didn't know the dimensions of the school grounds, and most didn't have a concept of *acre,* so their means-ends analysis was extensive. As students broke down the task into subgoals, they were working toward their final goal of determining the value of the school grounds.

Means-ends analyses can also be effective in solving ill-defined problems. Because one characteristic of ill-defined problems is an ambiguous goal, thinking about the problem in terms of subgoals that may need to be operationally defined helps the problem solver "get a handle" on the problem. In the case of the seventh graders who don't want to "think," for example, we might operationally define "thinking" as an inclination to search for relationships in the topics they study, to make conclusions on the basis of evidence, and to remain open-minded. We can then design learning activities that provide experiences for them in these areas.

Working Backward.   Suppose you're faced with the problem of running late for appointments and then feeling uneasy and stressed in the process. One person dealt with this problem by starting with the time of the appointment and backing up 45 minutes because, "It takes less than 45 minutes from where I work to anyplace else in town. Then if I get caught in traffic, I know I'll have a few extra minutes." This is a simple example of "working backward." As another example, suppose you're searching for an apartment, and you know you can spend $500 a month on rent and utilities. Working backward from this figure will put some limits on the amenities you might be able to have, whether you will need to search for a roommate, and perhaps even what location you will select.

Drawing Analogies.   **Drawing analogies** *is an attempt to solve unfamiliar problems by comparing them with familiar ones that have already been solved* (Mayer, 1992). Drawing analogies can be effective if the problem solver has some knowledge of both the problem domain and the analogy domain. Patty's students, for example, having solved the problem with the school grounds, would probably be able to solve area problems with other irregular plane figures by drawing analogies between the two.

8.22

Think again about the ill-defined problem of a personal relationship that is less satisfying than you would like it to be (see Note 8.17). Describe a means-ends analysis that might be used to "solve" the problem.

8.23

Students often have difficulty using drawing analogies as a strategy. What is the most likely reason they have this difficulty? Explain.

Small groups provide an effective means of teaching problem-solving heuristics.

Implementing the Strategy

The fourth step in the process is implementing the strategy. The key to successful implementation is clearly defining and representing the problem and selecting an appropriate algorithm or heuristic. If the initial phases of the process have been completed effectively, implementing the strategy is essentially routine. If problem solvers have difficulty implementing a strategy, they probably should back up and think about the original problem or the strategy they've selected.

Evaluating the Results

Evaluating results is the final step in problem solving. Although this step seems basic, it is often difficult for learners. Let's look at an example.

> One boy, quite a good student, was working on the problem "If you have 6 jugs, and you want to put ⅔ of a pint of lemonade into each jug, how much lemonade will you need?" His answer was 18 pints. I (Holt) said, "How much in each jug?" "Two-thirds of a pint." I said, "Is that more or less than a pint?" "Less." I said, "How many jugs are there?" "Six." I said, "But that doesn't make any sense." He shrugged his shoulders and said, "Well, that's the way the system worked out." (Holt, 1964, p. 18)

This case illustrates a common problem. Simply getting an answer, regardless of whether it makes sense, often seems to be the students' goal. In this last stage of problem solving, teachers are trying to help students change that goal. Evaluating results should be a reality check; students assess their answers in the light of what they know about the world and the problem. The message that teachers want to convey is that problem solving is a logical process that makes sense.

Research in metacognition (L. Baker, 1989) and self-regulation (Zimmerman, 1990) suggests that much of the developmental growth that occurs in problem solving results from effective evaluation. Young children in particular encounter difficulties at this stage, wanting to rush through, get on to the next problem, and finish the assignment (Schunk, 1994). This urge is not surprising if you recall how developmental factors influence impulsiveness and the ability of students to monitor their own cognitive processes.

Teachers can help in this process, particularly in math, by having students estimate answers before they begin. Estimates require careful thought, and they give students a benchmark for their answers. When answers and estimates are far apart, questions are raised. The habit of estimating is an important disposition that teachers should try to help students develop.

Expert-Novice Differences in Problem-Solving Ability

To this point, we have identified well-defined and ill-defined problems and looked at a general problem-solving model. As educators, however, we still have a "problem" of our own. Research indicates that many of our students are, in general, not very good at solving problems (Applebee, Langer, Mullis, & Jenkins, 1990; Bruer, 1993; Mullis & Jenkins, 1988, 1990). This is our "initial state." Our goal state is for them to be better problem solvers.

One way to approach this problem is to examine expert problem solvers, compare them with novices, and, keeping these differences in mind, guide learners as they try to develop expertise. An **expert** is an *"individual who is highly skilled or knowledgeable in a given domain"* (Bruer, 1993, p. 12), whereas a **novice** is an *individual who operates at a low skill level in a domain.* Research has identified four important differences between experts and novices in problem-solving ability (Bruning et al., 1995; Glaser & Chi, 1988): (a) differences in representing problems, (b) differences in problem-solving efficiency, (c) differences in monitoring problem solving, and (d) differences in domain-specific knowledge.

Expert-Novice Differences in Representing Problems

In representing problems, experts search for the context and relationships in problems; novices, in contrast, tend to see problems in isolated pieces. As a result, they often have difficulty effectively representing problems.

One reason that experts can represent problems more effectively than novices is the way they organize their knowledge in long-term memory. Experts' schemas are more complex and interrelated, allowing them to recognize patterns and to "chunk" large amounts of information into smaller units that don't exceed working memory's capacity. Novices tend to store more information as individual pieces; they see fewer relationships and patterns, and this results in ineffective problem representations.

Expert-Novice Differences in Problem-Solving Efficiency

Experts also solve problems much more rapidly than do novices. This rapidity occurs, in part, because experts have solved many, perhaps hundreds or more, similar problems in the past. As a result, they're able to use drawing analogies as a strategy to a much greater extent than can novices. "Specific experiences are represented in memory as 'cases' that are indexed and searched so that they can be applied analogically to new problems that occur" (Bransford, 1993 p. 4). In addition, much of experts' knowledge is automatic; this allows them to focus on the overall problem, rather than on specific mechanics (Bruer, 1993).

For instance, think again about Paula Waites's classroom management problem discussed earlier. She "thought and thought about it, and that's all I can come up with." In contrast, Linda quickly reacted to the problem, saying, "Whenever my students are acting up, the first thing I ask myself is whether I'm doing a good job of motivating and involving them in my lessons." She was able to analyze the problem in terms of her past experience.

When faced with unfamiliar problems, experts plan more carefully than do novices. For example, an expert mathematician faced with an unfamiliar problem spent more than

8.24

Suppose you have the experience described by Holt. Think about the boy's comment, "That's the way the system worked out." Describe specifically what you might do to help him arrive at a valid solution to the problem.

8.25

How could a teacher increase students' "expertise" about a topic without teaching any new information about it?

8.26

How do students develop automaticity? What might be an obstacle to the development of automaticity?

half of his allotted time trying to make sense of it, not beginning the actual solution until he was sure he was working in the right direction. In contrast, novices quickly selected an approach, took off in that direction, and continued despite evidence that they weren't making progress (Schoenfeld, 1989). Initially spending more time planning contributed to the expert's overall efficiency.

Expert-Novice Differences in Monitoring Problem Solving

Teachers bemoan learners' tendencies to accept any answer to a problem regardless of whether the answer "makes sense." An additional characteristic of experts is the ability and inclination to monitor the solutions to their problems.

The boy in the problem with the jugs, for example, would have demonstrated greater expertise if he had said to himself something such as, "I have 6 jugs and two thirds of a pint in each, so I know that I have less than 6 pints altogether." In general, experts have better metacognitive skills than do novices. Developing these skills is an important step in acquiring expertise.

Expert-Novice Differences in Domain-Specific Knowledge

Why do these differences between experts and novices exist? One explanation suggests that experts are "faster, more efficient, and more reflective *because of the depth and breadth of their knowledge*" (Bruning et al., 1995, p. 195). The need for thorough background knowledge is difficult to overstate. Effective problem solving involves access to much well-organized, domain-specific knowledge (Bransford, 1993; Mayer, 1992).

Developing Expertise: Role of Deliberate Practice

As we began this section, we said that one way to improve the problem-solving abilities of students is to examine expert problem solvers. But, how did these experts get that way? Research indicates that much of what characterizes expertise is teachable (E. Gagne et al., 1993). Researchers emphasize the importance of *deliberate practice*, which has four characteristics:

1. Learner motivation to attend to the task and exert effort
2. Instruction that takes learners' preexisting knowledge into account
3. Knowledge of results and feedback
4. Opportunities for learners to repeatedly perform similar tasks

You've already seen how important background knowledge is in acquiring expertise, and providing students with the opportunity to repeat tasks and receive feedback makes sense. One additional essential element is learner motivation.

Acquiring Expertise: Importance of Motivation

Research clearly indicates that if learners are to develop problem-solving expertise, they must acquire a great deal of experience in solving problems (Bransford, 1993; Bruning et al., 1995). To acquire this experience requires motivated students. Teachers may comment that this isn't realistic, knowing, for example, that some students complain about and try to avoid word problems in math. Unless teachers consciously plan for learner motivation in their efforts to improve problem solving, they are likely to have little success with all but the most

8.27 ▬
Using your understanding of working memory as a basis, explain why experts have better metacognitive skills than do novices.

8.28 ▬
Could two people have the same "amount" of knowledge, yet one be an expert and the other a novice? Explain.

8.29 ▬
Taking existing knowledge into account is identified as a characteristic of deliberate practice. Explain why this characteristic is important.

successful and highly motivated students (Pintrich, Marx, & Boyle, 1993). With these ideas in mind, we turn to suggestions for helping learners become better problem solvers.

Constructivist Approaches to Problem Solving: Helping Learners Become Better Problem Solvers

In Chapter 7 (Figure 7.11), we identified four characteristics of constructivism:

1. Learners construct their own understanding.
2. New knowledge depends on current understanding.
3. Learning is facilitated by social interaction.
4. Meaningful learning occurs within authentic learning tasks.

We discussed these characteristics in the context of learning theory, and we now apply them to problem solving. As you read the following sections, keep two questions in mind:

1. How are the characteristics incorporated into the suggestions for improving learner problem solving?
2. How effectively did Patty Kramer apply these characteristics in her lesson?

With these questions in mind, let's look at these suggestions as they are outlined in Figure 8.5.

Capitalize on Social Interaction

Social interaction facilitates learning. Research indicates that encouraging students to discuss and analyze problems during problem solving increases understanding and promotes transfer (M. Perry, Vanderstoep, & Yu, 1993; Stern, 1993). Teachers can apply this research in classrooms by arranging learning activities that encourage students to think about their problem-solving strategies and to share their thoughts with others. Patty, for example, had her students work cooperatively to both gather information and attempt solutions to problems. To see how social interaction facilitates problem solving, let's look again at some dialogue in Patty's lesson.

Eddy:	What do we do about this? (pointing to the irregular shape)
Aniva:	We have this graph paper. We could draw the thing on it. Then we could figure out the area for each square, and we could get the area.
Eddy:	Okay, let's try it. I'll get some paper.
Carol:	What about the line that goes partly through some squares? That's no good. We'll have to guess.

Figure 8.5

Improving learner problem solving

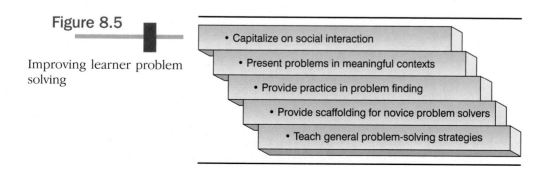

- Capitalize on social interaction
- Present problems in meaningful contexts
- Provide practice in problem finding
- Provide scaffolding for novice problem solvers
- Teach general problem-solving strategies

Eddy:	Well, how close do we have to come?
Carol:	I don't know, but this doesn't seem too good to me.
Aniva:	How about if we try this? (after looking at the drawing) If we draw lines through it like this, we have two rectangles and a triangle. That doesn't seem so hard.
Carol:	Hey, good idea!
Eddy:	All right.

The importance of student interaction was also illustrated as the students made their initial calculations and when Carol shared her strategy for finding the area of a triangle.

Patty also capitalized on social interaction when she reassembled the class and the groups shared their strategies for finding the area. Both the groupwork and the whole-class discussions made important contributions to the learning in her lesson by encouraging students to think about their problem-solving efforts and to share their thinking with others.

Present Problems in Meaningful Contexts

In looking at Patty's lesson again, you can see she attempted to reach her goal of finding the areas of irregular plane figures by embedding her learning activity in a problem about the value of the school grounds, which was an "authentic task." Embedding problems in concrete contexts can significantly improve problem-solving ability (Mayer, 1992).

In addition to providing context for problem solving, Patty's approach was motivating. The problem was concrete, and the school grounds were something the students could relate to personally. You could see Patty's conscious attention to motivation in her comment, "I bet they'll like it." As you saw in the section on deliberate practice, attention to motivation is critical if students are to persist in their efforts to develop problem-solving expertise.

You've seen how critical experience is in developing expertise. One way of acquiring experience is to solve a wide variety of examples embedded in meaningful contexts. For example, Patty's students need to solve other area problems, such as the surface areas of objects in the room or in their homes. A variety of contextualized problem-solving experiences provides opportunities for students to embed specific solutions in larger conceptual frameworks; this increases the chances for transfer (S. Reed, Willis, & Guarino, 1994).

Provide Practice in Problem Finding

Patty, even though she had clear goals for the lesson, helped her students identify and define the problem for themselves. Earlier, we said that learners get little practice in finding and identifying problems and that being able to define problems is one of the most important parts of the problem-solving process.

Let's look again at Patty's introduction to her lesson.

Patty:	I just read an article that says the cost of educating people like all of you is skyrocketing. What do you think are some of the things that contribute to that cost?
Jerome:	We have a nice school. I suppose schools are one thing.
Patty:	No question about it. The school itself and the land it sits on all cost a lot of money.
Eddy:	How much?
Patty:	The school cost about $5 million, but I don't know about the land. That's a very good question. How might we find it out?

8.30 ▬

Research indicates that discussing math problems qualitatively (without numbers) before attempting the actual solutions facilitates problem solving. Explain why this would happen.

8.31 ▬

You saw in Chapter 7 that context is important in helping students develop procedural knowledge. Explain why this is the case. Describe the declarative and procedural knowledge that Patty Kramer's students needed in order to solve the "school grounds" problem.

Segundo: Don't we have to know how much land we have before we can do anything else? Then, once we know how many acres we have, all we have to find out is how much an acre is worth, and we can figure it out.

By encouraging students to think about and explore problems, Patty provided her students with valuable experience in finding and framing problems.

Provide Scaffolding for Novice Problem Solvers

We introduced the concept of *scaffolding* in Chapter 2 when we discussed Vygotsky's work, and you saw in Tracey Stoddard's lesson in Chapter 7 how she provided enough but not too much scaffolding to keep her students on track. In the context of problem solving, scaffolding is the support teachers provide as novices attempt to solve specific problems. Scaffolding can easily be misinterpreted, however—for example, suggesting that an expert, such as a teacher, explain and model a problem solution while learners imitate the expert's behavior. Constructivist approaches to problem solving suggest that the expert provides only enough scaffolding to help novices progress *on their own*. A painter's scaffold supports the painter, but the painter does the painting; the teacher provides support, but the learner solves the problem.

You saw scaffolding illustrated in Patty's work. Her students had solved the problem with the school grounds, but many of them struggled with the next problem because the figure had a circular portion in it. She assisted those groups, again only enough to keep them on track, and finally, she again provided scaffolding for those who needed it when they did their seatwork.

Two forms of scaffolding can be particularly helpful: analyzing worked examples and visually representing problems.

Analyzing Worked Examples.   In traditional problem-solving instruction, teachers typically display one or more problems and present and model the solutions. Students then try to imitate the teacher's behavior, often with little understanding. In contrast, analyzing problems, discussing them in detail, and then relating the solutions to them makes the entire process much more meaningful.

This process is confirmed by research. Carroll (1994) found that students using worked examples made fewer errors, completed the work more rapidly, and required less assistance from the teacher than did students who received traditional explanations, even outperforming students who received individualized instruction. In addition to helping students solve the immediate problems, analyzing worked examples increases their understanding of the broader principles involved (S. Reed et al., 1994).

We emphasize that the combination of the worked examples *with discussion* is what makes the learning experience meaningful for students. Worked examples alone are insufficient; the discussion and analysis make the problem and solution meaningful for students (Chi, Bassok, Lewis, Reiman, & Glaser, 1989).

Visually Representing Problems.   Limitations of working memory are obstacles we all face when trying to solve problems. This obstacle is particularly important for novices because they represent problems less efficiently than do experts. Putting as much information as possible on paper helps reduce this load and improves problem-solving efficiency. Using drawings is particularly helpful because it often results in reconceptualizing the problem and allows the use of analogies as a strategy.

As Patty's students worked, they used the sketch she had prepared, and you saw how Carol, Eddy, and Aniva modified the sketch in their attempts to solve the problem.

8.32
Why do students in formal school settings get so little practice in finding and defining problems?

8.33
Both Piaget and Vygotsky are described as constructivist, yet the concept of *scaffolding* is only associated with Vygotsky's work. Why is this the case?

8.34
Using constructivism as a basis, explain why these discussions are so important.

8.35
We state in this section that novices represent problems "less efficiently" than do experts. Explain what this means.

You also saw how Sandra and Salvado modified the sketch in a different way because their strategy was different.

Cognitive Apprenticeship.   Scaffolding is described by some experts as a component of **cognitive apprenticeship,** *which occurs when a less skilled learner works at the side of an expert* (Collins, Brown & Holum, 1991; Collins, Brown & Newman, 1989). Cognitive apprenticeships include, in addition to scaffolding, other aspects of traditional apprenticeships, such as modeling, coaching, and gradually removing support as the apprentice becomes proficient. Because of the more abstract topics taught in classrooms, however, cognitive apprenticeships go beyond traditional apprenticeships to include teacher think-alouds and many teacher questions to promote active student involvement. (We discuss think alouds and coaching in more detail in the next section.) Also, teachers attempt to make tasks authentic to build on the motivation and meaningfulness that are characteristic of tasks situated in the work place outside of school (Good & Brophy, 1994). In this way we see how cognitive apprenticeship is consistent with constructivist approaches to problem solving.

We saw elements of cognitive apprenticeship in Patty's learning activity. Her task was authentic, a great deal of interaction took place, she modeled her own thinking, and she provided a considerable amount of scaffolding.

Teach General Problem-Solving Strategies

Research indicates that although general strategies in the absence of domain-specific knowledge are of limited value, within specific domains, such as mathematics, they can increase problem-solving abilities (Mayer, 1992; Resnick, 1987).

Teachers can help students think in terms of general strategies by modeling the thinking involved. Let's look at an example with the lemonade problem we presented earlier.

Mrs. Tate:	Hmmm, let's see. I know what my problem is. I want to find the profit for each glass. I need to keep this in mind as I think about a solution. Now, let's think about a strategy. What might we do?
Jenny:	I think I've got a way. We know that they sell it for $.10 per glass. Just find out how much it costs them a glass and subtract it from how much they make.
Mrs. Tate:	Interesting ideas, Jenny. What part of the problem-solving process are we in?
Jenny:	We're thinking about a strategy to solve our problem.
Mrs. Tate:	Good thinking, Jenny. Are there any other strategies we might consider?

8.36
Explain why general problem-solving strategies would be more effective within a particular domain than across domains.

Thinking aloud provides a model for students and also allows those less confident to see that it's all right to take risks and make mistakes. As with all forms of teaching, an accepting teacher attitude is essential. By inviting alternative solutions, emphasis is placed on the general problem-solving process, rather than on getting the answer to this specific problem.

Teachers can also help students acquire general problem-solving skills through explicit instruction in the form of "coaching" (Collins, Brown, & Newman, 1989). For example, as students work in small groups to solve problems, the teacher can ask questions to help the students develop an awareness of the problem-solving process:

What (exactly) are you doing?
   (Can you describe it precisely?)
Why are you doing it?

(How does it fit into the solution?)
How does it help you?
(What will you do with the outcome when you obtain it?)
(Shoenfeld, 1989, p. 98)

In time and with practice, students begin to think in terms of general problem-solving strategies, and their problem-solving skills improve.

This completes our discussion of problem solving. You can see how cognitive views of learning in general and constructivism in particular provide a conceptual foundation for helping students improve their problem-solving abilities. And you saw how Patty Kramer implemented these principles in her teaching. In the next section, we continue our discussion of cognitive applications by looking at learners as strategy users. As students become more strategic in their study, they can become more successful in all forms of learning, including concept learning and problem solving.

 # Classroom Connections

Teaching Problem Solving in Your Classroom

1. Teach students general problem-solving strategies.
   • A third-grade math teacher spends time at the beginning of the school year teaching her students to break down problems into subgoals; she uses categories such as "We know" and "We need to know." She provides practice and spends considerable class time discussing general approaches to problem solving.

2. Make problems as concrete as possible and discuss them qualitatively before attempting to solve them.
   • A middle school math teacher teaches the first stage of problem solving by having his students practice putting problems into their own words. He asks them to replace the variables in an equation by using a concrete description, such as a person's age or a number.

3. Put problems into meaningful contexts.
   • A second-grade teacher has a "problem of the week" activity. Each student in the class is required to bring in at least one "real world" problem each week. She selects from among them, and the class works on them in groups. She is careful to ensure that each student has problems that are selected during the year.

4. Provide students with practice in problem finding.
   • A second-grade teacher begins a lesson on graphing by asking the students how they might determine what people's favorite jelly beans are. She helps them identify a problem and guides their discussion of how to represent and solve it.

5. Teach students to evaluate the products of their problem solving.
   • A middle school math teacher requires his students to write down an estimate of the answer before actually solving the problem. After the problem is solved, he requires students to compare the two answers.
   • A science teacher requires her students to underline the part of the word problem that suggests or requests units, such as square centimeters and meters per second. After students solve the problem, they have to draw a line from their answer to the underlined part.

The Strategic Learner

In the first section of the chapter, we discussed concepts and the relationships among them. We then turned to problem solving, and the use of *strategies* for solving problems was an integral part of that discussion.

We now continue our discussion of strategies with a specific focus on learners. As learners improve in their abilities to use learning strategies, they become more and more capable of guiding their own learning; they make progress toward self-regulation, one of the most important goals in teaching.

Cognitive Strategies, Concept Learning, and Problem Solving: How Are They Different?

In Chapter 2, we defined **strategies** as *plans for accomplishing learning goals* that include cognitive operations above and beyond the processes directly entailed in carrying out a task (Pressley et al., 1990). You probably use a number of strategies in your own study. If you stop at the end of every third paragraph and ask yourself what you just read, you are using a strategy. It involves questioning yourself, a process above and beyond the normal processes involved in reading, and it reflects your conscious effort to increase your understanding of what you've read. Do you write notes in the margins as you read, highlight parts of the text, or reorganize your notes after class? These are also strategies designed to increase your understanding of the content.

Although cognitive strategies, concept learning, and problem solving are similar in several ways, they have two important differences. First, concepts, the relationships among them, and problems tend to be "domain-specific"; triangles, rectangles, and their areas, for example, fall into the domain of mathematics, or more specifically, the geometry of plane figures. In contrast, strategies can be used in a variety of situations. Once students have learned to monitor their comprehension, they can use the skill as a strategy in history, biology, or English classes, for example. The fact that cognitive strategies can be used in a variety of situations makes them one of the most powerful forms of school learning.

A second difference is that whereas learning concepts and solving problems are goals in themselves (unless the goal is to learn how to *use* a strategy), strategies are tools—means to ends. When students learn to summarize, for instance, the goal is to make other information meaningful, and summarizing is a tool used to reach the goal.

Although most research on strategy use has focused on reading (Duffy, 1992; Pressley, Johnson, Symons, McGoldrick, & Kurita, 1989), the characteristics of effective strategy users apply to all fields (C. Anderson & Roth, 1989; Schoenfeld, 1989). Let's examine these characteristics.

Characteristics of Effective Strategy Users

Effective strategy users display four characteristics: (a) They match tasks to goals, (b) they have well-developed metacognitive abilities, (c) they have a broad background of knowledge, and (d) they have a repertoire of strategies.

Effective Strategy Users Match Tasks to Goals

Effective strategy users possess *conditional knowledge* (Pressley, Borkowski, & Schneider, 1987), or the ability to know where and when to use a strategy. On the one hand, for

---

8.37

Think about the effort to acquire self-regulation as a problem. Is it well-defined or ill-defined? Explain. What is the initial state assumed to be in this problem?

8.38

Many students such as yourself take copious notes during college classes. Why is note taking considered to be a "strategy"? Under what conditions would it not be a strategy?

8.39

On the basis of the information in this section, the ability to match tasks to goals involves what kind of knowledge? How do you know?

example, if the goal in reading a passage is to get an overview of the content, good readers will often skim it, looking at headings and searching for major ideas. They've matched the strategy—skimming—to the goal—getting an overview of the content. On the other hand, if the goal is to acquire a deeper understanding of the content, good readers select a different strategy, such as note taking or outlining. They realize that the conditions are different and adapt their strategies accordingly.

Effective Strategy Users Have Well-Developed Metacognitive Abilities

Have you ever commented, "I studied all the wrong stuff for that test" or "I worked so hard, and I don't understand why I didn't do better"? Most people have. Unfortunately, people often fail to monitor their efforts to see whether their strategies are working.

Effective strategy users constantly monitor their progress to see whether the strategy they're using is as effective as it should be (Weinstein, 1994). Monitoring the effectiveness of a strategy involves *awareness* of and *control* over strategy use. These are metacognitive abilities.

Effective Strategy Users Have Broad Background Knowledge

The importance of a broad knowledge base has been emphasized repeatedly in both Chapter 7 and this chapter. It is no less important with effective strategy use. Trying to encode information and represent it in memory without an existing knowledge base as an anchor makes the use of strategies nearly impossible (Pressley et al., 1987). C. Anderson and Roth (1989) underscore this point in a study in which reciprocal teaching—a strategy we discuss later in this section—was used with science students. They found that, without sufficient background knowledge, students used the strategy to "predict trivia, to summarize details, and to clarify big words" (p. 300). Implementing strategies across the curriculum requires adequate background knowledge in students and a great deal of scaffolded instruction from the teacher.

> **8.40**
> Well-developed metacognitive abilities and background knowledge are described as characteristic of what other concept discussed in this chapter?

Effective Strategy Users Have a Repertoire of Strategies

Finally, learners won't be able to match strategies and goals if the strategies don't exist in the first place. Just as an effective problem solver has wide experience in solving problems, the effective strategy user has a variety of strategies from which to choose.

Research on good and poor readers corroborates these characteristics (Pressley et al., 1989; Wade, Trathen, & Schraw, 1990). Good readers possess more strategies and are more likely to use them spontaneously. Good readers also match the strategy to the task: They possess conditional knowledge. Finally, good readers continually evaluate whether their study skills are working and switch to others when they aren't. Their metacognitive abilities are well developed. Teachers can help students improve their metacognition and their use of strategies by encouraging them to think about and discuss when and why a specific strategy is effective (Carpenter, Levi, Fennema, Ansell, & Franke, 1995).

Having examined the characteristics of effective strategy users, let's turn now to some specific strategies.

Study Strategies

When students attempt to *increase their understanding of written materials and teacher presentations,* they commonly use **study strategies**. In this section, we examine different study strategies, beginning with basic study skills.

Basic Study Skills

Basic study skills are simple, commonly used ones, such as *highlighting* and *taking notes*. Highlighting is a popular strategy, and its value lies in the thought that goes into making the decision about what is important enough to highlight (T. Anderson & Armbruster, 1984). This, of course, is the most difficult part. Some students avoid the decision by highlighting entire sections, believing they're studying, when in fact the process is little more than the combined acts of reading and physically marking the text.

Students often have difficulty making decisions about what information is most important. They tend to focus on the first sentence of paragraphs; items that stand out, such as those in **bold face** or *italics* (Mayer, 1984); or those that are intrinsically interesting and often miss important ideas embedded in the body of a passage (Garner, Alexander, Gillingham, Kulikowich, & Brown, 1991).

As with highlighting, effective note taking depends on the learner's decision about what is important. Some students attempt to write down as much of what the teacher says as possible, and this in effect avoids analyzing the message and deciding what is important—the crux of note taking. Teachers can help students develop note-taking skills by modeling the process and by having students practice with specific topics (Deshler & Shumaker, 1993).

Research indicates that *effective* note taking significantly improves classroom learning and that it can be taught (Kiewra, 1989). Teachers can help students improve their note taking skills and ability to make decisions about what is important by providing them an outline or matrix to fill in and by modeling thinking while identifying important information. For example, a teacher discussing the characteristics of Eastern and Western Europe prior to the collapse of communism might present a skeleton matrix such as the one shown in Table 8.2. As information is discussed, students process and record it in the matrix. This process helps them learn to make comparisons, identify important information, and organize their note taking (Kiewra, 1989).

Other spacial representations, such as hierarchies, outlines, concept maps, networks, and even pictures, can help students in organizing information as they take notes and study written materials (Dansereau, 1985; Novak & Gowin, 1984). Again, teachers can help students learn how to do this by modeling and by making their own thinking public through think-alouds.

8.41 ▬
To what concept in Chapter 7 does the difference in effective compared with ineffective highlighting and note taking best relate? Explain.

8.42 ▬
On the basis of your study of Chapter 7, explain why organized note taking is important.

Comprehension Monitoring

Comprehension monitoring (Palincsar & Brown, 1984) *is the process of periodically checking to see whether you understand the material you're reading or hearing.* It is a

Table 8.2 ▮

Matrix used to guide note taking

	Economic Philosophy	Economic State	Political System	Other Factors
Western Europe				
Eastern Europe				

form of metacognition that we identified earlier as one characteristic of self-regulated learners, and it is an advanced study strategy. Low achievers and those lacking self-regulation seldom check themselves and fail to take action when they don't comprehend (L. Baker & Brown, 1984). Failure to monitor comprehension is a common problem, even with college students. You may have heard friends say something like, "I knew the stuff. The test was just so tricky." In fact, they probably didn't know the material because of ineffective comprehension monitoring (L. Baker, 1989; Mayer, 1992).

Let's look at two important comprehension monitoring strategies—self questioning and summarizing.

Self-Questioning. One of the most effective ways of learning to monitor comprehension is through self-questioning (Dole et al., 1991). It occurs when students stop periodically as they read and ask themselves questions about the material. **Elaborative questioning,** *which is the process of drawing inferences, citing examples, or identifying implications of the material being studied,* is a particularly effective form of self-questioning. You saw in Chapter 7 that elaboration was one way to promote meaningfulness, and students can also use the process as an effective comprehension-monitoring strategy. Although a number of elaborative questions exist, three important ones are as follows:

1. What is an additional example of this idea?
2. How is this topic similar to/different from the one in the previous section?
3. What is this a part of?

To illustrate these strategies, consider your own study of this chapter. As you were studying the section on the relationships among concepts, you could have asked yourself several questions:

What is another example of a generalization or academic rule?

How are generalizations and academic rules similar? How are they different?

Into what category do generalizations and academic rules fit?

Elaborative self-questioning creates links between new information and knowledge in long-term memory, improving both comprehension and learning (Dole et al., 1991).

Summarizing. Learning to **summarize,** or *prepare a concise statement of the essential meaning of a verbal or written passage,* is a second effective comprehension-monitoring strategy. One review concluded that "the evidence to date in favor of this strategy as a facilitator of comprehension and memory is so striking that we recommend the procedure without hesitation" (Pressley et al., 1989, p. 9). Summarizing is effective because it encourages students to

▌ Read for meaning
▌ Identify important ideas
▌ Transform content into their own words

Teaching students to summarize effectively takes time and requires training, but upper elementary students and higher can become skilled with it (Pressley et al., 1989). Training usually consists of walking students through a passage and helping them (a) identify and delete unimportant information, (b) construct general descriptions for lists of items, and (c) construct a topic sentence for each paragraph. Although time-consuming, training results in increased comprehension (T. Anderson & Armbruster, 1984; A. Brown & Palincsar, 1987).

Study strategies such as outlining are effectively learned through teacher modeling, think-alouds, and discussion.

8.43 ■
To what concept does "creates links between new information and knowledge in long-term memory" refer?

Table 8.3

The steps in SQ4R

S	Survey	Skim material. Use headings as guides.
Q	Question	Construct questions about material.
R	Read	Read, using questions as guides.
R	Reflect	Think about what has been read. Relate ideas to what is already known.
R	Recite	Answer questions. Relate information to headings.
R	Review	Organize information. Restudy difficult material.

Source: Improving Reading in Every Class: A Source Book for Teachers by E. Thomas and H. Robinson, 1972, Boston: Allyn & Bacon. Copyright 1972 by Allyn & Bacon. Adapted by permission of the publisher and the author.

Strategies for Improving Comprehension Monitoring

In an effort to help learners improve comprehension-monitoring abilities, researchers have developed comprehensive study systems specifically focusing on those abilities. Because the strategies are complex, they require extensive training.

8.44

Suppose in one situation, you're reading an article in a news magazine to prepare for a discussion in a world history class. In another, you're reading a unit on DNA in a biology text. For which of the two will SQ4R probably be more helpful? Explain.

SQ4R.   One of the oldest study systems, SQ4R (Survey, Question, Read, Reflect, Recite, Review) teaches students to attack a text and monitor comprehension in a series of sequential steps (Thomas & Robinson, 1972). A hybrid of an earlier system called SQ3R (the additional R is for *reflect*), SQ4R has proven effective for both learning and retention (A. Adams, Carnine, & Gersten, 1982). The steps in SQ4R are outlined in Table 8.3.

MURDER.   A more recent comprehension-monitoring system uses a mnemonic aid to help students remember the steps (Dansereau, 1985). The MURDER (Mood, Understanding, Recall, Digest, Expand, Review) system is more complex and specific than the SQ4R system. The steps are outlined in Table 8.4.

Research done with college students supports the effectiveness of the MURDER system. Trained students scored more than 30% higher than those in a control group on posttests and also reported favorable attitudes toward the system. Three-month follow-up questionnaires revealed continued use and favorable attitudes (Dansereau, 1985).

8.45

Think again about reading a topic in biology, such as genetics or DNA. Which of the strategies—SQ4R or MURDER—is probably better for helping you understand the content? Explain your answer, making specific reference to the characteristics of each strategy.

Reciprocal Teaching.   **Reciprocal teaching** (Palincsar & Brown, 1984) *is a teaching strategy specifically designed to help students learn to monitor their comprehension.* The strategy combines self-questioning and summarizing, together with clarifying and predicting, into a coherent sequence. These steps, which are to be applied to each paragraph students read, are outlined in Table 8.5. If students successfully complete the steps, they go on; if not, they reread the passage.

The designers of the strategy emphasize the importance of explicitly teaching the steps. In doing so, the teacher first describes and models each step. Then, students practice the skill and receive feedback. As they gradually internalize the strategy, more of the responsibility is released to them; they assume the role of the teacher as passages are read and discussed.

Table 8.4

Sequential steps in MURDER

M	Mood	Plan for study. Schedule time. Monitor concentration.
U	Understanding	Identify important and difficult ideas.
R	Recall	Paraphrase content. Map key concepts.
D	Digest	Reflect. Identify key points and trouble spots.
E	Expand	Ask how information is applied.
R	Review	Analyze errors on quizzes. Modify study methods.

Source: Learning Strategy Research by D. Dansereau. In J. Segal, S. Chipman, and R. Glaser (Eds.), *Thinking and Learning Skills* (Vol. I), 1985. Hillsdale, NJ: Erlbaum. Copyright 1985 by Lawrence Erlbaum. Reprinted by permission.

Let's look at the strategy in use with a group of first graders who have read a section of a story about aquanauts. The discussion begins with a student question:

Student 1: (Question) My question is, what does the aquanaut need when he goes under water?
Student 2: A watch.
Student 3: Flippers.
Student 4: A belt.
Student 1: Those are all good answers.
Teacher: (Question) Nice job! I have a question too. Why does the aquanaut wear a belt? What is so special about it?
Student 3: It's a heavy belt and keeps him from floating to the top again.
Teacher: Good for you.
Student 1: (Summary) For my summary now: This paragraph was about what aquanauts need to take when they go under the water.

8.46 What important characteristic of reciprocal teaching is missing in SQ4R and MURDER?

Table 8.5

Comprehension-monitoring steps in reciprocal teaching

1.	Summarize	the paragraph for the main idea.
2.	Construct a text question	that captures the essence of the passage.
3.	Clarify	any points in the passage that are not clear.
4.	Predict	what the author is going to say in the next paragraph.

Source: Reciprocal Teaching of Comprehension Strategies: A Natural History of One Program for Enhancing Learning by A. Brown and A. Palincsar, 1985, The Center for the Study of Reading. Copyright 1985 by The Center for the Study of Reading. Reprinted by permission.

Student 5:	(Summary) And also why they need those things.
Student 3:	(Clarify) I think we need to clarify gear.
Student 6:	That's the special things they need.
Teacher:	Another word for gear in this story might be equipment, the equipment that makes it easier for the aquanauts to do their job.
Student 1:	I don't think I have a prediction to make.
Teacher:	(Prediction) Well, in the story they tell us that there are "many strange and wonderful creatures" that the aquanauts see as they do their work. My prediction is that they'll describe some of these creatures. What are some of the strange creatures you already know about that live in the ocean?
Student 6:	Octopuses.
Student 3:	Whales?
Student 5:	Sharks?

(Palincsar & Brown, 1986, pp. 771–772)

Reciprocal teaching is one of the most thoroughly developed and researched study strategies and has been proven successful with both high and low achievers (Kelly, Moore, & Tuck, 1994; Rosenshine & Meister, 1994). One disadvantage of the strategy is that it is designed to be used with six to eight students at a time, as opposed to class-size groups. Also, some aspects of the strategy have proven difficult to implement in different content areas. For example, Brady (1990) found that clarifying and predicting were difficult in studying a social studies text because of the structure and density of the material. The benefits of question generating and summarizing, however, are well documented (Rosenshine & Meister, 1994).

Helping Students Become Effective Strategy Users

The most common approach to helping students become effective strategy users is to first explicitly teach the strategy by using modeling and think-alouds. Then the teacher guides students as they practice applying it and gradually withdraws support as the students become more competent (Rosenshine & Meister, 1994). Let's look at a teacher attempting to help her students become effective strategy users:

Donna Evans, a middle school geography teacher, began her lesson by saying, "We've been assigned to read the section of our text that describes the low-latitude climates, middle-latitude climates, and high-latitude climates. Let's talk for a few minutes about how we can help ourselves remember and understand what we've read.

"One way to help us be more effective readers is to summarize the information we read into a few short statements. This is a very useful reading skill. First, it makes the information easier to remember, and second, it helps us compare one climate region with another. We can use this skill whenever we're studying a specific topic, such as climates, and later when we study culture, economics, and imperialism. You can do the same thing when you study different classes of animals in biology or parts of the court system in your government class.

"Now, go ahead and read the passage and see if you can decide what makes a low-latitude climate a low-latitude climate," she said.

The class took a few minutes to read the section in the text.

After they had finished, Donna went on, "As I was reading, I kept asking myself what makes the low-latitude climates what they are. Here's how I thought about it. I read the section, and at first it looked as if the low-latitudes were hot and wet. Then, I saw that some of them are hot and dry. So, it looks like there are two major types: one humid and the other dry. Close to the equator, the humid tropical climate is hot and wet all year. A little farther away, it has wet summers and dry winters. For the dry tropical climate, high-pressure zones cause deserts, like the Sahara.

"Now, let's all give it a try with the section on the middle-latitude climates. Go ahead and read the section and see whether you can summarize it the way I did."

The class read the passage, and after they were finished, Donna began, "Okay. Give me a summary, someone. . . . Go ahead, Dana."

Dana offered her summary, and Donna and other class members responded, adding information and comments to what Dana said. They then practiced again with the section on the high-latitude climates.

Donna demonstrated several characteristics of effective strategy instruction:

- She explicitly taught the skill, explaining how it worked and why it was important. (She modified the skill slightly, focusing on the characteristics of the climate region, rather than merely identifying a topic sentence and supporting details. In this way, it better fit her content area.)
- She attempted to increase students' metacognitive awareness of the skill by identifying where it is useful, both in geography and in other parts of the curriculum.
- She modeled the skill with students.
- She had students practice the skill and gave them feedback in the process.

Notice also that although Donna focused explicitly on summarizing, she also modeled self-questioning when she said, "I kept asking myself, 'What makes the low-latitude climates what they are?'" Helping students see the larger picture by combining strategies in this way makes strategy instruction even more effective (Duffy, 1992).

8.47
Of the learning theories discussed in Chapters 6 and 7, to which is Donna's approach most closely related? Explain.

Critical Thinking

Developing critical and analytical learners is at the core of cognitive approaches to teaching. If learners are to be self-regulated, they must be able to use the information they possess to analyze and evaluate ideas and to construct solutions to problems. One approach to this challenge is through the development of students' critical thinking skills.

Critical thinking *is the ability to accurately and efficiently gather, interpret, and evaluate information* (Perkins, 1987). Interest in critical thinking has grown in recent years because of several factors, which are outlined in Table 8.6 (based on work by Bransford, Goldman, & Vye, 1991).

Although critical thinking skills are closely related to study skills, the two differ in scope. Study skills focus on learning from teacher presentations and written materials. Thinking skills are broader; they're used to process information in a general sense (E. Jones, 1995). For example, suppose you read a column in the editorial section of a newspaper. You might ask a question or summarize the passage to increase your comprehension of it. When you go beyond comprehension of the passage, however, to look for evidence for the author's position or to question whether the author is justified in taking the position he or she does, you are thinking critically.

Teaching Thinking: Within or Outside the Regular Curriculum?

Over the years, many programs have been developed to teach different aspects of thinking outside traditional content courses. Among them are the CoRT Thinking Program (de Bono, 1976), Philosophy for Children (Lipman, Sharp, & Oscanyan, 1980), and Project Intelligence/Odyssey (Hernstein, Nickerson, Sanchez, & Swets, 1986). The problem with these courses has been that the skills rarely transferred to the regular curriculum (Bransford et al., 1991).

8.48
Explain why the efforts to teach thinking outside the context of the regular curriculum have been generally unsuccessful. (Hint: Think about one of the themes of Chapters 7 and 8.)

Table 8.6

Factors contributing to the interest in teaching thinking

Factor	Description
Poor test scores	American students score poorly on tests that require thinking (e.g., writing persuasive essays, solving word problems in math, using formal and informal reasoning).
Concerns of business leaders	Business leaders believe that high school and college graduates cannot speak and write effectively, learn on the job, and use quantitative skills.
Increased need for thinking in the future	Many future jobs will require complex learning skills and the ability to adapt to rapid change. Thinking will no longer be in the domain of a select few.
National needs and personal rights	The primary weapon against being exploited by selfish leaders is the ability to think (Machado, 1980). A major impediment to peace in the world is irrational behavior (Nickerson, 1986).

A trend begun in the 1980s that continues today is the *explicit teaching of thinking* within the context of the *regular curriculum.* Emphasis on either without the other is likely to be less effective than combining the two. Nickerson (1988) summarizes this position:

> On the one hand, it is important to treat the skills, strategies, attitudes, and other targeted aspects of thinking in such a way that students come to understand their independence from specific domains and their applicability to many; on the other, it seems equally important to demonstrate their application in meaningful contexts so students witness their genuine usefulness. (p. 34)

Current approaches to teaching thinking skills vary but are generally organized around four basic elements. These are illustrated in Figure 8.6 (adapted from Nickerson, 1988).

Basic Processes

Basic processes *are the fundamental components of thinking.* They are thinking "tools." With some variation from one source to another (Beyer, 1988; Kneedler, 1985; Presseisen, 1986), most experts include the processes summarized in Table 8.7.

Figure 8.6

Elements of thinking

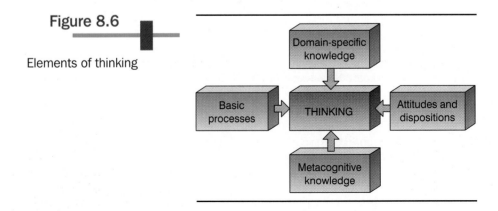

Table 8.7

Basic processes in thinking

Process	Subprocesses
Observing	Recalling Recognizing
Finding patterns and generalizing	Comparing and contrasting Classifying Identifying relevant and irrelevant information
Forming conclusions based on patterns	Inferring Predicting Hypothesizing Applying
Assessing conclusions based on observation	Checking consistency Identifying bias, stereotypes, clichés, and propaganda Identifying unstated assumptions Recognizing overgeneralizations or undergeneralizations Confirming conclusions with facts

You can think of these processes as the basic building blocks of thinking. By focusing on these processes and subprocesses, you are attempting to break the complex phenomenon of thinking into teachable and learnable parts.

Patty Kramer encouraged the use of these processes in her lesson. Her presentation and questioning led students to find patterns in each of the irregular figures; this achievement allowed the students to use familiar strategies to find the areas. David Shelton, in his astronomy lesson in the opening case study of Chapter 7, also emphasized these processes when he encouraged his students to explain different characteristics related to planets on the basis of the information the students had available to them.

Asking students to compare and contrast, analyze, and make predictions encourages them to use and develop higher level cognitive processes.

8.49 ▬

Which of the basic processes in thinking could a preoperational learner use? What processes would require concrete operational thinking? Formal operational thinking? Explain in each case.

Research on the teaching of thinking skills supports the idea of focusing on basic processes, which are specifically described, modeled, and practiced with feedback (Beyer, 1984). By integrating thinking skills into the regular school curriculum, teachers not only teach thinking but also help their students process information in a deeper, more meaningful way (Bransford et al., 1991; Van Leuvan et al., 1990).

Domain-Specific Knowledge

As with the other aspects of cognitive learning that we've discussed in Chapter 7 and in this chapter, domain-specific knowledge is critical to the teaching of thinking. To think, a person must think about something; domain-specific knowledge is the content in a given area on which a person focuses thinking skills. "The importance of domain-specific knowledge to thinking is not really debatable. To think effectively in any domain one must know something about the domain and, in general, the more one knows the better" (Nickerson, 1988, p. 13).

Metacognitive Knowledge

We emphasize metacognition throughout this text. In the context of thinking, metacognition means that the learner knows when to use the different basic processes, how they relate to domain-specific knowledge, and why they're being used. Effective thinkers not only find patterns and form conclusions based on evidence, for example, but also are keenly aware of what they're doing. Talking about thinking as it occurs in the classroom is an effective way to develop students' metacognitive knowledge (M. Adams, 1989).

Attitudes and Dispositions

Experts are becoming increasingly aware of the role attitudes play in thinking (Ennis, 1987; Resnick, 1987; Swartz, 1987). Attitudes are an essential component of thinking; they influence how and when thinking skills will be used. Examples include the inclination to rely on evidence in making conclusions; the ability to respect opinions that differ from your own; a sense of curiosity, inquisitiveness, and a desire to be informed; and a tendency to reflect before acting (Nickerson, 1988; Tishman, Perkins, & Jay, 1995). Each of these attitudes influences students' inclinations to use thinking strategies.

Much of a teacher's effort in teaching thinking is directed toward helping learners develop these inclinations. For example, we want our students to ask themselves, "Where is this person [the author] 'coming from'?" when they read a political commentary, knowing that political orientation will slant the author's opinion. In school, we want learners to be skeptical about the truth of rumors and in classroom settings to constantly wonder, "What does this relate to?" and, "How do we know?"

8.50 ▬

How do you know when students have a positive attitude toward something such as math? How about a positive attitude toward a specific thinking skill?

Attitudes and dispositions are admittedly difficult to define precisely, and they can't be taught directly. They're learned primarily by modeling; students disposed to think critically and accurately usually have teachers who demonstrate and set this tone for them.

This completes our discussion of critical thinking, the second major category of cognitive strategies emphasized in U.S. schools. We now turn our attention to *transfer,* a variable that influences how successfully concept learning, problem solving, and strategy use are applied in future learning situations.

Classroom Connections

Teaching Study Strategies in Your Classroom

1. Teach study strategies across the curriculum.
   - A sixth-grade teacher introduces note taking as a listening skill and then provides note-taking practice in science and social studies by using a skeletal outline to organize his presentations and by requiring students to take notes from his presentations.
   - A home economics teacher introduces outlining at the beginning of the school year. Later, she collects students' outline notes of her lectures and gives them feedback on the quality of the notes.

2. Teach students to analyze their study strategies and to match them to learning tasks.
   - A biology teacher reviews for a unit test by surveying the important concepts and then describing the types of items on the test, such as essay and multiple choice. Then, he asks for volunteers to share ways of studying that they have found effective.

Teaching Critical Thinking in Your Classroom

3. Plan and conduct lessons to promote thinking.
   - A first-grade teacher recaps every field trip by asking students to list things they saw on the trip.

Then, the class categorizes items and thinks of names for the categories.
   - A social studies teacher develops much of the content in her units with charts, graphs, and tables. She begins the units by asking her students first to make observations and then comparisons and conclusions based on the comparisons. Finally, they generalize whenever possible and analyze their thinking to see whether they have overgeneralized or undergeneralized.

4. Use questioning to promote thinking.
   - A fifth-grade teacher makes an effort to ask questions that promote thinking in his students. He has a list he calls "The Big Five," and he looks for opportunities to ask them whenever he can:

     What do you see? Notice? Observe?
     How are these alike? How are they different?
     Why?
     What would happen if . . . ?
     How do you know?

   - An English teacher attempts to help his students analyze literature. As they talk about a work, he constantly asks, "Why do you say that?" and, "What in the story supports your idea?"

Transfer of Learning

Consider the following situation:

> You get into your car, insert the key into the ignition, and the seat belt buzzer goes off. You quickly buckle the belt. Or, anticipating the buzzer, you buckle the belt before you insert the key.

Think now for a moment before reading further. What concept from behaviorism does your behavior—buckling the seat belt—best illustrate? Behaviorists would describe this as an example of *negative reinforcement*. If you identified it as such, you have demonstrated **transfer**, *which occurs when something learned at one time and place is applied in another setting*. You have applied your understanding of the concept of *negative reinforcement* to the situation with the seat belt.

Merely recalling information, however, doesn't involve transfer. If, for example, your instructor has previously discussed buckling the seat belt as an example of negative reinforcement and if you later identify it as such, there is no transfer. You merely remembered the information.

With respect to problem solving, transfer occurs when students are able to solve problems they haven't previously encountered, and in the case of study skills, transfer occurs when students use self-questioning—for example, in areas other than reading.

8.51
One learner transfers understanding of a topic to a new situation, whereas another learner does not. Describe the difference in the two learners' schemas.

Positive and Negative Transfer

Positive transfer occurs when learning in one situation *aids* learning in another, whereas negative transfer occurs when one situation *detracts from* learning in another. On the one hand, as a simple example, if students know that a mammal nurses its young and breathes through lungs and then conclude that a whale is a mammal, they demonstrate positive transfer. On the other hand, if they believe that a fish is an animal that lives in the sea and then conclude that a whale is a fish, negative transfer occurs.

General and Specific Transfer

At one time, educators believed that taking courses such as Latin, Greek, and mathematics were valuable not only for learning Latin, Greek, and math, per se, but also to "discipline" the mind. The hope was these courses would strengthen learners' general thinking ability. If these beliefs had been confirmed, they would involve **general transfer**, *which is the ability to take knowledge or skills learned in one situation and apply them in a broad range of different situations.* On the one hand, for example, if becoming an expert chess player would help a person learn math more easily because both require logic, general transfer

Students learn to transfer when teachers provide varied learning experiences and encourage students to make connections between classroom content and the real world.

would occur. On the other hand, if having learned that *photos* means "light" in Greek results in a learner better understanding words such as *photography* and *photosynthesis,* specific transfer occurs. **Specific transfer** *is the ability to use information in a setting similar to the one in which the information is originally learned.*

Unfortunately, as researchers found more than 70 years ago and have since confirmed repeatedly, transfer is quite specific (Driscoll, 1994; Perkins & Salomon, 1989; E. Thorndike, 1924). Studying Latin, for example, results in learners acquiring expertise in Latin and perhaps specific transfer to the Latin roots of English words; it does little to improve thinking in general. Teachers can, however, significantly increase their students' ability to transfer.

> **8.52**
> One of the themes of Chapters 7 and 8 can help in explaining why transfer tends to be more specific than general. Identify it, and offer an explanation.

Factors Affecting the Transfer of Learning

At least five factors affect students' ability to transfer: (a) the similarity between the two learning situations, (b) the variety of learners' experiences, (c) the quality of learners' experiences, (d) the context of learners' experiences, and (e) the depth of understanding and practice. Let's examine them.

Similarity Between the Two Learning Situations

As our discussion of general and specific transfer implies, the closer the two learning situations are related, the more likely transfer is to occur. On the one hand, for instance, if students have encountered examples of mammals such as dogs, cats, horses, and deer, they are likely to identify a cow as a mammal because cows are similar to the other examples. On the other hand, learners are less likely to transfer the concept of *mammal* to bats because bats aren't as closely related to the original examples.

With respect to problem solving, if first graders are given the following problem,

> *Angi has two pieces of candy. Kim gives her three more pieces of candy. How many pieces does Angi have now?*

they do well on this one:

> *Bruce had three pencils. His friend Orlando gave him two more. How many pencils does Bruce have now?*

When they're given the following problem, however,

> *Sophie has three cookies. Flavio has four cookies. How many do they have together?*

they perform less well (Riley, Greeno, & Heller, 1982). The first and second problems are more closely related than the first and third. These results demonstrate how specific transfer can be.

> **8.53**
> Think back to David Shelton's lesson at the beginning of Chapter 7. Describe the different knowledge representations he used. Do they represent adequate variety? Why or why not? Explain.

Variety of Learners' Experiences

The variety of learners' experiences is perhaps the most important factor affecting transfer. *Variety* means that a topic has been covered in several ways from a number of perspectives and is sometimes called "multiple knowledge representations" (Spiro, Feltovich, Jacobson, & Coulson, 1992). As learners construct understanding and prepare for transfer, each case or example adds different and useful connections that others miss. One way of visualizing this variety of examples is to think of "criss-crossing" a conceptual landscape, providing multiple paths for retrieval and connections to other ideas (Spiro et al., 1992). For instance, if the topic is reptiles, adequate variety means that examples of snakes, alligators, turtles, and lizards are included to help students in understanding the breadth and depth of the concept. Conversely, lack of variety can result in students undergeneralizing and forming an incomplete concept that fails to transfer. The same applies when teaching relationships among concepts, problem solving, and study skills: The greater the variety of applications, the greater the likelihood that students' understanding will transfer (B. Stein, 1989; Sternberg & Frensch, 1993).

Quality of Learners' Experiences

Quality refers to the extent that experiences are accessible and meaningful for learners (L. Brooks & Dansereau, 1987; Mayer, 1987). In the case of concept learning, this definition means the *essential characteristics of the concept are observable in the examples* and are understood by learners. In the case of the concept of *adverb,* for example, students should understand that the meaning of each verb, adjective, and adverb used as examples is being altered by the adverb modifying it.

In the case of principles, generalizations, or academic rules, *quality* refers to how clearly the *relationship* between the concepts is illustrated. Seeing a balloon actually expand over a heated bottle is a higher "quality" example than a picture or verbal statement when trying to teach the principle "Heat makes materials expand."

With respect to problem solving, high-quality problems have real-world applications and are meaningful to students' lives. Problems that students identify or generate themselves are particularly powerful. Patty Kramer capitalized on the value of real-world applications in guiding her students as they found the area of the school grounds.

Context of Learners' Experiences

In Chapter 7, we noted that learners don't merely encode information; they encode it together with the context in which it exists (J. Brown et al., 1989). The role of context has important implications for teaching in general and transfer in particular. For transfer to occur, knowledge and skills learned in one context must be applied in others. This is unlikely to happen unless learning experiences are embedded in varied contexts. Patty Kramer capitalized on this idea by embedding examples of triangles, rectangles, and circles in irregular figures. This tactic helped her students see how basic concepts could be used in real-life problem solving. She also embedded her entire problem-solving experience in the context of a practical problem that her students could directly relate to.

As with problem solving, applications of principles and generalizations should be made in real-world contexts. For instance, when teaching "Heat makes materials expand," students should have opportunities to examine applications, such as why an unopened can of pork and beans explodes when placed over a campfire and why bridges have "expansion" joints.

Similar situations exist for grammar and punctuation rules in language arts. Rather than isolated sentences, rules can be presented in the context of written passages, such as the following description designed to teach rules for forming plural nouns:

> Jefferson, one rural **county** among several *counties,* has six *schools*—one high school, two elementary *schools,* and one middle **school.** Five of the *schools* are in Brookesville, the largest **city** in Jefferson **county.** *Schools* in the three *cities* nearest

8.54
One teacher displays "Karen quickly jumped to her feet," whereas another displays "quickly," "very," "openly," and "rapidly" as examples of adverbs. Which display is of higher quality? Explain.

Brookesville are Brookesville's biggest rivals. The *schools* in all the *cities* hold an annual athletic and scholastic competition.

The two *women* advisors of the debate team and the **woman** who coached the softball team were proud of both the performance of the *students* from Big Tree High School and their appearance. (The school is named after a 600-year-old **tree** that stands prominently in a grove of oak *trees* near the school grounds.) One **student** took all-around honors, and four other *students* won medals. One **girl** and one **boy** were honored for their work in math, and two *boys* and two *girls* wrote exemplary *essays*. One **essay** was voted top of the competition. It described a **child** and how she helped several other *children* learn to cope with difficulty.

The students all looked the part of *ladies* and *gentlemen*. Each young **gentleman** wore a shirt and tie, and each young **lady** wore a dress or pant suit.

If explicit teaching of rules is a goal, embedding them in context makes sense. The goal in understanding rules is to help learners write correctly, and rules in context are more similar to writing than those presented in the abstract. Increasing the similarity of the learning situations increases the likelihood of transfer.

> **8.55** ▬
> Assess the variety and quality of the examples in the passage you've just read. Support your assessment with information taken directly from the passage.

Depth of Understanding and Practice

The more time learners spend studying a topic, the more likely transfer is to occur (Gick & Holyoak, 1987; Voss, 1987). The key here is *depth* of understanding (Brophy, 1992). Rutherford and Algren (1990) emphasized depth over breadth in saying, "Schools should pick the most important concepts and skills to emphasize so that they can concentrate on the quality of understanding rather than on the quantity of information presented" (p. 185).

Practice also influences depth of understanding. The more opportunities learners have to practice, the greater their depth of understanding, and again, the greater the likelihood of transfer (Cormier, 1987; Perkins & Salomon, 1987).

Student discussion also facilitates transfer; as students share ideas and analyze their interconnections, they gain insights into the ways ideas apply in different settings (Vanderstoep & Siefert, 1994).

Dispositions, Metacognition, and General Transfer

Although transfer of learning tends to be specific, *dispositions,* or the attitudinal element of learning, can transfer in a general sense (Prawat, 1989). A disposition to be open-minded, to reserve judgment, and to search for facts to support conclusions is a general disposition. Domain-specific knowledge is required for understanding the conclusion and the relevant facts, but the disposition is a general orientation. In addition, self-regulation can be a general disposition that transfers to a number of situations. Schoenfeld (1989), after acknowledging that much learning and problem solving is domain-specific, concludes:

> At the level of self-regulation, however, the issues appear to be the same across subject-matter boundaries. Are things going well as you perform a complex task? If yes, then leave well enough alone. If not, then there might be things you can do—and here, the details might be domain specific. (p. 95)

> **8.56** ▬
> Students most commonly learn dispositions in either or both of two ways. What are they?

Teachers encourage transfer of these dispositions through modeling across disciplines and by the day-in and day-out message that learning is a meaningful activity facilitated by cognitive monitoring.

Classroom Connections

Promoting Transfer in Your Classroom

1. Provide a wide range of examples and applications for the content you teach.
   - A fifth-grade teacher provides practice in writing paragraphs by requiring students to report their science experiments in paragraph form. She also requires appropriate paragraph structure in social studies reports and letters to foreign pen pals. Before each assignment, she reminds students of key points in paragraph structure before they begin their writing.
   - A geometry teacher illustrates applications of course content with examples from architecture. He also uses photographs from magazines and slides to illustrate how math concepts relate to the real world.

2. Plan representations that provide the information students need for understanding the topics they study.
   - A history teacher writes short cases to illustrate concepts, such as *mercantilism,* that are hard to understand from text alone. He guides students' analyses of the cases, helping them identify the essential characteristics of the concepts.
   - An English teacher prepares a matrix illustrating the characters, setting, and themes for several of Shakespeare's plays. Students use the information in summarizing and drawing conclusions from Shakespeare's work.

3. Embed information in meaningful contexts.
   - A fifth-grade teacher selects samples of student writing to teach grammar and punctuation rules. She copies samples onto overheads and uses the samples as the basis for her instruction.
   - A science teacher begins a discussion of light refraction by asking students why they can see better with their glasses on than they can without them. He tries to begin each new topic with a problem presented in a personalized way.

4. Use regular reviews to strengthen ideas and to provide practice with broad applications.
   - A chemistry teacher includes at least one problem from the previous topic on every new problem sheet. During the week before the grading period ends, she gives an assignment sheet containing problems from each topic covered during the grading period.
   - A fourth-grade social studies teacher caps each unit with the following questions:
     What have we learned in this unit?
     Why is it important?
     What does it have to do with our world today?

Windows on Classrooms

At the beginning of this chapter, you saw how Patty Kramer planned and conducted her lesson in an effort to promote thinking and problem solving in her students. Let's look now at a teacher with a group of second graders involved in a lesson on graphing. As you read the case study, consider the extent to which the teacher applied the information in this chapter in her lesson.

Suzanne Brush, a second-grade teacher at Webster Elementary School, has her students involved in a unit on graphing.

After the students settled down for math, she began, "I'm planning a party for us, and when I was doing that, a question came to my mind. I thought maybe you could help me solve it today. I need to know how I can figure out the class's favorite kind of jelly bean. If you can help me out with that, raise your hand."

Several students offered suggestions, and after considerable discussion, they finally settled on giving each student a variety of jelly beans and having them indicate which one was their favorite.

"It just so happens," Suzanne smiled as they decided on the idea, "that I did bring in some jelly beans today, and you'll be able to taste the jelly beans and vote for your favorite flavor."

She then handed out a baggy with seven different-flavored jelly beans in it to each student, in the process directing them not to open it until each person had one.

After Suzanne directed the students to taste all the jelly beans before they chose their favorite, the students opened the bags and began tasting them as Suzanne monitored the process and reminded them to taste all the jelly beans before selecting their favorite.

"Okay," she started when everyone seemed to be done with his or her tasting. "Right now I need your help. . . . Raise your hand, please, if you can tell me what we can do now that we have this information. . . . How can we organize it so that we can look at it as a whole group? We want the favorite flavor jelly bean. . . . Jacinta?"

"See how much people like the same one, and see how much people like other ones," Jacinta responded.

"Okay. . . . Can you add to that? . . . Josh?"

"You can like take, write their names down and see how many . . . like black, . . . how many ones are black," Josh answered uncertainly.

"That was right in line with what Jacinta said," Suzanne smiled and nodded. "Here's what we're going to do. Stacey and someone else, when we first started off, mentioned that we could graph the information, and so we have set up here. . . . We have an empty graph up in the front of the room," she continued, moving to the front of the room and displaying the outline of a graph that appeared as follows:

write it down; get all the colors and like red and like yellow, green, orange, black, yellow, white," he suggested haltingly, as Suzanne carefully monitored the attention of the rest of the students while Justin made his suggestion.

"That's a great idea," she smiled. "We're going to do that," and she then explained that she had a series of cardboard squares cut out that matched the colors for the graph. She directed the students to paste the color of square that represented their favorite color on the graph, and she called Table 4 to the front of the room.

"Robert, look at your card. Find your square and put it up there," she began, helping Robert put his square on the graph.

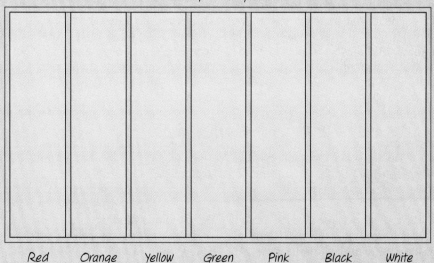

Most Popular Jelly Bean

Red   Orange   Yellow   Green   Pink   Black   White

"Yes, Justin," she nodded in response to his raised hand.

"See like which ones like, like red, get the people that like red and

She continued helping different students attach the cards to the graph.

After all the groups were done, the graph appeared as follows:

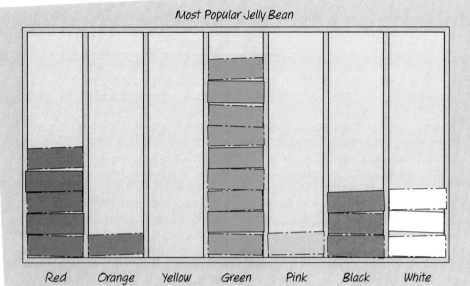

Most Popular Jelly Bean

Red   Orange   Yellow   Green   Pink   Black   White

"I need your attention back up here, please, for just a moment," she continued. "We collected the information and organized the information up here on the graph. Now, we need to look at and analyze the information. I need you to tell me what we know by looking at the graph up here. . . . What do we know? Please look at the graph up front. . . . Candice, what do we know?" she asked as she walked toward the middle of the room.

"People like green," Candice answered.

"Candice said most people like the green jelly beans. . . . Candice, how many people like green?"

" . . . Nine."

"Nine people like green. . . . And how did you find that out? Can you go up there and show us how you read the graph?"

Candice went up to the graph and moved her hand up from the bottom, counting the green squares as she went.

"What else do we know by just looking at the graph? . . . Justin? . . .

Thank you, Candice," she added as Candice moved back to her desk.

"There's three people that like black and three people that like white."

"Three people like black and three people like white," Suzanne repeated, pointing to the black and white columns on the graph. "Let's let Stacey add some more to that."

"No one liked yellow," Stacey answered.

"Nobody picked yellow," Suzanne repeated.

"Okay, what else do we know from looking at the bar graph? . . . Andrew?"

"One took orange."

"Only one person picked orange," Suzanne repeated.

"And one person picked pink. . . . Okay, here we go. . . . How many more people liked green than red?" she asked, changing the direction of the questioning. "How many more people liked the green jelly beans than the red? Look up at the graph. Try to find out the information, set up the problem, and then we'll see what

you come out with. You have to have a problem set up on your paper."

Suzanne watched as the students looked at the graph and began setting up the problem. She commented, "Quite a few hands, and a few people are still thinking," as she moved across the room. She stopped briefly to offer Carlos some help, continued watching the students as they finished, and then said, "I'm looking for a volunteer to share an answer with us. . . . Dominique?"

"Nine plus 5 is 14," Dominique answered.

"Dominique says 9 plus 5 is 14. Let's test it out," Suzanne said, asking Dominique to go up to the graph and show the class how she arrived at her answer.

Dominique went to the front of the room as Suzanne said, "We want to know the difference. . . . How many more people liked green than red, and you say 14 people, . . . 14 more people liked green. Does that work?" Suzanne said, pointing at the graph.

Dominique looked at the graph for a moment and then said, "I mean 9 take away 5."

"She got up here and she changed her mind," Suzanne said with a smile to the rest of the class after Dominique had made her comment. "Tell them."

"Nine take away 5 is 4," Dominique said.

"Nine take away 5 is 4," Suzanne continued, "so how many more people liked green than red? . . . Carlos?"

"Four," Carlos responded.

"Four, good, four," she smiled at him warmly. "The key was you had to find the difference between the two numbers.

"Raise your hand," she then continued, "if you can make up a problem like that, as I just set up and asked the whole class. . . . Okay, Jacinta."

"We could take pieces of paper and get all the students different colors . . . ," Jacinta began.

"Oh, I see. . . . You're giving me a different example of something that we could collect information on and graph. . . . Let's look at the one we have up there though. Could you just think of another problem that we could ask everyone to figure out?"

"How many more reds there are? . . . How many more people like red than black?" Jacinta responded haltingly.

"How many more people liked red than black?" Suzanne repeated. "Go ahead and do it," she said to the class.

She watched as the students solved the problem, and responding to Timmy energetically waving his hand, she nodded for him to answer.

"Two," he said.

"And how did you get your answer? What problem did you set up?"

"Five take away 3," Timmy explained.

Suzanne then continued, "I have one more question, and then we'll switch gears a little bit. How many people participated in this voting. How many people took part or participated in this voting?"

Suzanne watched as the students turned to the problem and then said, "Matt? . . . How many people?" she said as she saw that the students were finished and several had their hands raised.

"Twenty-four," Matt answered.

"Twenty-four," Suzanne repeated. "How many people in the room right now?"

"Uhmm, 25," he answered.

"Is that where you got your answer?" she asked, leaning over him and touching his shoulders. "What was the problem you set up?"

"How many people voted," he answered.

"Matt said 24. Did anyone get a different answer? So we'll compare. . . . I can't call on you if you're jumping up and ooing," she said as she walked among the students with their hands waving energetically.

"Robert?"

"Twenty-two."

"How many people got 22 for their answer?"

A number of hands went up, and Suzanne asked, "How many people got a different number?" which was followed by a few hands.

"How did you solve the problem?" she asked, walking past the table and motioning to Robert. "That's the most important thing."

"Nine plus 5 plus 3 plus 3 plus 1 plus 1 equals 22," he answered quickly.

"Where'd you get all those numbers?"

"There," he said, pointing to the graph.

"He went from the highest to the lowest, and the answer was 22. . . . Matt, why isn't it 24?" Suzanne asked walking back toward him, smiling.

" . . . "

"Raise your hand if you didn't put a square up there," she directed to the class, and she explained why the answer couldn't be 24.

" . . . Okay, I need your attention," she said changing the direction of the discussion, "so that I can explain to you six fun and exciting

centers that you're going to be working at this morning. You have in front of you your brown center folder. You'll start with your first center number. I'm going to explain the centers very quickly, and then you're going to break up into those groups and begin working."

The students then moved to the centers with Suzanne's reminder to use their manners and not interrupt each other.

The groups began their work. In one, the students attempted to flip a penny into a cup and fill in a bar graph comparing their attempts to their successful tries. In another, they tallied the number of students who had birthdays each month and entered the information on a bar graph. In a third, they placed pictures of the type of transportation they used to get to school and entered the information on a graph. In a fourth, they looked at a videotape of children at play and measured their times in different activities. A fifth group went out of the classroom, interviewed people about their favorite soft drinks, and tallied the results. A sixth group called four pizza delivery places, priced the cost of comparable pizzas, entered the information on a graph, and explained why they would choose a particular pizza place.

As time for lunch neared, Suzanne called the groups back together. After the students were settled, she said, "Raise your hand if you can tell me what you learned this morning in math."

"How to bar graph," Jenny responded.

"How to bar graph," Suzanne repeated. "More important, when we set up a problem, what do we have to do to solve the problem. . . . Timmy?"

"Add or subtract."

"Okay, but we have to decide *what,* before we add or subtract?"

"The numbers."

"So, we have to collect the information, then we have to organize it, and we organized it by setting up a bar graph, something that we can look at and talk about and decide what we need to do with the information, and we set up some problems, and we solved them, and it's a nice way to look at information and make decisions about certain things, and at your centers too. . . . Do you have any questions about your centers?" and she then ended the lesson.

Questions for Discussion and Analysis

Analyze Suzanne's lesson now in the context of the information in this chapter. In doing your analysis, you may want to consider the following questions. In each case, be specific and take information directly from the case study.

1. How effectively did Suzanne teach problem solving in her lesson? To what extent did she apply the suggestions for helping students become better problem solvers in her lesson? Explain, using information taken directly from the case study.

2. To what extent did Suzanne encourage critical thinking in her lesson? What could she have done to give the students more practice in developing critical thinking abilities? Explain.

3. How effective would Suzanne's lesson have been for promoting transfer? Explain, using information taken directly from the case.

4. Offer an overall assessment of Suzanne's lesson, based on the content of this chapter. What could she have done to improve the lesson? Be specific in any suggestions you make.

 # Summary

Concept Learning

Concepts help people make sense of the world by grouping stimuli with similar characteristics into classes. Concepts with few concrete characteristics are easier to learn than those with many more abstract characteristics. Learners construct an understanding of concepts by analyzing a wide variety of examples in which the characteristics are observable.

Principles, generalizations, and academic rules further simplify the world by describing relationships among concepts. Principles and generalizations describe observed relationships, principles being accepted as true and generalizations having known exceptions. Academic rules are relationships arbitrarily derived by people. As with concepts, each relationship is learned through a variety of examples followed by applications.

Problem Solving

Problems describe situations in which individuals are in one state and desire another state. Well-defined problems have clear goals and clear paths for achieving them; ill-defined problems have ambiguous goals and no clear means of achieving them.

Experts in any domain have thorough knowledge backgrounds organized into complex schemas that allow them to represent problems as relationships in context, to process problems quickly and in some cases automatically, and to monitor their problem-solving efforts effectively. Novices have schemas that are less well developed, often represent problems in isolated pieces, and don't monitor their efforts effectively. Experts spend more time thinking about and planning for problem solving than do novices. Teachers can help students become better problem solvers by helping them understand and acquire the problem-solving strategies of experts.

The Strategic Learner

A strategy is a plan or course of action for achieving a specific learning goal. Self-regulated learners, in addition to setting and monitoring goal attainment, assume responsibility for their learning and are effective strategy users. Effective strategy users have broad background knowledge and a repertoire of strategies to choose from in attempting to reach their goals.

Study skills are strategies used to increase comprehension of information in teacher presentations and written text. Self-questioning, summarizing, clarifying, and predicting are four strategies effective in monitoring and improving comprehension. Reciprocal teaching is a comprehensive study strategy that combines all four.

Critical thinking includes reflective strategies designed to improve understanding and decision making. Critical thinking requires thorough domain-specific knowledge, the ability to use basic cognitive processes, well-developed metacognitive ability, and dispositions for open-mindedness and a respect for evidence. Research indicates that critical thinking is most effectively developed in the context of specific topics.

Transfer of Learning

When learners are able to apply previously learned information to a new setting, transfer has occurred. Specific transfer occurs when the application is made in a situation closely related to the original; general transfer occurs when the two situations are quite different.

In addition to the relationship between learning and the applied situation, transfer depends on the amount of time and practice that learners spend on a topic, the quality and variety of the representations they study, and the context in which the learning experiences are embedded. Research indicates that transfer tends to be specific. Metacognitive and self-regulatory skills, however, may transfer across domains.

 # Important Concepts

academic rules (p. 295)

algorithm (p. 304)

basic processes (p. 322)

characteristics (p. 289)

cognitive apprenticeship (p. 312)

comprehension monitoring (p. 316)

concepts (p. 288)

concept mapping (p. 292)

convergent thinking (p. 302)

critical thinking (p. 321)

definition (p. 291)

divergent thinking (p. 302)

drawing analogies (p. 305)

elaborative questioning (p. 317)

examples (p. 290)

expert (p. 307)

functional fixedness (p. 303)

generalizations (p. 295)

general transfer (p. 326)

heuristics (p. 305)

ill-defined problem
  (p. 300)

means-ends analysis
  (p. 305)

novice (p. 307)

principles (p. 294)

problem (p. 300)

prototype (p. 290)

reciprocal teaching
  (p. 318)

specific transfer (p. 327)

strategies (p. 314)

study strategies (p. 315)

summarize (p. 317)

superordinate concept
  (p. 292)

transfer (p. 325)

well-defined problem
  (p. 300)

Chapter Outline

9

Increasing
Learner
Motivation

"We'd better get moving," Susan urged Jim as they approached the door of Kathy Brewster's classroom. "The bell is going to ring, and you know how Brewster is about this class. She thinks it's so important."

"Did you finish your homework?" Jim asked and then stopped himself. "What am I talking about? You've done your homework in every class since I've known you."

"I don't mind it all that much. Actually, it bothers me when I don't get something, and sometimes it's even sort of fun. My dad helps me quite a bit. He says he wants to keep up with the world," Susan explained with a laugh.

"In some classes, I just do enough to get a decent grade, but not in here," Jim responded. "I used to hate history, but it's sort of interesting the way Brewster's always telling us about the way we are 'cause of something that happened a zillion years ago. Besides, you miss a homework assignment in this class, and you're dead," He grinned wryly. "Nobody messes with Brewster."

"Gee, Mrs. Brewster, that assignment was impossible," Harvey grumbled as he walked in.

"That's good for you," Kathy smiled back. "I know it was a tough assignment, but it makes us think. It hurts my head too when I'm studying and trying to put together some new ideas, but if I hang in, I feel that I can usually get it."

"Aw, c'mon, Mrs. Brewster. I thought you knew everything."

"I wish. I have to study every night to keep up with you people, and the harder I study, the more I learn."

"But you make us work so hard," Harvey continued on in feigned complaint.

"Yes, but look what it's doing for you," Kathy smiled again, pointing her finger at him. "You've improved on each essay you've written. As a matter of fact, I think you hit a personal best on your last one. I believe that's the clearest essay you've written." She watched as Harvey smiled inwardly on his way to his desk.

Kathy turned to Jennifer as she walked in, and said quietly, "I pulled your desk over here, Jenny," motioning to a spot in the middle of the second row. "Go ahead and sit there. You've been a little quiet lately," and she touched Jennifer's arm, motioning her to the spot.

She finished taking roll and then pulled down a map in the front of the room. "Let's look again at the map and review for a moment to see where we are. We began our discussion of the Crusades yesterday. What was significant about them? . . . Gregory?"

" . . . You came in with pictures of the Crusaders and asked us to imagine what it would be like to be one of them. Antonio said he didn't think he'd like iron underwear." Gregory grinned at the titters of the rest of the class.

"All right, that's true." Kathy smiled back. "Now, how did we start the lesson? . . . Kim?"

" . . . "

"Remember, we started by imagining that we all left Lincoln High School and that it was taken over by people who believed that all extracurricular activities should be cut out. We then asked what we should do

about it, if anything. What did we decide we should do?"

" . . . We decided we'd go talk to them and try to change their minds," Kim responded hesitantly.

"Right. Exactly, Kim. Very good. We said that we would be on a 'crusade' to try to change the people's minds.

"Now, what were the actual Crusades all about? . . . Selena?"

" . . . The Christians wanted to get the Holy Land back from the Muslims."

"About when was this happening?"

" . . . I'm not sure."

"Look up at our time line."

" . . . Oh yeah, about 1100," Selena answered after peering at the time line.

"Good, and why did they want them back? . . . Becky?"

" . . . Well, they were the holy lands of Christianity. I s'pose they just wanted them because of that."

"Yes. Good, Becky," Kathy smiled. "Indeed, that was a factor. What else? . . . Anyone?"

After surveying the class and seeing uncertainty on students' faces, Kathy said, "You might not see what I'm driving at. Let's look at this," and she then displayed a map that illustrated the extent of Muslim influence in the Middle East, North Africa, and Europe.

"What do you see here? . . . Cynthia?"

Cynthia surveyed the map carefully and then said, "It looks like the Muslims are in control of more and more territory."

"Yes, very good. So, what implication did this have for the Europeans?"

" . . . They probably felt that the Muslims were a threat and would take over their lands," Scott volunteered.

"That's a good thought, Scott," Kathy responded. "They certainly were a military threat. In fact, the conflict in Bosnia is a present-day reminder of the clash between Christians and Muslims. How else might they have been threatening?"

"Maybe economically," Brad added. "You're always telling us how economics rules the world," he added with a grin.

"Brilliant, Brad," Kathy laughed. "I've taught you well. Indeed, economics was a factor. In fact, this is a little ahead of where we are, but we'll see that the military and economic threats of the Muslims, together with the religious issue, were also factors that led to Columbus's voyage to the New World. . . . Think about that. The Muslims in A.D. 1000 have had an influence on us here today."

"Now," Kathy said, "let's get back on track. Why do we study the Crusades? Who cares, anyway? . . . Toni?"

" . . . They were important to the development of Europe in the Middle Ages. They affected everything from fashion to the way the Europeans made war, all the way up to today. The Renaissance wouldn't have been as complete without them."

"Excellent, Toni! Very good analysis. Now, for today's assignment, you were asked to write a paragraph in which you were to answer the question, Were the Crusades a success or a failure? You could take either position. We want to learn how to make and defend an argument, so the quality of your paragraph depends on how you defended your position, not on the position itself. Remember, this is a skill that goes way beyond a specific topic, like the Crusades. This applies in everything we do.

"So, let's see how we made out. Go ahead. . . . Nikki?"

"I said they were a failure. They didn't . . . "

"Wait a minute!" Joe interrupted. "How about the new fighting techniques they learned?"

"Joe," Kathy began firmly, "what is one of the principles we operate on in here?"

"We don't have to agree with someone else's point, but we do have to listen. Sorry, Nikki. It just slipped out."

"Go on, Nikki," Kathy continued.

"That's okay, Joe. It seemed to me that militarily, at least, they were a failure because the Europeans failed in their goal to recapture the Holy Land for Christianity," Nikki said. "There were several Crusades, and after only one they did establish a foothold, and it only lasted about 50 years, I think."

"Okay. That's good, Nikki," Kathy responded. "You made your point and then supported it. That's what I wanted you to do in your paragraph."

"Now, go ahead, Joe. You were making a point," Kathy said, turning back to him.

"I made the argument that they were a success because the Europeans learned new military strategies that they later used on the Natives in the Americas, and they were good at it. If it hadn't been for the Crusades, they probably wouldn't have learned the techniques, at least not for a long time. At the time, only the Japanese were capable of the attacking techniques the Crusaders learned when they went to the Middle East. It has even affected our ideas about guerrilla warfare."

"Also good, Joe," Kathy responded, nodding and waving her hand for emphasis. "This is exactly what we're after. Nikki and Joe took opposite points of view in their paragraphs, but they each provided several details to support their positions. Again, I'm more concerned with the support you provide than with the actual position you take.

"Let's look at one more," she went on. "What was your position, Anita?"

"I took the position that they were a success," Anita responded. "Western Europe adopted a number of cultural features from the Middle East. For example, even some of the spices we eat today originally came to Europe from that time period."

"Now isn't that interesting!" Kathy enthused. "See, here's another case where we see ourselves in the 20th century finding a relationship to people who lived 1,000 years ago. That's what history is all about."

"Brewster loves this stuff," David whispered to Kelly, smiling slightly.

"Yeah," she replied. "History has never been my favorite subject, but it's sure a relief to be in here after sitting in Orr's class."

"Okay. One more," Kathy continued, giving David a knowing look, "and we'll move on."

The class reviewed another example, and then Kathy told the students to revise their paragraphs in the light of what they had discussed that day and to turn in a final product the following day.

When the period was nearly over, Kathy said, "Excuse me, everyone, but the bell is about to ring. I just want to remind you that for those of you who are making the group presentations on the Renaissance, we start next Wednesday and finish on Thursday. You need to decide what groups will be on each day. For those of you who chose to write the paper on the Middle Ages, remember that your papers are due next Friday. Remember, in both cases you have to identify any relationships you think exist between the Crusades and the Renaissance and how our lives have been affected by both."

In ideal classrooms, students pay attention, ask questions, and want to learn. They do their assignments without complaint and study without being coaxed or cajoled. But, teachers don't teach in an ideal world. They often have students who are not motivated; more accurately, students don't seem motivated to work on the tasks their teachers have set out for them.

A teacher contributes a great deal to students' desire to learn and to take responsibility and control for their own learning. A teacher won't be 100% successful all the time, but with a positive, proactive approach to motivation, he or she can influence the way students view themselves and learning.

In this chapter, we examine theory and research on student motivation, together with teacher characteristics, classroom climate variables, and instructional factors that can help make learning more positive for students.

After you've completed this chapter, you should be able to meet the following objectives:

- Explain learner motivation on the basis of behavioral, cognitive, and humanistic theories.
- Explain the role of motivation in developing self-regulation.
- Explain how teacher personal characteristics promote student motivation.
- Describe how classroom climate variables promote student motivation.
- Identify instructional factors that promote student motivation.

Motivation is a recurring dilemma for beginning and veteran teachers alike. In a review of more than 83 studies involving beginning teachers from nine countries, Veenman (1984) found that only classroom management ranked ahead of motivation as a concern. Experienced teachers usually come to grips with classroom management, but they continue to wrestle with the problem of motivation. It is a major factor influencing the difficulty and satisfaction that teachers experience in their jobs.

Motivation *is a force that energizes, sustains, and directs behavior toward a goal* (Baron, 1992; Schunk, 1990). Just as a force moves an object, motivation moves a person. When our students pay attention, turn in their work, and study for tests, we say they're motivated. If they don't do these things, we say they aren't. This notion isn't technically true, however. More accurately, they're not motivated to perform the tasks we set out for them; simply, their goals are not the same as our goals. Our job as teachers is to try to increase their inclination to perform meaningful learning tasks, and this is our frame of reference in this chapter.

Student motivation is critical for learning. Researchers have found a strong, positive correlation between motivation and achievement (Ugurogulu & Walberg, 1979; Wang, Haertel, & Walberg, 1993). Motivated students typically have positive attitudes toward school, cause fewer management problems, and describe school as satisfying. They are, not surprisingly, a primary source of job satisfaction for teachers.

Extrinsic and Intrinsic Motivation

Two students sit next to each other in a class. They look alike and are similar in ability but act very differently. One studies primarily to get high grades and seldom joins in discussions unless there is some "payoff"; the other jumps into assignments, participates eagerly in class, and seems to enjoy learning. Why the difference?

Motivation can be described in two broad categories. **Extrinsic motivation** *refers to motivation to engage in an activity as a means to an end,* whereas **intrinsic motivation** *is motivation to engage in an activity for its own sake* (Pintrich & Schunk, 1996). For example, extrinsically motivated learners may study hard for a test because they believe studying will lead to a high test score, teacher compliments, a good grade in the class, or some other reward or end. In contrast, intrinsically motivated learners study because studying is viewed as enjoyable or worthwhile in itself.

Although we tend to think of extrinsic and intrinsic motivation as two ends of a continuum, meaning the higher the extrinsic motivation, the lower the intrinsic motivation and vice versa, they are actually on separate continua (Pintrich & Schunk, 1996). One person might study hard, for example, both because it is enjoyable and because he or she wants a good grade in a class, and another person might study only to receive the good grade. The first is high in both extrinsic and intrinsic motivation, whereas the second is high in extrinsic motivation but low in intrinsic motivation. These relationships are illustrated in Figure 9.1.

9.1 ■
On the basis of the information in the case study, would you better describe Susan as being high in both extrinsic and intrinsic motivation, or high in one and low in another? Explain.

Extrinsic and intrinsic motivation also vary with the situation, and being contextual, they can change over time. Jim, in the opening case study, for example, demonstrated characteristics of extrinsic motivation in other classes—"In some classes, I just do enough to get a decent grade. . . ."— but intrinsic motivation in Kathy Brewster's history class—"I used to hate history, but it's sort of interesting the way Brewster's always telling us about the way we are 'cause of something that happened a zillion years ago."

Ideally, students will be intrinsically motivated, and much of a teacher's effort in planning learning activities and working with them is aimed at promoting intrinsic motivation. Further, research indicates that intrinsically motivated students achieve higher than those who are only extrinsically motivated (Gottfried, 1985). Jim's comments demonstrate how important teachers can be in promoting intrinsic motivation.

Theories of Motivation

In Chapters 6, 7, and 8, we examined different views of learning. These theories can also help in understanding motivation. In fact, some researchers argue that learning and motivation are so strongly interrelated that a person can't fully understand learning without considering the impact of motivation on it (Pintrich et al., 1993). We examine these views of motivation in the following sections.

Behaviorism: Motivation as Reinforcement

In our study of behaviorism in Chapter 6, you learned that reinforcement results in an increase in behavior. Praise, "happy faces," high test scores, and grades are all reinforcers

Figure 9.1

Extrinsic and intrinsic motivation

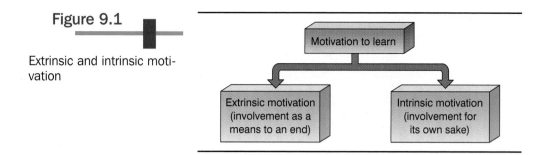

that can cause this increase. Because they are ends that result from student effort, they are potential extrinsic motivators. Jim's comment, "You miss a homework assignment in this class, and you're dead" is another example. Wanting to avoid the consequences for failing to do his homework suggests extrinsic motivation.

Effective Reinforcers

The effectiveness of a behavioral approach to motivation depends on effective reinforcers. Although the use of reinforcers has come under increasing criticism (M. Cohen, 1985; Harter & Jackson, 1992; Kohn, 1992), it is still quite common, especially in elementary classrooms. Examples of reinforcers used in elementary classrooms are listed in Table 9.1.

Reinforcers aren't as effective for junior high or high school students and underachievers. As you saw in our discussion of psychosocial development in Chapter 3, middle school students' orientation to adults declines in favor of peers and peer approval, and reinforcers provided by adults aren't as effective as they were with younger students. This

9.2
Jim demonstrated intrinsic motivation in Kathy's class, but his comment about missing a homework assignment implies extrinsic motivation. Are these two examples inconsistent? Explain.

Table 9.1

Potential reinforcers in elementary classrooms

Source	Examples
Consumable	M & M's Popcorn Soft drinks
Entertainment	Watching a favorite videotape Listening to the radio during project work
Independence	Free time
Adult approval	Teacher praise Comments on written work
Peer approval	Selection for teamwork Classmates asking for help
Competition	Highest grade in the class First to finish assignment correctly
Privilege or responsibility	Class monitor Directing class play

Identifying effective reinforcers that are grade-level appropriate can increase student motivation.

problem is compounded by the impersonal structure of middle, junior high, and high schools, in which a teacher sees a student for only 50 minutes a day in classes of 30 or more. These conditions make using personalized reinforcers difficult.

Criticisms of a Behavioral Approach to Motivation

Although the use of reinforcers is common in schools, behaviorism as an approach to motivation is controversial. Some of the opposition is philosophical, focusing on the assertion that schools should attempt to cultivate intrinsic interest in learning (Anderman & Maehr, 1994). Other criticisms are more pragmatic, arguing that using reinforcers is unwieldy and inefficient. Let's look at these arguments.

9.3

The research cited in this section suggests that the *offer* of a reward is more significant than the reward itself in decreasing intrinsic motivation. Offer an explanation for these research results.

Reinforcers Decrease Intrinsic Motivation.   One criticism of behavioral approaches to motivation is that *offering* reinforcers for engaging in intrinsically motivating tasks decreases interest in the tasks (Deci & Ryan, 1987; Kohn, 1993; Schwartz, 1990). In one study, fourth and fifth graders who were offered rewards for participating in an already interesting math task chose the task less often in free time than students who weren't rewarded (Greene, Sternberg, & Lepper, 1976), and the students who were rewarded for correct solutions to problems chose less difficult problems than those who were offered no rewards (Harter, 1978).

The problem here lies in how behavior is rewarded. Rewarding students for simply completing tasks rather than for making progress in learning detracts from motivation (Chance, 1992; Dickinson, 1989); the reward may act as a bribe for just completing work (Cameron & Pierce, 1994). For instance, giving all students A's for merely turning in a paper communicates that any level of performance is acceptable and that minimal effort will do. Students interpret the grades as rewards for compliance rather than for effort or quality, and motivation suffers.

Learners' Focus Is Narrowed.   Rewards also tend to narrow learners' focus. Students in lower grades say they engage in learning tasks to master the content; students in higher grades cite grades as motivators more often (deCharms, 1980). All teachers have been faced with the inevitable question, "Will this be on the test?" Although this query is unavoidable to a certain extent, emphasizing test scores and grades as reasons for studying instead of learning for its own sake exacerbates the problem (Ames, 1992; Crooks, 1988).

Rewards Present Logistical Problems.   Other criticisms of behavioral approaches involve logistical and practical concerns. Using reinforcers is demanding in terms of time and energy, and rewards given to some students may cause resentment in those who don't receive them, which in turn can lower motivation. Behavior modification, a widely used management and motivational strategy in the 1960s, lost popularity partially because of these factors. Now, "token economies," in which tokens or tickets can be exchanged for prizes at the end of a designated time period, are commonly used only with students having learning exceptionalities or to reward groups rather than individuals.

Finally, as you found in Chapter 6, constant and effusive praise or a barrage of positive comments on papers loses credibility with students, and their effectiveness as reinforcers is sharply reduced.

> **9.4** ▬
> What concept from behaviorism best explains why constant and effusive praise becomes ineffective as a reinforcer?

Rewards Ignore Student Cognitions.   Probably the biggest shortcoming of behaviorism as an approach to motivation is the fact that it considers only the application of reinforcers and ignores learners' perceptions and beliefs. For example, praise is a commonly used reinforcer, and its application appears straightforward—simply praise students for desired behavior.

The use of praise isn't that simple, however. Older students may perceive praise as reward for effort, rather than for accomplishment, or interpret praise for performance on easy tasks as an indication that the teacher believes they have low ability (Graham, 1991; Stipek, 1993; Weiner, Graham, Taylor, & Meyer, 1983), which in turn decreases intrinsic motivation. In these cases, praise intended as a reinforcer actually operates as a punisher. When you examine the concept of *self-efficacy* in the next section, you will better understand why this happens.

> **9.5** ▬
> On the basis of behaviorism, how would you know if praise acted as a punisher instead of a reinforcer?

Cognitive Theories of Motivation

> "C'mon, let's go," Melanie urged her friend Yelena as they were finishing a homework assignment.
>
> "Just a sec," Yelena waved. "I just can't seem to figure this out. I don't know why I missed this one. I thought I did the whole thing right, and it all made sense, but the answer turned out wrong."
>
> "Let's work on it tonight. Everybody's leaving," Melanie urged.
>
> "Go ahead, I'll catch up to you in a minute. I've gotta figure this out. . . . I just don't get it. This is the darndest problem I've ever seen."

As we examine this brief exchange, we find that we can't explain Yelena's behavior very well on the basis of behaviorism. Although getting the right answer would doubtless be reinforcing, it doesn't account for Yelena's effort to understand why the problem made sense but still came out wrong. It also doesn't help us understand why Yelena persisted in her efforts to solve the problem even though she is struggling with it.

Cognitive Theories: The Need to Understand

Cognitive theories of motivation *focus on learners' needs for order, predictability, and an understanding of events.* For example, why do young children so eagerly explore their environment? Why is the "play" of puzzles completely engrossing for a 4-year-old (and many adults)? Why was Yelena unable to leave until she solved the problem? Cognitive theorists suggest that each is motivated by the need for order and understanding.

Piaget's concept of *equilibrium,* which we discussed in Chapter 2, is an example of this need, and it is a cornerstone of his theory. When people's schemes are inadequate to explain events, they are motivated to modify the schemes, and this process results in development. Piaget (1952) also argued that humans are naturally inclined to practice their developing schemes. This inclination explains why children open and close doors repeatedly with no apparent desire to examine the contents inside and why they want the same story read over and over to the point of parental exasperation.

Cognitive theories help us explain a variety of other behaviors, such as the following:

▮ Why people are intrigued by brain teasers and other problems with no practical application
▮ Why people are curious when something occurs unexpectedly
▮ Why students ask questions about incidental and unrelated aspects of lessons
▮ Why people persevere on activities and then quit after they've mastered the task
▮ Why people want feedback about their performance, even if it's negative feedback

The items on the list all relate to a basic desire to simply understand "the way the world works." We relate back to these items as we describe different aspects of a cognitive view of motivation.

9.6

A father, reading his son a familiar story, sees that the child is getting sleepy, so he decides to skip a few pages. His son immediately corrects him and demands that all the pages be read. Explain the child's behavior on the basis of the information in this section.

Cognitive Theories: The Development of Self-Efficacy

You saw in Chapter 6 that social cognitive theory examines behavior, the environment, and personal factors in the learner. With respect to motivation, social cognitive theorists focus on two personal factors: expectations and beliefs.

The role of expectations can be explained with **expectancy × value theories** (Feather, 1982), *which suggest that learners are motivated to work on a task to the extent that they (a) expect to succeed on the task and (b) value task achievement or other potential outcomes.* If both are present, learners may develop a sense of **self-efficacy,** *which is learners' beliefs about their capability to succeed on specific tasks* (Schunk, 1994). To feel a sense of self-efficacy, learners must believe they are making genuine progress toward a worthwhile goal, not merely trying hard, doing as well or better than others, or succeeding on a trivial task.

Self-efficacy is a positive emotional experience. It can be exhilarating, for example, to solve a difficult algebra problem on your own, to make it to the bottom of a ski slope for the first time without falling, or even to repair your car. This feeling of self-efficacy results in an eagerness to work on other problems, to try a more difficult slope, or to tackle another repair job.

9.7

Think about the concept of *self-esteem,* presented in Chapter 3. Describe specifically how self-efficacy and self-esteem are different.

9.8

You saw in the previous section that praising students for performance on an easy task can lower intrinsic motivation. Explain why this could happen; use the concept of *self-efficacy* as the basis for your explanation.

Influence of Self-Efficacy on Behavior and Cognition

Self-efficacy affects several aspects of learner behavior and cognition, which are summarized in Table 9.2 (Bandura, 1993; Schunk, 1994). From the information in the table, you can see that learners high in self-efficacy approach learning activities willingly, expend greater effort and persist even in the face of difficulty, believe they can succeed, use strategies more effectively, and perform higher than their low-efficacy peers even when ability is similar. What can be done to increase self-efficacy?

Table 9.2

The influence of self-efficacy on behavior and cognition

	High Self-efficacy Learners	Low Self-efficacy Learners
Task orientation	Accept challenging tasks	Avoid challenging tasks
Effort	Expend high effort when faced with challenging tasks	Expend low effort when faced with challenging tasks
Persistence	Persist when goals aren't initially reached	Give up when goals aren't initially reached
Beliefs	Believe they will succeed	Focus on feelings of incompetence
	Control stress and anxiety when goals aren't met	Experience anxiety and depression when goals aren't met
	Believe they're in control of their environment	Believe they're not in control of their environment
Strategy use	Discard unproductive strategies	Persist with unproductive strategies
Performance	Perform higher than low-efficacy students of equal ability	Perform lower than high-efficacy students of equal ability

Factors Influencing Self-Efficacy

Four factors influence people's beliefs about their capability to perform (Bandura, 1986):

1. Past performance
2. Modeling
3. Verbal persuasion
4. Psychological state

As you would expect, past performance on similar tasks is the most important factor. A history of success in giving oral reports, for example, increases a person's self-efficacy for giving future reports. Modeling, such as observing others deliver excellent reports, also increases self-efficacy. Seeing others succeed raises expectations, provides information about how a skill is performed, and is motivating (Bandura, 1986).

Although somewhat limited, verbal persuasion, such as a teacher commenting, "I know you will give a fine report," can increase self-efficacy as well. It may improve self-efficacy indirectly by encouraging students to engage in demanding tasks, and if they're successful, efficacy increases.

Finally, factors such as fatigue or hunger can reduce efficacy even though they're unrelated to the task, and emotional arousal, such as anxiety, can reduce efficacy by filling working memory with thoughts of failure.

What can teachers do to help students increase their self-efficacy?

> Darren is a low achiever in Laura Cossey's seventh-grade math class. As Laura monitored the students during seatwork, she saw that Darren had made little progress on the word problems.
> "Come on, Darren. I know you can do this work," Laura whispered. "Read the problem carefully a few times. Then, break down the problem into parts and try drawing a picture of each part. I'm going to come back here in a few minutes to see how you're doing."

9.9 ■
What kind of peer model—one perceived to be of higher ability, of similar ability, or of lower ability—would increase an individual's self-efficacy the most? Explain.

In a few minutes, Laura returned, leaned over Darren, and said, "What do we have?"

Darren was still somewhat uncertain, but he obviously had gone over the problem and tried to get started. He pointed to the problem and said, "They want to know the overall percentage decrease in the cost."

"Good," Laura smiled. "Now, what else do you know?"

As Darren began explaining his understanding of the problem, Laura offered only as many suggestions as necessary to keep him on the right track. Finally, as he arrived at a solution, she said, "That's excellent thinking, Darren. . . . Now, look at the problem again to see whether it all makes sense. I'll be back in a minute to see your final solution. You be ready to explain to me exactly how you did it. Okay?" She smiled and moved on to another student.

9.10 ▬

What concept does "provided only enough guidance to be sure that he made genuine progress toward the solution—essentially on his own" best describe?

In this brief episode, you can see how Laura influenced Darren's self-efficacy. First, she used verbal persuasion, expressing her belief that he could solve the problem. Second, although she offered a strategy, she provided only enough guidance to be sure that he made genuine progress toward the solution—essentially on his own. Through her guidance, Darren saw evidence of his own progress; this is the most important influence on self-efficacy.

This example illustrates how important teachers can be in the development of student self-efficacy. Imagine the impact on Darren's self-efficacy if Laura Cossey had communicated low expectations for him instead, or suppose she had simply explained how to do the problem while Darren looked on passively or she provided "false" success by praising minimal effort. This would have been a good-faith attempt to be helpful, but it would have detracted from Darren's self-efficacy. He might have concluded, almost unconsciously, "Mrs. Cossey doesn't think I can do this on my own, so she has to do it for me," or, "She must not think I'm very smart if she compliments me for that." Social cognitive theory helps in understanding the important influence of teachers on learner beliefs and expectations.

Humanistic Views of Motivation

In Chapter 7, you saw that cognitive learning theory developed in response to the inadequacies of behaviorism. The beginnings of the "cognitive revolution" can be traced to the mid-1950s, and at about this time, another movement called **humanistic psychology** began, *which views motivation as people's attempts to fulfill their total potential as human beings* (Hamachek, 1987). This perspective on motivation is still popular.

Humanistic Psychology: Development of the Whole Person

9.11 ▬

Cognitive and humanistic views of motivation both have the notion of *needs* at their centers. Which of the two approaches views needs more broadly? Explain.

The first half of the 20th century was dominated by two major forces: behaviorism and psychoanalysis. As you know, behaviorism explains learning and motivation by using concepts such as *reinforcers* and *punishers*. Psychoanalysis, by comparison, focuses on unconscious drives and internal instincts and has contributed familiar concepts such as the *id, ego,* and *superego.* Humanistic psychology is a reaction against the kind of thinking that "reduces" human behavior to either a response to the environment or to internal instincts. Instead, it examines the total person—physical, intellectual, emotional, and interpersonal—and how these factors interact to affect learning and motivation. It focuses on individuals' perceptions, responses to internal needs, and the drive for "self-actualization," or becoming all that one can be (Maslow, 1968, 1954/1970). This was a new orientation at the time, and as a result, humanistic psychology became known as a "third force" alongside behaviorism and psychoanalysis.

Motivation as Growth

Humanistic approaches describe motivation as an integrative internal force that causes all human beings to grow, develop, and fulfill their potential. Each person has an innate "growth principle" that energizes and directs all human behavior (Combs & Avila, 1985). According to the humanistic view, there is no such thing as an unmotivated learner. The inattentive seventh grader who pokes the person in front of her is motivated; her motivation is just directed at nonacademic activities.

Promoting Growth: Implications for Teaching.   According to the humanistic view, learner motivation depends on how the learners view themselves as people and how they see the school contributing to their growth. If classes are personal and meaningful, students are motivated to learn; if not, they aren't. Good teaching is "the process of inviting students to see themselves as able, valuable, and self-directing, and of encouraging them to act in accordance with these self-perceptions" (W. Purkey & Novak, 1984, p. xiii). Teachers' ability to answer questions such as, "Why do we have to learn this stuff?" and to help students see the connection between what they're learning and their personal growth is critical to motivation and learning.

Two elements of the teaching-learning process are essential to humanistic psychologists: the *student-teacher relationship* and *classroom climate* (Hamachek, 1987). Supportive and caring teachers believe each student is important as an individual, and they consciously consider the learner's emotional well-being and personal growth in all they do.

Classroom climate is an outgrowth of the collective student-teacher relationships that form over time. Humanistic classrooms are safe environments where students believe they can learn and are expected to do so. Standards remain high but attainable. Each person is valued because he or she is an innately valuable human being. Convincing evidence supports the role of climate in both learning and motivation (C. Anderson, 1982; Brookover et al., 1978; Lezotte, 1981).

> **9.12**
> Identify an example in our introductory case study in which Kathy Brewster applied the student-teacher relationship element of the teaching-learning process. Then identify another example in which she promoted a positive classroom climate.

Classroom Connections

Applying Behavioral Approaches to Motivation in Your Classroom

1. Praise students appropriately for their accomplishments.

   • A fifth-grade teacher praises individual students specifically when they demonstrate clear understanding of a topic or problem solution. In each case, she identifies exactly what they have done that merits the praise. She praises trivial accomplishments sparingly.

• An English teacher underlines well-written passages in her students' essays, comments positively about them, and explains why the sections warrant the praise.

Applying Cognitive Approaches to Motivation in Your Classroom

2. Begin lessons with challenging questions and discrepant events.

   • A third-grade teacher drops an ice cube into a cup of alcohol (which the students initially think is

water), and the ice cube drops to the bottom of the cup. "We know that ice floats on water," she says. "How can we explain what just happened?"
- A math teacher has a "problem of the week." Once a week, the students are required to bring in a challenging, everyday problem for the class to solve.

3. Explain the reasons for dealing with the topics being studied.
   - A life science teacher introducing a unit on body systems says, "Understanding each of our body systems can help us lead healthier lives, and being healthy allows us to enjoy things more than if we're sick or hurt."

4. Provide clear and prompt feedback on assignments and tests.
   - A math teacher returns all tests and quizzes the following day and discusses and explains frequently missed problems.
   - An elementary teacher writes comments on students' papers, suggesting revisions. The originals and the revisions are then checked and placed in the students' portfolios.

5. Establish clear expectations for your students.
   - A geography teacher writes a letter to parents at the beginning of the school year. The letter tells parents how learning activities will be conducted, describes the procedures for turning in work, and states that all students in her class are expected to be involved and successful.

6. Develop self-efficacy by giving students only as much help as they need to make progress on challenging goals.

- After displaying a problem, a fifth-grade teacher asks students to suggest ways of solving it. Each strategy offered is taken seriously and discussed in detail.
- A seventh-grade English teacher returns students' essays with suggestions written on them. After students revise the essays, the teacher scans them, and they are reviewed by peers. When the students are satisfied with their revisions, they turn in their final drafts. The teacher makes comments identifying areas where the essays have been improved.

Applying Humanistic Approaches to Motivation in Your Classroom

7. Display a caring and empathetic manner with students.
   - A sixth-grade teacher spends time with students before and after school each day, helping them with problems and assignments.
   - An algebra teacher conducts a help session twice a week after school. He stays as long as any student wants to remain. Sometimes, conversations turn to school policy, and he listens intently when students express their views.

8. Create a supportive classroom climate for learners.
   - A fifth-grade teacher demands that all students treat each other with respect. Personal criticisms and sarcasm are forbidden. She carefully models these behaviors for students.
   - A first-grade teacher encourages and accepts all students' comments and questions. He tells students that mistakes are a part of learning and treats them that way in learning activities.

Personal Factors in Motivation

In the first section of the chapter, we examined three theories of motivation. Two of the theories—cognitive theory and humanistic psychology—focus on personal, or individual, factors in motivation, such as needs, expectations, and beliefs. The assumption involved in studying personal factors is that the better teachers understand student needs and beliefs, the more likely they'll be able to improve learning through increased motivation. In this section, we examine the following personal factors in more detail: arousal, needs, beliefs, goals, and self-regulation.

Motivation and Arousal

As former students, we've all had the experience of sitting nervously as an instructor hands out a test. Our blood pressure rises, our breath comes a little faster, and our hands may even sweat. We are alert and wide awake. Our motivation is high, and we could be described as being in a state of **arousal**, *which is a physical and psychological reaction to the environment.* Great coaches have reputations for being effective motivators because they are able to induce high levels of arousal in their players.

Arousal needs to be at an optimal level (Morris, 1988); too little or too much decreases performance. On the one hand, if we're exhausted coming into the test or if we have personal problems, for example, our level of arousal may be too low and we won't be at our best. On the other hand, if we're aroused to the point of anxiety, our performance may also suffer.

Anxiety, Motivation, and Performance

Anxiety *is arousal to the point of general uneasiness and tension,* and its relationship with motivation and performance is complex. For example, relatively high anxiety improves performance on simple, well-practiced tasks but lowers performance on new or difficult assignments (Covington & Omelich, 1987).

Also, anxiety results from a variety of factors. Some students are anxious because they are poorly prepared; others prepare but use ineffective strategies; still others prepare carefully but "choke" on tests. (In Chapter 13, we offer suggestions to teachers for reducing test anxiety in their students.)

The information-processing model in Chapter 7 helps teachers understand the relationship among motivation, arousal, and performance. On the one hand, if the task is difficult and arousal high (to the point of anxiety), thoughts such as "I'll never get this stuff"

Actively involving students in their own learning takes advantage of personal factors, such as goals, needs, and beliefs, in motivation.

and "I can't do this" lower performance by occupying working memory space and thus leave less space to devote to the task. On the other hand, simple tasks require limited working memory space, so arousal increases performance.

Capitalizing on Arousal: Curiosity Motivation

"**Curiosity** *is elicited by activities that present students with information or ideas that are discrepant from their present knowledge or beliefs and that appear surprising or incongruous*" (Pintrich & Schunk, 1996, p. 277). Curiosity induces arousal and can be a powerful source of intrinsic motivation (Lepper & Hodell, 1989).

Teachers can capitalize on curiosity motivation by asking paradoxical questions ("If Rome was such a powerful and advanced civilization, why did it fall apart?") or by using demonstrations with seemingly contradictory events (a bimetallic rod bends downward the first time when heated and upward the second, seemingly defying gravity). These discrepant events are designed to induce curiosity and pull students into the lesson.

9.13 ▬
Which theory of motivation best explains why curiosity motivation exists? Why are moderate discrepancies more effective than large discrepancies? Explain in each case.

Motivation and Needs

A **need** *is a real or perceived lack of something necessary or desirable.* On the one hand, needs can be simple and obvious, such as the need for food as signaled by hunger. Here, the need results from lacking something necessary—nourishment. On the other hand, needs can be complex and abstract, such as the need for order and understanding; this need is one cornerstone of cognitive theories of motivation. Here, need results from a desire to know or to eliminate uncertainty, which, though not necessary for survival, is beneficial.

In this section, we examine two perspectives on people's needs: humanistic and cognitive. We begin with Maslow's hierarchy.

Motivation as a Hierarchy of Needs: The Work of Maslow

Abraham Maslow (1968, 1954/1970), the father of the humanistic movement, described needs as existing in two groups, the first based on basic needs, such as survival and safety, and the second based on the desire for self-fulfillment and self-actualization. His work resulted in the hierarchy shown in Figure 9.2.

Deficiency Needs.   The bottom four categories of Maslow's hierarchy are called **deficiency needs**, *needs whose absence energizes or moves people to meet them.* Until a lower need is met, people aren't likely to move to a higher one. This assertion suggests that a person who doesn't feel safe, for example, won't be concerned with belonging, self-esteem, or any higher need.

Growth Needs.   If all deficiency needs are met, an individual can move to the top three levels, which are called growth needs, and according to Maslow, people respond to them differently than they do to deficiency needs. **Growth needs** are never "met" in the same sense as are the bottom four; rather, they *expand and grow as people have experiences with them.* For instance, as people's understanding of an area (e.g., literature) increases, their desire to learn and study actually increases, rather than decreases. This point explains why some people seem to have an insatiable desire for learning and are constantly involved in growth activities or why an individual never tires of quality art and music.

Figure 9.2

Maslow's hierarchy of needs

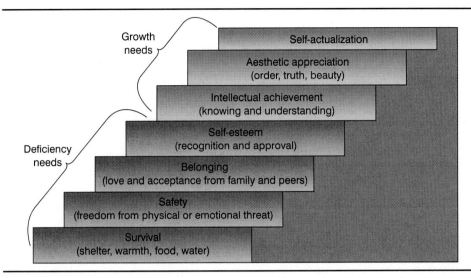

In an attempt to understand the process of self-actualization in people's lives, Maslow studied what he believed to be self-actualized people, such as Thomas Jefferson, Albert Einstein, and Eleanor Roosevelt. As he progressed in his work, he began to see patterns in the motivational needs of these people (see Figure 9.3). Although fewer than 1% of all people ever reach this level (Maslow, 1968), everyone strives for self-actualization, and Maslow concluded that it is reached by first satisfying deficiency needs so that one is free to reach for the higher ones.

Maslow's work has been criticized because his descriptions are imprecise and people don't always behave as would be predicted from the hierarchy. Michelangelo, for example, lay on his back for 4 years in enormous discomfort to create his masterpiece on the ceiling of the Sistine Chapel, a triumph of aesthetics at the expense of lower needs. At a more immediate level, you've no doubt heard of people who put themselves in grave danger to protect a loved one and others who sacrifice much in the name of principle. In Maslow's hierarchy, however, you can see the interrelationship of physical, emotional, intellectual, and aesthetic needs; together these describe the motivational needs of the "whole person" emphasized by humanistic thinkers.

Implications of Maslow's Work for Teachers. Maslow's work has important implications for education. When children come to school tired, hungry, or in extreme cases, abused, their desire to learn is certainly diminished. The hot breakfast and free lunch programs in schools are efforts to meet these deficiency needs, and teachers are now being trained to identify evidence of abuse so that counselors can respond immediately.

Kathy Brewster demonstrated an awareness of Maslow's work and consciously applied it in her teaching. Concerned that Jennifer might feel left out, she attempted to increase her feel-

9.14 ▬
On the basis of Maslow's work, would you conclude that people with high need for aesthetic appreciation have high self-esteem? Have they met their need for intellectual achievement? Explain in each case.

Figure 9.3

Characteristics of self-actualized individuals

- They have a clear perception of reality.
- They accept themselves, others, and the world for what they are.
- They are spontaneous in act and thought.
- They are problem-centered rather than self-centered.
- They are autonomous and independent.
- They are sympathetic to the condition of other human beings and seek to promote the common welfare.
- They have a democratic perspective of the world.
- They are creative.
- They establish deep and meaningful relationships with a few people rather than superficial bonds with a large number of people.
- They have peak experiences that are marked by feelings of great excitement, happiness, and insight.

ing of belonging by moving her into the middle of the class. This concern for students' emotional well-being lies at the core of the humanistic emphasis in teaching. When a deficiency need is met, it diminishes and the individual is freed to move to the next one on the hierarchy.

Maslow's work also suggests that teachers need to create learning environments where students are free from physical or emotional threat. Students who are threatened by potential embarrassment or who work in an otherwise unsafe and disorderly environment are less motivated to learn, and they achieve less than those whose learning situations are safe and stable (Blumenfeld, 1992; Brophy & Good, 1986; Doyle, 1986).

Cognitive Learning Needs

Although Maslow's work has humanistic psychology as its theoretical foundation, other needs can best be explained from a cognitive framework.

The Need for Competence.

> Larry, crying, came into the house. He had fallen off his bike again. His mother sympathetically put a bandage on his scraped knee and told him to wait and she would help him with the bike as soon as she finished writing a report for work. In a few minutes, however, Larry was back outside making another attempt at learning to ride a bike.

R. White (1959), in a classic paper, explains Larry's behavior as a response to the need for competence, and he argued that **competence motivation** *is an innate need in human beings that energizes people to master tasks and skills.* The need for competence is related to the basic need to "understand" as described by cognitive views of motivation. With increasing competence, an individual is more capable of coping with the environment, and according to White, this increasing capability is the source of competence motivation. Competence motivation is closely related to Piaget's concept of *equilibrium;* as schemes develop, competence increases and equilibrium is easier to achieve and maintain.

A teacher capitalizes on competence motivation when he or she emphasizes improvement and provides students with feedback suggesting they are increasing their

9.15 ▬
Explain competence motivation, using cognitive theories of motivation.

skills. It is a strong endorsement for a "learning-focused" classroom, which we discuss in the last section of the chapter.

The Need for Control and Self-Determination.   An alternative cognitive perspective links motivation to *control* and *self-determination*. According to this view, people have a need to control their environment, to be "Origins" of their fate, rather than "Pawns" to external forces (deCharms, 1968).

The need for control is a form of intrinsic motivation that is evidenced in both industrial settings and the classroom (Lepper & Hodell, 1989). Studies of stress in the workforce reveal that jobs having little authority or control, such as assembly line work, induce more stress in people than those with much more apparent responsibility and autonomy. Teachers can address this need for control by allowing student input in classroom decisions, such as the development of classroom rules or choices in learning activities (Ames, 1990).

For example, a ninth-grade biology teacher announced,

> I just want to remind you that we agreed to begin our presentations on genetics on Monday, so we need to sign up today. You all know what you have to do in your presentations. For those of you who chose to write a report on genetics instead, remember we discussed that your report must contain at least two common examples of genetic traits, one example of a trait that isn't genetic but is commonly thought to be, and one example in which scientists now think genetics may play a part but aren't sure. Your report is also due on Monday.

The teacher in this case did much to help students feel a sense of control over class requirements. She gave them an option of a group report or a written assignment, when the reports would begin, and the specifics of the reports. Opportunities such as these arise more often than we think, and when students feel in control of and responsible for their own learning, classroom climate improves and motivation to learn increases.

The Need to Achieve.   Student responses to the photograph on page 356 and questions in the caption are used to assess **achievement motivation**, *which is a drive to excel in learning tasks and the capacity to experience pride in accomplishment* (J. Atkinson, 1980, 1983). Achievement motivation is important in the classroom not only because it orients and energizes students toward positive accomplishments but also because it minimizes the need to avoid failure, which causes students to experience anxiety in testing situations and avoid challenging tasks.

To understand how achievement motivation operates, let's return to the photograph and questions in the caption. A student with a high need to achieve might respond to the questions in this way:

> "He's concerned about the C. He knows he can do better than that and should have studied harder."

In contrast, a student with a high need to avoid failure might decide:

> "He's not very good at science, and it was a hard test. He maybe shouldn't have taken this class."

These responses reveal differences in the need to achieve and the need to avoid failure. Students with a high need for achievement tend to be motivated by challenging assignments, high grading standards, explicit feedback, and the opportunity to try again. In contrast, students with a high need to avoid failure tend to avoid challenging tasks, experience anxiety in testing situations, and are motivated by liberal reinforcement for success, small clear steps in assignments, easy grading, and protection from embarrassment for failure.

9.16   In this section, we said that control is *another* source of intrinsic motivation. What is the first source that Lepper and Hodell (1989) identified?

9.17   Provide an explanation for achievement motivation from a behaviorist point of view. How would behaviorists measure achievement motivation?

9.18   Suppose a competitive diver was a failure-avoiding learner. How would this likely affect both her progress and her selection of dives to perform in competition?

Questions such as, "What is happening here?" "What happened in the past?" and "What is going to happen?" are used to measure students' achievement motivation.

9.19

Why is attributing failure to effort more desirable than attributing it to ability?

Attribution Theory.

> Three students eagerly waited as their teacher handed back a test.
> "How'd you do, Bob?" asked Anne.
> "Terrible," Bob answered somewhat sheepishly. "I just can't do this stuff. I'm no good at writing the kind of essays she wants."
> "I didn't do so well either," replied Anne, "but I knew I wouldn't. I just didn't study hard enough. I knew I was going to be in trouble."
> "Unbelievable!" Ronnie added. "I didn't know what the heck was going on, and I got a B+. I don't think she read mine."

Earlier, we said that cognitive views of motivation are based on the premise that people have a need for order and understanding. This view suggests that the students in the example have an intrinsic desire to understand why they got the grades they did. In response to that desire, they created *explanations (perceived causes) for their successes and failures,* which are called **attributions.** Bob suggested he wasn't good enough, Anne thought she hadn't tried hard enough, and Ronnie essentially wrote the issue off to luck. Attributions are important because they can focus students' motivational attention on effort, which is alterable, or on ability or luck, which are not.

The tendency to search for attributions is common in people's everyday lives. In response to something as simple as a headache, people say things such as, "I wonder if I'm coming down with something," or "Maybe it's something I ate." People instinctively search for an explanation for the headache. They may even ask, "What do you attribute that to?" in response to a person's description of some occurrence.

Attribution theory *is an attempt to systematically describe explanations for success and failure in classroom situations.* Weiner (1990) found that attributions fit general patterns and that people tend to view the causes of their successes and failures as being due to one or more factors. In achievement situations, common attributions include *ability, effort,* good or bad *luck,* and *task difficulty.* These attributions can be classified on three dimensions. The first is *locus of control* (Rotter, 1966), which is internal or external (I or E); the causes originate either within or outside the learner. The second dimension is *stability* (S or US), which is the likelihood of changing over time. The third is the extent to which students think they have *control* (C or UC) over the learning situation. Table 9.3 presents a summary of relationships among the attributions and dimensions.

Bob's "I just can't do this stuff" attributes his failure to lack of ability. Because it originates within the learner, it is internal (I); it is stable (S) because it is unlikely to change much over time; and it is out of his control (UC). Anne, in contrast, attributed her low score to lack of effort, which is internal (I), unstable (US), and controllable (C). Ronnie's luck is external (E), unstable (US), and uncontrollable (UC).

Table 9.3

Relationships among attributions and dimensions

	Locus of Control	Stability	Controllable
Ability	Internal (I)	Stable (S)	Uncontrollable (UC)
Effort	Internal (I)	Unstable (US)	Controllable (C)
Luck	External (E)	Unstable (US)	Uncontrollable (UC)
Task difficulty	External (E)	Stable (S)	Uncontrollable (UC)

Table 9.4

Cognitive and affective reactions to attributions

When Learners Are Successful			
Attribution	**Example**	**Affective Reaction**	**Cognitive Reaction**
Effort (I,US,C)	"I studied hard for this test."	Increased pride	Expectation of different performance
Ability (I,S,UC)	"I'm good at math."	Increased pride	Expectation of similar performance
Task difficulty (E,S,UC)	"The test was easy."	Decreased pride	Expectation of similar performance
Luck (E,US,UC)	"I guessed right."	Decreased pride	Expectation of different performance

When Learners Fail			
Attribution	**Example**	**Affective Reaction**	**Cognitive Reaction**
Effort (I,US,C)	"I didn't study enough."	Increased shame	Expectation of different performance
Ability (I,S,UC)	"I'm not good at math."	Increased shame	Expectation of similar performance
Task difficulty (E,S,UC)	"The test was hard."	Decreased shame	Expectation of similar performance
Luck (E,US,UC)	"I guessed wrong."	Decreased shame	Expectation of different performance

Attributions are important because they affect student reactions to success and failure. Locus of control attributions, for example, influence the sense of pride and self-esteem related to the experience, whereas stability leads to expectations for future performance. The control dimension is related to the "Pawns" and "Origins" we mentioned earlier. Table 9.4 presents a summary of students' attributions and reactions to success and failure.

Impact of Attributions on Behavior.   Let's look at the students' attributions again. Both Anne and Bob feel bad about their low scores because both effort and ability are internal, but Anne thinks she has control over her results, and she can expect the possibility of a different result on the next test. In contrast, Bob thinks he has no control and expects a similar result in the future. On the basis of their feelings and expectations, Anne would be apt to try harder the next time, but Bob may say, "What's the use? I won't do any better anyway."

In the extreme, Bob's attributions can lead to **learned helplessness**, *which is the feeling that no amount of effort can lead to success* (Seligman, 1975). This perspective leads to overwhelming feelings of shame and self-doubt that result in no effort. At-risk students with histories of failure are susceptible to learned helplessness.

Ronnie's situation is different. Although he was successful, the pride in his accomplishment was reduced, and he can't expect similar results in the future because luck is unstable and external. If he thinks the world is capricious, his motivation won't increase because he is not in control. His motivation would be greater if he could attribute his success to an internal source, such as effort or ability.

Attributions and Self-Efficacy.   Attributions are also related to self-efficacy. Students high in self-efficacy tend to attribute failure to lack of effort, poor approaches to the task, or use of an ineffective strategy, whereas students low in self-efficacy tend to attribute failure to lack of ability (Bruning et al., 1995). Anne displays the characteristics of high efficacy, whereas Bob appears low in self-efficacy.

Motivation and Beliefs

To this point, we have discussed two personal factors in motivation: arousal and needs. A third personal factor that affects people's motivation is their beliefs. You saw in our discussion of social cognitive theory that beliefs are basic to the concept of *self-efficacy*. We extend this discussion now.

Beliefs About Ability

Attribution theory views ability as a stable entity, and this is the way it is described in Tables 9.3 and 9.4. Other research, however, indicates that young children (Nicholls & Miller, 1984) and some adults (Dweck & Bempechat, 1983) view ability more as a skill and thus incremental; this view suggests that ability is alterable and controllable. This **incremental view of ability** *holds that ability can be improved with effort.* Others retain the view that ability is an entity. An **entity view of ability** *means that ability is stable and uncontrollable.*

Developmental differences exist in beliefs about ability. Young children tend to have an "optimistic" view of their ability, hold high expectations for success, and are quite resilient to failure. Also, through the early elementary grades, children tend to view effort and ability as synonymous. "They assume that smart people try hard and trying hard makes you smart. . . . If a person succeeds, then he must have tried hard and he must be smart. If he fails, he must not have tried and he must not be smart" (Stipek, 1993, p. 93).

Student beliefs about their own ability as students can be enhanced by experiences in which challenging tasks are successfully accomplished.

9.20
What evidence do you have that Anne has high self-efficacy? Use her comments and the characteristics of self-efficacy to provide an answer.

As learners progress through school, however, their perceptions of their ability decrease somewhat, and they tend to be more influenced by teachers' evaluations of their ability. They also react more strongly to failure and distinguish more strongly between effort and ability than do young children (Ames, 1990; Anderman & Maehr, 1994).

The Need to Protect Self-Worth

Covington (1992) asserts that the need for self-worth is a basic need of all individuals and that they instinctively strive to protect their self-worth when it is threatened, such as in the case of public failure. Covington notes that, for students, self-worth is often determined, at least in part, by their academic achievements.

Researchers have found relationships among learners' needs to protect their self-worth, their beliefs about ability, and achievement motivation (Ames, 1990; Covington, 1992; Covington & Omelich, 1987). This relationship is important in classrooms, particularly with older students. As students approach adolescence, they increasingly tend to view ability as stable (an entity) and less related to effort than they did earlier, and the perception of high ability increases in importance (Anderman & Maehr, 1994). As a result, putting forth effort can be risky because failure after working hard then suggests that one is "dumb."

Students may engage in "self-handicapping" behavior to protect their self-worth (Pintrich & Schunk, 1996)—for example, making a point of not trying ("Oh sure, I would get grades as good as yours if I studied half as hard as you do"), procrastinating ("I could have done a lot better, but I didn't start studying until midnight last night"), and blaming lack of performance on anxiety (Covington & Olemich, 1987; Mantzicopoulos, 1989). "From the students' points of view, failure without effort doesn't reflect on their ability. What they have achieved is 'failure with honor'" (Ames, 1990, p. 413).

Students with a high need for achievement, though, are more likely to see ability as incremental. Challenging goals allow them to improve their skills because improved skills mean they're "getting smarter." Failure is less likely to threaten their sense of competence or self-worth because it merely means that more work is needed. This pattern leads to sustained, successful learning (McClelland, 1985).

Needs, Beliefs, and Self-Worth: Conventional Wisdom and Research

As with many aspects of learning and behavior, the more we understand about motivation, the more complex we find it to be, and we also find that some of the "conventional wisdom" that guides teacher behavior is inconsistent with research results. Examples of this conventional wisdom (in italics), with related research results, are outlined as follows:

1. *Students who lack confidence in their ability should be given heavy doses of success.* Research indicates that success alone doesn't necessarily bolster confidence; it ignores students' attributions and perceptions of their experiences (Dweck, 1985). For self-efficacy to increase, students must perceive the task on which they're succeeding as challenging, meaningful, and important.
2. *Find something positive to say about a student's work.* Positive feedback is desirable, but praise for performance on easy tasks or praise that doesn't depend on accomplishment can detract from motivation, particularly in older students (Brophy, 1981; Ford, 1992). Again, self-efficacy requires genuine progress on meaningful and challenging tasks (Clifford, 1990).
3. *Reward students for desirable behavior.* If properly applied, reinforcers can be effective. Although they're usually intended to motivate the least attentive stu-

---

9.21
On the basis of the information in this section, which student is most likely to have an entity view of ability? Which is most likely to have an incremental view? Explain.

9.22
A student named Billy, seeing a C on a test, says, "That isn't bad, considering how much I studied. I didn't crack a book." Explain Billy's behavior on the basis of the information in this section.

9.23
Suppose you write a sentence on the chalkboard and ask the students to tell you what they see. One of your low achievers volunteers that it has a period at the end. On the basis of the information in this section, should you praise her for volunteering, or should you merely acknowledge her response? Defend your position.

dents or those who perform poorly, however, they're typically applied to the entire classroom or even the entire school (Ames, 1990).

4. *Give students choices and a sense of personal control in the classroom.* The problem here is that the structure of many classrooms involves competition and public comparisons of performance (Anderman & Maehr, 1994). In a competitive classroom, choices that ensure success and protection of ability will take precedence over interest, challenge, and task mastery (Maehr, 1992; Nicholls, 1989).

5. *Encourage students to attribute failure to lack of effort.* Many students believe that they are already trying hard, and telling them to try harder may actually decrease their self-efficacy. Further, impressing on students that sustained maximum effort is required to achieve success can lead to the feeling "I don't want to work that hard again" (Ames, 1990, p. 418), and they end up being discouraged. In most classrooms, students don't believe that those who are most successful are those who work the hardest, and trying to convince them otherwise has little credence (Nicholls, 1989). For effort feedback to be effective, it must be credible to students.

We emphasize that research doesn't imply that success isn't important, praise isn't valuable, students shouldn't be given choices, or effort shouldn't be encouraged. To the contrary, each is valuable and important. The key, however, is teacher judgment—how each is applied. This point leads us to the topic of our next section.

Motivation and Goals

We introduced the topic of goals in Chapter 6 and examined them again in Chapter 8 when we discussed matching cognitive strategies to them. For example, skimming a passage would be an effective strategy if the goal were to get an overview of the material, whereas summarizing would be a better strategy if the goal were comprehension.

Goals have been widely used to motivate workers and improve performance in the business world. They increase motivation and self-efficacy in at least three ways (Locke & Latham, 1990):

1. They give learners a standard against which to measure their progress; use of this "measuring stick" results in tangible evidence of learning.
2. They increase effort and persistence.
3. They encourage the development of new strategies when old ones are unsuccessful.

Despite these advantages, research indicates that many students—including those in college—study without clear goals in mind (Morgan, 1985). Students spend time copying and reorganizing their notes, for example, but don't consider how this task contributes to learning. They seem to tacitly think that spending time equals learning. After they are taught to set effective goals, achievement increases (Morgan, 1987).

Characteristics of Effective Goals

Effective goals have three characteristics:

1. Specific (vs. broad and general)
2. Immediate or close at hand (vs. distant)
3. Moderately difficult (vs. too easy or too hard) (Schunk, 1994)

Consider those characteristics as you examine the following goals:

1. To try harder on all my assignments
2. To learn algebra
3. To solve equations with one unknown

The problem with the first is that it is distant and not specific; it doesn't tell the student what to do next. The same is true for the second; it's also general and distant. In contrast, the third goal is specific, moderately difficult, and can be attacked immediately. Effective goals motivate students by providing concrete and challenging but achievable targets.

Learning Versus Performance Goals

For goals to work, learners must be committed to them (Pintrich & Schunk, 1996). One way of increasing commitment is to guide students in setting their own goals, rather than impose goals on them. In guiding students as they set goals, however, the distinction between those that are *learning oriented* and those that are *performance oriented* is important (Ames & Archer, 1988; Dweck, 1985). To illustrate these differences, consider the following goals:

1. To get at least a B on my essay
2. To score in the top fourth of the class on the next test
3. To identify a new example of every bold-faced topic in the next section of the chapter
4. To explain how I solved each of the problems on this assignment

The first and second are **performance goals**, *which focus on demonstrating high ability and avoiding failure.* In a "performance" orientation, learning isn't viewed as a goal in itself, but rather as a means toward an end, such as a high test score or good grade. Performance goals can lead to "getting by" or playing the game, rather than to genuine understanding.

Performance goals can also lead to feelings of anxiety about success and failure, loss of self-worth after failure (Dweck & Leggett, 1988), and an *ego orientation,* in which students are concerned about looking smarter or performing better than others, rather than about learning and understanding (Nicholls, 1984).

Third and fourth on the list, by contrast, are **learning goals**, *or goals that focus on the challenge and mastery of a task* (Pintrich & Garcia, 1991). Learning goals lead to a *task orientation* (Nicholls, 1984), in which students focus on understanding and don't worry about failure or comparisons with others. A task orientation can lead to selecting even more challenging activities (Ames, 1990), sustaining interest even after formal instruction has been completed (Maehr, 1976), using "deep processing" strategies such as comprehension monitoring and elaboration, and increasing self-efficacy. Performance goals and an ego orientation lead to an avoidance of challenging activities, limited effort, and surface strategies such as rehearsal (Meece, Blumenfeld, & Hoyle, 1988).

The difference between learning goals and performance goals is subtle but important. For example, the focus in the fourth goal on the list is in *explaining* how each problem was solved. Merely solving a number of problems isn't a true learning goal because it doesn't focus on strategies and an understanding of the problems. Focus on understanding is important both for achievement and for improved self-efficacy (Schunk, 1994). The same is true for the third goal on the list. Identifying a new example is a powerful learning strategy, which in turn can increase understanding and, with it, self-efficacy.

9.24
Suppose you are a sixth-grade math teacher working with a student who has very low self-efficacy. On the basis of the information in this section, offer a specific suggestion as to how you might try to improve his self-efficacy.

Although helping students set effective goals is not a panacea, it can reduce many of the problems involved in beliefs about ability that we discussed in the last section. Research indicates that students who adopt learning goals persist in the face of difficulty; attribute success to internal, alterable causes; take risks and accept academic challenges; and focus on personal mastery (Bruning et al., 1995). Teachers can help students develop this orientation by stressing content mastery and understanding, by de-emphasizing grading and competition, and by modeling their own search for understanding as they teach.

Motivation and Self-Regulated Learning

Most views of self-regulated learning suggest that it involves three components: metacognition, effective strategy use, and motivational control (Bruning et al., 1995). You saw in Chapter 6 that effective self-regulation includes goal setting, self-observation, and self-assessment. Self-observation and self-assessment are metacognitive processes. Self-regulated learners also make an effort to maintain their attention, perceive information accurately, and encode information in cohesive, integrated schemas. Awareness and control of these processes are also metacognitive.

In Chapter 8, you saw the value of a repertoire of strategies and the importance of matching strategies to goals. In this section, we complete the picture by discussing how motivational control contributes to self-regulated learning. The relationships among metacognition, strategy use, and motivational control are outlined in Figure 9.4.

Motivational Control

Motivation is an essential part of self-regulation. **Motivational control** *involves the inclination to set goals, evoke positive beliefs about one's skills and abilities, and adjust effort as learning progresses* (Bruning et al., 1995). Often, motivational control occurs through self-talk. For example, a student encountering a learning task might say something such as, "Let's see, what do I need to do here? Have I seen anything like this before? What should I do first?" As goal setting proceeds to selecting and implementing strategies, self-talk focuses on energizing and maintaining a direction, such as, "Hmm, can I do this? Yeah. I think it's like the one I did last week. One step at a time." Motivational control in the form of self-talk helps the learner maintain self-regulation during the process of learning.

> **9.25**
>
> In Chapter 6, you saw that self-regulated learning involved goal setting, self-observation, and self-assessment. To which component of self-regulation in Figure 9.4 does goal setting most closely relate? To which component do self-observation and self-assessment most closely relate? Explain.

Figure 9.4

Components of self-regulation

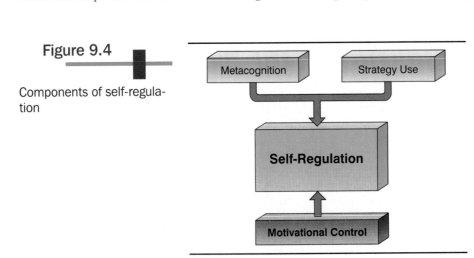

As students make progress toward learning goals, their sense of self-efficacy increases; we all feel good when we accomplish something. These feelings of efficacy then feed back and enhance learning. "Students who feel efficacious about learning choose to engage in tasks, select effective strategies, expend effort and persist when difficulties are encountered" (Schunk, 1994, p. 2). The development of motivational control through goal setting and self-monitoring not only enhances immediate learning but also contributes to the development of student self-regulation.

What does this discussion say to you as a teacher? First, as you teach, you should be clear about what your goals are and communicate them to students. Second, and even more important, you should help your students learn to set their own goals and help them develop a learning rather than a performance orientation. Third, you should help them select strategies to meet these goals and teach them to monitor their progress toward the goals. As the students become aware of these processes and their competence develops, self-regulation increases.

We have examined theoretical views of motivation—behavioral, cognitive, and humanistic—together with personal factors that affect people's motivation—arousal, needs, beliefs, goals, and self-regulation. In the next section, we combine all of these elements in a classroom model for promoting student motivation.

Classroom Connections

Applying an Understanding of Motivation and Arousal in Your Classroom

1. Begin classes with discrepant or eye-catching activities.
   - A third-grade teacher begins a study of animals with exoskeletons by bringing a lobster to class. She asks the students to compare the way the lobster feels and the way their own arms and legs feel.
   - A Spanish teacher periodically begins lessons with slides he's taken on trips to Mexico, emphasizing vocabulary and culture in each presentation.

Applying an Understanding of Motivation and Needs in Your Classroom

2. Attend to students' deficiency needs.
   - A seventh-grade teacher asks two of the more popular girls in her class to introduce a new girl to some of the other students and to take her under their wings until she gets acquainted.
   - A fifth-grade teacher calls on all students in her class to be certain they all feel that they're a part of the activity. She makes them feel safe by help-

ing them respond correctly when they are initially unable to answer.

3. Model growth needs with your students.
   - A social studies teacher brings in a newspaper columnist's political opinion piece and asks students for their opinions on the issue.
   - An English teacher comments to his class on an interesting television special about environmental issues and asks students what they think could be done about some of them.

4. Promote feelings of control by allowing students a voice in decision making.
   - A middle school teacher has students suggest classroom rules. He makes it a point to include some of them on his list.
   - A geography teacher allows students to decide the order in which they will study different cultural units.

5. Help students attribute achievement to effort.
   - A second-grade teacher carefully monitors student effort in seatwork. When she sees assignments that

indicate effort, she makes comments to individual students, such as, "Your work is improving all the time" or "Your hard work is paying off, isn't it?"

Applying an Understanding of Motivation and Beliefs in Your Classroom

6. Describe ability as incremental.
   • A sixth-grade English teacher comments, "I wasn't good at grammar for a long time. But I kept trying, and I found that I can do it. I'm good at grammar and writing now. You can get better at it too, but you have to practice."

Applying an Understanding of Motivation and Self-Regulation in Your Classroom

7. Promote self-efficacy through goal setting and modeling.

• A math teacher strongly stresses individual responsibility in learning. She has the students each set a weekly goal of the number of problems they can complete and explain. She encourages them to gradually increase the difficulty of the problems, and she then emphasizes their progress.
• A prealgebra teacher models persistence and statements of confidence in his ability to solve word problems. He thinks aloud in modeling problem solutions, purposely following dead-end approaches periodically to demonstrate persistence.

8. Avoid social comparisons among students.
   • An eighth-grade teacher writes test scores and grades on the last page of tests and papers. He comments, "Our grades are our own business. Please don't share them with your classmates."

The Classroom: A Model for Promoting Student Motivation

The earlier sections of the chapter provided you with the conceptual background to understand your students' motivation to learn. Our goal for this section is to present a model—synthesized from the information you've studied in the earlier sections—that teachers can use to promote motivation to learn in their classrooms. The model (see Figure 9.5) is not a set of rules to be applied without thinking, nor is it a list of teacher actions to be "checked off." The elements of the model interact with each other; the whole is greater than the sum of the individual parts. When implemented with professional judgment, the model components can significantly increase student motivation in classrooms.

Class Structure: Creating a Learning-Focused Framework for Motivation

To be effective, the model for promoting student motivation must be embedded in a learning-focused framework that emphasizes a task orientation, improvement and evidence of progress, and an incremental view of ability. As you saw previously, this approach to classroom goals contrasts with a performance orientation that emphasizes ability, an entity view of intelligence, an ego orientation, and social comparisons. Differences between a learning-focused and a performance- or ability-focused classroom are outlined in Table 9.5 (based on work by Maehr, 1992).

Let's look at some of the things Kathy Brewster did in her classroom to promote a learning-focused classroom.

Figure 9.5

A model for promoting student motivation

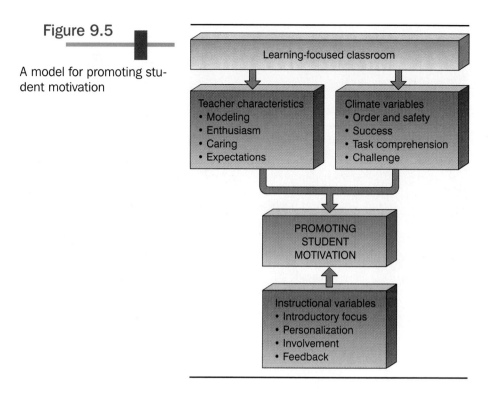

- She promoted a climate of cooperation rather than competition and avoided comparisons of performance among the students.
- She focused on improvement rather than ability, as indicated by her comment to Harvey, "I think you hit a personal best on your last one [essay]."
- She personalized her instruction by using a "crusade" to win back the school as context for her discussion of the Crusades.
- She gave her students the choice of either making a group presentation or writing a paper about the Renaissance.

In contrast, if she were performance focused, her emphasis would be on giving students high grades, comparing students' performances with each other, and attempting to motivate students with reminders of upcoming tests and threats of failure. Displays of grade distributions on the chalkboard, with or without names attached and comments, such as, "C'mon, there were only two A's on the last test," and "If you people don't get going, you'll be repeating this course next year," characterize this orientation.

Within this learning-oriented framework, the model for promoting student motivation has three parts:

1. *Teacher characteristics:* The teacher's personal orientations toward students, teaching, and learning
2. *Climate variables:* Teacher and classroom characteristics that promote feelings of security, understanding, and challenge
3. *Instructional variables:* Specific actions teachers can take to promote student motivation in specific lessons

A teacher's goal in applying the model to classroom learning is to increase learners' self-efficacy and help them develop self-regulation. Let's turn to specific components of the model.

9.26
A teacher says, "Excellent job on the last test, everyone. Over half the class got an A or a B." On the basis of the information in this section, how appropriate is this comment? Explain.

Groupwork within learning-focused classrooms provides opportunities for students to experience success in challenging tasks.

Teacher Characteristics

That teachers make a difference in student learning is a theme of this text, and it is certainly true for motivation. Teachers create learning environments, implement instruction, and establish learning-oriented or performance-oriented classrooms. None of the other components of the model are effective if the teacher characteristics—modeling, enthusiasm, caring, and positive expectations—are lacking. These characteristics are highlighted in Figure 9.6.

Table 9.5

Comparisons of learning-focused and performance-focused classrooms

	Learning-Focused	Performance-Focused
Definition of success	Improvement, progress, mastery	High grades, performance compared with that of others
Reasons for effort	Learn something new	High grades, demonstrate ability
Basis for satisfaction	Progress, challenge, mastery	Doing better than others, success with minimum effort
Evaluation criteria	Evidence of progress	Social comparisons
Interpretation of errors	Information, part of the learning process	Failure, lack of ability
Concept of ability	Incremental, improves with effort	Entity, fixed

Source: From *Transforming the school culture to enhance motivation.* Paper presented at the Annual Meeting of the American Educational Research Association, San Francisco, April, 1992. By M. Maehr. Adapted by permission.

Figure 9.6

Teacher characteristics in the model for promoting student motivation

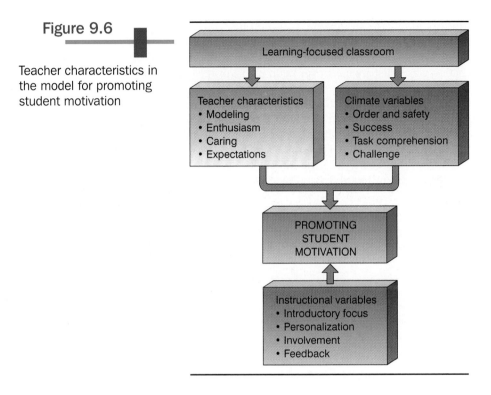

Teacher Modeling

Teachers' attitudes and beliefs about teaching and learning are communicated strongly through modeling. From studying Chapter 6, you know that teachers' behaviors, by themselves, have an important effect on students' learning. Student motivation to learn is virtually impossible if teachers model distaste or lack of interest in the topics they teach. Statements such as the following serve no useful purpose and are devastating for motivation:

"I know this stuff is boring, but we have to learn it."

"I know you hate proofs."

"This isn't my favorite topic either."

In contrast, even the most mundane topics can be made more palatable to students if the teacher models interest in them.

Modeling affects motivation in other ways as well. For example, Kathy Brewster modeled an incremental view of ability in saying, "I wish. I have to study every night to keep up with you people, and the harder I study, the more I learn." She also modeled effort attributions, and high self-efficacy in saying, " . . . but if I hang in, I feel that I can usually get it." Other than direct experience, modeling can be the most powerful factor affecting learners' self-efficacy (Bruning et al., 1995).

9.27
Explain how Kathy's interaction with Harvey near the beginning of the opening case study demonstrates effective modeling.

Teacher Enthusiasm: Communicating Genuine Interest

Research indicates that teachers who present information enthusiastically increase learners' self-efficacy, attributions of effort and ability, self-confidence, and achievement more than do less enthusiastic teachers (R. Perry, 1985; R. Perry, Magnusson, Parsonson, & Dickens, 1986).

In the opening case study, you saw the effect of enthusiasm in David and Kelly's behavior after Kathy commented, "Now isn't that interesting! . . . That's what history is all about." David's reaction was, "Brewster loves this stuff," and perhaps more significantly, Kelly's reaction was, "History has never been my favorite subject, but it's sure a relief to be in here. . . ."

The most significant aspect of Kathy's enthusiasm was that she demonstrated her own interest in the topic. It didn't include a pep talk or unnecessary theatrics; rather, it clearly identified why she found the topic interesting and meaningful to her, and she communicated those reasons to her students. A teacher's goal in projecting enthusiasm is to induce in students the feeling that the information is valuable and worth learning, not to amuse or entertain them (Good & Brophy, 1994).

Teacher Caring

- A first grader calls her teacher, "Mom."
- A fifth-grade teacher walks out on the playground during recess to talk with his students.
- A prealgebra teacher walks among the students as they do seatwork, pausing frequently to ask a question, make a comment, or simply say, "Good job."
- A high school teacher makes a special effort to make sure that Ngen Kao, a new student, feels welcome.

What do these incidents have in common? They all suggest that teaching is a human activity and that the teacher-student relationship is essential. Derived from humanistic views of motivation, emphasis on teacher caring should remind you that you are really teaching people and should focus on the learner as a whole person, including his or her emotional and social needs as well as intellectual ones.

Feelings of being cared about are important to all of us. (Recall in Maslow's hierarchy of needs how affective needs precede intellectual ones.) Advertisers inundate us with slogans: "Shop with the people who care" and "We care about you after the sale." We react when we go into a grocery or hardware store if the clerk seems to be genuinely helpful, rather than disinterested or too busy.

These factors also affect students directly. A fourth grader commented, "If a teacher doesn't care about you, it affects your mind. You feel like you're a nobody, and it makes you want to drop out of school" (Noblit, Rogers, & McCadden, 1995, p. 683). **Caring** *refers to teachers' abilities to empathize with and invest in the protection and development of young people* (Chaskin & Rauner, 1995). It's more than warm, fuzzy feelings that make people kind. In addition to understanding how students feel and where they're "coming from," caring teachers are committed to their students' growth and competence. They're attempting to do their very best for the people under their care (Noddings, 1995).

Communicating Caring.   How do teachers communicate caring to students? Although the ways are highly individual, research has identified several general characteristics, which are outlined in Table 9.6.

In examining these characteristics, you will see a thread running through them. This thread is *time*. We all react positively when someone is willing to spend time with us, and willingness to spend personal time with students communicates better than anything else that teachers care.

Caring exists at two levels. Spending time helping students who have problems with an assignment or calling a parent after school hours communicates that teachers care about student learning. A question about a baby brother or even a simple compliment

9.28 ▬
Which theoretical approach to motivation best explains the positive effects of enthusiasm? Offer an explanation based on that theoretical approach.

9.29 ▬
Research indicates that a negative emotional climate results in lowered student achievement. Using the information presented in this chapter, explain why this result could happen.

Table 9.6

Characteristics of caring teachers

Category	Description
Showing respect and politeness	Teachers are polite, treat students with respect, listen to their comments and questions, and are responsive to legitimate needs for second chances and extra help.
Valuing individuality	Teachers know students as human beings, noticing and commenting on changes in dress, habits, and behavior.
Helping with personal problems	Teachers are willing to listen to students' concerns about interpersonal relationships and nonacademic questions and problems.
Helping with schoolwork	Teachers are willing to help students, continually encourage students to do their best, and spend time in and out of class trying to explain material in understandable ways.
Going the "extra mile"	Teachers are willing to spend time with students to provide guidance in personal matters, help with difficult classwork, and work with students on extracurricular activities.

Source: Based on work by Bosworth (1995). Adapted with permission.

about a new hairstyle communicates caring about a student as a human being. The opposite is also true. Nothing offends people more than being brushed off as if they're not important enough to take up a person's time.

Teacher Expectations

"This is a new idea we've been working on, and it will be challenging, but I know you all can do the assignment. I want you to start right in while the ideas are still fresh in your mind. I'll be around in a moment to answer any questions. When you're done, you can choose a game until recess."

"This material is hard, but we've got to learn it. I want everyone to start right away, and no fooling around. Jesse, did you hear me? Some of you will have problems with this, and I'll be around as soon as I can to straighten you out. No messing around until I get there."

Teacher expectations for student behavior and achievement are communicated subtly (and not so subtly) every day. The first teacher in the examples above acknowledged that the assignment was difficult but that she expected students to successfully complete it. In addition, she promoted a climate of support. The second teacher, in contrast, implied that some students were less able than others and presented the entire assignment in a negative frame of reference.

How Teachers Form Expectations.   There is no doubt that teacher expectations influence student motivation, but the question of how teachers form expectations and the specific effects of those expectations is less clear and more controversial (Good & Brophy, 1994). One line of research has focused on studies in which teachers were asked to make predictions about fictional "students" on the basis of information they were provided, such as test scores and past performance. These studies indicate that, in addition to test scores, information about ability grouping, physical appearance, socioeconomic status

Positive teacher expectations communicate that all students can learn to their fullest potential.

(SES), race, and gender affect teacher expectations (Clifton, Perry, Parsonson, & Hryniuk, 1986; E. Jones, 1990; Jussim, 1989; Trujillo, 1986).

In the studies described above, however, the subjects, or teachers, had no opportunity to interact with real "students," and other research indicates that a teacher's perception of students are based primarily on their participation in learning activities and their performance on assignments and tests, rather than physical or status characteristics (Good & Brophy, 1994). These studies indicate that most teachers' perceptions of students are quite accurate, sometimes more accurate that predications based on test data (Helmke & Schrader, 1987; G. Short, 1985).

How Expectations Affect Teacher Behavior.   The effects of expectations on teachers' behaviors can be grouped into four categories: emotional support, teacher effort and demands, questioning, and feedback and evaluation. These four areas are summarized in Table 9.7.

You can see from the information in the table that teachers can be discriminatory, treating students they perceive to be high achievers more favorably than those they perceive as low achievers. Students are sensitive to these differences. In one study, researchers concluded that, "After ten seconds of seeing and/or hearing a teacher, even very young students could detect whether the teacher talked about or to an excellent or a weak student and could determine the extent to which that student was loved by the teacher" (Babad, Bernieri, & Rosenthal, 1991, p. 230).

Teacher Expectations: Implications for Motivation.   What does this research suggest to teachers? First, when teacher expectations are realistic, such as those based on student performance, they pose little problem. When they are based on something other than student performance, however, or are lower than past performance warrants, they can reduce both motivation and achievement.

Second, expectations tend to be self-fulfilling. "Sometimes our expectations about people cause us to treat them in ways that make them respond just as we expected they would" (Good & Brophy, 1994, p. 87).

9.30
The impact of teacher expectations on student motivation can be best explained on the basis of which theory of motivation? Provide an explanation based on this theory.

Table 9.7

Characteristics of differential teacher expectations

Characteristic	Teacher Behavior Favoring Perceived High Achievers
Emotional support	Have more interactions; interact more positively; give more smiles; make more eye contact; stand closer; orient body more directly; seat students closer to teacher
Teacher effort and demands	Give clearer and more thorough explanations; give more enthusiastic instruction; ask more follow-up questions; require more complete and accurate student answers
Questioning	Call on more often; allow more time to answer; give more encouragement; do more prompting
Feedback and evaluation	Give more praise; give less criticism; offer more complete and lengthier feedback and more conceptual evaluations

Source: Based on reviews by Good (1987a, 1987b) and Good and Brophy (1994).

Finally, differential treatment affects students' self-perceptions. If students are consistently left out of discussions, interactions are brief and cool, and feedback is cursory, they "learn" that they have lower ability than others treated better. As a result, healthy attributions for both success and failure are harder to develop. High expectations, in contrast, communicate that the teacher cares enough to make every possible effort on their behalf, and ultimately both motivation and self-worth are enhanced.

Our goal in writing this section is to increase *awareness.* Expectations are subtle and often out of teachers' conscious control. As you saw in Chapter 4, teachers often don't realize that they hold different expectations for their students. With awareness and effort, teachers will do their best to treat all students as fairly and equitably as possible. We examine specific instructional strategies to promote equitable treatment in Chapter 12.

Climate Variables

As students spend time in a classroom, they get a subjective feeling about whether they're safe and welcome and whether it will be a positive place to learn. **Classroom climate** *refers to teacher and classroom characteristics that promote students' feelings of safety and security, together with a sense of success, challenge, and understanding* (see Figure 9.7).

Climate is important because it creates an environment that encourages both motivation and achievement (Raviv, Raviv, & Reisel, 1990). Students learn best in a general atmosphere that is safe and orderly and that promotes success on tasks of worth and substance. In a healthy classroom climate, students are viewed and treated as competent people, and the students understand the requirements of learning tasks, perceive them as challenging, yet believe they will succeed if they make reasonable effort (Brophy, 1987b; Clifford, 1990). Let's look at specific ways to influence classroom climate.

Order and Safety: Classrooms as Secure Places to Learn

Cognitive and humanistic views of motivation, as well as research results, provide rationales for establishing a safe and orderly learning environment. Order helps create a sense of equilibrium in learners, and in Maslow's hierarchy, only survival precedes safety as a need. Effective schools are described as places of trust, order, cooperation, and high

Figure 9.7

Climate variables in the model for promoting student motivation

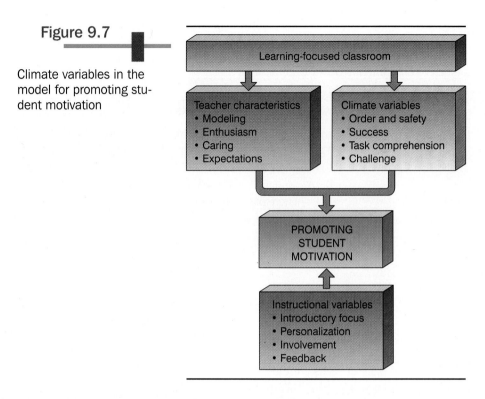

morale (Rutter, Maughn, Mortimore, Ouston, & Smith, 1979). For students to be motivated to learn, schools must be physically and psychologically safe places.

How does this idea translate into classroom practice? First, the teacher sets the tone by modeling respect and courtesy for learners. "Teachers who . . . avoid such negative practices as criticism of student behavior, screaming, sarcasm, scolding, and ridicule facilitate student learning" (J. Murphy et al., 1986, p. 86). Students who are criticized for venturing personal or creative thoughts about a topic are unlikely to take the risk a second time.

A practical way of creating a safe and orderly environment is to implement rules that are clearly stated and consistently enforced. Although rules vary according to classroom situations, one important rule needs to be considered here:

We will always treat each other with respect and courtesy.

This rule is essential for all ages and particularly for middle and junior high school students to help create a climate of safety and support. Breaking this rule should be the one capital crime in all classrooms.

Success

Once a safe and orderly environment is established, student expectation for success is the most important climate variable. This expectation for success is the expectancy component of expectancy × value theory. (Notice here that we're referring to the learners' expectation for success, not teacher expectation as we discussed in the previous section.)

Teachers can promote positive student expectations by using instructional strategies that maximize opportunities for success and that minimize possibilities for failures. For example:

▌ Begin lessons with open-ended questions. Build on students' existing understanding.
▌ Prompt students when they have difficulty answering questions.

9.31 ▬
Explain the negative effects of criticism; use behaviorism as a basis for your explanation. Explain, using social cognitive theory.

9.32 ▬
Identify a specific example in Kathy Brewster's lesson in which she promoted feelings of safety in her students.

▌ Use a wide variety of high-quality examples and demonstrations to promote understanding.

▌ Provide scaffolded practice before students are put on their own.

As with many aspects of teaching and learning, success isn't as simple as it appears. The teacher's motivational goal in promoting success is to create feelings of self-efficacy in learners, which means the success must be on tasks that learners perceive as substantial and worthwhile. Success on trivial tasks does little to create feelings of competence and self-efficacy. Some researchers argue that, by ignoring challenge, we create "artificial success" in classrooms, and they attribute student apathy to it (Clifford, 1990). Let's examine challenge further.

Challenge

Why do children persist in learning to ride a bicycle even though they fall repeatedly, and why does intrinsic interest in the skill decrease once it's been mastered? Children will stop riding a bicycle for its own sake, for example, and from that point on, use it only to be with friends or to ride to someone else's house.

In the previous section, we emphasized that students need to be successful. This emphasis doesn't imply, however, that constant success is necessary or even desirable. In fact, from a motivational perspective, success should occur in moderately difficult or truly challenging tasks, and it should be explained in terms of personal effort and well-chosen strategies (Clifford, 1990). A sense of challenge is needed if students are to experience feelings of satisfaction, competence, persistence, and control.

Clifford's (1990) assertion is supported by R. White's (1959) concept of *competence motivation,* Piaget's (1952) work, the concept of *self-efficacy,* and goal theory. According to White and Piaget, only increasing competence is emotionally satisfying, self-efficacy requires success on tasks of worth and substance, and moderate difficulty is one characteristic of effective goals (Schunk, 1994). Also, Lepper and Hodell (1989) identify *challenge* as one characteristic of intrinsically motivating activities.

Kathy Brewster capitalized on the motivational characteristics of challenge. She didn't limit her discussion of the Crusades to meaningless dates, times, and other facts, but instead focused on a thoughtful and intellectually stimulating discussion of the Crusades' success or failure. Some students, such as Harvey, initially perceived the assignment as difficult, but it was more intellectually satisfying than a hashing of the facts would have been. In pursuit of these challenging goals, Kathy provided enough scaffolding to ensure that her students could meet the challenge.

The idea of increasing challenge applies at all levels of schooling. In elementary schools, for example, once students have mastered a basic skill, such as their multiplication facts, using the facts to solve more difficult problems is more satisfying than continued drill.

As with most aspects of teaching and learning, however, the notion of challenge is subtler than it appears on the surface. For example, teachers must use careful judgment to identify the appropriate level of challenge. Unrealistic challenge or activities perceived as being overly difficult may lower student motivation because students become reluctant to be involved with them.

Task Comprehension

From expectancy × value theory, you know that to be motivated, learners must expect to succeed and also believe that what they're learning is important and valuable. Challenge

9.33
Suppose that you are teaching a lesson on "living things" to your first graders and that you have displayed for them a live hamster and a stone from the playground. Describe two open-ended questions you could use to begin the lesson.

9.34
In this chapter, we refer to two other characteristics that Lepper and Hodell (1989) have identified as characteristics of intrinsically motivating activities. What are they?

9.35
What concept best explains why activities perceived to be too difficult might lower student motivation? Provide an explanation based on the concept.

helps promote a sense of value. Sense of value is also enhanced when *students understand both what they're supposed to be learning and why they're learning it* (L. Anderson, 1989; Blumenfeld, 1992; Good & Brophy, 1994). This understanding is called **task comprehension.**

The "why they're learning it" aspect of task comprehension is critical for both teacher and learner. To provide an appropriate rationale for objectives and learning activities, teachers must think about what they want students to learn and why it is important. If students are to be motivated to learn, activities should teach things that are worth learning (Good & Brophy, 1994).

From the learners' perspectives, understanding what they're learning and why is critical in the development of self-regulation. They must understand "what" and "why" to identify appropriate goals, select effective strategies, and maintain their effort in the face of difficulty.

Kathy Brewster focused explicitly on the reasons for studying the Crusades when she asked, "Why do we study the Crusades? Who cares, anyway?" Later, she commented, "We want to learn how to make and defend an argument, so the quality of your paragraph depends on how you defended your position, not on the position itself. Remember, this is a skill that goes way beyond a specific topic, like the Crusades. This applies in everything we do." Questions and comments such as these help students understand the reasons why they are studying a particular topic. Further, when they see a link among the Crusades, the Renaissance, and their lives today, they are more likely to believe that what they're learning is worthwhile. This belief increases the "value" component of expectancy × value theory.

Compare Kathy's comments with the following statements actually made by teachers.

> Today's lesson is nothing new if you've been here.
>
> Get your nose in the book; otherwise, I'll give you a writing assignment.
>
> This test is to see who the really smart ones are. (Brophy, 1987a, p. 204)

9.36

On the basis of our earlier discussion of class structure, explain specifically why a statement such as, "This test is to see who the really smart ones are," could decrease motivation.

How motivated would you be if the teacher told you that you weren't going to learn anything new, the rationale for an activity is to avoid a different assignment, or a low score on a test means you aren't smart?

You can see now how climate variables interact to increase motivation to learn. Kathy's challenging assignment was an effective motivator only because the other variables were present. On the one hand, if her classroom had been emotionally threatening or if the students had been unable to succeed, the positive effects of challenge would have been lost. On the other hand, if her topic had been a dry coverage of facts or if the students hadn't known why they were studying it, no level of success or safety would have motivated them.

Instructional Variables

Teacher and climate variables influence learner motivation and form a general framework within which teachers can design motivating lessons. Within this context, the teacher can do much in specific learning activities to further enhance motivation. These instructional factors are illustrated in Figure 9.8.

One view of motivation to learn focuses on the extent to which students attend to instruction and become intellectually involved in learning activities (Wlodkowski, 1984). This view means that student attention must be initially captured and their involvement maintained. Motivation is also enhanced when students can relate to topics personally and receive feedback about their progress. These are the instructional variables that promote motivation to learn.

Figure 9.8

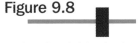

Instructional variables in the model for promoting student motivation

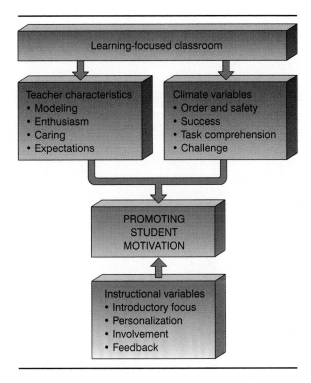

Introductory Focus: Attracting Students' Attention

As an introduction to the topic of cities and their locations, a social studies teacher hands out a map of a fictitious island. On it are physical features such as lakes, rivers, mountains, and bays. Also included is information about altitude, rainfall, and average seasonal temperature. The teacher begins, "Our class has just been sent to this island to settle it. We have this information about its climate and physical features. Our job is to decide where to make our first settlement."

A science teacher passes a baseball and a golf ball around the room and has the students feel them. After confirming that the baseball feels heavier, he climbs up onto one of the tables, holds the two balls in front of him, and as he prepares to drop them, says, "I'm going to drop these balls at the same time. What do you predict will happen?"

By beginning their lessons in these ways, the teachers were attempting to capitalize on **introductory focus,** *which is the teacher's method of attracting student attention and providing a framework for the lesson.* In our discussion of curiosity motivation, you saw that learners are motivated by unique, attractive, eye-catching, or discrepant experiences, and according to cognitive views of motivation, learners are motivated by a desire for an *understanding* of events. Introductory focus is intended to capitalize on the effects of arousal and the desire for understanding to attract students' attention and provide a framework for the lesson.

Unfortunately, conscious planning for lesson introductions occurs infrequently in classrooms; only 5% of teachers in one study made an explicit effort to draw students into the lesson (L. Anderson, Brubaker, Alleman-Brooks, & Duffy, 1984). Providing for effective introductory focus need not be difficult, however. All that is required is some conscious effort to connect the content of the lesson to students' backgrounds and interest. Some types and examples are provided in Table 9.8.

Although the types of introductory focus outlined in Table 9.8 are described independently, they are more effective when combined. For example, the picture of Heming-

9.37
Introductory focus performs two important functions. What are they?

Table 9.8

Types and examples of introductory focus

Type	Example
Discrepant (counterintuitive) events	Students blow between two pieces of paper. Instead of "blowing" apart, they come together.
Inductive sequences	Students see the following sentences "I had a ton of homework last night!" "That's the ugliest outfit ever!" "She's the most gorgeous girl in the world!" They find a pattern and develop a concept of *hyperbole*.
Attractive examples	A literature teacher shows the class a picture of Ernest Hemingway. An elementary teacher begins a unit on amphibians by bringing in a live frog.
Objectives and rationales	A math teacher begins, "Today, we want to learn about unit pricing. This will help us decide which product is a better buy. It will help us all save money and be better consumers."

way could be presented with the following description: "Here we see 'Papa' in all his splendor. He seemed to have everything—fame, adventure, romance. Yet, he took his own life. Why would this happen?" This description presents Hemingway's character as a discrepant puzzle, which provides students with a problem to solve.

Once students are attracted to the lesson and a conceptual framework is provided, the lesson then needs to maintain their attention and interest. This can be accomplished through personalization, involvement, and feedback.

Personalization: Links to Students' Lives

Let's look again at Kathy Brewster's lesson. Early in the process, she said, "Remember, we started by imagining that we all left Lincoln High School and that it was taken over by people who believed that all extracurricular activities should be cut out." She then used this example as a framework and an analogy to introduce her students to the Crusades. As another example, when introducing the topic of genetics, a teacher might say, "Once we understand genetics, we'll be able to figure out why Reeanne has blue eyes and Edward has brown."

These are both examples of personalization. **Personalization** *attempts to make topics meaningful by using intellectually and/or emotionally familiar examples.* Kathy used her school; she combined both intellectually and emotionally familiar examples. In the case with genetics, the teacher used two students in her class.

The value of *personalization* can be explained in several ways. First, relating content to students personally is one core element of humanistic views of motivation. Second, you saw in Chapter 7 that meaningfulness enhances learning; personalization is one way of increasing meaningfulness. Third, anything people can relate to personally is more concrete for them than distant or abstract information, and you saw in Chapter 2 how concrete experiences were an essential component of Piaget's work. Finally, research indicates that student engagement and attention increase when teachers refer to students and their daily lives (Lemke, 1982).

9.38
Look again at the example with Reeanne, Edward, and eye color. Explain how it might be used as an example of both introductory focus and personalization. Then describe how it might be used only as personalization.

When direct personalization is difficult, analogies can be used. You saw in Chapter 7 that analogies promote elaboration by linking new content to students' existing background experiences and that they can increase motivation by helping students see connections to their own lives. For instance, let's look at the way one teacher introduced *Julius Caesar,* a classic play about power and ambition, friendship and denial. Its message is as important today as when it was written more than 300 years ago. But how can teachers get students to relate to the play? Here's how one teacher did it:

> *Julius Caesar* is basically a play about internal conflicts, a moral decision for which there is really no wrong or right answer. If we kill this man, we might save our republic but we endanger ourselves. If we don't kill him, we could be endangered. [It focuses on one] man's struggle with a moral decision, the consequences of his actions, and how people turn against him.
>
> And so . . . I gave them an artificial scenario. I said, "You are the first officer on the Starship Enterprise. Captain Kirk has been getting out of hand. He's a good captain; he's been made Commander of the Fleet. But you, his closest friend, and your fellow officers have been noticing that he's been getting too risky, a little big-headed. You're afraid that he's going to endanger the Federation Fleet and might just seek glory in some farcical campaign."
>
> And they really took off on that . . . they said they found out there really wasn't a right answer. They argued back and forth. You couldn't just kill him because the whole fleet likes him. If you kill him, it's your head on the chopping block, too. But you also have a moral obligation to your country and you can't let him go on. What they finally came up with was that it's a pretty tough decision to make. (Wilson, Shulman, & Richert, 1987, p. 112)

By comparing *Julius Caesar* to characters on the *Starship Enterprise,* the teacher was able to relate the Shakespearean story to *Star Trek*—something real in students' lives.

Involvement

Introductory focus and personalization pull students into lessons, but unless a lesson or topic is particularly intriguing or timely, neither one alone nor the two in combination will sustain motivation. The key to maintaining motivation is **involvement**, *which means that students are actively participating in the learning activity.*

Think about your experience at lunch or a party. When you're talking and actively listening, you pay more attention to the conversation than you do when you're on its fringes. The same applies in classrooms. Conscious teacher efforts to promote involvement result in both increased participation and learning (Blumenfeld, 1992; Pratton & Hales, 1986). Let's look at some specific strategies for increasing student involvement.

Using Open-Ended Questioning to Promote Involvement.   The most generally applicable tool the teacher has to promote and maintain involvement is questioning. Student attention is at a peak when teachers ask questions but drops during teacher monologues (Lemke, 1982).

We discuss questioning in detail in Chapter 12, but we introduce one strategy here because it is particularly effective in improving involvement and motivation. This strategy is the open-ended question (Kauchak & Eggen, 1993). **Open-ended questions** *are those for which a variety of answers are acceptable.* For instance, in a lesson on amphibians, a teacher might begin by displaying a frog or a picture of a frog and asking,

"Look at the frog. What do you see in the picture?"

In the case of *Julius Caesar,* the teacher might ask,

9.39
Is the concept of *involvement* the same as the concept of *activity* as we discussed it in Chapter 7? If not, how are they different?

Effective teachers maintain students' motivation by actively involving them in lessons.

"What has happened so far in the play?"

"What are some of the major events?"

"Who is an important character and tell why he's important."

"What is one thing you can say about the play?"

These ask for simple observations of the topic. A second type of open-ended question asks for comparisons. For instance,

"How is the frog similar to a lizard?"

"How are the frog and a toad similar or different?"

"How are Brutus and Marc Antony similar? How are they different?"

"How does the setting for Act I compare with that for Act II?"

Open-ended questions capitalize on two of the climate variables we discussed earlier. When combined with a rule requiring students to treat each other with respect, they are safe, and because many answers are acceptable, they virtually ensure success. By combining safety and success, even the most reluctant student can be encouraged to respond without risk or fear of embarrassment.

Also, because they can be asked and answered quickly, open-ended questions can help solve the problem of involving 30 or more members of a class during a single lesson. Without the use of at least some open-ended questions, calling on reluctant responders often enough to significantly increase their level of attention is difficult if not impossible.

We emphasize, however, that "artificial" open-ended questions don't work. If students are asked to observe or compare but the teacher has a particular answer in mind, students quickly perceive that the questions aren't "truly" open-ended, and so their motivational effects are reduced.

Involving Students: Alternatives to Questioning. Although questioning is a powerful tool, it is demanding. Simultaneously maintaining the flow of the activity, keeping track of who has

9.40
What climate variable must exist before students will be willingly involved? Explain.

been called on, and continuing to generate questions even if they are open-ended requires a great deal of teacher skill and energy. Maintaining student involvement often requires additional strategies, some of which are outlined in Table 9.9. With each of these strategies, student involvement increases and the teacher is taken out of the center of the activity.

Some of these strategies are simple but clever. Improvement drills add an element of gamelike arousal to otherwise routine activities, and seeing improvement can increase self-efficacy. Using chalkboards is similar to having students solve problems at their desks by using notebook paper. The chalkboards, however, encourage individual effort, and students often will use them even when they won't try if only paper is used.

Groupwork can be particularly effective for promoting involvement. Both David Shelton in Chapter 7 and Patty Kramer in Chapter 8 used groupwork to promote student involvement. David had students work together to put information in a chart, and they worked together again to form explanations for some of the information. Patty had her students work in teams to measure the school grounds and find the area. In both cases, organizing and implementing the activities were relatively simple and didn't require an inordinate amount of teacher energy.

Feedback

Let's return to Kathy Brewster's lesson once more. In addition to everything else she did, Kathy gave students specific information about progress on their paragraphs. Research indicates that feedback used to improve future performance has powerful motivational value (Clifford, 1990). Feedback is particularly motivating when combined with clear student goals. Feedback gives learners information about the extent to which goals are being attained. If they are falling short, they can try harder or use a different strategy. If they have met or exceeded the goal, they get a feeling of accomplishment.

The need for feedback can be explained by cognitive theories of motivation. Not having a sense of "how you're doing" interferes with your equilibrium, and self-efficacy is impossible if you're not sure how you're performing. In our discussion of attribution theory, you also found that learners have a need to understand and explain why they are performing the way they are. Feedback helps them form accurate explanations.

Table 9.9

Strategies to promote involvement

Technique	Example
Improvement drills	Students are given a list of 10 multiplication facts on a sheet. Students are scored on speed and accuracy, and points are given for individual improvement.
Games	The class is divided equally according to ability, and the two groups respond in a game format to teacher questions.
Individual work spaces	Students are given their own chalkboards on which they solve math problems and identify examples of concepts. They hold the chalkboards up when they've solved the problem or when they think an example illustrates a concept. They also write or draw their own examples on the chalkboards.
Student groupwork	Student pairs observe a science demonstration and write down as many observations of it as they can.

9.41

On the basis of the information in this section, what should a teacher do after scoring a test and returning it to students?

Information about progress is lacking in a course that has only a midterm and a final exam or, even worse, just a final. Students don't know how they're doing, so they can't adjust their study strategies accordingly. As another example, imagine how you would feel if you were observed teaching a lesson and your observer left without saying anything to you. You would be left with an uneasy feeling.

When teachers provide feedback about performance, the emphasis should be on progress and mastery of the content, rather than on social comparisons (Crooks, 1988; Maehr, 1992; Schunk, 1994). This is especially important for less able students.

Kathy Brewster also used feedback to help students attribute their increased understanding to effort. When Harvey grumbled about how hard she worked them, Kathy quickly commented, "Yes, but look what it's doing for you. . . . You've improved on each essay you've written. As a matter of fact, I think you hit a personal best on your last one." He obviously thought the essays were challenging, and his improvement provided observable progress. The combination of the two works to increase self-efficacy.

Praise.   As you saw in Chapter 6, praise is perhaps the most common form of feedback. Used judiciously, praise can enhance motivation (Cameron & Pierce, 1994). Kathy was able to use praise effectively with Toni, Joe, Nikki, and Scott because she was able to elicit successful and substantive responses from them. She didn't praise them for trivial responses to easy questions. If the climate had been threatening, the content had been meaningless or unimportant, or the students had been generally uninvolved, efforts to use praise wouldn't have worked.

Combining Elements of the Model for Promoting Student Motivation

We have now examined the class structure and each of the 12 components of the model for promoting student motivation. We have described them separately for the sake of clarity, but we want to emphasize that as many components as possible should be combined in your teaching. For instance, one middle school teacher did the following:

> In beginning a unit on folktales, the teacher wrote three folktales about the school principal and two other teachers in the school. She began the lesson by telling the students that they would be given some brief stories and that they were to read them and find a pattern in them. The purpose was to give them some practice in becoming "good thinkers." She then asked the students to make observations about the stories by comparing them and looking for characteristics they had in common.

The teacher in this case capitalized on several elements of the model. She presented the folktales as a form of introductory focus, and her purpose and rationale for the lesson helped promote task comprehension. She used open-ended questioning to promote safety, success, and involvement, and her folktales capitalized on personalization. In this simple example, the teacher employed six features of the model, and it would have been easy to change the wording of her introduction slightly to increase the element of challenge. Assuming she has motivating personal characteristics, most of the model is employed in one simple yet creative lesson.

One of the most important messages we want to send in writing this chapter is that the roles of teachers involve much more than the simple delivery of content. One of those aspects is a conscious attempt to promote student motivation to learn.

Classroom Connections

Demonstrating the Personal Characteristics of the Model for Promoting Student Motivation in Your Classroom

1. Show students you care by giving them your personal time.
   - A geography teacher calls parents as soon as he sees a student having even minor academic or personal problems. He solicits their help in monitoring the student and solving the problem.

2. Display enthusiasm in your teaching.
   - During quiet reading time, a fourth-grade teacher comments on a book she's interested in and reads while the students are reading.

3. Model incremental views of ability.
   - An English teacher comments, "I've really studied a lot since I started teaching this class, and I have learned a lot more about American literature than I knew at the beginning of the year."

4. Maintain appropriately high expectations for all students.
   - A second-grade teacher makes a conscious attempt to treat all students in her class as equally as possible. She distributes her questions to them equally and is careful to demand as much as she can from each.

Applying the Climate Variables of the Model for Promoting Student Motivation in Your Classroom

5. Maintain a safe, orderly classroom environment.
   - In enforcing her rules, a fifth-grade teacher explains, "Our work in this class is important, and I will not allow any of you to rob others of their time by being disruptive."

6. Carefully describe objectives and rationales for your assignments.
   - A junior high English teacher carefully describes his assignment and due dates. Each time, he explains why the assignment is important.

7. Promote challenge and success in learning activities.
   - A fourth-grade teacher comments, "We've been doing so well, I have a problem that is going to make us all think. It will be tough, but I think we can do it."
   - An algebra teacher always has the class practice three or four seatwork exercises as a whole group and discusses them before students begin to work independently.

Applying the Instructional Variables of the Model for Promoting Student Motivation in Your Classroom

8. Plan lesson introductions to attract students' attention and to provide an umbrella for the lesson.
   - A middle school science teacher begins each class with a question or problem that leads into the lesson. She began one lesson on local geology by asking students to imagine what their area looked like 1 million, 10 million, and 100 million years earlier.
   - A fifth-grade teacher introduces concepts, principles, and rules inductively by beginning with examples, asking students to describe and compare the examples, and finding patterns that lead to each idea.

9. Promote involvement by eliciting responses from all students.
   - A language arts teacher randomly calls on all her students whether or not they raise their hands. At the beginning of the year, she explains that this would be her practice, that her intent is to encourage their participation, and that they will soon get over any uneasiness about being "put on the spot." Whenever students are unable to answer, she gives them extra support in the form of cues and prompts.

10. Personalize content.
    - A geography teacher begins a lesson on longitude and latitude by telling students to imagine that they have made a new friend from another country and that they want to be able to describe for the friend exactly where they live.

- A fifth-grade teacher begins a lesson on percentage by bringing in an advertisement for toys from a local newspaper. The ad says "10% to 25% off marked prices." After discussing how to compute percentage discounts, she returns to the ad and asks students to compute their savings on various items.

11. Provide prompt and informative feedback on student performance.

- A fourth-grade teacher responds, "You are following the steps in solving problems very well," in an effort to promote effective use of strategies for problem solving.

- A seventh-grade teacher comments, "You have some very good ideas. Now, you need to rework your essay so that it is grammatically correct. Look carefully at the notes I've made on your paper."

Motivation and Diversity

As you examine the research on the school success of ethnic minorities, you will see a pattern emerge. On most standard measures of school success—achievement test scores, retention in grade, and drop-out rates—many ethnic minorities in the United States perform less well than their majority counterparts (Macionis, 1994; Mullis, Dossey, Foertsh, Jones, & Gentile, 1991). Although several differences can be linked to SES, troubling disparities still remain. Many minority students leave school unprepared to participate in and benefit from the technologically oriented and skill-demanding world of today.

Educators have turned to motivational research in an attempt to address these problems. Unfortunately, the picture that appears remains cloudy. For example, researchers have attempted to explain why the achievement of African American students is lower than expected by hypothesizing deficits in need for achievement, internal locus of control, expectations for success, and academic self-concept, all motivational factors linked to achievement. In a comprehensive review of this literature, however, Graham (1994) concluded that deficits don't exist and that African American students "maintain a belief in personal control, have high expectance and enjoy positive self-regard" (p. 55). Researchers have also found that African American and Latina mothers have strong interest in their children's schooling, are enthusiastic about education, and hold high expectations for their children's future (Stevenson, Chen, & Uttal, 1990).

The picture is made more complex by research suggesting that motivation varies not only between minority groups but also within groups. For example, researchers have identified differences in the way different African American parents approach the task of motivating their children (Steinberg, Dornbusch, & Brown, 1992), and similar differences have been identified in Asian and Latino families. Peer groups within minority cultures also influence motivation differently, sometimes complementing school achievement, at other times detracting from it (Goodenow, 1992b; Steinberg et al., 1992). In addition, researchers have pointed out the considerable differences that exist among African American communities (Graham, 1994; Slaughter-Defoe, Nakagawa, Takanashi, & Johnson, 1990); motivational issues in an inner-city African American community are very different from those in suburban or rural ones.

9.42

From your study of the classroom model for promoting student motivation, what are some teacher characteristics, climate variables, and instructional variables that could influence minority students' motivation?

Motivational Problems: Student Perspectives

In attempting to understand how schools influence minority students' motivation and achievement, researchers have focused on students' perceptions of their school experiences and have identified the following problems:

▌ Lack of connection between classroom content and students' lives
▌ Alienation from school
▌ Disengagement and lack of involvement in classes
▌ Distant and inflexible teachers

Students report feeling alienated from school, like outsiders at a party. This feeling results from factors such as cultural discontinuities, language barriers, and academic problems (Ogbu 1992; Wong-Fillmore, 1992). In one study, researchers asked about connections between school and students' personal happiness:

Interviewer:	What do you really like about school? What makes you happy?
Diane:	Nothing really. I just come because I have to. Because I don't want to grow up being stupid.
Interviewer:	There's nothing you look forward to?
Diane:	Ummm . . . (defiantly stares; challenges.) Getting an education?
Interviewer:	Do you think there's a way to get an education without coming to school?
Diane:	(shakes her head no)
Interviewer:	It has to be this way?
Diane:	(softly; no eye contact) Yeah.

(Kramer & Colvin, 1991, p. 6)

Another student, who was discussing his decision to leave school at age 16, describes his alienation as follows:

Student:	I wouldn't go to nobody.
Interviewer:	Not even a counselor?
Student:	No.
Interviewer:	That seems funny. Don't you work in the office?
Student:	Yeah, but I don't *talk* to them [student emphasis].

(Kramer-Schlosser, 1992, p. 132)

Disengagement is another problem. Teachers report that students don't come to class or that when they do, they are reluctant to participate.

> They'll try to sit at the edges or the back of the classroom and they actually try to become less visible to me, or they'll act up so they get sent out of the classroom and there's less time, less chance I'll call on them or hold them accountable. . . . Usually they don't join the class. (Kramer & Colvin, 1991, p. 12)

Adding to these problem are student perceptions that teachers just don't care. One student described her teachers in this way:

Nichole:	People here don't have many people to talk to. I don't. The teachers . . . some of them don't care about their students. They say, "They [administrators] want me to teach and I'm going to do it no matter what." I don't like that. I like them to say, "I'm here to teach and help you because I care." That's what I like. But a lot of them are just saying, "I'm here to teach so I'm gonna teach." I don't think that's right.
Interviewer:	Do they actually say that?
Nichole:	It's more an attitude, and they do say it. Like Ms. G. She's like . . . she never says it, but you know, she's just there and she just wants to teach, but she doesn't want to explain the whole deal.
Interviewer:	How do you know that?

9.43
How does student disengagement relate to the concept of *involvement* discussed earlier? What questioning strategy suggested in this chapter and other parts of this text would be effective in increasing the involvement of cultural minorities?

> *Nichole:*   I could feel it. The way she acts and the way she does things. She's been here seven years and all the kids I've talked to that have had her before say, "Oooh! You have Ms. G.!" Just like that.
>
> *Interviewer:*   But a teacher who really cares, how do they act?
>
> *Nichole:*   Like Mr. P. He really cares about his students. He's helping me a lot and he tells me, "I'm not angry with you, I just care about you." He's real caring and he does teach me when he cares.
>
> (Kramer & Colvin, 1991, p. 13)

The pattern you see is a lack of connection to both school and classes. Students attend school, sit in classes, but don't feel a part of them. They question whether anyone cares about them, and from their perspective, the classes have little meaning for their daily lives.

Motivational Problems: Possible Solutions

Research suggests some possible solutions to student alienation and disengagement. Students must feel that they belong and can contribute to the classroom community. They need to value the classes they take and find them meaningful.

Teachers are critical to the success of the process, and research indicates that those who are effective at motivating at-risk and minority students have the following characteristics:

- They are enthusiastic, supportive, and have high expectations for student achievement.
- They create learner-centered classrooms with high levels of student involvement.
- They make a special effort to connect classroom content to students' lives (Kramer & Colvin, 1991; Kramer-Schlosser, 1992).

Teachers need to make a special effort to make all students feel welcome and to demonstrate that they sincerely care. They also need to communicate positive expectations and that they'll work with students if the students try. One teacher who was identified as effective in working with minority and at-risk students described his efforts in this way:

> I believe that marginal students who begin the year poorly and improved did so because they knew I would do all I could to help them to be a success in school. I told them I would explain, and explain, and explain until they understood. They were worth every moment it would take. No one ever has to fail. (Kramer-Schlosser, 1992, p. 137)

Because a focus on learners is a theme of this text, we emphasize two characteristics of teachers who support learners in their classrooms: First, they attempt to connect the topics they teach to the lives and concerns of students; second, they create learning activities that promote high levels of student involvement. Teacher questioning, discussions, small-group work, and group projects replace lectures and other teacher-centered approaches. They literally take the content to students, rather than say, "Here it is. Come and get it if you want it."

As you studied the chapter, you saw how it relates to the elements of the model for promoting student motivation. Teacher characteristics such as *caring, enthusiasm,* and *high expectations* were directly discussed, and the same is true for *personalization* and *involvement* in the instructional variables. Others, such as *order and safety, challenge, success,* and *feedback,* were less explicit but strongly implied. Conscious attention to these variables can reap positive results with all students, majority and minority alike.

Classroom Connections

Capitalizing on Diversity in Your Classroom

1. Communicate positive expectations for student success through your words and teaching strategies.

   • A math teacher responsible for basic math classes stresses at the beginning of the school year that she expects all students to succeed. She collects and grades homework every day and talks with students and their parents when it isn't handed in. She tests and quizzes frequently and gives detailed feedback to students about their performance.

2. Create learning environments that involve students in meaningful learning.

   • A social studies teacher supplements his units with student group projects. For example, in their study of World War II, he asked students to interview older neighbors, relatives, and friends about their memories of the war and had groups report on their findings on a class sharing day.

   • An English teacher redesigned his writing class to address issues that were important to his students. At the beginning of the term, he spent some time identifying issues that students wanted to talk and write about (e.g., dress codes, cafeteria food). He encouraged students to debate issues before writing about them and arranged with the school newspaper to publish some of the better ones in a pro and con editorial section.

3. Communicate caring by spending time with students, on both academic and personal topics.

   • A middle school science teacher contacts every student the first time he or she fails to turn in a homework assignment or scores poorly on a test. He has the student come in before or after school to discuss the problem and get extra help.

   • An elementary teacher regularly calls parents and other care givers, both to discuss attendance or academic problems and to congratulate them on special achievement improvements by their children.

Windows on Classrooms

At the beginning of the chapter, you saw how Kathy Brewster applied an understanding of student motivation in her teaching. She maintained high expectations for her students, accommodated their personal needs, promoted self-efficacy, and maintained a high level of student involvement in a safe and orderly learning environment.

We turn now to a case study that describes another teacher presenting the same topic to a different group of students. As you read this classroom episode, compare the approach with Kathy Brewster's work with her students.

"What are we up to today, Mr. Marcus?" Joe asked as he came into Damon Marcus's classroom Thursday morning.

"You'll see in a minute," Damon nodded and smiled. "Now, quickly, get to your seat so that we can get started."

Damon watched as the students took their seats, and he then announced, "Listen, everyone, I have your tests here from last Friday. Liora, Ivan, Lynn, and Segundo, super job on the test. They were the only A's in the class."

After he finished handing back the tests, Damon moved to the chalkboard and wrote the following:

A–4
B–7
C–11
D–4
F–3

"You people down here better get moving," Damon commented, pointing to the D's and F's on the chalkboard. "This wasn't that hard a test. Remember, we have another test in 2 weeks. Let's have some improvement. C'mon, now. I know you can do better. Let's give these four a run for their money," he finished with a wave.

"You can look over your papers, but be sure to turn them in by the end of the class period," Damon continued, as he turned to the day's lesson.

"Now, let's get going. We have a lot to cover today. . . . As you'll recall from yesterday, we began talking about the Crusades and said that they were an attempt by the Christian powers of Western Europe to wrest control of the traditional holy lands of Christianity away from the Muslims. Now, when was the first Crusade?" Damon asked, looking over the classroom.

"About 1500, I think," Clifton volunteered.

"No, no," Damon shook his head. "Remember that Columbus sailed in 1492, which was before 1500, so that doesn't make sense. It was well before 1500. . . . Wynetta?"

"It was about 1100, I think."

"Excellent, Wynetta. Now, remember, everyone, you need to know these dates, or otherwise you'll get confused just as Clifton did here. I know that learning dates and places isn't the most pleasant stuff, but you might as well get used to it because it will be on the next test."

While this was going on, Brad whispered to Donna, "Let me look at your test a sec. I got one point on this one, and I don't get it." Donna handed Brad her test, and he carefully read her answer and then read his own again.

"I still don't get it," he whispered and shrugged as he handed back her paper.

"Ask him about it," Donna suggested.

Damon continued, "The first Crusade was in 1095, and it was called the 'People's Crusade.' The Pope endorsed it. There were actually seven Crusades in all, ranging from the one in 1095 to the point where enthusiasm for them ended by 1300."

"The fourth Crusade was particularly notorious," he continued. "In it, the Crusaders sacked Constantinople in 1203, and the Greek Byzantine Church hated the Crusaders forever after that."

Damon continued, "The Crusades weren't just religiously motivated. The Muslim world was getting stronger and stronger, and it was posing a threat to Europe. For example, it had control of much of northern Africa, had expanded into southern Spain, and even was moving into other parts of southern Europe. So, it was a threat economically and militarily as well as religiously. This was also a factor in the Crusades."

Damon continued presenting information about the Crusades, including facts such as Richard the Lionheart's capture of Cyprus and the sponsorship of later Crusades by the French.

Seeing that about 20 minutes were left in the period, Damon then said, "Now, I want you to write a summary of the Crusades that outlines the major people and events and that tells why they were important. You should be able to finish by the end of the class period. If you don't, turn them in tomorrow at the beginning of the class period. You may use your notes. Go ahead and get started while I come around and collect your tests."

As Damon started to collect the students' tests, Brad came up to Damon's desk and said, "Mr. Marcus, I don't get this. I only got a 1 out of 5 on this one. But Donna got a 4 and the answers say almost the same thing."

"Let me look at Donna's," Damon requested.

Brad went back and got Donna's test. Damon looked at question 6 and turned to Brad, "Donna's answer was better organized and clearer than yours."

He then moved down the aisles, collecting students' tests. As he went by, he saw that Jeremy hadn't written anything on his paper. Damon finished collecting the papers and then went back to Jeremy's desk. Jeremy's paper was still blank.

"C'mon back here," Damon motioned to a table at the back of the room.

"Having trouble getting started?" Damon asked sympathetically. "I know you have a tough time with written assignments. Let me help you."

Damon then took a blank piece of paper and started writing as Jeremy watched. He wrote several sentences on the paper and then said, "See how easy that was. That's the kind of thing I want you to do. Go ahead. You can keep that so you can see what I'm looking for. Go back to your desk and give it another try."

Damon then went back to his desk at the front of the room and began arranging the students' tests in alphabetical order.

Questions for Discussion and Analysis

Compare Damon's lesson with Kathy's. In making your comparison, you may want to consider the following questions. In each case, be specific and take information directly from the case studies in making your comparisons.

1. Compare the two teachers' attempts to capitalize on the motivating effects of arousal. How were they alike and different?

2. Would Damon's handling of the lesson likely appeal to students with a high need for achievement? How appealing would the lesson be for students with a high need to avoid failure? Explain in both cases.

3. Assess Damon's lesson in terms of Maslow's hierarchy. How well did he meet needs at each level?

4. Would Damon's teaching more likely promote learning goals or performance goals? A task orientation or an ego orientation? Explain.

5. On the basis of Damon's remarks after he turned back the test, describe some possible attributions for students who did well on the test and some possible attributions for students who did poorly on the test.

6. Assess the effectiveness of Damon's lesson for students with diverse backgrounds. Make specific suggestions for improvement in instances for which you believe his teaching could be improved.

7. Assess Damon's instruction on the basis of each element of the model for promoting student motivation. In instances for which you believe he could have improved, offer specific suggestions for improvement.

Summary

Extrinsic and Intrinsic Motivation

Motivation is a force that energizes, sustains, and directs behavior toward a goal. Extrinsic motivation—the desire to engage in a task as a means to an end—comes from outside the learner in the form of high test scores, grades, and teacher compliments. Intrinsic motivation—the desire to engage in a task for its own sake—is a response to needs within the learner, such as curiosity, a desire for competence, and the feeling of being able to accomplish a goal. Fostering intrinsic motivation should be the goal of all teaching.

Theories of Motivation

Behaviorism suggests that motivation results from using reinforcers effectively. Critics of behavioral approaches to motivation suggest that using reinforcers detracts from intrinsic motivation and causes learners to focus on the reinforcers instead of learning.

Cognitive theories of motivation suggest that people have an innate need for order and predictability. Closely related to Piaget's concept of *equilibrium,* cognitive theories suggest that learners are motivated to resolve cognitive conflict when experiences don't make sense to them.

Humanistic views of motivation focus on the learner as a whole person and examine the relationships among physical, emotional, intellectual, and aesthetic needs. Classroom climate and the teacher-student relationship are central to the humanistic view.

Personal Factors in Motivation

Arousal is a physical or psychological reaction to the environment. Extreme arousal can result in anxiety, which is both a cause and a result of poor performance. Teachers can capitalize on the positive effects of arousal by using eye-catching or discrepant events in their teaching.

A need is a real or perceived lack of something desirable. From a humanistic perspective, Maslow described a hierarchy beginning with survival and safety needs, progressing through belonging and esteem needs, and ending with intellectual and aesthetic needs. Cognitive needs include needs for competence, control, and achievement. Attribution theory describes people's desire to understand and explain their performance on tasks.

Motivation is an important element of self-regulation. Self-regulated learners set challenging goals, persist in the face of difficulty, and adjust when strategies are ineffective. Learners high in self-efficacy also display characteristics of self-regulation.

A Classroom Model for Promoting Student Motivation

Within a learning-focused rather than a performance-focused classroom, teachers can do much to increase student motivation to learn. Teacher characteristics, including modeling, enthusiasm, caring, and high expectations, combine with classroom climate and instructional variables to enhance motivation.

Motivation is increased when students work in a safe and orderly classroom, experience success, understand tasks and the reasons for them, and experience optimal challenge. Teachers can increase motivation in their lessons by preparing attractive lesson beginnings, involving students, personalizing content, and providing informative feedback.

 # Important Concepts

achievement motivation
   (p. 355)

anxiety (p. 351)

arousal (p. 351)

attribution theory (p. 356)

attributions (p. 356)

caring (p. 368)

classroom climate (p. 371)

cognitive theories of motivation (p. 345)

competence motivation
   (p. 354)

curiosity (p. 352)

deficiency needs (p. 352)

entity view of ability
   (p. 358)

expectancy × value theories (p. 346)

extrinsic motivation
  (p. 342)

growth needs (p. 352)

humanistic psychology
  (p. 348)

incremental view of ability
  (p. 358)

intrinsic motivation
  (p. 342)

introductory focus (p. 375)

involvement (p. 377)

learned helplessness
  (p. 357)

learning goals (p. 361)

motivation (p. 341)

motivational control
  (p. 362)

need (p. 352)

open-ended questions
  (p. 377)

performance goals (p. 361)

personalization (p. 376)

self-efficacy (p. 346)

task comprehension
  (p. 374)

Chapter Outline

10
Managing the Learning Environment

Judy Harris is a ninth-grade geography teacher whose class is involved in a cultural unit on the Middle East. She has 32 students in a room designed for 24, so the students are sitting within arm's reach across the aisles.

As Ginger comes into the room, she sees a large map projected high on the screen at the front of the room. She quickly slides into her seat just as the bell stops ringing. Most of the students have already begun studying the map and the accompanying directions on the chalkboard: "Identify the longitude and latitude of Cairo and Damascus."

Judy takes roll and hands back a set of papers as students busy themselves with the task. As she hands Brad his paper, she touches him on the arm and points to the overhead, reminding him to return from his window-gazing.

She waits a moment for the students to finish and then pulls down a large map in the front of the classroom and begins a discussion with them.

"We've been studying the Middle East, and you just identified Damascus here in Syria," she notes, pointing at the map. "Now, think for a moment and make a prediction about the climate in Damascus."

Judy pauses, surveys the class, and says, "Bernice?" as she walks down one of the rows.

" . . . Damascus is about 34° north latitude, I think."

As soon as Judy walks past him, Kevin sticks his foot across the aisle, tapping Alison on the leg with his shoe while he watches Judy's back from the corner of his eye. "Stop it, Kevin," Alison mutters, swiping at him with her hand.

Judy turns, comes back up the aisle, and continues, "Good, Bernice. It's very close to 34°." Standing next to Kevin, she asks, "What would that indicate about its temperature at this time of the year? . . . Kevin?" she asks, looking directly at him.

" . . . I'm not sure."

"Warmer or colder than here?"

" . . . Warmer, I think."

"Okay. Good prediction, Kevin. And why might that be the case? . . . Jim?"

"Move up here," Judy says quietly to Sondra, who has been whispering and passing notes to Sherrill across the aisle. Judy nods to a desk at the front of the room as she waits for Jim to answer.

"What did I do?" Sondra protests.

Judy leans over Sondra's desk and points to a rule displayed on a poster:

LISTEN WHEN SOMEONE
ELSE IS TALKING.

"Quickly, now." She motions to the desk.

" . . . Damascus is south of us and also in a desert," Jim responds.

"I wasn't doing anything," Sondra protests.

"I have to interrupt my teaching when people aren't paying attention. I get worn out and frustrated when I'm interrupted. Please move," Judy says evenly, looking Sondra in the eye.

"Good analysis, Jim. Now let's look at Cairo," she continues as she watches Sondra move to the new desk.

From 1968 until 1986, those surveyed by the Gallup polls identified school discipline as the most important problem teachers face; from 1986 to 1992, discipline ranked second only to drugs and inadequate funding as the biggest educational problem. In 1994, lack of discipline was tied with violence and gangs as the number one problem again; in 1995, it surfaced again as the number one problem (Elam & Rose, 1995).

Like most issues in teaching, classroom management is complex, and skilled managers seem to have a "feel" for the process that their less effective colleagues often lack. In fact, some argue that capable management and discipline are functions of a teacher's personality and cannot be taught. Research results, however, counter that position. In this chapter, we examine the results of this research and analyze the strategies and actions of effective managers.

After you've completed this chapter, you should be able to meet the following objectives:

▌ Explain how effective planning can prevent management problems.
▌ Explain how developmental differences in students influence classroom management.

▌ Describe teacher characteristics associated with effective management.
▌ Identify examples of essential management skills in cases of classroom practice.
▌ Describe how effective intervention techniques can eliminate management problems.

Classroom Management and Discipline

Let's stop at this point and consider Judy's situation in the opening case. It typifies what many teachers face every day, all year long: Her class is too large, some of the students are only marginally interested in the content, her ninth graders are going through the turmoil of adolescence, and she is probably tired of constantly dealing with the annoyances of students like Kevin and Sondra.

Despite her less-than-ideal conditions, Judy demonstrated several characteristics of effective classroom managers. What are they? What do we mean by "discipline," and how does this differ from "management"?

Classroom Management

10.1

What's the difference between a good manager and a good disciplinarian? Which of the two will have students who learn more? Explain why you think so.

Classroom management *refers to the combination of teacher strategies and classroom organizational factors that lead to a productive learning environment.* This includes the established routines, school and classroom rules, teacher responses to student behavior, and instruction that promotes a climate conducive to student learning. **Discipline** *involves teacher actions in response to student behavior that detracts from the order and safety of the environment or that interferes with the opportunity to learn.* These behaviors, or misbehaviors, include talking or leaving desks without permission, tapping pencils, passing notes, poking or hitting other students, making hostile or sarcastic remarks, or more seriously, fighting, assaulting the teacher, and carrying weapons to school. In this chapter, we focus on the larger concept of *classroom management* and examine discipline within that context.

Persistence of Management Problems

Parents, school leaders, and teachers have all identified student discipline as a critical problem in schools, and observations in classrooms support this concern. Some investigators have found that students are off-task more than 50% of the time (F. Jones, 1979; Kounin, 1983), and teacher interventions that are used to maintain order occur about 16 times per hour in the typical classroom (M. White, 1975). Beginning teachers rate management as their number one problem (Veenman, 1984). At least three major reasons can be offered for the existence of these prevalent and persistent problems.

Sociological Factors

The social climate of American culture has changed. Most children are now raised either in families in which both mother and father work outside the home or by single parents. Many children spend more hours watching television each day than they spend on their studies, including time in school. Beginning in the 1960s, authority in general and teachers' authority in particular were questioned more often than at any earlier time. Students have been raised in more permissive environments, and their own rights and freedom of expression are emphasized to a greater extent than they were in the past. Many students are less compliant than they once were and are more likely to question a teacher's right or ability to manage them. One teacher in a national study commented,

> It's hard to punish a child for misbehaving when you understand his home situation directly causes him to behave the way he does. . . . Too much time must be spent counseling and teaching children better ways to handle anger, stress, and frustrations. The breakdown of families causes poor self-esteem and results in discipline problems. (Clapp, 1989, p. 32)

As you saw in earlier chapters, the home exerts a powerful influence not only on classroom learning but also on classroom management (Feldman & Wentzel, 1990; Wentzel, 1991).

Energy and Effort

The second reason for persistent management problems is that teachers sometimes feel overwhelmed by the effort required to maintain order. For some, it is simply easier to run a laissez-faire classroom. If students don't destroy the room and if some semblance of instruction exists, the teacher ignores misbehavior. The movie *Teachers*, popular in the mid-1980s, provided a caricature of this position at its extreme: A teacher died behind his mountain of dittos, and students didn't even notice.

Lack of Information

The third reason for persistent problems is that, historically, teachers have had only a few maxims (e.g., "Don't smile until Christmas," "Start tough and then ease up," "You gotta show 'em that you care about 'em"), together with their intuition, to guide them in making management decisions. More recently, though, effective management practices have been documented by research, and this body of knowledge is available to teachers to help them in developing successful strategies in this critical area.

10.2
Look again at Judy Harris's lesson. Do you see any evidence in it of a student's willingness to question the teacher's authority? If so, identify the example.

[handwritten margin note: Energy, effort — and effort feel overwhelmed by effort required to maintain order to instruction exists, the teacher ignores misbehavior]

Goals of Classroom Management

When teachers manage their classrooms, they have two important goals. The first is to create the best learning environment possible. Management in learning-oriented classrooms requires that teachers continually ask themselves how their management contributes to learning (Evertson & Randolph, 1995). For example, noise should not be a major criterion in judging the effectiveness of a learning-oriented classroom. Activities such as cooperative learning and group problem solving require student collaboration and interaction, and some noise will be part of these learning experiences. This point is a reminder that management goals must compliment learning goals (Morine-Dershimer & Reeve, 1994).

The second goal of classroom management is to develop student responsibility and self-regulation. Effective management systems help students grow in their ability to manage their own learning and to control their own behavior. Classroom management becomes "one vehicle for the enhancement of student self-understanding, self-evaluation, and the internalization of self-control" (McCaslin & Good, 1992, p. 8). This perspective views classroom management as one means to both an orderly classroom and self-regulated learners.

In obedience-oriented classrooms, teachers produce students who think about rules in absolute rather than functional ways. A "do it or else" orientation results in students who obey rules because they'll be rewarded or punished, not because the rules are needed to protect their rights and the rights of others. In contrast, responsibility-oriented teachers explain the reasons for rules and help students understand why order is necessary and how they are responsible for maintaining that order (Blumenfeld, Pintrich, & Hamilton, 1987).

Differences between these two orientations are summarized in Table 10.1. The obedience model stresses conformity and adherence to teacher authority (Curwin & Mendler, 1988); the responsibility model emphasizes self-regulation and attempts to help students understand the reasons for rules and the consequences for not following them. The differences in these approaches have important implications for teachers and students.

10.3
How did Judy Harris attempt to develop self-regulated learning in her students? Cite at least one specific example from the case study.

10.4
In what ways does an orderly and well-managed classroom contribute to learning? How do poorly managed classrooms detract from learning?

10.5
Think again about your study of theories of motivation in Chapter 9. Use your understanding of these theories to explain why a well-managed classroom is more motivating than a poorly managed one.

Outcomes of Effective Management

Increased Achievement

The relationship between management and achievement is well documented (Blumenfeld et al., 1987; Evertson, 1987). S. Purkey and Smith (1983) identified effective management as one of the four key characteristics of an effective school. Wang, Haertel, and Walberg (1993), in a comprehensive review of the literature on factors influencing learning conclude, "Effective classroom management has been shown to increase student engagement, decrease disruptive behaviors, and enhance use of instructional time, all of which results in improved student achievement" (p. 262). In short, effective management is an essential ingredient of effective teaching.

Improved Motivation

In Chapter 9, you found that order and safety are necessary to promote student motivation. Brophy (1987a) identified classroom management as an "essential precondition for motivating students" (p. 208). Classroom management is a foundation the teacher builds upon in creating motivating classrooms. In addition, by seeking student input on instructional and management issues, the teacher can promote student ownership and involvement, both of which positively influence student motivation (McLaughlin, 1994).

Table 10.1

The obedience and responsibility models of management

	Obedience Model	Responsibility Model
Goal	Teach students to follow orders.	Teach students to make responsible choices.
Organizing principle	Obey authority.	Learn from actions and decisions.
Teacher actions	Punish and reward.	Explain and apply logical consequences.
Student outcomes	Students learn obedience and conformity.	Students internalize the reasons for rules and learn to self-regulate.

Source: Adapted by permission from *Discipline with Dignity* by Richard Curwin and Allen Mendler, 1988, Alexandria, Va.: Assoc. for Supervision and Curriculum Development. Copyright 1988 by ASCD.

Well-managed classrooms contribute to student learning and motivation.

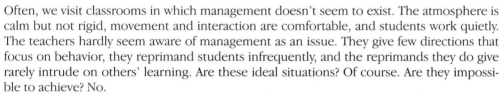

Planning: The Key to Preventing Management Problems

Often, we visit classrooms in which management doesn't seem to exist. The atmosphere is calm but not rigid, movement and interaction are comfortable, and students work quietly. The teachers hardly seem aware of management as an issue. They give few directions that focus on behavior, they reprimand students infrequently, and the reprimands they do give rarely intrude on others' learning. Are these ideal situations? Of course. Are they impossible to achieve? No.

Obviously, some classes are tougher to manage than others, and in a few cases, it may be difficult to reach the ideal described in the previous paragraph. In most instances, however, an orderly classroom is attainable, but it doesn't happen by accident. It requires careful planning, and research indicates that beginning teachers often underestimate the amount of planning it takes (Bullough, 1989; Weinstein, Woolfolk, Dittmeier, & Shankar, 1994).

Some of the first and most basic research in this area was done by Jacob Kounin, whose book *Discipline and Group Management in Classrooms* (1970) presented a summary of many years of extensive study. In analyzing the behaviors of effective and ineffective managers, Kounin concluded that the ways teachers handle misbehavior once it occurs are not the keys to successful classroom management. Changing his focus, he concluded that *teachers' preventive strategies were the keys to effective management.*

The cornerstone of an effective classroom management system is a well-conceived and administered set of procedures and rules (Emmer et al., 1994; Evertson, Emmer, Clements, Sanford, & Worsham, 1994). In planning procedures and rules, teachers must consider both the characteristics of their students and the physical environment of their classrooms. (The relationship among these factors is illustrated in Figure 10.1.)

Student Characteristics

Sam Cramer had completed his first semester's observation and tutoring in a high school, and it had been a terrific experience. He had taught several lessons, and except for the occasional rough spot, they had gone well. Students were interested and responded when involved. Management was not a problem.

Figure 10.1

Planning for effective class-room management

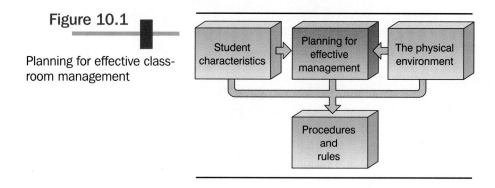

For his second semester, Sam moved to a junior high. It seemed like a different planet. Students were bubbling with excess energy. Giggling, whispering, and note passing were constant distractions. His first lesson was a disaster. They wouldn't let him teach!

From your study of Chapters 2 and 3, you know that students think, act, and feel differently at different stages of intellectual, psychosocial, and moral development. As Sam found out the hard way, students at different grade levels interpret and respond to rules and procedures differently, and teachers must anticipate these differences as they plan (Brophy & Evertson, 1976). These stages and related characteristics are outlined in Table 10.2.

In Table 10.2, you can see a pattern of increasing independence and self-regulation as students develop. In the process, they retreat somewhat from their reliance on and affection for teachers and become more likely to question authority. The process peaks during early adolescence when students' responses to their own physical, emotional, and intellectual changes are most uncertain. During the high school years, self-regulation matures, students begin to behave as young adults, and they respond well to being treated that way. Despite these developmental changes, however, students at all ages still need the emotional security of knowing that their teachers are genuinely interested in them as people and sincerely care about their learning.

> **10.6** ▬
> Explain differences in student characteristics for different ages using Piaget's and Erikson's work in Chapters 2 and 3 as a basis for your explanation.

Physical Environment

"I can't see the board."

"Fred tripped me."

"What? I can't hear."

As Judy's situation in the opening case study illustrates, few classrooms are ideal. Classes are too large, aisles are too narrow, work areas are too small, storage space is limited, and when used, maps or overhead projector screens cover half the chalkboard. For many teachers, planning the arrangement of desks and furnishings is a trade-off between what they would like and what is possible.

Evertson (1987) identifies three aspects of the physical environment that should be considered when teachers plan: (a) visibility, (b) accessibility, and (c) distractibility.

> **10.7** ▬
> Suppose you have made a transparency for your students but you're not sure the print is large enough for everyone in the class to see. Identify at least one simple thing you could do in your planning to check this visibility.

Visibility

The room must be arranged so that all students can see the chalkboard, overhead projector, or other displays. Although this seems self-evident, visibility is a surprisingly common problem, particularly with beginning teachers. Their writing on the chalkboard is too small or undecipherable, the image on the overhead is blurred, or poster displays aren't clear. These problems occur more often with students near the back of the room, who, because of their distance from the teacher, are most likely to be discipline problems in the first place. Judy anticipated this problem by having her screen mounted near the ceiling and by using a large map. Veterans usually display their materials before students come into the room and then walk to the back and personally check to see if they're clear. This is a simple example of the role planning plays in management.

Accessibility

The room should be designed with student traffic patterns in mind. Access to high traffic areas, such as the pencil sharpener, classroom door, and storage areas, should be kept clear and separated from each other. Elementary students must be able to deposit their work in trays or folders without distracting other students, students of all ages must be able to move in and out of the rooms without bumping each other, and the teacher must be able to move quickly and easily from one visual aid to another, such as from the overhead to the chalkboard.

Table 10.2

Student characteristics affecting classroom management

Stage	Student Characteristics
Stage 1: Kindergarten through grade 2	• are compliant, eager to please teachers • have short attention span, tire easily • are restless, wander around room • require close supervision • break rules because they forget • need rules and procedures to be explicitly taught, practiced, and reinforced
Stage 2: Grades 3 through 6	• are increasingly independent, but still like attention and affection from teachers • respond well to concrete incentives (e.g., stickers, free time), as well as praise and recognition • understand need for rules and accept consequences; enjoy participating in rule-making process • know how far they can push • need rules to be reviewed and consistently and impartially enforced
Stage 3: Grades 7, 8, and 9	• attempt to test independence; are sometimes rebellious and capricious • need firm foundation of stability; explicit boundaries and predictable outcomes are critical • need rules clearly stated and administered
Stage 4: Grades 10 and above	• behave more stably than in previous stage • communicate effectively adult to adult • respond to clear rationales for rules

Source: Learning from Teaching: A Developmental Perspective, by J. Brophy and C. Evertson, 1976, Boston: Allyn & Bacon. Copyright 1976 by Allyn & Bacon. Adapted with permission. Brophy, J., and Evertson, C. 1978. "Content Variables in Teaching," Educational Psychologist, 12, 310–316.

Distractibility

Elements of the environment that compete with the teacher for students' attention should be minimized. These include distractions outside the classroom, movement in the room, and student seating patterns. A teacher described one seating experiment as follows:

> I had 33 seventh graders in a room designed for 27. I experimented with different seating arrangements and tried a two-ring semicircle with the outer row behind the inner.
>
> My students weren't trying to be disruptive, but as they faced each other across the room, they would inaudibly mouth questions like "What are you doing tonight?" or they would be pinching each other on the rear ends. They just couldn't handle it. I soon had to go back to the old arrangement. (adapted from Kauchak & Eggen, 1993)

Optimal desk arrangement depends on the type of instruction. One study in fourth- and fifth-grade classrooms found that the quantity of work increased and behavior improved when students were seated in rows (N. Bennett & Blundell, 1983). For discussions in fifth- and sixth-grade classes, however, rows were the most disruptive, and a semicircle was best, allowing participants to see and communicate with each other (Rosenfield, Lambert, & Black, 1985).

These results suggest, first, that teachers should consider desk arrangement when they plan, and second, that no single arrangement is best for all situations. Teachers should experiment to see what works best for them.

Establishing Procedures

Having considered the characteristics of your students and your classroom environment, you're now ready to plan the procedures and rules for your classroom. Although the line between the two is not distinct, **procedures** *establish the routines students will follow in their daily activities,* such as how students pass in papers, sharpen their pencils, and make transitions from one activity to another. In comparison, **rules** *provide standards for acceptable behavior,* such as "Listen when someone else is talking."

Let's look again at Judy's work with her students. As they came into the room, they began her warm-up activity while she took roll and handed out a set of papers. Because this was part of a daily routine, students began immediately and without being told to do so. This simple activity both helped the students review earlier work and eliminated a period of time during which disruptions could occur. Procedures structure student activities and establish routines that promote order. By making the day predictable, such procedures maintain a form of regularity or equilibrium in the classroom environment.

Effective managers plan and teach procedures until they're essentially automatic. For example, teaching students what they will be allowed to do after completing assignments and how late or missing homework will be handled are important. These procedures may seem minor, but they affect the quality of classroom life and send larger messages about the purposes of school and learning. Table 10.3 illustrates some procedures in classrooms at different levels.

Creating Effective Rules

Rules that provide standards for student behavior are essential, and research confirms their value in creating an orderly environment (Emmer et al., 1994; Evertson et al., 1994); S. Purkey and Smith (1983) link them to effective schools: "Evidence exists indicating that clear, reasonable rules, fairly and consistently enforced, not only can reduce behavior

---

10.8 ▬

Suppose your classroom has a screen and chalkboard on the front wall, a chalkboard on the right wall, and windows overlooking a parking lot on the left wall. Under these conditions, what would probably be the best arrangement for students' desks?

10.9 ▬

What procedures govern the class in which this text is being used? Were these procedures explicitly discussed or implicitly assumed? Why do you think so?

Table 10.3

Sample classroom procedures

Elementary School Classrooms	
Student Behavior	**Sample Expectations**
Using worktables	Worktables are cleaned and materials stored in appropriate places at teacher signal.
Using bathroom and drinking fountain	Students always go to the bathroom and drinking fountain before entering the classroom.
Having access to pencil sharpener	Students sharpen two pencils after they've put their books on their desk or table.
Changing groups	Students go to their desks and begin assigned seatwork. The next group comes to the table.
Lining up for lunch and other transitions	Students quietly line up against the classroom wall when the teacher calls their row.

Middle, Junior High, and Secondary Classrooms	
Student Behavior	**Sample Expectations**
Completing homework assignments	On Monday, the students copy the assignments for the week on the front page of their notebooks. When the page is filled, they go to the next page.
Beginning a class period	Students complete a warm-up activity during the time roll is being taken.
Making a transition from class to seatwork	Students immediately begin homework assignment for the next day.
Getting assistance during seatwork	Students raise their hands and wait for the teacher to come to them during seatwork.
Following a format for tests and assignments	Students do tests and homework in pencil. They put their name, period, date, and assignment in the upper right-hand corner.

problems that interfere with learning but also can promote a feeling of pride and responsibility in the school community" (p. 445).

Students in effective schools see rules and teachers as fair and necessary even if they don't like some individual rules and penalties (Wayson & Lasley, 1984). Rules provide social structure both inside and outside the classroom and help create a positive framework for behavior. Some guidelines for establishing rules are outlined in Figure 10.2 (Evertson, 1987).

Class-School Consistency

Classroom and school rules must be consistent. This self-evident suggestion reminds teachers that they should review district and school rules before creating their own. For example, if the school requires hall passes when students are out of classrooms, individual teachers are obligated to enforce the rule.

Classroom rules establish standards for behavior that allow learning to take place.

Clarity

Rules must be stated clearly so that an inordinate amount of class time isn't used to interpret them. Researchers found that one ineffective manager had the rule "Be in the right place at the right time" (Emmer, Evertson, & Anderson, 1980). How much help would that rule be to a third grader wanting to do the right thing? As another example, contrast "Bring all needed materials to class each day" with "Always be prepared." In the latter case, students are left uncertain, and even in the former, the teacher needs to carefully discuss, explain, and illustrate the rule.

Rationales

Explaining why a rule is necessary is important for at least three reasons. First, it helps students understand that rules aren't arbitrary, and they help protect everyone's rights and interests. Second, discussing the need for a particular rule helps students think about rights and responsibilities, which helps in the development of self-regulation and moral reasoning. The third reason is pragmatic and simple: Students who understand reasons for rules are more likely to obey them.

Figure 10.2

Guidelines for preparing rules

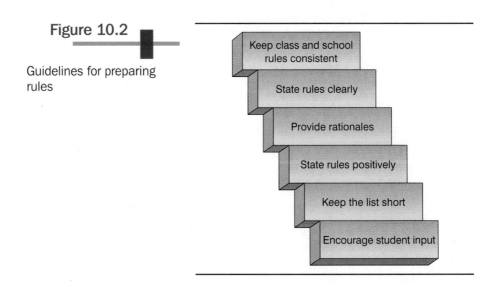

Keep class and school rules consistent

State rules clearly

Provide rationales

State rules positively

Keep the list short

Encourage student input

Positive Statements

"Listen when someone else is talking" is preferable to "Don't interrupt." Rules stated positively create a climate of positive expectations and encourage responsibility. Although the difference is subtle, rules stated negatively can contribute to an adversarial climate. Also, positively stated rules specify desired behavior; rules stated negatively only identify what students are not to do.

A Short List

Keep the list of rules short; four or five is a workable number. For rules to be effective, students must constantly be aware of them and must instantly know when they break one. The most common reason students break rules is that they simply forget! Although this is particularly true for young children, it applies to older ones as well.

Student Input

Allow student input in the rule-making process. Cooperative rule setting has several benefits:

- It promotes a feeling of ownership, which increases the likelihood that students will obey the rules.
- It emphasizes internal versus external control.
- It helps students see the values (e.g., respect and responsibility) behind rules.
- It treats students as moral thinkers and helps them develop better moral reasoning (Lickona, 1991).

Taking time to discuss and cooperatively plan rules provides teachers with opportunities to make management a learning rather than a custodial activity.

In evaluating the benefits of cooperative rule setting, other theorists emphasize students' need to exercise control over themselves and their environment (Glasser, 1969, 1985). Input into rules helps meet this need. Glasser advocates the use of classroom meetings throughout the school year to establish, monitor, and improve classroom rules. Through student-centered problem solving, these meetings stress student responsibility for making the classroom a livable place. The development of social responsibility is linked to both improved management and increased student achievement (Wentzel, 1991).

One teacher who tried this at the beginning of the year commented:

> The rules the students came up with are the ones I wanted anyway, and besides, they're often tougher on themselves than I would be. Actually, they handle it pretty well, so as I see it, I have nothing to lose by giving them a say in the process. They feel good about it.

Making Rules and Procedures Work

To this point, we have discussed effective teachers' efforts to prevent classroom management problems before they begin, and we have emphasized the critical role that planning plays in this process. In this section, we discuss putting these plans into practice. As we make the transition, we emphasize two important principles: (a) Rules and procedures must be carefully taught, and (b) once implemented, rules and procedures must be constantly monitored.

10.10 How does the rule "Listen when someone else is talking" illustrate the idea of students' rights and responsibilities? How did the way Judy handled the infraction of this rule help students understand the rationale behind it?

10.11 We said students "must instantly know when they break one." "Instantly knowing" relates to what concept from your study of information processing in Chapter 7?

10.12 How does cooperatively discussing classroom rules foster internal versus external control?

Teaching Rules and Procedures

Directly teaching rules and procedures to students is especially important for young students, who may not know or may have forgotten last year's rules. For older students, teaching provides opportunities to explain the reasons behind the rules. Rules should not merely be presented or announced; rules and procedures can't be learned from a simple statement any more than a concept is learned from a definition alone (F. Jones, 1987). They must be explicitly taught, as any concept or principle would be, and the reasons for their existence should be carefully explained.

The following describes how Martha Oakes, a first-grade teacher, taught one of her procedures.

> I put each of their names, as well as my own, on a cubby hole in a storage place on the wall of my room. I did a very short work sheet myself and literally walked it over and put it in my storage spot, thinking aloud as I went. "Hmm, I'm finished with my work sheet. . . . What do I do now? . . . I need to put it in my storage space so that my teacher can check it, and then I start on the next assignment." I then gave each of them the work sheet, directing them to take it to their file, quietly and individually, as soon as they were finished. After we had done one, I gave them another, asked them what they were going to do and why, and had them do it. I asked them to think what would happen if we didn't put papers where they belong. I asked them whether they had ever lost anything and how this was similar. After we had practiced a few times, I only had to remind them periodically.

Martha clearly understood the developmental characteristics of her first graders, realizing that unless she explicitly taught her procedures, the students were unlikely to understand or follow them. Her planning, modeling, dry runs, and actual practice helped make her classroom function like a well-oiled machine. Older students may not need a dry run, but a clear explanation of the procedure, the reasons for it, and examples are no less important.

In teaching rules and procedures, teachers should stress the logic behind each as they introduce it. This not only helps students understand the function of each but also involves them in a form of problem solving. Martha's use of verbal think-alouds provided her students with access to her own thinking and the logic of her actions.

Monitoring Rules and Procedures

Even if you do a superb job of teaching rules and procedures, consistently monitoring them will be necessary, just as practice and feedback are necessary in teaching any skill (Emmer et al., 1994; Evertson et al., 1994). Effective teachers react to misbehavior immediately, eliminate it, and refer students to the rule that was broken. In our opening case study, Judy did this skillfully in stopping Sondra's whispering and note passing. It was an example of effective rule monitoring because she called Sondra's attention to the rule and reminded her of its rationale as she enforced it.

The reasons for these principles are simple. A clearly taught rule will deter many students from misbehaving merely because the rule exists, and the students understand and appreciate the reasons for it regardless of consequences; this acceptance corresponds to Stage 4 of Kohlberg's descriptions of moral reasoning, which was discussed in Chapter 3. An additional number of students will obey the rules when they know the teacher monitors them. Because of these two reasons, many off-task and disruptive behaviors are prevented before they occur. This prospect simplifies the management process; dealing with 4 or 5 potential problems is much easier than dealing with 10, 12, or more.

10.13
Think about our discussion of concept teaching in Chapter 8. Based on the suggestions for teaching concepts, explain why Martha was effective in her procedure.

10.14
How does the way Martha taught her procedure involve her students in cognitive problem solving? What short- and long-term benefits might result from this approach?

Classroom Connections

Planning Procedures and Rules in Your Classroom

1. Carefully plan your classroom procedures and rules before the year begins.
   - A third-grade teacher prepares a handout for his students and their parents that describes procedures for making up work, how papers should be prepared, and how grades are determined.
   - A seventh-grade math teacher prepares a written list of rules before she starts class on the first day. She then asks students to suggest additional rules that will help make the classroom a positive place to learn.

2. Consider the developmental level of your students in preparing and teaching rules and procedures.
   - A first-grade teacher reviews her procedures for depositing seatwork for a few minutes each day until the students are able to follow the procedure without directions.
   - At the beginning of the school year, an eighth-grade teacher tries to establish a positive classroom climate by conducting a daily review of the rule requiring students to speak to each other

respectfully and by discussing the reasons for the rule in each review.

3. Consider your physical environment in planning procedures and rules.
   - A sixth-grade teacher arranges students' desks so that they are facing away from the classroom window, which looks out on the physical education field.
   - A geometry teacher has the custodian move her projection screen into the corner of the room so that it doesn't cover the chalkboard.

4. Explain and have the students practice your classroom procedures.
   - A kindergarten teacher carefully explains and has his students practice his procedures several times in dry runs during the first few days of school. He has them continue to practice until they follow the procedures without being told.
   - A ninth-grade physical science teacher takes a full class period to describe and explain safe lab procedures. She distributes to each student a handout describing them, models correct procedures, and explains the reasons behind each.

Preventing Problems: Putting Plans Into Action

In introducing the topics of management and discipline, our focus has been on preventing problems, and we suggested that rules and procedures, carefully planned, taught, and monitored, are the cornerstone of this process. In this section, we continue to emphasize prevention but shift to implementing the plans. The key elements of this process are (a) teacher characteristics, (b) the beginning of the school year, (c) essential management skills, and (d) communication with parents.

Teacher Characteristics

You saw in Chapter 9 that the teacher is an important factor in students' motivation to learn, and in Chapter 12 you'll see how the teacher is central to effective instruction and student learning. It's also the case in classroom management. We've all seen students go from one class, in which they're disruptive and out of hand, to another, in which they're orderly and on-task. The difference is the teacher. Because the teacher is central to a well-managed classroom, we begin our discussion here.

Effective managers cover a spectrum of personalities. Some appear quiet and unassuming; others have voices like a drill sergeant. Although one type isn't necessarily better than another, effective managers usually have three characteristics in common: they are (a) caring, (b) firm, and (c) democratic.

Caring: The Foundation of Positive Classroom Climate

Caring is a theme of this text. You found in Chapter 4 that sincere interest and caring were essential preconditions for working with at-risk students. You also found in Chapter 9 that caring increases student motivation. It is virtually impossible to manage a classroom successfully or succeed in any part of teaching without genuinely caring about students and their learning. In one study, researchers asked fourth graders how they knew whether their teacher cared (Rogers, 1991). They described a caring teacher as one who:

- Listens and tries to see things from a student's perspective
- Creates a safe and secure learning environment
- Helps with school work by making sense of learning tasks

A caring teacher creates an environment in which students feel secure and free to learn. This relates to Maslow's hierarchy of needs. Students can't focus their energies on intellectual achievement if their needs for safety, belonging, and self-esteem aren't met.

In the context of classroom management, caring goes further. Like Maslow, William Glasser (1969, 1985) argues that all students come to school with a set of innate needs, one of which is belonging, and he links disruptive behavior to unmet belonging needs. Glasser suggests that a truly caring teacher will not accept excuses for misbehavior, regardless of student background and experience. A caring teacher communicates, "I care too much about your learning to allow you to harm yourself by being disruptive." This leads us to the concept of firmness.

Firmness: Helping Students Develop Responsibility

Firmness *means viewing students as capable of exercising responsibility and holding them accountable for their actions.* A teacher who doesn't stand firm when a student breaks a rule communicates that the rule has no real purpose and that actions don't necessarily have consequences. These messages confuse students who are trying to make sense of the world. It is critical that a teacher follows through in making students responsible and accountable for their actions.

The Democratic Teacher: Combining Caring and Firmness

Rudolph Dreikurs (1968), a psychiatrist well known for his work in student discipline, argues that firmness combined with caring is one characteristic of a democratic teacher. Firmness indicates that teachers respect themselves, and caring shows respect for others. Dreikurs relates the two by connecting them in a democratic classroom. Let's look at an illustration.

Duranna Hamilton greets her students with a smile at the classroom door. She surveys them as they take their seats and says, "Rico and Steve," in response to the students' loud whispering after the bell stops ringing. "One of the rules we all agreed on was 'Be ready to work as soon as the bell stops ringing.'"

10.15
Think about the study of psychosocial development in Chapter 3. How would Erikson explain the disruptive behavior of a low-achieving fifth grader? Using Erikson's work as a guide, explain what you might do to help the student.

10.16
How did Judy Harris demonstrate firmness in her teaching? Identify a specific example in the case study.

The students quickly stop, and Duranna continues, "We have much to do today, so let's get started. Each of you was responsible for one part of your team's presentation. Please give me a report of your progress. Go ahead, Team 1."

In this brief episode, Duranna displayed several characteristics of a democratic teacher:

- Her class was orderly, and limits were established.
- Students had input into the rules.
- She provided leadership in both maintaining order and guiding learning.
- She used her learning activity to promote a sense of ownership and belonging.

From these characteristics, you again can see the close relationship between management and motivation.

Beginning of the School Year

Research consistently indicates that the beginning of the school year is a critical period during which classroom behavior patterns are established (W. Doyle, 1986; Evertson et al., 1994). Evertson (1987) stresses the precedent-setting nature of the first day:

> The first day of school has special significance for both teachers and students. It is at this time that rules, routines, and expectations are established. Students' first impressions about their classrooms, their teachers, and what standards are expected can have a lasting effect on their attitudes and on the ways they will engage in classroom tasks. (p. 69)

Effective teachers realize this and are ready to go from the first bell of the first day.

> Vicki Williams is organizing her handouts on the first day of class. Her eighth graders come into the room; some take their seats while others mill around talking in small groups. As the bell rings, she looks up and says over the hum of the students, "Everyone take your seats, please," and she turns back to finish organizing her materials.

> Donnell Alexander is waiting at the door for her eighth graders and has also prepared handouts. As the students come in, she smiles and says, "Take your seats quickly, please. You'll find your name on the desk. The bell is going to ring in less than a minute, and everyone must be at his or her desk and quiet when it does. Please read the handout while you're waiting." She is standing at the front of the room, surveying the class as the bell rings. When it stops, Donnell begins, "Good morning, everyone."

In the first few minutes of the year, Vicki and Donnell each taught their students some important ideas about the way their classes would be run. Vicki communicated, "Don't worry too much about whether or not you're in your seat at the beginning of the period," whereas, Donnell's clear message was, "Be ready to start when the bell rings." Students quickly pick up on these differences, and unless Vicki reverses her pattern, she will soon have problems—not dramatic perhaps, but chronic and low grade, like nagging sniffles that won't go away. Some guidelines for the first few days of school are summarized in Figure 10.3.

Essential Management Skills

Consider the following question: If you observed teachers with reputations as excellent managers, regardless of grade level, content area, or learning activity, what would you expect to see them doing? As we discussed earlier, we would expect them to be caring, yet firm and democratic, but beyond these general characteristics, what else would we look for?

10.17 ▬
Think about our discussion of Glasser's and Dreikurs' work. Would their approaches be called "behavioral"? Explain why or why not.

10.18 ▬
Suppose you want to teach the rule "Listen when others have the floor" on the first day of school. Describe precisely how you would teach this rule to a group of third graders. How would you teach it to a group of seventh graders?

Figure 10.3

Guidelines for beginning the school year

> 1. Plan initial class meetings for maximum contact and control. Use large-group instruction rather than small-group work; minimize work with individual students and keep the number of transitions from one activity to another as few as possible. Stay in the classroom and don't allow yourself to be distracted by parents or individual students.
>
> 2. Make explicit, positive statements about expectations for students' behavior. This helps establish a positive climate for management, motivation, and learning.
>
> 3. Begin teaching your rules and procedures the very first day. With young students, actively practice procedures. With older students, carefully discuss and illustrate rules and procedures.
>
> 4. Carefully explain course requirements and grading systems, particularly with older students. This helps clarify your expectations and establishes a climate of order and certainty.
>
> 5. Plan initial learning activities to promote maximum student motivation and success. Although this is always important, it is particularly critical at the beginning of the year to promote a positive climate, high expectations, and a sense of accomplishment. It sets the tone for the remainder of the year.
>
> 6. Monitor and enforce rules with complete consistency during this period. Your goal is to make the environment completely predictable. You want the students to know that you will intervene immediately and every time to establish the pattern for the remainder of the year.
>
> 7. Open lines of communication with parents.

Source: From Donald P. Kauchak and Paul D. Eggen, *Learning and Teaching: Research-based Methods,* Second Edition. Copyright © 1993 Allyn and Bacon. Adapted with permission.

Research helps us answer this question. These results are summarized as **essential management skills,** *which are the general strategies that effective managers use regardless of grade level or setting.* Essential management skills help maintain student involvement while minimizing off-task behaviors.

These skills fall into three categories: (a) organization, (b) lesson movement, and (c) communication.

Organization

Let's look back at Judy's class in our opening case study. When students walked into the room, they found a display and directions on the screen as Judy started her beginning-of-class routines. The class began working on her warm-up activity without being told, and Judy moved quickly and smoothly from it to her lesson for the day. She demonstrated four important characteristics of effective organization:

1. *Having materials and demonstrations prepared in advance:* Judy's display was prepared and waiting when the students came into the room.
2. *Starting on time:* Judy was taking roll before the bell rang.
3. *Having well-established routines:* Judy had a warm-up activity every day.

4. *Making transitions smoothly and quickly:* Judy moved quickly from her warm-up activity to her formal lesson.

The beginning of the class period and transitions from one activity to another are two times when students are apt to be off-task, and careful organization can eliminate the "dead time" during these periods (W. Doyle, 1986; Evertson, 1987). Careful organization maximizes opportunities for student involvement and learning and minimizes downtime that can lead to management problems.

10.19
Which would be more effective in dealing with classroom dead time—rules or procedures? Explain.

Lesson Movement

The second category of essential skills involves preventing misbehavior from disrupting the flow of a learning activity. Lesson movement emphasizes the strong relationship between effective management and effective instruction. Lesson movement is maintained through (a) withitness, (b) overlapping, and (c) momentum (Kounin, 1970).

Withitness.   As we began our discussion of management skills, we referred to the work of Jacob Kounin (1970). He found that effective managers had a characteristic he termed **withitness**, *which means the teacher knows what is going on in all parts of the classroom all the time and communicates this knowing both verbally and nonverbally.* Kounin described it as "having eyes in the back of the head." The label is intuitively sensible. We've all known people who seem oblivious to the world around them, and we may even have used the phrase, "He's out of it. He needs to get 'with it.'" Let's see what this concept looks like in the classroom:

Lesson movement draws students into classroom lessons; effective teachers maintain student attention through withitness, overlapping, and momentum.

Ron Ziers is explaining the procedure for finding percentages of numbers to his seventh graders. As he illustrates the procedure and answers questions, Kareem, in the second desk from the front of the room, is periodically poking Katilyna, who sits directly across from him. She retaliates by kicking him in the leg. Bill, sitting behind Katilyna, then pokes her in the arm with his pencil. Ron doesn't respond to the students' actions. After a second poke, Katilyna swings her arm back and catches Bill on the shoulder. "Katilyna!" Ron says sternly. "We keep our hands to ourselves! . . . Now, where were we?"

Karl Wickes, a seventh-grade life science teacher in the same school, has the same group of students. He puts a transparency displaying a flowering plant on the overhead. As he discusses the parts of the plant, he notices Barry whispering something to Julie, and he sees Kareem poke Katilyna, who kicks him and loudly whispers, "Stop it." As Karl asks, "What is the part of the plant that produces fruit?" he moves swiftly to Kareem's desk, leans over, and says quietly but firmly, "We keep our hands and materials to ourselves in here." He then moves to the front of the room, watches Kareem out of the corner of his eye, and says, "Barry, what other plant part do you see in the diagram?"

Karl skillfully demonstrated three important features of withitness. First, Karl *caught the misbehavior immediately;* he went at once to Kareem and intervened. Ron did nothing until the misbehavior had spread to other students. Second, Karl *caught the right one;* he knew that Kareem was the original cause of the incident. In addition to letting the misbehavior spread, Ron reprimanded Katilyna when she retaliated in frustration. This misdirected teacher response leaves other students with the sense that the teacher doesn't know what's going on. Third, Karl noted that two incidents of misbehavior were occurring at the same time, and he *responded to the more serious one first.* Barry's whispering was a minor incident. Kareem's poking was more flagrant and disruptive, and Karl accordingly responded to Kareem rather than Barry. Karl then further demonstrated his skill by calling on Barry, which got him back into the activity without Karl having to intervene in another way.

Overlapping.   **Overlapping** is related to withitness and *describes the teacher's ability to attend to two incidents at the same time without focusing exclusively on either one* (Kounin, 1970). For example, Karl moved quickly to Kareem, stopped the misbehavior, and moved back to the front of the classroom without disrupting the flow of his discussion. Ron, by contrast, stopped his lesson and then had to restart after he had reprimanded Katilyna. A second form of overlapping, common in elementary schools, is the ability to attend to two learning activities simultaneously. For instance,

Tara Goldstein is conducting a reading group at the back of the room when Andy comes back to get help with a seatwork assignment. She says, "Read the next paragraph for us, Tim," and then she quickly responds to Andy's question and turns back to the group before Tim is finished.

Skilled at overlapping activities, Tara was able to maintain the flow of her lesson and prevent interruptions and potential disruptions.

One caution: In their eagerness to maintain the flow of their lessons, beginning teachers sometimes turn back to their teaching before an off-task student has fully complied with the directive. This action communicates that the teacher wasn't really committed to the student's compliance, and the disruptive behavior is likely to recur. We discuss the issue of compliance again later in the chapter.

Momentum.   Think about some of the classes you're now taking. Do the instructors sometimes explain a topic longer than necessary, droning on and on? Do they speak so slowly and evenly that you have a hard time paying attention, or have you been put into

---

10.20

Identify an instance in Judy Harris's teaching in which she demonstrated withitness. Cite the example directly from the case study.

10.21

A teacher conducting a reading group says quietly, "Now, everyone read the next paragraph silently," and she then gets up and talks to two students who are talking when they are supposed to be doing seatwork. What does this teacher's behavior illustrate?

small groups to discuss a topic that would be more efficiently covered as a whole class? If your answers are yes, the instructors have been guilty of overdwelling, pacing their lessons too slowly, or fragmenting it, and as a result, the lessons lack momentum. In a college or university class, students drift off, and there are few consequences for the instructor. In public school classrooms, inattention can lead to behavior problems.

Momentum *refers to the force and flow of a lesson* (Kounin, 1970), and it is analogous to a steel marble rolling down a slope alongside a Styrofoam ball. The marble maintains its course and is not easily pushed aside, but the opposite is true for the ball. Similarly, lessons have momentum. An effective lesson pulls students along and maintains their interest, whereas lessons that lack momentum provide opportunities for students to be easily distracted. Veteran teachers develop a "feel" for a lesson's flow and make adjustments when it loses momentum. In contrast, inexperienced teachers often have trouble adapting when they run into problems. Table 10.4 provides examples of teacher behaviors that detract from lesson momentum.

Once again, you can see the close connection between instruction and management. The management skills of withitness, overlapping, and momentum all minimize management problems by strengthening instruction. We return to this topic in Chapter 12, where we discuss instruction in detail.

Communication With Learners

Earlier in the chapter, we said that management seems to be a non-issue in some classrooms. In them, the atmosphere is calm, but not rigid, and discipline rarely intrudes on the learning environment. "Calm but not rigid" is the key idea here. If a teacher is tough enough, students can be kept quiet. However, creating a safe and orderly classroom in

Table 10.4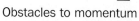

Obstacles to momentum

Behavior	Example
Content overdwelling	A biology teacher, in an effort to be thorough, continues explaining the process of photosynthesis long after the students indicate that they understand it.
Behavior overdwelling	As a teacher begins a lesson, she says, "I see that some of you still don't have your notebooks out. I've told you repeatedly that taking notes is an important part of learning. If you don't have your notebooks out, you can't possibly take notes efficiently."
Pacing	A world history teacher presents his information in a slow, deliberate manner, with frequent pauses to consult his notes. His questions are infrequent, slowly worded, and often confusing to the students.
Fragmentation	An art teacher says, "Now, Johnny, come up and get your brushes and paints. . . . Now, Kelly, get yours. Karin, you're next."

Source: From Donald P. Kauchak and Paul D. Eggen, *Learning and Teaching: Research-based Methods,* Second Edition. Copyright © 1993 by Allyn and Bacon. Reprinted by permission.

which students feel free to express their ideas requires a skilled teacher. Effective communication is important in this process. It has three characteristics: (a) verbal-nonverbal congruence, (b) "I-messages," and (c) active listening.

Verbal-Nonverbal Congruence.

Professor:	How do you know when your teacher really means what she says?
Third Grader:	Well, her eyes get big and round, and she looks right at us. She doesn't move and her voice is a little louder, but she talks kinda slowly. Sometimes she stands over us and looks down at us.
Professor:	What happens then?
Third Grader:	The class does what she wants!

(Woolfolk & Brooks, 1985, p. 514)

When we think of communication, we typically think of a conversation, in which two or more people have some kind of discussion. However, much of a receiver's perception of a message is derived from the way words are said and the way the speaker appears when saying them, rather than the words themselves. This fact is the source of the adage "It's not what you say, but how you say it." This channel of communication, called **nonverbal behavior**, *includes the tone of voice and the body language people use to convey unspoken messages.* Let's see how it works in a classroom.

> Karen Wilson's 10th graders are working on their next day's English homework as she circulates among them. She is helping Jasmine when Jeff and Mike begin whispering loudly behind her.
>
> "Jeff. Mike. Stop talking and get started on your homework," she says, glancing over her shoulder.
>
> The two slow their whispering, and Karen turns back to Jasmine. Soon, though, the boys are whispering as loudly as ever.
>
> "I thought I told you to stop talking," Karen says over her shoulder again, this time with a hint of irritation in her voice.
>
> The boys glance at her and quickly resume whispering.
>
> Isabelle Rodriguez is in a similar situation with her ninth-grade algebra class. As she is helping Vicki, Ken and Lance begin horsing around at the back of the room.
>
> Isabelle quickly excuses herself from Vicki, turns, and walks directly to the boys. Looking Lance in the eye, she says pleasantly but firmly, "Lance, we have plenty to do before lunch. You need to begin your homework now," and then looking directly at Ken, she continues, "Ken, you too. Quickly now. We have a lot to do." She stands facing them until they are working quietly. Then she returns to Vicki.

What did the two teachers communicate? The intent in their words was similar; they both wanted students to stop their off-task behavior and begin working. The effect of the communication, however, was quite different. Karen's message was, "I want you to stop, but I'm not committed to being sure you do." She issued her directive over her shoulder, didn't check for full compliance from the boys, and was almost pleading in her second reaction. Isabelle, in contrast, communicated, "I want you to stop, and I'm completely committed to being sure that you do." When the horseplay began, she responded immediately, faced the students directly, and made sure they had fully complied before she went back to Vicki.

Karen's communication was incongruent. Her words said one thing, but her body language said another. In cases of incongruent communication, words are virtually always the least credible part of the message. Mehrabian and Ferris (1967) developed a system for quantifying the process and found that 55% of a message's credibility is communicated with body language; 38% with the tone, pitch, and variation in voice quality; and a meager

---

10.22

What aspects of nonverbal communication did the third grader notice? How else do teachers use nonverbal communication to convey management messages?

10.23

We discussed the teacher characteristics of caring and firmness. Give an example of a teacher demonstrating these characteristics, including a description of the teacher's nonverbal behaviors.

10.24

Of the nonverbal behaviors in Table 10.5, which are easiest or most non-obtrusive to use? Which are more difficult or obtrusive?

7% through the actual words. Research in classrooms corroborates these findings: Direct eye contact and proximity both influence management messages (Houten & Doleys, 1983). In communicating with students, it is imperative that teachers keep their nonverbal behavior consistent with their words. Table 10.5 outlines some important features of nonverbal communication.

"I-Messages." That nonverbal behavior is critical doesn't imply that verbal messages are unimportant. For example, let's look again at the introductory case study and see how Judy handled Sondra's whispering and note passing. When Sondra protested, "What did I do?" Judy directed her to the rule, rather than say something such as, "You were whispering." When Sondra protested further, Judy responded with, "I get worn out and frustrated when I'm interrupted."

According to Thomas Gordon (1974), Judy demonstrated important communication skills. In dealing with disruptive behavior, Gordon advocates the use of **"I-messages,"** *which are verbal statements with three parts: (a) They address behavior rather than personality, (b) they describe the effects on the sender, and (c) they identify the feelings generated in the sender.*

Judy demonstrated these characteristics. First, by referring Sondra to the rule, Judy addressed the behavior, rather than Sondra's character or personality. When teachers say, "You're driving me up the wall," they're blaming the student and implying weaknesses in the students' characters. Instead, focusing on the incident communicates that students' intrinsic self-worth is unchanged but that the behavior is unacceptable.

Judy then demonstrated the second part of an "I-message" by saying, "I have to interrupt my teaching when people aren't paying attention." This describes the effect on the sender and helps students understand the link between their actions and the teacher's reaction.

Judy illustrated the third part of an "I-message" when she said, "I get worn out and frustrated." Again, the intent is to help students understand the effects their actions have on others—a step toward responsible behavior and self-regulation.

Table 10.5

Elements of nonverbal communication

Nonverbal Behavior	Example
Proximity	A teacher moves close to an inattentive student. In another case, a teacher moves to a student and touches her on the shoulder.
Eye contact	A teacher looks an off-task student directly in the eye when issuing a directive.
Body orientation	A teacher directs himself squarely to the learner, rather than over the shoulder or sideways.
Facial expression	A teacher frowns slightly at a disruption, brightens her face at a humorous incident, and smiles approvingly at a student's effort to help a classmate.
Gestures	A teacher puts her palm out (Stop!) to a student who interjects as another student is talking.
Vocal variation	A teacher varies the tone, pitch, and loudness of his voice for emphasis and displays energy and enthusiasm.

Active listening strengthens the teacher-student relationship by establishing and maintaining effective communication channels.

Active Listening.   "Communication is a two-way street" is another time-honored maxim. Teachers who effectively communicate with their students are also good listeners (Gordon, 1974). When students believe that teachers are listening rather than evaluating what they say, they begin to trust the teacher and feel free to communicate openly. For example,

> Gayle goes to Mrs. Cortez after class and says, "Mrs. Cortez, I don't think I should have gotten a zero on that last assignment."
>
> Mrs. Cortez sits down, focuses her attention on Gayle, and says evenly, "You don't think the grade was fair?"
>
> "No," Gayle says, squirming slightly.
>
> "Tell me why."
>
> "I was absent the day you assigned it, and I didn't know that it was due today."
>
> "I understand how you feel, Gayle," Mrs. Cortez responds, leaning forward. "I would feel bad too if I got a zero on an assignment. But I told you the day you got back that the assignment had been given and that it was due today. In the future, I would suggest that you write assignments down in your notebook so that you're less likely to forget them."

Mrs. Cortez sat down, gave Gayle her *full attention, and responded to both the intellectual and emotional content of the message.* These are essential characteristics of **active listening** (Sokolove, Garrett, Sadker, & Sadker, 1990). Notice also that Mrs. Cortez didn't acquiesce to Gayle's implication of unfairness. Active listening doesn't imply that standards are sacrificed or that rules and procedures are violated. Mrs. Cortez's willingness to take time to listen without defensiveness is the essence of active listening.

10.25 ▥

A student stops after class and comments, "Gee, Mrs. Taylor. That test was too hard. I studied for 3 days and still did terrible." The teacher glances up from her papers, smiles, and says, "It was designed to be challenging. I'm sure you'll do better on the next one," and then returns to her work. Is the teacher demonstrating the characteristics of active listening? Explain.

Classroom Connections

Establishing a Democratic Environment in Your Classroom

1. Allow students a voice in making classroom decisions.
   - An English teacher moving into a unit on American literature says, "We'll focus on three of the five authors I've listed here. Think about it and discuss it among yourselves before we decide which three."
   - A junior high science teacher meets with students at the beginning of the term and explains options in terms of science projects. Some students decide to work in teams on demonstrations and experiments; others choose to work alone on research papers.

2. Remain firm in agreed-on decisions.
   - A biology teacher's class tries to talk him into giving a test on Monday instead of Friday. "I'm sorry," he states firmly. "We agreed last week that the test would be Friday. If a special event had come up, I would be willing to compromise, but nothing has changed since we agreed on the date."

3. Demonstrate that you care about students and their learning.
   - A first-grade teacher makes it a point to call on each student at some point in all learning activities. She also devotes full attention to the students when they come to her for individual help.

- A prealgebra teacher schedules a help session after school every Tuesday and Thursday. "Be sure you come to the help session if you have any trouble on your homework," she reminds the students. "Remember, your homework has to be in on time."

Demonstrating Essential Management Skills in Your Classroom

4. Monitor students for verbal and nonverbal reactions during explanations and question-and-answer sessions.
   - In response to an uncertain look on students' faces, the teacher says, "Would you like another example?"
   - While continuing with an explanation, a teacher walks to some students involved in horseplay, makes a brief comment, and returns to the front of the room.

5. In dealing with students, be sure your verbal and nonverbal behaviors are congruent.
   - In response to an underachiever's attempts to answer a question, the teacher orients her body directly toward him, looks directly at him, and nods reassuringly.
   - In directing two students to quit whispering and begin working, a teacher moves close to them, looks them in the eye, and remains standing in front of them until they comply.

Accommodating Diversity: Communication With Parents

Although clear and positive communication with learners is important, it doesn't stop there. Communication with parents is equally important, and it is perhaps even more critical when working with students from diverse cultural, ethnic, and socioeconomic backgrounds. Because communication with parents is so critical to successful schooling, we devote a separate section of the chapter to this process.

Communication: Encouraging Parental Involvement

The relationship between home and school is emphasized more now than at any other point in the history of education. In a comprehensive review of variables affecting student learning, researchers concluded,

> Because of the importance of the home environment to school learning, teachers must also develop strategies to increase parent involvement in their children's academic life. This means teachers should go beyond traditional once-a-year parent/teacher conferences and work with parents to see that learning is valued in the home. Teachers should encourage parents to be involved with their children's academic pursuits on a day-to-day basis, helping them with homework, monitoring television viewing, reading to their young children, and simply expressing the expectation that their children will achieve academic success. (Wang et al., 1993, pp. 278–279)

Communication with parents or any other primary care giver is no longer an appendage of the teaching process; it is an integral part of the teacher's job.

Benefits of Communication

Research indicates that students benefit from home-school cooperation in at least four ways:

1. Higher academic achievement
2. More positive attitudes and behaviors
3. Better attendance rates
4. Greater willingness to do homework (Epstein, 1990; Weinstein & Mignano, 1993)

These outcomes probably result from parents' increased participation in school activities and their more positive attitudes about the process of schooling. There are classroom benefits as well (Weinstein & Mignano, 1993). A student's disruptive behavior is easier to understand and solve, for example, when his teachers learn that his mother or father has lost a job, his parents are going through a divorce, or there's a serious illness in the family. In addition, parents can help develop and reinforce behavior management plans. One teacher reported:

> I had this boy in my class who was extremely disruptive. He wouldn't work, kept "forgetting" his homework, distracted other children, wandered about the room. You name it; he did it. The three of us—the mother, the boy and I—talked about what we could do, and we decided to try a system of home rewards. We agreed that I would send a note home each day, reporting on the boy's behavior. For every week with at least three good notes, the mother added one Christmas present. In this way, what the child found under the tree on Christmas Day was directly dependent on his behavior. By Christmas, he had become so cooperative, I couldn't believe he was the same child! After Christmas, I observed some backsliding, so we all agreed to reverse the system: The mother took away one present each time a majority of the week's reports were negative. She didn't have to take many away! (Weinstein & Mignano, 1993, p. 226)

10.26
In addition to benefits to parents themselves, how else might improved parental involvement result in positive benefits to students?

Through combined efforts, parents and teachers can reach goals that neither could accomplish individually, and there are additional benefits for teachers. Those who encourage parental involvement report more positive feelings about teaching and their school. They also rate parents higher in helpfulness and follow-through and have higher expectations for parents (Epstein, 1990).

Barriers to Parental Involvement

Involving parents in the education of their children is a desired goal, but it doesn't happen automatically. Economic, cultural, and language barriers are often difficult to overcome. Understanding is the first step in resolving the difficulties.

Economic Barriers.   Communication and involvement take time, and other commitments often come first. First among these is employment; half the parents in one study indicated that their employment prevented them from helping their youngsters with homework (Ellis, Dowdy, Graham, & Jones, 1992). Other parents lack economic resources, such as child care, transportation, and telephones, that allow them to actively participate in school activities. These parents say they're willing to be involved in their children's schooling but schools need to be flexible and provide help and encouragement (Epstein, 1990).

Cultural Barriers.   Discontinuities between students' home cultures and the culture of the school can also be barriers (Delgado-Gaiton, 1992; Harry, 1992). Students may come from homes where the parents experienced school in a form different from current schools. Also, some parents may have only gone through the elementary grades or may have had negative school experiences. One researcher described the problem as follows:

> Underneath most parents is a student—someone who went to school, sometimes happily, sometimes unhappily. What often happens when the parent-as-adult returns to school, or has dealings with teachers, is that the parent as child/student returns. Many parents still enter school buildings flooded with old memories, angers, and disappointments. Their stomachs churn and flutter with butterflies, not because of what is happening today with their own children, but because of outdated memories and past behaviors. (Rich, 1987, p. 24)

Parents such as these will require encouragement and support to become involved.

In many Asian and Latino families, parents have mixed attitudes toward schools; they respect the teacher's authority but hesitate to become involved in matters they believe are best handled by the school (Harry, 1992). This deference to authority implies, "You're the teacher; do what is best," but it is often interpreted by teachers as apathy.

Teacher authority and management style can also be a source of cultural conflict. A study of Puerto Rican families found that parents thought U.S. schools were too impersonal—that teachers didn't "worry about" their children enough. One parent explained, "In the U.S. the teachers care about the education of the child, but they don't care about the child himself and his problems" (Harry, 1992, p. 479). These parents wanted teachers to act more like parents, providing both warmth and structure for their children.

Language Barriers.   Language provides another potential barrier to effective home-school cooperation. Many parents of bilingual students do not speak English; this makes home-school communication more difficult. Homework poses a special problem because parents are unable to interpret assignments or provide help (Delgado-Gaiton, 1992). In these situations, the child often has the responsibility of interpreting the message.

Schools also often compound the problem by using technical educational jargon when they send home letters or communiques. The problem is especially acute in special education, where legal and procedural safeguards can be bewildering. For example, studies indicate that parents often don't understand IEPs (Harry, 1992) or even remember that they've signed one (R. Stein, 1983). Other research indicates that many parents feel ill-prepared to assist their children with school-related tasks but that suggestions from school describing specific strategies in the home can be effective in bridging the home-school gap (Hoover-Dempsey, Bassler, & Burow, 1995).

10.27 ▬
Explain the feelings of the parents in the Rich (1987) quote; base your answer on our study of classical conditioning in Chapter 6.

10.28 ▬
Identify at least two specific things you as a teacher could use to overcome cultural and language barriers in communicating with the parents of your students.

Strategies for Involving Parents

Virtually all schools have formal communication processes, such as interim progress reports, that tell parents about their youngster's achievement at the midpoint of each grading period; open houses, during which teachers introduce themselves and describe general guidelines and procedures; parent-teacher conferences; and of course, report cards. Although these processes are schoolwide and necessary, as an individual teacher, you can do more to enhance the communication process.

Early Communication

Open the lines of communication immediately. Joan Williams, an eighth-grade English teacher, began the process on the first day by soliciting students' input, and with their help she prepared a description of her rules and procedures. On the second day, she had a letter prepared for her students to take home for their parents' signature. Because she had several native-Spanish-speaking students in her class, she enlisted the aid of another teacher and sent a copy, written in Spanish, to the parents of those students. The letter appears in Figure 10.4.

Joan's letter accomplished several things. Although not a Spanish-speaker, the fact that she prepared a letter in Spanish communicated a form of caring to her students, who in turn communicated this attitude to their parents. Joan's letter also included specific suggestions for parents. Even if parents cannot read a homework assignment, for example, asking their children to show it to them and explain it is worthwhile.

Further, the letter was written as a "contract" so that parents would make a commitment to the process, and the parent's signature further symbolized a commitment. Because student input was also part of the process of preparing the suggestions for parents, the students felt more ownership of the process and further pressured their parents to work with them in completing their homework.

Regardless of the approach, early and positive communication is essential. Don't wait until management problems arise to establish communication links with parents. Their support in the home will mean fewer management problems in the classroom.

10.29 ▬
How could teachers find out whether the letters and notes they are sending out make sense to parents? (Hint: Think back to Chapters 7 and 8 and the strategies teachers use to check comprehension.)

10.30 ▬
How does Joan Williams's approach, together with a letter like the one in Figure 10.4, demonstrate the teacher characteristics of being caring, firm, and democratic?

Teachers can involve parents in their children's learning through active communication strategies that express caring and concern.

Figure 10.4

Letter to parents

August 22, 1996

Dear Parents,

I am looking forward to a productive and exciting year, and I am writing this letter to encourage your involvement and support. You always have been and still are the most important people in your youngster's education. We cannot do the job without you.

For us to work together most effectively, some guidelines are necessary. With the students' help, we prepared the ones listed here. Please read this information carefully and sign where indicated. If you have any questions, please call me at Southside Junior High School (441-5935), or at home (221-8403) in the evenings.

Sincerely,

Joan Williams

AS A PARENT, I WILL TRY MY BEST TO DO THE FOLLOWING:

1. I will ask my youngsters about school every day. (Evening meal is a good time.) I will ask them about what they're studying and try to learn about it.
2. I will provide a quiet time and place each evening for homework. I will set an example by also working at that time or reading while my youngster is working.
3. Instead of asking if their homework is finished, I will ask to see it. I will have them explain some of the information to see if they understand it.

    Parent's Signature _____

STUDENT SURVIVAL GUIDELINES:

1. I will be in class and seated when the bell rings.
2. I will follow directions the first time they are given.
3. I will bring covered textbook, notebook, paper, and two sharpened pencils to class each day.
4. I will raise my hand for permission to speak or leave my seat.
5. I will keep my hands, feet, and objects to myself.

HOMEWORK GUIDELINES:

1. Our motto is I WILL ALWAYS TRY. I WILL NEVER GIVE UP.
2. I will complete all assignments. If an assignment is not finished or ready when called for, I understand that I get no credit for it.
3. If I am absent, it is my responsibility to come in before school in the morning (8:15–8:45) to make it up.
4. I know that I get one day to make up a test or turn in my work for each day I'm absent.
5. I understand that extra credit work is not given. If I do all the required work, extra credit isn't necessary.

    Student's Signature _____

Maintaining Communication

Early and positive communication helps get the year off to a good start. Continuing efforts help maintain the links you've established. Melissa Bolden, a sixth-grade teacher, took the following step.

> At the beginning of each grading period, Melissa sends a letter home to parents or care givers that describes the topics that will be covered, the tests and the approximate times they will be given, and any special projects that are required for the period. Because she speaks no language other than English, she asks her non-native-English-speaking students to rewrite the letter in their native language. She reports that the students take pride in writing the letters and even offer suggestions for changes that will better communicate with their parents or other care givers. She asks students to read the letters to their parents; this forms a link between home and school and better ensures that the message was understood.

Although Melissa's communique required considerable effort the first year, she reported that it became much easier. She had each of the letters in a computer file, which she pulled out and briefly edited in her second year. Now in her third year of using the process, she reports that the response of both her students and their parents makes the effort more than worthwhile.

Many schools now send packets of students' work home to parents, requiring that the packets be signed and returned. This gives parents both an ongoing record of student achievement and a continuing link between home and school.

10.31
In addition to initial classroom meetings, how else might teachers communicate to parents that they care about their children?

Classroom Connections

Capitalizing on Diversity in Your Classroom

1. Establish communication links between school and home during the first few days of school.
   - A kindergarten teacher makes a personal telephone call to the parents of each of her students during the first week of school. She tells the parents how happy she is to have their children in her class, encourages them to contact her at any time, and gives them her home phone number.

2. Maintain communication links throughout the year.
   - A fourth-grade teacher sends home a "class communicator" each month. It briefly describes the topics the students will be studying and suggestions parents might follow in helping their children. The students are required to write personal notes to their parents on the communicator, describing their efforts and progress.
   - A teacher calls a parent during the first week of school to report that her daughter didn't turn in her first two homework papers. "I want to catch these things early," she says on the phone. "Monica is a capable student, and I want her to get off to a good start."

3. Communicate in straightforward language. Avoid technical terms and educational jargon.
   - A second-grade teacher goes over a letter to parents with her students. She has them explain to her what each part says, and she then asks the students to read and explain the letter to their parents.

Interventions: Dealing With Misbehavior

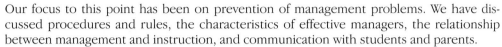

Our focus to this point has been on prevention of management problems. We have discussed procedures and rules, the characteristics of effective managers, the relationship between management and instruction, and communication with students and parents.

Despite teachers' best efforts, however, management problems will occur, and teachers must intervene in cases of disruptive behavior or chronic inattention. In this section, we discuss intervention strategies, examining each of the following: (a) behavioral approaches to intervention, (b) guidelines for successful intervention, (c) intervention techniques that vary according to the severity of the infraction (a continuum), and (d) violence and aggression.

Behavioral Approaches to Intervention

You found in Chapter 6 that behaviorism can be an effective tool for changing behavior. Although somewhat controversial, a judiciously applied system of reinforcement and punishment can be effective for teaching and sustaining desired behaviors, particularly at the elementary level.

Decisions About Behavioral Systems

Cindy Daines's first graders were sometimes frustrating. Although she tried "alerting" the groups and having the whole class make transitions at the same time, each one took 4 minutes or more.

In an effort to improve the situation, she made some "tickets" from construction paper, bought an assortment of small prizes, and displayed the items in a fishbowl on her desk the next day. She then explained, "We're going to play a little game to see how quiet we can be when we change lessons. . . . Whenever we change, such as from language arts to math, I'm going to give you 2 minutes and then I'm going to ring this bell," she continued, ringing the bell as a demonstration. "Students who have their books out and are waiting quietly when I ring the bell will get one of these tickets. On Friday afternoon, you can turn these in for prizes you see in this fishbowl. The more tickets you have, the better the prize will be."

During the next few days, Cindy moved around the room, handing out tickets and making comments such as, "I really like the way Merry is ready to work," "Ted already has his books out and is quiet," and "Thank you for moving to math so quickly."

She knew it was working when she heard "Shh" and "Be quiet!" from the students, and she moved from the prizes to allowing the students to "buy" free time with their tickets to finally giving them Friday afternoon parties as group rewards when the class had accumulated enough tickets. She gradually was able to space out the group rewards as the students' self-regulation developed.

Two decisions must be made when behavioral approaches to management interventions are considered. First, do the **consequences**—*outcomes following a behavior that influence future behaviors*—focus on desired behavior or on the elimination of undesired behavior? In essence, will the students be reinforced for following rules and procedures, or will they be punished for not following them? The second decision is whether the consequences will be individually or group administered.

Positive or Negative Consequences?   The first decision involves positive versus negative consequences. Positive reinforcement, as you saw in Chapter 6 and in Cindy's system,

10.32 ■
Cindy's comments, such as, "Ted already has his books out and is quiet," are an application of what concepts from your study of behaviorism in Chapter 6?

Figure 10.5

Guidelines for the use of punishment

- Use punishment sparingly to minimize negative emotional reactions.
- Be certain the punishment is directly related to the misbehavior and is applied immediately.
- Explain and model appropriate alternative behaviors.
- Keep negative consequences as mild and short as possible.
- Avoid using classwork or learning activities as punishers.
- Apply negative consequences logically, systematically, and dispassionately—not out of anger.

focuses on desired behavior. It can be effective in initiating new behaviors (McCaslin & Good, 1992). In planning for a positive reinforcement system, teachers identify the desired behaviors, link them to reinforcers, and then communicate both to the students. Cindy followed this process by explaining what students had to do to earn prizes.

Punishment, in contrast, presents the students with something undesired or takes something desired away when they behave inappropriately. Guidelines for its use are outlined in Figure 10.5.

Negative consequences can be effective in discouraging or suppressing specific, unwanted behaviors but should not form the core of a management system. Negative consequences suppress undesired behaviors but don't teach positive ones. Emphasizing positive behaviors is much more effective than focusing on eliminating unwanted ones (Sulzer-Azaroff & Mayer, 1986). The total system needs to be based more on caring and cooperation than on threats and fear.

Individual or Group Consequences?   The second decision involves individual versus group consequences. Individual consequences are useful when focusing on behaviors displayed by only a few students. The most extreme case of this is an individual behavior modification system designed for one student displaying chronic misbehavior (Sulzer-Azaroff & Mayer, 1986). Individual consequences concentrate efforts where they're most needed but are very demanding for the teacher.

Group systems link consequences to the behavior of the whole group. Cindy Daines's parties are examples; the whole class was given parties when they had accumulated enough points. The influence of peer pressure and the ease of administration are two advantages of group systems.

As Cindy found, logistics can be demanding when using a behavioral system. She managed hers by first using individual tokens and then switching to group rewards. Food, privileges, praise, stars, free time, and displays of work are all examples of rewards for desired behavior. Some are controversial, and careful judgment should be used in choosing them.

Although the use of group rewards can be effective, the effect of group punishment is different. Punishing the group for the misbehavior of a few leads to anger and resentment and is generally ineffective. If the problem lies with a small group of students and punishment is required, it should be administered individually.

On the surface, the application of behavioral consequences seems quite simple, but in practice it is difficult to plan for every contingency. As with other aspects of teaching, behavioral approaches to management require flexibility, sensibility, and sound judgment.

10.33
Even though emphasizing positive behaviors is preferred, many teachers largely ignore them and focus instead on undesirable behaviors. Why do you think this happens?

Assertive Discipline: A Structured Approach to Consequences

Lee and Marlene Canter (1992) have attempted to create a structured behavioral approach to management by carefully *stating rules and describing specific positive and negative consequences in their management system called* **assertive discipline**.

Assertive discipline is controversial. Critics charge that it is punitive, pits teachers against students, and stresses obedience and conformity over learning and self-control (Curwin & Mendler, 1988; McLaughlin, 1994). Proponents disagree and contend that its emphasis on positive reinforcement is effective (Canter, 1988). Despite this controversy, the program is popular and its use is widespread. It is difficult to find a school district in the country that hasn't had at least some exposure to assertive discipline; estimates suggest that more than 750,000 teachers have been trained in the program (D. Hill, 1990).

The Canters' Procedures.   As with other approaches to management, the Canters' program begins with a clearly specified set of rules that follow the suggestions outlined earlier in the chapter. Second, they suggest that the rules be prominently displayed so that students are constantly reminded that they exist. Third, although specifics may vary, the Canters suggest that teachers employ a simple and clearly stated process for applying consequences. Table 10.6 provides an outline of one fifth-grade teacher's implementation of the system (D. Hill, 1990).

The teacher reported that the system worked well, particularly with minor infractions such as talking and leaving seats without permission. She commented that, after a few weeks, most of the class were getting the free time at the end of the week. In fact, she needed to find a new reward because the students no longer valued the free time.

Putting students' names on a list is a form of presentation punishment. Removal punishment can be used as well. For example, as part of her daily routine, one teacher gives her students an envelope with three slips in it at the beginning of the day; she removes a slip for each rule infraction. The remaining slips can then be traded in on Friday for special privileges or prizes.

Table 10.6

Sample consequences in implementing assertive discipline

Consequences for Breaking Rules

First infraction	Name on list
Second infraction	Check by name
Third infraction	Second check by name
Fourth infraction	Half-hour detention
Fifth infraction	Call to parents

Consequences for Following Rules

A check is removed for each day that no infractions occur. If only a name remains, and no infractions occur, the name is removed.

All students without names on the list are given 45 minutes of free time Friday afternoon to do as they choose. The only restrictions are that they must stay in the classroom, and they must not disrupt the students who didn't earn the free time.

The choice of consequences depends on the teacher's judgment. Because the system is highly predictable, the Canters argue, it is effective for students with exceptionalities, in addition to regular classroom students.

Behavioral approaches to management offer teachers alternatives in dealing with management problems. They are particularly effective in initiating desired behaviors with young students. When misused, however, these approaches place too much emphasis on external control at the expense of developing student self-regulation and self-control. Effective teachers combine behavioral with other management approaches that stress individual decision making and responsibility.

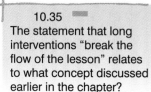

10.34
Why is assertive discipline called a "behavioral approach" to management?

Guidelines for Successful Interventions

Intervening in the case of classroom management problems is never easy. If it were, the issue of management wouldn't remain one of the most chronic problems teachers face. Some basic guidelines can help in the process.

Brevity

The first suggestion is keep the encounter as short as possible. Researchers have documented a negative relationship between time spent on discipline and student achievement; long interventions break the flow of the lesson and detract from instructional time (Crocker & Brooker, 1986; Evertson, Anderson, Anderson, & Brophy, 1980).

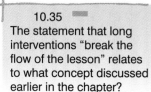

10.35
The statement that long interventions "break the flow of the lesson" relates to what concept discussed earlier in the chapter?

Let's see how Judy Harris applied this principle in her work with her ninth graders. First, she simply touched Brad on the arm. She used nonverbal communication to stop Kevin, and she spoke quietly to Sondra. In each case, she kept the encounter short and minimized its impact on the rest of the class.

Follow-Through

To illustrate the principle of follow-through, think again about the examples with Karen Wilson and Isabelle Rodriguez in our discussion of nonverbal communication on page 410.

Brief interventions that do not detract from instructional time maintain lesson focus while preventing more serious disruptions.

Karen told Jeff and Mike to stop whispering but turned back to Jasmine before she made certain they complied. Isabelle, in contrast, made sure Ken and Lance were working quietly before she turned back to Vicki.

Follow-through is difficult. As you saw at the beginning of the chapter, one reason management problems persist is that teachers sometimes simply give up. The effort it takes to follow through on each incident is often too much, and teachers are sometimes unable or unwilling to pay the price. Without follow-through, however, an entire management system breaks down because teachers communicate that they're not really serious about maintaining an orderly classroom. This is another reason that the first few days of the school year are so important. If you carefully follow through during this period, management becomes much easier during the rest of the year.

> **10.36** ▬
> Describe how Judy Harris demonstrated follow-through in dealing with Sondra in our opening case study.

Consistency

"Be consistent" is stated so often in reference to management that it has almost become a cliché. The need for consistency is obvious, but achieving complete consistency in the real world of teaching is virtually impossible. In fact, research indicates that interventions should be contextualized; they depend on the specific situation and student (W. Doyle, 1986).

Let's look at an example. Most classrooms have a rule "Speak only when recognized by the teacher." Suppose as you're monitoring seatwork, a student innocently asks a work-related question of another student and then quickly turns back to work. Do you intervene to let her know that you are "withit" and that talking is not allowed during seatwork? Failing to do so is technically inconsistent, but you don't intervene and you shouldn't. A student who repeatedly turns around and whispers, though, becomes a disruption. A "withit" teacher knows what is going on, discriminates between the two behaviors, and knows where to draw the line.

> **10.37** ▬
> What concept from Piaget's work (in Chapter 2) strongly relates to consistency? Explain how they are related.

Avoiding Arguments

Another important intervention principle is to avoid arguing with students. Teachers never "win" such arguments. They can assert their authority, but resentment is often the outcome, and the encounter may expand into a major incident. In the scenario that introduced this chapter, Judy handled this problem skillfully. In her encounter with Sondra, she simply restated her request and ensured that it was followed. In comparison, consider an alternative scenario.

> "I wasn't *speaking.*"
> "You were whispering."
> "It doesn't say *no whispering.*"
> "You know what the rule means. We've been over it again and again."
> "Well, it's not fair. I wasn't speaking. You don't make other students move when they whisper."
> "You were whispering, so move."

The student, of course, knew what the rule meant and was simply playing a game with the teacher, who allowed herself to be drawn into an argument. Judy didn't, and the incident was disarmed almost immediately.

Preserving Student Dignity

A final principle is to intervene in such a way that it preserves a student's dignity. Arguments, loud reprimands in front of the whole class, and public criticism and sarcasm all put students on the spot and can exacerbate misbehavior. Public interactions such as the following are unproductive.

"Janet, what are you doing?"
"Nothing."
"Yes you were. Speak up so that everyone can hear."
" . . . "
"You were talking. What's the rule about talking without permission?"
" . . . "
"Let's hear it. I want to hear you say the rule."
" . . . We don't talk until we're recognized."
"That's right. Do you understand that?"
" . . . Yes."

10.38
Put yourself in the role of the teacher and describe how you might later use Gordon's "I-messages" to deal with Janet.

This prolonged encounter was unnecessary. Janet knew exactly what she was doing. Although asking a student to state a rule sometimes makes sense, the tone in this encounter was negative, and the student was forced into a humiliating position. The exchange simply demonstrated the teacher's power over her. Janet's only alternatives were to acquiesce or to lash out. Either way, the student loses. Instead, the teacher could have identified the rule, enlisted compliance with it, and moved on with the lesson or spoken with the student privately (in the hall or after class).

With these principles in mind, let's look now at a series of interventions.

An Intervention Continuum

Disruptions vary widely, from an isolated incident, such as a student briefly whispering to a neighbor during quiet time, to chronic infractions, such as a student repeatedly poking, tapping, or kicking other students. Because the infractions vary, teachers' reactions should also vary. Management interventions occur on a continuum ranging from minor to serious infractions. In general, keep the intervention as short and nondisruptive as possible. The intervention continuum is described in Figure 10.6 and illustrated in Table 10.7.

Ignoring Inappropriate Behavior

10.39
Identify two or three examples of possible reinforcers for a student's inappropriate behavior. What must be done with these reinforcers if ignoring inappropriate behavior is going to work?

The simplest and least disruptive intervention is to simply ignore the misbehavior. In cases of minor or isolated incidents, this makes the most sense. It may also work if the student is being reinforced by the teacher's intervention, and ignoring eliminates the reinforcer. However, ignoring disruptive behavior to prevent positively reinforcing it often fails to recognize other reinforcers and motives operating in the classroom.

Praising Desired Behavior

10.40
Is praise for good behavior more effective at upper or lower grades? Explain your answer from a developmental perspective.

Teachers are urged to "catch 'em being good," and this is particularly effective as a method of prevention. Elementary teachers effectively use statements like, "I really like the way Jimmy is working quietly." From your study of Chapter 6, you know this is an example of directly reinforcing Jimmy and vicariously reinforcing the other students. In middle and secondary schools, a teacher who quietly comments to a student after class, "I'm extremely pleased with your effort this last week. I know you're trying hard. Keep it up," is also using positive reinforcement for desirable behavior. Using positive reinforcement or a combination of positive reinforcement and ignoring misbehavior works most effectively with minor disruptions (Pfiffer et al., 1985; Rosen et al., 1984).

Figure 10.6

An intervention continuum

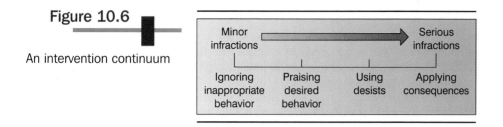

Using Desists

A **desist** *occurs when a teacher tells a student to stop a behavior* (Kounin, 1970). The phrases, "Glenys, we don't leave our seat without permission," "Glenys!" and "Class!" a finger to the lips, and even a stern facial expression are all desists and are the most common teacher reaction to misbehavior (Humphrey, 1979; Sieber, 1981).

Clarity and tone are important in the effectiveness of desists. For example, "Randy, what is the rule about touching other students in this class?" or, "Randy, how do you think that makes Willy feel?" are clearer than, "Randy, stop that," because they link the target behavior to either a rule or the consequences of the behavior and thus provide an additional opportunity to help students think about their behavior. Students react to these subtle differences, preferring rule and consequence reminders to teacher commands (Nucci, 1987).

The tone of desists should be firm but not hostile; angry desists should be avoided. Kounin (1970) found that kindergarten students handled with rough desists actually became more disruptive and that older students were uncomfortable in classes in which rough desists were used. Borg and Ascione (1982) found that gentle reprimands, together with the suggestion of alternative behaviors and effective questioning techniques, reduced time off-task by 20 minutes a day.

We emphasize here that clear communication (including congruence between verbal and nonverbal behavior), an awareness of what's happening in the classroom (withitness), and the other characteristics of effective lesson movement are critical in using desists to stop misbehavior. If these elements are missing, desists alone won't work.

> **10.41** ▄
> On the basis of your study of social cognitive theory in Chapter 6, explain why rough desists might result in students becoming more disruptive. What other explanations might there be?

Table 10.7

Applying the intervention continuum

Intervention	When Appropriate	Example
Ignoring inappropriate behavior	Short, nondisruptive behavior, or student "slips"	Teacher glances at Rosario whispering briefly to David but continues lesson.
Praising desired behavior	Compliance by most students, non-compliance by some	"I like the way Amad is working so quietly."
Using desists	Relatively minor infraction	"We're on page 31. Sal, please stop talking and turn to page 31 in your book."
Applying consequences	Serious or chronic misbehavior	Teacher removes a slip from Ron's packet.

Applying Consequences

Careful planning and effective instruction will eliminate most misbehavior before it starts. Some minor incidents can be ignored, and simple desists will stop others. When these strategies don't stop disruptions, however, you must apply consequences that are related to the problem.

Logical Consequences.   Logical consequences allow students to experience the results of noncompliance with established rules. For example, consider the case of a kindergarten teacher faced with the problem of several wet, dripping students.

> The kindergarten boys found a lovely mud puddle in the playground during recess. They had much fun running and splashing and then came back into the room wet and dripping, and they left muddy footprints all over the room.
>
> Their teacher called them aside for a conference. "Boys, we have two problems here. One is that the classroom is all dirty and it needs to be fixed so that the other children don't get wet and dirty. What can you do to fix it?"
>
> One little boy suggested that they could mop the floor.
>
> "Good idea," said the teacher. "Let's find our custodian, Mrs. Smith, and you can get a mop from her and mop the floor. Now what about our other problem, your dirty clothes?"
>
> "We could call our mothers and ask them to bring us clean clothes!" suggested one boy.
>
> "Another good idea," said the teacher. "But what if your mothers are not home?"
>
> This was a tougher problem. Finally, one boy said, "I know, we could borrow some clean clothes from the lost and found box!"
>
> "Good thinking," said the teacher. "And what can we do so that you don't lose so much time from class again?"
>
> "Stay out of mud puddles!" was the reply in unison. (J. McCarthy, 1991, p. 19)

10.42 ▬
How does the idea of logical consequences relate to the obedience and responsibility models outlined in Table 10.1?

By putting the students in a problem-solving role and helping them see cause-and-effect relationships between their actions and the problem, the teacher not only was solving the immediate problem but also was teaching students to take responsible ownership for their actions. Research indicates that children who learn to understand the effects of their actions on others become more altruistic and are more likely to take action to make up for their misbehavior (Berk, 1994).

Behavioral Consequences.   Classrooms are busy places, and it isn't always possible to solve problems the way the kindergarten teacher did in the previous section. In these instances, behavioral consequences offer an alternative:

> Jason was an intelligent and active fifth grader. He loved to talk and seemed to know just how far he could go before Mrs. Aguilar got exasperated with him. Ignoring him wasn't working. A call to his parents helped for a while, but soon he was back to his usual behavior—never quite enough to require a drastic response, but always a thorn in Mrs. Aguilar's side.
>
> Finally, she decided that she would give him one warning. At a second disruption, his name would go on her note pad. A third disruption would mean time out from regular instructional activities. She met with Jason and explained the new rules. The next day, he began to misbehave almost immediately.
>
> "Jason," she warned, "you can't work while you're talking. Please get busy."
>
> He stopped, but 10 minutes later, he was at it again. "Jason," she said calmly, "I've spoken to you once. You need to stop talking," and without another word, she wrote his name on her pad.
>
> A week later, Jason was working quietly and comfortably with the rest of the class.

10.43 ▬
Suppose Mrs. Aguilar has just begun implementing her system with Jason and she sees him briefly talk to one of his buddies. Should she ignore the behavior, or should she apply a consequence? Provide a rationale for your response.

Jason's behavior is common, particularly in the elementary and middle schools, and it is precisely this behavior that drives teachers up the wall. Students like Jason cause more teacher stress and burnout by far than do threats of violence and bodily harm. His behavior is impossible to ignore because it is disruptive; praise for good work helps to a certain extent, but much of his reinforcement comes from his buddies. Desists work briefly, but teachers simply play out constantly monitoring him. Mrs. Aguilar had no choice but to apply consequences.

The issue of consistency is important here, and as we said earlier, teacher judgment is essential. The key to handling students like Jason is predictability. He understands what he is doing, and he is capable of controlling himself. When he can unequivocally predict the consequences of his behavior, he will quit. The consequence might be his name on the chalkboard, loss of a slip of paper from his packet, or removal from the room. In Jason's case, Mrs. Aguilar briefly and calmly reminded him of the rule and applied consequences. There was no argument, little time was used, and the class wasn't disrupted. It was an effective solution to the problem.

Serious Management Problems: Violence and Aggression

Class is disrupted by a scuffle. You look up to see that Ron has left his seat and gone to Phil's desk, where he is punching and shouting at Phil. Phil is not so much fighting back as trying to protect himself. You don't know how this started, but you do know that Phil gets along well with other students and that Ron often starts fights and arguments without provocation. (Brophy & Rohrkemper, 1987, p. 60)

This morning several students excitedly tell you that on the way to school they saw Tom beating up Sam and taking his lunch money. Tom is the class bully and has done things like this many times. (Brophy & Rohrkemper, 1987, p. 53)

What would you do in these situations? What would be your immediate reaction? How would you follow through? What long-term strategies would you employ to ensure that these problems do not recur? Questions similar to these were asked of teachers identified by their principals as effective in dealing with serious management problems (Brophy & McCaslin, 1992). Their responses, together with other research examining violence and aggression in schools, form the focus of this section.

Problems of violence and aggression require both immediate actions and long-term solutions. First, the behavior must be stopped; second, the victim needs to be protected. Long-term strategies place the problem in a larger context and attempt to deal with possible causes.

Short-Term Strategies

Short term, experts recommend an immediate and assertive response to aggressive acts. Students must be confronted immediately and be told clearly that violence or aggression will not be allowed. In the incident with the lunch money, for example, Tom must be told that his actions were reported, that they are unacceptable, and that they will not be tolerated. In the case of the classroom scuffle, participants should be separated immediately (if possible) and be told that this kind of behavior is not permitted.

Experts suggest that students involved in incidents like these be immediately confronted with the problem and helped to understand the severity of their actions. In working with the student, it is important to communicate that the problem is serious, that it won't be tolerated, and that the student is being held accountable for his or her action.

10.44
Where on the intervention continuum would short-term actions be? Why would other interventions be skipped?

Long-Term Solutions

Expert teachers and their less effective counterparts differ in their long-term solutions (Brophy & McCaslin, 1992). Strategies of expert teachers are comprehensive and instructional; these teachers aren't satisfied with merely stopping the immediate behavior, but instead focus on long-term solutions. Less effective teachers, in contrast, are less systematic in their approaches, depending more on threats and coercion than long-term strategies.

Long term, students need to be taught ways other than fighting to solve problems. Students must learn to control their tempers and to cope with frustration. One promising approach uses problem-solving simulations to teach aggressive youth to understand the motives and intentions of other people. Research indicates that these youth often respond aggressively because they misread others' intentions as being hostile (Hudley, 1992). Following these problem-solving sessions, aggressive students were less hostile in their interpretation of ambiguous problem situations and were rated as less aggressive by their teachers. Other approaches include teaching aggressive students to solve conflicts through communication and negotiation rather than fighting and to express anger verbally rather than physically (Brophy & McCaslin, 1992).

Experts also suggest the involvement of others, including parents and school personnel (Brophy & McCaslin, 1992; Moles, 1992). Research indicates that a large majority of parents (88%) want to be notified immediately if school problems occur (Harris, Kagay, & Ross, 1987). In addition, school counselors, school psychologists, social workers, and principals have all been trained to deal with these problems and can provide advice and assistance. Experienced teachers can also provide a wealth of information about how they've handled similar problems. No one should face persistent or serious problems of violence or aggression alone.

In conclusion, we put problems of violence and aggression in a proper perspective. Even though they are possibilities, and you should understand options for dealing with them, the majority of your management problems will be issues of cooperation and motivation. Many can be prevented, others can be dealt with quickly, and some require individual attention. We all hear about students carrying guns to school, incidents of assault on teachers, and other news-making stories. However, we all should remember that, considering the huge numbers of students that pass through schools each day, these incidents remain statistically small in number.

10.45
Suppose you have just broken up a fight between two junior high boys. One of the boys has been in four fights in the past 2 months. Describe specifically what you might do to help change this behavior.

Classroom Connections

Using Successful Interventions in Your Classroom

1. Use positive reinforcement to initiate and teach positive behaviors.
   - A first-grade teacher, knowing that the times after recess and after lunch are difficult for many students, institutes a system in which the class has 1 minute to settle down and get out their materials after a timer goes off. When the class meets the requirement, they earn points toward free-time activities.

   - To encourage students to clean up quickly after labs, a junior high science teacher offers them a free 5 minutes of talk in their seats if the lab is cleaned up in time. Students who don't clean up in time are required to finish in silence.

2. Keep discipline encounters with students brief, clear, and to the point. Hold discussions regarding fairness or equity after class and in private.
   - After having been asked to stop whispering for the second time in a 10-minute period, a student protests that he has been asking about the assigned seatwork. The teacher reminds him of the two incidents in 10 minutes and that his whispering is disruptive. The teacher then removes a slip from his packet without further discussion. The teacher sits down with him after class to discuss the problem and work toward a solution.
   - A first-grade teacher tries to make interventions instructional. When she uses nonverbal cues to discipline, she points to the appropriate rule on the chalkboard. If students seem confused, she either bends down and quickly talks to them privately or makes a general reminder about the rule and its reason, such as "Class, there's too much noise in here, and I'm having trouble thinking."

3. Follow through consistently in the cases of disruptive behavior.
   - A teacher separates two boys who disrupt lessons with their horseplay, telling them the new seat assignments are theirs until further notice. The next day, they sit in their old seats as the bell is about to ring. "Do you know why I moved you two yesterday?" the teacher says immediately. After a momentary pause, both students nod. "Then move quickly now, and be certain you're in your new seats tomorrow. You come talk with me when you're ready to solve this horseplay problem."
   - A high school teacher reminds students about being seated when the bell rings. As the bell rings the next day, two girls are standing, having a conversation. The teacher turns to them and says, "I'm sorry, but you must not have understood me yesterday. To be counted on time, you need to be in your seats when the bell rings. Please go to the office and get a late admit pass. Please do it now . . . and if you want to talk with me about this, come in after class. Now, class, yesterday we were talking . . . "

4. Use problem-solving strategies to help students develop student responsibility.
   - A second-grade teacher uses Friday afternoons to do classroom chores. Two students begin a tug-of-war over a cleaning rag and knock over a potted plant. The teacher asks the two students what caused the problem and how they can solve it.

Windows on Classrooms

At the beginning of the chapter, you saw how Judy Harris managed her classroom in an effort to create an environment that promoted learning and student self-regulation. She had a set of well-planned rules and procedures, and she capitalized on the close relationship between management and instruction. She clearly communicated with her students and managed her classroom in an assertive but democratic way.

Let's look now at a case study that describes another teacher presenting the same topic to a different group of students. As you read, look for similarities and differences in the two teachers' approaches to the topic and their management of the students.

Janelle Powers is also a ninth-grade geography teacher who works in the same school as does Judy Harris. As with Judy's classroom, Janelle's room is crowded; she has 29 students.

Shiana came through the classroom doorway just as the tardy bell rang.

"Take your seat quickly, Shiana," Janelle directed. "You're just about late. All right. Listen up, everyone," she continued. "Ali?"

"Here."

"Gaelen?"

"Here."

"Chu?"

"Here."

Janelle finished taking the roll, and she then walked around the room and handed back a set of papers as she went.

"You did quite well on the assignment," she commented. "Let's keep up the good work. . . . Howard and Manny, please stop talking while I'm returning the papers. Can't you just sit quietly for 1 more minute?"

The boys, who were whispering, turned back to the front of the room.

"Now," Janelle continued, after handing back the last paper and returning to the front of the room, "we've been studying the Middle East, so let's review for a moment. . . . Look at the map and identify the longitude and latitude of Cairo. Take a minute and figure it out right now."

The students began as Janelle went to her file cabinet to get out some transparencies.

"Stop it, Damon," she heard Leila blurt out behind her.

"Leila," Janelle responded sternly, "we don't talk out like that in class."

"He's poking me, Mrs. Powers."

"Are you poking her, Damon?"

" . . . "

"Well?"

" . . . Not really."

"You did too," Leila complained.

"Both of you stop it," Janelle warned. "Another outburst like that, Leila, and your name goes on the chalkboard."

As the last students were finishing the problem, Janelle looked up from the materials on her desk to an example on the overhead and heard Howard and Manny talking and giggling at the back of the room.

"Are you boys finished?"

"Yes," Manny answered.

"Well, be quiet then until everyone is done," Janelle directed, and she went back to rearranging her materials.

"Quiet, everyone," she again directed as she looked up once more in response to a hum of voices around the room. "Is everyone finished? . . . Good. Pass your papers forward. . . . Remember, put your paper on the top of the stack. . . . Roberto, wait until the papers come from behind you before you pass yours forward."

Janelle collected the papers, put them on her desk, and then began, "We've talked about the geography of the Middle East, and now we want to look at the climate a bit more. It varies somewhat. For example, Syria is extremely hot in the summer but is actually quite cool in the winter. In fact, it will snow in some parts.

"Now, what did we find for the latitude of Cairo?"

" . . . Thirty degrees," Miguel volunteered.

"North or south, Miguel? . . . Wait a minute. Howard? . . . Manny? . . . This is the third time this period that I've had to say something to you about your talking and the period isn't even 20 minutes old yet. Get out your rules and read me the rule about talking without permission. . . . Howard?"

" . . . "

"It's supposed to be in the front of your notebook."

" . . . "

"Manny?"

" . . . 'No speaking without permission of the teacher,'" Manny read from the front page of his notebook.

"Howard, where are your rules?"

" . . . I don't know."

"Move up here," Janelle directed, pointing to an empty desk at the front of the room. "You've been bothering me all week. If you can't learn to be quiet, you will be up here for the rest of the year." Howard got up and slowly moved to the desk Janelle had pointed out.

After Howard was seated, Janelle began again, "Where were we before we were rudely interrupted? . . . Oh yes. What did you get for the latitude of Cairo?"

"Thirty degrees . . . north," Miguel again responded.

"Okay, good. . . . Now, Egypt also has a hot climate in the summer, in fact very hot. The summer temperatures will often go over 100° Fahrenheit. . . . Egypt is also mostly desert, so the people have trouble making a living. Their primary source of subsistence is the Nile River, which floods frequently. Most of the agriculture of the country is developed near the river."

Janelle continued presenting information to the students for the next several minutes.

"Andrew, are you listening to this?" Janelle interjected as she saw Andrew put his head down on his folded arms.

" . . . Yes," he responded, lifting up his head.

"I hope so, because all this will be on the next test, which is only a week away."

Janelle then continued with her presentation.

Let's compare Janelle's management of her class with Judy's. In analyzing the two classes, you may want to consider the following questions. In each case, be specific and take information directly from the case studies in making your comparisons.

1. What would you infer about Janelle's planning for classroom management, compared with Judy's? What seemed to be different about the two?

2. Although you don't have a lot of specific evidence about either teacher's rules, how do they compare on the basis of the evidence you do have?

3. Compare the two teachers' application of essential management skills. Be sure to provide evidence when the presence or absence of the skill is inferred rather than observed.

4. Compare the two teachers' communication with their students. Identify specific behaviors in the case studies in making your comparison.

5. Using the information from Chapter 10 as the basis for your assessment, assess Janelle Powers's overall management effectiveness. Consider your answers to Questions 1 through 4 as you make your analysis.

6. As in most classrooms, Janelle's class contains learners with diverse backgrounds. How effective would her management and instruction be for these students?

7. If, on the basis of the information in Chapter 10, you think Janelle's management or instruction could have been improved, what suggestions would you make? Again, be specific.

Summary

Classroom Management

Classroom management is a system of teacher strategies and organizational factors that contributes to productive learning environments. The goals of classroom management are to create environments that enhance learning and to develop student self-regulation. Students achieve more and are more motivated in well-managed classrooms.

Planning: The Key to Preventing Management Problems

Well-planned procedures and rules help establish and maintain orderly classrooms. The physical environment and students' developmental characteristics should be considered in planning procedures and rules.

Classroom rules provide a general framework for interacting in the classroom. Class rules must be consistent with those for the school and district. An effective list should be short, clear, and positive and include reasons for their existence. Allowing student input into rules promotes understanding and appreciation and gives the students a sense of control over their classroom environment.

Procedures provide structures for classroom activities. Each classroom will have a number of procedures that organize daily classroom routines. As with any concept or skill, rules and procedures must be carefully taught, monitored, and reviewed.

Preventing Problems: Putting Plans Into Action

Effective managers are democratic; they combine genuine caring for students and learning with firm enforcement of management decisions.

The first few days of the school year are critical in establishing expectations. Communication with parents should begin as soon as school opens and continue throughout the year.

Interventions: Dealing With Misbehavior

Effective managers keep their interventions brief, preserve student dignity, and follow through consistently on discipline decisions. Focusing on positive behavior, ignoring misbehavior, and simple desists can eliminate minor disruptions.

More lengthy interventions are sometimes necessary when misbehavior persists in frequency or duration. Logical consequences help students see the connection between their behaviors and the effects of their behaviors on others. Immediate intervention and holding students accountable is necessary in cases of chronic or serious misbehavior.

 **Important Concepts**

active listening (p. 412)

assertive discipline (p. 421)

classroom management (p. 392)

consequences (p. 419)

desist (p. 425)

discipline (p. 392)

essential management skills (p. 406)

firmness (p. 404)

"I-messages" (p. 411)

momentum (p. 409)

nonverbal behavior (p. 410)

overlapping (p. 408)

procedures (p. 398)

rules (p. 398)

withitness (p. 407)

Chapter Outline

11

Planning
for
Improved
Learning

"Good morning," Ron Adams, an eighth-grade science teacher, called out as he entered the faculty workroom of Prairie View Middle School. "How's it going?"

"Fine, I think," Mai Ling, an intern in sixth-grade math, responded. "I'm being observed today, and it's my slow math class, so I've really been preparing to be sure that I'm ready. What do you think?" asked Mai as she handed Ron a copy of a plan she was preparing.

Ron nodded. "Looks good to me, but frankly I think you've written down more material than necessary. Here, take a look at mine," and he handed her his plan book.

Heat, expansion, and pressure (pp. 28–35)

Monday (28 - 31)
Campfire Video (pretest)
Bottle, balloons, coffee pot

Tuesday (32-35)
Model

Wednesday
Egg and bottle (Boil eggs)

Thursday
Mass volume density (Ice cubes)

Friday
Summary, review

"Well," Mai responded, "we're required to write plans for our portfolio, and actually I'm more comfortable when I have it written out so that I know exactly what I'm going to do, and I follow it step-by-step."

"I used to do that, especially when I didn't have as much experience and wasn't quite sure about the material I was teaching," Ron shrugged. "Plus, I've been through this a bunch of times."

"What does all this—'Campfire video' and 'bottles, balloons, coffeepot' and 'model' and 'boil eggs'—

Unit: Decimals

Objectives: Students will know how to convert fractions to decimals so that when given different fractions, they'll describe the sequence of actions in their own words.

Students will understand how to convert fractions to decimals so that when given a series of fraction to decimal problems, they will solve each correctly.

Rationale: Converting fractions to decimals is a basic skill that will be used in everyday life. In addition, this skill deepens students' understanding of decimals, fractions, and division.

Procedures:

1. Show students different denominations of coins. Ask them why 25-cent pieces are called "quarters" and 50-cent pieces "half-dollars."
2. Write $1/4 = 25/100 = .25$ on the board.
   $1/2 = 50/100 = .50$
3. Review fractions, numerator, and denominator.
4. Do sample problem (#2). (Review division if necessary.) Have students do at desks. Compare answer to "quarters" example.
5. Review division with decimal point. Do sample problem (#3, p. 65).
6. Do another sample problem at board (#4). (Remember to think aloud!)
7. Give students problem to do at desk (#5). Call for show of hands to check for understanding.
8. Do problems 1–5, p. 239, as a class.
9. Assign problems 6–15 as seatwork.

Evaluation:

Present the students with a series of problems involving conversion to decimals and have them solve the problems.

Materials:

Text, worksheet with problems for homework.

all mean?" Mai asked, pointing at the notes in Ron's book.

"They're just reminders for the material I want to do when I do this unit on heat and expansion. We go camping some, so one time when we were out, I decided to videotape the 'naive Boy Scout trick,' so I heated some canned pork and beans on the fire until the can exploded, and I videotaped the whole thing. It really gets the students' attention . . . and it's a *real-world* problem. I start off by having the students write a paragraph explaining why they think the can of beans blew up. Some of the explanations they come up with are pretty cute."

"I apologize for being impudent," Mai said tentatively, "but I'm still not sure what you're trying to accomplish."

"No, not at all. That's a very good point . . . and I know it isn't clear from what you see here. . . . Anyway, my big goal is for them to be able to explain practical applications of heat, expansion, and pressure . . . such as why we're warned to not take the radiator cap off when a car is hot, and why bridges have expansion joints, and how pressure cookers work, and so on. As their background gets better, we link it to open and closed containers and mass, volume, and density, and then we hook

in some math when we do ratios, and we add some social studies when we talk about how technology applications affect the way we live.

"I know what I'm after with the students, but I don't have specific objectives down for each lesson because it depends on how they're coming along."

"So, what's the video for? To get their attention?"

"Well, yeah, . . . it's a jumping off point, but I also use it to get a feel for the ideas they already have about heat and everything. I start off by asking them to explain why they think it happened. Then, I work in the other points. I show them a simple demonstration of putting a balloon-covered soft drink bottle in a pot of hot water. The balloon pops up, and they love it. I use it with a drawing—that's the 'model'—to illustrate molecular behavior. And I have them do the egg and the bottle as an application. I've gathered up a bunch of cranberry juice jars, so we do that in teams. By the time we get into the 3rd or 4th day of the unit, they're really starting to understand what they're doing. Besides, all these things are simple and concrete. Students can get abstract ideas, like the materials we do with heat and molecules, but it first has to be hooked to something concrete if they're going

to really understand it. Otherwise, they just memorize strings of words and don't really get it.

"I make a big deal out of their understanding and tell them they're thinking like scientists. One thing I'm after is for them to get over their fear of science. They expect it to be so hard and boring. If they don't, they'll take only what's required in high school and get away from it as quickly as they can. I try to make what we do fairly challenging so that when they get to the point where they understand it, they feel 'smart' when we're finished," Ron smiled half self-consciously. "I'll show you what I mean if you'd like. I have my materials down in my room."

"Thanks, I would," Mai said eagerly. "Math is sort of the same way, although I think they start out scared and then get so that they don't like it. Besides, sometimes it is sort of boring. I can always use some ideas."

Ron continued as they walked out, "I used to present this material just about the same way as it was in the book, and it didn't work. The students didn't like it, and they didn't like science, so I said to myself, 'I'd better do something different.' Now, it's one of their favorite units. We have lots of discussions, and they really get into it."

Effective teaching has always required a thorough understanding of the learning process, characteristics of students at different stages of development, individual differences, factors that influence motivation, and procedures for maintaining orderly classrooms. Teachers have relied on this background when they've made decisions about what to teach, which points to emphasize, and how to present content to their students.

As research uncovers more about the complexities of learning and the implications they have for the teaching process, planning also becomes more complex. Teachers no longer simply identify objectives, the learning activities to meet them, and assessments. They now consider the learning environment more carefully than they have in the past, and they consciously plan to capitalize on factors such as the social nature of learning.

The first three parts of this text have been designed to help provide the background that allows teachers to make informed decisions when they plan experiences for their students. Now, we move on to the process of planning for learning in classrooms.

After you've completed your study of this chapter, you should be able to meet the following objectives:

▌ Explain the different uses for planning.
▌ Describe the role of learner goals and outcomes in planning.
▌ Identify learner outcomes in the three domains of learning.
▌ Identify differences between teacher-centered and learner-centered approaches to planning.
▌ Describe the results of planning research.

Teacher Planning

Careful planning is essential for beginning teachers because it helps simplify the complex task of teaching. But how much planning is enough? Were Mai's and Ron's lessons both well planned? Was one more prepared than the other? What does planning mean? We answer these questions in this chapter.

11.1
Give a probable reason for Mai Ling's lesson plan being so much more detailed than Ron Adams's.

Concepts of planning range from the simple concrete products that appear on paper, such as Mai's and Ron's written plans, to abstract processes that include all the decisions teachers make when they teach. Beginning education students tend to produce the former and often think of planning as a written document that includes objectives, topics, procedures, and sometimes more. This was Mai's notion of planning, reflected by her comment, "So I've really been preparing to be sure that I'm ready."

Planning is much more complex than that, however, and its complexity is increasing. To be most effective, **planning** *takes into account the classroom environment, social forces, and students' cultural and intellectual backgrounds, their expectations and beliefs, as well as content, goals, and learning activities.* Historically, behaviorists and even cognitive psychologists ignored most factors other than selecting and organizing content (Pintrich et al., 1993). The complexity of effective instruction makes planning even more important than it has been in the past.

Planning Functions

All teachers—rookies and veterans alike—plan even though their written products may vary greatly. To understand these variations, let's look at the role that planning plays in the overall process of teaching. It fulfills three primary functions: (a) emotional security, (b) organization, and (c) reflection.

Emotional Security

Planning helps reduce teacher anxiety by making the classroom more orderly and predictable (C. Clark, 1988). In our opening case study, Mai's effort is an example of how planning provides security for teachers. She is an intern and somewhat unsure of herself, and careful planning provides her with a measure of security that reduces the normal anxiety a new teacher experiences (McCutcheon, 1982). As indicated by her comment, "So I know exactly what I'm going to do, and I follow it step-by-step," Mai's plan provides a "script" that helps guide her interaction with the students. As teachers, we all periodically feel shaky in anticipating some lessons. The content may be unfamiliar, we're uneasy with the audience, or we've had a bad experience in the past. In these cases, we tend to plan in more detail and write more information on paper. Because of his experience, Ron is more secure, and his written plan serves more as a reminder than as a form of security. This is typical of experienced teachers; they can rely on previous experience to shape the form of classroom interaction (Brown-Claridge, Stein, & Berliner, 1988; Sardo-Brown, 1994).

Organization

11.2 ▬

Think about your study of Chapter 10. Describe specifically how planning is involved in effective classroom management.

Planning also serves the very practical function of helping teachers organize their work. As you saw in Chapter 10, organization helps both classroom management and instruction. As they plan, teachers identify topics, make decisions about sequencing learning activities, and gather needed materials. Even though Ron's written plan was less detailed than Mai's, his notes reminded him of the material he needed for his unit. Teachers recognize these practical functions—organizing content and gathering instructional materials—as important.

Beginning teachers often learn how much planning is necessary by trial and error. One 1st-year teacher contrasted her planning with what she did during student teaching:

> I do more lesson plans, but they look kind of funny in my book because lots of times I'll use one of those sticky papers and stick it on top of the assignment . . . like tomorrow we are going to play a game . . . when the time comes [for me to begin the game] I might get flustered and set it up wrong. [To prevent that] I now tend to write things down . . . like "choose an umpire," "write their names on the board." Just little things like that help me. (Bullough, 1989, p. 37)

These written reminders free the teacher to focus on other, more important aspects of teaching, such as whether the students are understanding the content.

Experience is important for subsequent planning; teachers use the experience they gain as a basis for modifying and shaping future lessons. Research suggests that successful plans are stored in memory in terms of the goals they satisfy and the problems they avoid (Hammond, 1990). Failures and the conditions that caused them are also stored as reminders for future planning.

11.3 ▬

Describe a specific example in which a teacher would consciously plan for student motivation.

Increased teacher organization can also have beneficial results on students. In one study, students taught in well-planned lessons spent less time on non-instructional activities, less time waiting their turns, and less time off-task during instructional activities (Byra & Coulon, 1992). These findings have important implications for classroom management: Well-planned learning activities actively involve students in learning and minimize opportunities for disruptions.

Reflection

The third planning function—reflection—is more elusive and abstract than the other two. Let's look again at Ron's planning. He noted, "I used to present this material just about the same way as it was in the book, and it didn't work. . . . so I said to myself, 'I'd better do something different.'" His comment suggests that he didn't merely teach as he had been teaching or simply go through the motions, but rather he "reflected" on his work and concluded that he needed to make some adjustments.

Reflection *involves asking basic questions of ourselves about our teaching* [italics added]. The basic and comprehensive question during reflection is, What am I doing and why? . . . Reflection, then, is an individual's needs assessment and continued self-monitoring or satisfaction with effectiveness. (Valverde, 1982, p. 86)

Reflective teachers constantly think about their teaching and the effect it is having on student learning (D. Ross, 1989).

Ron's inclination to be reflective is a credit to him as a professional. Through reflection, he made important changes in his planning, which in turn improved his teaching. As he planned, he consciously considered goals, his students' current knowledge, their motivation, and the connection between what they were learning and the real world. He also considered their emotional reactions to science as indicated by his desire to make them feel "smart." These actions were the outcomes of his planning and the result of his reflection. He had a ready answer for Mai's question, " . . . but I'm still not sure what you're trying to accomplish," and he knew why he approached his unit in that way. These are outcomes of teacher reflection.

Mai's planning also indicated reflection. She understood how beginning her lesson with a question or problem could increase her students' motivation, and she planned her lesson accordingly. This point suggests that Mai was also thinking about what she was doing.

> **11.4**
> Suppose that a teacher is following a plan step-by-step and that the lesson isn't going well. Would you predict that the teacher would be more likely to abandon the plan in an effort to improve the lesson or to continue to follow the plan anyway? Why do you think so?

Prerequisites to Effective Planning

From our discussion to this point, you can see that the relationship between planning and instruction is complex and interconnected. As you have seen in other parts of this book, *knowledge* is important for most aspects of learning and teaching, and the same is true for planning. Effective planning requires at least three kinds of teacher knowledge:

- Knowledge of content
- Pedagogical content knowledge
- Knowledge of learners and learning

Knowledge of Content

"We can't teach what we don't understand ourselves." This statement is self-evident. To be effective, teachers must thoroughly understand the content they're teaching.

Knowledge of content has important implications for planning because teachers won't be expert in every topic they teach and because they don't want to limit their instruction to only those topics they know well. When they're uncertain, they need to spend more time studying and planning. As Kathy Brewster commented to Harvey at the beginning of Chapter 9, " . . . I have to study every night to keep up with you people, and the harder I study, the more I learn."

Pedagogical Content Knowledge

Knowledge of content alone, however, is not enough. As you saw in Chapter 1, teachers must also have **pedagogical content knowledge** (L. Shulman, 1986), *or knowledge of ways to represent topics for learners, plus an understanding of what makes topics difficult or easy for them to learn.* As teachers move away from "transmission models of instruction" (Bransford, 1993), or simply lecturing and explaining, toward guiding and

Experienced or expert teachers rely on previous experiences organized in schemas to help novice teachers understand the complexities of teaching when they plan.

scaffolding students' efforts to construct their own understanding, pedagogical content knowledge becomes even more important.

Ron demonstrated thorough pedagogical content knowledge in his conversation with Mai. He knew he couldn't simply explain heat and expansion and expect understanding beyond mere memorization. Instead, he had considered how he could represent these concepts with a video, demonstration, model, and hands-on activity. As the students worked with these representations, and with his guidance, their current understanding would gradually evolve.

Knowledge of Learners and Learning

As we said in the introduction to the chapter, teachers' understanding of learning and the factors that influence it are increasing. To be effective, teachers must take these factors into account when they plan. For example, Ron understood that his sixth graders " . . . can get abstract ideas, like the material we do with heat and molecules, but it has to be hooked to something concrete if they're going to really understand it," and that, "they expect it to be so hard and boring." He was taking both the development of his students and their expectations into account as he planned. His desire to help them feel "smart" by making the unit challenging yet practical indicates that he was aware of his students' motivation and self-efficacy, and he consciously planned for them. Finally, by using his pretest to get some information about their current understanding and by acknowledging the social nature of learning, as evidenced by, "We have lots of discussions, and they really get into it," he indicated insight into social factors that influence learning. His planning was student centered. In contrast, Mai's planning was more content centered. She had specific objectives she wanted the students to meet, and these objectives were based on the established curriculum.

Domains of Instruction

> Three physical education teachers were comparing their objectives for a unit on exercise. Carol commented, "I'm trying to develop muscle tone, strength, and flexibility so that no matter how they use their bodies in other activities, they'll have a good foundation."
>
> "I'm interested in that, too," Sharon, a second-year teacher, added, "but I'm more concerned that they know about the different kinds of exercise. They need to know the difference between aerobic and anaerobic exercise and how each affects their bodies."
>
> "Both of those are important," Tanya agreed, "but I'm concerned about what happens after they leave school. We've got too many couch potatoes out there already. I'm trying to get them turned on to exercise so that they'll exercise for the rest of their lives." (Kauchak & Eggen, 1993, p. 69)

What are we all as teachers attempting to do when we plan for instruction? Are we trying to make our students more knowledgeable, or are we trying to change the way they think about the world? What about attitudes and values; how can our instruction influence the way our students feel about themselves and other people? What should be the role of our instruction in changing the ways our students' bodies develop? Answers to these questions can be found in the three areas or domains of learning: *cognitive, affective,* and *psychomotor.*

From the introductory example, you can see that Ron and Mai wanted their students to understand heat and expansion and fractions and decimals, respectively. These are goals in the cognitive domain, but Ron and Mai had other goals as well. Ron was concerned with students' adverse reaction to science, and Mai wanted to help students get

11.5 ▬
Could teachers have thorough knowledge of content and inadequate pedagogical content knowledge? Explain. Could teachers have pedagogical content knowledge without knowledge of content? Explain.

11.6 ▬
Give a probable reason for why Ron's planning was student centered, whereas Mai's tended to be content centered. How do these differences relate to the information-processing model in Chapter 7?

11.7 ▬
How does the emphasis on the three domains change as students progress through the grades? Is there a shift away from one domain and toward another? Do you think this shift is a positive or negative trend? Explain.

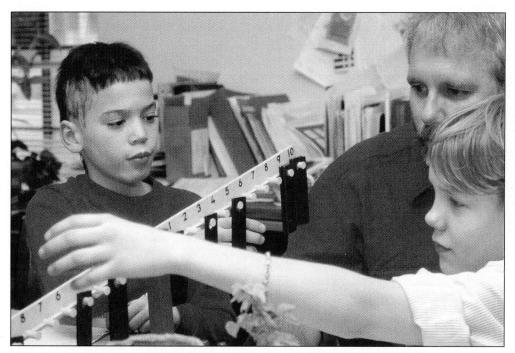

The different levels of the cognitive domain help teachers design learning activities that emphasize problem solving and critical thinking.

over their fear of math—goals in the affective domain. Teachers in the lower grades and in performance areas such as physical education also have goals related to their students' physical development. These are goals in the psychomotor domain.

Cognitive Domain

Most goals and outcomes that appear in state, district, and school curriculum guides are in the **cognitive domain**, *which focuses on knowledge and understanding of facts, concepts, principles, rules, skills, and problem solving.* It is the intellectual dimension of schooling.

Let's look again at Mai Ling's lesson plan. She had two objectives; both were related to converting fractions to decimals but were quite different in what they required of students. The same is true for nearly all objectives. For instance, a lesson focusing on adjectives could have any or all of the following objectives:

> To define adjectives
>
> To identify examples of adjectives in sentences in order to write sentences properly using adjectives
>
> To make writing attractive with the creative use of adjectives

Although each of these objectives fits the general goal of understanding adjectives, they vary in their demands on learners, in how they should be taught, and in how they would be assessed.

In response to the variation in levels of objectives, researchers developed a system for their classification (B. Bloom, Englehart, Furst, Hill, & Krathwohl, 1956). The results of this effort are well known in education and are commonly referred to as Bloom's taxon-

11.8
Classify Mai Ling's objectives into one of the levels of the taxonomy in Table 11.1.

Table 11.1

Levels, outcomes, and examples in the cognitive domain

Level	Outcome	Example
Knowledge	Knows terms, facts, rules, classifications, generalizations, principles, algorithms, and methods	States the definition of figurative language
Comprehension	Translates, interprets, predicts, generalizes, explains, identifies examples	Identifies statements that are similes and metaphors
Application	Applies rules, methods, and principles to unique situations	Rewrites a passage and increases expressiveness using figurative language
Analysis	Breaks communication into parts, determines point of view, recognizes bias, specifies implications, identifies theme	Identifies author intent in use of figurative language
Synthesis	Creates new products, methods, and patterns, from constituent elements	Creates an original work using figurative language
Evaluation	Judges on the basis of evidence and criteria	Assesses quality of a piece of writing in which the author has used figurative language

From: Taxonomy of Educational Objectives: Book 1: Cognitive Domain edited by Benjamin S. Bloom. Copyright © 1956, 1984 by Longman Publishing Group.

omy. **Bloom's taxonomy** *is a classification system developed to help teachers think about the objectives they write, the questions they ask, and the assessments they prepare.* It has six levels ranging from memory to higher order operations. These levels are outlined in Table 11.1.

Although the taxonomy is historically significant and widely used, it is difficult to reliably classify objectives into one of the six levels (Fairbrother, 1975), the question whether or not the levels represent a hierarchy has never been satisfactorily answered (Ormell, 1979; Seddon, 1978), and with the increasing influence of cognitive and constructivist views of learning, the taxonomy has been criticized as behaviorist in its orientation.

Despite these criticisms, the taxonomy serves an important function: It reminds teachers that they want students to have more than mere knowledge and simple recall of the topics they teach and that teachers must make conscious efforts to help students reach the higher levels. The goal of raising instruction beyond the knowledge level is even more important as the 21st century approaches, with the increased emphasis on student thinking and decision making. Success in schooling and later life increasingly depends on students not only knowing something but also being able to use that information in problem-solving situations. In this sense, the taxonomy is compatible with cognitive and constructivist perspectives of learning.

Affective Domain

The cognitive domain is important, and most formal school goals focus on it. Alone, however, it is incomplete. For instance, if Ron's students understand the relationship between heat and expansion but at the same time develop an aversion to science, he will have gained something but lost something even more important. The **affective domain** *focuses* *on the teaching of attitudes and values and the development of students' personal and emotional growth.* Mai and Ron both had goals in this domain even though they weren't explicitly stated.

Objectives in the affective domain can also be classified, and an affective taxonomy similar in structure to the one in the cognitive domain has been developed (Krathwohl, Bloom, & Masia, 1964). The guiding principle behind the affective domain is *internalization,* or the extent to which an attitude or value has been incorporated into a student's total value structure. The system is outlined in Table 11.2 and is illustrated with an example from Ron's science class.

Sometimes, teachers will specifically target the affective domain in their lessons. For example, you saw in Chapter 5 that learning about physical disabilities helped students develop more positive attitudes toward people with disabilities (T. Jones et al., 1981). In addition, many multicultural lessons have as their goal increased awareness of and appreciation for other cultures' values and customs.

Effective teachers also use affective goals to promote students' personal and emotional growth. By creating safe and nurturant learning environments, teachers address Maslow's needs of safety, belonging, and self-esteem and help students develop a feeling of industry as they learn specific content.

Effective teachers are aware of the critical role student attitudes play in the teaching-learning process, and they consider affective goals when they plan. The taxonomy underscores the importance of keeping affective dimensions of learning in mind when teachers plan and teach their lessons.

11.9
On the basis of Mai and Ron's conversation, at what level in the affective taxonomy would you classify their goals?

Psychomotor Domain

The **psychomotor domain** *focuses on the development of students' physical abilities and skills.* The psychomotor domain has historically received the least formal emphasis of the three—in areas other than physical education—and taxonomies in this area weren't developed until the 1970s (Harrow, 1972; Simpson, 1972). However, schools are increasing their

Table 11.2

Levels, outcomes, and examples in the affective domain

Level	Outcome	Example
Receiving	Is willing to listen, open-minded	Pays attention in science class
Responding	Demonstrates new behavior, volunteers involvement	Volunteers answers, asks questions
Valuing	Shows commitment, maintains involvement	Reads ahead in text, watches science-oriented programs on television
Organizing	Integrates new value into personal structure	Chooses to take 4 years of science in high school because of interest in science
Characterizing by value	Gains open, firm, and long-range commitment to value	Chooses a branch of science as a career field

Source: Taxonomy of Educational Objectives: Handbook II: Affective Domain by D. Krathwohl, B. Bloom, and B. Masia, 1964, New York: David McKay. Copyright 1964 by David McKay. Adapted by permission.

Encouraging growth in the affective domain promotes personal and emotional development that leads to student self-regulation.

emphasis on physical development in early learning experiences as its role in overall development becomes better understood. For instance, kindergarten children practice tying their shoes, and classrooms often have a puppet whose coat they button and unbutton. In the early school years, the ability to physically manipulate a pencil is considered in assessing a child's readiness for writing. In addition, science requires using equipment such as microscopes and balances, some math courses require constructions with compasses and rulers, word processing and driver's training require physical skills, and fine motor movements are critical in art and music. These are all activities in the psychomotor domain.

Table 11.3

Levels, outcomes, and examples in the psychomotor domain

Level	Outcome	Examples
Reflex movements	Involuntary responses	Blinking, knee jerks
Basic fundamental movements	Innate movements, combinations of reflexes	Eating, running, physically tracking an object
Perceptual abilities	Movement following interpretation of stimuli	Walking a balance beam, skipping rope, writing p and q
Physical abilities	Endurance, strength, flexibility, agility	Pull-ups, toe touching, distance bicycling
Skilled movements	Efficiency in complex movement tasks	Hitting a tennis ball, jazz dancing
Nondiscursive communication	Communication with physical movement, body language	Pleasure, authority, warmth, and other emotions demonstrated with body language

Source: A Taxonomy of the Psychomotor Domain: A Guide for Developing Behavioral Objectives by A. Harrow, 1972, New York: David McKay. Copyright 1972 by David McKay. Adapted by permission.

Table 11.3 presents a description and illustration of the psychomotor taxonomy using Harrow's (1972) conception as a framework.

Considering the psychomotor domain provides teachers a more complete picture of their students as developing human beings. In addition to helping them grow cognitively and affectively, teachers also want their students to develop healthy bodies. In areas where physical skills are necessary and potentially underdeveloped, an understanding of the psychomotor taxonomy can help teachers as they make planning decisions.

To this point, we've considered the functions that planning serves, the prerequisites to effective planning, and different domains in which planning occurs. We now turn our attention to the actual planning process.

11.10 ▬
Lifestyle research indicates that weight training is beneficial to a person's overall health and well-being. Where would it be classified in the psychomotor taxonomy?

Classroom Connections

Using Taxonomies in Your Teaching

1. Carefully consider the level of your instruction. Make an effort to focus your goals on meaningful activities that encourage student thinking.
   - A fourth-grade teacher comments after giving a quiz on body parts, "I give them a drawing and have them identify the parts in the drawing. It's much better than having them just memorize the definitions."
   - In a geography lesson, the teacher wants her students to understand how climate is influenced by the interaction of a number of variables. She does this by giving students a map of a fictitious island, together with longitude, latitude, topography, and wind direction. She then gears her instruction around the conclusions they can make about the climate of the island.

2. Consciously plan for goals in the affective domain and, where appropriate, in the psychomotor domain.
   - A physics teacher plans her initial presentation of vector problems around soccer players kicking the ball and moving to it. "I want them to see that vectors apply to 'where they live.'"
   - A music teacher dislikes rock music but plans to begin her unit on different musical forms with songs by prominent rock stars. "Students appreciate the classics once they find out that a lot of rock stars first got their ideas from them," she notes.

Approaches to Planning

In most teacher-training programs, considerable time and effort are devoted to learning how to plan effectively. Methods textbooks used in these programs devote considerable space to discussions of planning (Jacobsen, Eggen, & Kauchak, 1993).

Teacher-Centered Approaches to Planning: Linear Rational Model

The approaches to planning most often presented are grounded in a model created by Ralph Tyler and described in his book *Basic Principles of Curriculum and Instruction,*

Growth in the psychomotor domain contributes to healthy self-concepts and increased physical well-being in students.

first published in 1950. This text is a classic, and over the years it has had more impact on the way teachers are taught to plan and organize instruction than any other work.

Tyler described the relationship between planning and instruction in four logical and sequential steps, hence the name *linear rational model*. The **linear rational model of planning** *begins by specifying objectives, follows with selecting and organizing learning activities, and ends with designing assessments.* The steps in this model are illustrated in Figure 11.1.

You can see that Mai Ling used this model in her planning, and this likely reflects her recent teacher-education experience. Tyler's model was so influential that it was not critically studied for more than 20 years, and literally hundreds of thousands of teachers and educational leaders were trained in its use. Not until the 1970s did researchers begin to study planning and to compare teachers' practices to Tyler's prescriptions. We examine these research results later in the chapter, but first let's look more closely at the components of the model.

11.11
Offer an explanation for why Tyler's model was so influential and why it was not critically examined for so long.

Figure 11.1

The linear rational model

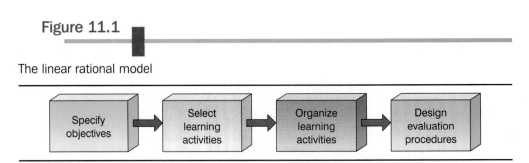

Objectives

The linear rational model begins with teachers specifying objectives. Tyler (1950) suggested that the most useful form for stating objectives was "to express them in terms which identify both the kind of behavior to be developed in the student and the content or area of life in which this behavior is to operate" (p. 46). Thus, *behavioral objectives*—statements that specify learning outcomes in terms of observable student behaviors—were born, and because of Tyler's influence, the ability to write behavioral objectives comprises an important component of teacher preparation courses.

Two approaches to preparing objectives have historically dominated the field: Mager's behavioral objectives and Gronlund's instructional objectives.

Mager's Behavioral Objectives. Another powerful teacher-training influence followed Tyler's work when Robert Mager published *Preparing Instructional Objectives* in 1962. In his short and highly readable book, Mager suggested that an objective ought to describe "what the student will be doing when demonstrating his achievement and how you will know he is doing it" (p. 53). **Mager's behavioral objectives** have three parts:

1. An observable behavior
2. The conditions under which the behavior will occur
3. Criteria for acceptable performance

Examples of objectives written according to Mager's format are listed in Table 11.4.

Gronlund's Instructional Objectives. An alternate and very popular approach to preparing objectives has been suggested by Norman Gronlund (1995). **Gronlund's instructional objectives** *include a general term, such as* know, understand, *or* apply, *followed by specific learning outcomes that operationally define what we mean when we say a learner*

11.12
Suppose you want your students to understand the main ideas in a passage. Using Mager's format, write an objective that would reflect this goal.

Table 11.4

Objectives using Mager's approach

Objective	Condition	Performance	Criteria
Given a list of sentences, the student will identify the adjective in each.	given a list of sentences	identify	each
Given 10 problems involving subtraction with regrouping, the student will correctly solve 7.	given 10 problems	solve	7 of 10
Given a ruler and compass, the student will construct the bisector of an angle to within 1°.	given a ruler and compass	construct	within 1°

Table 11.5

Objectives using Gronlund's format

General Objective	Specific Learning Outcome
Understands concepts	1. Writes definitions of concepts 2. Identifies examples of concepts 3. Generates examples of concepts 4. Identifies coordinate concepts
Solves problems	1. Identifies information relevant to the problem 2. Describes problem qualitatively 3. Translates qualitative description into numerical symbols 4. Estimates answer 5. Generates solution to problem

11.13
Using Gronlund's format, rewrite your objective that focuses on "main ideas" from Note 11.12.

"knows," "understands" or "applies," for example. Objectives written according to Gronlund's format are illustrated in Table 11.5.

In comparing Mager's and Gronlund's formats, you can see that Gronlund's objectives don't include conditions and criteria. He directly addresses the issue, stating that they "are especially useful for programmed instruction and for mastery testing in simple training programs. When used for regular classroom instruction, however, they result in long cumbersome lists that restrict the freedom of the teacher" (Gronlund, 1995, p. 10). Classroom experience supports Gronlund's position. Rarely do teachers specify conditions and criteria in their objectives, although thinking about both of these helps teachers design effective assessments. Mager's work is significant because of his historical impact, but most of the curriculum materials you'll encounter use a modification of Gronlund's approach.

Preparing Learning Activities

Once objectives have been specified, the next step is for the teacher to design ways of helping students reach them. This step involves selecting learning activities. For instance, Mai's goal was for students to understand how to convert fractions to decimals. She planned to help students reach her goal by presenting problems, explaining how they are solved, and having students practice solving them. These were her learning activities.

11.14
Suppose your objective is for first graders to improve their awareness of whether or not they're paying attention in lessons. Describe how you would prepare and organize learning activities to reach this goal.

Organizing Learning Activities

Merely selecting learning activities isn't enough. The activities must be organized and sequenced to be most effective. For instance, Mai began her lesson with a familiar example using coins. This progression from the familiar to the abstract was designed to show her low-ability students how math relates to their world. Her decision to sequence the activity this way took motivation into account and was part of the organizational process. Decisions such as these are conscious decisions teachers make as they plan ways of helping students attain objectives.

Task Analysis: A Behavioral Planning Tool.

> Kelly Ryan stared at the second-grade math book and didn't know where to start. Her assignment in her methods class was to identify a topic in the area of math, plan a lesson, and teach it to a small group of second-graders. She had met with Mrs. Ramirez, her cooperating teacher, and they had identified two-digit subtraction with regrouping as a topic that needed more work. Mrs. Ramirez had even given her some work sheets with subtraction problems:

$$
\begin{array}{ccccc}
98 & 27 & 25 & 72 & 45 \\
-19 & -18 & -16 & -13 & -36 \\
\hline
\end{array}
$$

> Kelly sat a bit bewildered, not knowing where to begin.

Task analysis can be a valuable planning tool when teachers are uncertain about all the elements involved in learning a concept or skill. **Task analysis** *is the process of taking a skill or other form of content and breaking it down into its component parts* (M. Gardner, 1985; Merrill, 1983). Breaking a complex skill into simpler subskills helps the teacher plan for instruction; it also helps the learner by breaking a large task into smaller steps. (Basic steps in doing a task analysis are outlined in Figure 11.2.)

Teachers begin a task analysis by specifying the "terminal behavior," the behavior students will be able to demonstrate when the lesson is finished. This is stated in the objective, such as "converting fractions to decimals" in Mai Ling's case, or "solving two-digit subtraction problems that require regrouping" in Kelly Ryan's.

Task analysis helps in the planning process by *identifying the prerequisite skills* needed to reach the final objective. Some prerequisite skills for performing two-digit subtraction with borrowing are as follows:

- Knowing basic subtraction facts (e.g., 7 – 5)
- Understanding place value (e.g., 15 is really 1 "ten" plus 5 "ones")
- Being able to do two-column subtraction with no regrouping when the bottom number is a single digit (e.g., 15 – 4)

You can see the influence of behaviorism in this process; the emphasis is on discrete, observable behaviors, which are to be mastered before complex behaviors are tackled.

Once identified, subskills must be put in a sequence. R. Gagne (1985) describes this sequence as a learning hierarchy and presents evidence that learning prerequisite skills does facilitate learning target skills (R. Gagne & Dick, 1983). The sequence in Kelly Ryan's case is straightforward: Students must first know basic facts and place value, then one-digit from two-digit subtraction, and two-digit from two-digit subtraction without regrouping before they can understand subtraction with regrouping.

Figure 11.2

Performing a task analysis

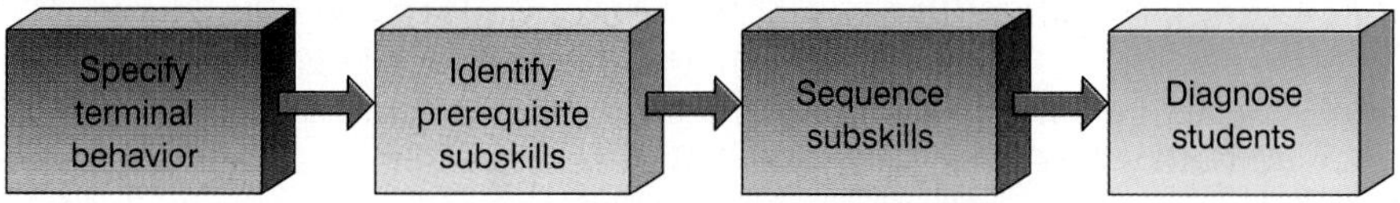

11.15

Suppose you want your students to be able to write sentences using adverbs properly. Design a brief task analysis for this skill.

Having sequenced the skills, teachers determine which of these the students lack; this determination is usually done by pretesting at the beginning of a unit. Kelly's instruction will depend, for example, on whether her students understand subtraction without regrouping. If they do not, the topic will need to be reviewed or even formally retaught before she moves to regrouping (Rosenshine & Stevens, 1986).

Whether or not teachers adhere to a behavioral view of learning, task analysis has value in the planning process. First, it encourages them to think about their goals in concrete terms. By carefully thinking about their goals, they can identify the specific outcomes they want for their students. In doing this, task analysis helps shift teachers' attention away from content to students and what they need to do to be successful. By encouraging teachers to ask, "What do students already know, and how can I design learning activities to build on this knowledge," task analysis helps in the designing of lessons that help students learn.

Assessment

The final phase of the Tyler model calls for specifying assessment procedures. Mai followed the model by stating in advance how her students would be assessed. Notice also that the objective specified the assessment at the outset and that the objective, learning activity, and assessment procedure were all consistent. This is the ideal that Tyler advocated as he conceived his model. Ron, in contrast, didn't specify any assessment, and his plan gives no insight into how his students would be assessed. A major advantage of specifying objectives during the planning process is that they provide a blueprint for assessments. We discuss this idea further in Chapter 13 when we describe assessment procedures in detail.

In reviewing the linear rational model, you can see that it is a logical and focused framework for planning instruction. It makes sense to consider first what you want students to learn, then to select ways of helping them learn it, and finally to establish a means of determining the extent to which the learning has taken place. This is the logical aspect of the model. The focused aspect of the model is its emphasis on student content and skill outcomes.

Learner-Centered Planning: Psychological Principles

11.16

To what theory of learning do the learner-centered psychological principles most closely relate? Explain, citing evidence from the principles themselves.

Because of its emphasis on specific objectives and observable behaviors, the linear rational model is commonly described as a behaviorist approach to planning. As you saw in Chapters 7 and 8, however, a growing body of research now suggests that learning doesn't necessarily proceed in discrete and isolated steps that must be mastered before moving to more complex behaviors, but rather that knowledge is constructed by individual learners and that it depends on the context in which it is learned and the real-world application to which it is put (Brophy, 1992; J. Brown et al., 1989; Marshall, 1992). This view of learning shifts the focus away from the teacher and a predetermined curriculum and toward the learner. It has resulted in a number of learner-centered initiatives, among them the American Psychological Association's *Learner-Centered Psychological Principles: Guidelines for School Redesign and Reform* (Presidential Task Force on Psychology in Education, 1993). In addition to guiding the reform of U.S. schools, the "learner-centered psychological principles" are also having an important influence on the way teachers are prepared. These principles are outlined in Table 11.5; they have important implications for planning and instruction. We turn now to planning based on them.

Table 11.6

APA learner-centered psychological principles

Principle	Description
1: The nature of the learning process	Learning is a natural process of pursuing personally meaningful goals, and it is active, volitional, and internally mediated; it is a process of discovering and constructing meaning from information and experience, filtered through the learner's unique perceptions, thoughts, and beliefs.
2: Goals of the learning process	The learner seeks to create meaningful, coherent representations of knowledge regardless of the quantity and quality of data available.
3: The construction of knowledge	The learner links new information with existing and future-oriented knowledge in uniquely meaningful ways.
4: Higher-order thinking	Higher-order strategies for "thinking about thinking"—for overseeing and monitoring mental operations—facilitate creative and critical thinking and the development of expertise.
5: Motivational influences on learning	The depth and breadth of information processed, and what and how much is learned and remembered, are influenced by (a) self-awareness and beliefs about personal control, competence, and ability; (b) clarity and saliency of personal values, interests, and goals; (c) personal expectations for success or failure; (d) affect, emotion, and general states of mind; and (e) the resulting motivation to learn.
6: Intrinsic motivation to learn	Individuals are naturally curious and enjoy learning, but intense negative cognitions and emotions (e.g., feeling insecure, worrying about failure, being self-conscious or shy, and fearing corporal punishment, ridicule, or stigmatizing labels) thwarts this enthusiasm.
7: Characteristics of motivation-enhancing learning tasks	Curiosity, creativity, and higher-order thinking are stimulated by relevant, authentic learning tasks of optimal difficulty and novelty for each student.
8: Developmental constraints and opportunities	Individuals progress through states of physical, intellectual, emotional, and social development that are a function of unique genetic and environmental factors.
9: Social and cultural diversity	Learning is facilitated by social interactions and communication with others in flexible, diverse (e.g., in age, culture, family background), and adaptive instructional settings.
10: Social acceptance, self-esteem, and learning	Learning and self-esteem are heightened when individuals are in respectful and caring relationships with others who see their potential, genuinely appreciate their unique talents, and accept them as individuals.
11: Individual differences in learning	Although basic principles of learning, motivation, and effective instruction apply to all learners (regardless of ethnicity, race, gender, physical ability, religion, or socioeconomic status), learners have different capabilities and preferences for learning mode and strategies. These differences are a function of environment (what is learned and communicated in different cultures or other social groups) and heredity (what occurs naturally as a function of genes).
12: Cognitive filters	Personal beliefs, thoughts, and understandings resulting from prior learning and interpretations become the individual's basis for constructing reality and interpreting life experience.

Learner-Centered Planning: A Contextual Planning Model

Learner-centered planning is reflected in the **contextual planning model,** *which considers the traditional questions of teaching such as goals, learning activities, student motivation, and assessment but answers the questions by focusing on guiding learners' own construction of understanding and helping them learn to monitor their own thinking and learning, rather than simply "transmitting" knowledge* (Bransford, 1993; Resnick & Klopfer, 1989). Let's look now at these planning elements.

Stating Goals and Outcomes

In planning for learner-centered instruction, goals and outcomes are as—or even more—important as they would be when using a teacher-centered approach, but stating them is a bit more complex. The teacher is no longer thinking of specific behaviors that can be practiced to mastery, with appropriate reinforcement along the way. Rather, knowledge acquisition is demonstrated in the context of real-world problems. For example, Ron Adams wanted his students to be able to explain why the can of pork and beans burst when left too long in a campfire, why people are warned to avoid removing the radiator cap from a hot engine, and why bridges have expansion joints. All these explanations relate to his goal of having the students understand the relationships between heat, expansion, pressure, and the movement of molecules. Each new experience is woven into this general goal and contextually embedded.

Although goals are important, teachers must also remain flexible. Students' responses and their current understanding may require that goals and instructional strategies be altered, sometimes in the middle of a lesson (Brooks & Brooks, 1993). You saw this in Tracey Stoddard's lesson in Chapter 7. Her students' current understanding of heat resulted in changing the direction of her lesson to conduct a series of experiments that resulted in them acquiring a more sophisticated understanding of heat. You also saw it in Ron's planning. As he said, "I know what I'm after with the students, but I don't have specific objectives down for each lesson because it depends on how they're coming along." In addition, learner-centered psychological principles suggest that learning is increased when students are aware of and develop control over their own thinking as they work. This then becomes an additional goal that is woven through all learning activities. Content outcomes are only part of the goal; the processes the students use to get there and the depth of their understanding are equally important.

> **11.17**
>
> To what concept does students becoming "aware of and developing control over their own thinking" refer?

Designing and Organizing Learning Activities

As with goal setting, designing learning activities may be even more critical when planning for learner-centered instruction. Two components are essential when designing learning activities: authentic tasks and multiple representations of content. Let's look at them.

Authentic Tasks.   You saw in Chapter 7 that one characteristic of constructivism was that "meaningful learning occurs within authentic learning tasks." **Authentic tasks** *are classroom learning activities that require understanding similar to the understanding that would be used in the world outside the classroom* (Needels & Knapp, 1994). This definition suggests that as teachers plan, they should make an effort to embed learning activities in real-world tasks and problems. Ron Adams consciously planned for an authentic task with his videotape of the pork and beans in the campfire, commenting on it both as an attention getter and a "real world" problem. Having his students explain why people shouldn't take the cap off a hot car radiator is also an authentic task.

As teachers acquire experience, authentic tasks can be developed in a variety of areas. Patty Kramer, in Chapter 8, who had her students find the area of the school grounds to determine the cost, used an authentic task. Having students in an English class write an opinion column about a public issue and having history students conduct interviews to develop oral histories of past events are also examples of authentic tasks in other subject areas.

Multiple Representations of Content.   Placing students at the center of the learning process acknowledges that knowledge construction is a personal process and that students construct understanding that makes sense to them. Ensuring individual understanding requires multiple representations of topics, or "criss-crossing a conceptual landscape" (Spiro et al., 1992), as we discussed in Chapter 8. Certain ways of representing ideas are meaningful to some students, and different representations will be meaningful to others. Providing an array of representations acknowledges the uniqueness of students and provides multiple paths for making ideas meaningful.

Let's look again at the way Ron Adams planned to represent his content. He included the following:

- The video of the pork and beans in the campfire
- A demonstration of heat and expansion with the balloon-covered soft-drink bottle in hot water
- A model illustrating the influence of heat on molecular motion
- A hands-on activity where a hard-boiled egg is pushed into a jar to illustrate the effect of heat and pressure in an open system
- A demonstration illustrating the relationship among mass, volume, and density

He used five different representations, all of which related to his goal of understanding heat, expansion, and pressure. Studying each representation and how it relates to the others resulted in a deeper understanding of the topic (Spiro et al., 1992). Preparing different ways of representing content is perhaps the most difficult planning task a teacher has. It

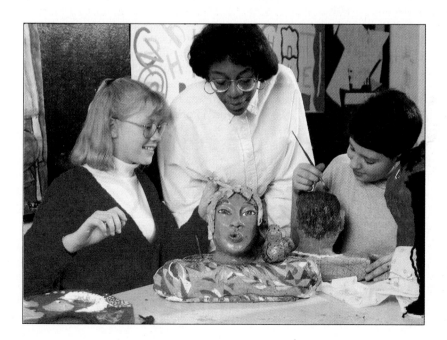

11.18

If a teacher cannot prepare a learning activity that involves an authentic task, does this imply that the activity or goal to which it is related is inappropriate? Explain.

Authentic tasks and multiple representations of content help students see how abstract ideas relate to their lives.

requires both a thorough knowledge of the topic and thorough pedagogical content knowledge. Ron demonstrated both in his planning.

Assessing Current Understanding

You saw in Chapter 7 that an additional characteristic of constructivism is "new learning depends on current understanding," and the third learner-centered principle (see Table 11.5) stresses the importance of linking new to existing information. These points mean that teachers need to consciously plan to gain insight into students' current understanding.

Assessing current understanding can be accomplished in a number of relatively easy ways, each of which involves some planning. For example, teachers can give formal pretests, they might simply ask students to describe their current understanding of a topic, or they might begin a lesson and informally assess the students' understanding on the basis of their comments and responses to questions.

Ron Adams used a particularly effective form of pre-assessment with his students. He presented his video and had students describe in writing their understanding of why the can burst. This approach was effective for at least three reasons. First, the students described their understanding of a specific event—the bursting can. Beginning with a concrete demonstration and having students describe their understanding of it provides students an opportunity to demonstrate their understanding in a meaningful, real-world context. Second, by having the students write their explanations, he assessed each individual's understanding. Third, his assessment was easy to prepare and thus saved valuable planning and teaching time.

Planning for Social Interaction

In Chapter 7, you saw that "learning is facilitated by social interaction" is one characteristic of constructivism, and you see this same statement in the ninth learner-centered principle (see Table 11.5). This point suggests that teachers should consciously plan to capitalize on the social nature of learning.

To teachers, planning for social interaction often means "put the students into groups." It isn't quite that simple, however. If student groupwork isn't carefully planned, it can result in student confusion and a great deal of wasted time. Effective groupwork requires clearly specified tasks, learning how to work together, and careful teacher monitoring.

In whole-group activities, social interaction is facilitated by teacher questioning. If teachers are not skilled in questioning, they tend to revert to mini-lectures, and the benefits of social interaction are lost. (We discuss the characteristics of effective groupwork and teacher questioning in Chapter 12.)

A critical part of the process is the quality of the representations teachers use. You saw earlier that "multiple representations of content" are critical in student-centered learning, and they are critical if teachers are to capitalize on the benefits of social interaction. If representations are clear and meaningful, students will be both able and inclined to be involved in discussions. If the representations are ineffective, virtually no amount of teacher guidance will result in meaningful discussions.

Planning the Learning Environment

Learner-centered instruction requires a classroom environment in which students feel free to take risks and offer conclusions, conjectures, and evidence without fear of criticism or embarrassment. It also requires students who are willing to listen to each other, wait their

---

11.19
Assessing current understanding on the basis of students' comments is time-efficient and relatively simple. However, this process can easily lead to erroneous conclusions on the part of the teacher. Explain why.

11.20
What does "clear" and "meaningful" knowledge representations mean? Illustrate your explanation with at least two different examples.

turn, and remain attentive while others are talking. Students may not have these abilities or inclinations when learner-centered instruction is first introduced. If this is the case, teachers need to help students develop as independent learners and assist them in accepting responsibility for their own behavior when groupwork discussions are taking place. Conscious planning will help identify the specific skills to be developed and the strategies, such as modeling, that will be used to teach them.

Planning for Assessment

Learner-centered instruction also has implications for assessment. Rather than answer questions on abstract and isolated problems, students will be asked to demonstrate understanding in realistic, lifelike contexts. In addition to assessing students' ability to apply the information they've learned, teachers will gather information about the students' thinking in the process. (We discuss these "alternative" or "authentic" assessments in detail in Chapter 13.)

From this discussion, you can see that learner-centered instruction requires planning that involves goals, organizing and sequencing learning activities, and assessments as much as do teacher-centered approaches. Learner-centered approaches, however, require more care in the way content is represented, as well as conscious planning for the learning environment and the social interaction that takes place within it. In addition, teachers need to be more flexible in their planning, adapting goals and strategies as instruction unfolds.

> **11.21** ▬
> Explain why planning based on a behaviorist approach would be simpler than learner-centered planning.

Classroom Connections

Using Planning to Make Your Teaching Effective

1. Identify what you want your students to be able to do after you're finished with a lesson or unit and let this be your guide for planning.
    - A geometry teacher emphasizes the importance of proofs to her students and their parents. She then spends much of her planning time creating problems and examples to help the students learn to do proofs.
    - An elementary teacher wants her students to become skilled writers. She keeps this goal in mind as she designs thematic, interdisciplinary units that require written communication in a number of areas. For example, in a unit on community helpers, she has students write letters to police officers and fire fighters, plan presentations in writ-

ing, and design and construct posters to illustrate what they've learned.

2. Adapt your planning to the task demands of the situation.
    - In a social studies lesson, the teacher is teaching a unit on the American Depression. He modifies plans he used when he taught in a rural, agricultural setting to focus on his present situation which is urban and industrial. He changes the focus from implications of the Depression for farmers to how the Depression affected factory workers and their lives.
    - A veteran teacher is beginning a new unit on pollution. Because it's new, she goes to the library and curriculum lab for materials and talks with other teachers about her ideas. Her plans for this unit are more detailed than those for other units.

3. Prepare a variety of representations of the content you want students to understand.

- A social studies teacher involved in a unit on war and conflict as instruments of social change has students read information about the American, French, and Russian Revolutions. She also prepares a matrix in which excerpts from the students' reading are placed. Then, she prepares a series of case studies illustrating the thinking of different people in each of the countries during these time periods.

- A second-grade teacher doing a unit on chemical and physical change plans to have the students melt ice, crumple paper, dissolve sugar, break toothpicks, and make Kool-Aid all to illustrate phys-

ical change. She also plans to have them watch a laser disc that describes physical change. She further plans to have them melt sugar, burn paper, pour vinegar into baking soda, and chew soda crackers to illustrate chemical change.

4. Plan for social interaction.

- A geography teacher involved in a lesson on the geography and economy of different regions in the United States plans to have students work in groups of three to identify similarities and differences in the regions. As students work in groups, they develop a chart comparing the different regions, and these charts form the basis for a whole-class discussion.

 ## Planning to Accommodate Learner Diversity

As you've seen throughout this text, student populations are becoming increasingly diverse. Students bring with them different ways of interacting, studying, and learning, all of which are influenced by their homes, neighborhoods, and cultures. In this section, we examine the implications this diversity has for teacher planning, particularly for learner-centered instruction, which is built on student interaction.

Classroom Interaction: Research Results

Classroom interaction patterns are amazingly homogeneous across the United States, both over time and across grade levels (Cazden, 1986; Cuban, 1984):

> [T]he dominant form of interaction is the teacher-directed lesson in which the instructor is in control, determining the topics of discussion, allocating turns at speaking, and deciding what qualifies as a correct response. Verbal participation is required of students. Implicitly, teaching and learning are equated with talking, and silence is interpreted as the absence of knowledge. Students are questioned in public and bid for the floor by raising their hands. They are expected to wait until the teacher awards the floor to one of them before answering. Speaking in turn is the rule, unless the teacher specifically asks for choral responses. Display questions prevail. Individual competition is preferred to group cooperation. Topics are normally introduced in small and carefully sequenced steps, with the overall picture emerging only at the end of the teaching sequence. (Villegas, 1991, p. 20)

11.22 ■
What theory of learning is implied in this quote? Explain and document your explanation with information taken from the quote.

Although this form of interaction may be functional for some students, research indicates it may be inappropriate for others. Many students come from cultures in which adults and children interact in ways that differ from the patterns found in most classrooms. Let's look at these differences and ways that teachers can plan to accommodate this diversity.

Accommodating Diversity: Experimental Programs

KEEP: The Kamehameha Early Education Program

Teachers working with Hawaiian students noticed these youngsters' inability to effectively interact in regular classroom lessons; either they didn't participate at all, or they participated in inappropriate ways, breaking in and interrupting other participants (Au, 1992; Tharp, 1989). These behavior patterns and their consequences have resulted in lowered achievement and lowered self-esteem.

Researchers attempting to explain this problem went into Hawaiian homes and observed the children as they interacted with adults, siblings, and peers. They observed a conversational style incompatible with school settings. In homes, Hawaiian children jumped into conversations, contributing freely as an adult or other child spoke. There were no clear turns marked by pauses; instead, several people talked at once, and overlapping speech was common. As a result, school felt strange to the children when teachers didn't allow them to join in whenever they wanted.

Working with these differences, researchers helped teachers adjust their questioning strategies to the Hawaiian students. Here's how one group reading lesson sounded. (The brackets indicate people speaking at the same time.)

Teacher:	Why do you think the author wrote this story? What did he want—what did he want you to learn from it?
Chad:	About moths
Teacher:	About moths. What—what else?
Natasha:	[Caterpillars
Kamalu:	[You can't keep things in
	you can't keep things [forever
Chad:	[in jars
Kamalu:	They have to come [like moths
Darralyn:	[how to take care of it
Kamalu:	[You can't keep them in a glass jar forever
Natasha:	[You can keep a dog or cat forever
	but like insects you cannot keep 'em [forever
Teacher:	[Okay
Natasha:	they have to be [free
Chad:	[Hey, once
	I kept one lizard forever
Keala:	[Born to be free
Teacher:	[Excuse me
	Is there anything else that they were telling us?
	[she was trying to tell us
Keala:	[Yeah
Teacher:	about? (Au, 1992, pp. 10–11)

Notice how the interaction patterns overlapped, with students joining in to help with each other's thoughts. Also, many interchanges went from student to student. The teacher intervened only when necessary to clarify a point. Both adjustments made the classroom interaction more like the conversation patterns in the Hawaiian home.

The results in terms of student achievement are positive. "Hawaiian children in regular classrooms are among the lower achieving minorities in the United States; in Kame-

> **11.23**
> Research with low-achieving students in small reading groups found a positive correlation between call-outs and achievement. How might you explain this finding and the one from the KEEP project?

hameha Schools KEEP classrooms, they approach national norms on standard achievement tests" (Tharp, 1989, p. 350).

Wait-Time: Working With Native American Students

11.24
Wait-time was discussed but not defined in this section. What is meant by "wait-time"?

Similar efforts to make questioning strategies compatible with Native American interaction patterns have also been successful (Tharp, 1989). Researchers noticed differences between the wait-times of Anglo and Navajo teachers. Anglo teachers would interpret pauses in a Navajo student's response as a sign of a completed answer, not realizing that long pauses (by Anglos' standards) and silences were a regular part of Navajo conversation. Interrupted in this way, Navajo students felt unappreciated and uncomfortable, and they became less willing to participate. Adjusting wait-times produced expected results; in one study of Pueblo Indian children, students in longer wait-time classes participated twice as frequently as those in shorter wait-time classes (Winterton, 1977).

Strategies for Accommodating Diversity: Implications for Planning

As you saw in the examples with Hawaiian and Native American students, what works with one group may not with another, so prescribing guidelines is difficult. In addition, broad prescriptions for a cultural group may be inappropriate for individuals within it (e.g., extroverted or shy) or subgroups (e.g., females, gifted students) within that group. Teachers need general strategies that can be applied according to their best professional judgment. Two important ones are (a) learning about student interaction patterns and (b) planning for student involvement and success.

Learning About Student Interaction Patterns

Teachers need to consciously plan to learn about the cultures of their students. For example, as teachers interact with their students, they should consciously listen to students from different cultures to understand how they interact with their peers and other adults. Research indicates that teachers who understand their students' speech patterns accept and use student responses more frequently than those who lack this understanding (Washington & Miller-Jones, 1989).

Teachers can gain valuable information about student interaction patterns by working with them in extracurricular activities, talking with students outside class, and even eating lunch with them periodically. Developing lines of communication with parents and talking with colleagues from other cultures can also provide valuable insights into ways to make classroom interactions more culturally compatible.

Planning for Student Involvement and Success

11.25
Why are high-quality content representations so important for students with diverse backgrounds? Think again about your response to Note 11.20 when you answer.

Two ways to consciously plan for involvement and success are (a) use high-quality content representations as focal points for discussion and (b) use open-ended questioning to encourage student involvement. Let's examine these strategies.

Use High-Quality Content Representations.   High-quality content representations provide a concrete frame of reference that the teacher can use in engaging students in meaningful dialogue. For instance, Jenny Newhall, in Chapter 2, represented the idea that air takes up space with her demonstration. Diane Smith, in Chapter 4, used concrete examples and their descriptions (pencils of different lengths and hair of different colors) to help her students talk about and understand comparative and superlative adjectives. Suzanne Brush, in Chapter 8, used the students' preferences for colors of jelly beans to help her students understand how the data for her graph related to their worlds. Kathy Brewster, in Chapter 9, used a simulation to represent the idea of a Crusade. These high-quality representations provided concrete reference points for meaningful classroom dialogue about important abstract ideas.

Use Open-Ended Questioning.   In Chapter 9, we emphasized the role of open-ended questions as a tool for involving all students, and they are particularly valuable when working with cultural minorities (Kasten, 1992). When combined with high-quality representations, open-ended questioning can invite broad student participation, ensure success for all students, and promote a positive classroom climate.

As an example, let's consider Ron Adams's demonstration with the bottles, balloons, and hot water again. After doing the demonstration, he could simply have the students *observe* and *describe* it and *compare* the heated bottle with an identical, unheated one. A wide variety of responses are possible:

"The bottles are the same size."

"The one on the right is hot."

"The balloon on the heated one is sticking up."

"The air in the one on the right has expanded."

"The volume of the air has increased."

Open-ended questions, in addition to ensuring success, also provide information about students' thinking. It is an excellent strategy for accommodating diversity, and it is consistent with constructivist views of learning and the learner-centered psychological principles that emphasize building upon students' existing knowledge base.

Open-ended questioning doesn't have to involve making observations and comparison, however. One project on the Navajo Reservation encouraged teachers to use a more student-centered approach to instruction incorporating open-ended questioning into an integrated unit on communities. In one lesson, as students studied photographs depicting local scenes, the teacher asked them to suggest items in the pictures that they needed in their community.

> Several students quickly jumped from their seats, calling out: "Houses!" "Sheep!" "Grazing (grass)!" "The school!" "Clinic!" "Chidis (automobiles)!" "Your relatives!" Though he periodically requested clarification, the teacher-demonstrator accepted all responses. Within minutes, students had volunteered so many ideas that he ran out of chalkboard space to write them all down. (McCarty, Lynch, Wallace, & Benally, 1991, p. 48)

By asking students open-ended questions that capitalized on their background knowledge, the teacher promoted student motivation through active involvement. These same strategies, together with extending wait-times and making an extra effort to prompt students from different cultures or those whose English is limited, help ensure success for all students (Boyle & Peregoy, 1990; Sutton, 1989).

Combining high-quality content representations and open-ended questions has three additional benefits. First, it accommodates differences in learners' backgrounds, perceptions, and ways of communicating. Second, it uses social interaction as a learning tool.

For instance, Ron could have his students work in pairs or small groups to make observations and comparisons with the bottles. Collaboration allows the students to benefit from each others' thinking, and he could strategically organize the groups so that members of different cultures work together.

Third, they provide opportunities for all students to learn alternative ways of expressing themselves.

> All of us, regardless of class or cultural background, have to acquire literacies that go beyond our home-based ways of making sense and using language. . . . The key challenge for schools is to introduce and enculturate students into these school-based discourses, without denigrating their culturally specific values and ways of using language. (Michaels & O'Connor, 1990, p. 18)

Because they ensure success and high levels of involvement, activities that combine concrete representations and open-ended questioning help students learn to use school-based language and different ways of interacting with each other.

Classroom Connections

Capitalizing on Diversity in Your Classroom

1. Learn about the interaction patterns of your students.
   - A fourth-grade teacher invites the parents, guardians, or caretakers of her students to a special evening session of her class. She asks the students to introduce the adult with them and to tell something about each. In turn, she asks each adult to say something about the child in his or her care.
   - A junior high teacher volunteers to co-sponsor a school club. He uses the club meetings to observe the way the students interact with each other.

2. Prepare high-quality representations of the content you're teaching.
   - An English teacher illustrates the concept of *verbal irony* with the description:
     Cal said, "I decided to overpower him with my knowledge of politics," when in reality Cal had virtually no understanding of politics.
   - A kindergarten teacher, wanting her students to understand the processes of following directions and sharing in cooperative groups, illustrates the processes by modeling listening, following directions, and sharing with a parent volunteer and aides.

3. Use open-ended questioning to promote involvement and success.
   - A physical science teacher starts many of her lessons with a demonstration and then begins the discussion with the question, "What did you observe here?"
   - A math teacher begins each of her reviews with a problem and the statement, "Who can describe this problem for us?"

4. To ensure success, prompt students when they are unable or are reluctant to answer.
   - A fourth-grade teacher working on adverbs with her class displays this sentence: "Jane's eyes moved quickly across the paper." She asks, "What is the adverb in the sentence? . . . Suzy?" When the student doesn't answer, she says, "How did Jane's eyes move?"
   - A seventh-grade math teacher displays a problem and asks, "What is the first step in the problem? . . . Jamaal?"
     Jamaal responds, "I don't know."
     The teacher continues, "What do you see in the problem, Jamaal?"

Planning: Research Results

Research Examining Objectives

When objectives first came into widespread use, they were enormously controversial. Proponents offered objectives as a panacea for all of education's ills; opponents criticized them with equal vigor. Proponents claimed clearly specifying objectives would help teachers keep their instruction focused. Critics countered on two points.

First, they argued that explicitly stating objectives would be unnecessarily time-consuming. According to one estimate, for example, more than 10,000 objectives would be needed to specify all the desired outcomes from studying an educational psychology text, such as the one you're now reading (McDonald-Ross, 1974). Second, critics suggested that many learner outcomes, such as the development of self-esteem or aesthetic appreciation, aren't conducive to description in an objective. Further, with the emphasis on students' construction of their own understanding, how can teachers write behavioral objectives that describe a student's thinking?

Despite criticisms, however, objectives are widely used because they provide a way for educators to communicate with each other. It is a rare elementary or secondary school textbook program that doesn't include them in the teacher's edition. For instance, the following objectives are taken from a recent eighth-grade physical science text.

1. **Distinguish** between kinetic and potential energy.
2. **Recognize** that energy can change from one form to other forms with no loss of total energy.
3. **Compare** the scientific meaning of *work* with its everyday meaning. (Thompson, McLaughlin, & Smith, 1995, p. 108A)

In addition, although the trend is away from objectives and instruction based on behavioral views of learning, most states and districts continue to use objectives in their curriculum standards and guidelines. For all intents and purposes, objectives are a fact of professional life. Teachers report using them as guides in their own planning (Sardo-Brown, 1988), and many teachers share their objectives with their students.

> **11.26**
> Predict what effects on learning sharing objectives with students has, compared with not sharing objectives with students. Explain your prediction.

Research and Teacher Planning

Now, let's look at teachers in their individual classrooms. In this section, we address two questions. First, how do teachers actually plan; second, how does planning affect teacher behavior? We've partially answered the second question by suggesting that planning promotes a feeling of professional security, helps organize instruction, and encourages the process of reflection. We further examine research into the planning process and compare these results with suggestions Tyler made in presenting the linear rational model.

Research Examining the Products of Teacher Planning

Products refers to the actual planning documents that teachers prepare. Mai's detailed plan, for instance, was her product, and Ron's notes were his.

Research examining teacher planning reveals some interesting patterns with respect to products. Students in teacher-training programs spend considerable time and effort learning to write objectives and detailed lesson plans. In other words, there is a heavy emphasis on producing written products.

11.27
If teachers don't write objectives and detailed lesson plans in the real world, what is the point in learning to write them in a teacher-training program?

Research indicates that these products are useful primarily because they allow the process of planning to be analyzed and developed. They are a way of helping preservice teachers learn to think systematically about planning and instruction. Once they get into the field and begin working with students, however, teachers often stop writing objectives and detailed plans (Morine-Dershimer & Vallance, 1976; Peterson, Marx, & Clark, 1978).

Mai Ling's and Ron Adams's approaches to planning illustrate these findings. As an intern, Mai planned in detail and wrote much of it down. Ron, a veteran, put less on paper, and what he did write was a brief sketch of topics and materials, which he used as a reminder. His goals and procedures already existed in his head, and all he needed were reminders to activate his long-term memory. When veterans write down more details, it typically appears as a sequenced list of activities and topics, rather than as objectives and procedures (C. Clark & Yinger, 1979; McCutcheon, 1982; Sardo-Brown, 1988).

Why don't veteran teachers write objectives and detailed plans? One reason is that putting written objectives and detailed procedures on paper is time-consuming. With the many and varied demands they face, teachers simply do not view the process of writing objectives and detailed plans as an efficient use of their time.

Another reason for not writing down lesson plans and objectives is that planning is often not a linear process. Rather than start with an objective that is followed by a learning activity, teachers commonly begin with a topic (Morine-Dershimer & Vallance, 1976; Peterson et al., 1978) or learning activity (C. Clark & Peterson, 1986; Sardo, 1982). This finding doesn't mean that objectives are ignored. Rather, they come later in the process (Peterson et al., 1978; Zahorik, 1975). The process is continuous, cyclical, and nested in past experience, rather than linear. A teacher in one study described daily lesson planning in this way: "In order to do this planning (for tomorrow), I have to remember what I did today and what I wanted to do when I made my unit plan" (Sardo-Brown, 1988, p. 74). This is what *cyclical* and *nested* mean.

11.28
Suppose all teachers were required to write detailed lesson plans. Do you think this would improve the quality of their instruction? Why or why not?

A third reason why planning doesn't begin with writing objectives is that objectives are often implicit in learning activities. A kindergarten lesson on geometric shapes would certainly have students' ability to identify the shapes as a goal for the activity. Also, objectives are often embedded in criterion-referenced math and reading tests. One teacher observed: "It seems ludicrous to list objectives. They wouldn't be doing the work unless it was aimed at an objective, because the test is all objectives based" (McCutcheon, 1982, p. 263).

Research Examining the Processes of Teacher Planning

The fact that veteran teachers don't prepare detailed written products doesn't imply that they don't go through the mental process of planning. Effective teachers are acutely aware of their goals and objectives, and because planning doesn't begin with objectives doesn't mean that goals and objectives don't serve as guides for teachers' thinking.

Ron, for example, was very aware of his goals, and he planned carefully, but most of it was internal and mental rather than external (preparing a written product). Because of his experience, it probably wasn't necessary to commit details to paper. This is typical. Veteran teachers rely strongly on past experience in planning future activities (Sardo, 1982). This ability to analyze lesson plans from a "what worked and what didn't work" perspective is one major difference between experienced and inexperienced teachers (Borko & Livingston, 1989).

11.29
What concepts from your study of information processing in Chapter 7 help you understand why Ron was able to consider his students' "motivation, their self-esteem, their long-range interest in science" without committing any of this information to paper?

Further, as you saw earlier in this section, Ron's brief notes belie the complexity of his planning. As he planned, he considered his students' motivation, their self-esteem, their long-range interest in science, and their level of development. These complex factors were not reflected in his written materials; they were revealed only in his conversation.

From this information, you can see that planning does indeed serve an important practical function in teaching and that effective planning involves much more than selecting, organizing, and sequencing content. It also includes decisions about the emotional

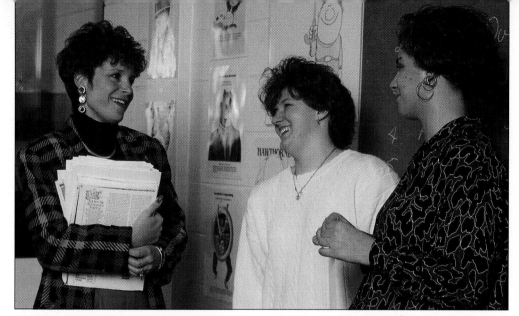

Research shows that teacher planning is a complex phenomenon that depends on the teacher's personality and level of experience.

characteristics of the students, their motivation, and their background and development. Plans help reduce the complexity of the teaching-learning process, and once made, teachers tend to follow them.

Planning: Implications for Teacher Training and Practice

Where does this discussion leave us? We've found that preservice teachers are trained to use a model that isn't explicitly followed by veteran teachers. Because this is the case, should the practice be stopped, and should teacher-training institutions stop requiring that students prepare written plans?

Probably not. An important argument can be made for continuing to study planning, including the Tyler model. It provides perspective; it is a historical frame of reference that teachers can use as they move to more student-centered approaches to planning.

For instance, in comparing the Tyler and contextual planning models, you can see that both focus on goals, designing and organizing learning activities, and assessments. The way they look at these planning elements differs: The contextual model provides for decisions, such as planning for authentic tasks, social interaction, and the creation of productive learning environments; the Tyler model doesn't address these. Nevertheless, goals, learning activities, and assessments are a part of both models.

This discussion suggests that teacher trainers should still help preservice teachers think in terms of goals and ways to help students reach them. In this process, trainers might de-emphasize discrete and decontextualized performances as goals and emphasize instead deep and interrelated understandings of topics that relate to the real world.

A similar comparison can be made with designing learning activities. Although effective learning activities have always been important, teachers now emphasize multiple representations of content, recognizing that a single representation probably won't be meaningful to all learners. This means that when teachers plan, they have to give more thought to the way they represent the topics they teach.

Teachers' Use of Textbooks: Implications for Practice

Textbooks are a fact of teaching life. Research indicates that teachers depend heavily on them; texts are involved, in some form, more than 75% of the time students spend in

11.30
Research cited by Sardo-Brown (1994) indicates that overrelying on textbooks can have a negative influence on the quality of instruction. Offer an explanation for this research result.

classrooms. Further, student teachers use them even when they experience teacher-training programs that devalue the use of textbooks (Zahorik, 1991).

Teachers' tendencies to rely on textbooks have implications for teacher training and practice (Sardo-Brown, 1994). Devaluing textbooks and encouraging teachers to abandon them isn't realistic. "Conceptions of teaching that do not include a place for textbooks and other classroom realities are likely to have questionable success in illuminating teaching" (Zahorik, 1992, p. 399). Instead, teachers should learn how to use textbooks and other materials in more effective ways. Three ways to use textbooks more effectively and improve your planning in general are (a) be selective in the topics you teach, (b) think about your reasons for selecting topics, and (c) think in terms of goals and representations of knowledge. Let's look at them.

Be Selective in the Topics You Teach.   As you saw earlier, teachers often begin their planning by considering topics, and textbooks and curriculum guides are the most common source of those topics. This finding doesn't mean, however, that every topic that exists in the textbook (or curriculum guide) should be formally taught (plus, you may want to include others you think are important). The content in a typical textbook has expanded dramatically over the last two decades, and it has become literally impossible to adequately "cover" all the topics that exist. "Parsimony is essential in setting out educational goals. Schools should pick the most important concepts and skills to emphasize so that they can concentrate on the quality of understanding rather than on the quantity of information presented" (Rutherford & Algren, 1990, p. 185).

Think About Your Reasons for Selecting Topics.   In other words, have a rationale for selecting the topics you teach. Because of the demands on their time and effort, teachers tend to select topics with little thought—they like the topic, they've taught it before, or it appears next in the book. These aren't adequate reasons.

Having rationales for teaching requires thoughtful reflection and perhaps some consultation with other teachers. It will pay off in learning that is more meaningful for students.

Think in Terms of Goals and Representations of Knowledge.   To consider goals and representations, let's look at Ron Adams's planning again. His topic was "heat, expansion, and pressure," but the topic alone didn't give him enough information to guide his planning. He asked himself, "What do I want the students to understand about heat, pressure, and expansion?" Having a clear goal in mind helped him prepare the "multiple representations of knowledge" that learners need to construct their understanding.

Thinking in terms of goals and representations of content is critical if teachers are to use learner-centered approaches to instruction. This thinking also has implications for the way teachers use textbooks. Rarely do books include enough representations to make the content meaningful, so teachers will have to provide additional ones if learners are to develop deep understanding of topics.

Instructional Alignment: A Key to Learning

The outcome of careful planning is **instructional alignment,** *which is the match between goals, learning activities, and assessment.* You saw alignment in both Mai Ling's and Ron Adams's planning even though Mai's approach tended to be teacher centered, whereas Ron's was more learner centered. Both had thought about their goals and had designed learning activities and assessments to be congruent with them.

Alignment is critical if learning is to be maximized. It is every bit as important when teaching is learner centered and based on constructivist views of learning as it is when more traditional approaches are used. This is why thinking in terms of goals and representations of knowledge is so important, and this also is why thoughtful planning is crucial.

11.31 ▬
Do you think that lack of instructional alignment is a common problem for teachers? Explain why you believe that it is or is not.

Classroom Connections

Applying Planning Research in Your Teaching

1. Reflect on past experience and use this information to make decisions about goals and learning activities.

   • A life science teacher who has had students memorize technical terms in the past analyzes past tests, talks with other teachers, and looks at future courses his students will be taking, and decides to focus more on the ecological relationships among living things.

   • A first-grade teacher makes the development of writing and communication skills a priority. She decides to have the students do at least one writing activity each day throughout the year.

2. Make conscious decisions about the topics you select from textbooks and other resources.

   • An American history teacher puts more emphasis on the French and Indian War than is presented in the text: "It was an important factor leading up to the American Revolutionary War, and students need to understand that."

   • A second-grade teacher skips several of the exercises on subtraction in the math text, instead focusing on applications in word problems: "I want students to understand what subtraction means and to be able to estimate and evaluate their answers to word problems. We'll do the computation on calculators."

Windows on Classrooms

At the beginning of the chapter, you saw how Mai Ling and Ron Adams planned for their teaching. Although they differed in their planning, they were both well organized, and they both considered the cognitive and affective aspects of their teaching. Both consciously planned for factors other than the mere delivery of content. The differences in their planning probably reflected the fact that Ron was more experienced than was Mai Ling.

Let's look now at a case study that describes another teacher also planning to teach the conversion of fractions to decimals. As you read the case study, compare the teacher's planning with Mai Ling's and Ron Adams's.

Kimberly Zibisky sat at her desk on Friday afternoon, getting ready for Monday.

"I'm going to start in a different place," she thought to herself as she got up to retrieve a packet of graph paper out of her filing cabinet and remembered the last time she taught fractions and decimals. "I thought I was so clear in showing them the steps that there was no way they could miss . . . but they did. It didn't work."

As Kimberly turned to her desk, she peered at the paper and thought to herself, "The squares are big enough, I believe. . . . We'll see how it works."

She semi-nodded to herself as she looked again at the graph paper and thought, "This should be enough for everybody."

Kimberly then began jotting some notes on a pad on her desk:

1. Graph paper—10 x 10 square
2. Mark off 25—make fraction
3. Do again with 50, 33—Make fractions
4. Work in pairs—turn around—1/8, 2/3
5. Show algorithm—compare to graph paper

Just as she finished writing the last line, Hattie Jordan, a colleague from across the hall, stuck her head in Kimberly's room, saw the packet, and said, "Hang it up. There's nothing worth graphing on a Friday afternoon. . . . We're all going out for a little TGIF. Want to come?"

"I'd love to," Kimberly smiled, "but I want to get myself ready for Monday before I come."

"What's so interesting?" Hattie wondered, looking over Kimberly's shoulder at her notes. "I don't mean to be nosy, but this is Friday afternoon. What's all that scratching?"

"My students are going to understand converting fractions to decimals this year," Kimberly said with determination. "Here, see whether this makes sense."

Kimberly then drew an outline around 100 squares on the graph paper so that it appeared as follows:

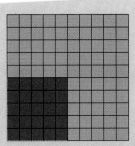

"See," she went on. "I give them the graph paper. They draw a 10 x 10 box so that they have 100 squares. Then, we color in 25 so that we have a fraction and the fraction is 25 100ths, which is a direct link to decimals. That's what this 10 x 10 stuff is here (pointing to her notes). The whole idea is to give them something tangible so that when they see 25%, it means something to them other than a number and a percent sign."

"Makes sense to me," Hattie shrugged. "It's clear as a bell. . . . What's this?" she asked, pointing to the 'Work in pairs—turn around' in Kimberly's notes.

"Oh, . . . after we mark off 25 squares to show 25 over 100 and then to 25%, we do the same thing by marking off 50 squares and 33 squares and getting the fractions from them. . . . The getting to one third from the 33 squares will probably take a little doing. . . . Then, I'm going to put the students in pairs and have them try to figure out

how many squares they will have when they have 1/8 and 2/3 as fractions.

"Some of them seem to be more willing to talk to a partner than they are to talk to the whole class," she added. "That's why I do that as often as I can. We'll discuss what each group comes up with as a whole group, and when they describe what they did, I'll find out something about their thinking. . . . Finally, when I think it makes sense to them, I'll show them the algorithm and show them how it relates to what they were doing with the graph paper. We probably won't get that far on Monday, but that's fine."

"Clever," Hattie nodded. "I'm impressed . . . but I'll be even more impressed if we get going."

"One more second. I want to write one more note. This morning's newspaper had some information on percentages, and I want to bring it in to class. I want to make some test questions out of it too. I'm writing a note to remind myself.

"Okay," Kimberly said finally. "I think I'm ready."

She picked up her notes, muttering, "I'll stick these in my book over the weekend."

She then pulled her plan book out of her desk, stuck her notes inside the front cover, and the two of them headed out the door.

Questions for Discussion and Analysis

Analyze Kimberly's planning now. In doing your analysis, you may want to consider the following questions. In each case, be specific and take information directly from the case study to defend your conclusions.

1. Of the planning functions—security, organization, and reflection—which was most evident in Kimberly's planning? Which was least evident?

2. On the basis of Kimberly's planning processes, which of the following would you say is the best estimate of the number of years she has taught prior to this year—1, 3, or more than 3?

3. On the basis of her planning, would you say Kimberly had a clear goal for her lesson? Why or why not?

4. Was Kimberly's primarily a teacher-centered or a student-centered approach to planning? How could she change her planning to reflect a different approach? Be specific in your suggestions.

5. Compare Kimberly's planning with that of Mai Ling and Ron Adams. On the basis of their planning, which of the three would you say is most student centered in her or his approach to planning? Which is most teacher centered? Defend your conclusion with information taken from the case studies.

6. Compare Kimberly's emphasis on the affective domain with that of Mai and Ron. Did she emphasize it more or less than they did? Defend your conclusion with information from the case studies.

7. Consider Kimberly's planning in the context of student diversity. How well did she accommodate diversity in her planning? Explain specifically.

8. Assess Kimberly's planning on the basis of the content of this chapter. If you believe her planning could have been improved, offer specific suggestions for improvement.

 ## Summary

Teacher Planning

Planning is a complex process. Effective teachers consider the classroom environment, students' cultural and intellectual backgrounds together with their expectations and beliefs, in addition to organizing content and designing learning activities when they plan.

Planning helps teachers organize their instruction, makes them feel more secure in difficult situations, and encourages them to reflect on their own teaching. Careful planning results in more focused lessons, greater learner participation, and less off-task behavior.

Prerequisites to Effective Planning

To plan effectively, teachers must understand the content they want to teach, know how to represent topics for learners, and understand the learning characteristics of their students. When topics are new or when teachers lack personal background, more study and effort are required.

Domains of Instruction

Teachers' goals may fall in the cognitive domain, which focuses on knowledge, understanding, and intellectual skills; the affective domain, which includes attitudes and values; or the psychomotor domain, which analyzes physical skills and abilities. Objectives in each domain can be classified into different levels, each of which requires different learner behaviors.

Domains of instruction are valuable because they help teachers in considering different levels of understanding, which can result in emphasis on goals that go beyond knowledge and memorization. The affective and psychomotor domains remind teachers that the development of attitudes, values, dispositions, and physical skills is part of students' total learning experience.

Approaches to Planning

Teacher-centered approaches to planning involve identifying objectives, preparing and organizing learning activities consistent with the objectives, and designing assessments that match both the objectives and the learning activities.

Learner-centered approaches to planning also involve goals, learning activities, and assessments, but in addition they also consider ways of making tasks authentic, how to represent content in a variety of ways, learners' current understanding, social interaction, and the learning environment.

Planning to Accommodate Learner Diversity

Teachers plan to accommodate learner diversity by learning about student interaction patterns and planning for student involvement and success through the use of high-quality content representations combined with open-ended questioning. This combination accommodates learner background differences and ways of communicating, capitalizes on the social nature of learning, and helps students learn to use school-based language and ways of interacting with each other.

Research Results on Planning

Teachers usually start the planning process with a topic or learning activity, and objectives follow. They also depend heavily on textbooks and curriculum guides for making planning decisions. Planning research suggests that teachers should be selective in the topics they teach and that they should think in terms of goals, knowledge representations, reasons for selecting topics and instructional alignment.

 # Important Concepts

affective domain (p. 442)

authentic tasks (p. 452)

Bloom's taxonomy (p. 442)

cognitive domain (p. 441)

contextual planning model (p. 452)

Gronlund's instructional objectives (p. 447)

instructional alignment (p. 464)

linear rational model of planning (p. 446)

Mager's behavioral objectives (p. 447)

pedagogical content knowledge (p. 439)

planning (p. 437)

psychomotor domain (p. 443)

reflection (p. 438)

task analysis (p. 449)

goats know

*C*hapter Outline

12

Teachers
and
Learners

"What are you doing with those cake pans?" Jim Barton asked his wife, Shirley, as he walked into the kitchen and saw her hard at work at the table.

"What do you think?" she grinned at him. "Do they look like cake?" she asked, holding up rectangular cardboard pieces drawn to resemble two cakes cut into pieces.

"Actually, they almost do," he responded, a bit impressed with her work.

"My students didn't score as well as I would have liked on the fractions part of the Stanford Achievement Test last year, and I promised myself that they were going to do better this year."

"But you said the students aren't as sharp this year."

"That doesn't matter. I'm pushing them harder. I think I could have done a better job last year, so I swore I was really going to be ready for them this time."

As Jim walked back into the living room with a slight smile on his face, he mumbled something about thinking that teachers who have taught for 11 years were supposed to burn out.

The next day, Shirley met with her 28 fourth graders, and they began their day, which usually follows this schedule:

8:30–10:00	Language arts (spelling, writing, grammar)
10:00–10:55	Math
10:55–11:05	Break
11:05–11:35	Science
11:35–12:00	Lunch
12:00–1:30	Reading
1:30–2:00	Social Studies
2:00–3:00	Rotating subjects (art, music, P.E., computer)

As Shirley walked up and down the aisles, she put two pieces of paper on each student's desk and stopped periodically to comment on someone's work or offer reassurance as the class completed a writing assignment. When she glanced at her watch and saw that it was 9:58, she announced, "Quickly put your writing in your folders and get out your math homework. We're running a little late today."

The students stopped their writing and passed the papers forward. She collected them from the first person in each row, and as she walked by Shelli, she paused and asked, "How are you feeling today, Shelli? Is your cold better?"

"A lot better," Shelli replied. "I've just got some sniffles now."

Shirley put the papers into a folder and stepped to the chalkboard as she watched the students put their reading materials away and pull out their math books. She wrote the following problems on the chalkboard:

$$\frac{3}{8} + \frac{2}{8} = \qquad \frac{3}{7} + \frac{4}{7} =$$

$$\frac{5}{12} + \frac{6}{12} =$$

At 10:01, the students had their math books out and were waiting.

"Now," she began as she pulled out two drawings designed to look like pizzas, each cut into eight parts, "We've been adding fractions, so for a moment, let's look again at what we've been doing. What does the 8 mean in the first problem? . . . Dean?"

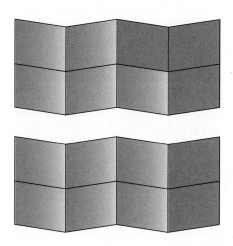

"We have eight parts of something altogether."

"Parts of what?"

" . . . Supposed to be pizza."

"And what kind of parts? . . . Emerson?"

" . . . "

"How do the parts compare with each other?"

" . . . They're all equal."

"How do you know?"

" . . . I . . . I can see them. . . . They look equal."

"Okay. Good," Shirley smiled. "We have two pizzas, both cut into 8 equal parts."

Shirley continued, asking Nel what the top numbers meant in the first problem. She then asked, "How much pizza did we eat altogether? . . . Gayle?"

"Five pieces."

"What part of a whole pizza did we eat?"

"I. . . . think . . . ⅝ of it."

"Good. And how did Gayle get that? . . . Estella?"

" . . . She added them up."

"How might we prove that adding them up is the thing to do? . . . Anyone?"

After a short pause, Natasha finally said, "We have three pieces there (pointing to the first drawing), and if we had two more pieces, we would have five altogether, so it would be ⅜ and ⅖, which would be ⅝ altogether."

"What do the rest of you think about that?" Shirley queried.

"I don't think so," Adam shook his head. "It looks like 5/16 to me."

"No, look," Natasha countered, pointing to the drawing. "We have only eight pieces altogether."

"What about the other drawing?"

"We're not on the other drawing. We're on this one. I said put two more pieces on this one."

Shirley watched as other students joined the discussion, which continued for a few more minutes, but didn't intervene. Finally, the students agreed that Natasha's "proof" seemed to make sense.

Shirley then continued with the second and third problems on the chalkboard and finished by saying as she tapped her knuckle on the chalkboard, "Now, let's think about these problems. What is similar about them, like pretend that they're all pizzas and we're adding pieces of them."

" . . . They all have the same pieces," Karen noted.

"I'm not sure what you mean," Shirley queried.

" . . . Like 7 and 7, and 12 and 12."

"Ahh, I see," Shirley nodded. "Each of these problems has the same denominator." She pointed respectively to the 8s, the 7s, and the 12s. "Yes," she said raising her voice, "let's keep that in mind as we study some more problems.

"Now," she continued as she strode vigorously across the front of the room, "we're going to shift gears because I've got another, different kind of problem." She pulled out the two cardboard rectangles drawn to resemble the cake that she had made the night before, one divided into thirds and the other divided in half.

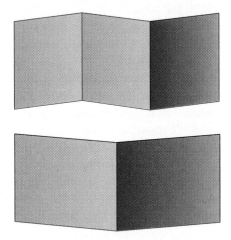

"Now, we have cakes instead of pizza," she smiled, "and I'm still hungry, so I eat this piece," she said, pointing to the third. "Then I go sort of wild and eat this piece too," pointing to the half. "How much cake have I eaten?"

"A third of one and a half of the other," Tenisha volunteered.

"Makes sense, . . . but is that more than a whole cake, less than a whole cake, or what part of a cake?"

" . . . I'm pretty sure less," Adam offered, peering at the two cakes.

"How do you think we could find out for sure?" Shirley wondered. She paused and then said, "To help us, take two of the pieces of paper from the copying room that I put on your desks while you were working on your writing and carefully fold them like our cakes here."

The students quickly took the papers from their desks and began folding. Shirley helped some of them who had trouble folding their papers into thirds.

"Now, we have two whole papers, which we'll pretend are our cakes. Let's think about our problem again. If we eat a third of one and a half of the other one, how much have we eaten altogether? . . . How can we figure that out?"

" . . . Let's lay one on top of the other," Jan suggested, after thinking for several seconds.

"Good idea. . . . Go ahead and try it."

" . . . It's less than a whole cake," Tanya offered after peering carefully at the papers.

"How much less?"

Tanya thought about it and gestured and shrugged an 'I don't know.'

"How about some other ideas? . . . Anyone?"

The students offered a few uncertain suggestions, and Shirley then asked, "Let's think about the work we've been doing. What did we just review?" pointing at the chalkboard.

"Adding up the pizzas," Juan offered.

"And what do we know about them?"

" . . . They weren't like the cakes," Bryan added.

"In what way?" Shirley asked with a quizzical shrug.

"They were the same. . . . They had the same-size parts. . . . And . . . these are different," he pointed to the cakes.

"Maybe we need to cut them different so they're the same," Enrico suggested.

This response prompted some additional discussion, after which Shirley offered, "Let me make a suggestion how we can get them to be the same, using Enrico's idea."

She continued, "How much cake do we have here? . . . Tim?"

" . . . A third."

"Fine," Shirley smiled. "Now, let's all fold our 'cakes' this way," and she folded the cardboard in half along the opposite axis as she watched the students. "How many pieces do I have altogether now? . . . Karen?"

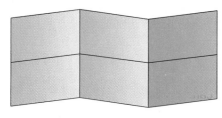

" . . . It looks like six," she responded uncertainly.

"Yes. Good, Karen. I saw you actually counting them," Shirley noted and then counted the six squares again herself. "So what portion is now shaded? . . . Jon?"

" . . . Two sixths."

"Excellent, Jon!" and she moved to the chalkboard and wrote ⅓ and ²⁄₆ alongside each other with an equal sign between.

"Now, how do we know that the ⅓ and ²⁄₆ are equal?"

"It's the same amount of cake," Dan shrugged.

Shirley then continued by having the students fold the second 'cake' into thirds so that they appeared as follows:

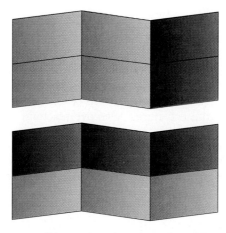

"Now, what do we see here?"

" . . . They both have the same number of pieces," Lorraine noted.

"And all the pieces are the same size," Crystal added.

"Ooh, ooh, I know!" Adam said excitedly. "We've eaten ⁵⁄₆ of the cake."

"That's an interesting thought, Adam. Would you explain that for us please?"

" . . . It's like the pizza. We have two pieces there, and three pieces there, so it's ⁵⁄₆ of the pizza, ah cake."

"I don't get that," Mike shook his head.

" . . . What if we cut them out, to see how many we have," Gail suggested.

"Good thought, Gail," Shirley nodded. "Let's do it. . . . Everybody cut out these pieces," she said, pointing to the marked pieces in the 'cake' on the top.

She watched as the students took out scissors from their desks and cut out the pieces.

"Now, go ahead and lay them over the other 'cake.' . . . What do you see there?"

"There are five pieces covered," John observed. "We ate ⁵⁄₆ of the cake alright."

"Now, let's think about what we did," Shirley continued. "What was our problem?"

" . . . We were trying to figure out how much cake we ate," Lakesha offered.

"Why was that a problem?"

"The pieces weren't the same size."

"So, what did we do about it? . . . Karen?"

" . . . We fixed them so they were the same size."

"And exactly how did we do that? . . . Bryan?"

" . . . We made the ⅓ of a cake into ²⁄₆, and we made the ½ a cake into ³⁄₆, and then we could just add them up."

Shirley then said with a grin, "You're all pretty clever. . . . Let's see how you do now," and she pulled out two more pieces of cardboard, one of which was divided into thirds and the other into fourths. She then guided the students' analysis of the second problem in the same way she had done with the first.

They then reviewed the problem as they did the first one, and Shirley said, "Tomorrow, I'll show you how we can figure out a little more quickly how to make the parts equal so that we don't have to work as hard as we did with the ⅓ and ¼."

Finally, seeing that it was 10:52, Shirley said, "It's nearly time for science. Put your math books and materials away, and we'll have our recess break."

In Chapter 9, you found that although some students are more intrinsically motivated than others, teachers have a powerful influence on all students' motivation to learn. Similarly, although some students are more capable learners than others, teachers strongly affect their students' achievement. A line of research that gathered momentum in the 1970s and 1980s identified patterns of teacher behavior that increase student achievement and labeled these patterns "effective teaching" (Brophy & Good, 1986). The later 1980s and 1990s, with the greater influence of cognitive psychology and increased understanding of learning, have marked a trend toward more student-centered instruction (Good & Brophy, 1994; Marshall, 1992). This chapter focuses on both the teacher effectiveness literature and the more recent research that has taken the profession "beyond effective teaching" to emphasize learner-centered instruction.

After you've completed your study of this chapter, you should be able to meet the following objectives:

▌ Identify examples of essential teaching skills in classroom settings.
▌ Identify characteristics of teacher-centered approaches to instruction.
▌ Identify characteristics of learner-centered approaches to instruction.
▌ Discuss the relationship between constructivist views of learning and learner-centered appraoches to instruction.
▌ Describe procedures for organizing and implementing student groupwork and cooperative learning.

 ## Teaching and Learning◀━━

In her lesson, Shirley did a number of things to promote learning. Some were overt and specific, such as the way she used concrete examples to illustrate her topic; others were subtler, such as her attitude and general orientation toward her work. Most of her actions are documented by research as being effective (Brophy & Good, 1986). In the next section, we examine this research.

Teacher Effectiveness: Defining Teaching Competence

12.1
What does the inability to find "universally effective methods" imply about teaching methodology? Explain.

Although research in teaching has a long history, evidence of a link between teacher actions and student achievement is relatively recent. Before the 1970s, researchers attempted to find connections between student achievement and teacher traits, such as a sense of humor or a particular personality type, as well as links between achievement and "universally effective methods," such as discovery learning or inquiry. Both proved fruitless (Dunkin & Biddle, 1974).

Then, a reanalysis of the data from the famous Coleman Report (Coleman et al., 1966), which had originally concluded that students' socioeconomic status (SES) was the primary factor influencing achievement, found that students in some classes learned much more than would be expected for their grade level and ability, whereas others achieved as expected or less. In trying to explain these differences, investigators videotaped and analyzed literally thousands of lessons, focusing on teachers' behaviors in both high- and low-achieving classes. After ensuring that students and resources were comparable, they found that teachers of high-achieving classes taught differently than did teachers of low-achieving ones (Gage, 1985; Good & Brophy, 1986, 1994). A description of these differences resulted in a body of knowledge called the **teacher effectiveness literature**, *which describes patterns of teacher behavior that are associated with high student achievement.* Since the 1970s, the teacher effectiveness literature has been influential in staff development, teacher evaluation, and teacher education programs.

The teacher effectiveness literature made an invaluable contribution to education; for the first time, the profession had a body of knowledge that was grounded in research. It was limited, however, in two important respects. First, it focused on basic aspects of teaching, which differentiated the least effective teachers from others, but it didn't identify the characteristics of outstanding teachers. Second, because it used standardized tests to assess effectiveness, it often measured isolated student knowledge instead of students' ability to apply their learning outside the classroom (Brophy, 1992).

In response to these limitations, research emerged during the 1980s that emphasized teaching for understanding and application in real-world settings (Brophy, 1992; Marshall, 1992; Perkins & Blythe, 1994; Resnick & Klopfer, 1989). Strongly influenced by constructivism (which we discussed in Chapters 2, 7, and 8), this research retained its emphasis on the vital role teachers play in student learning while recognizing students as active participants in the process. This is where we are today.

> **12.2**
> On what theory of learning is an emphasis on "isolated student knowledge" based? Explain.

Essential Teaching Skills

Suppose you sit in the back of any classroom, regardless of grade level or topic being taught. What would you expect to see in all effective teachers? Just as we're all familiar with the basic skills in reading, writing, and math that all learners need, in order to promote learning, there are *essential abilities that all teachers should have,* called **essential teaching skills**. Derived from the teacher effectiveness literature, these are the basic abilities one expects to see in all teachers, even those in their first year of teaching. These essential teaching skills are outlined in Figure 12.1.

Although for the sake of clarity we discuss the skills separately, they are interdependent, and none is as effective alone as it is in combination with the others. The balance and blend of these characteristics and skills are critical.

> **12.3**
> Think back to your study of Chapter 8 and identify one important skill that you would expect to see in expert teachers that you wouldn't expect to see in novices. How did the experts acquire these skills?

Figure 12.1

Essential teaching skills

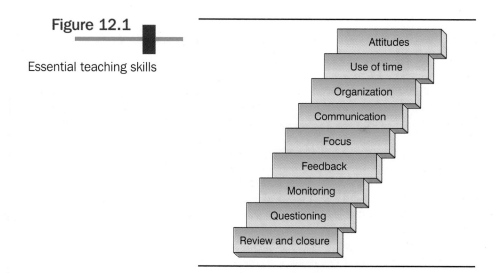

Attitudes

12.4

Shirley also demonstrated the caring, high expectations, enthusiasm, and modeling that you saw in the model for promoting student motivation in Chapter 9. Identify in the case study an example of each of these variables.

Although, admittedly, "attitude" is not a skill, we begin our discussion of essential teaching skills to emphasize how fundamental positive attitudes are to effective teaching. To see why, let's turn again to Shirley Barton and think about her general orientation to teaching. She believed that she could make a difference in her students' learning and that it was her responsibility to do so. She was able and willing to conclude, "I could have done a better job last year," and she expected to improve this year. Shirley was high in **teaching efficacy**, *which is the belief that teachers and schools have an important positive effect on students* (Bruning et al., 1995). Teachers high in efficacy, in addition to increasing student achievement, tend to use praise rather then criticism, to persevere with low achievers, to use their time effectively, and to be accepting of students and their answers. This characterization is in contrast with low-efficacy teachers, who spend less time on learning activities, "give up" on low achievers, and use criticism more than do high-efficacy teachers (D. Kagan, 1992a). High-efficacy teachers also tend to be more flexible, adopting new curriculum materials and changing strategies more readily than do low-efficacy teachers (Poole, Okeafor, & Sloan, 1989).

Use of Time

You saw in the previous section that high-efficacy teachers use their time effectively. It isn't quite as simple as it appears on the surface, however, because different levels of classroom time influence learning in different ways. They are outlined in Table 12.1.

As one moves from allocated time to academic learning time, the relationship with learning becomes stronger (Nystrand & Gamoran, 1989). In classrooms where students are engaged and successful, high levels of learning occur, and learners feel good about themselves and the material they're learning (Fisher et al., 1980).

12.5

What is the allocated time for the class you're now in? Of this time, how much does your instructor typically devote to instruction?

The goal of teachers is to increase each of the levels to the point where it's as close to allocated time as possible. Shirley's students, for instance, having made a quick and smooth transition from reading, had their math books out and were waiting at 10:01. The class lost only 1 minute of their allocated time at the beginning of the class, and they continued until 10:52. Of the 55 minutes allocated to math, Shirley devoted 52 minutes to instruction. Understanding how important it is for learning, Shirley used her time very effectively.

Table 12.1

Levels of classroom time

Level	Description
Allocated time	The amount of time a teacher or school designates for a content area or topic
Instructional time	The amount left for teaching after routine management and administrative tasks are completed
Engaged time	The amount of time students are actively involved in learning activities
Academic learning time	The amount of time students are actively involved in learning activities *during which they're successful*

Although one can't be sure from a written case study, Shirley's students also appeared to be engaged for most of her lesson, and comparisons of high and low achievers demonstrate the importance of such engaged time. In studies at both the elementary and high school levels, high-achieving students were on-task more than 75% of the time, compared with less than 50% of the time for low achievers (Evertson, 1980; Frederick, 1977). These results are intuitively sensible. If we go into a class to observe a teacher, one of the first things we would look for is whether students are paying attention.

Finally, your study of self-efficacy in Chapter 9 helps you understand the importance of academic learning time. There, you saw how important success is in maintaining motivation, and you know that motivation and achievement are closely linked. Effective teachers create learning activities in which students are both engaged and successful.

Organization

How many times do you put something away and later can't locate it? Have you ever said, "I've simply got to get organized," or, "If he'd just get organized, he could be so effective"? Organization affects the way people live because it determines how effectively they use time, and it is no less the case in teaching. Teachers who are "organized" have students who learn more than students of their less-organized counterparts (S. Bennett, 1978; Rutter et al., 1979).

Organization *includes the set of teacher actions that increase instructional time,* and this increase, in turn, increases learning. (You also saw in Chapter 10 that effective organization helps prevent classroom management problems.) The characteristics of effective organization are outlined in Table 12.2.

Shirley's organization resulted in effective use of students' time, and equally important, it saved her energy. Teachers who have their materials prepared and have established efficient routines can devote their working-memory space and physical energy to thinking about and guiding instruction. This time use is essential if they are going to regularly con-

> **12.6**
> You found in Chapter 9 that another factor, in addition to success, is necessary for students to feel good about themselves and the material they're learning. What is this factor? Why is it important?

Effective organization allows teachers to make the best use of instructional time.

Table 12.2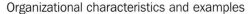

Organizational characteristics and examples

Dimension	Example
Starting on time	Shirley's students had their math books out and were waiting by 10:01.
Preparing materials in advance	Shirley had her cardboard "cakes" prepared and waiting.
Established routines	At Shirley's signal, the students passed their papers forward without having to be told specifically to do so.

duct engaging and meaningful learning activities. Organization is also important from the learners' perspective. Well-established routines are predictable and give learners a sense of order and equilibrium, all of which help create an environment conducive to learning.

Communication

Teacher language is one of the earliest and most widely researched variables in the teacher effectiveness literature, (Rosenshine & Furst, 1971). The link between effective communication and both student achievement and student satisfaction with instruction is well established (Cruickshank, 1985; Snyder et al., 1991). In this section, we examine four aspects of effective communication: (a) precise terminology, (b) connected discourse, (c) transition signals, and (d) emphasis.

Precise Terminology.   Precise terminology *means that teachers eliminate vague terms (e.g., perhaps, maybe, might, and so on, usually) from presentations.* When teachers use these seemingly innocuous terms in their explanations and responses to students' questions, students are left with a sense of uncertainty about the topics they're studying; this uncertainty detracts from learning (Smith & Cotten, 1980). For example, suppose you asked, "What do high-efficacy teachers do that promotes learning?" and your instructor responded, "Usually, they use their time somewhat better and so on," in comparison with, "They believe they can increase learning, and one of their characteristics is the effective use of time." The first response contains uncertainty, whereas the second is clear and precise.

Connected Discourse: Making Relationships Clear.   Connected discourse *means the teacher's lesson is thematic and leads to a point.* If the point in the lesson isn't clear, if it is sequenced inappropriately, or if incidental information is added without indicating how it relates to the topic, the classroom discourse becomes "disconnected" or "scrambled." Effective teachers keep their lessons on track and spend less time on matters unrelated to the topic than do their less effective counterparts (Coker, Lorentz, & Coker, 1980; Smith & Cotten, 1980).

Transition Signals.   Transition signals *are forms of verbal communication that remind students that one idea is ending and another is beginning.* When Shirley said, "Now, we're going to shift gears because I've got another, different kind of problem," or if an American government teacher said, "We've been talking about the Senate, which is one house of Congress. We're going to turn now to the House of Representatives," they were

---

12.7

To which level of classroom time (see Table 12.1) does precise terminology most closely relate?

12.8

Does the information in this section imply that teachers should avoid interjecting additional material into lessons—yes or no? Explain.

signaling a transition. Because not all students are at the same place mentally, a transition signal alerts them that they are making a conceptual change—moving to a new topic—and allows them to prepare for it.

Emphasis: Signaling Important Ideas.

Emphasis, a fourth aspect of effective communication, *alerts students to important information in a lesson and is communicated through verbal and vocal cues and repetition.* For example, Shirley raised her voice—a form of vocal emphasis—in saying, "Let's keep that in mind as we study some more problems." When teachers say, "Now remember, everyone, this is very important . . . ," or, "Listen carefully now," they're using verbal emphasis.

Repeating a point is also a form of emphasis. For instance, "What did we say earlier that these problems had in common?" reminds students of an important feature in the problems and aids cognitive elaboration by helping them link new to past information.

Focus

Let's review for a moment some of the ideas we've discussed so far. In discussing the essential teaching skills, we've concentrated on attitudes, use of time, organization, and clear communication. For any of these to influence student learning, students must be engaged in the lesson. Lesson focus attracts and holds students' attention throughout the learning activity.

You saw in Chapter 9 that **introductory focus** *attracts students' attention and provides a framework for the lesson.* In addition to attracting attention, it is designed to enhance motivation by arousing curiosity and making lesson content attractive.

Shirley provided introductory focus for her students by showing them the two "cakes" and saying, " . . . I've got a problem," and, "How much cake have I eaten?" Her "cakes," together with her problem, attracted students' attention and provided a context for the rest of the lesson.

Shirley's "cakes" also acted as a form of **sensory focus**, which is *the use of stimuli— concrete objects, pictures, models, materials displayed on the overhead, and even information written on the chalkboard—to maintain attention.* Her "cakes" gave students something to look at and provided a mental model to help them conceptualize an abstract idea. In looking back at some of the lessons you've already seen, Jenny Newhall's demonstration with the cup and water in Chapter 2, David Shelton's chart in Chapter 7, and Suzanne Brush's graph in Chapter 8 all provided forms of sensory focus. Sensory focus serves as a continual reminder of the lesson's topic and direction.

Feedback

Feedback, another essential teaching component, *is information about the accuracy or appropriateness of a response.* In Chapter 6, you found that effective feedback is *immediate* and *specific,* that it *provides corrective information* for the *learner,* and that it has a *positive emotional tone.* In Chapter 9, you found that it also increases motivation to learn (Clifford, 1990). Its role in improving learning is clear and well documented (Brophy & Good, 1986; Rosenshine & Stevens, 1986).

Information-processing theory and constructivism both help teachers understand the need for feedback. It gives learners information they can use to check the accuracy of their background knowledge, and it helps them create additional associations that result in more meaningful learning through elaboration. It also helps students determine whether their constructions or interpretations of content make sense.

12.9
One teacher clearly understands the topic she's teaching, whereas a second teacher's understanding is less certain. Will there be any difference in the clarity of the two teachers' communication? Explain.

12.10
Focus relates most closely to which level of classroom time discussed earlier?

12.11
Identify one important difference between introductory and sensory focus.

12.12
Social cognitive theory also points out the importance of feedback. Explain why feedback is important; base your answer on social cognitive theory.

Written Feedback.   Because so much time and effort are required to write detailed comments on student papers and essays, providing written feedback is a problem for teachers, and as a result, they often compromise. Feedback becomes brief and sketchy, and students get little useful information (B. Bloom & Bourdon, 1980).

A partial solution to this dilemma is to provide students with a written ideal, or model response to written assignments. For instance, to help students evaluate their answers to essay items on tests, the teacher could write an ideal answer and share it with the students, thus allowing them to compare their answers with the model. Seeing an ideal answer, combined with class discussion and time available for individual help after school, provides adequate feedback yet is manageable for the teacher.

Verbal Feedback.   Verbal feedback is delivered in question-and-answer sessions and varies from a simple acknowledgment of an answer, such as "Okay" and "Good," to extended responses about the accuracy of the answers. In providing verbal feedback, the informational value of the teacher's response is crucial. For instance, suppose a teacher displays the following sentence: "Running is a very good form of exercise" and this exchange takes place:

T:	How is the word *running* used in the sentence? . . . Mylan?
M:	It's a verb.
T:	Not quite, Mylan. Can someone help him out?

Even though the feedback was immediate, it was not specific and provided Mylan with no additional information. Contrast that response with the following:

T:	How is the word *running* used in the sentence? . . . Emilio?
E:	It's a verb.
T:	Look again, Emilio. Running is the topic of the sentence. So how is it used?
E:	. . . It's the subject.

In the second example, the teacher supplied a specific response based on Emilio's answer and provided information that allowed him to answer correctly. He was helped to understand why his first answer was incorrect and was given a chance to think through and correct it.

Monitoring: Being Responsive to Students

Monitoring *involves checking students' verbal and nonverbal behavior for evidence of learning progress.* Monitoring gives the teacher information about the progress of the lesson, and it is especially important when students work independently, because chances for confusion and error increase. Shirley monitored her students as she "walked up and down the aisles . . . and stopped periodically to comment on someone's work or offer reassurance," and she again monitored when they began their homework.

Monitoring also includes being aware of inattention and different students' reactions during learning activities. Alert teachers notice inattentive students and walk over to them or call on them to bring them back into the lesson. They also gauge students' nonverbal behaviors and respond by asking questions such as, "I see uncertain looks on some of your faces. Do you want me to rephrase that question?"

Monitoring and responding to students can simultaneously contribute to a climate of support and demonstrate high expectations for student achievement. The positive effects of the other essential skills are increased when the teacher is constantly aware of and sensitive to student behavior (Duffy, Roehler, Meloth, & Vavrus, 1985; O'Keefe & Johnston, 1987).

12.13 ▬
Research indicates that the emotional tone of feedback is important. On the basis of the model for promoting student motivation (in Chapter 9), explain why a positive emotional tone is important.

12.14 ▬
To which of the essential management skills discussed in Chapter 10 does monitoring most closely relate? Explain.

Questioning

Although the cognitive revolution in general and constructivism in particular have shifted the focus in the teaching-learning process away from the teacher and toward the students, it has also redirected attention to the powerful effects that teacher actions, such as questioning, can have on learning (Wang et al., 1993).

> Today's cognitive science . . . is concerned with all of the traditional questions of teaching: how to present and sequence information, how to organize practice and feedback, how to motivate students. . . . But each of these questions is addressed differently than in traditional instructional theory, for it is assumed that the goal of all of these instructional activities is to stimulate and nourish students' own mental elaborations of knowledge and to help them grow in their capacity to monitor and guide their own learning and thinking. (Resnick & Klopfer, 1989, p. 4)

Teacher questioning is one of the most powerful tools available for guiding and stimulating students' constructions and elaborations of knowledge. A teacher skilled in questioning can stimulate thought, help students form relationships, promote success, involve shy or reticent students, recapture students' attention, and enhance self-esteem.

Becoming skilled in questioning takes practice and hard work. To avoid overloading their own working memories, teachers need to practice questioning skills to the point that they are nearly automatic; thus, working-memory space is left available to monitor student behavior and to assess lesson progress. Although difficult, research indicates that, with effort and experience, teachers can and do become expert at it (Kerman, 1979; Rowe, 1986).

Effective questioning has four characteristics, which are outlined in Table 12.3 and discussed below.

Shirley skillfully applied the questioning strategies in Table 12.3 in her teaching. She asked many questions; in fact, she developed her entire lesson with questioning. She practiced *equitable distribution,* calling on a wide variety of students; she addressed all students by name; and she never strayed from the goal of her lesson.

You can also see that, as a pattern, Shirley asked the question first and selected the student second. By first asking the question, all students knew that they could be called on and, as a result, were more attentive. With the reversed pattern, as soon as a student is identified, the rest of the class knows they are "off the hook," and attention can suffer.

At this point, you might wonder, "I'm supposed to call on all the students, but what do I do if they can't answer?" One solution is **prompting,** *which is the process of helping students respond by providing cues after an incorrect or incomplete answer or silence.*

> **12.15**
> Why are equitable distribution and calling on students by name important? To which of the teacher characteristics discussed in Chapter 9 does equitable distribution most closely relate?

Table 12.3

Characteristics of effective questioning

Characteristic	Description
Frequency	The number of questions teachers ask
Equitable distribution	A pattern in which all students in the class are called on as equally as possible
Prompting	A teacher question or cue that elicits a response after a student has failed to answer or has given an incorrect or incomplete answer
Wait-time	The period of silence before or after a student response

12.16 ▬
Most teachers, instead of prompting, turn the question to another student, and the student initially asked the question becomes even more reluctant to respond. What concept from behaviorism explains this increasing reluctance?

For example, when Shirley first asked Emerson, "And what kind of parts?" and he was unable to answer, she continued, "How do the parts compare with each other?" which elicited his answer, "They're all equal." Her prompt took little time and helped ensure a successful response.

Prompting is also valuable because it keeps other students active, a factor that promotes meaningfulness and encoding. Prompts facilitate learning, probably as much by helping other students think through the question as by helping the individual being prompted (O'Flahavan, Hartman, & Pearson, 1988).

Finally, students' learning is enhanced when they're given **wait-time**, which is *a period of silence before or after a student is asked a question.* It increases learning by giving students time to think. In most classrooms—regardless of grade or ability levels—wait-times are very short, often less than 1 second (Rowe, 1986).

Increasing wait-time to about 3 to 5 seconds increases learning in three ways:

12.17 ▬
When would it be appropriate—even desirable—to keep wait-times shorter than 3 to 5 seconds? Give at least two examples.

1. The length and quality of student responses improve.
2. Failures to respond are reduced, and voluntary participation increases.
3. Equitable distribution and participation from minority students improve. (Rowe, 1986; Tobin, 1987)

Cognitive Levels of Questions.   Which are better—questions that are low level, requiring mere recall, or those that demand considerable student thought? The cognitive levels of teacher questions have been widely researched, but surprisingly, the results are mixed. Both low-level, such as *knowledge* on the Bloom taxonomy (B. Bloom et al., 1956), and high-level questions, such as *application* and *synthesis,* correlate positively with achievement, depending on the teaching situation (Good & Brophy, 1994).

These seemingly contradictory results again remind us of the importance of context and clear goals. On the one hand, if the goal is automaticity with basic skills, low-level questions may be most effective. On the other hand, if the goal is for students to analyze factors leading up to the Revolutionary War, for example, high-level questions are desirable. The teachers' first concern should be what they are trying to accomplish—their goals, not the level of questions they choose to ask. When goals are clear, appropriate questions will follow.

Review and Closure

Review *summarizes previous work and helps students link what has been learned to what is coming.* It can occur at any point in a lesson, although it is most common at the beginning and end. Effective reviews emphasize important points and encourage elaboration; in Shirley's lesson, the students reviewed adding fractions with like denominators and then used this information to understand the need for making the pieces of "cake" equal, as a step toward learning to add fractions with unlike denominators. Effective reviews involve more than simple rehearsal; they shift the learner's attention away from verbatim details to the deeper conceptual structure of the material being studied (Dempster, 1991).

Closure *is a form of review that occurs at the end of a lesson;* in it, topics are summarized, structured, and integrated. The notion of closure is common and intuitively sensible; it pulls together and signals the end of a lesson. Perhaps you have even used the term in a conversation, saying something like, "Let's try and get to closure on this."

12.18 ▬
Describe Shirley's closure in her lesson.

When concepts, principles, generalizations, and rules are being taught, an effective form of closure is to have students state a definition of the concept or state the principle,

Review provides opportunities for teachers to emphasize important points and to help students organize information in meaningful ways.

generalization, or rule in their own words. This action leaves them with the essence of the topic, from which they can elaborate in the next lesson.

This completes our discussion of the essential teaching skills based on the teacher effectiveness literature. In the following sections, we examine specific approaches to instruction. As you study these sections, think about how the essential teaching skills can be incorporated into each approach.

Classroom Connections

Demonstrating Professional Attitudes in Your Classroom

1. Have high expectations for your students and show them you are committed to their learning.
   - A geometry teacher, knowing that her students initially have trouble with proofs, offers help sessions twice a week after school.
   - A third-grade teacher calls a student's parents and solicits their help as soon as the student fails to turn in an assignment or receives an unsatisfactory grade on a quiz or test.

2. Commit yourself to being a role model for students.
   - A seventh-grade teacher displays the statement "I will always try to behave in the way I expect you to behave in this class" on the bulletin board, and she uses it as a guiding principle in her class.

Maximizing Instructional Time in Your Classroom

3. Carefully plan and organize materials to maximize instructional time. Avoid spending class time gathering and displaying materials.
   - A first-grade teacher has several boxes filled with frequently used science materials, such as soft drink bottles, balloons, matches, baking soda, vinegar, funnels, and a hot plate. The night before a science demonstration, she spends a few minutes selecting her materials from the boxes and sets them on the shelf near her desk so that she'll have everything ready at the beginning of the lesson.

4. Begin lessons on time; give students a short assignment or problem while you conduct your beginning routines.

- An English teacher displays a paragraph on the overhead at the beginning of the class period and asks students to identify and correct all the mechanical errors in it.
- An algebra teacher gives students a problem that is slightly more difficult than their homework assignment and has them solve it while he takes roll.

Demonstrating Essential Teaching Skills in Your Classroom

5. Monitor your communication to be certain your presentations are clear and concise.
   - A second-grade teacher videotapes a lesson she conducts with her students and then studies the tape to check her language and nonverbal communication.
   - A ninth-grade American government teacher asks colleagues to visit his class and check whether he emphasizes the important points in the lesson, sequences the presentation logically, and clearly communicates changes in topics.

6. Begin your lessons with problems, demonstrations, and displays.
   - A science teacher dealing with the concept of *kindling temperature* soaks a cloth in a water-alcohol mix, ignites it, and asks, "Why isn't the cloth burning?"
   - A second-grade teacher introducing the concept of *verb* has a student walk across the room, writes "Kelly walked across the room" on the chalkboard, and begins her lesson from that point.
   - A life science teacher beginning a study of arthropods brings a live lobster to class and builds the lesson around the lobster's characteristics.

7. Provide feedback on student written work as soon as possible after it's been completed.
   - An English teacher writes an "ideal" answer to each essay question she gives her students. She carefully goes over the model answer, explaining its elements, and asks students to compare it with the answers they've written.

8. Begin and end each class with a short review.
   - An English teacher begins, "We studied pronoun-antecedent agreement yesterday. Give me an example that illustrates the idea and explain why it is correct."
   - A fifth-grade teacher whose class is studying different types of boundaries says, "We've looked at three kinds of boundaries between the states so far today. What are the three?"

Teacher-Centered Approaches to Instruction

Having examined specific effective teaching skills, we now move on to more general approaches to instruction. To begin this section, let's look at another math teacher and compare his instruction with what we saw in Shirley Barton's lesson.

Sam Barnett began math with his second graders by saying, "Class, today we are going to go a step farther with our work in addition so that we'll be able to solve problems like this," and he then displayed the following on the overhead. "Jana and Patti are friends. They were saving special soda cans to get a free compact disc. Jana had 15 cans and Patti had 12. How many did they have together?"

After pausing briefly to give students a chance to read, Sam continued. "You can see that problems like this are important. It's important for Jana and Patti to know how many cans they have, and it's important for us too.

"We'll come back to the problem in a minute, but before we do, let's review. Everyone take out your bean sticks and beans and do this problem."

Sam then put the following problem on the chalkboard and watched as the students used their sticks and beans to demonstrate their answer.

$$\begin{array}{r} 8 \\ + 7 \\ \hline \end{array}$$

"Very good," Sam smiled as students laid a stick with 10 beans glued on it and 5 more beans on the centers of their desks.

Sam had the students do two more problems with their sticks and beans, and he then went on, "Let's begin by looking at our problem again."

With that, he returned to the problem with Jana and Patti, and said, "Everyone look at the overhead. Good. Now what does the problem ask us? . . . Shalinda?"

" . . . How many they have together?" Shalinda responded hesitantly.

"Okay, so let's put the problem on the chalkboard like this," Sam continued, writing the following on the chalkboard.

$$\begin{array}{r} 15 \\ + 12 \\ \hline \end{array}$$

"Now, I'd like everyone to show me how to make a 15 at your desk by using your sticks and beans."

Sam paused as they class worked at their desks.

"Does everyone's look like this?" Sam asked as he did the same at the flannel board.

They did the same with the 12, and Sam then said, "Now, watch what I do here. . . . When I add 5 and 2, what do I get? Hmm, let me think about that . . . 5 and 2 are 7. Let's put a 7 up on the chalkboard," Sam said as he walked to the chalkboard and added a 7.

$$\begin{array}{r} 15 \\ + 12 \\ \hline 7 \end{array}$$

"Now, show me that with your beans," and he watched as the students combined seven beans on their desks.

"Now, we still have to add the 10s. What do we get when we add two 10s? Hmm, that should be easy. One 10 and one 10 is two 10s. Now, look where I have to put the 2 up here. It is under the 10s column because the 2 means two 10s." With that, he wrote the following on the chalkboard.

$$\begin{array}{r} 15 \\ + 12 \\ \hline 27 \end{array}$$

"So, how many cans did Jana and Patti have together? . . . Alesha?"

"27?"

"Good, Alesha. They had 27 altogether. Now, with your beans, what is this 7?" he asked, pointing to the 7 on the chalkboard. ". . . Carol?"

" . . . It's this," she said, motioning to the seven beans on her desk.

"Good, yes it is. It's the seven individual beans. . . . Now, . . . what is this 2? . . . Jeremy?" Sam went on, pointing to the numeral on the chalkboard.

" . . . It's these two," Jeremy answered, holding up the two sticks with the beans glued on them.

"Now, we saw that I added the 5 and the 2 before I added the two 1s. Why do you suppose I did that? . . . Anyone?"

" . . . Maybe . . . you have to find out how many you have by themselves first," Callie offered.

"That's excellent thinking, Callie. That's exactly right. We'll see why again tomorrow when we have some problems in which we'll have to regroup, and that will be just a little tougher, but for now let's remember what Callie said.

"Now, let's describe in words for us what the 2 means. . . . Leroy?"

"It's . . . two, ah, two . . . bunches or something like that of 10 beans."

"Yes, that's correct, Leroy. It's two groups of 10 beans, or in the case of Jana and Patti, it's two groups of 10 soda cans.

"So, let's look again. There is an important difference between this 2," pointing to the 10s column, "and this 2," pointing to the 2 in the 12. "What is this difference? . . . Katrina?"

" . . . That 2 . . . is . . . two groups of 10, and that one is just 2 . . . by themselves."

"Yes, that's excellent. Good work, everyone. . . . Show me this 2," pointing to the 10s column.

The students held up two sticks with the beans glued on them.

"Good, and show me this 2," pointing to the 2 in the 12, and the students held up two beans.

"Great," Sam nodded. "Now, let's try another one," and he then displayed the following problem on the chalkboard.

$$\begin{array}{r} 23 \\ + 12 \\ \hline \end{array}$$

He watched as the students used their beans and sticks to make 35, and again they discussed the problem. They did two more, and then Sam gave the students an assignment of 10 more problems to do for seatwork.

Let's take a look at Sam's lesson. He began by reviewing the previous day's work and then turned to his new topic, introducing it in a way designed to pique students' interest. He went on to model the process of adding two-digit numbers and had the students demonstrate it with their sticks and beans. Finally, he had students practice adding two-digit numbers, first under his guidance and later, independently, while he monitored their work.

Direct Instruction

Sam demonstrated the essential features of an approach to teaching called **direct instruction** (Rosenshine, 1979). Also called "explicit teaching" (Rosenshine, 1986, 1987), *this strategy is a highly structured approach to teaching procedural skills, characterized by teacher modeling and student practice.*

Procedural Skills

Direct instruction is particularly effective for teaching **procedural skills**, *which are forms of content that have three essential characteristics:*

1. They have a specific set of identifiable operations or procedures (which is why they're called procedural skills).
2. They can be illustrated with a large and varied number of examples.
3. They are developed through practice (W. Doyle, 1983).

Adding two-digit numbers is a procedural skill. Others include adding fractions with unlike denominators, punctuating sentences, finding coordinates on a map, and balancing chemical equations. Each of the procedural skills has an unlimited number of examples, they follow specific procedures, and students develop facility with them through practice.

Phases of Direct Instruction

The phases of direct instruction are (a) introduction and review, (b) presentation, (c) guided practice, and (d) independent practice. In the first two phases, the teacher

12.19 ▬
Punctuating sentences is identified as a procedural skill. Are procedural skills and rules the same thing? If not, how are they different?

Direct instruction provides opportunities for students to actively encode information during guided and independent practice.

explains and models the skill; in the last two, students practice it under decreasing amounts of teacher guidance. The phases and corresponding teacher actions are summarized in Figure 12.2 and described in the sections that follow.

Introduction and Review.　A direct instruction lesson begins with a review of the previous day's work, including a discussion of students' homework. The teacher then attempts to draw the students into the lesson by describing the objective and explaining why studying the topic is important. Although this procedure may seem obvious, 21% of all skills lessons begin with little or no introduction (Brophy, 1982).

Presentation.　Having introduced his lesson, Sam used both modeling and students' hands-on experiences to explain the procedure for adding two-digit numbers. Modeling provided a specific set of actions students could imitate, the examples provided concrete experiences, and Sam proceeded in short steps to avoid overloading the students' working memories.

　　Sam also encouraged a great deal of interaction in his lesson. He asked students to verbally explain what the 7 and 2 meant, he had them demonstrate each with their sticks and beans, and he also asked them to explain the difference between the 2 in the 27 and the 2 in the 12. Verbalizing and explaining procedures is a subtle but important part of learning activities and one that teachers sometimes miss. They often involve students in a hands-on activity but then fail to make the connection between it and the abstractions they represent.

Guided Practice.　Guided practice applies the concept of *scaffolding,* which we discussed in Chapters 2 and 8. After the presentation, students practice under the watchful eye of the teacher, who applies enough scaffolding support to ensure success, but not so much that students' sense of accomplishment and self-efficacy is reduced. For example, Sam had his students work a problem, and they discussed it carefully, with Sam monitoring their progress. He had them work on their own only after he was sure they were ready.

12.20 ▬
Explain why these introductory activities are important, using information-processing theory as a basis for your explanation. Also explain their importance, using motivation theory as a basis.

12.21 ▬
Sam was thorough and effective in the presentation phase of the lesson. Predict how less effective teachers might conduct this phase.

Figure 12.2

Phases of direct instruction

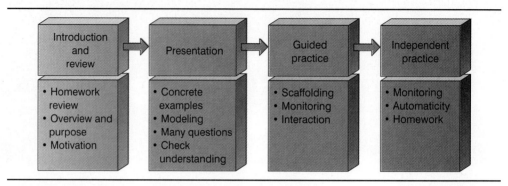

Independent Practice.   In the independent practice phase, teacher support (scaffolding) is removed, and responsibility is shifted to the students. At this point, they're expected to perform the skill on their own, perhaps with some initial hesitancy, but later with ease and fluency. The goal is automaticity, intended to free working memory to focus on application, such as solving future word problems.

Teacher monitoring is still important during independent practice. As students work on the assignment, effective teachers move around the room, checking student work and offering assistance.

Homework.   Homework is a common form of independent practice, and its effect on learning is positive, especially if teachers grade and comment on it. The effects of homework are especially strong at the high school and junior high level. Research also indicates that frequency is important. For example, 5 problems every night are more effective than 25 once a week (Cooper, 1989).

Effective homework has at least four characteristics, which are outlined in Table 12.4, based on work by Walberg, Paschal, and Weinstein (1985) and Berliner (1984).

These characteristics emphasize how important instructional alignment is in planning and teaching. Homework should be an extension of instruction, and although grading homework can be time-consuming, some mechanism for providing feedback on it is critical if students are expected to take it seriously and use it as a learning tool.

Lectures and Lecture-Recitation

Organized Bodies of Knowledge

In the previous section, we examined direct instruction and emphasized its use in teaching procedural skills—forms of content, such as adding two-digit numbers, that can be illustrated with a variety of examples and developed by practicing a specific set of operations.

An English teacher involved in a unit on 20th-century American literature, for example, has different goals. A specific relationship, set of characteristics, or procedures doesn't exist. The topic can't be illustrated with precise examples. Instead, the teacher's goal might be for students to understand how concepts such as *plot, setting,* and *character*

12.22
Which phase of direct instruction is most important in ensuring successful independent practice? Explain.

12.23
Using social cognitive theory as a basis, explain why assigning but not collecting homework is ineffective practice.

Table 12.4

Characteristics of effective homework

Characteristic	Rationale
Extension of classwork	The teacher teaches; homework reinforces.
High success rates	Success is motivating. Success leads to automaticity. No one is available to provide help if students encounter problems.
Part of class routines; assignments written on chalkboard	Becomes a part of student expectations, increases likelihood of students completing assignments.
Graded	Increases accountability and provides feedback.

development interact in a work, as well as generalizations such as "Authors' works are influenced by their personal experiences." However, the lesson wouldn't focus exclusively or even primarily on these topics. Rather, the goal would be for students to understand the relationships among the concepts and generalizations in comparing one author's work with another's.

Although labels vary, the term *organized bodies of knowledge* can be used to describe this type of content (Calfee, 1986; Rosenshine, 1986). **Organized bodies of knowledge** *are topics that examine facts, concepts, generalizations, and principles, and the relationships among them.*

Because organized bodies of knowledge can't be illustrated with precise examples, practice—as you found in skills instruction—can't be used to develop student understanding. As a result, direct instruction doesn't apply, and alternative instructional formats are used. Most common among them are lecture and lecture-recitation.

Lecture

The prevalence of the lecture as a teaching method is paradoxical. Although it is and historically has been the most widely criticized of all teaching methods, it continues to be the most commonly used (Cuban, 1984). At least three reasons are given for its durability:

1. Lectures are efficient; planning time is devoted to organizing content.
2. Lectures are flexible; they can be applied to virtually any content area.
3. Lectures are relatively simple to implement.

Despite their wide use, lectures have some important disadvantages. Most important is the fact that lecturing puts students in a passive mode, which is inconsistent with nearly everything known about information processing and constructivism. Constructing understanding and encoding information into long-term memory requires active learners.

The ineffectiveness of lecture as a teaching method is well documented. In seven comparisons of lecture to discussion, discussion was superior in all seven on measures of retention and higher order thinking. In addition, discussion was superior in seven of nine studies on measures of student attitude and motivation (McKeachie & Kulik, 1975).

It isn't that lectures, in themselves, are always inappropriate, however; it is that they are often ineffectively or inappropriately used. As with all aspects of instruction, the key is clear goals. Ausubel (1963) argued that effective lectures provide students with informa-

12.24
Think about some of the case studies in other chapters in this text. Identify two of these in which an organized body of knowledge was being taught.

12.25
Using information processing as a basis for your explanation, explain why the simplicity of lectures is important to teachers (particularly beginning teachers).

tion that would take them hours to find on their own. Others suggest that lectures are appropriate if the teacher's goals include the following:

▌ To acquire information not readily accessible in other ways
▌ To integrate information from a variety of sources
▌ To understand different points of view
▌ To understand complex topics that students have difficulty learning on their own (Henson, 1988; McMann, 1979)

If teachers are clear about their goals and if their goals can be met with lectures, their periodic use is appropriate.

Lecture-Recitation

One of the most effective ways to overcome the weaknesses of lectures is to use **lecture-recitations**, *a combination of short lectures supplemented with teacher questioning* (Eggen & Kauchak, 1996).

Lecture-recitations are conducted in three sequential steps. The teacher begins by *presenting information.* After a brief presentation, she pauses and asks students a series of clarifying questions to *monitor comprehension.* For instance, after presenting information about the conflict between the British and the French prior to the Revolutionary War, a teacher would ask questions such as, "How might we summarize what we know about the British to this point?" "How was the French involvement in North America different from the British involvement?" and, "What does this information suggest to us?"

The teacher then presents additional information followed by another period of comprehension monitoring. At this point, she asks the students to extend their understanding with questions such as, "What were the key factors that caused conflicts between

12.26 ▬
Incorporating the essential teaching skills into lecture-recitations is critical if students are to stay involved and acquire meaningful information. Using the conflict between the British and the French as a framework, describe specifically how each of the essential teaching skills would be incorporated into the lesson. Include specific examples in your description.

During lecture-recitations, teachers monitor student comprehension through frequent questions.

the French and the British?" and, "What do we see in North America today that relates back to the time we're discussing?" These questions encourage students to go beyond comprehension monitoring and promote *integration* by having them describe cause-and-effect relationships that the teacher hasn't offered.

The line between comprehension monitoring and integration isn't distinct, and there is often overlap. We discuss them separately to emphasize that the interactive phases of lecture-recitations involve more than asking students to simply restate or summarize what the teacher has said. Lecture-recitations require careful planning to encourage student involvement and thinking and, when properly done, can promote meaningful learning.

Classroom Connections

Using Direct Instruction Effectively in Your Classroom

1. Introduce lessons with a demonstration, question, or problem that promotes student interest.
   - A third-grade teacher comes into class and writes on the chalkboard, "The animal most likely to survive on Earth is the INSECT!" He then says, "Let's keep this statement in mind as we begin our study of insects today."
   - A math teacher beginning a unit on percentages and decimals comments that the star quarterback for the state university has a completion rate of 58%. "What does that mean?" she asks. "How can we figure it out?"

2. Provide as much guided practice as necessary to ensure students' successful transition from your presentation to independent practice.
   - A fifth-grade teacher, wanting students to understand similes and metaphors, begins by saying, "All right. Everyone write a sentence with at least one simile or metaphor in it." She then circulates among the students, examining their sentences. She has several students share their sentences by writing them on the chalkboard. The class discusses whether these are similes or metaphors and then continues writing and sharing others until the teacher is sure the students can proceed on their own.

3. Monitor students during independent practice.
   - A first-grade teacher has assigned a series of problems involving addition and subtraction. As students work the problems, he walks up and down the rows to check each student's progress. He periodically stops and offers suggestions as he checks their work.

Using Lecture-Recitation Effectively in Your Classroom

4. Organize information in the form of charts, outlines, or hierarchies.
   - A sixth-grade science teacher is beginning a discussion of controlled and experimental variables. She begins by drawing the following figure on the chalkboard. She continually refers to the figure when she explores relationships between the variables.

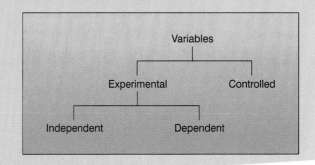

5. Incorporate as many concrete examples as possible in the lesson.
   • An American history teacher discussing immigration in the 19th and early 20th centuries compares these immigrant groups with the Cuban population in Miami, Florida; and the Mexican immigrants in San Antonio, Texas. He examines the difficulties immigrants encounter in their efforts to assimilate into mainstream American culture.

6. Keep the presentation of information short, review frequently, and examine relationships among items of information.
   • A biology teacher is presenting information related to cellular transport, identifying and illustrating several of the concepts in the process. About 5 minutes into the presentation, she stops and asks, "Suppose a cell is in a hypotonic solution in one case and a hypertonic solution in another. What's the difference between the two? What would happen to the cell in each case?"

Learner-Centered Approaches to Instruction

The teacher effectiveness literature made an invaluable contribution to education because it both confirmed the critical role teachers play in student learning and provided "the field of education with a knowledge base capable of moving the field beyond testimonials and unsupported claims toward scientific statements based on credible data" (Brophy, 1992, p. 5). It provides, however, only a baseline above which all teachers should be. Expert teachers go beyond this threshold to present lessons that help students develop deep understandings of the topics they study. In addition, many recommendations derived from the effectiveness research tend to be teacher centered, and teacher-centered approaches in general and direct instruction in particular are being increasingly criticized. Let's look at some of these criticisms.

Criticisms of Direct Instruction

Critics of direct instruction charge that it focuses on lower level objectives and breaks content into small pieces, thus reinforcing or correcting students for desired performances. This technique is based on a behaviorist view of learning that emphasizes *performance* more than *understanding,* they argue. Further, this emphasis runs counter to the current focus on conceptual growth and learners as active constructors of their own understanding (Marshall, 1992; Stoddart, Connell, Stofflett, & Peck, 1993).

The following example illustrates this criticism. A teacher is attempting to teach place value to her third graders. On the basis of directions given in the teacher's manual, she begins by putting 45 tally marks on the chalkboard and circling four groups of 10. Let's look at the interaction that followed:

Teacher:	How many groups of 10 do we have there, boys and girls?
Children:	4.
Teacher:	We have 4 groups of 10, and how many left over?
Children:	5.
Teacher:	We had 4 tens and how many left over?
Beth:	4 tens.
Sarah:	5.

Teacher:	5. Now, can anybody tell me what number that could be? We have 4 tens and 5 ones. What is that number? Ann?
Ann:	(Remains silent)
Teacher:	If we have 4 tens and 5 ones, what is that number?
Ann:	9.
Teacher:	Look at how many we have there (points to the 4 groups of ten) and 5 ones. If we have 4 tens and 5 ones we have? (slight pause) 45.
Children:	45.
Teacher:	Very good.

(Wood, Cobb, & Yackel, 1992, p. 180)

This pattern of focusing on student verbalization or performance rather than understanding is typical in many classrooms (Goodlad, 1984; Stodolsky, 1988). It's obvious from the dialogue that Ann, and probably several others, didn't understand the relationship between the place values of 10s and 1s and that the teacher did little to change their misunderstandings. Once they gave the desired response, the teacher reinforced (praised) them and moved on.

> **12.27**
> Describe specifically what the teacher might have done to increase the students' understanding of place value in this lesson.

Characteristics of Learner-Centered Approaches to Instruction

As we better understand learning, we begin to appreciate how complex it is, with social interaction, learner motivation, learner beliefs and expectations, and other individual differences all influencing the process (Alexander & Murphy, 1994; Nuthall & Alton-Lee, 1993; Pintrich et al., 1993).

The foundation of learner-centered approaches to instruction is a constructivist view of learning, and you saw in Chapter 7 that learners constructing their own understanding is the essence of constructivism. Errors from an adult point of view are children's expressions of their current understanding, and substantive learning takes place over a long period of time and often occurs during periods of confusion and conflict (J. Brooks & Brooks, 1993; Clements & Batista, 1990).

Based on constructivist views of learning, three characteristics of learner-centered instruction are illustrated in Figure 12.3 and discussed below. Let's look at them.

Learners at the Center of the Learning Process

Research examining the thought processes of experts, the expanding influence of constructivism, and the increasing criticisms of direct instruction have resulted in a much greater

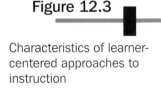

Figure 12.3

Characteristics of learner-centered approaches to instruction

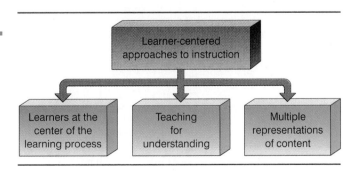

emphasis on the central role of the student in the learning process. You saw this emphasis reflected in the American Psychological Association's learner-centered principles (Alexander & Murphy, 1994), which we discussed in Chapter 11. It's also the basis for the theme "A focus on learners" that we introduced in Chapter 1 and illustrate throughout the text.

Implications of Student-Centered Learning for Teachers.   Placing students at the center of learning involves a subtle but important shift in teaching emphasis. It makes the teacher's role more complex and demanding and has important implications for the way instruction is conducted.

Let's look at an example of learner-centered instruction and compare it with the episode on place value that we just presented.

> As a homework assignment, Keisha Coleman gives her third graders a worksheet with a number line on it that appears as follows:

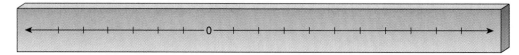

> She had asked students to put numbers on the number line representing positive and negative numbers. She also had given them 12 problems, some of which involved adding and subtracting negative numbers. Keisha and her students spend half an hour discussing the following problem:

$$-10 + 10 = ?\text{ How do you know?}$$

> In introducing these problems, Keisha emphasizes that students are supposed to not only give an answer but also explain why their answer was correct.

Keisha:	Would someone like to give us an answer?
Marta:	Zero.
Keisha:	Negative 10 plus 10 equals zero (writing $-10 + 10 = 0$ on the chalkboard). Now, can you explain how you know that, Marta?
Marta:	(Nods yes.)
Keisha:	Good, Marta. Go ahead and do that. I would like for the rest of you to listen very carefully because I want you to be able to tell Marta whether you agree with what she says.
Marta:	You have to count 10 numbers to the right.
Keisha:	(Writing Marta's exact words on the chalkboard) All right. Marta says that negative 10 plus 10 equals zero, so you have to count 10 numbers to the right. What do you people think about that? . . . Harold?
Harold:	I think it's easy, but I don't understand how she explained it.
Keisha:	Does anyone else have a comment on that? . . . Tessa?
Tessa:	I think it's zero 'cause negative 10 plus 10 equals zero.
Keisha:	Okay. But now let's focus on what Marta said.
Tessa:	There's not . . . I don't agree.
Keisha:	What do you disagree with?
Tessa:	You have to count numbers to the right. Then you have to count back to the left. If you just count to the right you won't get to zero. You have to count to the left.
Keisha:	Could you explain a little bit more about what you mean by that? I'm not sure if I follow you. And the rest of you need to listen very carefully so you can see whether you agree or disagree.
Tessa:	Because if you went that way (pointing to the right), then it would have to be a higher number.

To this point in the dialogue, the interaction has been mostly teacher-student-teacher-student. Keisha then makes an effort to turn the dialogue to student-student. She does this by nodding to Chang and encouraging him to respond to Tessa.

12.28

What principle in making information meaningful, which we discussed in Chapter 7, is best illustrated in this dialogue?

Chang:	Tessa says if you're counting right, then the number is . . . I don't understand. I don't know what she's talking about. Negative 10 plus 10 is zero.
Keisha:	Do you want to ask her?
Chang:	What do you mean by counting to the right?
Tessa:	If you count from 10 up, you can't get zero. If you just count from 10 left, you can get zero.
Chang:	Well, negative 10 is a negative number, . . . smaller than zero.
Tessa:	I know.
Chang:	Then why do you say you can't get to zero when you're adding to negative 10, which is smaller than zero?
Tessa:	OHH! I get it! This is positive.
Keisha:	Excuse me?
Tessa:	If it's positive, you have to count right (motioning).
Keisha:	You're saying in order to get to zero, you have to count to the right? From where, Tessa?
Tessa:	Negative 10.

(Adapted from Peterson, 1992, with permission)

This episode illustrates both the students' struggle to understand the topic they were studying and the teacher's crucial role in guiding learning. Two aspects of this process are important. First, explanations and understanding evolved on the basis of students' developing understanding, not Keisha's explanation; second, Keisha carefully monitored and guided the process to be sure it remained meaningful for students.

This is extremely sophisticated instruction. Some guidance is necessary to maintain learning progress and to prevent students from developing misconceptions, but too much prevents them from developing their own understanding. Unfortunately, no rules exist to tell teachers whether they should intervene or when. Further, although two students are involved in a dialogue, other students may not be understanding or even attending. If they're not, the teacher must intervene and bring the rest of the class back into the lesson. It's easy to see why teacher-centered approaches, which are much easier to implement, have been popular for so long.

Teaching for Understanding

The phrase "teaching for understanding" seems like a paradox; no teacher consciously teaches for lack of understanding. As you saw in the example with place value, however, understanding isn't always an outcome of instruction, and teaching for "understanding" isn't as simple as it appears. Understanding involves thought-demanding processes, such as explaining, finding evidence, providing unique examples, generalizing, and the ability to relate parts to wholes (Knapp, Shields, & Turnbull, 1995; Perkins & Blythe, 1994). You saw few of these processes in the place value lesson, whereas you saw a great deal of explaining and providing evidence in Keisha Coleman's instruction and in Shirley Barton's as well.

Let's return to Shirley's lesson again with this idea in mind. First, she promoted "understanding" with questions such as:

"How do you know?" (That the parts are equal)

"And how did Gayle get that?"

"How might we prove that adding them up is the thing to do?"

"How do you think we could find out for sure?"

Each question required students to explain and provide evidence, or "justify their thinking," in making their conclusions.

In addition to focusing on understanding, she moved students to the center of the learning process as illustrated by the following:

Shirley:	How might we prove that adding the top numbers is the thing to do? . . . Anyone?
Natasha:	We have three pieces there (pointing to the first drawing), and if we had two more pieces, we would have five altogether, so it would be ⅜ and ⅖, which would be ⅝ altogether.
Shirley:	What do the rest of you think about that?
Adam:	I don't think so. It looks like ⁵⁄₁₆ to me.
Natasha:	No, look. We have only eight pieces altogether.
Adam:	What about the other drawing?
Natasha:	We're not on the other drawing. We're on this one. I said put two more pieces on this one.

By focusing on understanding and placing students in the center of the process, teachers communicate that students must take responsibility for constructing and verifying their own conclusions. Taking responsibility leads to self-regulated learning, a concept we've emphasized repeatedly.

Multiple Representations of Content

In Chapter 11, we said that putting students at the center of the learning process acknowledges that knowledge construction is a personal process that requires multiple representations of content. This statement has implications for both planning and instruction.

To illustrate the idea of multiple representations, think back to some of the teachers you've studied so far. In Chapter 2, you saw that Jenny Newhall first did a demonstration illustrating that air takes up space and followed her demonstration by allowing her first graders to directly experiment with the same phenomenon themselves. David Shelton, in Chapter 7, represented information about the solar system by using demonstrations, models, and charts. Suzanne Brush, with her second graders in Chapter 8, used jelly beans together with numerical data, graphs, and follow-up activities to represent the topic of graphing. Kathy Brewster, in Chapter 9, used both her personalized "crusade" information and the students' essays to provide different forms of information for her high school students, and Shirley Barton used her initial problem, "cakes," and numerical examples. Each teacher—ranging from first grade through high school—used multiple representations of content to facilitate meaningful encoding. In each instance, the teacher capitalized on the powerful influence that demonstrations and concrete illustrations have on learning (Nuthall & Alton-Lee, 1993).

Misconceptions About Student-Centered Approaches to Instruction.

Studying student-centered approaches to instruction can sometimes lead to misconceptions. First, because students are constructing their own understanding, one might infer that a clear goal and careful preparation are less important when using student-centered approaches. Nothing could be farther from the truth. In fact, clear goals are even more important because

---

12.29

What process and what subprocess from the basic processes in thinking (in Table 8.7 on p. 323) does "justifying thinking" best illustrate? Explain.

12.30

Consider the concept of *transfer,* which you studied in Chapter 8. To what feature that promotes transfer does the concept of *multiple representations of content* most closely relate?

they give teachers points of focus as they guide the interaction. As students build on their current understanding, teachers may modify their own goals, as Tracey Stoddard did in her lesson on heat in Chapter 7. However, teachers begin their lessons with clear goals in mind.

Second, one might conclude that if the students are involved in discussions and other forms of social interaction, learning is automatically taking place. Again, this isn't necessarily true. As you saw with Keisha's and Shirley's lessons, the teacher must carefully monitor the discussions, and if students head down "blind alleys" or develop misunderstandings about the topic, the teacher needs to intervene and redirect the discussion (A. Brown & Campione, 1994). The teacher wants students to construct understandings that make sense to them, but these understandings must also be valid. For instance, in Chapter 2, you saw how a cup was inverted into a container of water to help students understand that air takes up space. To first graders, it makes sense that the cup itself (and not air) kept the water out. However, we can't leave the lesson at this point because the students' understanding is incomplete.

Third, because they are not lecturing and explaining, one might conclude that teachers have a less important role in student-centered learning than in a traditional classroom. This is also false. As you saw earlier, their role is both more important and more difficult. Learning to guide students into genuine understanding is a sophisticated process; there are no rules that tell when to intervene or how extensive the intervention should be. Teachers must make these decisions on their own on the basis of their knowledge of the content and their past experiences.

With the characteristics of learner-centered approaches to instruction in mind, let's look at some specific learner-centered strategies.

12.31
What did Jenny Newhall, on page 69, do to help the students understand that air, rather than the cup itself, kept the water out? (You might want to look at the case study again.)

Discovery Approaches to Instruction

Discovery learning *is an instructional approach that provides students with information they use to construct understanding.* Discovery learning was first made popular by Jerome Bruner (1960, 1966, 1971), who spoke persuasively in the 1960s and 1970s for student autonomy and initiative. In this regard, many of his views about learning are similar to those of the constructivists today.

Types of Discovery

Discovery learning generated a considerable amount of research that helped clarify some of the issues involved, such as the distinction between unstructured and guided discovery (Keislar & Shulman, 1966). "Pure discovery," or **unstructured discovery,** *occurs in a natural setting where learners construct understanding on their own,* such as a scientist making a unique discovery in a research project. **Guided discovery** *occurs when the teacher identifies a content goal, arranges the information so that patterns can be found, and guides the students to the goal.*

Research on Discovery Learning

Even though a faithful application of Piaget's and Bruner's ideas suggests an unstructured discovery approach (Resnick & Klopfer, 1989), research indicates that it is generally ineffective (Anastasiow, Bibley, Leonhardt, & Borish, 1970; R. Gagne & Brown, 1961). Students in unstructured discovery activities become lost and frustrated; this confusion sometimes leads to misconceptions (A. Brown & Campione, 1994). Consequently, other than student projects and investigations, unstructured discovery activities are rarely seen in classrooms today.

Through guided discovery, teachers use constructivist learning principles to help students form concepts through hands-on experiences.

Guided discovery is quite another matter. It is consistent with learner-centered approaches to instruction and constructivist views of learning (Bransford, 1993), and it provides a role for teachers that cognitive research supports (A. Brown & Campione, 1994; Resnick & Klopfer, 1989). For example, a meta-analysis of research on writing instruction indicated that students taught with a guided-discovery approach showed three times more improvement than those taught with a natural process (similar to unstructured discovery) and four times more improvement than those taught with a traditional, teacher-oriented expository approach (Hillocks, 1984).

A more recent study compared guided discovery and direct instruction in the teaching of science concepts and principles to learners with mild disability and learners without disability. Results indicated that guided discovery resulted in more transfer and greater long-term retention than did the direct instruction approach (Bay, Staver, Bryan, & Hale, 1992). In comparing guided discovery to direct instruction, researchers found that teachers spent less time lecturing and explaining and more time asking questions during guided discovery. In addition, they found that students were more involved and had more opportunities to practice higher order thinking, both learner-centered principles (Alexander & Murphy, 1994).

12.32 ▬
On the basis of the information in this section, what principle of "making information meaningful" from Chapter 7 does guided discovery apply to a greater extent than does direct instruction?

Guided Discovery: An Application

Let's see what guided discovery might look like in the classroom.

Judy Nelson is beginning the study of longitude and latitude in social studies with her sixth graders. In preparation, she buys a beach ball, finds an old tennis ball, and checks her wall maps and globes.

To begin her lesson, she has the students identify where they live on the wall map. She then says, "Suppose you made some new friends on your summer vacation and you want to describe for them exactly where you live. How might we do that?"

She gets a number of suggestions from the class and asks whether the suggestions are precise enough to pinpoint their exact location. The students, after additional discussion, conclude that they aren't.

She continues, "It looks as if we have a problem. We want to be able to tell our new friends exactly where we live, but we don't quite have a way of doing it. Let's see whether we can figure this out."

She then holds up the beach ball and globe and asks her students to observe and compare the two. In the process, they identify north, south, east, and west on the beach ball, and she draws a circle around the center of the ball, which they identify as the equator. They do the same with the tennis ball, which she then cuts in half and thus allows them to see that the ball is in two hemispheres.

Judy continues by drawing other lines on the beach ball and then says, "Now, compare the lines with each other."

". . . They're all even," Kathy volunteers.

"Go ahead, Kathy. What do you mean by 'even,'" Judy encourages.

". . . They don't cross each other," Kathy explains, motioning with her hands.

"Okay," Judy nods smiling.

Judy asks for and gets additional comparisons, such as, "The lines all run east and west," and, "They get shorter as they move away from the equator." Judy writes them on the chalkboard. After the class is done making comparisons, Judy introduces the term *latitude* to refer to the lines they have been discussing.

She continues by drawing lines of longitude on the beach ball and identifies them as shown below:

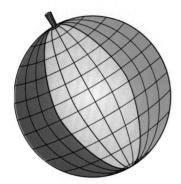

Let's look now at the dialogue that follows.

Judy:	How do these lines compare with the lines of latitude?
Tricia:	. . . They go all around the ball.
Judy:	Good. And what else?
Elliot:	The lengths are the same.
Thomas:	Lengths of what?
Elliot:	The up-and-down lines and the cross ones.
Judy:	What did we call the cross ones?
Elliot:	. . . Latitude.
Jime:	We said that they got shorter. . . . So, how can they be the same length?
Tabatha:	I think those are longer (pointing to the longitude lines).
Judy:	How might we check to see about the lengths?
Jime:	We could measure the lines, like with a tape or string or something.
Judy:	What do you think of Jime's idea?

The students agree that it seems to be a good idea, so Judy helps hold pieces of string in place while Jime wraps them around the ball at different points, and the class compares the lengths.

> *Chris:*   These are the same (holding up two "longitude" strings).
> *Nicole:*   These aren't (holding two "latitude" strings).

After looking at all the strings, Judy then asks the students to work in pairs to summarize what they found. They make the following conclusions.

Longitude lines are farthest apart at the equator; latitude lines are the same distance apart everywhere.

Lines of longitude are the same length; latitude lines get shorter north and south of the equator.

Lines of longitude intersect each other at the poles; lines of latitude and longitude intersect each other all over the globe.

Judy continues, asking, "Now, how does this help us solve our problem of identifying an exact location?" and with some guidance from her, the class concludes that location can be pinpointed by where the lines cross, and she points out that this is what they will focus on the next day. (Eggen & Kauchak, 1996, adapted with permission)

In this guided-discovery lesson, you saw several characteristics of learner-centered instruction. Students were at the center of the learning process, they interacted both with Judy and with each other as they constructed their understanding of longitude and latitude, and her focus was on understanding rather than performance. Judy's instruction also provided for multiple representations of content; she used the beach ball, tennis ball, globe, and strings, and she planned to use maps the following day to represent content in a variety of ways. Undoubtedly, her approach, such as using the strings to measure the lines, took more time than direct instruction would have, but without this time and effort, students like Elliot would probably leave the lesson with incomplete understandings.

Several of the case studies you've already read used guided discovery to varying degrees, such as Jenny Newhall in Chapter 2, David Shelton and Tracey Stoddard in Chapter 7, Patty Kramer and Suzanne Brush in Chapter 8, and Shirley Barton in this chapter. You may want to refer again to these lessons as you develop your understanding of teaching using guided discovery.

Discussions

In looking back at Shirley Barton's and Keisha Coleman's lessons, you can see that their teaching incorporated elements of **discussions**, *which are instructional approaches designed to stimulate thinking, challenge attitudes and beliefs, and develop interpersonal skills* (Oser, 1986). These thinking and interpersonal skills include:

▮ Learning to listen to others
▮ Developing tolerance for dissenting views
▮ Learning democratic processes
▮ Critically examining one's understanding, attitudes, and values, as well as those of one's peers

As with guided discovery, discussions incorporate characteristics of student-centered teaching; they differ from guided discovery in that they typically do not have a specific concept, generalization, principle, or rule as their goal.

Characteristics of Effective Discussions

Discussions have four essential characteristics: (a) focus, (b) sufficient student background knowledge, (c) emphasis on understanding, and (d) student-student interaction.

12.33 ▬
In the dialogue, Judy said, "It looks like we have a problem. We want to be able to tell our new friends exactly where we live, but we don't quite have a way of doing it. Let's see whether we can figure this out." What essential teaching skill does this statement best illustrate?

12.34 ▬
Your use of the case studies to develop your understanding of guided discovery illustrates one characteristic of learner-centered approaches to instruction. Identify this characteristic.

12.35 ▬
If they're properly done, discussion, guided discovery, direct instruction, and lecture-recitation have an important element in common. What is this element?

Focus.   The teacher provides focus in discussions by posing a question or problem and then maintains this focus with questions and comments (Krabbe & Polivka, 1990). Students have a tendency to "wander" in discussions, and without guidance, an animated discussion can develop over an irrelevant issue. Keeping students focused and helping them recognize when they are making irrelevant arguments is an important part of the teacher's role. In addition, as you saw in Chapter 8, developing the ability to separate relevant from irrelevant information is a higher order thinking skill.

Sufficient Student Background Knowledge.   We have emphasized the importance of background knowledge at several points in this text, and it is critical for discussions as well. To allow students to focus on problem solving, discussions should follow lessons in which content background has been developed. If students' backgrounds are inadequate, discussions disintegrate into random conjectures, uninformed opinions, and "pooled ignorance." We've probably all been in situations where we've been asked to discuss a problem or issue with insufficient background. It is a waste of time at best.

Emphasis on Understanding.   Discussions are best used to explore relationships, to integrate ideas, and to promote higher order thinking, all factors that help develop deep understanding. They are not effective for acquiring initial knowledge. Successful discussions invite students to identify links between ideas and to construct understandings that make sense to them. Uncertainty, conjecture, and healthy disagreement are all part of this process. The end product should be a deeper understanding of the topic.

Student-Student Interaction.   Students must be involved to benefit from discussions (Dillon, 1987; Krabbe & Polivka, 1990). Ideally, as much student-student interaction as possible is desirable. This interaction allows students to learn to explain and defend their own reasoning, to challenge others' thinking, and to respond on the basis of what they really think, rather than answer according to feedback they get from the teacher. All of these elements are consistent with student-centered instruction.

   In addition, during discussions, students learn to respect others' opinions and right to speak, to wait their turn, and to remain open-minded in the face of new evidence. Development of these interpersonal skills is often as important as the content they're learning.

Student Groupwork

Although not necessary, guided discovery and discussions are often conducted as whole-group activities. Judy Nelson, for example, conducted the first part of her lesson as a whole-group activity. At times, however, teachers have goals that can't be met in large groups, such as helping students learn to work together. To reach these goals, *student groupwork* and *cooperative learning* can be effective.

   Although the two are not identical, clear distinctions between groupwork and cooperative learning don't exist, and the terms are often used interchangeably. On the one hand, for example, Cohen (1986) defines **student groupwork** as *"students working together in a group small enough so that everyone can participate on a task that has been clearly assigned"* (pp. 1–2). On the other hand, D. Johnson and Johnson (1994) define cooperative learning as students working together to accomplish shared goals. Common to both are that they place students in small groups, thus emphasizing student interaction and common goals. We begin with a discussion of simple groupwork, and then we turn to some specifics about cooperative learning.

12.36
Both Shirley Barton's and Keisha Coleman's lessons contained elements of discussion. Identify specifically how Shirley and Keisha each provided *focus* in their lessons.

12.37
Identify specific examples of student-student dialogue in Shirley's and Keisha's lessons.

Groupwork: Promoting Student Involvement

Stacy Sims organizes her third graders in groups of three. She gives each group bar and horseshoe magnets and a packet of common items, including a dime, metal spoon, piece of aluminum foil, rubber band, wooden pencil, paper clip, ballpoint pen, and nails. She directs the groups to experiment with the magnets and items for 10 minutes and to write their observations and findings on a sheet of paper. As they work, she responds to questions and makes periodic comments. The groups report their findings, and the class discusses them as a whole group.

David Brosky has his eighth-grade American history students break into pairs. He gives each pair a chart that lists facts about the Jamestown and Plymouth colonies and asks them to identify and write down as many similarities and differences between the two as they can in 5 minutes. He circulates among the students as they work, and at the end of the allotted time, they report to the class and identify patterns in the descriptions.

Mary Willis's students are working on word problems involving areas of geometric shapes. She divides the class into teams of three and asks each team to work on the problems. As they work, she checks on their progress, offering brief suggestions when she sees errors that point them down "blind alleys." After the groups finish, they take turns explaining how they solved the problems. Mary encourages the rest of the class to raise additional questions, to ask the presenters to justify their thinking, and to volunteer alternative explanations.

In whole-group activities, it's easy for quiet or less confident students to become uninvolved. Students learn that opportunities for participation are limited, and some drift off, even in stimulating discussions. In addition, individual students often don't get the chance to construct and defend their own conclusions and to share them with others. To encourage the involvement of all learners, student groupwork can be an effective alternative.

Several of the teachers in the cases you've already studied used groupwork as an integral part of their instruction. Jan Davis in Chapter 1, Jenny Newhall in Chapter 2, David Shelton and Sue Southam in Chapter 7, and Patty Kramer and Suzanne Brush in Chapter 8 all used groupwork during their learning activities. Groupwork's primary advantage is that it applies the constructivist principle of learning being facilitated by social interaction. Although whole-group activities can include a great deal of social interaction, the opportunity for all students to be involved increases during groupwork.

Planning and Conducting Groupwork Activities

The key to effective groupwork is organization. Tasks must be designed that promote learning and encourage student interaction (Cohen, 1994). Materials must be readily available and quickly distributed to each group, and students must be able to get into and out of groups easily and quickly. If the process isn't well organized, instructional time is lost in transitions. Goals and directions must be very clear to prevent activities from disintegrating into aimless "bull sessions."

Suggestions for planning and organizing effective groupwork include the following:

12.38
Identify the task that each of the three teachers at the beginning of this section specified for their students. What was the product that each of the groups had to provide?

▌ Train students in groupwork with short, simple tasks, such as the ones Stacy Sims and David Brosky used. (Mary Willis's was more difficult; her students had to generate specific solutions to problems.)

▌ Have students practice moving into and out of the groups quickly. Group members can be seated together prior to the activity to make the transition from the whole-class activity to student groups and back again with little disruption.

▌ Give students a clear and specific task to accomplish in the groups.

- Specify the amount of time students are allowed to accomplish the task (and keep it short).
- Require that students produce a product as a result of the groupwork.
- Monitor the groups while they're involved in the activity.

Effective use of student groups requires that all of the elements be employed. Seating students together prevents loss of instructional time in transitions. Clear directions, a short and specific time limit, a required product, and monitoring all help keep students on task.

Cooperative Learning

In comparing groupwork to cooperative learning, you can see they're similar, differing primarily in structure. Groupwork typically involves students simply working collaboratively on some task, whereas cooperative learning is more highly structured, and the mix of students in the groups is more carefully specified.

Cooperative learning *is a set of teaching strategies used to help learners meet specific learning and interpersonal goals in highly structured groups.* Groups of three, four, or five are common, with four often described as the ideal. Groups larger than five are unwieldy; they limit individual participation and are generally not recommended (Cohen, 1986; Slavin, 1995). To facilitate interpersonal goals, attempts are also made to balance the groups by ability, gender, ethnicity, and special needs.

Researchers have identified specific characteristics or elements of effective cooperative learning activities (D. Johnson & Johnson, 1994; Slavin, 1995):

- *Positive interdependence:* Activities are structured so that students must depend on each other to successfully reach their goals. Interdependence can be promoted by giving students different tasks, materials or information, and roles or by establishing group rather than individual rewards.
- *Face-to-face interaction:* Activities should require students to interact. Activities that can be done as effectively alone as in a group, such as learning to use a microscope, are not well suited for cooperative learning.
- *Individual accountability:* One purpose of cooperative learning is to increase the achievement of each student, and every group member is responsible for learning the content.
- *Interpersonal skills:* The development of interpersonal skills is an important goal for cooperative learning. Interpersonal skills are explicitly taught and monitored.

Let's look at two cooperative learning models.

> 12.39
> How will individual accountability in cooperative learning most commonly be accomplished? What does this imply about students receiving group grades (all students in a group receiving the same grade)?

Student Teams Achievement Divisions (STAD)

Created by Robert Slavin (1995), **STAD** *implements cooperative learning by using a structured system of reinforcers to promote concept, skill, and fact learning.* STAD typically follows a direct instruction format, but in place of solitary independent practice, *team study* is used. During team study, students complete exercises on teacher-prepared work sheets and compare their results with those of their teammates. The teacher intervenes only if team members are unable to resolve disagreements about answers. Team study is complete when all teammates understand and can explain the problems or exercises.

Team study is followed by quizzes, which are scored as they would be in any other situation. Individuals contribute to team rewards by improving their performance, compared with past quizzes and tests.

Although reinforcers are used with STAD, teachers can reduce the emphasis on them by focusing on personal improvement and by stressing that teams do not compete with each other. All groups can achieve the highest group rewards if they improve enough or have high enough averages.

Jigsaw II

12.40
Positive interdependence is one characteristic of cooperative learning. What type of interdependence is promoted with STAD? What kind is promoted with Jigsaw II? Explain.

Jigsaw II *is a form of cooperative learning in which individual students become experts on subsections of a topic and teach that subsection to others.* In contrast with STAD, which is most effective in teaching procedural skills, Jigsaw II is designed to teach organized bodies of knowledge. In a unit on Central America, for instance, a social studies teacher may have one student from each team focus on the geography, another the climate, a third the economy, and a fourth the political system of each country. Individuals study their topics and then attend "expert meetings," in which all students assigned to a particular topic (e.g., the climate) meet, compare notes, and clarify their understanding. "Experts" then teach the members of their teams. Each member contributes a different piece of the knowledge puzzle; thus, the name Jigsaw. All members are held accountable for the content of each area.

Research on Cooperative Learning

Research indicates that cooperative learning methods have been effective in increasing achievement—including higher level outcomes, such as problem solving—in a variety of content areas, the results appear on both teacher-made and standardized tests, and they've been found at all grade levels (Cohen, 1994; O'Donnell & Dansereau, 1992; Quin, Johnson, & Johnson, 1995; Slavin, 1995).

Research also indicates that cooperative learning can promote friendships and positive attitudes toward students differing in achievement, ethnicity, and gender, in addition to fostering the acceptance of mainstreamed students with exceptionalities (Slavin, 1995).

Cooperative Learning: A Tool for Capitalizing on Diversity

You saw earlier that cooperative learning methods, in addition to increasing achievement, are effective for promoting friendships and positive attitudes toward students who differ in achievement, ethnicity, gender, and exceptionality (Slavin, 1995). Let's see how a teacher uses cooperative learning to improve interpersonal relations among a group of students with diverse backgrounds.

As Maria Sanchez watched her third graders bent over their work, she was simultaneously pleased and uneasy. On the one hand, they had made huge strides in their math and reading abilities since the beginning of the year, but on the other hand, they still didn't feel like a group. There was little mixing among her minority and non-minority students, she worried about the six in ESL who were still struggling with English, and then there were the four resource students who left her class every day for extra help. She could tell they felt different from the others and didn't want to leave.

Maria decided to try cooperative learning to see whether she could help the class become more cohesive. Because of her ESL students and the range of abilities in reading, she chose it as a beginning point. Over the weekend, she used comments from their previous year's teacher, their performance on her tests, and her own judgment to organize the students into groups of four, with equal numbers of high- and low-ability readers in each group. She also mixed the students by race and gender, and she put each ESL student and each student with exceptionalities into different groups. Then, she gathered materials that she would use with the groups.

On Monday, she began. She directed her students to their groups and explained how they were to work together. She sat with a group and modeled cooperation and being helpful for the rest of the students.

Then, she sent each group to a different part of the room to begin working on specific tasks to help them become better acquainted. When they moved to the reading groups, one student from each group would read a paragraph, and another student would ask the other members of the group questions, using stems that Maria had provided. As they worked, Maria moved around the room, promoting cooperation, ensuring that all students were involved, and preventing individuals from dominating the groups.

After a demanding but fairly successful session, Maria sent her students outside for recess.

"Phew," she thought to herself as she surveyed the classroom. "This sure isn't any easier, but it already seems to be a little better."

The benefits of having diverse students work together don't just happen; they require careful planning and monitoring, particularly when students are first introduced to the process. To maximize the benefits of cooperative learning, teachers need to organize groups carefully, structure tasks to promote interaction, train groups to function effectively, and monitor group progress (Cohen, 1994). Let's look at these tasks.

Grouping

As you saw in Maria's case, cooperative learning groups should have equal numbers of high- and low-ability students, boys and girls, ethnic minorities, and students with exceptionalities, particularly when the goal is to promote positive relationships among students.

Learning Tasks

To be successful in promoting acceptance of diversity, cooperative learning tasks must require cooperation and communication (Cohen, 1994; Good, McCaslin, & Reys, 1992). Maria accomplished this by providing question stems for each group and by having students take turns reading paragraphs and asking and answering questions. By rotating students through these roles, Maria encouraged participation from all group members and helped prevent the more aggressive students from dominating the activity. Other tasks that can be used to encourage communication and cooperation include presenting and checking math problems, practicing spelling and grammar exercises in which students take turns as students and tutors, and providing open-ended problems (Cohen, 1994; Quin et al., 1995).

Training

Effective group interaction doesn't just happen; it must be planned for and taught to students. Effective helping behaviors can be taught, and these skills appear especially valuable for minority students, who are often hesitant about seeking and giving help (Webb & Farivar, 1994). Effective group interaction skills include the following (S. Kagan, 1994; Webb & Farivar, 1994):

- *Listening and questioning skills:* Helping other students verbalize and express their ideas and learning to listen to others' ideas without judging them
- *Checking for understanding:* Asking for elaboration when answers are incomplete
- *Staying on-task:* Making sure the discussion remains focused and time limits are met
- *Emotional support:* Supportive comments for incorrect answers (e.g., "That's okay. I don't always get it the first time either.")

12.41
Provide a specific explanation for why students are more likely to develop more positive attitudes toward students different from themselves in cooperative learning groups than in whole-group activities.

12.42
Describe an open-ended problem from your content area that might be effective with a diverse group of students.

Cooperative learning involves students in small-group learning activities that teach both content and interpersonal skills.

Role playing, teacher modeling, and videotapes of effective groups are all effective in teaching these skills (Fitch & Semb, 1992).

Monitoring

As Maria found, groups need constant monitoring and support, especially in the beginning. Research indicates that student achievement is directly related to the quality of interaction within groups (Cohen, 1991), which influences group cohesion and intragroup relations. Teachers can deal with problems in individual groups or, if the problem persists, can reconvene the class for discussion, additional modeling, and role playing.

Classroom
Connections

Capitalizing on Diversity in Your Classroom

1. Use the composition of cooperative learning groups to capitalize on the strengths of diverse students.
   • A first-grade teacher waits for several weeks into the school year to form cooperative learning groups in her classroom. She uses this time to observe her students and to gather data about student interests and talents, as well as peer-group friendships. Using this information, she forms groups that are diverse in terms of ability, ethnicity, and gender.

2. Design learning tasks that require group interaction and cooperation.
   • A sixth-grade math teacher uses cooperative learning groups to provide practice and feedback in his class. When he assigns word problems, he asks students to work in pairs and to compare and explain their answers to the other students in the

pair before checking their answers on an answer sheet.

- A high school English teacher uses cooperative learning as a way to provide student reactions and responses to each other's writing. Students in each group take turns reading and reacting to each other's works on the basis of elements of style and clarity and make suggestions for the next revision.

3. Use warm-up, introductory, and team-building exercises to promote interaction within groups.
    - A junior high social studies teacher encourages cooperative learning group solidarity by having members interview each other about such things as their favorite food, hobby, song, or vacation. Each interviewer then presents this information to other members of the group in a round-robin format.
    - A high school teacher starts her cooperative learning activities with an icebreaker called "Truth and Lies." Each person in the group says four things about him- or herself, three of which are true and one of which is a lie. The others try to guess which one is the lie.

4. Provide feedback to students about their interactions within the group.

- A high school English teacher walks around the room during reader response sessions and joins in with the students during the groups. Comments such as, "I really like the way you used examples from his writing to tell him what you liked," help students understand how to give constructive feedback.
- A kindergarten teacher sometimes interrupts cooperative learning activities when she detects problems, such as students arguing about who gets to perform a certain task. She tells them they must learn to cooperatively solve their problem, and she models cooperation in a simulation and think-aloud.

5. Evaluate cooperative learning groups to determine their effectiveness.
    - A fourth-grade teacher asks her students to fill out evaluation forms after cooperative group activities. On the half-sheet of paper, she asks students to tell her:
      a. What I learned
      b. What I liked about working in the group
      c. How the group could help me learn better

Individualized Instruction

In our discussion of learner-centered approaches to instruction, we examined guided discovery, discussions, groupwork, and cooperative learning, which involve a trend from whole-group to small-group instruction. We complete the trend in this section with a discussion of individualization.

Individualization *is a form of instruction adapted to meet the specific learning needs of each student.* Three ways of individualizing are (a) varying time available for learning, (b) varying learning activities, and (c) varying instructional materials.

Varying Time Available for Learning

Learners differ in the amount of time needed to master a topic, with high achievers needing less time than do low achievers (Slavin, 1987). Teachers often accommodate this difference by giving common assignments and then providing extra instruction for small groups while the majority of the students work on seatwork or enrichment activities.

In skill areas, a technique called *team-assisted individualization* (Slavin, 1985) keeps objectives constant but varies the time and resources available to students. In it, students work on individualized learning materials in mixed-ability teams. Similar to STAD, it differs primarily in the fact that, with team-assisted individualization, the teacher provides direct instruction to small groups.

Varying Learning Activities

12.43 ▰
Identify a topic area in which student choice would be effective and desirable, and identify another topic area in which it wouldn't be advisable.

Varying learning activities provides a second way of individualizing. For instance, an English teacher might allow students to write a paper, give an oral report, or prepare a multimedia presentation about an author. A science teacher may allow students to prepare written reports or to conduct an investigation. Allowing students choices in learning activities provides opportunities for students to pursue topics of individual interest, and this pursuit can greatly increase motivation.

Varying Instructional Materials

12.44 ▰
Suppose you have students of widely varying ability in your groups. Which type of activity—David Brosky's or Mary Willis's—would be more effective for these students? Explain why.

Individualization has become easier in recent years, with the increased availability of audiovisual materials (audio- and videotaped instruction, filmstrips, and computer software), together with advice on how to select appropriate media (Good & Brophy, 1994). If these materials are not available, reading passages can be made more accessible by providing study guides and by conducting prereading discussions that focus on key ideas (T. Anderson & Armbruster, 1984).

Research on Individualized Instruction

Research results examining individualized instruction are mixed. Individualization appears to be most effective when assessment is frequent and opportunities for student choice, self-regulation, and peer cooperation exist (Good & Brophy, 1994). Although acknowledging that some students need more time and instruction than others, Good and Brophy (1994) conclude, "It seems more appropriate to develop high-quality instructional materials and methods intended for all students than to set out from the beginning to develop different materials and methods for various students" (p. 333). Further, they note, although individualization is well suited to practice on basic skills, it is not well suited to higher order thinking and problem solving.

Teacher-Centered and Learner-Centered Approaches to Instruction: A Final Look

In this chapter, we have attempted to present a balanced look at teacher-centered and learner-centered approaches to instruction. We end this chapter with three final reminders.

First, teachers need to keep in mind that all approaches to instruction are intended to help students reach goals; they are not goals in themselves. This statement may seem self-evident, but instructional strategies sometimes "take on a life of their own": The strategy becomes the goal. For example, putting students into groups is not an appropriate goal. One goal might be to help students develop interpersonal skills, and if that's the case, cooperative learning can be effective. Don't use cooperative learning for the sake of using cooperative learning.

This advice applies to all forms of student-centered approaches to instruction. We encourage their use because research indicates that they are often more effective than teacher-centered approaches for helping students acquire a deep understanding of content (the goal). Don't use them for their own sake.

Second, regardless of approach, effective instruction is aligned. Teachers must be clear about their goals and design learning activities to reach them. Learner-centered approaches to instruction do not in any way reduce the need for instructional alignment. Shirley Barton began her lesson with a problem, for example, and used a hands-on activity to help her students understand the concept of *equivalent fractions*. She chose this approach because it was aligned with her goal. She didn't use a hands-on approach for its own sake.

Third, no strategy is any better than the teacher using it. The real issue is not the effectiveness of direct instruction or guided discovery as methods, for example; it is the ability of the teacher using them. For some goals, direct instruction may be the most effective method; for others, guided discovery may be better. In the past, experts and researchers tried to develop "teacher proof" methods and curricula. They were unsuccessful. We would be better served trying to prepare teachers capable of exercising sound judgment, flexibility, and sensitivity (Michaels & O'Connor, 1990). Nothing substitutes for the expertise of the teacher.

Classroom Connections

Using Learner-Centered Approaches to Instruction in Your Classroom

1. Focus on deep understanding of topics.
   - A fifth-grade teacher involved in a discussion of force puts a book on a table and asks questions such as:
     "Is the table exerting a force on the book?"
     "Is the book exerting a force on the table?"
     "Why or why not?"
     "Suppose I lift the book off the table. Am I exerting a force on the book? Is it exerting a force on me? If the answer to these two questions is yes, which force is greater? How do you know?"
     She then leads a discussion of these questions in which she attempts to reconcile different student positions.

2. Use a variety of examples and representations of the topics you teach.
   - A sixth-grade teacher beginning a unit on folktales writes a series of "folktales" about the school principal and other teachers. She also has students read folktales about characters such as John Bunyon and Pecos Bill and provides a matrix linking folktales to true historical events. She then discusses some contemporary figures that have been described in the media as "folk heroes" and how they may have achieved that status. Finally, she has the students write their own "folktales" about anyone they choose.

3. Use guided-discovery approaches to instruction.
   - A fourth-grade teacher embeds illustrations of possessive pronouns and singular and plural possessive nouns in the context of a paragraph. He then guides the students' discussion as they develop explanations for why sentences such as "The girls' and boys' accomplishments in the middle school were noteworthy, as were the children's feats in the elementary school" were punctuated the way they were.
   - A first-grade teacher begins a unit on reptiles by bringing a snake and a turtle to class. She then includes colored pictures of lizards, alligators, and sea turtles. She has the students describe the live animals and the pictures and then guides them to the essential characteristics of reptiles.

Conducting Effective Discussions in Your Classroom

4. Ensure that students have a solid informational background before conducting a discussion.
   - A biology teacher is planning a discussion of global warming. Before the discussion, she presents information about the depletion of the Amazon rain forest, U.S. data on carbon dioxide emissions, and Eastern European countries' records on air emissions.

5. Begin discussions with a clear issue or problem and keep the discussion focused on the issue.
   - A history teacher involved in a discussion of the efficacy of the U.S. involvement in Vietnam asks simply, "Considering the historical context, was America's decision to go into Vietnam a wise one?" He then keeps the students focused on America's initial decision to begin the conflict. When they discuss the war's outcome, he refocuses them on the original decision.

Using Groupwork Effectively in Your Classroom

6. Introduce students to groupwork by using simple, open-ended tasks.
   - A second-grade teacher gives her students a cup of materials (containing sand, iron filings, salt; and aluminum foil, water, and a magnet). She directs the students to experiment with the materials and to make as many observations as possible.

Using Individualization Effectively in Your Classroom

7. Vary objectives and learning activities.
   - To increase students' interest in art, a teacher provides watercolors and clay and allows students to work on individual projects within these different media.
   - A social studies teacher uses a unit on American immigrants to allow her students to explore their own cultural and ethnic backgrounds. After introducing the topic, she has students work individually or in groups exploring the history of their ethnic group in the United States, as well as their own family histories. At the end of the unit, students share their findings.

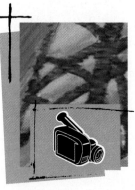

Windows on Classrooms

In studying this chapter, we've examined essential teaching skills and both teacher-centered and learner-centered approaches to instruction. At the beginning of this chapter, you saw how Shirley Barton planned and conducted her lesson in an effort to actively involve her students in learning and to place them at the center of the learning process.

Let's look now at another teacher working with a class of ninth-grade geography students. As you read the case study, consider the extent to which the teacher applied in her lesson the information you've studied in this chapter.

Judy Holmquist, a ninth-grade geography teacher at Lakeside Junior High School, is involved in a unit on climate regions of the United States. To begin the unit, she divided the class into groups, and each group gathered information about the geography, economy, ethnic groups, and future issues of Florida, California, New York, and Alaska. She then put into the matrix the information the students had gathered (see p. 511):

Judy began the day's lesson by referring the class to information they had gathered and put on the chart and reminded them they would be looking for similarities and differences in the information. After focusing their attention on the information in the first column, she began by saying, "What I want you to do is get with your partner and write down three differences and similarities on just the geography portion of the chart. I want three, and I

	Geography	**Economy**	**Ethnic Groups**	**Future Issues**
	Coastal plain	Citrus industry	Native Americans	Population explosion
F	Florida uplands	Tourism	Spanish	Immigration problems
L	Hurricane season	Fishing	Cubans	Pollution
O	Warm ocean currents	Forestry	Haitians	Tax revisions
R	Temp. Moisture	Cattle	African American	Money for education
I	Dec. 69 1.8			
D	March 72 2.4			
A	June 81 9.3			
	Sept 82 7.6			

	Geography	**Economy**	**Ethnic Groups**	**Future Issues**
C	Coastal ranges	Citrus industry	Spanish	Earthquakes
A	Cascades	Wine/vineyards	Mexican	Deforestation
L	Sierra Nevadas	Fishing	Asian	Population explosion
I	Central Valley	Lumber	African American	Pollution
F	Desert	Television/Hollywood		Immigration problems
O	Temp. Moisture	Tourism		
R	Dec. 54 2.5	Computers		
N	March 57 2.8			
I	June 66 T			
A	Sept. 69 .3			

	Geography	**Economy**	**Ethnic Groups**	**Future Issues**
N	Atlantic Coastal Plain	Vegetables	Dutch	Industrial decline
E	New England uplands	Fishing	Native Americans	Decaying urban areas
W	Appalachian Plateau	Apples	Italians	Waste disposal
	Adirondack Mts.	Forestry	French	Crime
Y	Temp. Moisture	Light manufacturing	Polish	Homelessness
O	Dec. 37 3.9	Entertainment/TV	Puerto Rican	Crowded schools
R	March 42 4.1		African American	
K	June 72 3.7		English	
	Sept. 68 3.9		Irish	
			Russian	

	Geography	**Economy**	**Ethnic Groups**	**Future Issues**
	Rocky Mountains	Mining	Eskimo (Inuit)	Unemployment
	Brooks Range	Fishing	Native Americans	Cost of living
A	Panhandle area	Trapping	Russian	Oil spills
L	Plateaus between mountains	Lumbering/forestry		Pollution
A	Islands/treeless	Oil/pipeline		
S	Warm ocean currents	Tourism		
K	Temp. Moisture			
A	Dec -7 .9			
	March 11 .4			
	June 60 1.4			
	Sept. 46 1.0			

want them written down on this paper, and I want you to each write them down so that if I call on one or the other of you, you've got the information right in front of you. . . . So get together with your partner."

As Judy moved among the groups, offering help and answering questions, Chris raised his hand and said, "I don't understand exactly what we're supposed to do."

"Okay, you take a look at the geography column. . . . You give me three things that are alike and three things that are different," Judy explained quietly.

"All right, in all four of them or in two of them?" Matt continued.

"In all four of the regions. Yes. From all four of the regions. Yes. You got it," she confirmed, and they went to work.

"Three things that are similar; three differences," she repeated in response to a question from another group, and she repeated it a second and a third time in response to other questions, in the process reminding the class that they had 4 minutes to complete the task.

"The temperature like in September in New York and California. Can I put that down as the same, cuz they're like 68 in California and 69 in New York?" Kiki asked as they were working.

"Yes," Judy nodded, "and you might think about why, too," and she reminded the class that they could use the climate and physical maps in their books as additional sources of information.

"Okay, Ann," she said in response to another question.

"Like for similarities, do they have to be like in all of them?"

"Not necessarily, no. It could be in just two of them."

"Okay," Ann said brightly.

Judy continued to respond to questions as the students worked,

gave them another minute, and then called them back together.

"You look like you're doing a good job. . . . Okay, I think we're ready."

The class turned their attention to the front of the room, and Judy began, "Give me a piece of information, Jackie," she began, "about the geography column."

"Mmm, they all have mountains except for Florida."

"Okay, they all have mountains except for Florida," Judy repeated and wrote it under "Similarities" on the chalkboard.

"Give me something else. . . . Jeff?"

"They all touch the oceans in places."

"Okay, what else? Give me something else. Go ahead, Todd."

"They're all in four corners."

"Okay, we have four corners."

"What else? . . . Missy?"

"New York and Florida both have coastal plains."

"Okay, New York and Florida both have coastal plains," she again repeated, writing the information on the chalkboard.

"Okay, you two in the back. I can hear you. Scott, give me something."

"They all have cold weather in December."

"Aha," Judy chuckled, "We're going to look at that one. Cold weather in December."

"Okay. . . . Tim?"

"All the summer temperatures are above 50% . . . er 50°," Tim answered to some laughter from the rest of the class.

"What else can you tell me? How about some differences?" Judy encouraged. "Okay, Chris?"

"The temperature ranges a lot."

"All right. . . . John?"

"Different climate zones."

The students offered several additional differences, and Judy then continued, "Okay, Kiki?"

"Alaska gets below zero. It's the only . . . is the only one that gets below zero."

"It's the only one that gets below zero in winter. Is that what you said, Sweetheart?" Judy asked to confirm Kiki's response, and Kiki nodded.

"Okay, let's have a little bit more. I know you've got some more. I see it written on your paper."

"Carnisha, do you have anything to add, Sweetheart?"

"All except Alaska have less than 4 inches of moisture in the winter," Carnisha offered.

"Okay, have we exhausted your lists? Anyone else have anything more to add?"

Judy waited a few seconds and then said, "Okay, now I want you to look at the economy, and I want you to write down three similarities and three differences in terms of the economy. And you have 3 minutes."

The students again went back to work, and Judy monitored the students as she had done during the first part of the lesson.

After they finished, she again called for and received a number of similarities and differences based on the information in the "Economy" column.

She then shifted the direction of the lesson, saying, "Okay, great. . . . Okay, let's take a look at this. Now, . . . why in terms of a similarity do they all have fishing?" she asked, waving her hand across the class as she walked toward the back of the room. "John?"

"They're all near the coast."

"Okay, why do they all have forestry? . . . Okay, Jeremy?"

"They all have lots of trees," he answered to smiles from the rest of the class.

"Now, if they have lots of trees, what does this tell you about their climate?"

"It's warm enough for them to grow."

"But along with being warm enough, it has . . . ?"

"Fertile soil."

"And?"

"Moisture."

"Great, Okay.

"Now, let's take a look. We have fruit in California and Florida. Why do we have the citrus industry there?"

"Okay, Jackie, good," she said, seeing Jackie's raised hand.

"Never mind."

"Pardon?"

"Never mind."

"Oh, you know," Judy encouraged.

"No."

"Why do we grow oranges down here?"

"It's the climate."

"All right, because of the climate. Okay, now. Jackie says it's because of the climate. What kind of climate allows the citrus industry? . . . Tim?"

" . . . Humid subtropical."

"Okay, humid subtropical. Humid subtropical means that we have what? . . . Go ahead."

"Long humid summers, short mild winters," he replied, reading from the book.

"Does California have the same thing?"

"No."

"What does it say about California?"

"Tropical and subtropical desert," Tim answered.

"Okay. Tourism. Why does each area have tourism?" Judy continued. "Okay, Lance?"

"Because they're all spread out. They're each at four corners, and they have different seasons that they're popular in."

Judy then asked what made Alaska popular, and in response to a statement about mountains and dog sled racing, she diverged to a comment about the Iditarod dog sled race in Alaska, to some giggles from the class.

She then said, "Okay, back on-task. . . . We have tourism in all four areas. Now, in terms of differences, Alaska also has trapping. Can anyone tell me what trapping is? Go ahead, Jeff in back."

"That's like where they trap beavers and stuff and sell their hides."

"Okay, within conservation practices, this is where you get your fur coat, if you're brave enough to wear them in the colder climates," Judy acknowledged.

Then, seeing that the period was nearing a close, she said, "Okay, let's deal with one issue. I want to know what effect. . . . Listen up. I want to know what effect the climate has on the economy of those regions."

She gave the class 1 minute to work again in their pairs, announcing that she expected to hear from as many people as possible.

"Let's see what you've got for an answer," she said after the minute had passed. "Braden, you had one. . . . Okay, I want to know what effect, . . . listen up, excuse me, Brooks, . . . I want to know what effect geography, which is climate and landforms, has on the economy," she said, pointing at Braden.

"If you have mountains in the area, you can't have farmland," he responded.

"Okay, what else? . . . Becky?"

"The climate affects like what's grown and like what's done inside the section."

"Okay, great. Climate affects what's grown and what was the last part of that?"

"Like what's done," Becky repeated as the bell rang.

Judy waved, "Okay, great. Class dismissed," as the students began gathering their materials to move to their next class period.

Questions for Discussion and Analysis

Analyze Judy's lesson now in the context of the information in this chapter. In doing your analysis, you may want to consider the following questions. In each case, be specific and take information directly from the case study.

1. Which essential teaching skills did Judy Holmquist demonstrate in her lesson? Confirm your conclusions with information taken directly from the case study.

2. Did Judy use primarily a teacher-centered or a learner-centered approach to instruction in her lesson? Explain, using information taken directly from the case study.

3. To what extent did Judy apply constructivist principles of learning in her lesson? Explain, using information taken from the case study.

4. How effectively did Judy use groupwork to promote learning? Assess her use of groupwork, using the following criteria: (a) clearly specified task, (b) concrete product, and (c) teacher monitoring.

5. Now, provide an overall assessment of the lesson. Provide evidence taken from the case study in making your assessment. What could Judy have done to make the lesson more effective? Be specific in making your suggestions.

 **Summary**

Teacher Effectiveness and Essential Teaching Skills

Essential teaching skills are the teaching behaviors that promote student learning. Effective teachers are high in efficacy; they believe they are responsible for student learning and can increase it. In addition, they are caring, enthusiastic, good role models, and have high expectations for their students.

Effective teachers are well organized, use their time well, communicate clearly, and carefully monitor their students' verbal and nonverbal behavior. They represent content in attention-getting ways, provide clear and informative feedback to students, and review important ideas.

Effective teachers use effective questioning strategies. They ask many questions, prompt students who don't answer successfully, employ equitable distribution, and give students time to think about their answers.

Teacher-Centered Approaches to Instruction

When teaching procedural skills, such as grammar and punctuation rules or the solving of algebraic equations, direct instruction can be effective. When teaching organized bodies of knowledge, lectures and lecture-recitations can be used. Lecture-recitations help overcome some of the weaknesses of lectures by placing students in an active role during the lesson. Effective lecture-recitations ensure that students comprehend the information being presented and integrate it with what they already know in a cyclic process.

Student-Centered Approaches to Instruction

Improvements in the understanding of learning, together with criticisms of teacher-centered approaches to instruction, have led to an increased focus on learners in the learning process. Characterized by emphasis on deep understanding of topics and constructivist views of learning, learner-centered approaches require expert teachers and include guided discovery, discussions, groupwork and cooperative learning, and individualization.

A Final Look at Teacher-Centered and Learner-Centered Approaches to Instruction

The approach to instruction that teachers use should depend on their goals. Effective teachers have clear goals and present learning activities that are aligned with them. Effective teachers remember that the approach to instruction is a means to reaching the goal; it isn't the goal itself.

 **Important Concepts**

closure (p. 482)

cooperative learning (p. 503)

connected discourse (p. 478)

direct instruction (p. 486)

discovery learning (p. 497)

discussions (p. 500)

emphasis (p. 479)

essential teaching skills (p. 475)

feedback (p. 479)

guided discovery (p. 497)

individualization (p. 507)

introductory focus (p. 479)

Jigsaw II (p. 504)

lecture-recitations (p. 490)

monitoring (p. 480)

organization (p. 477)

organized bodies of knowledge (p. 489)

precise terminology (p. 478)

procedural skills (p. 486)

prompting (p. 481)

review (p. 482)

sensory focus (p. 479)

STAD (p. 503)

student groupwork (p. 501)

teacher effectiveness literature (p. 475)

teaching efficacy (p. 476)

transition signals (p. 478)

unstructured discovery (p. 497)

wait-time (p. 482)

Chapter Outline

13 Assessing Classroom Learning

Kathy Stevens walked among the desks of her seventh graders as they worked on their seatwork assignment. "Check that one again," she whispered as she passed Kim. She continued this process for another 5 minutes, checking each student's work as she walked by. She then called for the students' attention.

"Let me hand back your quizzes," she announced. "You did fine on today's. You seem to understand when you explain your solutions, and you're doing okay on your homework, so we're going to have our test

Thursday. We'll review a little more tomorrow to be sure you understand the word problems," she smiled.

"Now, let's take a look at a few items that a few of you missed on the quiz," she continued as she finished handing the papers back to the students.

Later, as she worked on her test in the faculty lounge, Ken Allen, another math teacher, walked by. "How's your new system working?" he asked.

"Good," she returned. "Since I've been giving the short quiz every

day, they're more conscientious about their homework, and they did better on the last test."

"Tell me again exactly what you're doing."

"I just give them a problem or two every day that's based on their homework. I score it while they begin the next day's assignment, and I hand it back at the end of the period. If we have an extra-tough topic, I don't get a quiz in every day, but they get at least three a week."

The following quote, contained in a review of research on teachers' classroom evaluation practices, underscores the powerful effect that teachers' quizzes, tests, and other assessments have on the learning behavior of students.

> Here is something approaching a law of learning behavior for students: namely that the quickest way to change learning is to change the assessment system. (Elton & Laurillard, 1979, p. 100)

Despite its importance, teachers often feel ill-prepared to deal with the complexities of classroom assessment (R. Linn, 1990). Experienced teachers express concerns about their ability to write individual assessment items, to construct valid assessments, and to assign grades (Crooks, 1988; Haertel, 1986). Beginning teachers also express concerns about their ability to assess student progress (Lomax, 1994), ranking this problem fourth, after management, motivation, and dealing with individual differences (Veenman, 1984).

In this chapter, we address these concerns by examining the effects of assessment on learning and motivation, analyzing teachers' assessment patterns, and describing ways to design effective classroom assessments.

After you've completed this chapter, you should be able to meet the following objectives:

- Describe and explain basic assessment concepts.
- Describe classroom teachers' assessment patterns.
- Identify characteristics in specific assessment items that detract from their validity.
- Construct alternative assessments in your content area or grade level.
- Apply effective assessment procedures in classrooms.

Classroom Assessment

The case study at the beginning of the chapter illustrates one of the most basic and difficult tasks teachers face in their work: assessment. **Classroom assessment** *involves all the*

processes and tools teachers use to make decisions about their students' progress. These include observations of students' seatwork and homework, their voluntary responses and answers to questions, and their results on teacher-made and standardized tests. It includes authentic assessments, such as watching first graders print, observing a word-processing class type a letter, and having auto mechanics students actually repair an engine. It also involves decisions, such as assigning grades, reteaching a topic, and providing supplementary instruction. When combined, *these elements make up the teacher's* **assessment system.** In Kathy's case, her system included monitoring her students' progress by using their homework, her quizzes, and her tests.

Functions of Classroom Assessment

13.1 ▬
How would a behaviorist explain the advantage of frequent, announced quizzes over those given infrequently? (Hint: Think about the concept of *reinforcement schedules* from Chapter 6.)

In addition to gathering information and making decisions about learning progress, assessment accomplishes two other important goals: (a) increasing learning and (b) increasing motivation (Crooks, 1988).

The relationship between learning and assessment is strong and robust. Students learn more in classes where assessment is an integral part of instruction than in those where it isn't, and brief, frequent assessments are more effective than long, infrequent ones (Bangert-Drowns, Kulik, & Kulik, 1991; Dempster, 1991; Kika, McLaughlin, & Dixon, 1992).

Implying a link between testing and motivation is somewhat controversial because, ideally, students should be motivated to learn for its own sake. Critics even argue that assessment can detract from motivation. In the real world, however, evidence runs counter to these arguments (Crooks, 1988). Think about your own experiences. In which classes did you learn the most, and for which did you study the hardest? For most students, those classes are the ones in which they're frequently and thoroughly assessed.

13.2 ▬
Should you describe for your students precisely what your tests will cover? Why or why not? Should you go over tests item by item once they've been taken and scored? Again, why or why not?

In recalling your study of Chapter 9, you can see an additional link between assessment and motivation. There, you found that learners have a need to know what they are supposed to learn, why they are learning it, and how they are progressing. Assessment is a vehicle for providing this information, and it exerts a powerful influence not only on how much students study but also on the way they study (Crooks, 1988).

Measurement and Evaluation

Two fundamental processes are involved in assessment: **measurement,** *which includes all the information teachers gather as part of the assessment process,* and **evaluation,** *which refers to the decisions teachers make on the basis of the measurements.*

Effective teachers use a range of measurement tools to capture different aspects of student learning. Some, as listed in Figure 13.1, use traditional paper-and-pencil formats, whereas others employ alternative formats to assess higher order thinking and problem-solving ability.

13.3 ▬
Identify an important similarity and an important difference between traditional and alternative measurement formats. Also identify an advantage and a disadvantage of each.

The process of assigning grades is what teachers commonly think of as evaluation, and this is an important part of the process, but evaluation also includes other decisions, such as when to assess, what form the assessment will take, and whether to reteach a topic. Kathy's decision to give her test on Thursday was an evaluation, and the students' oral responses, their homework, and the quiz scores were the measurements she used to help her reach that decision.

Figure 13.1

Traditional and alternative measurement formats

Traditional Measurement Formats	Alternative Measurement Formats
True-false	Specific performance task
Multiple choice	Timed trial
Matching	Exhibition of work
Fill in the blank	Reflective journal entry
Short, open-ended answer	Open-ended oral presentation
Paragraph response to specific question	Oral response to specific question
Paragraph response to open-ended question	Collaborative group project
	Audiovisual presentation
Essay	Debate
	Simulation

Source: Adapted from Cheek (1993).

Formal and Informal Measurement

Informal measurements *are measurements gathered in an incidental way,* such as listening to students' comments and answers to questions, noticing puzzled looks, and seeing that a student isn't paying attention. In contrast, *the process of systematically gathering information is called* **formal measurement**. Tests and quizzes are formal measurements, as are performance observations, such as a physical education teacher observing the number of sit-ups a student can do.

The Need for Systematic Assessment

Informal measurements are essential in helping teachers make the frequent instructional decisions required in every class. Kathy used them to help her decide when to stop seatwork and when to schedule her test. Teachers also use informal measurements to decide how fast they can cover a topic, whom they should call on, and when they should stop one activity and move on to the next.

Informal measurements have an important drawback, however. Because teachers don't get the same information from each student, they don't know about individual students' progress. Concluding that the whole class understands an idea on the basis of responses from only a few can be a mistake.

Without realizing it, teachers sometimes make decisions as important as assigning grades on the basis of informal measurements. Students who respond readily and have engaging personalities are often awarded higher grades than their less outgoing peers. Further, students who are physically attractive are often judged more favorably by teachers than are their less attractive peers (Ritts, Patterson, & Tubbs, 1992). Gathering systematic information about each student's progress is one way to prevent these biases.

13.4
Identify an example of informal measurement in the case study illustrating Kathy Stevens's work with her students.

Gathering systematic information about each student and keeping current records about students' learning progress help ensure accurate assessment.

13.5

What would be an example of a systematic assessment in the class you're in now? What makes it systematic? What would be an example of an assessment that would not be called systematic?

13.6

Describe an example of a measurement that might be invalid for a student from a minority group. Why would it be invalid?

13.7

A junior high teacher gave her students the following writing assignment: "Describe a room in your home. Check to make sure your writing is correct in terms of grammar and punctuation." When she returned the papers, they had two grades: one for creativity and one for punctuation and grammar. Are both of these two grades valid? Explain.

13.8

Research indicates that increasing the length of a test increases reliability, but studies of child development indicate that attention spans of young children are limited. How can teachers reconcile these two findings?

Systematic assessment is particularly important in the lower elementary grades, where teachers often rely on performance assessments, such as handwriting samples and verbal identification of written numerals, to make evaluation decisions. The question "Could I defend and document this decision to a parent if necessary?" is a helpful guideline in this process.

Validity: Making Appropriate Evaluation Decisions

Validity *means that the assessment measures what it is supposed to measure.* It involves "the adequacy and appropriateness of the interpretations made from assessments, with regard to a particular use" (Gronlund & Linn, 1995, p. 47). Validity describes the link between the information gathered and the decisions made from that information (Shepard, 1993). From an instructional point of view, validity is the extent to which a measurement is congruent with goals and instruction.

The concept of *validity* is at the heart of many controversies in assessment. For example, many critics argue that standardized tests are culturally biased and, as a result, are invalid for minority students (Helms, 1992). Other critics assert that responses to questions measuring isolated and decontextualized skills—typical of standardized tests—give an incomplete and therefore invalid picture of student understanding. This assertion has contributed to the movement toward "alternative," or "authentic," assessment (Herman, Aschbacher, & Winters, 1992; Moss, 1992; we examine authentic assessment in detail later in the chapter).

In classrooms, validity suffers when assessment decisions are made on the basis of personality, appearance, or other factors not related to a lesson's goals. Also, teachers who give lower scores on essay items because of messy handwriting are using invalid criteria. Unfortunately, these actions are often unconscious; without realizing it, teachers base their assessments on appearance, rather than on substance.

None of this discussion implies, however, that teachers are doomed to using invalid assessments. The purpose of this discussion is to emphasize that awareness and careful judgment are required in the measurement process. Teachers who continually look for ways to improve their assessments, analyze patterns in student responses, and revise their measurements will increase the validity of their assessment system. These actions are a part of the reflective attitude that we emphasize throughout this text.

Reliability: Consistency in Measurement

Reliability, an intuitively sensible concept, *describes the extent to which measurements are consistent.* For instance, your bathroom scale might be no longer reliable; its readings vary whether your weight does or not. You are aggravated by people who are unreliable because you can't count on them to follow through on what they agree to do. Your old scale and those people are inconsistent. Unreliable measurements cannot be valid even if the measurements are consistent with the teacher's goals.

The influence of scoring consistency on reliability can be illustrated with essay tests, which are notoriously unreliable. Studies indicate that different instructors with similar backgrounds, ostensibly using the same criteria, have awarded grades ranging from excellent to failure on the same essay (Lindeman & Merenda, 1979). When this inconsistency occurs, lack of reliability makes the item invalid.

Similarly, informal measurements are often unreliable because, for example, not all students can respond to the same question. Uncertainty on one student's face doesn't necessarily mean the other students are confused; likewise, a quick, confident answer

from one student doesn't necessarily mean the entire class understands the topic. The solution is the use of formal, more reliable assessments.

Traditional Assessment

The way teachers historically have assessed learning, and the way a major part of learning will continue to be assessed, is through the use of teacher-made tests. When well designed and constructed, these tests provide valid assessments of many aspects of student progress (Gronlund & Linn, 1995). In this section, we examine teachers' assessment patterns and discuss ways of constructing different types of traditional measurement items to make them as valid and reliable as possible.

Teachers' Assessment Patterns

Laura Brinson's second graders are working on subtracting one-digit from two-digit numbers where regrouping is required. She has put a series of problems on the chalkboard, and the students are now busily involved in their solutions as Laura circulates among them.

"Check this one again, Kelly," she says, seeing that Kelly had written

$$\begin{array}{r} 24 \\ -\ 9 \\ \hline 25 \end{array}$$

on her paper.

"I think I'll take a grade on this one," Laura says to herself. She collects the papers after the students finish, scores them, and writes "90" in her grade book for Kelly because she missed one of the 10 problems from the chalkboard.

Table 13.1

Elementary teachers' assessment patterns

Characteristic	Description
Performance measures	Primary teachers rely heavily on actual samples of student work (e.g., the ability to form letters or write numerals) to evaluate student learning (Marso & Pigge, 1992).
Informal measurements	Measurement is often informal, as was the case in Laura's class. She comments, "I take a grade a few times a week. I don't really have a regular schedule that I follow for grading." Further, teachers sometimes give social and background characteristics greater emphasis than ability (Marso & Pigge, 1992; Salmon-Cox, 1981).
Commercially prepared tests	When they do test, elementary teachers depend heavily on commercially prepared and published tests. Teachers in the primary grades rarely prepare their own formal tests, instead using informal assessments or using exercises from texts or teachers' editions.
Emphasis on affective goals	Primary teachers emphasize affective goals, such as "Gets along well with others" (Salmon-Cox, 1981). In one analysis of kindergarten progress reports sent home to parents, over a third of the categories were devoted to intrapersonal or interpersonal factors (Freeman & Hatch, 1989).

Laura's assessment of her second graders is typical of elementary teachers, particularly at the primary level. She relies heavily on informal measures versus formal, teacher-made tests (see Table 13.1). In addition, elementary teachers tend to use commercially prepared items, such as those that come with textbook series, and they emphasize affective goals (Marso & Pigge, 1992; Stiggins & Conklin, 1992).

Middle school and senior high teachers' assessment practices differ in at least two ways from those of elementary teachers. They depend more on traditional tests than on performance measures, and they prepare their own items instead of relying on published tests. Table 13.2 presents characteristics of these teacher-made items (Boothroyd, McMorris, & Pruzek, 1992; Frary, Cross, & Weber, 1992; Marso & Pigge, 1992).

Two important factors help explain the patterns in Table 13.2. First, teachers' jobs are complex and demanding, and teachers respond by simplifying their work (Stiggins, Conklin, & Bridgeford, 1986). Reusing an item is simpler than revising it, for example. Essay items are easy to write but difficult and time-consuming to score; multiple-choice items are just the opposite. The simplest alternatives are the completion and matching formats, which are most popular with teachers. Further, knowledge and recall items are easy to construct, score, and defend.

Second, teachers lack confidence about their ability to write good test items and to improve test quality (Marso & Pigge, 1992). Because of inadequate training, teachers have difficulty writing unambiguous test items at a level above knowledge and recall (Carter, 1984; Fleming & Chambers, 1983).

13.9

Offer an explanation as to why elementary teachers tend to rely on performance measures to a greater extent than do middle and secondary teachers.

13.10

Explain why most test items written above the knowledge level are in math and science.

Table 13.2

Characteristics of teacher-made test items

1. Teachers commonly use test items containing many technical errors.

2. Teachers rarely use techniques such as item analysis and tables of specifications to improve the quality of their items. Once items are constructed, teachers tend to reuse them without revision.

3. Even though teachers state that higher order objectives are important, over three fourths of all items are written at the knowledge/recall level, and most of those above the knowledge level are in math and science. In other areas, 90% to 100% of the items are written at the knowledge level.

4. About 1% of all teacher-made test items use the essay format. This figure is higher in English classes.

5. The short-answer format is used most frequently, such as:

   a. Which two countries border on Mexico? _____

   _____

   b. Why does a cactus have needles, whereas an oak tree has broad leaves?

   _____

6. Matching items are common, for example:

_____ A quadrilateral with one pair of opposite equal sides	a. Parallelogram
_____ A three-sided plane figure with two sides equal in length	b. Pentagon
_____ A quadrilateral with opposite sides equal in length	c. Rhombus
	d. Scalene triangle
	e. Square
	f. Isosceles triangle

These results indicate a need for better quality assessments, "particularly items that are less ambiguous and require more of students than the simple recall of facts and information" (Stiggins et al., 1986, p. 9).

Designing Valid Test Items

We introduced the concept of *validity* earlier in the chapter, and we reexamine it now, focusing on specific test items. An item is valid if students who understand the content answer the item correctly and if those who don't understand it get the item wrong. For instance, if you've given a multiple-choice item with *a* as the right answer and if most of the class chose *c*, the item may indicate a general misconception or a difficult idea, you may not have taught it well, or the item may have been misleading. If it's misleading, it's invalid; the other alternatives do not indicate problems with validity. The only way you will know is to discuss the item with your class and determine why so many people selected the incorrect choice.

If clues to the correct answer are included in the item, though, students may answer correctly without understanding the topic, and that item would also be invalid. Students as young as fifth and sixth graders can use item clues to identify correct choices (Sudweeks, Baird, & Petersen, 1990). Teachers confess that they have trouble writing effective items but believe that many of these problems could be eliminated through training and awareness (Carter, 1986). Our goal for this section is to provide some of this training and awareness.

Using the concept of *validity* as our framework, we now turn to a discussion of specific item formats. Item formats can be classified in two ways. First, *selected-response formats* require learners to select the correct answer from a list of alternatives—multiple-choice, true-false, and matching; *supply formats* require learners to produce their own answers—completion and essay (Stiggins, 1994). Second, an objective measure is one "on which equally competent examinees will obtain the same scores (e.g., multiple-choice test), whereas a subjective test is one where the scores are influenced by the opinion or judgement of the person doing the scoring (e.g., essay test)" (Gronlund & Linn, 1995, p. 20). Let's examine objective, selected-response formats first.

13.11 ▬
Suppose you've found that most of students in your class chose *d* on a multiple-choice item when the correct answer was *b*. In discussing the item with the class, you find that it was indeed ambiguous. Is the item valid? Is it reliable? What should you do?

13.12 ▬
Completion formats have been described as supply-type items. Would you classify them as objective or subjective? When and why?

Multiple-Choice Items

The multiple-choice format is one of the most effective for preparing valid and reliable items at different levels of thinking; this is demonstrated by the fact that most standardized tests are written in this format. Gronlund (1993) suggests that teachers should first try writing multiple-choice items and then switch to another format only if the objectives or content require it.

We have all had a great deal of experience responding to multiple-choice items, so the basic format requires little explanation. **Multiple-choice items** *contain a stem, composed of a question or incomplete statement, and several alternatives that require students to choose the best one.* The incorrect alternatives are called **distracters** *because they are designed to "distract" students who don't understand the content being measured in the item.*

Items may be written in which only one choice is correct, or they may be in a "best-answer" form, in which more than one choice is partially correct but one is clearly better than the others. The best-answer form is more demanding, promotes higher level thinking, and measures more complex and subtle achievement. Guidelines for preparing multiple-choice items are summarized in Table 13.3.

Table 13.3

Guidelines for preparing multiple-choice items

1. Present one clear problem in the stem of the item.
2. Make all distracters plausible and attractive to the uninformed.
3. Vary the position of the correct choice randomly. Be careful to avoid overusing choice *c*.
4. Avoid similar wording in the stem and the correct choice.
5. Avoid phrasing the correct choice in more technical terms than distracters.
6. Keep the correct answer and the distracters similar in length. A longer or shorter answer should usually be used as an incorrect choice.
7. Avoid using absolute terms (e.g., *always, never*) in the incorrect choices.
8. Keep the stem and distracters grammatically consistent.
9. Avoid using two distracters with the same meaning.
10. Emphasize *negative wording* by underlining if it is used.
11. Use "none of the above" with care, and avoid "all of the above" as a choice.

Source: How to Construct Achievement Tests, 4th ed., by N. Gronlund, 1988. Upper Saddle River, NJ: Prentice Hall. Copyright 1988 by Prentice Hall. Adapted by permission.

The Stem.   The stem should pose one question or problem for students to consider. With this guideline in mind, compare the items in Figure 13.2.

The first item is essentially a series of true-false statements linked only by the fact that they fall under the same stem. The second item presents two problems. If students select choice *b,* for example, it could be they don't know that the veins are part of the circulatory system, or it could be they don't realize that veins carry blood back to the heart rather than away from it. The third item, in comparison, presents a single, clearly stated problem. The distracters merely provide possible alternatives.

13.13

What is the simplest and most effective way to correct Item 2 in Figure 13.2?

Distracters.   Although carefully written stems are important, good distracters are the critical elements of multiple-choice items. One way to generate effective distracters is to first include the stem on a test as a short answer or fill-in-the-blank item. As students respond, you can use incorrect answers as the distracters for future tests, knowing that these are viable alternatives for some students (Stiggins, 1994).

Many of the problems with faulty multiple-choice items involve clues in distracters that allow students to answer the question correctly without knowing the content. Figure 13.3 contains six items with faulty distracters. See whether you can identify features in them that are inconsistent with the guidelines. Then turn to the discussion that follows.

What kinds of problems did you find with the distracters? In Item 1, you can see that forms of the same term—*circulate*—appear in both the stem and the correct answer.

The correct choice is written in more technical terms than the distracters in Item 2. Teachers fall into this trap when they take the correct choice directly from the text and then make up the distracters. Their language appears in the distracters, whereas text language appears in the correct answer.

The correct choice in Item 3 is significantly longer than the incorrect choices. A similar clue is given when the correct choice is shorter than the distracters. If one choice must be significantly longer or shorter than the others, it should be a distracter.

In Item 4, choices *a* and *c,* which are stated in absolute terms, send up a flag to a test-wise student. Absolute terms, such as *all, always, none,* and *never,* are usually associated with incorrect answers. If used, they should be in the correct answer, such as "All algae contain chlorophyll."

The stem in Item 5 is stated in negative terms without it being emphasized. Also, choice *a* is grammatically inconsistent with the stem. One solution to the problem of consistency is to avoid ending the stem with *a* or *an.* Another is to end it with *a(n),* thereby preserving grammatical consistency.

In Item 6, choices *a* and *c* are automatically eliminated because both are gerunds and only one answer can be correct. Also, Item 6 uses "all of the above" as a choice; it can't be correct if *a* and *c* are eliminated. That makes *b* the only possible choice. A student could get the item right and have no idea what a participle is.

As you can see, preparing good items requires thought and care. With effort and practice, however, you can become skilled at writing good multiple-choice items, and when you do, you have a powerful learning and measurement tool.

13.14
Rewrite each of the six items in Figure 13.3 so that they are consistent with the guidelines.

Measuring Higher Level Learning.   Although most of the examples presented to this point measure low-level outcomes, the multiple-choice format can be effectively used to assess higher order thinking as well. In a procedure called an "interpretive exercise," students are presented with material similar, but not identical, to information presented in class and are asked to analyze it in some way (Gronlund, 1993). The material may be in the form of a graph, chart, table, map, picture, or case study. Figure 13.4 contains an example from the area of science.

Figure 13.2

The stems of multiple-choice items

1. The circulatory system is the system that
    *a. transports blood throughout the body
    b. includes the lungs
    c. protects the vital organs of the body
    d. turns the food we eat into energy
2. Which of the following is a part and function of the circulatory system?
    *a. The blood vessels that carry food and oxygen to the body cells
    b. The blood veins that carry blood away from the heart
    c. The lungs that pump blood to all parts of the body
    d. The muscles that help move a person from one place to another
3. Which of the following describes the function of the circulatory system?
    *a. It moves blood from your heart to other parts of your body.
    b. It turns the sandwich you eat into energy you need to keep you going throughout the day.
    c. It removes solid and liquid waste materials from your body.
    d. It protects your heart, brain, and other body parts from being injured.

Figure 13.3

Choosing distracters for multiple-choice items

1. Which of the following is a function of the circulatory system?
    a. to support the vital organs of the body
    *b. to circulate the blood throughout the body
    c. to transfer nerve impulses from the brain to the muscles
    d. to provide for the movement of the body's large muscles

2. Of the following, the definition of *population density* is
    a. the number of people who live in your city or town
    b. the number of people who voted in the last presidential election
    *c. the number of people per square mile in a country
    d. the number of people in cities compared to small towns

3. Of the following, the most significant cause of World War II was
    a. American aid to Great Britain
    b. Italy's conquering of Ethiopia.
    c. Japan's war on China
    *d. the devastation of the German economy as a result of the Treaty of Versailles.

4. Which of the following is the best description of an insect?
    a. It always has one pair of antennae on its head.
    *b. It has three body parts.
    c. None lives in water.
    d. It breathes through lungs.

5. The one of the following that is not a reptile is a
    a. alligator.
    b. lizard.
    *c. frog.
    d. turtle.

6. Which of the following illustrates a verb form used as a participle?
    a. Running is good exercise.
    *b. I saw a jumping frog contest on TV yesterday.
    c. Thinking is hard for many of us.
    d. All of the above.

Figure 13.4

Interpretive exercise used with the multiple-choice format

Look at the drawings above. They represent two identical soft drink bottles covered with identical balloons sitting side-by-side on a table. Bottle A was then heated. Which of the following is the most accurate statement?
a. The density of the air in Bottle A is greater than the density of the air in Bottle B.
b. The density of the air in Bottle A is less than the density of the air in Bottle B.
c. The density of the air in Bottle A is equal to the density of the air in Bottle B.
d. We don't have enough information to compare the density of the air in Bottle A to the density of the air in Bottle B.

In this case, the teacher's goal was for science students to be able to apply information about heat, expansion, mass, volume, and density to a familiar but unique situation. This type of exercise promotes transfer and helps develop thinking skills, and once students develop facility with the process, it can increase learner motivation.

True-False Items

As we all know from experience, the **true-false format** *involves statements of varying complexity that learners have to judge as being correct or incorrect.* Because of the guessing factor and the tendency to use these items to measure lower level outcomes, true-false items should be used sparingly (Gronlund & Linn, 1995). As with the multiple-choice format, guidelines can help teachers improve their effectiveness. Figure 13.5 presents an outline of guidelines for preparing true-false items.

Figure 13.5

Guidelines for preparing
true-false items

1. When using the format, write slightly more false than true statements. (Teachers tend to write more true than false statements, and students tend to mark answers they're unsure of as "true.")
2. Make each item one clear statement.
3. Avoid clues that may allow students to answer correctly without fully understanding the content.

Look at the examples presented below and analyze them according to the guidelines. See whether you can identify problems with the items, and then turn to the discussion that follows.

1. Mammals are animals with four-chambered hearts and that bear live young.
2. Most protists have only one cell.
3. Negative wording should never be used when writing multiple-choice items.
4. All spiders have exoskeletons.

13.15
Using teachers' assessment patterns as a frame of reference, what is another problem that the four sample items have in common?

Item 1 contains two ideas: (a) Mammals have four-chambered hearts and (b) they bear live young. The first is true, but the second is not true in all cases because some mammals, such as the duck-billed platypus, are egg layers. Therefore, the item must be marked false. If both ideas are important, they should be written in two separate items.

The qualifying word *most,* which is a clue that the statement is true, appears in Item 2. In comparison, Item 3 uses the term *never.* As you saw in the previous section, negative wording should be used with caution in multiple-choice items, but to say it should "never" be used is a false statement.

In general, true-false items should be free of qualifying terms such as *may, most, usually, possible,* and *often,* and of absolutes such as *always, never, all,* and *none.* If a qualifier is used, it should typically be used in a false statement; similarly, absolutes would be most appropriate in true statements. For instance, Item 4 uses the absolute *all,* but the statement is true.

You saw how interpretive exercises can be used with multiple-choice items. This procedure can also be used with the true-false format. In this case, students are presented with a situation and are asked to assess the truth of a series of statements related to it. The exercise in Figure 13.4 could easily be turned from a multiple-choice into a true-false format, for example. The students would be shown the same drawing with the same information and then would be asked to mark true or false statements such as:

- The mass of the air in Bottle A is greater than the mass of the air in Bottle B.
- The volume of the air in Bottle A is greater than the volume of the air in Bottle B.
- The density of the air in Bottle A is greater than the density of the air in Bottle B.

Matching Items

The **matching format** *is a variation on multiple-choice questions and is most effective when the same alternatives are used in a series of items* (Stiggins, 1994). For instance, consider the following items:

1. The statement "Understanding is like a light bulb coming on in your head" is an example of
   *a. simile.
   b. metaphor.
   c. hyperbole.
   d. personification.
2. The statement "That's the most brilliant comment ever made" is a statement of
   a. simile.
   b. metaphor.
   *c. hyperbole.
   d. personification.

Combining the items into a single matching format is more efficient than writing a series of statements, as the following example illustrates:

Match the following statements with the figures of speech by writing the letter of the appropriate figure of speech in the blank next to each statement. Each figure of speech may be used *once, more than once,* or *not at all*.

_____	1. Understanding is like a light bulb coming on in your head.	a.	alliteration
_____		b.	hyperbole
_____	2. That's the most brilliant comment ever made.	c.	metaphor
_____		d.	personification
_____	3. His oratory was a belch from the bowels of his soul.	e.	simile
_____	4. Appropriate attitudes are always advantageous.		
_____	5. Her eyes are limpid pools of longing.		
_____	6. He stood as straight as a rod.		
_____	7. I'll never get this stuff, no matter what I do.		
_____	8. The colors of his shirt described the world in which he lived.		

Several characteristics of matching items are illustrated in the item. First, the material is homogeneous; all the statements are figures of speech, and only figures of speech are given as alternatives. Other content areas for which matching items might be used include persons and their achievements, historical events and dates, terms and definitions, authors and their works, and principles and their illustrations (Gronlund & Linn, 1995). Homogeneity is necessary if all alternatives are to be plausible.

Second, you can see that there are only eight statements and five possible alternatives (these numbers reduce the chances of correctly guessing the answer), the directions state that the alternatives may be used more than once or not at all, and the entire item fits on a single page. Lists of more that 10 statements should be broken into two items, and items that partially appear on two pages require students to flip back and forth; this necessity increases the likelihood of accidental error.

13.16
What are some other topics with homogeneous material that could be appropriately measured with the matching format?

Completion Items

1. What is an opinion _____ ?
2. What is the capital of Canada _____ ?

Completion items *include a question or an incomplete statement that requires the learner to supply appropriate words, numbers, or symbols.* As you saw earlier, the completion format is one of the most popular with teachers, probably because such questions seem easy to construct. This advantage is illusory, however, because the completion format has two serious disadvantages.

First, it is very difficult to phrase a question so that only one possible answer is correct. A number of defensible responses could be given to Question 1, for example. Overuse of the completion format puts students in the position of trying to predict the answer the teacher wants, rather than giving the one they think is the most correct. Second, unless the question involves the solution to a problem, it is usually used to measure simple knowledge-level outcomes. Because of these weaknesses, completion formats should be used sparingly (Gronlund, 1993). Table 13.4 presents guidelines for preparing items using this format.

Essay Items: Measuring Complex Outcomes

Often, "the ability to organize ideas," "the ability to make and defend an argument," or "the ability to express ideas" is a desired outcome for students. As with other goals, teachers need a way to measure them.

Essay items *require students to make extended written responses to questions or problems.* Essay questions are valuable for two reasons. First, the goals in the previous paragraph are integral to higher order and critical thinking; second, the essay format is often the only way they can be measured (Sabban & Kay, 1987). In addition, when students study for an essay exam, they are more likely to organize information in a meaningful way (Foos, 1992).

Despite the need for them, essay items have several disadvantages:

▌ Scoring is very time-consuming.
▌ Scoring is highly subjective and notoriously unreliable.
▌ Essay items are strongly influenced by writing skill. If writing skill is a desired outcome, this influence is appropriate. If not, it detracts from the validity of the items.
▌ Grammar, spelling errors, and handwriting tend to artificially influence scores.

Because essay items appear easy to write, they are often ambiguous and so leave students uncertain about how to respond. The result is that the student's ability to interpret the teacher's question is often the outcome that is measured.

13.17
Rewrite the two sample completion items so that only one defensible response can be given.

13.18
Suppose your written response to an essay item contains several grammatical errors and a number of misspelled words. Your instructor takes off points for these errors. Is he or she making a valid decision in doing so? Why or why not?

Table 13.4

Guidelines for preparing completion items

Guideline	Rationale
1. Use only one blank and relate it to the main point of the statement.	Several blanks are confusing, and one answer may depend on another.
2. Use complete sentences followed by a question mark or period and place the blanks to the left of the question statements.	Complete sentences allow students to more nearly grasp the full meaning of the statement. Scoring is easier when all responses are to the left.
3. Keep blanks the same length. Use "a(an)" at the end of the statement or eliminate indefinite articles.	A long blank for a long word or a particular indefinite article commonly provides clues to the answer.
4. For numerical answers, indicate the degree of precision and the units desired.	Degree of precision and units clarify the task for students and prevent them from spending more time than necessary on an item.

Table 13.5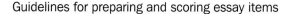

Guidelines for preparing and scoring essay items

1. Elicit higher order thinking by using such terms as *explain* and *compare*. Have students defend their responses with facts.
2. Write a model answer for each item. This can be used both for scoring and for providing feedback.
3. Require all students to answer all items. Allowing students to select particular items prevents comparisons and detracts from reliability.
4. Prepare criteria for scoring in advance.
5. Score all students' answers to a single item before moving to the next item.
6. Score all responses to a single item in one sitting if possible. This increases reliability.
7. Score answers without knowing the identity of the student. This helps reduce the influence of past performance and expectations.

Because of these limitations, essay items should be reserved for complex and high-level learning outcomes that cannot be measured with other formats (Gronlund, 1993). Table 13.5 presents guidelines for preparing and scoring essay items.

Probably the most essential component involved in scoring is establishing grading criteria. Criteria should be prepared prior to scoring and applied uniformly throughout the process. One way to establish criteria is to use a rubric such as the one in Figure 13.6 that links the criteria to points.

This rubric is content free, referring to general, organizational criteria; similar rubrics can be constructed that focus on specific concepts or topics. By referring to this rubric during scoring, teachers can increase consistency and reliability.

Figure 13.6

Rubric for scoring essay items

High Score	5	The response is clear, focused, and accurate. Relevant points are made with good support (derived from the content to be used, again as spelled out in the exercise). Good connections are drawn, and important insights are evident.
	3	The answer is clear and somewhat focused, but not compelling. Support of points made is limited. Connections are fuzzy and lead to few important insights.
Low Score	1	The response either misses the point, contains inaccurate information, or otherwise demonstrates a lack of mastery of the material. Points are unclear, support is missing, and/or no insights are included.

Source: Adapted from Stiggins (1994, p. 153).

Using Commercially Prepared Test Items

As you saw earlier, many teachers depend on the tests included in textbooks, teachers' guides, and other curriculum materials in commercially prepared programs. Although using these tests obviously saves time, they should be used with caution for at least three reasons:

1. *Goals:* The goals as conceived by the curriculum developers may not be the same as the goals you have for your students. If the tests don't reflect the goals and instruction in your course, they are invalid.
2. *Emphasis:* The tests reflect the emphasis of the curriculum developers, and even if your goals are similar to theirs, the emphasis reflected on the commercially prepared test may not parallel yours.
3. *Quality:* This factor is perhaps most important. Many commercially prepared tests are of low quality and are written at low levels, tapping student memorization rather than higher order thinking.

These results suggest that teachers should exercise caution in using tests supplied by textbook publishers. They often are little, if any, better than the items teachers prepare themselves, and they are less likely to be congruent with teachers' goals and instruction than are teacher-prepared items. Although writing quality test items is demanding, the instructional benefits make it worth the effort. As you saw earlier in the chapter, students study and learn according to the way they're assessed. An important way of improving learning in classrooms is to improve the quality of assessments.

13.19

We identified three problems with the use of commercially prepared tests: goals, emphasis, and quality. Which do these problems affect more—validity or reliability? Explain.

Authentic Assessment

As you've seen, traditional assessment remains popular and widely used. Despite this popularity, traditional assessments, often in multiple-choice formats, are being increasingly criticized. Some reasons given are:

- Test content focuses on knowledge of low-level, discrete content and skills.
- Tests measure only outcomes, providing no insight into learners' thinking and problem-solving skills.
- Objective formats, such as multiple-choice, don't measure learners' ability to apply understanding in the real world (Herman et al., 1992).

In response to these criticisms, the use of authentic assessments, or "direct examination of student performance on significant tasks that are relevant to life outside of school" (Worthen, 1993, p. 445), is being urged. The terms **alternative assessment, authentic assessment,** and **performance assessment** are used interchangeably in describing *assessments that directly measure student performance through "real life" tasks* (Herman et al., 1992; Worthen, 1993).

Examples include:

- Designing and conducting an experiment to measure the effects of different levels of exercise on hamsters
- Writing a persuasive essay
- Designing menus for a week's worth of nutritionally balanced meals
- Identifying and fixing the problems with a lawn mower engine that won't start
- Creating an original piece of pottery

In addition to products, such as the results of the experiment, the essay, and the piece of pottery, teachers using authentic assessments are also interested in the processes students use to prepare the products (Gronlund, 1993). For example, a structured interview might be used to gain insight into students' thinking as they design their experiments. In addition, a portfolio of writing samples, or systematic observation of students as they work, could be used to document their process growth.

Alternative assessments have at least three advantages over traditional paper-and-pencil measures:

1. They tap higher level thinking and problem-solving skills.
2. They invoke real-world applications.
3. They ask students to perform, create, produce, or do something (Herman et al., 1992).

Alternative assessments are consistent with constructivist views of learning, which recognize that learning is holistic and should be contextualized within authentic tasks (Camp, 1992).

Let's look at two forms of authentic assessments: performance assessments and the use of portfolios.

13.20
Construct an authentic assessment for Shirley Barton in our opening case study on teaching fractions in Chapter 12. What makes it "authentic"?

Performance Assessments

A middle school science teacher notices that her students have difficulty applying scientific principles to everyday events. In an attempt to improve their abilities, she focuses on everyday problems (e.g., why an ice cube floated in one cup of clear liquid but sank in another), which the students have to solve in groups and discuss as a class. On Fridays, she presents another problem (e.g., why two clear liquids of the same volume, when put on a balance, don't have the same mass), and the students have to solve it in groups. As they work, she circulates among them, taking notes that will be used for assessment and feedback.

A health teacher reads in a professional journal that the biggest problem people have in applying first aid is not the mechanics per se, but knowing what to do and when. In an attempt to address this problem, the teacher has a periodic unannounced "catastrophe" day. Students entering the classroom encounter a catastrophe victim with an unspecified injury. Each time, they must first diagnose the problem and then apply first-aid interventions.

These teachers are using performance assessments to gather information about students' abilities to apply information in realistic settings. **Performance assessments** *are authentic assessments that measure skill and understanding by directly measuring student performance in a natural setting.* Performance assessments attempt to increase validity by placing students in as lifelike an assessment situation as possible and evaluating student performance against realistic criteria.

13.21
Are essay items performance assessments? Defend your answer, using the information from this section.

Designing Performance Assessments

Experts have identified four steps in designing classroom performance assessments (based on work by Gronlund, 1993): (a) specifying desired outcomes, (b) selecting the focus of evaluation, (c) determining the appropriate degree of realism, and (d) selecting evaluation procedures.

Specifying Desired Outcomes.   The first step in any assessment is to develop a clear idea of what you're trying to measure. A clear description of the skill or process helps students understand what is required and helps the teacher design appropriate instruction. An example of an attempt to specify the desired performance outcomes in the area of speech is outlined in Figure 13.7 (based on work by Gronlund, 1993).

Performance assessments measure students' ability to demonstrate skills similar to those required in real-world settings.

Selecting the Focus of Evaluation.   Having specified the performance outcomes, teachers must then decide whether assessment will focus on processes or products. Processes may be the initial focus, with a shift to products after procedures are mastered (Gronlund, 1993). Examples of both processes and products as components of performance assessments are found in Table 13.6.

Determining the Appropriate Degree of Realism.   The strength of performance assessments lies in their link to realistic tasks. Ultimately, teachers want students to use the skill

Figure 13.7

Performance outcomes in speech

Oral Presentation
1.   Stands naturally.
2.   Maintains eye contact.
3.   Uses gestures effectively.
4.   Uses clear language.
5.   Has adequate volume.
6.   Speaks at an appropriate rate.
7.   Topics are well organized.
8.   Maintains interest of the group.

Table 13.6

Processes and products as components of performance

Content Area	Product	Process
Math	Correct answer	Problem-solving steps leading to the correct solution
Music	Performance of a work on an instrument	Correct fingering and breathing that produces the performance
English Composition	Essay, term paper, or composition	Preparation of drafts and thought processes that produce the product
Word Processing	Letter or copy of final draft	Proper stroking and techniques for presenting the paper
Science	Explanation for the outcomes of a demonstration	Thought processes involved in preparing the explanation

in the real world. Time, expense, and safety may prevent the "real thing," however, and intermediate steps might be necessary.

For example, in driver education, the goal is to produce safe drivers. However, putting students in heavy traffic to assess how well they function behind the wheel is both unrealistic and unwise. Figure 13.8 contains evaluation options ranging from low to high realism.

Simulations provide opportunities for teachers to measure performance with intermediate degrees of realism in cases in which high realism is impossible. For instance, a geography teacher wanting to measure students' understanding of the role climate and geography play in where cities are located might display the information shown in Figure 13.9. The students would then be asked to identify the best location for a city on a map and the criteria they used in determining the location. Their ability to state defensible criteria provides the teacher with insight into their understanding and thought processes.

Selecting Evaluation Procedures. The final step in the design of performance assessments is selecting (or constructing) evaluation procedures. Reliability is the primary concern when designing and implementing evaluation procedures; research indicates that performance assessments are often unreliable (Baxter & Shavelson, 1992; Madaus & Tan, 1993). However, although achieving the reliability of objective paper-and-pencil measures

> **13.22**
> How does realism influence validity and reliability? Explain, using the driver education example as a frame of reference.

Figure 13.8

Continuum of realism on performance tasks

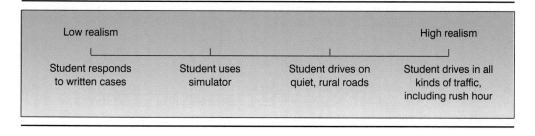

Figure 13.9

Simulation in geography

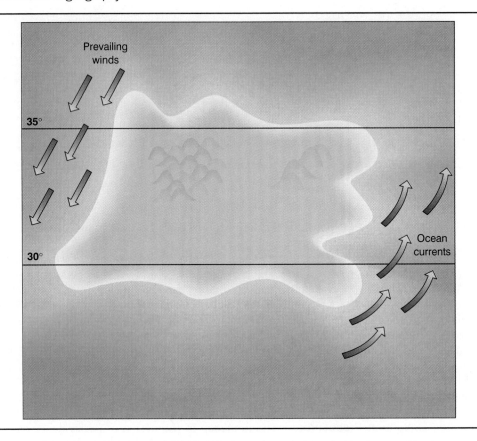

is probably impossible, acceptable levels of reliability can be achieved if care is taken (Nystrand, Cohen, & Dowling, 1992).

To achieve acceptable levels of reliability, well-defined criteria are needed. Effective criteria have four elements (Herman et al., 1992):

1. One or more dimensions that serve as a basis for assessing student performance
2. A description of each dimension
3. A scale of values on which each dimension is rated
4. Definitions of each value on the scale

Let's look now at three methods of evaluation used with performance assessments: (a) systematic observation, (b) checklists, and (c) rating scales.

Evaluation Methods With Performance Assessments

Teachers observe students in classroom settings all the time. Observations typically are not systematic, however, and records are rarely kept. **Systematic observations** are intended to solve these problems *by specifying criteria and taking notes based on the criteria*. For example, a science teacher attempting to teach her students scientific problem solving might establish the following criteria.

1. Have stated problem or question
2. Have stated hypotheses
3. Have identified independent, dependent, and controlled variables
4. Have described the way data will be gathered
5. Have ordered and displayed data
6. Have evaluated hypotheses based on the data

The teacher's notes would then refer directly to the criteria, making them reasonably consistent for all groups. The notes could be used to provide feedback for the students and provide information that could be used in future planning.

Checklists extend systematic observation by specifying important aspects of an activity and by sharing them with students. **Checklists** *are written descriptions of dimensions that must be present in an acceptable performance.* They differ from systematic observations in that observations of desired performances are typically "checked off," rather than described in notes. For example, the science teacher wanting to assess scientific problem-solving ability might prepare a checklist such as the one in Figure 13.10. (Notes could be added to each dimension on a checklist if the teacher so desired; this would have the effect of combining checklists and systematic observations.)

Checklists are useful when meeting a criterion can be determined with a yes-or-no answer, such as "Specifies values for controlled variables," because students either did or did not specify the values. In other cases, however, such as "Draws conclusions consistent with the data in the chart," the results aren't cut-and-dried. Conclusions aren't merely consistent or inconsistent with the data; some conclusions are more thorough or insightful than others. This discussion leads us to rating scales.

Rating scales *are written descriptions of dimensions and scales of values on which each dimension is rated.* They allow more precise information to be gathered than is possible with checklists. A sample rating scale, again based on students' performance of experimental procedures, is illustrated in Figure 13.11. Notice that although our example

13.23
Create a rating scale that would allow you to assess someone's performance in creating high-quality multiple-choice test items.

Systematic observation incorporating checklists and rating scales allows teachers to assess accurately and to provide valuable information to students about their performance.

Figure 13.10

Checklist for evaluating experimental technique

DIRECTIONS: Place a check in the blank for each step performed.

_____ 1. Writes problem at the top of the report.

_____ 2. States hypothesis(es).

_____ 3. Specifies values for controlled variables.

_____ 4. Makes at least two measurements of each value of the dependent variable.

_____ 5. Presents data in a chart.

_____ 6. Draws conclusions consistent with the data in the chart.

is designed to rate a performance, rating scales for assessing the quality of products can also be developed.

The rating scale in Figure 13.11 contains three of the four elements of effective criteria listed earlier. Six dimensions are identified, the dimensions are described, and a scale of values is provided on which each dimension rated is included. The values are not defined, however. For example, how does one know whether "States problem or question clearly and accurately" warrants a rating of 4 or 3? To be complete, definitions of values, such as the following, should be included.

Rating = 4

Problem is stated in clear, complete, and observable language; communicates clearly with reader; indicates understanding of content by specifying significance and importance of problem; provides a clear basis for hypothesizing solution.

Figure 13.11

Rating scale for evaluating experimental technique

DIRECTIONS: Rate each of the following items by circling 4 for an *excellent* performance, 3 for a *good* performance, 2 for *fair*, 1 for *poor*, and 0 for *nonexistent.*

4 3 2 1 0   1. States problem or question clearly and accurately.

4 3 2 1 0   2. States hypothesis that clearly answers the question.

4 3 2 1 0   3. Controls variables.

4 3 2 1 0   4. Uses appropriate data-gathering procedures.

4 3 2 1 0   5. Displays gathered data accurately and clearly.

4 3 2 1 0   6. Draws appropriate conclusions.

Rating = 3

Problem is stated reasonably clearly. Problem is appropriate and significant, but more significant problems exist within the context of the topic. A clear basis for hypothesizing solution is provided.

Rating = 2

Ambiguous problem is stated; basis for hypothesizing solution is uncertain.

Rating = 1

Statement is made, but is unclear whether it is a problem; learner indicates uncertainty about the relationship between problem and hypotheses.

Rating = 0

No problem stated.

Definitions for values of each of the other dimensions would also be described. With these descriptions as guides, trained observers can achieve acceptable levels of reliability for both student performance and products.

13.24
How do systematic observations, checklists, and rating scales influence validity and reliability? Explain.

Portfolio Assessment: Involving Students in Authentic Assessment

The use of portfolios, another form of alternative assessment, has the additional advantage of involving students in the design, collection, and evaluation of learning products. **Portfolios** *are collections of work that are reviewed against preset criteria to judge a student*

Portfolios foster self-regulation by providing opportunities for students to become actively involved in assessing their own learning progress.

Table 13.7

Portfolio samples in different content areas

Content Area	Example
Elementary Math	Samples of computation and problem papers.
Writing	Drafts of narrative, descriptive, and persuasive essays. Samples of poetry.
Art	Examples of art projects over the course of the year.
Science	Drawings and written explanations for the behavior of objects in demonstrations and hands-on activities. Collections of lab reports.

or program (Herman et al., 1992). The portfolio per se is not the assessment; it is a collection of different students' products, such as essays, journal entries, artwork, and videotapes. The assessments are the teachers' and students' judgments of learning progress.

Two features distinguish portfolios from other forms of assessment:

1. Portfolios collect work samples over time, reflecting developmental changes.
2. Portfolios involve students in design, collection, and evaluation.

Examples of portfolio assessments in different content areas are found in Table 13.7.

Portfolios are designed to reflect student growth. For example, writing samples can document the changes that occur over a term or course. This documentation can then be used as a basis for communicating with parents and for helping students observe their own progress.

Two questions are involved when portfolio assessment is used. First, how do teachers decide what goes into the portfolio; second, on what criteria will the students' work be evaluated? Student involvement in selecting portfolio content provides opportunities for students to reflect on their own learning progress. One seventh-grade language arts teacher shared her experience in involving students:

> I introduced the idea that their portfolios might present a broader picture—how students have changed or improved, what their particular interests are, and areas where they still have difficulties. This comment led my students to suggest including the following items: an early and a later piece of writing, a rewrite of something, examples of what they like and don't like, a list of books they like and don't, and reading logs that show how their thinking about books has changed. (Case, 1994, p. 46)

Criteria were also jointly established and included (a) how well students explained why particular pieces were selected, (b) the actual pieces, (c) clarity and completeness of the cover letter describing the contents, and (d) neatness and organization. As the class struggled with what to include in the portfolio, the issue of including only high-quality pieces versus pieces demonstrating growth came up. One student commented,

> We could all just turn in the papers that got the best grades. But we already got those grades, so what would be the point of making a portfolio? (Case, 1994, p. 46)

By involving students in these decisions, teachers help students become aware of options in evaluating their own growth and lay the foundation for student self-regulation.

13.25
Suppose you want to use portfolio assessment in a fifth-grade math class. Identify at least three types of items that might be included in the portfolio.

Classroom Connections

Creating Valid and Reliable Assessments in Your Classroom

1. Be sure objectives and tests are congruent.
   - A life science teacher compares items on his tests to the objectives in the curriculum guide and unit plan to be sure all the appropriate objectives are covered.

2. Write individual test items soon after material has been presented. Write as many items as possible above the knowledge/recall level.
   - A social studies teacher writes a draft of one test item at the end of each day to be certain the emphasis on her tests is consistent with her instruction. She reports that she can now write a good item in less than 5 minutes.

3. Analyze test items after they have been written to make sure they measure intended outcomes.
   - A second-grade teacher rereads the items she has written to eliminate wording that might be confusing or too advanced for her students.

4. Construct scoring rubrics for essay items. Score essays by using the rubric as the criterion.
   - A high school economics teacher writes an "ideal" response to each essay item she prepares. She then awards points to students for each element of the model demonstrated in their answers.

5. Use commercially prepared items with caution.
   - A third-grade teacher comments, "I look at the tests they send with the book. I find the good ones and use them. Then I make up the rest of the items myself."

6. Use alternative assessments to increase validity.
   - A fifth-grade math teacher assigns his students the task of going to three supermarkets and comparing prices on a list of five household items. They are required to determine which store provided the best bargains and what the difference was among the stores on each item.
   - A fourth-grade teacher uses portfolios to evaluate students' writing progress during the school year. Students are required to keep a weekly journal describing their work and noting accomplishments.

Effective Assessment Practices

In the previous section, we examined both traditional and alternative assessment in detail. However, even though good items and performance measures are essential, there is more to effective assessment. Individual items must be combined into tests, performance assessments must be designed, students need to be prepared, and assessment must be administered, scored, and discussed to maximize learning. We look now at four processes in effective assessment: (a) designing assessments, (b) preparing students for assessments, (c) administering assessments, and (d) analyzing results.

Designing Assessments

In designing an assessment, the first task is to be certain it is consistent with your goals and instruction. Although this appears obvious, many teachers fail to do so. For example, because tests are typically prepared some time after instruction is completed, a topic given little emphasis in class might have several items related to it, whereas another, given much stronger emphasis, is covered less thoroughly on the test. A topic may be discussed in class at the application or analysis level, but test items related to the topic are at a knowledge level. The goal may call for an observable performance, but the assessment is a series of multiple-choice questions. Each of these factors reduces the validity of a test.

Tables of Specifications: Increasing Validity Through Planning

One way to help ensure that goals and tests are consistent is to prepare a table of specifications. A **table of specifications** *is a matrix derived from the teacher's objectives that classifies topics measured on the test by cognitive level, such as knowledge and comprehension, or by specific outcomes.* For example, a geography teacher has been basing her instruction in a unit on the Middle East on the following list of objectives:

Understands location of cities

1. States location
2. Identifies historical factors in settlement

Understands climate

1. Identifies major climate regions
2. Explains reasons for existing climates

Understands influence of physical features

1. Describes topography
2. Relates physical features to climate
3. Explains impact of physical features on location of cities
4. Analyzes impact of physical features on economy

Understands factors influencing economy

1. Describes economies of countries in the region
2. Identifies characteristics of each economy
3. Explains how economies relate to climate and physical features

Table 13.8 presents a table of specifications in a topic-cognitive-level matrix based on the objectives. You can see that the teacher has a mix of items, with more emphasis placed on physical features than the others. This emphasis reflects the teacher's objectives, which emphasize the influence of physical features on the location of cities, the climate, and the economy of the region. In addition, this emphasis presumably also reflects the time and effort spent in class on each area. Ensuring this match among goals, instruction, and assessment procedures is a primary function of a table of specifications.

For alternative assessments, establishing criteria as discussed in the section on systematic observations, checklists, and rating scales serve somewhat the same function as tables of specifications. They identify performance, determine emphasis, and attempt to ensure congruence between goals and assessments.

Preparing Students for Assessments

Let's begin this section by looking at a brief case study in which a teacher is preparing her students for an upcoming test.

> Tanya Erickson is making the transition from reading to math on a Wednesday. She is standing in front of the room with a transparency in her hand at 10:02 as the last of the students gets out their math books.

13.26 ▅

Two teachers were arguing about the best time to construct a table of specifications—during planning, before teaching a unit, or after a unit. What are the advantages and disadvantages of each approach? Explain.

13.27 ▅

A teacher closely follows her curriculum guide, checks off objectives, and writes at least one test item related to each objective as soon as she's finished covering it with her students. Is she being consistent with the idea of tables of specifications by using this procedure? Why or why not?

Table 13.8

Sample table of specifications

Content	Outcomes		
	Knowledge	Comprehension	Higher-Order Thinking and Problem-Solving
Cities	4	2	2
Climate	4	2	2
Economy	2	2	
Physical features	4	9	7
Total items	14	15	11

"Get out your chalkboards and chalk," she reminds them, referring to small individual chalkboards she had made for each of them at the beginning of the year.

"Look up here at the chalkboard," she begins, pointing to the chalkboard at the front of the room. "I just want to remind you again that we're having a test tomorrow on finding equivalent fractions and adding fractions with unlike denominators, and we decided that the test will go in your math portfolios. On the test, you will have to add some fractions in which the denominators are the same and others in which the denominators are different. Then there will be some word problems in which you will need to do the same thing. I'll give the test back Friday, and if we all do well, we won't have any homework over the weekend."

"YEAH!" the students shout in unison, and Tanya smiles at their response.

She holds up her hand, they quiet down, and she continues. "I have some problems on the test that are going to make you think." She smiles. "But we've all been working hard, and you know that if you work hard enough, you'll be able to do it. You're my team, and I know you'll come through," she continues energetically.

"To be sure we're okay," she goes on, "I have a few problems that are just like those on the test, so let's see how we do. Write these first two on your chalkboards."

$$\tfrac{1}{3} + \tfrac{3}{4} = ? \qquad \tfrac{2}{7} + \tfrac{4}{7} = ?$$

Tanya watches as they work on the problems and hold their chalkboards up when they're finished. Seeing that three of the students miss the first problem, she carefully goes through it with the class, comparing it with the second problem.

She then displays the following three problems:

$$\tfrac{2}{3} + \tfrac{1}{6} = ? \qquad \tfrac{4}{9} + \tfrac{1}{6} = ? \qquad \tfrac{2}{9} + \tfrac{4}{9} = ?$$

Two students miss the second one, so again she goes through this problem carefully.

"Now, let's try one more," she continues, displaying the following problem on the overhead. "You are at a pizza party with five other people, and you order two pizzas. The two pizzas are the same size, but one is cut into four pieces and the other is cut into eight pieces. You eat one piece from each pizza. How much pizza do you eat altogether?"

Again, Tanya watches as the students work on the problem, and she discusses it and reviews the solution with them when they are finished. In the process, she asks questions such as, "What information in the problem is particularly important, and how do we know?" "What do we see in the problem that's irrelevant?" and, "What should we do first in solving the problem?"

She displays two more word problems for them and then says, "The problems on the test are like the ones we practiced in here today." She responds to additional questions from the students and concludes her review with the following interchange.

"All right, when we take a test, what do we always do?"

"WE READ THE DIRECTIONS CAREFULLY!" the students shout in unison.

"Okay, good," Tanya smiles. "Now, remember, what will you do if you get stuck on a problem?"

"Go on to the next one so we don't run out of time."

"And what will we be sure not to do?"

"We won't forget to go back to the one we skipped."

In preparing students for tests, teachers have long- and short-term goals. Long term, they want students to understand test-taking procedures and strategies and to enter testing situations with a minimum of anxiety. Short term, they want students to understand the test format and the content being tested. By preparing students, teachers increase the probability that test scores accurately reflect student achievement, thus increasing validity.

Teaching Test-Taking Strategies

13.28 ▬
What did Tanya Erickson do to promote test-taking skills in her students? Identify at least two specific examples in the case study.

Teaching test-taking strategies is a long-term effort to improve student performance in testing situations. They include:

▌ Using time efficiently
▌ Reading directions carefully
▌ Identifying the important information in questions
▌ Understanding the characteristics of different testing formats

For the strategy to be most effective, students should be reminded of the strategies throughout the school year, concrete examples should be linked to the strategies, and students should be given practice with a variety of formats and testing situations. Research indicates that strategy instruction significantly improves test-taking performance and that young, low-ability, and minority students who have limited test-taking experience benefit the most (Anastasi, 1988; Mehrens & Lehmann, 1987).

Reducing Test Anxiety

Listen my children and you shall hear. . . .

Listen my children and you shall hear. . . .

Rats! I knew it this morning in front of Mom.

13.29 ▬
Using classical conditioning as a basis, explain the emotional component—such as feelings of dread—of test anxiety. Using information processing as a basis, explain why the worry component of test anxiety can lower test performance.

As with this student, many of us have experienced the negative effects of anxiety in a testing situation. For most of us, the adverse effects of pressure are momentary and minor, with little impairment of performance. For a portion of the school population, however (estimates run as high as 10%), anxiety during testing situations is a serious problem (K. Hill & Wigfield, 1984; J. Williams, 1992).

Test anxiety *is a relatively stable, unpleasant reaction to testing situations that lowers performance.* Most theories of test anxiety suggest that it consists of two components (Pintrich & Schunk, 1996). Its *emotional component* can include physiological symptoms, such as faster pulse rate, dry mouth, and headache, as well as feelings of dread and helplessness and sometimes "going blank." Its *cognitive, or worry, component* involves thoughts such as worrying about failure (e.g., parents being upset, having to retake the course) and being embarrassed by a low score. During tests, test-anxious students tend to be preoccupied with test difficulty and are often unable to focus on the individual items.

Test anxiety is triggered by testing situations that (a) involve pressure to succeed, (b) are perceived as difficult, (c) impose time limits, and (d) contain unfamiliar items or formats (Wigfield & Eccles, 1989). Unannounced or surprise tests can have an especially adverse effect on test anxiety (Saigh, 1984).

Teachers can do much to minimize test anxiety (Everson, Tobias, Hartman, & Gourgey, 1991), and the most successful of these efforts are usually aimed at the worry component (Pintrich & Schunk, 1996). Some suggestions follow:

- Use criterion-referenced measures to minimize the competitive aspects of tests.
- Avoid social comparisons, such as public displays of test scores and grades.
- Increase the frequency of quizzes and tests.
- Teach students test-taking skills.
- Discuss test content and procedures prior to testing.
- Give clear directions and be sure students understand the test.
- Use a variety of measures, including alternative assessments, to measure students' understanding and skills.
- Provide students with ample time to take tests.

> **13.30**
> Suppose you have an extremely test-anxious student in your class. State specifically what you would do to reduce her anxiety. What should you do if you think her anxiety is a danger to her emotional health?

Specific Test-Preparation Procedures

Before any test, teachers want to be as sure as possible that students understand test content and procedures and that they expect to succeed on the exam. In preparing students for her test, Tanya Erickson did three important things:

1. She specified precisely what would be on the test.
2. She gave students a chance to practice the items under testlike conditions.
3. She established positive expectations in her students and encouraged them to link success and effort.

Clarifying test format and content establishes structure for students; this structure, in turn, reduces test anxiety (Szafran, 1981). Research indicates that providing this structure leads to higher achievement for all students, particularly those of low ability (Carrier & Titus, 1981).

Merely specifying the content often isn't enough, however, particularly with elementary students, so Tanya actually gave students practice exercises and presented them in a way that paralleled the way they would be presented on her test. In initially learning math skills, for instance, the students first practiced adding fractions with like denominators, then learned to find equivalent fractions, and finally added fractions with unlike denominators, each in separate lessons. On the test, however, the problems were mixed. This mixing requires an additional integration of the skills, and Tanya provided students a chance to practice the behaviors required of them on the test. The benefits of this practice are particularly important for young (Kalechstein, Kalechstein, & Doctor, 1981) and minority (Dreisbach & Keogh, 1982) students.

Finally, Tanya clearly communicated that she expected the students to do well on the test. The benefits of establishing positive expectations have been confirmed by two decades of research (Good, 1987b).

Tanya also encouraged attributions of effort for success by saying, "You know that if you work hard enough, you'll be able to do it." In recalling your study of Chapter 9, you know that helping students see links between effort and success benefits both performance and long-term motivation.

Preparing students for alternative assessments can actually be easier than preparing for traditional testing. For example, systematic observation of student behavior can be conducted during learning activities, and products from learning activities can be put into portfolios so that instruction and assessment are strongly integrated. The biggest task teachers face is becoming personally comfortable and confident with alternative assessments. Relinquishing the security that results from using objective tests and their cut-and-dried answers requires some adjustment.

Administering Assessments

Let's return again to Tanya Erickson and her class at 10:00 the next morning.

> Tanya had opened a window before school started, but she shuts it now because delivery trucks are driving back and forth outside. She had considered rearranging the desks in the room but decided to wait until after the test.
>
> "Okay, everyone," she calls. "Let's get ready for our math test." With that, the students put their books under their desks.
>
> She waits a moment, sees that everyone's desk is clear, and says, "When you're finished with the test, turn it over, and I'll come and get it. Now, look at the chalkboard. After you're done, work on the assignment listed there until everyone else is finished. Then, we'll start reading."
>
> As she hands out the tests, she says, "If you get too warm, raise your hand, and I'll turn on the air conditioner. I shut the window because of the noise outside.
>
> "Work carefully," she says after everyone has a copy of the test. "We've all been working hard, and I know you will do well. You have as much time as you need. Now go ahead and get started."
>
> The students quickly begin working, and Tanya stands near the door, watching their efforts.
>
> After several minutes, she notices Dean repeatedly doodling at the top of his paper and periodically glancing around the room. She goes to him, puts an arm around his shoulders, and says, "It looks like you're doing fine on these problems," and she points to some near the top of the paper. "Now concentrate a little harder. I'll bet you can do most of the others." She smiles reassuringly and again stands near the door.
>
> Tanya moves over to Chao in response to his raised hand. "The lead on my pencil broke, Mrs. Erickson," he whispers.
>
> "Take this one," Tanya responds, handing him one. "Come and get yours after the test."
>
> As the students finish, Tanya picks up their papers, and they begin the assignment written on the chalkboard.

Let's look now at how Tanya administered the test. First, she arranged the environment to be comfortable, free from distractions and similar to the way it was when the students learned the skills. Distractions can depress test performance, particularly in young or low-ability students (Trentham, 1975).

Second, Tanya gave precise directions about taking the test, collecting the papers, and spending their time afterward. This direction reinforced the order in the room and further prevented distractions for late-finishing students.

Finally, Tanya carefully monitored the test during the entire time the students worked on it. This not only allowed her to encourage students who became lost or distracted but also discouraged cheating. In the real world, unfortunately, some students will cheat if given the opportunity. However, classroom climate and external factors, such as the teacher leaving the room, influence cheating more than whether students are inherently inclined to do so (Bushway & Nash, 1977). Careful monitoring during tests also helps students learn to monitor their own test-taking behaviors.

13.31

In an effort to keep his students informed about the amount of time left during a test, a teacher reminds them of the time every 10 minutes. Is this a good idea? How will it affect test anxiety? If at all possible, what should teachers do in scheduling the amount of time students have to take a test?

Teacher monitoring of student progress during assessment provides opportunities for teachers to encourage students, to answer questions, and to clear up misunderstandings or confusion.

In Tanya's case, monitoring was more a form of giving support than of being a watchdog. When she saw that Dean was distracted, she quickly intervened, offered him encouragement, and urged him to increase his concentration. This encouragement is particularly important for underachieving and test-anxious students, who tend to become distracted and have lapses in their effort (Nottelman & Hill, 1977).

Analyzing Results

Let's return to Tanya's class once more as she gives back the tests on Friday morning.

"Do you have our tests finished, Mrs. Erickson?" the students ask as they get out their math books.

"Of course!" She smiles at them. "Here they are," and with that, she hands back their papers.

"Overall, you did very well on the test, and I'm very proud of you. I knew all that hard work would pay off.

"There are a few items I want to go over, though," she continues. "Five of you had trouble with Number 8, and you all made nearly the same mistake, so let's take a look at it."

She waits a moment while the students read the problem and then asks, "Now, what are we given in the problem? . . . Hannah?"

"There's a drawing of two cakes. One is cut into 12 pieces, and the other is cut into 6 pieces."

"Okay. Good. And what else do we know? . . . Shareef?"

Tanya continues the discussion and explanation of the problem. She then carefully discusses two other problems that were frequently missed. In the process, she makes some notes at the top of her copy, identifying the problems that were difficult. She writes "Ambiguous" by one problem and underlines some of the wording in it. By another, she writes, "Teach them how to draw diagrams of the problem." Finally, she puts her copy of the test in a file folder, lays it on her desk to be filed, and turns back to the class.

Tanya's efforts didn't end with administering the test. She scored it and returned it the next day, discussed the results, and provided students with feedback as quickly as possible. This process is important for both achievement and motivation (Bangert-Drowns, Kulik, Kulik, & Morgan, 1991). The feedback allowed students to identify and correct com-

13.32 ▬
Why is knowledge of results important for motivation? (Hint: Think about the behaviorist, humanistic, and cognitive views of motivation discussed in Chapter 9.

mon misconceptions, and as you saw in Chapter 9, knowledge of results is one variable that promotes student motivation. Virtually all teachers provide feedback after a test, and many take up to half a class period to do so (Haertel, 1986). Because student motivation is high, many teachers believe that the instruction in these postmortems is more valuable than the original instruction.

In addition, Tanya made positive comments about the general performance of the class on the test. In a study examining this factor, students who were told they did well on a test performed better on a subsequent measure than those who were told they did poorly, even though the two groups did equally well on the first test (Bridgeman, 1974). Research also supports the benefits of individual feedback on tests; students who receive comments such as, "Excellent! Keep it up!" and, "Good work, keep at it!" do better on subsequent work (Page, 1992). The effects of these short, personalized comments justify the extra work involved.

Finally, Tanya made notes on her copy of the test and filed the copy. Her notes reminded her that the wording on one of her problems was misleading, so she could revise the problem before she gave it again. This, plus other information gleaned from the test, will assist her in future planning for both instruction and assessment.

Accommodating Diversity in Classrooms: Reducing Bias in Assessment

When teachers assess their students, they gather data that are used to make decisions about student progress and to help them in improving their instruction. The diversity in classrooms, however, often complicates this process. A teacher may have students, for example, who are unfamiliar with standard assessment practices such as tests and quizzes. They may not understand the purpose of these assessments or have effective test-taking strategies. Also, because most assessments are strongly language-based, language may present another obstacle. In this section, we examine strategies to accommodate this diversity.

First, students with diverse backgrounds may lack experience with general testing procedures, different test formats, and test-taking strategies, so the effective testing practices we discussed in the previous section are particularly important for them. In addition, teachers can respond to diversity in assessment in at least three other ways: (a) being careful with wording in assessment items, (b) making provisions for non-native English speakers, and (c) accommodating diversity in scoring.

Being Careful With Wording in Assessment Items

13.33
Is content bias more a problem with validity or reliability? Explain.

Content bias is always a possibility when assessing students with diverse backgrounds. For example, students can have difficulties with items containing information uncommon in their culture, such as transportation (e.g., ambulances, cable cars, garbage trucks), sports (e.g., football, hockey, skiing, surfing), and musical instruments (e.g., banjo, guitar, harmonica; Cheng, 1987). In addition, holidays such as Thanksgiving or people such as Abraham Lincoln and Franklin D. Roosevelt, which most people in American culture take for granted, may be unfamiliar to them. When these terms and events are included in assessment items, teachers are measuring both the intended topic and students' understanding of American vocabulary and culture.

There is no easy solution to this problem, but teacher awareness and sensitivity are starting points. In addition, encouraging students to ask questions and discussing tests thoroughly after they are given can help uncover unintended bias.

Making Provisions for Non-Native English Speakers

How would you do if your next exam in this class were presented in Spanish, French, or German? This prospect gives you some idea of the problems facing non-native English-speaking students during tests.

Ways to accommodate these differences include translating tests into the student's native language, using a student interpreter, providing extra time to take the exam, and making sure that directions and items are clear. The last suggestion is particularly important because language barriers or cultural norms might make non-native English speakers reluctant to ask questions (Cheng, 1987). Teachers can't assume that silence means understanding; they need to make an extra effort to ensure that test content and procedures are understood.

Accommodating Diversity in Scoring

As you saw earlier in the chapter, essay exams and alternative assessments that involve oral descriptions are effective for measuring students' ability to organize information, to think analytically, and to apply their understanding to real-world problems. However, they also place an extra burden on students who are wrestling with both content and language.

What can teachers do? Valid assessment often requires the use of essays and alternative formats, and teachers cannot ignore students' grammatical errors. One solution is to evaluate essays and performance assessments with two grades: one for content and another for grammar, spelling, and punctuation (Hamp-Lyons, 1992; Scarcella, 1990). **Multiple trait scoring** *creates different criteria for different dimensions of a product, whether it is an essay or some other alternative assessment product.* For example, an item in science that asks students to propose a solution to the problem of water pollution might be scored on three criteria: (a) solution to the problem, (b) understanding of content, and (c) way the ideas are developed (Hamp-Lyons, 1992). Breaking the score into three areas allows the teacher to discriminate among understanding of content, problem solving, and ability to use language.

Each of these suggestions is designed to ensure, as much as possible, that test scores reflect differences in achievement and not cultural bias related to background knowledge, vocabulary, or testing sophistication.

Classroom Connections

Capitalizing on Diversity in Your Classroom.

1. Be continually aware of the effect that diversity can have on assessment.
   - At the beginning of the school year, a math teacher in an inner-city school carefully explains her grading system and what it requires of students. She emphasizes that it is designed to promote learning.

   - A first-grade teacher takes extra time and effort during parent-teacher conferences to explain how she arrives at grades for her students. She saves students' work samples and shares them with the parents during conferences.

2. Adapt testing procedures to meet the needs of all students.

- A history teacher encourages her students to ask her about any terms on the test that they don't understand. Unless measuring their understanding of the term is part of what she is measuring, she defines and illustrates the term for the students.
- A second-grade teacher adjusts her testing procedures for her non-native English speakers. She arranges to give the students extra time, and she provides for an older student as a translator for those whose command of English is still rudimentary.

3. Thoroughly discuss results after tests have been scored and returned.

- A science teacher discusses all of the frequently missed items on his tests. He asks students why they responded as they did and what their thinking was. He writes notes during the discussion to revise items that may have been ambiguous or that required knowledge not all students should be expected to know.

Grading and Reporting: The Total Assessment System

To this point, we have discussed the preparation of traditional test items, the design of alternative assessments, and the assessment process itself, which includes preparing students, administering assessments, and analyzing results. Some additional issues must also be considered, however, such as:

- How many tests and quizzes should be given?
- How will alternative assessments be used?
- How will homework be counted?
- How is missed work made up?
- How are affective dimensions, such as cooperation and effort, reported in the overall assessment?
- How is performance reported (e.g., letter grade, percentage, descriptive statement)?

These decisions are largely the teacher's responsibility, and this is significant for beginning teachers, who have no experience to fall back on. Merely knowing that the decisions are the teacher's, however, removes some of the uncertainty in the process. We examine these decisions and offer some suggestions in the following sections.

Designing a Grading System

Designing a grading system is an important task. The format of this system will influence both student learning and teacher workload. Some guidelines can help you in this process.

1. Your system must be consistent with school and district policies.
2. Your system should be designed to gather frequent and systematic information from each student.
3. In most situations, homework should be an integral part of the assessment system.
4. You should be able to confidently defend the system to a parent or administrator if necessary.

With these guidelines in mind, let's look at the elements of an effective system.

Formative and Summative Evaluation

The way a teacher uses quizzes and tests affects their influence on learning. Although a teacher typically thinks of giving tests and quizzes to assign grades, they can be given to simply provide the teacher and students with feedback about learning progress—perhaps a more important function. In this case, they are given, scored, and discussed just as any other quiz or test would be, but they are not included in any grading decision. This process is called **formative evaluation** *because it is used only to provide feedback to the learner.*

Tests, quizzes, homework, and alternative assessments that are used to make grading decisions, however, are part of the process called **summative evaluation**, *which is evaluation used for grading purposes.* In public schools, most assessments are used for summative evaluations, but formative evaluations can be helpful in making instructional decisions and in providing incentives for student effort.

Norm-Referenced and Criterion-Referenced Evaluation

An important part of a teacher's job is to assign value to students' work. This task is as diverse as giving smiley faces, writing comments on papers, and assigning grades. Norm-referenced and criterion-referenced evaluations are two ways to assign value to a measurement. **Norm referencing** *means that decisions about students' performances are based on comparisons with their peers;* **criterion referencing** *means that a decision is made according to a predetermined standard.* A comparison of norm and criterion referencing is found in Table 13.9.

Criterion-referenced evaluation has two important advantages. First, because it reflects the extent to which goals are met, it is more effective in describing content mastery. Second, criterion referencing de-emphasizes competition, and competitive environments can discourage students from helping each other, threaten peer relationships, detract from intrinsic motivation, and encourage students to attribute success and failure to ability rather than to effort (Ames, 1992; Crooks, 1988; Maehr, 1992). Although criterion referencing alone does not eliminate all these problems, it is usually preferable to norm referencing.

> **13.34**
> Think about the effects of formative evaluation on elementary, junior high, and high school students. With which group would formative evaluation be most important? Least important? Explain why this would be the case.

> **13.35**
> Is the assessment system for the class you're in norm referenced or criterion referenced? What makes it that way?

Table 13.9

A comparison of norm referencing and criterion referencing

	Examples	Characteristics
Norm referencing	Grading on the curve: 15% of students get *A*s 15% get *B*s 40% get *C*s 15% get *D*s 15% get *F*s	Compares students' performances to each other Creates a competitive environment
Criterion referencing	94–100 = A 86–93 = B Performance assessments (e.g., recognizes shapes, knows rhyming sounds, knows directions)	Reflects extent to which course goals are being met Reduces student competitiveness

Tests and Quizzes

For teachers in the upper elementary, middle, and secondary schools, tests and quizzes form the cornerstone of the grading system. Some teachers add tests and quizzes together and count them as a certain percentage of the overall grade. Others weigh them differently in assigning grades. Both methods are appropriate, depending on the teacher's goals.

The design of the curriculum often influences the use of tests and quizzes. For example, one teacher gives a quiz at the end of each chapter and a test at the end of each unit in the text. Another gives weekly quizzes, with tests at midterm and the end of the grading period. However it is done, frequent monitoring of progress with feedback to students is important for both achievement and motivation.

Alternative Assessments

If you're using alternative assessments, they should be included in your grading system. To do otherwise communicates that they are less important than the traditional measures you're using. If you rate student performance on the basis of well-established criteria, scoring will have acceptable reliability and alternative assessments can then be used in the same way as tests and quizzes.

Homework

In Chapter 12, you found that properly designed and used homework contributes to learning. To be most effective, homework should be collected, scored, and included in the grading system (Cooper, 1989). Beyond this point, however, research provides little guidance as to how it should be managed. Accountability, feedback, and your own workload are factors that will influence this decision. Table 13.10 outlines some options.

As you can see, each option has advantages and disadvantages. The best strategy is one that results in your students making the most consistent and conscientious effort on their homework without costing you an inordinate amount of time.

13.36
Using social cognitive theory as a basis, explain why it is important that homework be scored and included in the grading system. What can you do about the possibility that students will copy their homework from others?

Assigning Grades: Increasing Learning and Motivation

Having made decisions about tests, quizzes, alternative assessments, and homework, you are now ready to design your total grading system. At this point, you must make two decisions: (a) what to include and (b) the weight to assign each component. Earlier, you saw that tests, quizzes, alternative assessments, and homework should each be included in most cases. Some teachers build in additional factors, such as effort, class participation, and attitude. This practice, though common in classrooms, is discouraged by assessment experts (Gronlund & Linn, 1995). Gathering systematic information about affective variables is difficult, so assessing them is highly subjective. Factors such as effort, cooperation, preparedness, and class attendance should be reflected in a separate section of the report card.

Here are two teachers' systems for assigning grades:

Sun Ngin		**Lea DeLong**	
Tests and Quizzes	50%	Tests	45%
Homework	20%	Quizzes	45%
Observation	20%	Homework	10%
Projects	10%		

Table 13.10

Homework assessment options

Option	Advantages	Disadvantages
Grade it yourself	Promotes learning. Allows diagnosis of students. Increases student effort.	Is very demanding for the teacher.
Grade samples	Reduces teacher work, compared with first option.	Doesn't give the teacher a total picture of student performance.
Collect at random intervals	Reduces teacher workload.	Reduces student effort unless homework is frequently collected.
Change papers, students grade	Provides feedback with minimal teacher effort.	Consumes class time. Doesn't give students feedback on their own work.
Students score own papers	Is the same as changing papers. Lets students see their own mistakes.	Is inaccurate for purposes of evaluation. Lets students not do the work and copy in class as it's being discussed.
Students get credit for completing assignment	Gives students feedback on their work when it's discussed in class.	Reduces effort of unmotivated students.
No graded homework, frequent short quizzes	Is effective with older and motivated students.	Reduces effort of unmotivated students.

In examining these two examples, you can see that the two teachers' systems are quite different. Sun Ngin, an eighth-grade physical science teacher, emphasizes both homework and alternative assessments, which include projects and what he calls "observation." Traditional tests and quizzes count only 50% in his system. Lea DeLong emphasizes tests and quizzes much more heavily; they count 90% in her system. The rationale in each case was straightforward. Sun indicated that the homework was important to student learning and believed that unless it was emphasized, students wouldn't do it. He also included projects as an important part of his grades. In his judgment, projects involved his students in the study of science, and he used systematic observation to chart their progress as they worked on the projects and other hands-on activities. Lea, a secondary Algebra II teacher, thought that students fully understood the need to do their homework in order to be successful on the tests and quizzes. She gave a weekly quiz and three tests during a 9-week grading period.

For it to be effective in promoting learning, students must understand the assessment system. On the one hand, if they are quizzed frequently and if their homework is scored and returned quickly, even young students learn to understand the relationship between effort and grades. On the other hand, even high school students have problems understanding a grading system if it is too complex (Evans & Engelberg, 1988).

Raw Points or Percentage?

In assigning scores to assignments, quizzes, or tests, teachers have two options. In a percentage system, they convert each score to a percentage and then average the percentages as the grading period progresses. In the other system, they accumulate raw points and convert to a percentage only at the end of the period.

To illustrate these options, let's think back to Laura Brinson's work with her second graders, first presented in our discussion of teachers' assessment patterns. Kelly, one of her students, missed 1 of 10 problems on a seatwork assignment. As is typical of many teachers, Laura used a percentage system, and because 9 correct out of 10 is 90%, she wrote 90 for Kelly on this assignment. This is a straightforward and simple process.

Suppose now that students are graded on another assignment; this time, it is five items long and Kelly gets three of the five correct. Her grade on this assignment would be 60. Teachers then typically average the assignments, meaning that Kelly's average at this point is 75 because the average of 90 and 60 is 75.

This process is flawed. By finding the percentage for each assignment and averaging them, the two are given equal weight. In fact, on the two assignments, Kelly has correctly responded to 12 of 15 problems. If Laura had recorded Kelly's raw points for each assignment, her average at that point would be 80 (12/15 x 100), 5 points higher than the average gotten by using a percentage system.

If averaging percentages is flawed, why is it so common? The primary reason is simplicity. In addition to being simpler for teachers to manage, it is easier to communicate to students and parents. Many teachers, particularly those in the elementary and middle schools, have attempted point systems and later went back to percentage systems because of pressure from students, who believe they better understand percentage systems.

As with many other aspects of teaching, the option is your choice. On the one hand, a percentage system is fair if assignments are similar in length, tests are also similar in length, and tests are given more weight than quizzes and assignments. On the other hand, a point system can work if the teacher simply has the students keep a running total of their points and then communicates the number they must have for an A, a B, and so on at any point in the grading period.

> **13.37**
> What kind of grading system is used in the class you're taking? Is it a point, percentage, or some other system? Is the system clear? Do you know where you stand at all times during the semester or quarter?

Classroom Connections

Using Effective Assessment in Your Classroom

1. Be explicit about what will be covered on assessments.
   - A social studies teacher announces to her class, "On Thursday's test, you will be asked to explain in an essay question how the characteristics of the northern, middle, and southern colonies affected the economy of each region." On the test, one of the subsections includes an essay item on this topic.

2. Provide practice for your students under testlike conditions.
   - As she prepares her class for an essay exam, a social studies teacher displays the following question on the overhead: "The southern colonies were primarily agricultural rather than industrial. Using the characteristics of the region, explain why this would be the case." She gives the students a few minutes to respond. She then discusses the item and appropriate responses to it, again reminding the students that this is the type of question they will have on the test.

3. Prepare a test-item file.
   - A fourth-grade teacher writes items for science and social studies and stores them in a computer file, classified according to topic. When he begins to prepare a test, he goes back into the file to retrieve and review the items.

4. Do an item analysis of test items.
   - After giving a test, a sixth-grade teacher surveys the distribution of student responses. She then revises items that are misleading or that have ineffective distracters. The revisions are stored in the computer for next time.

5. Hand back tests, discuss them, and collect them for later use.

- A second-grade teacher discusses each problem on a math test and then asks the students to rework the problems that were frequently missed.

6. Consider the effects of the total assessment system on learning and motivation.
   - A history teacher gives frequent quizzes between major tests. He notices a decrease in test anxiety, as well as an increase in the amount of time students spend studying for his classes.

Windows on Classrooms

At the beginning of the chapter, you saw how Kathy Stevens used her understanding of assessment to help increase both her students' achievement and motivation. In studying the chapter, you've seen how assessment, in both traditional and alternative forms, can help teachers make strategic decisions about their students' learning progress.

Let's look now at another teacher working with a group of students. As you read the case study, compare the teacher's approach with the suggestions you've studied in the chapter.

Donald Hawkins is a 10th-grade English teacher at Brentwood High School. He teaches three sections of standard English and two sections of English Honors II.

We look in now at his third period on Monday as he begins a unit on pronoun cases with one of his standard classes.

The tardy bell rings at 9:10 as Donald begins, "All right, listen, everyone. . . . Today, we're going to begin a study of cases of pronouns. Everybody turn to page 484 in your text. . . . We see at the top of the page that we're dealing with pronoun cases. This is very important in our writing. We want to be able to write and use Standard English correctly, and this is one of the places where people often get mixed up. So, when we're finished with our study here,

you'll all be able to use pronouns correctly in your writing."

He then wrote the following on the chalkboard:

Pronouns use the nominative case when they're subjects and predicate nominatives.

Pronouns use the objective case when they're direct objects, indirect objects, or objects of prepositions.

"Let's review briefly," Donald continued. "Give me a sentence that has

both a direct and indirect object in it. . . . Anyone?"

"Mr. Hawkins gives us too much homework," Amato offered jokingly.

Donald wrote the sentence on the chalkboard amid laughter from the students and then smiled and continued, "Okay, Amato. Good sentence, even though it's incorrect. I don't give you *enough* work. . . . What's the subject in the sentence?"

" . . . "

"Go ahead, Amato."

"Oh, I'm sorry. . . . *Mr. Hawkins.*"

"Yes, good. *Mr. Hawkins* is the subject," and Donald then underlined *Mr. Hawkins* in the sentence.

"Now, what's the direct object? . . . Helen?"

" . . . *Homework.*"

"All right, good. And what's the indirect object? . . . Anya?"

" . . . *Us.*"

"Excellent, everybody." Donald proceeded by reviewing predicate nominatives and objects of prepositions.

He then continued, "Now, let's look at some additional examples. Look what I have displayed on the overhead."

He then uncovered an overhead with 10 sentences written on it. The following were the first four.

1. Did you get the card from Esteban and (I, me)?
2. Will Meg and (she, her) run the concession stand?
3. They treat (whoever, whomever) they hire very well.
4. I looked for someone (who, whom) could give me directions to the theater.

"Okay, look at the first one. Which is correct? . . . Omar?"

" . . . *Me.*"

"Good, Omar. How about the second one? . . . Lonnie?"

" . . . *Her.*"

"Not quite, Lonnie. Listen to this. . . . Suppose I turn the sentence around a little and say, 'Meg and her will run the concession stand.' See, that doesn't sound right, does it? *Meg and she* is a compound subject, and when we have a subject, we use the nominative case. . . . Are you okay on that, Lonnie?"

Lonnie nodded and Donald went on, "Look at the third one. . . . Cheny."

" . . . I don't know. . . . *whoever,* I guess."

"This one is tricky all right," Donald nodded. "When we use *whoever* and *whomever, whoever* is the nominative case, and *whomever* is the objective case. So, we see in this sentence that *whomever* is a direct object, so it is the correct form."

Donald then continued with the rest of the sentences as he had with the first four. After he finished, he gave the students another list of sentences in which they were to select the correct form of the pronoun.

On Tuesday, Donald first went over the exercises the students had completed for homework and then continued with some additional examples of using *who, whom, whoever,* and *whomever.* He then went on to discuss the rules for pronoun-antecedent agreement (Pronouns must agree with their antecedents in gender and number) and again had the students work examples as he had done with pronoun cases. He continued with pronouns and their antecedents on Wednesday and began a discussion of indefinite pronouns as antecedents for personal pronouns—*anybody, either, each, one, someone*—and had the students work examples as he had done before.

Near the end of class on Thursday, Donald announced, "Tomorrow, we're going to have a test on this material—pronoun cases, pronouns and their antecedents, and indefinite pronouns. You have your notes, so study hard . . . Are there any questions? . . . Good. I expect you all to do well. I'll see you tomorrow."

On Friday morning, the students filed into class, and as the bell rang, Donald picked up a stack of tests from his desk.

"Everybody ready?" he asked, and amid some mock groans and murmurs each student took a test copy and began working.

The test was composed of 30 sentences, 10 of which dealt with case, 10 more with antecedents, and the final 10 with indefinite pronouns. The final part of the test directed the students to write a paragraph.

The following are some sample items from the test:

> For each of the items below, mark A on your answer sheet if the pronoun case is correct in the sentence, and mark B if it is incorrect. If it is incorrect, supply the correct pronoun.
>
> 1. Be careful who you tell.
> 2. Will Rennee and I be in the outfield?
> 3. My brother and me like water skiing.

Write the pronoun that correctly completes the sentence.

11. Arlene told us about _____ visit to the dentist to have braces put on.
12. The Wilsons planted a garden in _____ backyard.
13. Cal read the recipe and put _____ in the file.
21. Each of the girls on the team wore _____ school sweater to the game.
22. None of the brass has lost _____ shine yet.
23. Few of the boys on the team have taken _____ physicals yet.

The directions for the final part of the test were as follows:

> Write a short paragraph that contains at least two examples of pronouns in the nominative case and two examples of pronouns in the objective case.

Include also at least two examples of pronouns that agree with their antecedents. Remember!! The paragraph must make sense. It cannot just be a series of sentences.

Donald watched as his students took the test, periodically walking up and down the aisles. Seeing that 15 minutes remained in the period and that some students were only starting on their paragraphs, he announced, "You only have 15 minutes left. Watch your time and work quickly. You must be finished by the end of the period."

He then continued monitoring the students, again reminding them to work quickly when 10 minutes were left and again when 5 minutes were left.

Luis, Simao, Moy, and Rudy were hastily finishing the last few words of their tests as the bell rang. Luis finally turned in his paper as Donald's fourth-period students were filing into the room.

"Here," Donald said. "This pass will get you into Mrs. Washington's class if you're late. . . . How did you do?"

"Okay, I think," Luis said over his shoulder as he scurried out of the room, "except for the last part. It was hard. I couldn't get started."

"I'll look at it," Donald said. "Scoot now."

On Monday, Donald returned the papers, and as he handed them back, he said, "Here are your papers. You did fine on the sentences, but your paragraphs need a lot of work. Why did you have so much trouble with them, when we had so much practice?"

"It was hard, Mr. Hawkins."

"Not enough time."

"I hate to write."

Donald listened patiently and then said, "Be sure you write your scores in your notebooks. . . . Okay. . . . You have them all written down? . . . Are there any questions?"

"Number 8," Enrique asked.

"Okay, let's look at 8. It says, 'I didn't know to (who, whom) to give the letter.' There, the pronoun is the object of a preposition, so it's *whom*.

"Any others?"

A sprinkling of questions came from around the room, and Donald responded, "We don't have time to go over all of them. I'll discuss three more."

He then responded to three students who seemed to be most urgent in waving their hands. He then collected their tests and began a discussion of adjective and adverb clauses.

Questions for Discussion and Analysis

Analyze Donald's lesson now in the context of the information in this chapter. In doing your analysis, consider the following questions. In each case, be specific and take information directly from the case study in making your comparison.

1. Alternative, authentic, or performance assessment (depending on the label you choose) was discussed in the chapter. How "authentic" was Donald's assessment?

2. How well was Donald's curriculum aligned? Explain specifically. What could he have done to increase curricular alignment?

3. In the section on effective testing practices, we discussed preparing students for tests, administering tests, and analyzing results. How effectively did Donald conduct each part? Describe specifically what he might have done to be more effective in these areas.

4. As in most classrooms, Donald's class is composed of learners with diverse backgrounds. How effective was his teaching and assessment for these students?

5. What were the primary strengths of Donald's teaching and assessment? What were the primary weaknesses? If you think Donald's teaching and assessment could have been improved on the basis of information in this chapter, what suggestions would you make? Be specific.

6. Was Donald's teaching primarily behaviorist in its orientation, or was it more constructivist? Explain. How might he change his orientation?

 **Summary**

Classroom Assessment

Classroom assessment includes the data teachers gather through tests, quizzes, homework, and classroom observations, as well as the decisions teachers make about student progress. Effective assessment results in increased learning, as well as improved motivation.

Teachers informally measure student understanding during classroom activities and discussions. Formal measurements are attempts to systematically gather information for grading and reporting.

Validity involves the appropriateness of interpretations made from measurements. Reliability describes the extent to which measurements are consistently interpreted. Both concepts provide standards for effective assessment.

Traditional Assessment

Teachers in elementary schools rely on performance measures and commercially prepared items, and they focus on affective goals more than do teachers of older students. Teachers of older students tend to use completion items more than other formats, and their assessments overemphasize memory and low-level outcomes.

Teachers can improve the effectiveness of their assessments by using guidelines and by keeping validity and reliability in mind when they construct items. Multiple choice, true-false, matching, completion, and essay items all have strengths and weaknesses that can be addressed through thoughtful item writing.

Authentic Assessment

Authentic assessments, including performance assessments and portfolios, ask students to perform complex tasks similar to those found in the real world. In designing alternative assessments, teachers attempt to place students in realistic settings, asking them to perform high-level tasks involving problem solving in various content areas. Portfolio assessment involves students in the construction of a collection of work samples that documents learning progress. The reliability of alternative assessments can be improved through careful application of predetermined criteria and the use of systematic observation, checklists, and rating scales to evaluate products.

Effective Assessment Practices

Effective assessments are congruent with goals and instruction, and effective teachers communicate what will be covered on assessments, allow students to practice on items similar to those that will appear on tests, teach test-taking skills, and state positive expectations for student performance. Increasing testing frequency, using criterion referencing, providing clear information about tests, and giving students ample time help reduce test anxiety.

Grading and Reporting: The Total Assessment System

Grading and reporting are important functions of an assessment system. Formative evaluation provides feedback about learning, whereas summative evaluations are used for grading purposes. Norm-referenced evaluation compares a learner's performance with that of peers, whereas criterion-referenced evaluation compares students' performance with a standard.

 **Important Concepts**

alternative assessment (p. 532)

assessment system (p. 518)

authentic assessment (p. 532)

checklists (p. 537)

classroom assessment (p. 517)

completion items (p. 529)

criterion referencing (p. 551)

distracters (p. 523)

essay items (p. 530)

evaluation (p. 518)

formal measurement (p. 519)

formative evaluation (p. 551)

informal measurements (p. 519)

matching format (p. 528)

measurement (p. 518)

multiple-choice items (p. 523)

multiple trait scoring (p. 549)

norm referencing (p. 551)

performance assessments (pp. 532, 533)

portfolios (p. 539)

rating scales (p. 537)

reliability (p. 520)

summative evaluation (p. 551)

systematic observations (p. 536)

table of specifications (p. 542)

test anxiety (p. 544)

true-false format (p. 527)

validity (p. 520)

Chapter Outline

14

S tandardized
T esting

"Hello, Mrs. Palmer. I'm glad you could come in. It's good to see you again," Danny Chavez, a fourth-grade teacher, said as he offered his hand in greeting.

"Thank you," Doris Palmer responded. "I'm anxious to see how David's doing. His sister always did so well."

"Let's take a look," Danny said as he motioned for Mrs. Palmer to take a seat next to his desk. "Here are the results from the Stanford Achievement Test that David took earlier this spring. There's quite a bit of information here, so let me walk you through it" (see Figure 14.1).

After giving Mrs. Palmer a chance to look at the report for a few moments, Danny began by pointing to the reading scores, "Let's take a look at reading first. . . . David is quite strong there."

"He loves to read. I'm amazed, but he loves going to the library."

"Yes, he always has a book out when he has free time in class. You can see three reading scores—vocabulary, reading comprehension, and total reading. Reading comprehension is especially strong. David's at the 80th percentile there."

"What does this 5.6 mean?" Mrs. Palmer interjected, pointing to the 'grade equivalent' column. Should he be in the fifth grade?"

"Not really," Danny smiled. "It really means that David scored very

well on the reading portion of the test. Technically, in standardized testing lingo, it means that David's performance on this part of the test was about the same as that of the average fifth grader in the sixth month of school. You should be very pleased, . . . but tests like these don't tell us where students should be placed in school.

"You already know he's in our top reading group," Danny continued. "This test confirms that he's properly placed. I have some other materials from his portfolio that give us some more information."

"So, what's the point in the tests if we already know that he's good at reading? They seem to make him nervous," commented Mrs. Palmer.

"Good question. We actually use the tests for several reasons. One is they help us understand how our students are doing, compared with other students around the country. They give us an objective, outside measure. Second, these tests can help us pinpoint some problem areas. . . . Like here in math," Danny continued, pointing at the report. "David isn't quite as strong in math as in reading."

"He says he doesn't like math."

Danny smiled, "That's what he says, but I'm not sure that's the whole picture. Look here on the test. Notice how his lowest math score is on concepts of numbers. His per-

centile rank there is 20. . . . And, look over here. Notice how this band is lower than most of his others. This could suggest he has difficulty understanding math concepts."

"You're telling me. Sometimes he comes home and complains about all the problems you have him do. He says he knows the answer but you keep asking him 'why?'"

"That's interesting, Mrs. Palmer, because the test is telling us something that I could see in his work. His work in my class, which I'll show you in a minute," he said, motioning to a folder, "suggests that maybe David tended to memorize quite a bit in his earlier math classes. He knew a lot but probably wasn't asked to think that much about what he was learning. Now that he's in fourth grade, I'm trying to help him understand *why* he's doing what he's doing. I really believe that it will pay off if he sticks with it—and if you and I encourage him to stick with it."

"Well," she responded uncertainly, "if you're sure, we'll hang in there."

"Overall, Mrs. Palmer, I'm very pleased with David's performance," Danny interjected, sensing her uncertainty. "If he can keep his reading scores up and work to get those math scores up some by next year, he will be making excellent progress."

Standardized tests have become a familiar part of the educational landscape. Most of us have taken standardized achievement tests as we moved through school, and the SAT or ACT has become an accepted rite of passage from high school to college.

Teachers, such as Danny Chavez in the opening case, play an important role in determining whether standardized tests are used effectively; they help select and administer the

Figure 14.1

David Palmer's achievement test report

STANFORD

ACHIEVEMENT TEST SERIES, EIGHTH EDITION

TEACHER:	DANNY CHAVEZ		1988 NORMS:	STANFORD GRADE 4	OLSAT GRADE 4	STUDENT SKILLS ANALYSIS FOR DAVID PALMER
SCHOOL:	LAKESIDE ELEMENTARY	GRADE: 4 TEST DATE:	SPRING	NATIONAL INTER 1	NATIONAL E	
DISTRICT:	NEWTOWN	4/96	LEVEL: FORM:	J	1	

TESTS	NO. OF ITEMS	RAW SCORE	NATL PR-S	LOCAL PR-S	GRADE EQUIV	NATIONAL GRADE PERCENTILE BANDS
Total Reading	94	70	65–6	75–6	5.6	
Vocabulary	40	27	54–5	59–5	5.0	
Reading Comp.	54	43	72–6	80–7	6.7	
Total Math	118	58	28–4	29–4	4.2	
Concepts of No.	34	14	20–3	21–3	3.6	
Computation	44	22	28–4	29–4	4.0	
Applications	40	22	37–4	38–4	4.3	
Total Language	60	47	64–6	60–6	5.8	
Lang. Mechanics	30	21	41–5	38–4	4.4	
Lang. Expression	30	26	80–7	75–6	9.7	
Spelling	40	22	37–4	37–4	4.2	
Study Skills	30	21	53–5	55–5	5.2	
Science	50	31	60–6	80–7	5.5	
Social Science	50	42	88–7	90–8	8.7	
Listening	45	25	34–4	35–4	3.9	
Using Information	70	35	24–4	25–4	3.5	
Thinking Skills	101	45	27–4	30–4	3.5	
Basic Battery	387	243	44–5	45–5	4.6	
Complete Battery	487	316	52–5	55–5	5.1	

National Grade Percentile Band scale markings: 1 10 30 50 70 90 99

AGE 10 YRS 2 MOS   READING GROUP   LANGUAGE ARTS GROUP   MATHEMATICS GROUP   COMMUNICATIONS GROUP

H REGULAR INSTRUCTION   SPELLING   CONCEPTS   LISTENING

COPY XX

PROCESS NO. X–(SSAI)–X REVISED 09/29/89

THE PSYCHOLOGICAL CORPORATION
HARCOURT BRACE JOVANOVICH, INC.

Source: Stanford Achievement Test: 8th Edition. Copyright © 1989 by Harcourt Brace & Company. Reproduced by permission. All rights reserved.

tests, and they interpret results for both students and their parents. Their roles and responsibilities in the wise use of standardized tests are very important.

The goal of this chapter is to provide you with information that will help you make sound decisions about using standardized tests. After you've completed your study of this chapter, you should be able to meet the following objectives:

- Describe different uses for standardized tests and explain how they influence educational decision making.
- Discuss the different types of standardized tests on the basis of their educational use.
- Explain how different types of validity can be used to evaluate standardized tests.
- Discuss different issues involving standardized testing and explain how they influence classroom teachers.
- Explain how student diversity influences measurement validity and discuss strategies that teachers can use to minimize measurement bias.

Standardized Tests

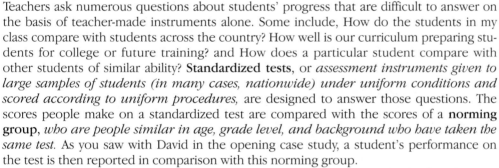

Teachers ask numerous questions about students' progress that are difficult to answer on the basis of teacher-made instruments alone. Some include, How do the students in my class compare with students across the country? How well is our curriculum preparing students for college or future training? and How does a particular student compare with other students of similar ability? **Standardized tests**, or *assessment instruments given to large samples of students (in many cases, nationwide) under uniform conditions and scored according to uniform procedures,* are designed to answer those questions. The scores people make on a standardized test are compared with the scores of a **norming group**, *who are people similar in age, grade level, and background who have taken the same test.* As you saw with David in the opening case study, a student's performance on the test is then reported in comparison with this norming group.

14.1
Identify at least two similarities and at least two differences between standardized tests and teacher-made tests.

The influence of standardized testing can hardly be overstated. The fact that students in other industrialized countries, such as Japan and Germany, score higher than U.S. students on some of these tests has alarmed many in this country. The "reform movement" that began in the early 1980s was largely a result of standardized test results. Few of the concerns you may have heard and read so much about would be voiced without the information gathered from standardized tests. Standardized tests also influence individual students. "The results of a morning's testing often become a powerful factor in decisions about the future of each student" (H. Gardner, 1992, p. 77).

Standardized testing is also controversial. In a given year, 127 million students take state-mandated tests at a cost of between $725 and $915 million annually (National Commission on Testing and Public Policy, 1990). In addition, standardized tests are often used to compare students' performance in different schools, districts, states, and even countries. Many teachers believe that standardized testing is overemphasized and adversely affects a balanced school curriculum (Herman, Abedi, & Golan, 1994; Urdan & Paris, 1991). Before examining this controversy further, let's look at some uses of standardized tests.

Functions of Standardized Tests

Standardized tests serve several functions. They can be used to gather information about learning progress, to diagnose an individual students' strengths and weaknesses, and to make

Standardized tests can provide valuable information to students and their parents about learning progress.

selection and placement decisions in instructional programs. They also help school personnel in measuring the effectiveness of specific programs, as well as overall performance.

Student Assessment

14.2
Identify at least one advantage and at least one disadvantage of using standardized tests for the purpose of student assessment.

Probably the most common function of standardized testing is to provide an external, objective picture of student progress. In our opening case study, for example, David has consistently received A's in his reading classes, but his parents, teachers, and school administrators want to know how he and his peers compare with other students at his grade level. Standardized tests provide one means of comparison, and when combined with teacher-made assessments and other measures of classroom performance, they can help provide a complete picture of student progress.

Diagnosis

Standardized tests are also used to diagnose student strengths and weaknesses. For example, having found that David scored low on the math section of his achievement test, a diagnostic test could be used to gather detailed information about his strengths and weaknesses in math. These tests are usually administered individually, with the intent of getting specific information about a student's achievement in particular aspects of a content area.

Placement and Selection

Placing students and selecting students for programs where the number of available slots are limited are two other uses of standardized tests. For instance, a math faculty will have students coming to their high school from "feeder" junior high schools, private schools, and schools outside the district. Scores from the math section of a standardized test can help these professionals place students in classes that will best match their backgrounds and capabilities.

Standardized test results can also be used to place students in advanced programs, such as programs for the gifted, and they are used as one basis for university selection. Most of us, for instance, have taken either the *Scholastic Aptitude Test* (SAT) or the *American College Testing Program* (ACT) during our junior or senior year in high school. These are standardized tests, the results of which played an important part in determining whether we were accepted by the college of our choice. Because college students come from different parts of the country and because their backgrounds are diverse, these tests provide a basis for uniform comparison.

14.3
Identify at least one advantage and at least one disadvantage of using standardized tests for placement purposes.

Program Evaluation and Improvement

Suppose an elementary school moves from a traditional reading program to one that emphasizes writing and children's literature. To assess the effectiveness of this change, the faculty use teacher-made assessments, student work samples, and the perceptions of teachers and parents. However, the faculty still don't know how the students' performance compares with their performance when the old curriculum was in place or with the performance of peers in other reading programs. Standardized test results can help in answering these questions.

Accountability

Increasingly, schools and teachers are being held responsible for student learning (Darling-Hammond & Snyder, 1992). Parents, school board members, state officials, and decision makers at the federal level are demanding evidence that tax dollars are being used efficiently. Standardized test scores provide one indicator of this effectiveness.

The accountability movement is controversial. Critics, for example, contend that misuse of standardized test scores can result in narrowing the curriculum and give an inaccurate picture of student learning (E. Baker, 1989). We examine this controversy later in the chapter when we discuss issues in standardized testing.

Types of Standardized Tests

Achievement Tests

Achievement tests, the most widely used type of standardized tests, *are designed to measure and communicate how much students have learned in different content areas.* Although most common in reading and math, they also measure learning in science, social studies, computer literacy, and other content areas. Popular achievement tests include the *Iowa Test of Basic Skills,* the *California Achievement Test,* the *Stanford Achievement Test,* the *Comprehensive Test of Basic Skills,* and the *Metropolitan Achievement Test,* as well as individual statewide assessments and minimum-level skills tests.

Standardized achievement tests serve several purposes:

▌ Determining how well students have mastered a content area
▌ Comparing the performance of students with others across the country
▌ Tracking student progress over time
▌ Determining whether students have the background knowledge to begin instruction in particular areas
▌ Identifying learning problems

Most standardized achievement tests come as batteries of specific tests administered over several days. These tests are intended to reflect a curriculum common to most schools, and thus they will assess some, but not all, of the goals of a specific school. This is both a strength and a weakness. On the one hand, because they are designed for a range of schools, they can be used in a variety of locations. On the other hand, this "one size fits all" approach may not accurately measure achievement for a specific curriculum. For example, one study found that only 47% to 71% of the math content measured on commonly used standardized achievement batteries was the same as content covered in popular elementary math textbooks (Berliner, 1984). In a worst-case scenario, this means that students might have covered less than half the content measured on the test.

Schools and teachers should be cautious in selecting and interpreting standardized achievement tests for their students. When selecting a test, it is important to go beyond the name and to examine the specific contents described in the testing manual's table of specifications. Comparing the content of the test with your curriculum objectives will help you in deciding whether the test is valid for your use.

Diagnostic Tests

Whereas achievement tests measure students' progress in a variety of curriculum areas, **diagnostic tests** *provide a detailed description of learners' strengths and weaknesses in specific skill areas.* They are common in the primary grades, where instruction is designed to match the developmental level of the child, as well as math and reading across several levels. Diagnostic tests are usually administered individually, and compared with achievement tests, they include a larger number of items, use more subtests, and report scores in more specific areas (Gronlund & Linn, 1995). A diagnostic test in reading, for example, might include letter recognition, word analysis skills, sight vocabulary, vocabulary in context, and reading comprehension. Commonly used diagnostic tests include the *Metropolitan Achievement Tests,* the *Detroit Test of Learning Aptitude,* the *Durrell Analysis of Reading Difficulty,* and the *Stanford Diagnostic Reading Test.*

Intelligence Tests

In Chapter 4, we discussed intelligence in the context of individual differences and defined it as *the capacity to acquire knowledge, the ability to think and reason in the abstract, and the capability for solving problems.* **Intelligence tests** are designed to measure those abilities. Attempts to measure intelligence in a valid and reliable way were among the first in the history of standardized testing.

A Short History of Intelligence Tests. Standardized intelligence tests originated in the early 1900s when Alfred Binet was asked by the French minister of public instruction to assist in developing an instrument to be used in the education of students with mental disabilities. He selected a number of school-related skills, such as defining words and making change, and with his partner, Theodore Simon, developed a series of tests based on these skills. They gave the tests to heterogeneous groups of children, eliminating items so difficult that no students passed or so easy that all did. The result was an objective instrument, essentially independent of social class or the person administering the test, that could be passed by the average child of a given age.

Although intelligence tests were first developed to measure the capabilities of learners with disabilities, they were later broadened to describe the performance of a variety of people. Initially, performance was described as a mental age; for example, a child succeeding on tasks designed for a typical 8-year-old had a mental age of 8 years.

14.4

Describe what a teacher might do if a lack of fit is uncovered between a standardized achievement test and a teacher's curriculum.

14.5

Is the issue of "fit" more or less important when using diagnostic tests than when using achievement tests? Explain.

To overcome problems with older populations—describing a 20-year-old as functioning like a 30-year-old wasn't meaningful, for example—the mental age (M.A.) was divided by the chronological age (C.A.) and multiplied by 100 and resulted in the familiar ratio IQ (intelligence quotient). For example, a 6-year-old with an M.A. of an 8-year-old would have an IQ of 133 (8/6 = 1.33 x 100 = 133).

The importance of Binet and Simon's pioneering work is hard to overstate. For the first time, educators had an objective way of predicting school success; students who performed well on the test usually did well in school and vice versa. The predictions weren't perfect, but they were a vast improvement over people's intuition. The test was translated and brought to the United States by Lewis Terman, a professor at Stanford, and it then became the famous Stanford-Binet. The updated version is one of the two most widely used intelligence tests in schools today.

The Stanford-Binet.   The Stanford-Binet is an individually administered instrument composed of subtests, much like Binet's original. It comes in a kit that includes a box of standard toy objects for young children, booklets of printed cards for older subjects, a large picture of a unisex and multicultural doll, a recording booklet, and a test manual. Earlier versions heavily emphasized verbal tasks, but the most recent edition is more diverse, including performance items not requiring verbal skills (R. Thorndike, Hagen, & Sattler, 1986). Table 14.1 presents descriptions of some sample subtests in the latest revision.

The Stanford-Binet is a technically sound instrument second only to the Wechsler scales (described in the next section) in popularity. It has been revised and renormed a number of times over the years, most recently in 1986, using 5,000 schoolchildren in 47 states, grades 3 through 12, stratified by economic status, geographic region, and community size. Members of the White, African American, Hispanic, Asian, and Asian/Pacific Islander subcultures were all represented in proportion to their membership in the total population.

14.6

Suppose a 10-year-old had an M.A. of an 8-year-old. What would the child's IQ be?

14.7

What does the term *renormed* mean? Why is it important that minorities were used in revising and renorming the latest Stanford-Binet?

Table 14.1

Sample subtests from the revised (4th edition) Stanford-Binet

Subtest	Example/Description
Comprehension (Verbal reasoning)	Students are asked to explain facets of everyday life (e.g., "Why do people wear sunglasses?" or "Why do we go to the doctor?"). This subtest measures the ability to use and reason with words.
Number series (Quantitative reasoning)	Students are presented with a numerical sequence such as 1, 4, 7, and are expected to provide the next number. This subtest measures students' ability to find abstract patterns in numbers.
Abstract/visual reasoning (Copying)	Pictures of block designs are shown to students, and they are asked to copy them either with blocks (young children) or with paper and pencil (older children). This subtest measures students' ability to visualize and reproduce abstract patterns.

Source: Adapted with permission of The Riverside Publishing Company from *Stanford-Binet Intelligence Scale Technical Manual: Fourth Edition* by R. L. Thorndike, E. P. Hagen, and J. M. Sattler. The Riverside Publishing Company, 8420 W. Bryn Mawr Avenue, Chicago, IL 60631. Copyright 1986.

Teachers should consider the norming population for a test because similarities between that population and their own influences test validity.

The Wechsler Scales.   Developed by David Wechsler over a period of 40 years, the Weschler scales are the most popular intelligence tests in use today (Salvia & Ysseldyke, 1988). The three Wechsler tests, aimed at preschool-primary, elementary, and adult populations, have two main parts: verbal and performance. The Wechsler Intelligence Scale for Children–Third Edition (WISC-III; Wechsler, 1991) is an individually administered intelligence test with 13 subtests, of which 6 are verbal and 7 are performance (Table 14.2 presents some sample subtests). The performance sections were added because of dissatisfaction with the strong verbal emphasis of earlier intelligence tests. As with the Stanford-Binet, the Wechsler scales are considered technically sound by testing experts (Anastasi, 1988; Kaplan & Saccuzzo, 1993).

The Wechsler's two subtests, yielding separate verbal and performance scores, are an asset. For example, a substantially higher score on the performance compared with the verbal subtest could indicate a language problem related to poor reading or language-based cultural differences (Kaplan & Saccuzzo, 1993). Performance tasks are helpful in studying students who resist school-like tasks, learners with disabilities, and persons with limited education, because these subtests demand a minimum of verbal ability.

Individual Versus Group Intelligence Tests.   Individually administered intelligence tests include a wide variety of tasks, and they have an appropriate mix of verbal and performance subtests. Because both the directions and responses are oral, no opportunity for an error on an answer sheet exists, and the test administrator can seek clarification of uncertain answers and spot signs of fatigue, worry, or anxiety. Also, by observing carefully, the test administrator can often determine why the student gave the answer he or she did. These factors are important in interpreting a student's score. Experts emphasize that attentiveness, motivation, and anxiety can all have powerful effects on intelligence test performance (Snyderman & Rothman, 1987).

14.8
How do the subtests of the WISC-III compare with the Stanford-Binet? What does this comparison tell you about the two tests' views of intelligence?

14.9
Group intelligence tests are considered to be particularly inappropriate for young children. Identify at least two reasons for this.

Table 14.2

Sample items from the WISC-III

VERBAL SECTION	
Subtest	**Description/Examples**
Information	This subtest taps general knowledge common to American culture: a. How many minutes are there in an hour? b. Who was the first president of the United States?
Arithmetic	This subtest is a test of basic mathematical knowledge and skills, including counting and addition through division: a. Ted had three cookies but gave one to his friend. How many did he have then? b. There were six balls to play with and two teams. How many balls could each team have?
Similarities	This subtest is designed to measure abstract and logical thinking through use of analogies: a. How are a dog and a tree alike? b. How are books and newspapers alike?

PERFORMANCE SECTION	
Subtest	**Description/Examples**
Picture completion	Students are shown a picture with elements missing, which they are required to identify. This subtest measures general knowledge as well as visual comprehension.
Block design	This subtest focuses on a number of abstract figures. Designed to measure visual-motor coordination, it requires students to match patterns displayed by the examiner.

Top

Left face

Right face

Front and back face

Bottom

Student given blocks of this configuration

In contrast with individually administered tests, group tests are heavily weighted toward verbal skills, and they are susceptible to motivational, test-taking, and language problems. Because test data are so important in decision making and because individual tests are clearly superior, the use of group tests for individual diagnosis and placement is suspect. Because group tests require less time and administrative effort, however, their continued use is likely.

Aptitude Tests

Although *aptitude* and *intelligence* are often used synonymously, aptitude is only one characteristic of intelligence—the capacity to acquire knowledge. **Aptitude tests *are designed to predict the potential for future learning and to measure general abilities developed over long periods of time.*** Aptitude tests are commonly used in selection, placement, and assessment decisions, and they correlate highly with achievement tests. The concept of *aptitude* is intuitively sensible; for example, people will say, "I just don't have any aptitude for math," implying that their potential for learning math is limited.

The two most common aptitude tests at the high school level are the SAT and the ACT, mentioned earlier in the chapter. They are designed to measure a student's potential for success in college. This potential is heavily influenced by previous experience, however; classroom-related knowledge, particularly in language and mathematics, is critical for success on the tests. But because the tests are objective and reliable, they eliminate teacher bias and the unevenness of grades from different teachers and different schools. In this regard, they add valuable additional information in predicting future success.

The Scholastic Assessment Test (SAT I) is a revised version of the original Scholastic Aptitude Test (SAT), which contains six subsections: three verbal and three math. The verbal subtests include analogies, sentence completion (vocabulary and sentence structure), and critical reasoning; math subtests include standard computation, estimation, and student-produced response questions. Calculators are now allowed for use during the test.

The American College Testing Program (ACT) consists of tests in four areas: English, math, reading, and science reasoning. The total test takes about 3 hours, and calculators are not allowed.

14.10 ▬
Are aptitude and intelligence synonymous? If not, how are they different?

Evaluating Standardized Tests: Validity Revisited

Wendy Klopman was a little nervous. She had been asked to serve on a districtwide committee to select a new standardized achievement test battery for the elementary grades. Her task was to get feedback from the faculty at her school about two options: the Stanford Achievement Test and the California Achievement Test.

After giving a brief overview of the two tests during a faculty meeting, Wendy opened the floor for questions.

"How much do the two tests cover problem solving?" a fifth-grade teacher asked.

"We're moving our language arts curriculum more in the direction of writing. What about it?" a first-grade teacher wondered.

As the discussion continued, a confused and exasperated colleague asked, "Which one is better? That's really the bottom line. How about a simple answer?"

Wendy couldn't offer a simple answer, not because she was unprepared, but because she was asked to make a judgment about validity.

In Chapter 13, you saw that validity involves "the adequacy and appropriateness of the interpretations made from assessments, with regard to a particular use" (Gronlund & Linn,

1995, p. 47), and we emphasized the importance of matching assessments and goals. For teacher-made tests, validity is influenced by the kinds of assessments teachers construct and how the assessments are used.

In the case of standardized tests, validity is a bit different because the tests have already been constructed. Here, the teacher is asked to judge the suitability of a test for a specific purpose. Validity resides in the appropriate use of a test, not in the test itself (Messick, 1989; Shepard, 1993).

Experts describe three kinds of validity: (a) content, (b) predictive, and (c) construct, and each provides a different perspective on the issue of appropriate use.

Content Validity

Content validity *represents the overlap between what is taught and what is tested.* Content validity is determined by comparing test content with curriculum objectives, and it is a primary concern when considering standardized achievement tests. The question Wendy was asked about which test was "better" addressed content validity. The "better" test is the one with the closer match between the school's goals and the content of the test.

14.11
How does a teacher ensure content validity in a teacher-made test? How is the process similar to or different from that with standardized tests?

Predictive Validity

Often, teachers use standardized tests in an attempt to predict how students will do in a future course or program of study. **Predictive validity** *is an indicator of a test's ability to gauge future performance.* It is central to the SAT and the ACT; these tests are designed to measure a student's potential to do college work. Predictive validity is also the focus of tests that gauge students' readiness for the academic tasks of kindergarten and first grade.

Predictive validity is usually quantified by correlating a test and some other criterion, such as grades. For example, a correlation of .42 exists between the SAT and college grades (Shepard, 1993). High school grades is the only predictor that is better (a correlation of .48).

Why isn't the correlation between tests and college performance higher? The primary reason is that the SAT is designed to predict "general readiness" for college; other factors, such as motivation, study habits, and specific content background, strongly affect performance.

14.12
Describe a situation in which predictive validity would apply to the use of a standardized achievement test. (Think about the uses of achievement tests that were described earlier in the chapter.)

14.13
Suppose a standardized test was a "perfect predictor" of college success. What would the correlation between college performance and the test score be? What if there were no relationship between the score and performance in college?

Construct Validity

Finally, **construct validity** *is an indicator of the connection between a test and what it is designed to measure.* It is somewhat abstract but important in understanding the total concept of *validity* (Messick, 1989; Shepard, 1993). It answers the question, Do these items actually measure the ideas the test is designed to measure?

For instance, in examining the SAT, you can see that many of the items do indeed tap the ability to do abstract thinking about words and numbers—tasks that students are likely to face in their college experience. Because of this, the test has construct validity.

For a complete review of more than 1,400 standardized tests of achievement, aptitude, diagnosis, and personality, an excellent source is the *Mental Measurements Yearbook* (Conoley & Kramer, 1989). Originally edited by Oscar Buros, the yearbook provides accurate and critical reviews of all major standardized tests and is an important source of information for selecting and using these tests.

Understanding and Interpreting Standardized Test Scores

We said earlier in the chapter that standardized tests are given to literally thousands of students. To deal with the vast amount of information gathered and to describe individuals' performances compared with others', statistical methods are used in summarizing test information.

Descriptive Statistics

To illustrate the use of statistics in summarizing information, examine the following scores made by two classes of 31 students on a 50-item test. (As you examine this information, keep in mind that a standardized test would have a sample much larger than 31 and would probably contain a larger number of items. We use a class-size example here for the sake of illustration.)

The scores for the two classes, including the mean, median, and mode for each class, are displayed in Table 14.3 and are ranked from the highest to the lowest score. (We discuss the mean, median, and mode in the sections that follow.) As you can see in the table, the simple array of scores is somewhat cumbersome and doesn't tell you much, even when the scores are ranked. An efficient way of summarizing the information is needed.

Frequency Distributions

14.14

If the scores in Figure 14.2 reflected ability, which of the two classes would be easier to teach? Why?

One way of summarizing test data is to simply count the number of people who obtained each score; this is called a **frequency distribution**. It can be represented as a graph with the possible scores on the horizontal (x) axis and the frequency, or the number of students who got each score, on the vertical (y) axis. The frequency distributions for the two classes are shown in Figure 14.2.

This information is still in rough form, but you can already begin to see some differences in the two classes. For instance, the scores from the first class are spread out over a wider range than the scores of the second class, and there is a greater grouping of scores near the middle of the second distribution. Beyond this qualitative description, however, the distribution isn't particularly helpful. A more quantitative summary of the information is needed.

Measures of Central Tendency

14.15

Why is the title of this section—"Descriptive Statistics"—an appropriate label? What are the "statistics" in the label "Descriptive Statistics"?

Measures of central tendency—*the mean, median, and mode—are quantitative descriptions of how the group performed as a whole.* The **mean** is *the average score,* the **median** is *the middle score in the distribution,* and the **mode** is *the most frequent score.*

To obtain a mean, simply add the scores and divide by the number of scores. As it turns out, both distributions have $1302 / 31 = 42$. The class average of 42 is one indicator of how each group performed as a whole.

The median for the first distribution is 43 because half the scores (15) fall equal to or above 43 and the other half are equal to or below 43. Using the same process, you can find that the median for the second distribution is 42.

The median is useful when extremely high or low scores skew the mean and give a false picture of the sample. For example, you commonly hear or read demographic statistics such as "The median income for families of four in this country went from . . . in 1986 to . . . in 1996." The *median* income is used because a few billionaires would make the average (mean) income quite high and give an artificial indicator of typical families' stan-

Table 14.3

Scores of two classes on a 50-item test

Class #1	Class #2
50	48
49	47
49	46
48	46
47	45
47	45
46	44 ⌉
46	44
45	44 │ mode
45	44
45	44 ⌋
44 ⌉	43
44 │ mode	43
44 │	43
44 ⌋	43
43— median	42— median & mean
42— mean	42
41	42
41	42
40	41
40	41
39	41
39	40
38	40
37	39
37	39
36	38
35	38
34	37
34	36
33	35

dards of living. The median, in contrast, is not affected by these extremes and gives a more realistic picture of the typical American family's economic status. The median provides this same type of accuracy when used with test scores.

Looking once more at the two samples, you can see that the most frequent score for each is 44, which is the mode. Small samples, such as here, will often have more than one mode, and those cases have a "bimodal" or even "trimodal" distribution.

Using our measures of central tendency, you can see that the two samples are very much alike: the same mean, nearly the same median, and the same mode. As you saw from examining the frequency distribution, however, this doesn't give a complete picture of the two. A measure of their variability or "spread" is also needed.

Measures of Variability

To get a more accurate picture of the samples, you need to find out how much the scores in the sample vary, or what the spread is. One measure of variability is the **range**—*the distance between the top and bottom scores.* In the first class, the range is 17; in the second

14.16
Sketch a frequency distribution in which the mean, median, and mode differ significantly. What might this type of distribution suggest about the students in that class?

Figure 14.2

Frequency distributions for two classes on a 50-item test

Class 1

														X						
														X	X					
				X			X		X	X	X			X	X	X	X		X	
			X	X	X	X	X	X	X	X	X	X	X	X	X	X	X	X	X	X
30	31	32	33	34	35	36	37	38	39	40	41	42	43	44	45	46	47	48	49	50

Class 2

														X						
												X	X	X						
											X	X	X	X						
								X	X	X	X	X	X	X	X	X				
					X	X	X	X	X	X	X	X	X	X	X	X	X	X		
30	31	32	33	34	35	36	37	38	39	40	41	42	43	44	45	46	47	48	49	50

class, the range is 13. This finding confirms what you saw earlier in the frequency distribution. Although simple to compute, the range suffers from the problem of being overly influenced by one or more extreme scores. Another measure of variability that minimizes the problem is the **standard deviation**, which is *a statistical measure of the spread of scores.* With the use of computers, teachers rarely have to calculate a standard deviation manually, but we briefly describe the procedure here to help you understand the concept. To find the standard deviation:

1. Calculate the mean.
2. Subtract the mean from each of the individual scores.
3. Square each of these values. (This eliminates negative numbers.)
4. Add the squared values.
5. Divide by the total number of scores (31 in our samples).
6. Take the square root.

In our samples, the standard deviations are 4.8 and 3.1, respectively. You saw from merely observing the two distributions that the first was more spread out; the standard deviation gives a quantitative measure of that spread.

> 14.17
> Try this analogy: Range:Mode::Standard Deviation:_____. (Range is to mode as standard deviation is to ?)

Normal Distribution

Standardized tests are administered to large (in the thousands) samples of students, and the distribution of scores often approximates a normal distribution. To understand this concept, look again at our two distributions of scores and then focus specifically on the second one. If you drew a line over the top of the frequency distribution, it would appear as shown in Figure 14.3.

> 14.18
> In Figure 14.4, what does the height of the curve at any point represent? What is represented along the horizontal (*x*) axis?

Now, imagine a very large sample of scores, such as you would find from a typical standardized test. The curve would approximate the one shown in Figure 14.4. This is a **normal distribution,** *which is a distribution of scores in which the mean, median, and mode are all the same score, and the scores distribute themselves in a "bell-shaped" curve.* Many large samples of human characteristics, such as height and weight, tend to distribute themselves in this way, as do the large samples of most standardized tests.

Our sample has both a mean and median of 42 but a mode of 44, so its measures of central tendency don't quite fit the normal curve. Also, as you can see from Figure 14.4, 68% of all the scores fall within one standard deviation from the mean, but in the distribution, about 71% of the scores are within one standard deviation above and below the mean. You can see from these illustrations that the samples aren't quite normal distributions; this is typical of the smaller samples found in most classrooms.

14.19

Reexamine Figure 14.2. Is the first class more or less like a normal distribution than the second class? Why?

Interpreting Standardized Test Results

Using our two small samples, we have illustrated techniques that statisticians use to summarize standardized test score results. Again, keep in mind that data gathered from standardized tests come from literally thousands of students, rather than from the small number we used in our illustrations. A goal for standardized test users is to compare individual students with other students from around a state, a nation, or even the world. To make these comparisons, test makers use raw scores, percentiles, stanines, and grade equivalents. Some of these scores are illustrated in Figure 14.1 on David Palmer's report from the Stanford Achievement Test.

Raw Scores

All standardized tests begin with and are based on raw scores. A **raw score** *is simply the number of items the individual answered correctly.* For example, in looking back to Figure 14.1, you can see that David's raw score for reading comprehension was a 43: Of a possible 54 items, David answered 43 of them correctly. But what does this mean? Was the test easy or difficult? How did he do, compared with others taking the exam? As you can see, this score doesn't tell you much until you compare it with others. Percentiles, stanines, grade equivalents, and standard scores help you do that.

Percentiles

The percentile is one of the most commonly reported scores on standardized tests. The **percentile (PR)** *is a ranking that compares an individual's score with the scores of all the others who have taken the test.* For instance, David's raw score of 43 in reading comprehension placed him in the 72nd percentile nationally and the 80th percentile locally. That find-

Figure 14.3

Frequency distribution for the second class

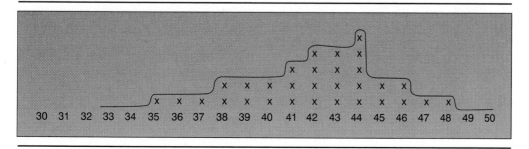

Figure 14.4

Normal distribution

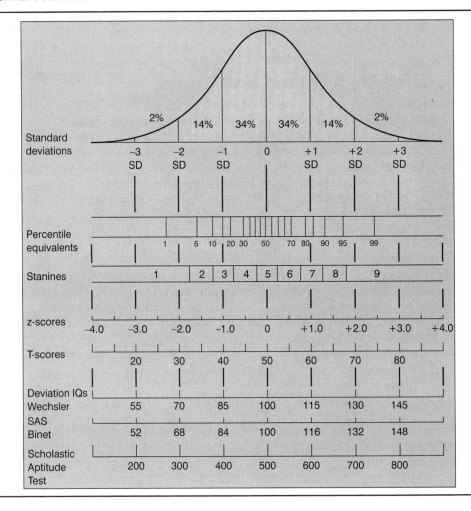

ing means his score was as high or higher than 72% of the scores of people who took the test across the nation and 80% of the scores of people who took the test in his district.

Parents and students often confuse percentiles with *percentages*. Percentages reflect the number correct, compared with the total number possible. Percentile rank, in contrast, tells how a student did in comparison with other students taking the test.

Percentiles are used because they are simple and straightforward. One thing should be kept in mind, however: These are *rankings,* and the differences between the ranks are not equal. For instance, in our first distribution of 31 students, a score of 48 would be in the 90th percentile, 46 in the 80th, 44 in the 60th, and 43 in the 50th percentile. You can see that the difference between the 90th and 80th percentiles is twice as great (2 points) in our sample as the difference between the 60th and 50th percentiles (1 point). With large samples, this difference can be even more pronounced. Students who score at the extremes in the sample vary more from their counterparts than do those who score near the middle of the distribution. This finding is confirmed in Figure 14.4, where you can see that the range of scores from the 50th to the 60th percentile is much smaller than the range from the 90th to the 99th percentile.

Percentile bands *describe standardized test score performance in percentile ranges, rather than as precise percentages.* Their advantage is that they acknowledge the possibility of measurement error by presenting a range of percentile scores (Lyman, 1991). In this respect, percentile bands function somewhat like stanines. (Percentile bands for David Palmer's results are illustrated in Figure 14.1.)

Stanines

The stanine is another score shown in David's achievement test results. For example, his reading comprehension score placed him in stanine 6 nationally and stanine 7 locally. The **stanine (S),** *or "standard nine," describes a range of scores.* Stanine 5 is in the center of the distribution and includes all the scores within one fourth of a standard deviation on either side of the mean. Stanines 4, 3, and 2 are each a band of scores half a standard deviation in width extending below stanine 5, and stanines 6, 7, and 8 are also a half standard deviation in width extending above stanine 5. Stanines 1 and 9 cover the tails of the distribution. A student with a score that falls one standard deviation above the mean will have a stanine score of 7, and a score two standard deviations above the mean will have a stanine score of 9. Figure 14.4 shows how stanines correspond to other measures we've discussed.

The stanine is widely used because it is simple and because it encourages teachers and parents to interpret scores based on a range instead of fine distinctions that may be artificial. For instance, a score in the 57th percentile may be the result of one or two extra points on a subtest, compared with a score in the 52nd percentile, and the student may have guessed the answer correctly, so the difference between the two wouldn't be meaningful. Both scores would fall in stanine 5, which is probably a more realistic indicator of performance.

Reducing the scores to a simple 9-point band, however, sacrifices considerable information. For instance, in our first distribution, with a standard deviation of 4.8, a score of 40 would be in stanine 4 because 40 is slightly more than one-fourth standard deviation below the mean. A score of 44 would be in stanine 6 because it is slightly more than one-fourth standard deviation above the mean. However, a 40 is in the 35th percentile, and a 44 is in the 65th, a considerable difference. It is important to keep the advantages and disadvantages of stanines in mind as you help parents and students interpret standardized test scores.

Grade Equivalents

A third commonly reported score is called the grade equivalent. **Grade equivalents** *compare an individual's score with those of a particular age-group.* For example, David's grade equivalent for total reading is 5.6. This means he scored as well on the test as the average score for those students taking the test who are in the sixth month of the fifth grade.

As you saw with David Palmer's mother, reporting results in this way can be misleading because it oversimplifies results and suggests comparisons that are not necessarily valid. They tell that David is somewhat advanced in reading. They do not suggest that he should be promoted to fifth grade, nor do they necessarily suggest that he should be reading with fifth graders. Other factors, such as maturity, psychosocial development, and motivation, must be considered in making decisions about students. Because of these limitations and the possibility for misinterpretation, grade equivalents should be used cautiously and never in isolation from other measures (Mehrens & Lehmann, 1987).

14.20
Suppose a student named Carol is at the 96th percentile rank in number concepts; her friends Marsha and Lenore are at the 86th and 76th, respectively. Is the difference between Carol and Marsha greater than the difference between Marsha and Lenore, or vice versa? Explain.

14.21
Imagine that, in our first class (illustrated in Table 14.3 and Figure 14.2), a student got a score of 47 on the test. In what stanine would this put that student? What stanine would a score of 47 be in the second class?

14.22
A fourth grader has taken a standardized test, and the summary described his grade equivalent as 6.7. What does this mean? What implications does this have for your teaching?

Standard Scores

As you saw in our discussion of percentiles, differences in raw scores don't result in comparable differences in the percentile rank. For instance, you saw that it took only 1 raw score point difference—43, compared with 42—to move from the 50th to the 60th percentile but that it took a 2-point difference—48, compared with 46—to move from the 80th to the 90th percentile in our first distribution in Figure 14.2. To deal with this discrepancy, standard scores were developed.

Standard scores *express test performance in standard deviations units* (Gronlund & Linn, 1995). Standardized test makers operationally define the mean and standard deviation and report standard scores by using these definitions.

One type of standard score is the **z-score**, which is *the number of standard deviation units from the mean.* A z-score of 2 is two standard deviations above the mean, for example, and a z-score of –1 is one standard deviation below the mean. The **T-score**, *with the mean defined as 50 and the standard deviation defined as 10, is another standard score.* A T-score of 70 would be two standard deviations above the mean and would correspond to a z-score of 2.

Standard scores are useful because they make comparisons convenient. Because they are based on equal units of measurement throughout the distribution, intergroup and intertest comparisons are possible (Lyman, 1991).

Standard Error of Measurement

Although standardized tests are technically sophisticated, they still contain measurement error; scores only reflect an approximation of a student's "true" score. If it were possible to give a student the same test over and over, for example, the scores would vary. If you averaged those scores, you would have a good estimate of the student's "true" score. Although it's impractical to give a person the same test repeatedly, you can get an estimate of the true score by using the **standard error of measurement**, which *describes a range of scores within which a person's true score is likely to fall.* This range is sometimes termed the *confidence interval, score band,* or *profile band.* For example, suppose Ben has a raw score of 46 and Kim has a raw score of 52 on a test with a standard error of 4. This means that Ben's true score is between 42 and 50 and that Kim's is between 48 and 56. At first glance, Kim appears to have scored significantly higher than Ben, but considering the standard error, their scores may be equal, or Ben's true score may even be higher than Kim's. Understanding the concept of *standard error* is important when you make decisions based on standardized tests. For instance, it would be unwise to place Ben and Kim in different ability groups solely on the basis of the results illustrated here.

Issues in Standardized Testing

Earlier in the chapter, we presented a brief history of intelligence testing. The success of these tests resulted in increased use of standardized testing in schools, colleges, and industry. Experts estimate that between 100 and 500 million standardized tests are administered annually, with total sales of $128 million in 1990 (Haney, Madaus, & Lyons, 1993). Two thirds of the states have statewide assessment programs, and almost that many have minimum competency tests (E. Baker, 1989; Haney et al., 1993). Although experts may disagree on specifics, they generally agree that the influence of standardized testing has grown.

Concern over the widespread use of standardized tests has also grown. In an overview of the subject, Nickerson (1989) reached this conclusion:

14.23
The SAT has a mean defined as 500 and a standard deviation defined as 100. Suppose you scored a 1,050 on the SAT—500 on the math portion and 550 on the verbal section. You scored as well or better than approximately what percentage of the people who took the test in each case?

14.24
A person scored a 45 on the second class test in Figure 14.2. If the standard deviation were rounded off to an even 3 for this sample, what would the person's z-score and T-score be?

14.25
Suppose Nathan scores a 62 and Jerome scores a 67 on a test with a standard error of 3. Is Jerome's true score higher than Nathan's? Explain.

To say that testing is controversial is to oversimplify the complex melange of attitudes that exist toward the subject. Some people object to testing in principle; others believe that too little of it is done. Many have ambivalent feelings on the matter, believing that testing can serve important purposes but that it is often used in inappropriate or objectionable ways. (p. 6)

In the following sections, we briefly examine some of the issues that have made standardized testing so controversial.

The Accountability Movement: Holding Teachers and Students Responsible for Learning

Accountability has become a driving force in the growth of standardized testing. **Accountability** *consists of setting goals and making both students and educators responsible for attaining them* (Darling-Hammond & Snyder, 1992).

The accountability movement originated in public dissatisfaction with the quality of education. Some researchers trace its beginning to the 1960s, when interest in mastery learning and criterion-referenced testing focused on the measurement of specific learning outcomes (Stiggins, 1994). During the 1970s, behavioral objectives emphasized the importance of translating abstract goals into measurable student performances. Concern over the quality of U.S. schooling intensified with the publication of *A Nation at Risk* (National Commission on Excellence in Education, 1983), which reported that an alarming number of Americans were functionally illiterate. American students' mediocre performance on standardized tests, compared with the performance of students in other industrialized countries, suggested links between the quality of education and the nation's economic development (Berryman, 1988). One of the more prominent outcomes of the accountability movement has been the growth of minimum competency testing.

> **14.26** ▥
> Identify at least two positive and at least two negative aspects of the accountability movement.

Minimum Competency Testing

Minimum competency testing, *in which graduation from school or admission into advanced programs is determined by a passing score on a test,* is one solution offered for the quality problem. This process has public support; 65% of the people responding to a 1995 Gallup poll endorsed the idea of testing students to determine whether educational standards were being met (Elam & Rose, 1995). Minimum competency tests are being used in 40 states, and in some of those states, the tests are used to determine who graduates with a high school diploma (Geisinger, 1992).

Minimum competency programs have the following characteristics:

▥ All students of designated grades are required to take paper-and-pencil tests designed to measure basic academic skills.
▥ A standard for acceptable levels of performance has been established.
▥ Test results are used for decisions about promotion and graduation (Mehrens & Lehmann, 1987).

Minimum competency tests take many forms. In some states, the testing is centralized, with all students in all districts receiving the same test at the same level. In other states, districts are responsible for designing and implementing their own tests.

Advocates of minimum competency tests claim the tests help clarify the major goals of a school system, send clear messages to students about what they should be learning, and provide the public with hard evidence about school effectiveness (Popham, 1993). Oppo-

> **14.27** ▥
> Compared with aptitude, achievement, and diagnostic tests, which of the three are minimum competency tests most like? Explain.

nents contend that the cutoff scores are arbitrary, that the instruments are too crude to be used in making crucial decisions about people, that teaching is reduced to minimums or "teaching to the test," and that the tests have a disproportionately adverse impact on minorities (E. Baker, 1989), particularly those with limited proficiency in English (Geisinger, 1992).

Standardized Testing With Alternative Formats

While demands for accountability have increased, traditional multiple-choice formats have also come under fire. Critics contend that "familiar assessment formats and procedures, . . . give only a single-dimensional indication of what a student can do at the end-point of a learning experience. At best, they allow opportunity only for highly constrained simulations of the actual performances in which we want students to engage, either in the classroom or the world beyond" (Camp, 1992, p. 243). Critics are calling for more authentic assessments that measure students' ability to use information in real-life settings.

The use of alternative assessments with large samples of students is a monumental task. Worthen (1993) identifies at least three issues that must be resolved if alternative assessments are to be successful on a large scale.

1. *Goals and criteria:* Agreement must be reached about what constitutes a valid measure of predetermined goals. Research indicates that different alternative assessments are often not exchangeable (Baxter & Shavelson, 1992; Madaus & Tan, 1993).
2. *Logistics:* Administering and scoring alternative assessments are enormously time-consuming. Further, because alternative assessments are not machine scored, all performances must be judged by at least two people to maintain reliability. This process doubles the number of hours required to score an individual response.
3. *Validity:* Because alternative assessments are necessarily subjective, the assessments are susceptible to questions about their validity.

Despite these issues, one thing is clear: Asking students to perform tasks similar to those required in a real-world setting gives educators better information than does a score on a multiple-choice test. Thus, alternative assessments are now being used in place of or in addition to traditional standardized testing in some places across the country (Camp, 1992; Madaus & Tan, 1993). Even though traditional testing will always be an integral part of standardized testing, alternative assessments are occupying an increasingly prominent place in the process.

Student Diversity and Standardized Testing

As we've presented the topics in this book, we've examined different dimensions of diversity and their implications for teaching and learning. We now extend this discussion to consider the implications of diversity for standardized testing.

Bias in Measurement

An important question to anyone testing students with diverse backgrounds is whether the instruments and procedures he or she uses are fair for all students. Measurement experts have identified at least three types of testing bias (Gronlund & Linn, 1995; Kaplan & Saccuzzo, 1993): (a) bias in content, (b) bias in testing procedures, and (c) bias in test use.

14.28
Suppose minimum competency testing were eliminated and decisions about promotion and graduation were left to individual teachers. What advantages and disadvantages would this system have? Could the system work on a national level? Why or why not?

14.29
How do alternative assessment formats increase validity? Explain your answer, using the three types of validity discussed earlier.

Bias in Content

Critics contend that the content of standardized tests is geared to White, middle-class American students and thus places minorities at a disadvantage. For example, one item on a standardized intelligence test asks, "From what animal do we get bacon?" First- or second-generation Portuguese children would likely have difficulty with this question because most are unfamiliar with the term *bacon* (Cummins, 1984). They would have little problem, however, if asked, "From what animal do we get sausages (*chouricos*)?" because sausage is a staple in the meals of Portuguese families.

Bias can also occur in math word problems (Gronlund & Linn, 1995). For example, consider the following percentage problem:

> *John Carey is presently batting 300 after 100 trips to the plate. In his next three times at bat, he gets a single, a double, and a home run. What is his batting average now?*

Word problems using content that not all children can be expected to know (e.g., how are batting averages computed, do doubles and home runs count more than singles) can unfairly penalize females or minorities who don't have the necessary background knowledge. Math word problems can also be biased if students miss the problem because of limited reading skills, rather than lack of conceptual or computational skills in math.

Even the content of pictures used in testing situations can be a source of bias. In one test of English proficiency, students are shown the picture of a smiling boy and are asked to describe the picture. The expected response is that the boy is happy. Researchers working with Vietnamese students, however, have found that a smiling Vietnamese boy may not be happy; he may be embarrassed, confused, or even angry (Cargill, 1987). Responding with any one of these answers would result in an incorrect response—not from lack of knowledge, but from cultural differences.

Bias in Testing Procedures

Bias can also occur in testing procedures (Mehrens & Lehmann, 1987). Students from different cultures respond to testing situations in different ways. Students generally become more knowledgeable about testing as they move through the grades and gain experience with different tests. However, if exposure to testing is limited or if the process of testing isn't compatible with students' cultures, their performance can be hampered. For example, a study of Navajo test-taking strategies found that students treated tests as gamelike events and were unaware of the role that tests played in measuring learning or the long-term effects of poor test performance (Deyhle, 1987).

Timed tests are another source of possible bias in testing procedures, particularly for students with limited English proficiency (Scarcella, 1990). Our study of information processing in Chapter 7 helps in understanding why. Students with limited knowledge of English will require extra time and working-memory space to decode the words and to comprehend questions. A time limit makes this process more difficult for them and can lower test performance.

Bias in Test Result Use

Bias can also occur in the use of test results. Experts are concerned about the adverse effects of testing on minority students' progress through public schools and entrance into college (National Commission on Testing and Public Policy, 1990). Evidence suggests that test results are sometimes used in ways that discriminate against minorities and non-Eng-

Traditional standardized test formats have come under increased criticism; critics suggest alternative formats that require students to demonstrate mastery of higher level and problem-solving strategies in realistic settings.

14.30
Is content bias more of a problem with validity or with reliability? Explain.

14.31
Explain how a teacher might use information gathered from other teachers or students to ensure that test content is unbiased.

14.32
Describe at least two things teachers can do to minimize the potential effects of bias in testing procedures.

14.33
Identify at least three things teachers can do to help students with limited English respond as successfully as possible in testing situations.

lish-speaking students. For example, a study of 812 residents classified as having mental retardation found 300% more Mexican Americans and 50% more African Americans but 40% fewer Anglo Americans labeled as having mental retardation than would be expected from their numbers in the general population. Further, people in lower income brackets were overrepresented, whereas people in the upper income brackets were underrepresented (J. Mercer, 1973).

Alternative Tests

14.34
Why might social adaptability, medical history, and scores on nonverbal tests be of interest to consumers of intelligence test scores?

In response to problems identified in testing students from different cultures and different socioeconomic backgrounds, alternative intelligence tests have been developed. These tests attempt to provide a more comprehensive picture of intelligence by

- Including nonverbal scales that minimize the influence of language
- Using measures of social adaptability to augment traditional IQ scales
- Focusing on medical aspects that could influence intellectual functioning
- Using norms that compare students who are similar in racial, ethnic, and socioeconomic background

Let's examine two of these tests.

System of Multicultural Pluralistic Assessment (SOMPA)

The System of Multicultural Pluralistic Assessment (SOMPA; J. Mercer, 1979) was developed by combining the Wechsler Intelligence Scale for Children (WISC) with other sources of information about the child "to provide comprehensive, nondiscriminatory assessment of public school pupils between the ages of 5 and 11" (Salvia & Ysseldyke, 1988, p. 460). The supplementary sources include medical and social components and sociocultural scales that take cultural, ethnic, and socioeconomic background into account when interpreting scores on the WISC. The medical component examines factors such as visual and auditory acuity, weight and height, physical dexterity, and a comprehensive health history. The social component examines general adaptive behavior such as peer relations, grooming, dress, and other aspects of out-of-school performance. The intent is to provide a comprehensive assessment of children from varying social, cultural, and ethnic backgrounds.

Kaufman Assessment Battery for Children (KABC)

The Kaufman Assessment Battery for Children (KABC; Kaufman & Kaufman, 1983) is another attempt to gather additional information for use in assessment and placement. Individually administered, the test examines aptitude and achievement for children between the ages of 2 and 12.

The test includes a nonverbal scale, which uses tasks such as pattern recognition, matrix analogies, and replication of hand movements to assess intellectual potential. This subtest is valuable for testing "deaf, hearing impaired, speech- or language-disordered, autistic and non-English-speaking children" (Kaufman & Kaufman, 1983, p. 35). As with the SOMPA, sociocultural norms compare a student's performance on different subtests with other students of similar ethnic and socioeconomic status.

Both the SOMPA and the KABC have generated considerable interest in the educational community (Kaplan & Saccuzzo, 1993). Despite some fundamental questions about their reliability and validity, these tests are important because they attempt to identify indicators of ability not found on most other tests and because they are useful with non-White, non-middle-class school populations (Salvia & Ysseldyke, 1988; R. Taylor, 1989).

Clinical Approaches

In addition to the strategies already discussed, experts now recommend clinical approaches to assessment that combine standardized test results with other data sources, such as grades, samples of student work, and input from teachers and parents (Anastasi, 1988). The goal of this approach is to gather as much information as possible about other aspects of competence, such as motivation and social skills, which are not tapped by standardized intelligence tests.

> **14.35**
> What are one advantage and one disadvantage of the clinical approach to assessment currently being advocated in the field of special education?

Classroom Connections

Capitalizing on Diversity in Your Classroom

1. Be sensitive to the effects that diversity can have on assessment.
   - Before any of her non-native English-speaking students are referred for special education testing, a first-grade teacher talks with the testing expert and describes the student's background and language patterns.

2. Adapt testing procedures to meet the needs of all students.

- A third-grade teacher who teaches in an urban school takes extra time prior to standardized testing to explain the purpose of the tests and to provide opportunities for students to practice. She states positive expectations for all students and carefully monitors them to be sure the students understand what is required in responding to the items.
- A high school social studies teacher makes a special effort to ensure that the vocabulary on the test is understood. If questions arise about terms, he puts the terms and the definitions on the chalkboard.

Windows on Classrooms

At the beginning of the chapter, you saw how Danny Chavez used standardized testing and interpreted test scores for a parent. Let's look now at another teacher involved in a situation where the use of standardized tests could be an issue.

Peggy Barret looked up from the stack of algebra tests that she was grading as her colleague Stan Witzel walked into the teacher's lounge.

"How's it going?" Stan asked.

"Fine . . . I think. I'm scoring tests from my Algebra I class. That's the one where I'm trying to put more emphasis on problem solving and not so much on the mechanics. I took a class last summer in which the instructor emphasized problem solving, and I'm giving it a try. Quite a few of the students are actually getting into the applications now, and they like the problem solving when they do their small-group work. The trouble is, some of the others are really struggling, so . . . I'm not so sure about it all."

"I wish I had your problems. It sounds like your students are learning, and at least some of them even like it. What more could you want?" Stan asked, with a puzzled look on his face.

"Yeah, I know," Peggy replied. "Getting these students to like any kind of math is a major accomplishment, but still I wonder. It's just that I'm not sure whether they're getting all that they should," she continued. "I don't know whether this class is *really* doing better than last year . . . or even my other classes this year, for that matter. The tests I give are quite different in the different classes. I think—or at least I'd like to believe—that they're doing better on problem solving, but to be honest about it, I see quite a few of them struggling with the mechanics at times. I work on them, the mechanics, but not as much as in the other classes. . . . I guess what I'm saying is that I'm not sure whether I've drawn the line in the right place as far as the emphasis I'm placing on each part of the class."

"Good question," Stan shrugged. "I always wonder when I make changes if they're missing out on something."

"As important," Peggy continued, "I wonder how they'll do when they go off to college . . . if they go to college. Actually, quite a few of them in this class will be going," she said, commenting more to herself than to Stan.

"Anyway," she looked over at him, "that's what I'm thinking about. . . . Got any good ideas?"

"Good questions, Peggy. I wish I knew, but . . . I guess that's part of teaching."

"Yeah," she said with her voice trailing off, "it seems like we should be able to get some better information. I can see that some of the students just don't seem to get it. I would say their background is weak; they seem to be trying. On the other hand, I checked out some of their old standardized test scores, and their math scores weren't that bad. Maybe it's not background. Maybe they just don't belong in my class."

"Say more," Stan encouraged. "Tell me about the students who are struggling."

"I've got several students who really struggle with word problems. They do fine on computation but fall apart when I ask them to solve word problems. They do fine when they work in small groups but sometimes don't even finish the tests I give them, like this one."

"Anything that they have in common?" Stan continued.

"Not really. They're as different as can be. Jacinta struggles but tries really hard. Quan is a whiz at computation but struggles when I ask him to think. Carlos actually seems to do fairly well with the problems, but his mechanics aren't so good."

"Maybe you ought to talk to Yalanda," Stan suggested. "She's been in this game awhile and might know about some tests that are available that you could give to help you answer some of your questions."

Questions for Discussion and Analysis

1. What type of standardized test would help Peggy determine the answer to her own question: "I don't know whether this class is *really* doing better than last year, . . . or even my other classes this year, for that matter"?

2. In the selection of a standardized test to answer Question 1, what type of validity would be a primary concern? How might Peggy answer the question about validity?

3. One of Peggy's concerns was the background knowledge of her students: "I would say their background is weak." What type of standardized test might Peggy use to gather data related to this concern?

4. In investigating the problems that her students were having in math, Peggy checked out their overall test scores from past standardized tests. What else might she have done?

5. Using the information in this chapter, how might you diagnose the problems that Jacinta and Quan are having with word problems? What suggestions do you have for Peggy?

 Summary

Standardized Tests

Standardized tests can be used to assess student academic progress, diagnose strengths and weaknesses, and place students in appropriate instructional programs. These tests can also be used to provide information for program evaluation and improvement.

Achievement tests provide information about what students have learned; diagnostic tests provide in-depth analysis of specific strengths and weaknesses; intelligence tests are designed to measure students' capacity to acquire knowledge, the ability to think in the abstract, and the capability for solving problems; and aptitude tests are designed to predict potential for future learning.

Validity measures the appropriateness of a test for a specific purpose and includes content, predictive, and construct validity.

Understanding and Interpreting Standardized Test Scores

Standardized test scores are interpreted by using descriptive statistics to compare a person's performance with the performance of a norm group or some criterion. Percentiles, stanines, grade equivalents, and standard scores all compare a student's score against comparable students in a norm group.

Issues in Standardized Testing

Accountability, minimum competency testing, and other forms of high-stakes testing point to the increased use of standardized tests for both policy making and individual decisions. Advocates argue that standardized tests efficiently assess the educational achievements of large numbers of students. Critics counter that misuse of standardized tests discourages innovation, encourages teaching to low-level skills, and discriminates against cultural minorities and non-native English speakers. Including performance assessments in standardized testing is seen as one possible solution to the problem of low-level outcomes.

Student Diversity and Standardized Testing

Bias in standardized testing can occur in the content of tests, in testing procedures, and in test results use. Alternative test formats, including clinical approaches, are seen as possible solutions to this problem.

 # Important Concepts

accountability (p. 579)

achievement tests (p. 565)

aptitude tests (p. 570)

construct validity (p. 571)

content validity (p. 571)

diagnostic tests (p. 566)

frequency distribution (p. 572)

grade equivalents (p. 577)

intelligence tests (p. 566)

mean (p. 572)

measures of central tendency (p. 572)

median (p. 572)

minimum competency testing (p. 579)

mode (p. 572)

normal distribution (p. 574)

norming group (p. 563)

percentile (p. 575)

percentile bands (p. 577)

predictive validity (p. 571)

range (p. 573)

raw score (p. 575)

standardized tests (p. 563)

standard deviation (p. 574)

standard error of measurement (p. 578)

standard scores (p. 578)

stanine (p. 577)

T-score (p. 578)

z-score (p. 578)

References

AAAMR Ad Hoc Committee on Terminology and Classification. (1992). *Mental retardation: Definition, classification, and systems of support* (9th ed.). Washington, DC: American Association on Mental Retardation.

Aboud, F., & Skerry, S. (1984). The development of ethnic identity: A critical review. *Journal of Cross-Cultural Psychology, 15,* 3–34.

Adams, A., Carnine, D., & Gersten, R. (1982). Instructional strategies for studying content area texts in the intermediate grades. *Reading Research Quarterly, 18,* 27–53.

Adams, M. (1989). Thinking skills curricula. *Educational Psychologist, 24,* 25–77.

Adamson, H. (1993). *Academic competence, theory, and practice: Preparing ESL students for content courses.* White Plains, NY: Longman.

Alberto, P., & Troutman, A. (1990). *Applied behavior analysis for teachers* (2nd ed.). Upper Saddle River, NJ: Merrill/Prentice Hall.

Alexander, P., & Murphy, P. (1994, April). *The research base for APA's learner-centered psychological principles.* Paper presented at the Annual Meeting of the American Educational Research Association, New Orleans.

Allen, R. (1976). *Language experience in communication.* Boston: Houghton Mifflin.

Allen, V. (1992). Teaching bilingual and ESL children. In J. Flood, J. J. Jensen, D. Lapp, & J. Squire (Eds.), *Handbook of research on teaching the English language arts* (pp. 356–364). New York: Macmillan.

American Association for the Advancement of Science (AAAS). (1993). *Benchmarks for science literacy.* Washington, DC: Author.

American Association of University Women. (1992). *How schools shortchange girls.* Annapolis Junction, MD: Author.

Ames, C. (1990). Motivation: What teachers need to know. *Teachers College Record, 91,* 409–421.

Ames, C. (1992). Classrooms: Goals, structures, and student motivation. *Journal of Educational Psychology, 84*(3), 261–271.

Ames, C., & Archer, J. (1988). Achievement goals in the classroom: Students' learning strategies and motivation processes. *Journal of Educational Psychology, 80,* 260–267.

Anastasi, A. (1988). *Psychological testing* (6th ed.). New York: Macmillan.

Anastasiow, N., Bibley, S., Leonhardt, T., & Borish, G. (1970). A comparison of guided discovery, discovery, and didactic teaching of math to kindergarten poverty children. *American Educational Research Journal, 7,* 493–510.

Anderman, E., & Maehr, M. (1994). Motivation and schooling in the middle grades. *Review of Educational Research, 64,* 287–309.

Anderson, C. (1982). The search for school climate: A review of research. *Review of Educational Research, 52,* 368–420.

Anderson, C., & Roth, K. (1989). Teaching for meaningful and self-regulated learning in science. In J. Brophy (Ed.), *Advances in research on teaching* (Vol. 1, pp. 265–309). Greenwich, CT: JAI Press.

Anderson, J. (1990). *Cognitive psychology and its implications* (3rd ed.). New York: Freeman.

Anderson, L. (1989). Learners and learning. In M. Reynolds (Ed.), *Knowledge base for the beginning teacher* (pp. 85–100). New York: Pergamon Press.

Anderson, L., Brubaker, N., Alleman-Brooks, J., & Duffy, G. (1984). *Making seatwork work* (Research Series No. 142). East Lansing: Michigan State University, Institute for Research on Teaching.

Anderson, L., Evertson, C., & Brophy, J. (1979). An experimental study of effective teaching in first-grade reading groups. *Elementary School Journal, 79,* 193–223.

Anderson, M., Nelson, L., Fox, R., & Gruber, S. (1988). Integrating cooperative learning and structured learning: Effective approaches to teaching social skills. *Focus on Exceptional Children, 20*(9), 1–8.

Anderson, R., Hiebert, E., Scott, J., & Wilkinson, I. (1985). *Becoming a nation of readers.* Washington, DC: National Institute of Education.

Anderson, T., & Armbruster, B. (1984). Studying. In D. Pearson (Ed.), *Handbook of reading research* (pp. 657–679). White Plains, NY: Longman.

Applebee, A., Langer, J., Mullis, I., & Jenkins, L. (1990). *The writing report card, 1984–88: Findings from the Nation's Report Card.* Washington, DC: U.S. Department of Education, Office of Educational Research and Improvement.

Arias, M., & Casanova, U. (Eds.). (1993). *Bilingual education: Politics, practice, and research. Ninety-second yearbook of the National Society for the Study of Education, Part 2.* Chicago: University of Chicago Press.

Armstrong, T. (1994). Multiple intelligences: Seven ways to approach curriculum. *Educational Leadership, 52*(3), 26–27.

Arnold, D., Lonigan, C., Whitehurst, G., & Epstein, J. (1994). Accelerating language development through picture book reading: Replication and extension to a videotape learning format. *Journal of Educational Psychology, 86*(2), 235–243.

Ashcraft, M. (1989). *Human memory and cognition.* Glenview, IL: Scott, Foresman.

Atkinson, J. (1980). Motivational effects in so-called tests of ability and educational achievement. In L. Fyans (Ed.), *Achievement motivation: Recent trends in theory and research.* New York: Plenum Press.

Atkinson, J. (1983). *Personality, motivation, and action.* New York: Praeger.

Atkinson, R., & Shiffrin, R. (1968). Human memory: A proposed system and its control processes. In K. Spence & J. Spence (Eds.), *The psychology of learning and motivation: Advances in research and theory* (Vol. 2). San Diego: Academic Press.

Au, K. (1992, April). *"There's almost a lesson here": Teacher and students' purposes in constructing the theme of a story.* Paper presented at the Annual Meeting of the American Educational Research Association, San Francisco.

Ausubel, D. (1963). *The psychology of meaningful verbal learning.* New York: Grune & Stratton.

Babad, E., Bernieri, F., & Rosenthal, R. (1991). Students as judges of teachers' verbal and nonverbal behavior. *American Educational Research Journal, 28*(1), 211–234.

Baker, D., & Stevenson, D. (1986). Mothers' strategies for children's school achievement: Managing the transition to high school. *Sociology of Education, 59,* 156–166.

Baker, E. (1989). Mandated tests: Educational reform or quality indicator? In B. Gifford (Ed.), *Test policy and test performance: Education, language, and culture* (pp. 3–23). Boston: Kluwer.

Baker, L. (1989). Metacognition, comprehension monitoring, and the adult reader. *Educational Psychology Review, 1,* 3–38.

Baker, L., & Brown, A. (1984). Metacognitive skills of reading. In D. Pearson (Ed.), *Handbook of reading research.* White Plains, NY: Longman.

Ball, D. (1992, Summer). Magical hopes: Manipulatives and the reform of math education. *American Educator,* pp. 28–33.

Ballantine, J. (1989). *The sociology of education.* Upper Saddle River, NJ: Prentice Hall.

Bandura, A. (1977). *Social learning theory.* Upper Saddle River, NJ: Prentice Hall.

Bandura, A. (1986). *Social foundations of thought and action: A social cognitive theory.* Upper Saddle River, NJ: Prentice Hall.

Bandura, A. (1989). Social cognitive theory. In R. Vasta (Ed.), *Annals of child development* (Vol. 6, pp. 1–60). Greenwich, CT: JAI Press.

Bandura, A. (1993). Perceived self-efficacy in cognitive development and functioning. *Educational Psychologist, 28*(2), 117–148.

Bangert-Drowns, R., Kulik, C., Kulik, J., & Morgan, M. (1991). The instructional effect of feedback in test-like events. *Review of Educational Research, 61*(2), 213–238.

Bangert-Drowns, R., Kulik, J., & Kulik, C. (1991). Effects of frequent classroom testing. *Journal of Educational Research, 85,* 89–99.

Barbetta, P., & Heron, T. (1991). Project Shine: Summer home instruction and evaluation. *Intervention in School and Clinics, 26,* 276–281.

Baron, R. (1992). *Psychology* (2nd ed.). Needham Heights, MA: Allyn & Bacon.

Baxter, G., & Shavelson, R. (1992, April). *Exchangeability of science performance assessment.* Paper presented at the Annual Meeting of the American Educational Research Association, San Francisco.

Bay, M., Staver, J., Bryan, T., & Hale, J. (1992). Science instruction for the mildly handicapped: Direct instruction versus discovery teaching. *Journal of Research in Science Teaching, 29,* 555–570.

Beane, J., & Lipka, R. (1986). *Self-concept, self-esteem, and the curriculum.* New York: Teachers College Press.

Bee, H. (1989). *The developing child* (5th ed.). New York: Harper & Row.

Behrend, D., Rosengren, K., & Perlmutter, M. (1992). The relation between private speech and parental interactive style. In R. Díaz & L. Berk (Eds.), *Private speech: From social interaction to self-regulation* (pp. 85–100). Hillsdale, NJ: Erlbaum.

Benard, B. (1993). Fostering resilience in kids. *Educational Leadership, 51*(3), 44–48.

Benard, B. (1994). *Fostering resilience in urban schools.* San Francisco: Far West Laboratory.

Bennett, N., & Blundel, D. (1983). Quantity and quality of work in rows of classroom groups. *Educational Psychology, 3,* 93–105.

Bennett, S. (1978). Recent research on teaching: A dream, a belief, and a model. *British Journal of Educational Psychology, 48,* 27–147.

Berk, L. (1994). *Child development* (3rd ed.). Needham Heights, MA: Allyn & Bacon.

Berliner, D. (1984). *Making our schools more effective: Proceedings of three state conferences.* San Francisco: Far West Laboratory.

Berliner, D. (1987). Simple views of effective teaching and a simple theory of classroom instruction. In D. Berliner & B. Rosenshine (Eds.), *Talks to teachers* (pp. 93–110). New York: Random House.

Bernardo, A. (1994). Problem-specific information and the development of problem-type schemata. *Journal of Experimental Psychology: Learning, Memory & Cognition, 20*(2), 379–395.

Berryman, S. (1988, August). *Education and the economy: A diagnostic review and implications for the federal role.* Paper presented at the Seminar on the Federal Role in Education, The Aspen Institute, Aspen, CO.

Best, J. (1992). *Cognitive psychology* (3rd ed.). St. Paul, MN: West.

Beyer, B. (1984). Improving thinking skills: A practical approach. *Phi Delta Kappan, 65,* 556–560.

Beyer, B. (1988). Developing a scope and sequence for thinking skills instruction. *Educational Leadership, 45*(7), 26–30.

Bloom, A. (1987). *The closing of the American mind.* New York: Simon & Schuster.

Bloom, B. (1981). *All our children learning.* New York: McGraw-Hill.

Bloom, B. (1984a). The search for methods of group instruction as effective as one-to-one tutoring. *Educational Leadership, 41*(8), 4–17.

Bloom, B. (Ed.). (1984b). *Taxonomy of educational objectives: Book 1. Cognitive domain.* White Plains, NY: Longman. (Original work published 1956)

Bloom, B., & Bourdon, L. (1980). Types and frequencies of teachers' written instructional feedback. *Journal of Educational Research, 74,* 13–15.

Bloom, B., Englehart, M., Furst, E., Hill, W., & Krathwohl, O. (1956). *Taxonomy of educational objectives: The classification of educational goals: Handbook 1. The cognitive domain.* White Plains, NY: Longman.

Blumenfeld, P. (1992). Classroom learning and motivation: Clarifying and expanding goal theory. *Journal of Educational Psychology, 84*(3), 272–281.

Blumenfeld, P., Pintrich, P., & Hamilton, V. L. (1987). Teacher talk and students' reasoning about morals, conventions, and achievement. *Child Development, 58,* 1389–1401.

Boothroyd, R., McMorris, R., & Pruzek, R. (1992, April). *What do teachers know about measurement, and how did they find out?* Paper presented at

the Annual Meeting of the National Council on Measurement in Education, San Francisco.

Borg, W., & Ascione, F. (1982). Classroom management in elementary mainstreaming classrooms. *Journal of Educational Psychology, 74,* 85–95.

Borko, H., & Livingston, C. (1989). Cognition and improvisation: Differences in mathematics instruction by expert and novice teachers. *American Educational Research Journal, 26,* 473–498.

Bosworth, K. (1995). Caring for others and being cared for: Students talk caring in school. *Phi Delta Kappan, 76,* 686–693.

Bower, G., Clark, M., Lesgold, A., & Winzenz, D. (1969). Hierarchical retrieval schemes in recall of categorized word lists. *Journal of Verbal Learning and Verbal Behavior, 8,* 323–343.

Bowie, R., & Bond, C. (1994). Influencing future teachers' attitudes toward Black English: Are we making a difference? *Journal of Teacher Education, 45*(2), 112–118.

Boyle, G., & Peregoy, S. (1990). Literacy scaffolds: Strategies for first- and second-language readers and writers. *Reading Teacher, 44*(3), 194–199.

Braddock, J. (1990). Tracking the middle grades: National patterns of grouping for instruction. *Phi Delta Kappan, 71*(6), 445–449.

Brady, P. (1990). *Improving the reading comprehension of middle school students through reciprocal teaching and semantic mapping strategies.* Unpublished doctoral dissertation, University of Oregon, Eugene.

Brandes, A. (1995, April). *Barriers to conceptual change in a sixth-grade classroom.* Paper presented at the Annual Meeting of the American Educational Research Association, San Francisco.

Bransford, J. (1993). Who ya gonna call? Thoughts about teaching problem solving. In P. Hallinger, K. Leithwood, & J. Murphy (Eds.), *Cognitive perspectives on educational*

leadership (pp. 2–30). New York: Teachers College Press.

Bransford, J., Goldman, S., & Vye, N. (1991). Making a difference in people's abilities to think: Reflections on a decade of work and some hopes for the future. In L. Okagaki & R. Sternberg (Eds.), *Directors of development* (pp. 147–180). Hillsdale, NJ: Erlbaum.

Bransford, J., & Stein, B. (1984). *The IDEAL problem solver.* New York: Freeman.

Bridgeman, B. (1974). Effects of test score feedback on immediately subsequent test performance. *Journal of Educational Psychology, 66,* 62–66.

Brookover, W., Schweitzer, J., Schneider, J., Beady, C., Flood, P., & Wisenbaker, J. (1978). Elementary school social climate and school achievement. *American Educational Research Journal, 15,* 301–318.

Brooks, J. (1990). Teachers and students: Constructivists forging connections. *Educational Leadership, 47*(5), 68–71.

Brooks, J., & Brooks, M. (1993). *In search of understanding: The case for constructivist classrooms.* Alexandria, VA: Association for Supervision and Curriculum Development.

Brooks, L., & Dansereau, D. (1987). Transfer of information: An instructional perspective. In S. Cormier & J. Hagman (Eds.), *Transfer of learning: Contemporary research and applications.* San Diego: Academic Press.

Brophy, J. (1981). On praising effectively. *Elementary School Journal, 81,* 269–278.

Brophy, J. (1982). *Fostering student learning and motivation in the elementary school classroom.* East Lansing: Michigan State University, Institute for Research on Teaching.

Brophy, J. (1986). Research linking teacher behavior to student achievement: Potential implications for instruction of Chapter 1 students. In B. Williams, P. Richmond, & B. Mason (Eds.), *Designs for Compensatory Education Conference proceedings and papers* (pp. IV-121–IV-179).

Washington, DC: Research and Evaluation Associates.

Brophy, J. (1987a). On motivating students. In D. Berliner & B. Rosenshine (Eds.), *Talks to teachers* (pp. 201–245). New York: Random House.

Brophy, J. (1987b). Syntheses of research on strategies for motivating students to learn. *Educational Leadership, 45*(2), 40–48.

Brophy, J. (1990). Teaching social studies for understanding and higher order applications. *Elementary School Journal, 90,* 351–418.

Brophy, J. (1992). Probing the subtleties of subject-matter teaching. *Educational Leadership, 49*(7), 4–8.

Brophy, J., & Evertson, C. (1976). *Learning from teaching: A developmental perspective.* Needham Heights, MA: Allyn & Bacon.

Brophy, J., & Evertson, C. (1978). Context variables in teaching. *Educational Psychologist, 12,* 310–316.

Brophy, J., & Good, T. (1986). Teacher behavior and student achievement. In M. Wittrock (Ed.), *Handbook of research on teaching* (3rd ed., pp. 328–375). New York: Macmillan.

Brophy, J., & McCaslin, M. (1992). Teachers' reports of how they perceive and cope with problem students. *Elementary School Journal, 93*(1), 3–68.

Brophy, J., & Rohrkemper, M. (1987). *Teachers' strategies for coping with hostile-aggressive students.* East Lansing: Michigan State University, Institute for Research on Teaching.

Brown, A. (1994). The advancement of learning. *Educational Researcher, 23,* 4–12.

Brown, A., Bransford, J., Ferrara, R., & Campione, J. (1983). Learning, remembering, and understanding. In J. Flavell & E. Markman (Eds.), *Handbook of child psychology: Vol. 3. Cognitive development* (4th ed., pp. 77–166). New York: Wiley.

Brown, A., & Campione, J. (1986). Psychological theory and the study of learning disabilities. *American Psychologist, 41,* 1059–1068.

Brown, A., & Campione, J. (1994). Guided discovery in a community of learners. In K. McGilly (Ed.), *Classroom lessons: Integrating cognitive theory and classroom practice* (pp. 229–270). Cambridge: MIT Press.

Brown, A., & Palincsar, A. (1985). *Reciprocal teaching of comprehension strategies: A natural history of one program for enhancing learning* (Tech. Rep. No. 334). Champaign-Urbana: University of Illinois, Center for the Study of Reading.

Brown, A., & Palincsar, A. (1987). Reciprocal teaching of comprehension strategies: A natural history of one program for enhancing learning. In J. Borkowski & J. Day (Eds.), *Cognition in special education: Comparative approaches to retardation, learning disabilities, and giftedness.* Norwood, NJ: Ablex.

Brown, J., Collins, A., & Duguid, P. (1989). Situated cognition and the culture of learning. *Educational Researcher, 18,* 32–42.

Brown, R., & McNeill, D. (1966). The "tip-of-the-tongue" phenomenon. *Journal of Verbal Learning and Verbal Behavior, 5,* 325–337.

Brown-Claridge, P., Stein, P., & Berliner, D. (1988, April). *Lesson planning by expert, novice, and postulant teachers.* Paper presented at the Annual Meeting of the American Educational Research Association, New Orleans.

Bruer, J. (1993). *Schools for thought: A science of learning for the classroom.* Cambridge: MIT Press.

Bruner, J. (1960). *Process of education.* Cambridge, MA: Harvard University Press.

Bruner, J. (1966). *Toward a theory of instruction.* New York: Norton.

Bruner, J. (1971). *Relevance of education.* New York: Norton.

Bruner, J. (1985). Vygotsky: A historical and conceptual perspective. In J. Wertsch (Ed.), *Culture, communication, and cognition: Vygotskian perspectives* (pp. 21–34). New York: Cambridge University Press.

Bruning, R., Schraw, G., & Ronning, R. (1995). *Cognitive psychology and instruction* (2nd ed.). Upper Saddle River, NJ: Prentice Hall.

Bullough, R. (1989). *First-year teacher.* New York: Teachers College Press.

Bushway, A., & Nash, W. (1977). School cheating behavior. *Review of Educational Research, 47,* 623–632.

Busmeyer, J., & Myung, I. (1988). A new method for investigating prototype learning. *Journal of Experimental Psychology: Learning, Memory & Cognition, 14,* 1292–1302.

Butler-Por, N. (1987). *Underachievers in school: Issues and intervention.* New York: Wiley.

Byra, M., & Coulon, S. (1992, April). *Preservice teachers' in-class behaviors: The effect of planning and not planning.* Paper presented at the Annual Meeting of the American Educational Research Association, San Francisco.

Byrne, B. (1984). The general/academic self-concept nomological network: A review of construct validation research. *Review of Educational Research, 54,* 427–456.

Byrnes, J. (1988). Formal operations: A systematic reformulation. *Developmental Review, 8,* 66–87.

Calderhead, J., & Robson, M. (1991). Images of teaching: Student teachers' early conceptions of classroom practice. *Teaching and Teacher Education, 7,* 1–8.

Calfee, R. (1986, April). *Those who can explain teach.* Paper presented at the Annual Meeting of the American Educational Research Association, San Francisco.

Cameron, J., & Pierce, D. (1994). Reinforcement, reward, and intrinsic motivation: A meta-analysis. *Review of Educational Research, 64,* 363–423.

Camp, R. (1992). Assessment in the context of schools and school change. In H. Marshall (Ed.), *Redefining student learning: Roots of educational change* (pp. 241–263). Norwood, NJ: Ablex.

Canter, L. (1988). Let the educator beware: A response to Curwin and

Mendler. *Educational Leadership, 46*(2), 71–73.

Canter, L., & Canter, M. (1992). *Assertive discipline.* Santa Monica, CA: Lee Canter & Associates.

Caplan, N., Choy, M., & Whitmore, J. (1992). Indochinese refugee families and academic achievement. *Scientific American, 266*(2), 36–42.

Cargill, C. (1987). Cultural bias in testing ESL. In C. Cargill (Ed.), *A TESOL professional anthology: Culture.* Lincolnwood, IL: National Textbook.

Carnegie Foundation. (1988). *The conditions of teaching: A state-by-state analysis.* Lawrenceville, NJ: Princeton.

Carpenter, T., Levi, L., Fennema, E., Ansell, E., & Franke, M. (1995, April). *Discussing alternative strategies as a context for developing understanding in primary grade mathematics classrooms.* Paper presented at the Annual Meeting of the American Educational Research Association, San Francisco.

Carrier, C., & Titus, A. (1981). Effects of notetaking pretraining and text mode expectations on learning from lectures. *American Educational Research Journal, 18,* 385–397.

Carrol, J. (1963). A model of school learning. *Teachers College Record, 64,* 723–733.

Carrol, W. (1994). Using worked examples as an instructional support in the algebra classroom. *Journal of Educational Psychology, 86*(3), 360–367.

Carter, K. (1984). Do teachers understand the principles for writing tests? *Journal of Teacher Education, 35*(6), 57–60.

Carter, K. (1986). Test-wiseness for teachers and students. *Educational Measurement: Issues and Practice, 5*(6), 20–23.

Carter, K. (1990). Teachers' knowledge and learning to teach. In R. Houston (Ed.), *Handbook of research on teacher education* (pp. 291–310). New York: Macmillan.

Case, S. (1994). Will mandating portfolios undermine their value? *Educational Leadership, 52*(2), 46–47.

Cattell, R. (1963). Theory of fluid and crystallized intelligence: A critical experiment. *Journal of Educational Psychology, 54,* 1–22.

Cattell, R. (1971). *Abilities: Their structure, growth, and action.* Boston: Houghton Mifflin.

Catterall, J., & Cota-Robles, E. (1988). *The educationally at-risk: What the numbers mean.* Palo Alto, CA: Stanford University Press.

Cazden, C. (1986). Classroom discourse. In M. Wittrock (Ed.), *Handbook of research on teaching* (3rd ed., pp. 432–464). New York: Macmillan.

Cazden, C. (1988). *Classroom discourse.* Portsmouth, NH: Heinemann.

Cermak, L., & Craik, F. (1979). *Levels of processing in human memory.* Hillsdale, NJ: Erlbaum.

Chance, P. (1992). The rewards of learning. *Phi Delta Kappan, 74*(3), 200–207.

Chapman, J. (1988). Learning-disabled children's self-concept. *Review of Educational Research, 58,* 347–371.

Chaskin, R., & Rauner, D. (1995). Youth and caring: An introduction. *Phi Delta Kappan, 76,* 667–674.

Cheek, D. (1993). Plain talk about alternative assessment. *Middle School Journal, 25*(2), 6–10.

Cheng, L. R. (1987). *Assessing Asian language performance.* Rockville, MD: Aspen.

Chi, M., Bassok, M., Lewis, M., Reimann, P., & Glaser, R. (1989). Self-explanations: How students study and use examples in learning to solve problems. *Cognitive Science, 5,* 121–152.

Chinn, C., & Brewer, W. (1993). The role of anomalous data in knowledge acquisition: A theoretical framework and implications for science instruction. *Review of Educational Research, 63,* 1–49.

Chomsky, N. (1972). *Language and mind* (2nd ed.). Orlando, FL: Harcourt Brace.

Clapp, B. (1989). The discipline challenge. *Instructor, 99*(2), 32–34.

Clark, C. (1988). Teacher preparation: Contribution of research on teacher thinking. *Educational Researcher, 17,* 5–12.

Clark, C., & Peterson, P. (1986). Teachers' thought processes. In M. Wittrock (Ed.), *Handbook of research on teaching* (3rd ed., pp. 255–296). New York: Macmillan.

Clark, C., & Yinger, R. (1979). *Three studies of teacher planning* (Research Series No. 55). East Lansing: Michigan State University, Institute for Research on Teaching.

Clark, J., & Paivio, A. (1991). Dual coding theory and education. *Educational Psychology Review, 3,* 149–210.

Clark, K., & Clark, M. (1939). The development of consciousness of self and the emergence of racial identification in Negro preschool children. *Journal of Social Psychology, 10,* 591–599.

Clarke-Stewart, A., & Friedman, S. (1987). *Child development: Infancy through adolescence.* New York: Wiley.

Clements, B., & Evertson, C. (1982, March). *Orchestrating small-group instruction in the elementary school classroom.* Paper presented at the Annual Meeting of the American Educational Research Association, New York.

Clements, D., & Battista, M. (1990). Constructivist learning and teaching. *Arithmetic Teacher, 38,* 34–35.

Clifford, M. (1990). Students need challenge, not easy success. *Educational Leadership, 48*(1), 22–26.

Clifton, R., Perry, R., Parsonson, K., & Hryniuk, S. (1986). Effects of ethnicity and sex on teachers' expectations of junior high school students. *Sociology of Education, 59,* 58–67.

Clinkenbeard, P. (1992, April). *Motivation and gifted adolescents: Learning from observing practice.* Paper presented at the Annual Meeting of the American Educational Research Association, San Francisco.

Cobb, P. (1994). Where is the mind? Constructivist and sociocultural perspectives on mathematical development, *Educational Researcher, 23.*

Cohen, E. (1986). *Designing groupwork: Strategies for the heterogeneous classroom.* New York: Teachers College Press.

Cohen, E. (1991). Strategies for creating a multiability classroom. *Cooperative Learning, 12*(1), 4–7.

Cohen, E. (1994). Restructuring the classroom: Conditions for productive small groups. *Review of Educational Research, 64*(1), 1–35.

Cohen, M. (1985). Extrinsic reinforcers and intrinsic motivation. In M. Alderman & M. Cohen (Eds.), *Motivation theory and practice for preservice teachers* (pp. 6–15). Washington, DC: American Association of Colleges of Teacher Education.

Coker, H., Lorentz, C., & Coker, J. (1980, April). *Teacher behavior and student outcomes in the Georgia study.* Paper presented at the Annual Meeting of the American Educational Research Association, Boston.

Cole, D. (1991). Change in perceived competence as a function of peer and teacher evaluation. *Developmental Psychology, 27,* 682–688.

Cole, D., Vandercook, T., & Rynders, J. (1988). Comparison of two peer interaction programs: Children with and without severe disabilities. *American Educational Research Journal, 25,* 415–439.

Cole, M. (1991). Conclusion. In L. Resnick, J. Levine, & S. Teasley (Eds.), *Perspectives on socially shared cognition* (pp. 398–417). Washington, DC: American Psychological Association.

Coleman, J., Campbell, E., Hobson, D., McPortland, J., Mood, A., Weinfield, F., & York, R. (1966). *Equality of educational opportunity.* Washington, DC: U.S. Department of Health, Education and Welfare.

Collins, A., Brown, J., & Newman, S. (1989). Cognitive apprenticeship: Teaching the crafts of reading, writing, and mathematics. In L. Resnick (Ed.), *Knowing, learning, and instruction: Essays in honor of Robert Glaser* (pp. 453–494). Hillsdale, NJ: Erlbaum.

Combs, A., & Avila, D. (1985). *Helping relationships* (3rd ed.). Needham Heights, MA: Allyn & Bacon.

Conger, R., Conger, K., Elder, G., Lorenz, F., Simons, R., & Whitbeck, L. (1992). A family process model of economic hardship and adjustment of early adolescent boys. *Child Development, 63,* 526–541.

Conoley, J., & Kramer, J. (1989). *Mental measurements yearbook* (19th ed.). Lincoln: University of Nebraska, Buros Institute of Mental Measurement.

Consortium for Longitudinal Studies. (1983). *As the twig is bent: Lasting effects of preschool programs.* Hillsdale, NJ: Erlbaum.

Cooper, H. (1989). Synthesis of research on homework. *Educational Leadership, 47*(3), 85–91.

Copeland, W., & Decker, D. (1995, April). *Video cases and the development of meaning making in preservice teachers.* Paper presented at the Annual Meeting of the American Educational Research Association, San Francisco.

Cormier, S. (1987). The structural processes underlying transfer of training. In S. Cormier & J. Hagman (Eds.), *Transfer of learning: Contemporary research and applications.* San Diego: Academic Press.

Corno, L., & Snow, R. (1986). Adapting teaching to individual differences among learners. In M. Wittrock (Ed.), *Handbook of research on teaching* (3rd ed., pp. 605–629). New York: Macmillan.

Cortes, C. E. (1986). The education of language-minority students: A contextual interaction model. In *Beyond language: Social and cultural factors in schooling language-minority students* (pp. 299–343). Los Angeles: California State University, Evaluation, Dissemination, and Assessment Center.

Cotton, K., & Savard, W. (1981). *Instructional grouping: Ability grouping.* Portland, OR: Northwest Regional Laboratory.

Covington, M. (1992). *Making the grade: A self-worth perspective on motivation and school reform.* Cambridge, MA: Harvard University Press.

Covington, M., & Omelich, C. (1987). "I knew it cold before the exam": A test of the anxiety blockage hypothesis. *Journal of Educational Psychology, 79,* 393–400.

Cowan, S. (1988). Coping strategies of university students with learning disabilities. *Journal of Learning Disabilities, 21,* 161–164.

Craik, F., & Lockhart, R. (1972). Levels of processing: A framework for memory research. *Journal of Verbal Learning and Verbal Behavior, 11,* 671–680.

Crocker, R., & Brooker, G. (1986). Classroom control and student outcomes in grades 2 and 5. *American Educational Research Journal, 23,* 1–11.

Crooks, T. (1988). The impact of classroom evaluation practices on students. *Review of Educational Research, 58,* 438–481.

Cruickshank, D. (1985). Applying research on teacher clarity. *Journal of Teacher Education, 35*(2), 44–48.

Cruickshank, D. (1987). *Reflective teaching: The preparation of students of teaching.* Reston, VA: Association of Teacher Educators.

Cuban, L. (1984). *How teachers taught: Constancy and change in American classrooms: 1890-1980.* White Plains, NY: Longman.

Cummins, J. (1984). *Bilingualism and special education: Issues in assessment and pedagogy.* Clevedon, UK: Multilingual Matters.

Curwin, R., & Mendler, A. (1988). Packaged discipline programs: Let the buyer beware. *Educational Leadership, 46*(2), 68–71.

Cushner, K., McClelland, A., & Safford, P. (1992). *Human diversity in education.* New York: McGraw-Hill.

Dansereau, D. (1985). Learning strategy research. In J. Segal, S. Chipman, & R. Glaser (Eds.), *Thinking and learning skills* (Vol. 1, pp. 209–239). Hillsdale, NJ: Erlbaum.

Darling-Hammond, L., & Snyder, J. (1992). Reframing accountability: Creating learner-centered schools. In A. Lieberman (Ed.), *The changing contexts of teaching* (pp. 3–17). Chicago: University of Chicago Press.

Darling-Hammond, L., Wise, A., & Pease, S. (1983). Teacher evaluation in the organizational context: A review of the literature. *Review of Educational Research, 53,* 285–328.

Davis, G. (1989). Testing for creative potential. *Contemporary Educational Psychology, 14,* 257–274.

Davis, G., & Rimm, S. (1993). *Education of the gifted and talented* (3rd ed.). Upper Saddle River, NJ: Prentice Hall.

de Bono, E. (1976). *Teaching thinking.* London: Temple Smith.

deCharms, R. (1968). *Personal causation.* San Diego: Academic Press.

deCharms, R. (1980). The origins of competence and achievement motivation in personal causation. In L. Fyans (Ed.), *Achievement motivation: Recent trends in theory and research.* New York: Plenum Press.

Deci, E., & Ryan, R. (1987). The support of autonomy and the control of behavior. *Journal of Personality and Social Psychology, 53,* 1024–1037.

Delgado-Gaiton, C. (1992). School matters in the Mexican American home: Socializing children to education. *American Educational Research Journal, 29*(3), 495–516.

Delisle, J. (1984). *Gifted children speak out.* New York: Walker.

Dempster, F. (1991). Synthesis of research on reviews and tests. *Educational Leadership, 48*(7), 71–76.

Derry, S. (1992). Beyond symbolic processing: Expanding horizons for educational psychology. *Journal of Educational Psychology, 84,* 413–419.

Deshler, D., & Schumaker, J. (1993). Strategy mastery by at-risk students: Not a simple matter. *Elementary School Journal, 94*(2), 153–166.

DeVries, R., & Zan, B. (1995, April). *The sociomoral atmosphere: The first principle of constructivist education.* Paper presented at the Annual Meeting

of the American Educational Research Association, San Francisco.

Deyhle, D. (1987). Learning failure: Tests as gatekeepers and the culturally different child. In H. Trueba (Ed.), *Success or failure?* (pp. 85–108). Cambridge, MA: Newberry.

Díaz, R. (1983). Thought and two languages: The impact of bilingualism. In E. Gordon (Ed.), *Review of research in education* (Vol. 10). Washington, DC: American Educational Research Association.

Díaz, R. (1990). Bilingualism and cognitive ability: Theory, research, and controversy. In A. Barona & E. Garcia (Eds.), *Children at risk: Poverty, minority status, and other issues of educational equity* (pp. 91–102). Washington, DC: National Association of School Psychologists.

Dickinson, A. (1989). The detrimental effects of extrinsic reinforcement on intrinsic motivation. *Behavior Analyst, 12,* 1–15.

Dillon, D. (1989). Showing them that I want them to learn and that I care about who they are: A microethnography of the social organization of a secondary low-track English reading classroom. *American Educational Research Journal, 26*(2), 227–259.

Dillon, J. (1987). *Questioning and discussion: A multidisciplinary study.* Norwood, NJ: Ablex.

Dole, J., Duffy, G., Roehler, L., & Pearson, D. (1991). Moving from the old to the new: Research on reading comprehension instruction. *Review of Educational Research, 61,* 239–264.

Dolgins, J., Myers, M., Flynn, P., & Moore, J. (1984). How do we help the learning disabled? *Instructor, 93*(7), 29–36.

Doyle, R. (1989). The resistance of conventional wisdom to research evidence: The case of retention in grade. *Phi Delta Kappan, 71,* 215–220.

Doyle, W. (1983). Academic work. *Review of Educational Research, 53,* 159–199.

Doyle, W. (1986). Classroom organization and management. In M. Wittrock (Ed.),

Handbook of research on teaching (3rd ed., pp. 392–431). New York: Macmillan.

Dreikurs, R. (1968). *Psychology in the classroom* (2nd ed.). New York: Harper & Row.

Dreisbach, M., & Keogh, B. (1982). Test-wiseness as a factor in readiness test performance of young Mexican American children. *Journal of Educational Psychology, 74,* 224–229.

Driscoll, M. (1994). *Psychology of learning for instruction.* Needham Heights, MA: Allyn & Bacon.

Driver, R., Asoko, H., Leach, J., Mortimer, E., & Scott, P. (1994). Constructing scientific knowledge in the classroom. *Educational Researcher, 23*(7), 5–12.

Duffy, G. (1992, April). *Learning from the study of practice: Where we must go with strategy instruction.* Paper presented at the Annual Meeting of the American Educational Research Association, San Francisco.

Duffy, G., Roehler, L., Meloth, M., & Vavrus, L. (1985, April). *Conceptualizing instructional explanation.* Paper presented at the Annual Meeting of the American Educational Research Association, Chicago.

Duncker, K. (1945). On problem solving [Special issue]. *Psychological Monographs, 58*(270).

Dunkin, M., & Biddle, B. (1974). *The study of teaching.* New York: Holt, Rinehart & Winston.

Dunkle, M., Schraw, G., & Bendixon, L. (1995, April). *Cognitive processes in well-defined and ill-defined problem solving.* Paper presented at the Annual Meeting of the American Educational Research Association, San Francisco.

Dweck, C. (1985). Motivation. In R. Glaser & A. Lesgold (Eds.), *Handbook of psychology and education.* Hillsdale, NJ: Erlbaum.

Dweck, C., & Bempechat, J. (1983). Children's theories of intelligence: Consequences for learning. In S. Paris, G. Olson, & H. Stevenson (Eds.), *Learning and motivation in the classroom* (pp. 239–255). Hillsdale, NJ: Erlbaum.

Dweck, C., & Leggett, E. (1988). A social-cognitive approach to motivation and personality. *Psychological Review, 95,* 256–273.

Eggen, P., & Kauchak, D. (1996). *Strategies for teachers: Teaching content and thinking skills* (3rd ed.). Needham Heights, MA: Allyn & Bacon.

Eggen, P., Kauchak, D., & Kirk, S. (1978). Hierarchical cues and the learning of concepts from prose materials. *Journal of Experimental Education, 46*(4), 7–10.

Eggen, P., & McDonald, S. (1987, April). *Student misconceptions of physical science concepts: Implications for science instruction.* Paper presented at the Annual Meeting of the National Association for Research in Science Teaching, Washington, DC.

Elam, S., & Rose, L. (1995). The 27th annual Phi Delta Kappa/Gallup poll. *Phi Delta Kappan, 77*(1), 41–49.

Ellis, S., Dowdy, B., Graham, P., & Jones, R. (1992, April). *Parental support of planning skills in the context of homework and family demands.* Paper presented at the Annual Meeting of the American Educational Research Association, San Francisco.

Elton, L., & Laurillard, D. (1979). Trends in research on student learning. *Studies in Higher Education, 4,* 87–102.

Emmer, E. (1988). Praise and the instructional process. *Journal of Classroom Interaction, 23,* 32–39.

Emmer, E., Evertson, C., & Anderson, L. (1980). Effective classroom management at the beginning of the school year. *Elementary School Journal, 80,* 219–231.

Emmer, E., Evertson, C., Sanford, J., Clements, B., & Worsham, M. (1994). *Classroom management for secondary teachers* (3rd ed.). Upper Saddle River, NJ: Prentice Hall.

Englert, C., Raphael, T., & Anderson, L. (1989). *Cognitive Strategy Instruction in Writing Project.* East Lansing: Michigan State University, Institute for Research on Teaching.

Ennis, R. (1987). A taxonomy of critical thinking dispositions and abilities. In J. Baron & R. Sternberg (Eds.), *Teaching thinking skills.* New York: Freeman.

Epstein, J. (1990). School and family connections: Theory, research, and implications for integrating sociologies of education and family. In D. Unger & M. Sussman (Eds.), *Families in community settings: Interdisciplinary perspectives* (pp. 99–126). New York: Haworth Press.

Erikson, E. (1968). *Identity: Youth and crisis.* New York: Norton.

Erikson, E. (1980). *Identity and the life cycle* (2nd ed.). New York: Norton.

Escalante, J., & Dirmann, J. (1990). The Jaime Escalante Math Program. *Journal of Negro Education, 59*(3), 407–423.

Evans, E., & Engelberg, R. (1988). Student perceptions of school grading. *Journal of Research and Development in Education, 21*(2), 45–54.

Everson, H., Tobias, S., Hartman, H., & Gourgey, A. (1991, April). *Text anxiety in different curricular areas: An exploratory analysis of the role of subject matter.* Paper presented at the Annual Meeting of the American Educational Research Association, Chicago.

Evertson, C. (1980, April). *Differences in instructional activities in high- and low-achieving junior high classes.* Paper presented at the Annual Meeting of the American Educational Research Association, Boston.

Evertson, C. (1987). Managing classrooms: A framework for teachers. In D. Berliner & B. Rosenshine (Eds.), *Talks to teachers* (pp. 54–74). New York: Random House.

Evertson, C., Anderson, C., Anderson, L., & Brophy, J. (1980). Relationship between classroom behaviors and student outcomes in junior high mathematics and English classes. *American Educational Research Journal, 17,* 43–60.

Evertson, C., Emmer, E., Clements, B., Sanford, J., & Worsham, M. (1994). *Classroom management for*

elementary teachers (3rd ed.). Upper Saddle River, NJ: Prentice Hall.

Evertson, C., & Randolph, C. (1995). Classroom management in the learning-centered classroom. In A. Ornstein (Ed.), *Teaching: Theory and practice.* Needham.Heights, MA: Allyn & Bacon.

Eysenck, M., & Keane, M. (1990). *Cognitive psychology: A student's handbook.* Hillsdale, NJ: Erlbaum.

Fairbrother, R. (1975). The reliability of teachers' judgments of the abilities being tested by multiple-choice items. *Educational Research, 17,* 202–210.

Faw, T., & Belkin, G. (1989). *Child psychology.* New York: McGraw-Hill.

Feather, N. (Ed.). (1982). *Expectations and actions.* Hillsdale, NJ: Erlbaum.

Feldhusen, J. (1989). Synthesis of research on gifted youth. *Educational Leadership, 46*(6), 6–11.

Feldman, S., & Wentzel, K. (1990). Relations among family interaction patterns, classroom self-restraint, and academic achievement in preadolescent boys. *Journal of Educational Psychology, 82*(4), 813–819.

Fennema, E. (1987). Sex-related differences in education: Myths, realities, and interventions. In V. Richardson-Koehler (Ed.), *Educators' handbook* (pp. 329–347). White Plains, NY: Longman.

Fennema, E., & Koehler, M. (1983). Expectations and feelings about females' and males' achievement in mathematics. In E. Fennema (Ed.), *Research on relationship of spatial visualization and confidence of male/female achievement in grades 6–8* (Final Report, National Science Foundation Project No. SED78-17330). Washington, DC: National Science Foundation.

Fennema, E., & Peterson, P. (1987). Effective teaching for girls and boys: The same or different? In D. Berliner & B. Rosenshine (Eds.), *Talks to teachers* (pp. 111–125). New York: Random House.

Fernald, L. (1989). Tales in a textbook: Learning in the traditional and narrative modes. *Teaching of Psychology, 16*(3), 121–124.

Finn, C., Dulberg, L., & Reis, J. (1979). Sex differences in educational attainment: A cross-national perspective. *Harvard Educational Review, 49,* 477–503.

Fisher, C., Berliner, D., Filby, N., Marliave, R., Cohen, K., & Dishaw, M. (1980). Teaching behaviors, academic learning time, and student achievement: An overview. In C. Denham & A. Lieberman (Eds.), *Time to learn* (pp. 7–32). Washington, DC: National Institute of Education.

Fitch, M., & Semb, M. (1992, April). *Peer teacher learning: A comparison of role playing and video evaluation for effects on peer teacher outcomes.* Paper presented at the Annual Meeting of the American Educational Research Association, San Francisco.

Fitzgerald, J. (1995). English-as-a-second-language learners' cognitive reading processes: A review of research in the United States. *Review of Educational Research, 65*(2), 145–190.

Flavell, J. (1963). *Developmental psychology of Jean Piaget.* Princeton, NJ: Van Nostrand.

Flavell, J. (1985). *Cognitive development* (2nd ed.). Upper Saddle River, NJ: Prentice Hall.

Flavell, J., Friedrichs, A., & Hoyt, J. (1970). Developmental changes in memorization processes. *Cognitive Psychology, 1,* 324–340.

Fleming, M., & Chambers, B. (1983). Teacher-made tests: Windows on the classrooms. In W. Hathaway (Ed.), *Testing in the schools: New directions for testing and measurement* (No. 19). San Francisco: Jossey-Bass.

Foos, P. (1992). Test performance as a function of expected form and difficulty. *Journal of Experimental Education, 60*(3), 205–211.

Ford, M. (1992). *Motivating humans: Goals, emotions, and personal agency beliefs.* Newbury Park, CA: Sage.

Fowler, R. (1994, April). *Piagetian versus Vygotskian perspectives on development and education.* Paper presented at the Annual Meeting of the American Educational Research Association, New Orleans.

Frary, R., Cross, L., & Weber, L. (1992, April). *Testing and grading practices and opinions in the nineties: 1890s or 1990s?* Paper presented at the Annual Meeting of the American Educational Research Association, San Francisco.

Frederick, W. (1977). The use of classroom time in high schools above or below the median reading score. *Urban Education, 11,* 459–464.

Freeman, E., & Hatch, J. (1989). What schools expect young children to know: An analysis of kindergarten report cards. *Elementary School Journal, 89,* 595–605.

Frey, K., & Ruble, D. (1987). What children say about classroom performance: Sex and grade difference in perceived competence. *Child Development, 58,* 1068–1080.

Fuchs, L., Fuchs, D., Bentz, J., Phillips, N., & Hamlett, C. (1994). The nature of student interactions during peer tutoring with and without prior training and experience. *American Educational Research Journal, 31*(1), 75–103.

Gage, N. (1985). *Hard gains in the soft sciences: The case of pedagogy.* Bloomington, IN: Phi Delta Kappa.

Gage, N., & Berliner, D. (1989). Nurturing the critical, practical, and artistic thinking of teachers. *Phi Delta Kappan, 71,* 212–214.

Gagne, E., Yekovich, C., & Yekovich, F. (1993). *The cognitive psychology of school learning* (2nd ed.). New York: HarperCollins.

Gagne, R. (1985). *The conditions of learning and a theory of instruction* (4th ed.). New York: Holt, Rinehart & Winston.

Gagne, R., & Brown, L. (1961). Some factors in the programming of conceptual learning. *Journal of Experimental Psychology, 62,* 313–321.

Gagne, R., & Dick, W. (1983). Instructional psychology. In M. Rosenzweig & L. Porter (Eds.), *Annual review of psychology.* Palo Alto, CA: Annual Reviews.

Gall, M. (1984). Synthesis of research on teachers' questioning. *Educational Leadership, 42*(3), 40–47.

Gallagher, J., & Reid, D. (1981). *Learning theory of Piaget and Inhelder.* Pacific Grove, CA: Brooks/Cole.

Garber, H. (1988). *Milwaukee Project: Preventing mental retardation in children at risk.* Washington, DC: American Association on Mental Retardation.

Gardner, H. (1983). *Frames of mind: The theory of multiple intelligences.* New York: Basic Books.

Gardner, H. (1992). Assessment in context: The alternative to standardized testing. In B. Gifford (Ed.), *Changing assessments: Alternate views of aptitude, achievement, and instruction* (pp. 77–119). Boston: Kluwer.

Gardner, H. (1993). *Creating minds: An anatomy of creativity seen through the lives of Freud, Einstein, Picasso, Stravinsky, Elliot, Graham, and Gandhi.* New York: Basic Books.

Gardner, H. (1995). Reflections on multiple intelligences: Myths and messages. *Phi Delta Kappan, 77,* 200–209.

Gardner, H., & Hatch, T. (1989). Multiple intelligences go to school. *Educational Researcher, 18*(8), 4–10.

Gardner, M. (1985). Cognitive psychological approaches to instructional task analysis. In E. Gordon (Ed.), *Review of research in education* (Vol. 12, pp. 157–195). Washington, DC: American Educational Research Association.

Garner, R., Alexander, P., Gillingham, M., Kulikowich, J., & Brown, R. (1991). Interest and learning from text. *American Educational Research Journal, 28,* 643–659.

Geisinger, K. (1992). Testing L.E.P. students for minimum competency and high school graduation. In *Focus on evaluation and measurement* (Vol. 2, pp. 33–68). Washington, DC: U.S. Department of Education.

Gelfand, D., Jenson, W., & Drew, C. (1988). *Understanding child behavior disorders* (2nd ed.). New York: Holt, Rinehart & Winston.

Gelman, R., Meck, E., & Merkin, S. (1986). Young children's numerical competence. *Cognitive Development, 1,* 1–29.

Genishi, C. (1992, April). *Oral language and communicative competence.* Paper presented at the Annual Meeting of the American Educational Research Association, San Francisco.

Gersten, R., & Woodward, J. (1995). A longitudinal study of transitional and immersion bilingual education programs in one district. *Elementary School Journal, 95*(3), 223–239.

Gilligan, C. (1982). *In a different voice: Psychological theory and women's development.* Cambridge, MA: Harvard University Press.

Gilligan, C., & Attanucci, J. (1988). Two moral orientations: Gender differences and similarities. *Merrill-Palmer Quarterly, 34,* 223–237.

Glaser, R., & Chi, M. (1988). Overview. In M. Chi, R. Glaser, & M. Farr (Eds.), *The nature of expertise* (pp. xv–xxviii). Hillsdale, NJ: Erlbaum.

Glasser, W. (1969). *Schools without failure.* New York: Harper & Row.

Glasser, W. (1985). *Control theory in the classroom.* New York: Perennial Library.

Glick, M., & Holyoak, K. (1987). The cognitive basis of knowledge transfer. In S. Cormier & J. Hagman (Eds.), *Transfer of learning: Contemporary research and applications.* San Diego: Academic Press.

Glickman, C., & Bey, T. (1990). Supervision. In R. Houston (Ed.), *Handbook of research on teacher education* (pp. 549–568). New York: Macmillan.

Glover, J., Ronning, R., & Bruning, R. (1990). *Cognitive psychology for teachers.* New York: Macmillan.

Glynn, S., Duit, R., & Thiele, R. (in press). Teaching science with analogies: A strategy for constructing knowledge. In S. Glynn & R. Duit (Eds.), *Learning science in the schools: Research reforming practice.* Hillsdale, NJ: Erlbaum.

Gollnick, D., & Chinn, P. (1986). *Multicultural education in a pluralistic society* (2nd ed.). New York: Merrill/Macmillan.

Gollnick, D., & Chinn, P. (1994). *Multicultural education in a pluralistic society* (4th ed.). New York: Merrill/Macmillan.

Good, T. (1987a). Teacher expectations. In D. Berliner & B. Rosenshine (Eds.), *Talks to teachers* (pp. 159–200). New York: Random House.

Good, T. (1987b). Two decades of research on teacher expectations: Findings and future directions. *Journal of Teacher Education, 37*(4), 32–47.

Good, T., & Brophy, J. (1986). School effects. In M. Wittrock (Ed.), *Handbook of research on teaching* (3rd ed., pp. 570–604). New York: Macmillan.

Good, T., & Brophy, J. (1994). *Looking in classrooms* (6th ed.). New York: HarperCollins.

Good, T., & Marshall, S. (1984). Do students learn more in heterogeneous or homogeneous groups? In P. Peterson, L. Wilkinson, & M. Hallinan (Eds.), *The social context of instruction: Group organization and group process* (pp. 15–38). San Diego: Academic Press.

Good, T., McCaslin, M., & Reys, B. (1992). Investigating work groups to promote problem solving in mathematics. In J. Brophy (Ed.), *Advances in research on teaching* (Vol. 3, pp. 115–160). Greenwich, CT: JAI Press.

Goodenow, C. (1992a, April). *School motivation, engagement, and sense of belonging among urban adolescent students.* Paper presented at the Annual Meeting of the American Educational Research Association, San Francisco.

Goodenow, C. (1992b). Strengthening the links between educational psychology and the study of social contexts. *Educational Psychologist, 27*(2), 177–196.

Goodlad, J. (1984). *A place called school.* New York: McGraw-Hill.

Gordon, T. (1974). *Teacher effectiveness training.* New York: Wyden.

Gottfried, A. (1985). Academic intrinsic motivation in elementary and junior high students. *Journal of Educational Psychology, 82,* 525–538.

Graham, S. (1991). A review of attribution theory in achievement contexts. *Educational Psychology Review, 3*(1), 5–39.

Graham, S. (1994). Motivation in African Americans. *Review of Educational Research, 64*(1), 55–117.

Graham, S., & Johnson, L. (1989). Teaching reading to learning disabled students: A review of research-supported procedures. *Focus on Exceptional Children, 21*(6), 1–9.

Grant, L. (1984). Black females' "place" in desegregated classrooms. *Sociology of Education, 57,* 98–111.

Grant, L., & Rothenberg, J. (1986). The social enhancement of ability differences: Teacher-student interactions in first- and second-grade reading groups. *Elementary School Journal, 87,* 29–49.

Greene, D., Sternberg, B., & Lepper, M. (1976). Overjustification in a token economy. *Journal of Personality and Social Psychology, 34,* 1219–1234.

Greenleof, C. (1995, April). *You feel like you belong: Student perspectives on becoming a community of learners.* Paper presented at the Annual Meeting of the American Educational Research Association, San Francisco.

Gresham, F., Evans, S., & Elliott, S. (1988). Self-efficacy differences among mildly handicapped, gifted, and non-handicapped students. *Journal of Special Education, 22,* 231–241.

Griffith, D. (1992, April). Prenatal exposure to cocaine and other drugs: Developmental and educational prognoses. *Phi Delta Kappan, 74,* 30–34.

Gronlund, N. (1988). *How to construct achievement tests* (4th ed.). Upper Saddle River, NJ: Prentice Hall.

Gronlund, N. (1993). *How to make achievement tests and assessments.* Needham Heights, MA: Allyn & Bacon.

Gronlund, N. (1995). *How to write and use instructional objectives* (5th ed.). Upper Saddle River, NJ: Merrill/Prentice Hall.

Gronlund, N., & Linn, R. (1995). *Measurement and evaluation in teaching* (7th ed.). Upper Saddle River, NJ: Prentice Hall.

Guilford, J. (1967). *The nature of human intelligence.* New York: McGraw-Hill.

Guilford, J. (1988). Some changes in the structure-of-intellect model. *Educational and Psychological Measurement, 48,* 1–4.

Haan, N., Smith, M., & Block, J. (1968). Moral reasoning of young adults: Political-social behavior, family background, and personality correlates. *Journal of Personality and Social Psychology, 10,* 183–201.

Haertel, E. (1986, April). *Choosing and using classroom tests: Teachers' perspectives on assessment.* Paper presented at the Annual Meeting of the American Educational Research Association, San Francisco.

Hakuta, K., & Garcia, E. (1989). Bilingualism and education. *American Psychologist, 44*(2), 374–379.

Hall, C., & Lindzey, G. (1978). *Theories of personality.* New York: Wiley.

Hall, R. J., Gerber, M. M., & Stricker, A. G. (1989). Cognitive training: Implications for spelling instruction. In J. N. Hughes & R. J. Hall (Eds.), *Cognitive-behavioral psychology in the schools: A comprehensive handbook* (pp. 347–388). New York: Guilford Press.

Hallahan, D., Hall, R., Ianno, S., Kneedler, R., Lloyd, J., Loper, A., & Reeve, R. (1983). Summary of research findings at the University of Virginia Learning Disabilities Research Institute. *Exceptional Education Quarterly, 4*(1), 95–114.

Hallahan, D., & Kauffman, J. (1994). *Exceptional children* (6th ed.). Needham Heights, MA: Allyn & Bacon.

Hallinan, M. (1984). Summary and implications. In P. Peterson, L. Wilkinson, & M. Hallinan (Eds.), *The social context of instruction: Group organization and group processes* (pp. 229–240). San Diego: Academic Press.

Hamachek, D. (1987). Humanistic psychology: Theory, postulates, and implications for educational processes. In J. Glover & R. Ronning (Eds.), *Historical foundations of educational psychology* (pp. 159–182). New York: Plenum Press.

Hammond, K. (1990). Case-based planning: A framework for planning from experience. *Cognitive Science, 14,* 385–443.

Hamp-Lyons, L. (1992). Holistic writing assessment for L.E.P. students. In *Focus on evaluation and measurement* (Vol. 2, pp. 317–358). Washington, DC: U.S. Department of Education.

Haney, W., Madaus, G., & Lyons, R. (1993). *The fractured marketplace for standardized testing.* Boston: Kluwer.

Hardman, M., Drew, C., & Egan, W. (1996). *Human exceptionality* (5th ed.). Needham Heights, MA: Allyn & Bacon.

Harris, L., Kagay, M., & Ross, J. (1987). *The Metropolitan Life survey of the American teacher: Strengthening links between home and school.* New York: Louis Harris & Associates.

Harrow, A. (1972). *A taxonomy of the psychomotor domain: A guide for developing behavioral objectives.* New York: McKay.

Harry, B. (1992). An ethnographic study of cross-cultural communication with Puerto Rican American families in the special education system. *American Educational Research Journal, 29*(3), 471–488.

Harter, S. (1978). Pleasure derived from challenge and the effects of receiving grades on children's difficulty level choices. *Child Development, 49,* 788–789.

Harter, S., & Connell, J. (1984). A comparison of alternative models of the relationships between academic achievement and children's perceptions of competence, control, and motivational orientation. In J. Nicholls (Ed.), *Development of achievement-related cognitions and behavior.* Greenwich, CT: JAI Press.

Harter, S., & Jackson, B. (1992). Trait versus nontrait conceptualizations of intrinsic/extrinsic motivational orientation. Special issue: Perspectives on intrinsic motivation. *Motivation and Emotion, 16,* 209–230.

Hayes, J. (1988). *The complete problem solver* (2nd ed.). Hillsdale, NJ: Erlbaum.

Hayes, S., Rosenfarb, I., Wulfert, E., Munt, E., Korn, Z., & Zettle, R. (1985). Self-reinforcement effects: An artifact of social standard setting? *Journal of Applied Behavior Analysis, 18,* 201–214.

Haynes, N., & Comer, J. (1995, April). *The School Development Program (SDP): Lessons from the past.* Paper presented at the Annual Meeting of the American Educational Research Association, San Francisco.

Heath, S. (1982). Questioning at home and at school: A comparative study. In G. Spindler (Ed.), *Doing the ethnography of schooling.* New York: Holt, Rinehart & Winston.

Helmke, A., & Schrader, F. (1987). Interactional effects of instructional quality and teacher judgment accuracy on achievement. *Teaching and Teacher Education, 3,* 91–98.

Helms, J. (1992). Why is there no study of cultural equivalence in standardized cognitive ability testing? *American Psychologist, 47*(9), 1083–1101.

Henson, K. (1988). *Methods and strategies for teaching in secondary and middle schools.* White Plains, NY: Longman.

Herman, J., Abedi, J., & Golan, S. (1994). Assessing the effects of standardized testing on schools. *Educational and Psychological Measurement, 54*(2), 471–482.

Herman, J., Aschbacher, P., & Winters, L. (1992). *A practical guide to alternative assessment.* Alexandria, VA: Association for Supervision and Curriculum Development.

Hernstein, R., Nickerson, R., Sanchez, M., & Swets, J. (1986). Teaching thinking skills. *American Psychologist, 41,* 1279–1289.

Hess, R., & McDevitt, T. (1984). Some cognitive consequences of maternal intervention techniques: A longitudinal study. *Child Development, 55,* 2017–2020.

Heward, W. (1996). *Exceptional children* (5th ed.). Upper Saddle River, NJ: Merrill/Prentice Hall.

Hill, D. (1990). Order in the classroom. *Teacher, 1*(7), 70–77.

Hill, J., Holmbeck, G., Marlow, L., Green, T., & Lynch, M. (1985). Menarchal status and parent-child relations in families of seventh-grade girls. *Journal of Youth and Adolescence, 14,* 301–316.

Hill, K., & Wigfield, A. (1984). Test anxiety: A major educational problem and what can be done about it. *Elementary School Journal, 85,* 105–126.

Hillocks, G. (1984). What works in teaching composition: A meta-analysis of experimental treatment studies. *American Journal of Education, 93,* 133–170.

Hmelo, C. (1995, April). *The effect of problem-based learning on the early development of medical expertise.* Paper presented at the Annual Meeting of the American Educational Research Association, San Francisco.

Hodgkinson, H. (1991). Reform vs. reality. *Phi Delta Kappan, 73*(1), 8–16.

Holstein, C. (1976). Irreversible, stepwise sequence in the development of moral judgment: A longitudinal study of males and females. *Child Development, 47,* 51–61.

Holt, J. (1964). *How children fail.* New York: Putnam.

Hoover-Dempsey, K., Bassler, O., & Burow, R. (1995). Parents' reported involvement in students' homework: Strategies and practices. *Elementary School Journal, 95*(5), 435–449.

Hornberger, N. (1989). Continua of biliteracy. *Review of Educational Research, 59,* 271–296.

Houten, R., & Doleys, D. (1983). Are social reprimands effective? In S. Axelrod & J. Apache (Eds.), *The effects of punishment on human behavior* (pp. 45–70). San Diego: Academic Press.

Hudley, C. (1992, April). *The reduction of peer-directed aggression among highly aggressive African American boys.* Paper presented at the Annual Meeting of the American Educational Research Association, San Francisco.

Humphrey, F. (1979). *"Shh!" A sociolinguistic study of teachers' turn-taking sanctions in primary school lessons.* Unpublished doctoral dissertation, Georgetown University, Washington, DC.

Hvitfeldt, C. (1986). Traditional culture, perceptual style, and learning: The classroom behavior of Hmong adults. *Adult Education Quarterly, 36*(2), 65–77.

Isabella, R., & Belsky, J. (1991). Interactional synchrony and the origins of infant-mother attachment: A replication study. *Child Development, 62,* 373, 384.

Jacobsen, D., Eggen, P., & Kauchak, D. (1993). *Methods for teachers: A skills approach* (4th ed.). New York: Macmillan.

Jensen, A. (1987). Individual differences in mental ability. In J. Glover & R. Ronning (Eds.), *Historical foundations of educational psychology.* New York: Plenum Press.

Jenson, W., Sloane, H., & Young, K. (1988). *Applied behavior analysis in education.* Upper Saddle River, NJ: Prentice Hall.

Johnson, D., & Johnson, R. (1994). *Learning together and alone: Cooperation, competition, and individualization* (4th ed.). Needham Heights, MA: Allyn & Bacon.

Johnson, J. (1972). Punishment of human behavior. *American Psychologist, 27,* 1033–1054.

Jones, E. (1990). *Interpersonal perception.* New York: Freeman.

Jones, E. (1995, April). *Defining essential critical thinking skills for college students.* Paper presented at the Annual Meeting of the American Educational Research Association, San Francisco.

Jones, F. (1979). The gentle art of classroom discipline. *National Elementary Principal, 58,* 26–32.

Jones, F. (1987). *Positive classroom discipline.* New York: McGraw-Hill.

Jones, T., Sowell, V., Jones, J., & Butler, L. (1981). Changing children's perceptions of handicapped people. *Exceptional Children, 47,* 365–368.

Jussim, L. (1989). Teacher expectations: Self-fulfilling prophecies, perceptual biases, and accuracy. *Journal of Personality and Social Psychology, 57,* 469–480.

Kagan, D. (1992a). Implications of research on teacher belief. *Educational Psychologist, 27,* 65–90.

Kagan, D. (1992b). Professional growth among preservice and beginning teachers. *Review of Educational Research, 62,* 129–169.

Kagan, S. (1994). *Cooperative learning.* San Juan Capistrano, CA: Resources for Teachers.

Kail, R., & Bisanz, J. (1992). The information-processing perspective on cognitive development in childhood and adolescence. In R. Sternberg & C. Berg (Eds.), *Intellectual development* (pp. 229–260). New York: Cambridge University Press.

Kalechstein, P., Kalechstein, M., & Doctor, R. (1981). The effects of instruction on test-taking skills in second-grade Black children. *Measurement and Evaluation in Guidance, 13,* 198–202.

Kaplan, R., & Saccuzzo, D. (1993). *Psychological testing* (3rd ed.). Pacific Grove, CA: Brooks/Cole.

Karplus, R., Karplus, E., Formisano, M., & Paulsen, A. (1979). Proportional reasoning and control of variables in seven countries. In J. Lockheed & M. Clements (Eds.), *Cognitive process instruction: Research on teaching thinking skills.* Philadelphia: Franklin Institute Press.

Kasten, W. (1992). Bridging the horizon: American Indian beliefs and whole language learning. *Anthropology and Education Quarterly, 23*(2), 108–119.

Kauchak, D., & Eggen, P. (1993). *Teaching and learning: Research-based methods* (2nd ed.). Needham Heights, MA: Allyn & Bacon.

Kaufman, A., & Kaufman, N. (1983). *Kaufman Assessment Battery for Children: Interpretive manual.* Circle Pines, MN: American Guidance Service.

Keislar, E., & Shulman, L. (Eds.). (1966). *Learning by discovery: A critical appraisal.* Chicago: Rand McNally.

Kellogg, J. (1988). Forces of change. *Phi Delta Kappan, 70,* 199–204.

Kelly, M., Moore, D., & Tuck, B. (1994). Reciprocal teaching in a regular primary school classroom. *Journal of Educational Research, 88*(1), 53–59.

Kerman, S. (1979). Teacher expectations and student achievement. *Phi Delta Kappan, 60,* 70–72.

Kiewra, K. (1989). A review of note-taking: The encoding-storage paradigm and beyond. *Educational Psychology Review, 1,* 147–172.

Kika, F., McLaughlin, T., & Dixon, J. (1992). Effects of frequent testing of secondary algebra students. *Journal of Educational Research, 85,* 159–162.

Kim, D., Solomon, D., & Roberts, W. (1995, April). *Classroom practices that enhance students' sense of community.* Paper presented at the Annual Meeting of the American Educational Research Association, San Francisco.

Kirk, S., & Gallagher, J. (1989). *Educating exceptional students* (6th ed.). Boston: Houghton Mifflin.

Knapp, M., Shields, P., & Turnbull, B. (1995). Academic challenge in high-poverty classrooms. *Phi Delta Kappan, 76,* 770–776.

Kneedler, P. (1985). California assesses critical thinking. In A. Costa (Ed.), *Developing minds: A resource book for teaching thinking* (pp. 276–282). Alexandria, VA: Association for Supervision and Curriculum Development.

Kochenberger-Stroeher, S. (1994). Sixteen kindergartners' gender-related views of careers. *Elementary School Journal, 95*(1), 95–103.

Kohlberg, L. (1963). The development of children's orientation toward moral order: Sequence in the development of human thought. *Vita Humana, 6,* 11–33.

Kohlberg, L. (1969). Stage and sequence: The cognitive-developmental approach to socialization. In D. Goslin (Ed.), *Handbook of socialization theory and research.* Chicago: Rand McNally.

Kohlberg, L. (1975). The cognitive-developmental approach to moral education. *Phi Delta Kappan, 56,* 670–677.

Kohlberg, L. (1981). *Philosophy of moral development.* New York: Harper & Row.

Kohlberg, L. (1984). *Essays on moral development: Vol. 2. The psychology of moral development.* New York: Harper & Row.

Kohn, A. (1992). *No contest: The case against competition.* Boston: Houghton Mifflin.

Kohn, A. (1993). Why incentive plans cannot work. *Harvard Business Review, 71,* 54–63.

Kounin, J. (1970). *Discipline and group management in classrooms.* New York: Holt, Rinehart & Winston.

Kounin, J. (1983). *Classrooms: Individuals or behavior settings* (Monographs in Teaching and Learning No. 1). Bloomington: Indiana University, School of Education.

Kozulin, A. (1990). *Vygotsky's psychology: A biography of ideas.* Cambridge, MA: Harvard University Press.

Krabbe, M., & Polivka, J. (1990, April). *An analysis of students' perceptions of effective teaching behaviors during discussion activity.* Paper presented at the Annual Meeting of the American Educational Research Association, Boston.

Kramer, L., & Colvin, C. (1991, April). *Rules, responsibilities, and respect: The school lives of marginal students.* Paper presented at the Annual Meeting of the American Educational Research Association, Chicago.

Kramer-Schlosser, L. (1992). Teacher distance and student disengagement: School lives on the margin. *Journal of Teacher Education, 43*(2), 128–140.

Krathwohl, D., Bloom, B., & Masia, B. (1964). *Taxonomy of educational objectives: The classification of educational goals: Handbook 2. Affective domain.* New York: McKay.

Kreutzer, M., Leonard, C., & Flavell, J. (1975). An interview study of children's knowledge about memory. *Monographs of the Society for Research in Child Development, 40*(1, Serial No. 15).

Kruger, A. (1992). The effect of peer and adult-child transactive discussions on moral reasoning. *Merrill-Palmer Quarterly, 38*(2), 191–211.

Kulik, J., & Kulik, C. (1984). Effects of accelerated instruction on students. *Review of Educational Research, 54,* 409–425.

LaBerge, D., & Samuels, S. (1974). Toward a theory of automatic information processing in reading. *Cognitive Psychology, 6,* 293–323.

Labov, W. (1972). *Language in the inner city: Studies in the "Black" English vernacular.* Philadelphia: University of Pennsylvania Press.

Lane, D., & Pearson, D. (1982). The development of selective attention. *Merrill-Palmer Quarterly, 28,* 317–337.

Langer, J., Bartolome, L., Vasquez, O., & Lucas, T. (1990). Meaning construction in school literacy tasks: A study of bilingual students. *American Educational Research Journal, 27,* 427–471.

Lawler-Prince, D., & Holloway, D. (1992). The family dynamics and characteristics of homeless children: Barriers to education. *National Forum of Teaching Education Journal, 2*(1), 49–53.

Lawson, A., & Snitgren, D. (1982). Teaching formal reasoning in a college biology course for preservice teachers. *Journal of Research in Science Teaching, 19,* 233–248.

Lawson, M., & Chinnappan, M. (1994). Generative activity during problem solving: Comparison of the performance of high-achieving and low-achieving high school students. *Cognition & Instruction, 12*(1), 61–93.

Leahey, T., & Harris, R. (1993). *Learning and cognition* (3rd ed.). Upper Saddle River, NJ: Prentice Hall.

Lemke, J. (1982, April). *Classroom communication of science* (Final report to NSF/RISE). Washington, DC: National Science Foundation. (ERIC Document Reproduction Service No. ED 222 346)

Lepper, M., & Hodell, M. (1989). Intrinsic motivation in the classroom. In C. Ames & R. Ames (Eds.), *Research on motivation in education* (Vol. 3, pp. 73–105). San Diego: Academic Press.

Levin, H. (1988, April). *Structuring schools for greater effectiveness with educationally disadvantaged or at-risk students.* Paper presented at the Annual Meeting of the American Educational Research Association, San Francisco.

Lezotte, L. (1981). Climate characteristics in instructionally effective schools. *Impact on Instructional Improvement, 16,* 26–31.

Lickona, T. (1991). *Educating for character.* New York: Bantam.

Lindeman, R., & Merenda, P. (1979). *Educational measurement.* Glenview, IL: Scott, Foresman.

Linn, M., & Hyde, J. (1989). Gender, mathematics, and science. *Educational Researcher, 18*(8), 17–19, 22–27.

Linn, R. (1990). Essentials of student assessment: From accountability to instructional aid. *Teachers College Record, 91,* 422–436.

Lipman, M., Sharp, A., & Oscanyan, F. (1980). *Philosophy in the classroom.* Philadelphia: Temple University Press.

Locke, E., & Latham, G. (1990). *A theory of goal setting and performance.* Upper Saddle River, NJ: Prentice Hall.

Lohman, D. (1995, April). *Intelligences as an outcome of schooling: Some prescriptions for developing and testing the fluidization of abilities.* Paper presented at the Annual Meeting of the American Educational Research Association, San Francisco.

Lomax, R. (1994, April). *On becoming assessment literate. Preservice teachers' beliefs and practices.* Paper presented at the Annual Meeting of the American Educational Research Association, New Orleans.

Lovett, M., & Anderson, J. (1994). Effects of solving related proofs on memory and transfer in geometry problem solving. *Journal of Experimental Psychology, 20*(2), 366–378.

Luckasson, R., Coulter, D., Pollaway, E., Reiss, A., Shalock, R., Snell, M., Spitalnik, D., & Stark, J. (1992). *Mental retardation: Definition, classification, and systems of supports.* Washington, DC: American Association on Mental Retardation.

Lyman, H. (1991). *Test scores and what they mean* (5th ed.). Upper Saddle River, NJ: Prentice Hall.

Maccoby, E., & Jacklin, C. (1974). *The psychology of sex differences.* Palo Alto, CA: Stanford University Press.

Mace, F., Belfiore, P., & Shea, M. (1989). Operant theory and research on self-regulation. In B. Zimmerman & D. Schunk (Eds.), *Self-regulated learning and academic achievement: Theory, research, and practice.* New York: Springer-Verlag.

Mace, F., & Kratochwill, T. (1988). Self-monitoring. In J. Witt, S. Elliot, & F. Gresham (Eds.), *Handbook of behavior therapy in education.* New York: Plenum Press.

Machado, L. (1980). *The right to be intelligent.* New York: Pergamon Press.

Macionis, J. (1994). *Sociology* (4th ed.). Upper Saddle River, NJ: Prentice Hall.

MacKenzie, B. (1984). Explaining race difference in IQ: The logic, the methodology, the evidence. *American Psychologist, 39,* 1214–1233.

Macmillan, D., Keogh, B., & Jones, R. (1986). Special educational research on mildly handicapped learners. In M. Wittrock (Ed.), *Handbook of research on teaching* (3rd ed., pp. 686–726). New York: Macmillan.

Madaus, G., & Tan, A. (1993). The growth of assessment. In G. Cawelti (Ed.), *Challenges and achievements of American education* (pp. 53–79). Alexandria, VA: Association for Supervision and Curriculum Development.

Maehr, M. (1976). Continuing motivation: An analysis of a seldom considered educational outcome. *Review of Educational Research, 46,* 443–462.

Maehr, M. (1992, April). *Transforming the school culture to enhance motivation.* Paper presented at the Annual Meeting of the American Educational Research Association, San Francisco.

Mager, R. (1962). *Preparing instructional objectives.* Palo Alto, CA: Fearon.

Maheady, L., Sacca, M., & Harper, G. (1987). Classwide student tutoring teams: The effects of peer-mediated instruction on the academic performance of secondary mainstreamed students. *Journal of Special Education, 21*(3), 107–121.

Mantzicopoulos, P. (1989, April). *Coping with school failure: The relationship of children's coping strategies to academic achievement, self-concept, behavior, and locus of control.* Paper presented at the Annual Meeting of the American Educational Research Association, San Francisco.

Marcia, J. (1980). Identity in adolescence. In J. Adelson (Ed.), *Handbook of adolescent psychology.* New York: Wiley.

Marcia, J. (1987). The identity status approach to the study of ego identity development. In T. Honess & K. Yardley (Eds.), *Self and identity: Perspectives across the life span.* London: Routledge & Kegan Paul.

Marsh, H. (1989). Age and sex effects in multiple dimensions of self-concept: Preadolescence to early adulthood. *Journal of Educational Psychology, 81,* 417–430.

Marsh, H. (1992). Content specificity of relations between academic achievement and academic self-concept. *Journal of Educational Psychology, 84*(1), 34–52.

Marsh, H., & Shavelson, R. (1985). Self-concept: Its multifaceted hierarchical structure. *Educational Psychologist, 20,* 107–123.

Marshall, H. (1992). Seeing, redefining, and supporting student learning. In H. Marshall (Ed.), *Redefining student learning: Roots of educational change* (pp. 1–32). Norwood, NJ: Ablex.

Marso, R., & Pigge, F. (1992, April). *A summary of published research: Classroom teachers' knowledge and skills related to the development and use of teacher-made tests.* Paper presented at the Annual Meeting of the American Educational Research Association, San Francisco.

Maslow, A. (1968). *Toward a psychology of being* (2nd ed.). New York: Van Nostrand.

Maslow, A. (1970). *Motivation and personality* (2nd ed.). New York: Harper & Row. (Original work published 1954)

Mason, C., & Kahle, J. (1989). Student attitudes toward science and science-related careers: A program designed to promote a stimulating gender-free learning environment. *Journal of Research in Science Teaching, 26,* 25–40.

Masten, A., Morison, P., Pelligrini, D., & Tellegen, A. (1990). Competence under stress: Risk and protective factors. In J. Rolf, A. Masten, D. Cicchetti, K. Nuechterlein, & P. Weintraub (Eds.), *Risk and protective factors in the development of psychopathology* (pp. 236–256). New York: Cambridge University Press.

Matute-Bianchi, M. (1986). Ethnic identities and patterns of school success and failure among Mexican-descent and Japanese American students in a California high school: An ethnographic analysis. *American Journal of Education, 95,* 233–255.

May, B. (1990). *Reading as communication* (3rd ed.). Upper Saddle River, NJ: Merrill/Prentice Hall.

Mayer, R. (1984). Aids to text comprehension. *Educational Psychologist, 19,* 30–42.

Mayer, R. (1987). *Educational psychology: A cognitive approach.* Boston: Little, Brown.

Mayer, R. (1992). *Thinking, problem solving, cognition* (2nd ed.). New York: Freeman.

Mazur, J. (1994). *Learning and behavior* (3rd ed.). Upper Saddle River, NJ: Prentice Hall.

McCall, R., Appelbaum, M., & Hogarty, P. (1973). Developmental changes in mental performance. *Monographs of the Society for Research in Child Development, 38*(3, Serial No. 150).

McCarthy, J. (1991, April). *Classroom environments which facilitate innovative strategies for teaching and learning.* Paper presented at the Annual Meeting of the American Educational Research Association, Chicago.

McCarthy, S. (1994). Authors, text, and talk: The internalization of dialogue from social interaction during writing. *Reading Research Quarterly, 29,* 201–231.

McCarty, T., Lynch, R., Wallace, S., & Benally, A. (1991). Classroom inquiry and Navajo learning styles: A call for reassessment. *Anthropology and Education Quarterly, 22*(1), 42–59.

McCaslin, M., & Good, T. (1992). Compliant cognition: The misalliance of management and instructional goals in current school reform. *Educational Researcher, 21*(3), 4–17.

McClelland, D. (1985). *Human motivation.* Glenview, IL: Scott, Foresman.

McCutcheon, G. (1982). How do elementary school teachers plan? The nature of planning and influences on it. In W. Doyle & T. Good (Eds.), *Focus on teaching.* Chicago: University of Chicago Press.

McDonald-Ross, M. (1974). Behavioral objectives: A critical review. *Instructional Science, 2,* 1–51.

McKeachie, W., & Kulik, J. (1975). Effective college teaching. In F. Kerlinger (Ed.), *Review of research in education* (Vol. 3). Washington, DC: American Educational Research Association.

McLaughlin, H. J. (1994). From negation to negotiation: Moving away from the management metaphor. *Action in Teacher Education, 16*(1), 75–84.

McMann, R. (1979). In defense of lecture. *Social Studies, 70,* 270–274.

Means, B., & Knapp, M. (1991). Introduction: Rethinking teaching for disadvantaged students. In B. Means, C. Chelemer, & M. Knapp (Eds.), *Teaching advanced skills to at-risk students* (pp. 1–27). San Francisco: Jossey-Bass.

Meece, J., Blumenfeld, P., & Hoyle, R. (1988). Students' goal orientations and cognitive engagement in classroom activities. *Journal of Educational Psychology, 80,* 514–523.

Mehrabian, A., & Ferris, S. (1967). Inference of attitude from nonverbal behavior in two channels. *Journal of Consulting Psychology, 31,* 248–252.

Mehrens, W., & Lehmann, I. (1987). *Using standardized tests in education* (4th ed.). White Plains, NY: Longman.

Mercer, C., & Mercer, A. (1993). *Teaching students with learning problems* (3rd ed.). New York: Macmillan.

Mercer, J. (1973). *Labeling the mentally retarded.* Berkeley: University of California Press.

Mercer, J. (1979). *System of Multicultural Pluralistic Assessment: Technical manual.* Cleveland, OH: Psychological Corporation.

Merrill, M. (1983). Component display theory. In C. Reigeluth (Ed.), *Instructional design theories and models: An overview of their current status.* Hillsdale, NJ: Erlbaum.

Messick, S. (1989). Validity. In R. Linn (Ed.), *Educational measurement* (3rd ed., pp. 13–103). New York: Macmillan.

Meyer, C., & Foster, S. (1988). The effect of teacher self-efficacy on referral chance. *Journal of Special Education, 22,* 378–385.

Michaels, S., & O'Connor, M. (1990, Summer). *Literacy as reasoning within multiple discourses: Implications for policy and educational reform.* Paper presented at the Council of Chief State School Officers 1990 Summer Institute.

Miller, D., Barbetta, P., & Heron, T. (1994). START tutoring: Designing, training, implementing, adapting, and evaluating tutoring programs for school and home settings. In R. Gardner, D. Sianato, J. Cooper, W. Heward, T. Heron, J. Eshleman, & T.

Grossi (Eds.), *Behavior analysis in education: Focus on measurably superior instruction* (pp. 265–282). Pacific Grove, CA: Brooks/Cole.

Miller, G. (1956). Human memory and the storage of information. *IRE Transactions of Information Theory, 2-3,* 129–137.

Miller, G. (1990, April). *Critical factors in the design of successful self-instruction with disabled readers.* Paper presented at the Annual Meeting of the American Educational Research Association, Boston.

Miller, P. (1983). *Theories of developmental psychology.* New York: Freeman.

Miller, P. (1985). Metacognition and instruction. In D. Forrest-Pressley, G. MacKinnon, & T. Waller (Eds.), *Metacognition, cognition, and human performance: Vol. 2. Instructional practices.* San Diego: Academic Press.

Miller, S., Leinhardt, G., & Zigmond, N. (1988). Influencing engagement through accommodation: An ethnographic study of at-risk students. *American Educational Research Journal, 25,* 465–487.

Mishel, L., & Frankel, D. (1991). *The state of working America: 1990-1991 edition.* Armonk, NY: M. E. Sharpe.

Mitchell, R., & Pietkowska, O. (1974). Characteristics associated with underachievement. *Australian Psychologist, 9,* 19–41.

Moles, O. (1992, April). *Parental contacts about classroom behavior problems.* Paper presented at the Annual Meeting of the American Educational Research Association, San Francisco.

Monroe, S., Goldman, P., & Smith, U. (1988). *Brothers: Black and poor—A true story of courage and survivors.* New York: Morrow.

Montague, M. (1990, April). *Mathematical problem-solving characteristics of middle school students with learning disabilities.* Paper presented at the Annual Meeting of the American Educational Research Association, Boston.

Moore, T. (1990). Problem finding and teacher experience. *Journal of Creative Behavior, 24,* 39–58.

Morgan, M. (1984). Reward-induced decrements and increments in intrinsic motivation. *Review of Educational Research, 54,* 5–30.

Morgan, M. (1985). Self-monitoring of attained subgoals in private study. *Journal of Educational Psychology, 77,* 623–630.

Morgan, M. (1987). Self-monitoring and goal setting in private study. *Contemporary Educational Psychology, 12,* 1–6.

Morine-Dershimer, G., & Reeve, P. (1994). Prospective teachers' images of management. *Action in Teacher Education, 16*(1), 29–40.

Morine-Dershimer, G., & Vallance, C. (1976). *Teacher planning* (Beginning Teacher Evaluation Study, Special Report C). San Francisco: Far West Laboratory.

Morris, C. (1988). *Psychology: An introduction* (6th ed.). Upper Saddle River, NJ: Prentice Hall.

Moshman, D. (1982). Exogenous, endogenous, and dialectical constructivism. *Developmental Review, 2,* 371–384.

Moss, P. (1992, April). *Shifting conceptions of validity in educational measurement: Implications for performance assessment.* Paper presented at the Annual Meeting of the American Educational Research Association, San Francisco.

Mousavi, S., Low, R., & Sweller, J. (1995). Reducing cognitive load by mixing auditory and visual presentation modes. *Journal of Education Psychology, 87*(2), 319–334.

Mullis, I., Dossey, J., Foertsh, M., Jones, L., & Gentile, C. (1991). *Trends in academic progress.* Washington, DC: U.S. Department of Education, National Center for Education Statistics.

Mullis, I., & Jenkins, L. (1988). *The science report card: Elements of risk and recovery.* Princeton, NJ: Educational Testing Service.

Mullis, I., & Jenkins, L. (1990). *The reading report card, 1971–88: Findings from the Nation's Report Card.*

Washington, DC: U.S. Department of Education, Office of Educational Research and Improvement.

Murphy, G., & Allopena, P. (1994). The locus of knowledge effects in concept learning. *Journal of Educational Psychology, 20*(4), 904–919.

Murphy, J., Weil, M., & McGreal, T. (1986). The basic practice model of instruction. *Elementary School Journal, 87,* 83–95.

Myers, C. (1970). Journal citations and scientific eminence in contemporary psychology. *American Psychologist, 25,* 1041–1048.

Nagy-Jacklin, C. (1989). Female and male: Issues of gender. *American Psychologist, 44*(2), 127–133.

Nahmias, M. (1995). Including a child who has ADHD. *Early Childhood Today, 10*(1), 21–22.

National Center for Research on Teacher Learning. (1993). *Findings on learning to teach.* East Lansing: Michigan State University, National Center for Research on Teacher Learning.

National Commission on Excellence in Education. (1983). *A nation at risk: The imperative for educational reform.* Washington, DC: Government Printing Office.

National Commission on Testing and Public Policy. (1990). *From gatekeeper to gateway.* Chestnut Hill, MA: Boston College Press.

National Council for the Social Studies. (1984). Scope and sequences in the social studies. *Social Education, 48,* 249–262.

National Council of Teachers of Mathematics (NCTM). (1989). *Curriculum and evaluation standards for school mathematics.* Reston, VA: Author.

National Council of Teachers of Mathematics (NCTM). (1991). *Professional standards for teaching mathematics.* Reston, VA: Author.

National Joint Committee on Learning Disabilities. (1994). Learning disabilities: Issues on definition. A position paper of the National Joint

Committee in Learning Disabilities. In *Collective perspectives on issues affecting learning disability: Position papers and statements.* Austin, TX: PRO-ED.

National Research Council. (1980). *Science and engineering doctorates in the United States.* Washington, DC: National Academy of Sciences.

Needels, M., & Knapp, M. (1994). Teaching writing to children who are underserved. *Journal of Educational Psychology, 86*(3), 339–349.

Neisser, U. (1967). *Cognitive psychology.* New York: Appleton-Century-Crofts.

Nicholls, J. (1984). Achievement motivation: Conceptions of ability, subjective experience, task choice, and performance. *Psychological Review, 91,* 328–346.

Nicholls, J. (1989). *The competitive ethos and democratic education.* Cambridge, MA: Harvard University Press.

Nicholls, J., & Miller, A. (1984). Conceptions of ability and achievement motivation. In R. Ames & C. Ames (Eds.), *Research on motivation in education: Vol. 1. Student motivation* (pp. 39–73). San Diego: Academic Press.

Nickerson, R. (1986). Why teach thinking? In J. Baron & R. Sternberg (Eds.), *Teaching thinking skills: Theory and practice* (pp. 27–38). New York: Freeman.

Nickerson, R. (1988). On improving thinking through instruction. In E. Rothkopf (Ed.), *Review of research in education* (pp. 3–57). Washington, DC: American Educational Research Association.

Nickerson, R. (1989). New directions in educational assessment. *Educational Researcher, 18*(9), 3–7.

Noblit, G., Rogers, D., & McCadden, B. (1995). In the meantime: The possibilities of caring. *Phi Delta Kappan, 76,* 680–685.

Noddings, N. (1995). Teaching the themes of care. *Phi Delta Kappan, 76,* 675–679.

Nosofsky, R. (1988). Similarity, frequency, and category representations. *Journal*

of Experimental Psychology: Learning, Memory & Cognition, 14, 54–65.

Nottelman, E., & Hill, K. (1977). Test anxiety and off-task behavior in evaluative situations. *Child Development, 48,* 225–231.

Novak, J., & Gowin, B. (1984). *Learning how to learn.* New York: Cambridge University Press.

Novak, J. D., & Musonda, D. (1991). A twelve-year longitudinal study of science concept learning. *American Educational Research Journal, 28*(1), 117–153.

Nucci, L. (1987). Synthesis of research on moral development. *Educational Leadership, 44*(5), 86–92.

Nuthall, G., & Alton-Lee, A. (1993). Predicting student learning from student experience of teaching: A theory of student knowledge in classrooms. *American Educational Research Journal, 30,* 799–840.

Nystrand, M., Cohen, A., & Dowling, N. (1992, April). *Reliability of portfolio assessment for measuring verbal outcomes.* Paper presented at the Annual Meeting of the American Educational Research Association, San Francisco.

Nystrand, M., & Gamoran, A. (1989, March). *Instructional discourse and student engagement.* Paper presented at the Annual Meeting of the American Educational Research Association, San Francisco.

Oakes, J. (1990). *Multiplying inequalities: The effects of race, social class, and tracking on opportunities to learn math and science.* Santa Monica, CA: RAND.

Oakes, J. (1992). Can tracking research inform practice? *Educational Researcher, 21*(4), 12–21.

O'Donnell, A., & Dansereau, D. (1992). Scripted cooperation in student dyads: A method for analyzing and enhancing academic learning and performance. In R. Hertz-Lazarowitz & N. Miller (Eds.), *Interaction in cooperative groups: The theoretical anatomy of group learning.* Cambridge, MA: Harvard University Press.

O'Flahavan, J., Hartman, D., & Pearson, D. (1988). Teacher questioning and

feedback practices: A twenty-year retrospective. In J. Readence, R. Baldwin, J. Konopak, & P. O'Keefe (Eds.), *Dialogues in literacy research* (pp. 183–208). Chicago: National Reading Conference.

Ogbu, J. (1987). Variability in minority school performance: A problem in search of an explanation. *Anthropology and Education Quarterly, 18,* 312–334.

Ogbu, J. (1992). Understanding cultural diversity and learning. *Educational Researcher, 21*(8), 5–14.

O'Keefe, P., & Johnston, M. (1987, April). *Teachers' abilities to understand the perspectives of students: A case study of two teachers.* Paper presented at the Annual Meeting of the American Educational Research Association, Washington, DC.

Ormell, C. (1979). The problem of analyzing understanding. *Educational Research, 22,* 32–38.

Ormrod, J. (1995). *Human learning* (2nd ed.). Upper Saddle River, NJ: Merrill/Prentice Hall.

Oser, F. (1986). Moral education and values education: The discourse perspective. In M. Wittrock (Ed.), *Handbook of research on teaching* (3rd ed., pp. 917–941). New York: Macmillan.

Overton, F. (1984). Worldviews and their influence on psychological theory and research. In H. Reese (Ed.), *Advances in child development and behavior.* San Diego: Academic Press.

Page, E. B. (1992). Is the world an orderly place? A review of teacher comments and student achievement. *Journal of Experimental Education, 60*(2), 161–181.

Pajares, M. (1992). Teachers' beliefs and educational research: Cleaning up a messy construct. *Review of Educational Research, 62,* 307–322.

Palincsar, A. (1987, April). *Reciprocal teaching: Field evaluations in remedial and content area reading.* Paper presented at the Annual Meeting of the American Educational Research Association, Washington, DC.

Palincsar, A., & Brown, A. (1984). Reciprocal teaching of comprehension-fostering and comprehension-monitoring activities. *Cognition and Instruction, 2,* 117–175.

Palincsar, A., & Brown, A. (1986). Interactive teaching to promote individual learning from text. *Reading Teacher, 39,* 771–777.

Palincsar, A., & Brown, A. (1987). Advances in improving the cognitive performance of handicapped students. In M. Wang, M. Reynolds, & H. Walberg (Eds.), *Handbook of special education, research, and practice: Vol. 1. Learner characteristics and adaptive education* (pp. 93–112). New York: Pergamon Press.

Pallas, A., & Alexander, K. (1983). Sex differences in quantitative SAT performance: New evidence on the differential coursework hypothesis. *American Educational Research Journal, 20,* 165–182.

Pallas, A., Natriello, G., & McDill, E. (1989). The changing nature of the disadvantaged population: Current dimensions and future trends. *Educational Researcher, 18*(5), 16–22.

Papalia, D., & Wendkos-Olds, S. (1992). *Human development* (5th ed.). New York: McGraw-Hill.

Pavlov, I. (1928). *Lectures on conditioned reflexes* (W. Gantt, Trans.). New York: International Universities Press.

Peng, S., & Lee, R. (1992, April). *Home variables, parent-child activities, and academic achievement: A study of 1988 eighth graders.* Paper presented at the Annual Meeting of the American Educational Research Association, San Francisco.

Perkins, D. (1987). Thinking frames: An integrated perspective on teaching cognitive skills. In J. Baron & R. Sternberg (Eds.), *Teaching thinking skills: Theory and practice* (pp. 41–61). New York: Freeman.

Perkins, D. (1995). *Outsmarting IQ.* New York: Free Press.

Perkins, D., & Blythe, T. (1994). Putting understanding up front. *Educational Leadership, 51,* 4–7.

Perkins, D., Jay, E., & Tishman, S. (1993). Now conceptions of thinking: From

ontology to education. *Educational Psychologist, 28,* 67–85.

Perkins, D., & Salomon, G. (1987). Transfer and teaching thinking. In D. Perkins, J. Lochhead, & J. Bishop (Eds.), *Thinking: The Second International Conference.* Hillsdale, NJ: Erlbaum.

Perkins, D., & Salomon, G. (1989). Are cognitive skills context-bound? *Educational Researcher, 18,* 16–25.

Perry, M., Vanderstoep, S., & Yu, S. (1993). Asking questions in first-grade mathematics classes: Potential influences on mathematical thought. *Journal of Educational Psychology, 85*(1), 31–40.

Perry, R. (1985). Instructor expressiveness: Implications for improving teaching. In J. Donald & A. Sullivan (Eds.), *Using research to improve teaching* (pp. 35–49). San Francisco: Jossey-Bass.

Perry, R., Magnusson, J., Parsonson, K., & Dickens, W. (1986). Perceived control in the college classroom: Limitations in instructor expressiveness due to noncontingent feedback and lecture content. *Journal of Educational Psychology, 78,* 96–107.

Peterson, P. (1986). Selecting students and services for compensatory education: Lessons from aptitude-treatment interaction research. In B. Williams, P. Richmond, & B. Mason (Eds.), *Designs for Compensatory Education Conference: Proceedings and papers.* Washington, DC: Research and Evaluation Associates.

Peterson, P. (1992). Revising their thinking: Keisha Coleman and her third-grade mathematics class. In H. Marshall (Ed.), *Redefining student learning: Roots of educational change* (pp. 151–176). Norwood, NJ: Ablex.

Peterson, P., Marx, A., & Clark, C. (1978). Teacher planning, teacher behavior, and student achievement. *American Educational Research Journal, 15,* 417–432.

Pfiffer, L., Rosen, L., & O'Leary, S. (1985). The efficacy of an all-positive approach to classroom management. *Journal of Applied Behavior Analysis, 18,* 257–261.

Phillips, D. (1990, April). *Parents' beliefs and beyond: Contributions to children's academic self-perceptions.* Paper presented at the Annual Meeting of the American Educational Research Association, Boston.

Phillips, S. (1983). *The invisible culture: Communication in classroom and community on the Warm Springs Indian Reservation.* White Plains, NY: Longman.

Phinney, J. (1989). Stages of ethnic identity development in minority group adolescents. *Journal of Early Adolescence, 9,* 34–39.

Phinney, J., & Alipuria, L. (1990). Ethnic identity in college students from four ethnic groups. *Journal of Adolescence, 13,* 171–183.

Piaget, J. (1926). *The language and thought of the child.* New York: Harcourt, Brace & World.

Piaget, J. (1952). *Origins of intelligence in children.* New York: International Universities Press.

Piaget, J. (1959). *Language and thought of the child* (M. Grabain, Trans.). New York: Humanities Press.

Piaget, J. (1965). *The moral judgment of the child.* New York: Free Press. (Original work published 1932)

Piaget, J. (1970). *The science of education and the psychology of the child.* New York: Orion Press.

Piaget, J. (1977). Problems in equilibration. In M. Appel & L. Goldberg (Eds.), *Topics in cognitive development: Vol. 1. Equilibration: Theory, research, and application* (pp. 3–13). New York: Plenum Press.

Pintrich, P., & Garcia, T. (1991). Student goal orientation and self-regulation in the college classroom. In M. Maehr & P. Pintrich (Eds.), *Advances in motivation and achievement* (Vol. 7, pp. 371–402). Greenwich, CT: JAI Press.

Pintrich, P., Marx, R., & Boyle, R. (1993). Beyond cold conceptual change: The role of motivational beliefs and classroom contextual factors in the process of conceptual change. *Review of Educational Research, 63,* 167–199.

Pintrich, P., & Schunk, D. (1996). *Motivation in education: Theory, research, and applications.* Upper Saddle River, NJ: Prentice Hall.

Pogrow, S. (1990). Challenging at-risk students: Findings from the HOTS Program. *Phi Delta Kappan, 71*(5), 389–397.

Poole, M., Okeafor, K., & Sloan, E. (1989, April). *Teachers' interactions, personal efficacy, and change implementation.* Paper presented at the Annual Meeting of the American Educational Research Association, San Francisco.

Popham, J. (1993). Measurement-driven instruction as a "quick-fix" reform strategy. *Measurement and Evaluation in Counseling and Development, 26,* 31–34.

Porter, A. (1989). A curriculum out of balance. *Educational Researcher, 18*(5), 9–15.

Postman, L., & Underwood, B. (1973). Critical issues in interference theory. *Memory and Cognition, 1,* 19–40.

Pratton, J., & Hales, L. (1986). The effects of active participation on student learning. *Journal of Educational Research, 79,* 210–215.

Prawat, R. (1989). Promoting access to knowledge, strategy, and disposition in students: A research synthesis. *Review of Educational Research, 59,* 1–41.

Premack, D. (1965). Reinforcement theory. In D. Levine (Ed.), *Nebraska Symposium on Motivation* (Vol. 13, pp. 3–41). Lincoln: University of Nebraska Press.

Presidential Task Force on Psychology in Education. (1993). *Learner-centered psychological principles: Guidelines for school redesign and reform.* Washington, DC: American Psychological Association.

Presseisen, B. (1986). *Thinking skills: Research and practice.* Washington, DC: National Education Association.

Pressley, M., Borkowski, J., & Schneider, W. (1987). Cognitive strategies: Good strategies users coordinate metacognition and knowledge. In R. Vasta & G. Whitehurst (Eds.), *Annals of child development* (Vol. 5, pp. 89–129) Greenwich, CT: JAI Press.

Pressley, M., Harris, K., & Marks, M. (1992). But good strategy users are constructivists! *Educational Psychology Review, 4,* 3–31.

Pressley, M., Johnson, C., Symons, S., McGoldrick, J., & Kurita, J. (1989). Strategies that improve children's memory and comprehension of text. *Elementary School Journal, 90,* 3–31.

Pressley, M., Woloshyn, V., Lysynchuk, L., Martin, V., Wood, E., & Willoughby, T. (1990). A primer of research on cognitive strategy instruction: The important issues and how to address them. *Educational Psychology Review, 2,* 1–58.

Pugach, M., & Wesson, C. (1995). Teachers' and students' views of team teaching of general education and learning-disabled students in two fifth-grade classes. *Elementary School Journal, 95*(3), 279–295.

Purkey, S., & Smith, M. (1983). Effective schools: A review. *Elementary School Journal, 83,* 427–452.

Purkey, W., & Novak, J. (1984). *Inviting school success* (2nd ed.). Belmont, CA: Wadsworth.

Quin, Z., Johnson, D., & Johnson, R. (1995). Cooperative versus competitive efforts and problem solving. *Review of Educational Research, 65*(2), 129–143.

Ravetta, M., & Brunn, M. (1995, April). *Language learning, literacy, and cultural background: Second-language acquisition in a mainstreamed classroom.* Paper presented at the Annual Meeting of the American Educational Research Association, San Francisco.

Raviv, A., Raviv, A., & Reisel, E. (1990). Teachers and students: Two different perspectives? Measuring social climate in the classroom. *American Educational Research Journal, 27,* 141–157.

Reed, R. (1992, April). *Self-monitoring of attention versus self-monitoring of performance: Effect on attention and academic performance.* Paper presented at the Annual Meeting of the American Educational Research Association, San Francisco.

Reed, S., Willis, D., & Guarino, J. (1994). Selecting examples for solving word problems. *Journal of Educational Psychology, 86*(3), 380–388.

Reis, S. (1992, April). *The Curriculum Compacting Study.* Paper presented at the Annual Meeting of the American Educational Research Association, San Francisco.

Reis, S., & Purcell, J. (1992). *An analysis of content elimination and strategies used by elementary classroom teachers in the curriculum compacting process.* Storrs: University of Connecticut, National Research Center on the Gifted and Talented.

Renzulli, J. (1986). The three-ring conception of giftedness: A developmental model for creative productivity. In R. Sternberg & J. Davidson (Eds.), *Conceptions of giftedness.* Cambridge, MA: Harvard University Press.

Renzulli, J., Smith, L., & Reis, S. (1982). Curriculum compacting: An essential strategy for working with gifted students. *Elementary School Journal, 82*(3), 185–194.

Resnick, L. (1987). *Education and learning to think.* Washington, DC: National Academy Press.

Resnick, L., & Klopfer, L. (1989). Toward the thinking curriculum: An overview. In L. Resnick & L. Klopfer (Eds.), *Toward the thinking curriculum: Current cognitive research* (pp. 1–18). Alexandria, VA: Association for Supervision and Curriculum Development.

Rich, D. (1987). *Teachers and parents: An adult-to-adult approach.* Washington, DC: National Education Association.

Riley, M., Greeno, J., & Heller, J. (1982). The development of children's problem-solving ability in arithmetic. In H. Ginsburg (Ed.), *Development of mathematical thinking.* San Diego: Academic Press.

Ringness, T. (1965). Affective differences between successful and non-successful bright ninth-grade boys. *Personnel and Guidance Journal, 43,* 600–606.

Ritts, V., Patterson, M., & Tubbs, M. (1992). Expectations, impressions, and judgments of physically attractive students: A review. *Review of Educational Research, 62,* 413–426.

Roberts, W., Horn, A., & Battistich, V. (1995, April). *Assessing students' and teachers' sense of the school as a caring community.* Paper presented at the Annual Meeting of the American Educational Research Association, San Francisco.

Robins, S., & Mayer, R. (1993). Schema training in analogical reasoning. *Journal of Educational Psychology, 85*(3), 529–538.

Rogers, D. (1991, April). *Conceptions of caring in a fourth-grade classroom.* Paper presented at the Annual Meeting of the American Educational Research Association, Chicago.

Rogoff, B. (1990). *Apprenticeship in thinking: Cognitive development in social context.* New York: Oxford University Press.

Rosen, L., O'Leary, S., Joyce, S., Conway, G., & Pfiffer, L. (1984). The importance of prudent negative consequences for maintaining the appropriate behavior of hyperactive students. *Journal of Abnormal Child Psychology, 12,* 581–604.

Rosenberg, M. (1989). The effects of daily homework assignments on the acquisition of basic skills by students with learning disabilities. *Journal of Learning Disabilities, 22,* 314–323.

Rosenfield, P., Lambert, S., & Black, R. (1985). Desk arrangement effects on pupil classroom behavior. *Journal of Educational Psychology, 77,* 101–108.

Rosenshine, B. (1979). Content, time, and direct instruction. In P. Peterson & H. Walberg (Eds.), *Research on teaching: Concepts, findings, and implications* (pp. 28–56). Berkeley, CA: McCutchan.

Rosenshine, B. (1983). Teaching functions in instructional programs. *Elementary School Journal, 83,* 335–351.

Rosenshine, B. (1986). Synthesis of research on explicit teaching. *Educational Leadership, 43*(7), 60–69.

Rosenshine, B. (1987). Explicit teaching. In D. Berliner & B. Rosenshine (Eds.), *Talks to teachers.* New York: Random House.

Rosenshine, B., & Furst, N. (1971). Research on teacher performance criteria. In B. Smith (Ed.), *Research in teacher education.* Upper Saddle River, NJ: Prentice Hall.

Rosenshine, B., & Meister, C. (1992, April). *The use of scaffolds for teaching less structured academic tasks.* Paper presented at the Annual Meeting of the American Educational Research Association, San Francisco.

Rosenshine, B., & Meister, C. (1994). Reciprocal teaching: A review of the research. *Review of Educational Research, 64,* 479–530.

Rosenshine, B., & Stevens, R. (1986). Teaching functions. In M. Wittrock (Ed.), *Handbook of research on teaching* (3rd ed., pp. 376–391). New York: Macmillan.

Ross, S., Smith, L., Loks, L., & McNelie, M. (1994). Math and reading instruction in tracked first-grade classes. *Elementary School Journal, 95*(2), 105–118.

Rothenberg, J. (1989). The open classroom reconsidered. *Elementary School Journal, 90,* 68–86.

Rothman, R. (1990). New study confirms income, education linked to parent involvement in schools. *Education Week, 9*(31), 10.

Rothman, R. (1991). Schools stress speeding up, not slowing down. *Education Week, 9*(1), 11, 15.

Rotter, J. (1966). Generalized expectancies for internal versus external control of reinforcement. *Psychological Monographs, 1*(609).

Rowe, M. (1974). Relation of wait-time and rewards to the development of language, logic, and fate control: Part 1. Wait-time. *Journal of Research in Science Teaching, 11,* 81–94.

Rowe, M. (1986). Wait-time: Slowing down may be a way of speeding up. *Journal of Teacher Education, 37*(1), 43–50.

Rubin, L. (1985). *Artistry in teaching.* New York: McGraw-Hill.

Rubin, R., & Balow, B. (1978). Prevalence of teacher-identified behavior problems: A longitudinal study. *Exceptional Children, 45,* 102–111.

Ruble, D. (1988). Sex-role development. In M. Bornstein & M. Lamb (Eds.), *Developmental psychology: An advanced textbook* (2nd ed., pp. 411–460). Hillsdale, NJ: Erlbaum.

Rutherford, F., & Algren, A. (1990). *Science for all Americans.* New York: Oxford University Press.

Rutter, M., Maughan, B., Mortimore, P., Ouston, J., & Smith, A. (1979). *Fifteen thousand hours.* Cambridge, MA: Harvard University Press.

Sabban, Y., & Kay, P. (1987). Distinction between essay and objective tests in assessing writing skills of underprepared college students. *Journal of Research and Development in Education, 21*(1), 61–68.

Sadker, M., & Sadker, D. (1985, March). Sexism in the schoolroom of the 80's. *Psychology Today,* pp. 54–57.

Sadker, M., & Sadker, D. (1994). *Failing at fairness: How America's schools cheat girls.* New York: Scribner's.

Sadker, M., Sadker, D., & Klein, S. (1991). The issue of gender in elementary and secondary education. In G. Grant (Ed.), *Review of research in education* (Vol. 17, pp. 269–334). Washington, DC: American Educational Research Association.

Saigh, P. (1984). Unscheduled assessment: Test anxiety, academic achievement, and social validity. *Educational Research Quarterly, 9*(4), 6–11.

Salmon-Cox, L. (1981). Teachers and standardized achievement tests: What's really happening? *Phi Delta Kappan, 62,* 631–634.

Salvia, J., & Ysseldyke, J. (1988). *Assessment in special and remedial education* (4th ed.). Boston: Houghton Mifflin.

Samuels, S. (1988). Decoding and automaticity: Helping poor readers become automatic at word recognition. *Reading Teacher, 41*(8), 756–760.

Sardo, D. (1982, October). *Teacher planning styles in the middle school.* Paper presented at the Annual Meeting of the Eastern Educational Research Association, Ellenville, NY.

Sardo-Brown, D. (1988). Teacher's planning. *Elementary School Journal, 89,* 68–87.

Sardo-Brown, D. (1994, April). *A longitudinal study of novice secondary teachers' planning: Year two.* Paper presented at the Annual Meeting of the American Educational Research Association, New Orleans.

Scarcella, R. (1990). *Teaching language-minority students in the multicultural classroom.* Upper Saddle River, NJ: Prentice Hall.

Scheirer, M., & Kraut, R. (1979). Improving educational achievement via self-concept change. *Review of Educational Research, 49,* 131–150.

Schiff, M., Duyme, M., Dumaret, A., & Tomkiewicz, S. (1982). How much could we boost scholastic achievement and IQ scores? A direct answer from a French adoption agency. *Cognition, 12,* 165–192.

Schmidt, P. (1992). Gap cited in awareness of students' home languages. *Education Week, 11*(32), 11.

Schneider, W., & Shiffrin, R. (1977). Controlled and automatic human information processing: Detection, search, and attention. *Psychological Review, 84,* 1–66.

Schoenfeld, A. (1989). Teaching mathematical thinking and problem solving. In L. Resnick & L. Klopfer (Eds.), *Toward the thinking curriculum: Current cognitive research* (pp. 83–103). Alexandria, VA: Association for Supervision and Curriculum Development.

Schon, D. (1983). *The reflective practitioner: How professionals think in action.* New York: Basic Books.

Schunk, D. (1987). Peer models and children's behavioral change. *Review of Educational Research, 57,* 149–174.

Schunk, D. (1990). Introduction to the special section on motivation and efficacy. *Journal of Educational Psychology, 82,* 1–6.

Schunk, D. (1991). *Learning theories: An educational perspective.* Upper Saddle River, NJ: Merrill/Prentice Hall.

Schunk, D. (1994, April). *Goal and self-evaluative influences during children's mathematical skill acquisition.* Paper presented at the Annual Meeting of the American Educational Research Association, New Orleans.

Schwartz, B. (1990). The creation and destruction of value. *American Psychologist, 45,* 7–15.

Schwartz, B., & Reisberg, D. (1991). *Learning and memory.* New York: Norton.

Scott, M. (1988, April). *Analysis of the rising tide of "at-risk" students from a developmental framework.* Paper presented at the Annual Meeting of the American Educational Research Association, New Orleans.

Sears, R., Maccoby, E., & Levin, H. (1957). *Patterns of child rearing.* Evanston, IL: Row, Peterson.

Seddon, G. (1978). The properties of Bloom's taxonomy of educational objectives for the cognitive domain. *Review of Educational Research, 48,* 303–323.

Seifert, T. (1993). Effects of elaborative interrogation with prose passages. *Journal of Educational Psychology, 85*(4), 642–651.

Seligman, D. (1975). *Helplessness.* San Francisco: Freeman.

Shepard, L. (1993). Evaluating test validity. In L. Darling-Hammond (Ed.), *Review of research in education* (Vol. 19, pp. 405–450). Washington, DC: American Educational Research Association.

Sherwood, R., Kinzer, C., Bransford, J., & Franks, J. (1987). Some benefits of creating macro-contexts for science instruction: Initial findings. *Journal of Research in Science Teaching, 24,* 417–435.

Shields, P., & Shaver, D. (1990, April). *The mismatch between the school and home cultures of academically at-risk students.* Paper presented at the Annual Meeting of the American Educational Research Association, Boston.

Shinn, M., & Hubbard, D. (1992). Curriculum-based measurement and problem-solving assessment: Basic procedures and outcomes. *Focus on Exceptional Children, 24*(5), 1–2.

Short, E., Schatschneider, C., & Friebert, S. (1993). Relationship between memory and metamemory performance: A comparison of specific and general strategy knowledge. *Journal of Educational Psychology, 85*(3), 412–423.

Short, G. (1985). Teacher expectation and West Indian underachievement. *Educational Researcher, 63,* 95–101.

Shulman, J. (Ed.). (1992). *Case methods in teacher education.* New York: Teachers College Press.

Shulman, L. (1986). Those who understand: Knowledge growth in teaching. *Educational Researcher, 15*(2), 4–14.

Sieber, R. (1981). Socialization implications of school discipline, or how first graders are taught to "listen." In R. Sieber & A. Gordon (Eds.), *Children and their organizations: Investigations in American culture* (pp. 18–43). Boston: G. K. Hall.

Siegler, R. (1991). *Children's thinking* (2nd ed.). Upper Saddle River, NJ: Prentice Hall.

Simon, H. (1978). Information-processing theory of human problem solving. In W. Estes (Ed.), *Handbook of learning and cognitive processes: Vol. 5. Human information processing.* Hillsdale, NJ: Erlbaum.

Simpson, E. (1972). *The classification of educational objectives: Psychomotor domain.* Urbana: University of Illinois Press.

Simpson, J., Olejnik, S., Tam, A., & Suprattathum, S. (1994). Elaborative verbal rehearsals and college students' cognitive performance. *Journal of Educational Psychology, 86*(2), 267–278.

Skiba, R., & Raison, J. (1990). Relationship between the use of timeout and academic achievement. *Exceptional Children, 57,* 36–47.

Skinner, B. (1953). *Science and human behavior.* New York: Macmillan.

Skinner, B. (1957). *Verbal behavior.* Upper Saddle River, NJ: Prentice Hall.

Skoe, E., & Dressner, R. (1994). Ethics of care, justice, identity, and gender: An extension and replication. *Merrill-Palmer Quarterly, 40*(2), 272–289.

Slaughter-Defoe, D., Nakagawa, K., Takanashi, R., & Johnson, D. (1990). Toward cultural/ecological perspectives on schooling and achievement in African and Asian American children. *Child Development,* pp. 363–383.

Slavin, R. (1985). Team-assisted individualization: A cooperative learning solution for adaptive instruction in mathematics. In M. Wang & H. Walberg (Eds.), *Adapting instruction to individual differences.* Berkeley, CA: McCutchan.

Slavin, R. (1987). Ability grouping and student achievement in elementary schools: A best-evidence synthesis. *Review of Educational Research, 57,* 293–336.

Slavin, R. (1995). *Cooperative learning* (2nd ed.). Needham Heights, MA: Allyn & Bacon.

Slavin, R., & Karweit, N. (1982, April). *School organizational vs. developmental effects on attendance among young adolescents.* Paper presented at the Annual Meeting of the American Psychological Association, Washington, DC.

Slavin, R., Karweit, N., & Madden, N. (Eds.). (1989). *Effective programs for students at risk.* Needham Heights, MA: Allyn & Bacon.

Slavin, R., Madden, N., Karweit, N., Dolan, L., & Wasik, B. (1992). *Success for all: A relentless approach to prevention and early intervention in elementary schools.* Arlington, VA: Educational Research Service.

Smith, L., & Cotten, M. (1980). Effect of lesson vagueness and discontinuity on student achievement and attitude. *Journal of Educational Psychology, 72,* 670–675.

Smylie, M. (1989). Teachers' views of the effectiveness of sources of learning to teach. *Elementary School Journal, 89,* 543–548.

Snyder, S., Bushur, L., Hoeksema, P., Olson, M., Clark, S., & Snyder, J. (1991, April). *The effect of instructional clarity and concept structure on students' achievement and perception.* Paper presented at the Annual Meeting of the American Educational Research Association, Chicago.

Snyderman, M., & Rothman, S. (1987). Survey of expert opinion on intelligence and aptitude testing. *American Psychologist, 42,* 137–144.

Sokolove, S., Garrett, S., Sadker, M., & Sadker, D. (1990). Interpersonal communication skills. In J. Cooper (Ed.), *Classroom teaching skills* (pp. 185–228). Lexington, MA: Heath.

Spaulding, C. (1992). *Motivation in the classroom.* New York: McGraw-Hill.

Spearman, C. (1927). *The abilities of man: Their nature and measurement.* New York: Macmillan.

Spector, J. C. (1992). Predicting progress in beginning reading: Dynamic assessment of phonemic awareness. *Journal of Educational Psychology, 84*(3), 353–363.

Speidel, G. (1987). Conversation and language learning in the classroom. In K. Nelson & A. Van Kleeck (Eds.), *Children's language* (Vol. 6, pp. 99–135). Hillsdale, NJ: Erlbaum.

Spencer, D. (1988). Transitional bilingual education and the socialization of immigrants. *Harvard Educational Review, 58*(2), 133–153.

Spiro, R., Feltovich, P., Jacobson, M., & Coulson, R. (1992). Knowledge representation, content specification, and the development of skill in situation-specific knowledge assembly: Some constructivist issues as they relate to cognitive flexibility theory and hypertext. In T. Duffy & D. Jonassen (Eds.), *Constructivism and the technology of instruction: A conversation* (pp. 121–127). Hillsdale, NJ: Erlbaum.

Sprigle, J., & Schoefer, L. (1985). Longitudinal evaluation of the effects of two compensatory preschool programs on fourth-through sixth-grade students. *Developmental Psychology, 21,* 702–708.

Stahl, S., & Miller, P. (1989). Whole language and language experience approaches for beginning reading: A quantitative research synthesis. *Review of Educational Research, 59,* 87–116.

Stein, B. (1989). Memory and creativity. In J. Glover, R. Ronning, & C. Reynolds (Eds.), *Handbook of creativity.* New York: Plenum Press.

Stein, R. (1983). Hispanic parents' perspectives and participation in their children's special education program: Comparisons by program and race. *Learning Disability Quarterly, 6,* 432–439.

Steinberg, L. (1987). *Pubertal status, hormonal levels, and family relations: The distancing hypothesis.* Baltimore: Society for Research in Child Development.

Steinberg, L., Dornbusch, S., & Brown, B. (1992). Ethnic differences in adolescent achievement. *American Psychologist, 47*(6), 723–729.

Stern, E. (1993). What makes certain arithmetic word problems involving the comparison of sets so difficult for children? *Journal of Educational Psychology, 85*(1), 7–23.

Sternberg, R. (1986). *Intelligence applied: Understanding and increasing your intellectual skills.* Orlando, FL: Harcourt Brace.

Sternberg, R. (1988). *The triarchic mind.* New York: Viking.

Sternberg, R. (1989). Intelligence, wisdom, and creativity: Their natures and interrelationships. In R. Linn (Ed.), *Intelligence: Measurement, theory, and public policy* (pp. 119–146). Chicago: University of Illinois Press.

Sternberg, R. (1990). *Metaphors of mind: Conceptions of the nature of intelligence.* New York: Cambridge University Press.

Sternberg, R. (1994). Allowing for thinking styles. *Educational Leadership, 52,* 36–40.

Sternberg, R., & Frensch, P. (1993). Mechanisms of transfer. In D. Detterman & R. Sternberg (Eds.), *Transfer on trial: Intelligence, cognition, and instruction.* Norwood, NJ: Ablex.

Sternberg, R., & Lubart R. (1995). *Defying the crowd.* New York: Free Press.

Stevenson, H., Chen, C., & Uttal, D. (1990). Beliefs and achievements: A study of Black, White, and Hispanic children. *Child Development, 61,* 508–523.

Stevenson, H., & Fantuzzo, J. (1986). The generality and social validity of a competency-based self-control training intervention for underachieving students. *Journal of Applied Behavior Analysis, 19,* 269–276.

Stevenson, H., Lee, S., & Stigler, J. (1986). Mathematics achievement of Chinese, Japanese, and American children. *Science, 231,* 693–699.

Stiggins, R. (1994). *Student-centered classroom assessment.* Upper Saddle River, NJ: Merrill/Prentice Hall.

Stiggins, R., & Conklin, N. (1992). *In teachers' hands.* Albany: State University of New York Press.

Stiggins, R., Conklin, N., & Bridgeford, N. (1986). Classroom assessment: A key to effective education. *Educational Measurement: Issues and Practice, 5*(2), 5–17.

Stipek, D. (1984). The development of achievement motivation. In R. Ames & C. Ames (Eds.), *Research on motivation in education: Vol. 1. Student motivation.* San Diego: Academic Press.

Stipek, D. (1993). *Motivation to learn* (2nd ed.). Needham Heights, MA: Allyn & Bacon.

Stipek, D., & Gralinski, H. (1991, April). *Gender differences in children's achievement-related beliefs and emotional responses to success and failure in math.* Paper presented at the Annual Meeting of the American Educational Research Association, Boston.

Stoddart, T., Connell, M., Stofflett, R., & Peck, D. (1993). Reconstructing elementary teacher candidates' understanding of mathematics and science content. *Teaching and Teacher Education, 9,* 229–241.

Stodolsky, S. (1988). *The subject matters: Classroom activity in math and social studies.* Chicago: University of Chicago Press.

Stowe, C. (1992, April). *At-risk language-minority preschool children.* Paper presented at the Annual Meeting of the American Educational Research Association, San Francisco.

Strickland, B. B., & Turnbull, A. P. (1990). *Developing and implementing individualized education programs* (3rd ed.). New York: Macmillan.

Strom, B. (1990, April). *Teacher perceptions of talented and gifted minority children: An exploration.* Paper presented at the Annual Meeting of the American Educational Research Association, Boston.

Strom, S. (1989). The ethical dimension of teaching. In M. Reynolds (Ed.), *Knowledge base for the beginning teacher* (pp. 267–276). New York: Pergamon Press.

Sudweeks, R., Baird, J., & Petersen, G. (1990, April). *Test-wise responses of third-, fifth-, and sixth-grade students to clued and unclued multiple-choice science items.* Paper presented at the Annual Meeting of the American Educational Research Association, Boston.

Sulzer-Azaroff, B., & Mayer, G. (1986). *Achieving educational excellence using behavioral strategies.* New York: Holt, Rinehart & Winston.

Sutton, C. (1989). Helping the nonnative English speaker with reading. *Reading Teacher, 42*(9), 684–688.

Svenson, A. (1971). *Relative achievement: School performance in relation to intelligence, sex, and home environment.* Stockholm: Almquist & Wiksell.

Swartz, R. (1987). Critical thinking, the curriculum, and the problem of transfer. In D. Perkins, J. Lochhead, & J. Bishop (Eds.), *Thinking: Progress in research and teaching.* Hillsdale, NJ: Erlbaum.

Swialth, M., & Benbow, C. (1991). Ten-year longitudinal follow-up of ability-match accelerated and unaccelerated gifted students. *Journal of Educational Psychology, 83*(4), 528–538.

Szafran, R. (1981). Question-pool study guides: Effects on test anxiety and learning retention. *Teaching Sociology, 9,* 31–43.

Tatsuoka, K. K., & Tatsuoka, M. M. (1987). Bug distribution and statistical pattern classification. *Psychometrika, 52,* 193–206.

Taylor, J. (1983). Influence of speech variety on teachers' evaluation of reading comprehension. *Journal of Educational Psychology, 75,* 662–667.

Taylor, R. (1987, March). *Knowledge for critical thinking.* Paper presented at the meeting of the Near East South Asia Council for Overseas Schools, Nairobi, Kenya.

Taylor, R. (1989). *Assessment of exceptional children* (2nd ed.). Upper Saddle River, NJ: Prentice Hall.

Tennyson, R., & Cocchiarella, M. (1986). An empirically based instructional design theory for teaching concepts. *Review of Educational Research, 56,* 40–71.

Terman, L., Baldwin, B., & Bronson, E. (1925). Mental and physical traits of a thousand gifted children. In L. Terman (Ed.), *Genetic studies of genius* (Vol. 1). Stanford, CA: Stanford University Press.

Terman, L., & Oden, M. (1947). The gifted child grows up. In L. Terman (Ed.), *Genetic studies of genius* (Vol. 4). Stanford, CA: Stanford University Press.

Terman, L., & Oden, M. (1959). The gifted group in mid-life. In L. Terman (Ed.), *Genetic studies of genius* (Vol. 5). Stanford, CA: Stanford University Press.

Tharp, R. (1989). Psychocultural variables and constants: Effects on teaching and learning in schools. *American Psychologist, 44*(2), 349–359.

Thomas, E., & Robinson, H. (1972). *Improving reading in every class: A source book for teachers.* Needham Heights, MA: Allyn & Bacon.

Thompson, M., McLaughlin, C., & Smith, R. (1995). *Merrill physical science.* Westerville, OH: Glencoe.

Thorndike, E. (1924). Mental discipline in high school studies. *Journal of Educational Psychology, 15,* 1–2, 83–98.

Thorndike, R., Hagen, E., & Sattler, J. (1986). *The Stanford-Binet Intelligence Scale* (4th ed.). Chicago: Riverside.

Thornton, M., & Fuller, R. (1981). How do college students solve proportion problems? *Journal of Research in Science Teaching, 18,* 335–340.

Tishman, S., Perkins, D., & Jay, E. (1995). *The thinking classroom: Creating a culture of thinking.* Needham Heights, MA: Allyn & Bacon.

Tobin, K. (1987). Role of wait-time in higher cognitive level learning. *Review of Educational Research, 57*(1), 69–95.

Top, B., & Osgthorpe, R. (1987). Reverse-role tutoring: The effects of handicapped students tutoring regular class students. *Elementary School Journal, 87*(4), 413–423.

Torrance, E. (1983). Status of creative women past, present, future. *Creative Child and Adult Quarterly, 8,* 135–144.

Torrance, E. (1984). Some products of 25 years of creativity research. *Educational Perspectives, 22*(3), 3–8.

Torrance, E. (1986). Teaching creative and gifted learners. In M. Wittrock (Ed.), *Handbook of research on teaching* (3rd ed., pp. 630–647). New York: Macmillan.

Trentham, L. (1975). The effect of distractions on sixth-grade students in a testing situation. *Psychology in the Schools, 16,* 439–443.

Trujillo, C. (1986). A comparative examination of classroom interactions between professors and minority and non-minority college students. *American Educational Research Journal, 23,* 629–642.

Tulving, E. (1979). Relation between encoding specificity and level of processing. In L. Cermak & F. Craik (Eds.), *Levels of processing and human memory* (pp. 405–428). Hillsdale, NJ: Erlbaum.

Turiel, E. (1973). Stage transitions in moral development. In R. Travers (Ed.), *Second handbook of research on teaching* (pp. 732–758). Chicago: Rand McNally.

Turnbull, A., Turnbull, H. R., Shank, M., & Leal, D. (1995). *Exceptional lives.* Upper Saddle River, NJ: Prentice Hall.

Turner, J. (1995). The influence of classroom contexts on young children's motivation for literacy. *Reading Research Quarterly, 30,* 410–441.

Tyler, R. (1950). *Basic principles of curriculum and instruction.* Chicago: University of Chicago Press.

Ugurogulu, M., & Walberg, H. (1979). Motivation and achievement: A quantitative synthesis. *American Educational Research Journal, 16,* 375–389.

Urdan, T., & Paris, S. (1991). Teachers' perceptions of standardized achievement tests. *Educational Policy, 8*(2) 137–156.

U.S. Bureau of the Census. (1992). *Statistics.* Washington, DC: Author.

U.S. Congress. (1978). Educational Amendment of 1978, P.L. 95–561, IX(A).

U.S. Department of Education. (1988, June 20). Final research priorities establishment. *Federal Register, 23,* 192–193, 195.

U.S. Department of Education. (1993). *Fifteenth annual report to Congress on the implementation of the Individuals With Disabilities Act.* Washington, DC: Government Printing Office.

U.S. Department of Education. (1994). *Sixteenth annual report to Congress on the implementation of the Individuals With Disabilities Act.* Washington, DC: Government Printing Office.

Vaillant, G., & Vaillant, C. (1981). Natural history of male psychological health: Work as a predictor of positive mental health. *American Journal of Psychiatry, 138,* 1433–1440.

Valverde, L. (1982). The self-evolving supervisor. In T. Sergiovanni (Ed.), *Supervision of teaching* (pp. 81–89). Alexandria, VA: Association for Supervision and Curriculum Development.

Vanderstoep, S., & Seifert, C. (1994). Problem solving, transfer, and thinking. In P. Pintrich, D. Brown, & C. Weinstein (Eds.), *Student motivation, cognition, and learning* (pp. 27–49). Hillsdale, NJ: Erlbaum.

Van Leuvan, P., Wang, M., & Hildebrandt, L. (1990, April). *Students' use of self-instructive processes in the first and second grade.* Paper presented at the Annual Meeting of the American Educational Research Association, Boston.

VanTassel-Baska, J., Patton, J., & Prillaman, D. (1989). Disadvantaged gifted learners at risk for educational attention. *Focus on Exceptional Children, 22*(3), 2–3.

Vaughn, S., McIntosh, R., Spencer, R., & Rowe, T. (1990, April). *Increasing peer acceptance with low-accepted LD students: An intervention model.* Paper presented at the Annual Meeting of the American Educational Research Association, Boston.

Veenman, S. (1984). Perceived problems of beginning teachers. *Review of Educational Research, 54,* 143–178.

Villegas, A. (1991). *Culturally responsive pedagogy for the 1990s and beyond.* Princeton, NJ: Educational Testing Service.

Vito, R., & Connell, J. (1988, April). *A longitudinal study of at-risk high school students: A theory-based description and intervention.* Paper presented at the Annual Meeting of the American Educational Research Association, New Orleans.

Voss, J. (1987). Learning and transfer in subject-matter learning: A problem-solving model. *International Journal of Educational Research, 11,* 607–622.

Vygotsky, L. (1978). *Mind in society: The development of higher psychological processes* (M. Cole, V. John-Steiner, S. Scribner, & E. Souberman, Eds. & Trans.). Cambridge, MA: Harvard University Press.

Vygotsky, L. (1986). *Thought and language.* Cambridge: MIT Press.

Wade, S., Trathen, W., & Schraw, G. (1990). An analysis of spontaneous study strategies. *Reading Research Quarterly, 25,* 147–166.

Wadsworth, B. (1996). *Piaget's theory of cognitive and affective development* (5th ed.). White Plains, NY: Longman.

Wagner, R., & Sternberg, R. (1985). Practical intelligence in real-world pursuits: The role of tacit knowledge. *Journal of Personality and Social Psychology, 52,* 1236–1247.

Walberg, H. (1984). Improving the productivity of America's schools. *Educational Leadership, 41*(8), 19–27.

Walberg, H. (1991). Improving school science in advanced and developing countries. *Review of Educational Research, 61,* 25–70.

Walberg, H., Paschal, R., & Weinstein, T. (1985). Homework's powerful effects on learning. *Educational Leadership, 42*(7), 76–79.

Walker, D., Greenwood, C., Hart, B., & Carta, J. (1994). Prediction of school outcomes based on early language production and socioeconomic factors. *Child Development, 65,* 606–621.

Walker, H., & Bullis, M. (1991). Behavior disorder and the social context of regular class integration: A conceptual dilemma. In J. Lloyd, N. Singh, & A. Repp (Eds.), *The regular education initiative: Alternative perspectives on concepts, issues, and models* (pp. 75–94). Sycamore, IL: Sycamore.

Walker, J. (1996). *The psychology of learning: Principles and processes.* Upper Saddle River, NJ: Prentice Hall.

Walsh, D. (1991). Extending the discourse on developmental appropriateness: A developmental perspective. *Early Education and Development, 2*(2), 109–119.

Wang, M., Haertel, G., & Walberg, H. (1993). Toward a knowledge base for school learning. *Review of Educational Research, 63*(3), 249–294.

Wang, M., Haertel, G., & Walberg, H. (1995, April). *Educational resilience: An emerging construct.* Paper presented at the Annual Meeting of the American Educational Research Association, San Francisco.

Ward, T., Ward, S., Landrum, M., & Patton, J. (1992, April). *Examination of a new protocol for the identification of at-risk gifted learners.* Paper presented at the Annual Meeting of the American Educational Research Association, San Francisco.

Washington, V., & Miller-Jones, D. (1989). Teacher interactions with non-Standard-English speakers during reading instruction. *Contemporary Child Psychology, 14,* 280–312.

Waterman, A. (1985). Identity in the context of adolescent psychology. *New Directions for Child Development, 30,* 5–24.

Watson, B., & Konicek, R. (1990). Teaching for conceptual change: Confronting children's experience. *Phi Delta Kappan, 71,* 680–685.

Wayson, W., & Lasley, T. (1984). Climates for excellence: Schools that foster self-discipline. *Phi Delta Kappan, 65,* 419–421.

Webb, N., Farivar, S. (1994). Promoting helping behavior in cooperative small groups in middle school mathematics, *American Educational Research Journal, 31*(2), 369–395.

Wechsler, D. (1991). *The Wechsler Intelligence Scale for Children—Third Edition—WISC-III.* San Antonio, TX: Psychological Corporation.

Weiland, A., & Coughlin, R. (1979). Self-identification and preferences: A comparison of White and Mexican American first and third graders. *Journal of Social Psychology, 10,* 356–365.

Weinberg, R. (1989). Intelligence and IQ. *American Psychologist, 44,* 98–104.

Weiner, B. (1990). History of motivational research in education. *Journal of Educational Psychology, 82,* 616–622.

Weiner, B., Graham, S., Taylor, S., & Meyer, W. (1983). Social cognition in the classroom. *Educational Psychologist, 18,* 109–124.

Weinstein, C. (1994). Strategic learning/strategic teaching: Flip sides of a coin. In P. Pintrich, D. Brown, & C. Weinstein (Eds.), *Student motivation, cognition, and learning* (pp. 257–273). Hillsdale, NJ: Erlbaum.

Weinstein, C., & Mignano, A. (1993). *Elementary classroom management.* New York: McGraw-Hill.

Weinstein, C., Woolfolk, A., Dittmeier, L., & Shankar, U. (1994). Protector or prison guard? Using metaphors and media to explore student teachers' thinking about classroom management. *Action in Teacher Education, 16*(1), 41–54.

Wentzel, K. (1991). Social competence at school: Relation between social responsibility and academic achievement. *Review of Educational Research, 61*(1), 1–24.

Whimbey, A. (1980). Students can learn to be better problem solvers. *Educational Leadership, 37,* 560–565.

White, A., & Bailey, J. (1990). Reducing disruptive behaviors of elementary physical education students with sit and watch. *Journal of Applied Behavior Analysis, 23,* 353–359.

White, M. (1975). Natural rates of teacher approval and disapproval in the classroom. *Journal of Applied Behavior Analysis, 8,* 367–372.

White, R. (1959). Motivation reconsidered: The concept of competence. *Psychological Review, 66,* 297–333.

Wigfield, A., & Eccles, J. (1989). Test anxiety in elementary and secondary school students. *Educational Psychologist, 24,* 159–183.

Wilkie, V. (1985). Richardson Study, Q's & A's. *G/C/T, 36,* 2–9.

Williams, J. (1992, April). *Effects of test anxiety and self-concept on performance across curricular areas.* Paper presented at the Annual Meeting of the American Educational Research Association, San Francisco.

Williams, R. (1987). Current issues in classroom behavior management. In J. Glover & R. Ronning (Eds.), *Historical foundations of educational psychology* (pp. 297–325). New York: Plenum Press.

Willoughby, T., Wood, E., & Khan, M. (1994). Isolating variables that impact on or detract from the effectiveness of elaboration strategies. *Journal of Educational Psychology, 86*(2), 279–289.

Wilson, S., Shulman, L., & Richert, A. (1987). 150 different ways of knowing: Representations of knowledge in teaching. In J. Calderhead (Ed.), *Exploring teacher thinking* (pp. 104–124). London: Cassel.

Winitzky, N. (1991). Multicultural and mainstreamed classrooms. In R.

Arends, *Learning to teach* (2nd ed., pp. 125–148). New York: McGraw-Hill.

Winn, J. (1992, April). *The promises and challenges of scaffolded instruction.* Paper presented at the Annual Meeting of the American Educational Research Association, San Francisco.

Winterton, W. A. (1977). The effect of extended wait-time on selected verbal response characteristics of some Pueblo Indian children (Doctoral dissertation, University of New Mexico, 1976). *Dissertation Abstracts International, 38,* 620-A. (University Microfilms No. 77-16, 130)

Wlodkowski, R. (1984). *Motivation and teaching.* Washington, DC: National Education Association.

Wolfram, W. (1991). *Dialects and American English.* Upper Saddle River, NJ: Prentice Hall.

Wong-Fillmore, L. (1992). When learning a second language means losing the first. *Education, 6*(2), 4–11.

Wood, T., Cobb, P., & Yackel, E. (1992). Change in learning mathematics: Change in teaching mathematics. In H. Marshall (Ed.), *Redefining student learning: Roots of educational change* (pp. 177–205). Norwood, NJ: Ablex.

Woodcock, R. (1995, April). *Conceptualizations of intelligence and their implications for education.* Paper presented at the Annual Meeting of the American Educational Research Association, San Francisco.

Woolfolk, A., & Brooks, D. (1985). The influence of teachers' nonverbal behaviors on students' perceptions and performance. *Elementary School Journal, 85,* 514–528.

Worthen, B. (1993). Critical issues that will determine the future of alternative assessment. *Phi Delta Kappan, 74,* 444–454.

Wright, S., & Taylor, D. (1995). Identity and the language of the classroom: Investigating the impact of heritage versus second-language instruction on personal and collective self-esteem. *Journal of Educational Psychology, 87*(2), 241–252.

Ysseldyke, J., O'Sullivan, P., Thurlow, M., & Christenson, S. (1989). Qualitative differences in reading and math instruction received by handicapped students. *Remediate and Special Education, 10*(1), 14–20.

Yussen, S., & Levy, V. (1975). Developmental changes in predicting one's own span of short-term memory. *Journal of Experimental Child Psychology, 19,* 502–508.

Zahorik, J. (1975, April). *Teachers' planning models.* Paper presented at the Annual Meeting of the American Educational Research Association, Washington, DC.

Zahorik, J. (1991). Teaching style and textbooks. *Teaching and Teacher Education, 7,* 185–196.

Zahorik, J. (1992). Good teaching and supervision. *Journal of Curriculum and Supervision, 7,* 393–404.

Zens, J., Curtis, M., Graden, J., & Ponti, C. (1988). *Helping students succeed in the regular classroom.* San Francisco: Jossey-Bass.

Zimmerman, B. (1990). Self-regulated academic learning and achievement: The emergence of a social cognitive perspective. *Educational Psychology Review, 2,* 173–201.

Zimmerman, B., & Blotner, R. (1979). Effects of model persistence and success on children's problem solving. *Journal of Educational Psychology, 71,* 508–513.

Glossary

ability grouping The placing of students of similar abilities and backgrounds in the same class or subject for instruction.

academic rules A type of cognitive learning that describes a relationship between two concepts which has been arbitrarily derived by people.

academic self-concept The part of general self-concept that deals with our perception of our competence as students.

acceleration An educational program that provides the same basic academic menu but allows more academically advanced students to move through the curriculum at a faster rate.

accommodation A form of adaptation in which an existing scheme is changed in response to new experiences or information.

accountability In standardized testing, it consists of setting goals and making both students and educators responsible for attaining them.

achievement motivation The drive to excel at learning tasks; related to the learner's capacity to experience pride in accomplishment.

achievement tests Tests designed to measure how much students have learned in different content areas.

active listening Listening characterized by devoting full attention to the speaker, responding to both the intellectual and emotional content of the message.

adaptation The process of adjusting our schemes and experiences to each other in order to maintain a state of equilibrium.

adaptive fit The degree to which a learner is able to cope with the requirements of a school setting and the extent to which the school accommodates the student's special needs.

affective domain The part of the school curriculum dealing with students' attitudes and values.

algorithm A specified set of steps for solving problems.

alternative assessment The direct examination of student performance on significant tasks that are relevant to life outside of school.

analogy A comparison in which some likeness exists between otherwise dissimilar ideas.

anxiety Emotional arousal to the point of general uneasiness and tension.

application The direct use of concepts and principles in the classroom; the third level of Bloom's cognitive taxonomy.

aptitude tests Tests designed to predict the potential for future learning.

arousal A physical and psychological reaction to the environment.

assertive discipline A discipline program based on behavioral principles that carefully specifies rules as well as positive and negative consequences for student behaviors.

assessment system The combined and coordinated elements of classroom assessment, including observations of students' seatwork and homework, voluntary responses and answers to questions, teacher-made and standardized tests, performance observations, and instructional decisions, such as assigning grades, reteaching a topic, or providing supplementary instruction.

assimilation A form of adaptation in which an experience in the environment is incorporated to fit an existing scheme.

at-risk students Children in danger of failing to complete their education with the skills necessary to survive in a modern technological society.

attention The cognitive process that is an organism's orienting response to a stimulus or stimuli. (Also, the first step in the observational learning process, during which learners focus on a model's behavior.)

attention deficit/hyperactivity disorder (AD/HD) A type of learning problem in which students experience difficulties because of an inability to focus their attention on the learning task at hand; often characterized by failure to finish tasks, failure to listen, easy distractibility, difficulty in concentrating, impulsiveness, and a high need for supervision.

attributions Explanations (perceived causes) created to account for a student's successes and failures.

attribution theory A cognitive view of motivation that focuses on students' explanations for their own successes and failures in classroom situations.

authentic assessment Assessments that directly measure student performance through "real life" tasks.

authentic task A classroom learning activity that requires understanding similar to understanding that would be used in the world outside the classroom.

automaticity   A process that occurs when information or operations are overlearned and can be retrieved and used with little mental effort.

autonomous morality   A type of moral thinking that includes rational ideas of fairness and a view of justice as a reciprocal process of treating others as they would want to be treated.

autonomy   Erikson's state of psychosocial development in toddlerhood (1–3 years), in which independence is developed through successful experiences fostered by support and structure.

basic processes   The fundamental constituents of thinking; thinking "tools."

behavior disorder (BD)   A type of exceptionality characterized by the display of serious and persistent age-inappropriate behaviors that result in social conflict, personal unhappiness, and school failure; sometimes referred to as emotionally disturbed or emotionally handicapped.

bidialecticism   The ability to switch back and forth between a dialect and Standard English.

Bloom's taxonomy   A system for the classification of cognitive teaching objectives that includes six levels: knowledge, comprehension, application, analysis, synthesis, and evaluation.

body of knowledge   An integrated system of information; the content of educational psychology that can help teachers improve their teaching.

caring   The ability to empathize with and invest in the protection and development of young people.

case studies   Segments of teachers' professional lives that focus on specific features of classroom activities or professional events, deal with the classroom and teachers' interactions with students or with larger issues such as learning to teach and professional growth, and are designed to provide the reader with a realistic segment of the real world of teaching.

centration   The tendency to focus on one perceptual aspect of an event to the exclusion of all others.

characteristics   A concept's defining features.

checklists   An assessment procedure using a list of observable criteria used to determine whether or not students demonstrate an expected performance, e.g., to assess students' ability to properly design a laboratory procedure when given an outline of specific directions.

chunking   The process of combining separate items into larger, and usually more meaningful, units.

classical conditioning   Respondent learning in which a previously neutral stimulus is paired with an unconditioned stimulus to produce a conditioned response.

classification   The grouping of objects that are alike into categories according to common characteristics.

classroom assessment   Involves all the processes and tools teachers use to make decisions about their students' progress; it includes observations of students' seatwork and homework, voluntary responses and answers to questions, and results on teacher-made and standardized tests.

classroom climate   The atmosphere in a classroom that is influenced by teacher affective behaviors, teacher expectations, management, and interaction patterns.

classroom management   All the teacher behaviors and classroom organizational factors that lead to an orderly learning environment.

closure   A form of review that occurs at the end of a lesson.

cognitive apprenticeship   Occurs when a less skilled learner works at the side of an expert.

cognitive domain   The intellectual dimension of schooling; objectives that deal with knowledge and understanding of facts, concepts, principles, rules, skills, and problem-solving abilities.

cognitive learning theories   Explanations for learning that focus on the internal mental processes people use in their effort to make sense of the world.

cognitive modeling   Modeled demonstrations, together with verbal descriptions of the model's thoughts and actions.

cognitive processes   Internal, intellectual actions that transform information and transfer it from one storage place to another.

cognitive theories of motivation   Theories of motivation dealing with our need to understand the world, to have control over our lives, and to be self-directed.

collective self-esteem   Children's perceptions of the relative worth of the groups to which they belong.

competence motivation   An innate characteristic of human beings that energizes people to master tasks and skills.

completion items   A testing method that includes a question or incomplete statement that requires the learner to supply appropriate words, numbers, or symbols.

comprehension monitoring   The phase of the lecture-recitation cycle used to assess students' understanding of information that has been presented.

concept   An abstraction, category, or set that groups objects, events, or ideas based on common characteristics.

concept mapping   A teaching strategy in which pictures or diagrams are used to illustrate the logical relations represented in a concept analysis.

concrete operational stage   Piaget's third stage of development (approximately 7–11 years), characterized by operating logically with concrete, visual materials and by classifying and ordering serially.

conditioned response   In classical conditioning, the consistent result or reaction to a previously neutral stimulus that has been paired with an unconditioned stimulus.

conditioned stimulus   Particular situations or events that induce a conditioned response.

connected discourse   A positive characteristic of lessons that increases learning through thematic organization that leads to a point.

consequence   In operant conditioning, an outcome that occurs after a behavior is demonstrated; reinforced behaviors are strengthened and punished behaviors are weakened.

conservation   The idea that the "amount" of a substance stays the same regardless of its shape or the number of pieces into which it is divided.

construct validity   The conceptual connection between a test and what it is designed to measure.

constructivism   A growing movement in education that places primary importance on direct experience and students' active construction of mental structures, and that de-emphasizes lecturing and "telling" as instructional tools.

content validity   The overlap between what is taught and what is tested.

context   The surrounding or environment in which an individual, object, or idea exists.

contextual planning model   A model which considers the traditional questions of teaching, such as goals, learning activities, student motivation, and assessment but answers the questions by focusing on guiding learners' own constructions and understandings and helping them learn to monitor their own thinking and learning, rather than simply "transmitting" knowledge.

contiguity   A behavioral view of learning which emphasizes simple stimulus-response (S-R) pairings through which associative learning occurs.

continuous reinforcement   A schedule in which a learner is reinforced for every desired response.

convergent thinking   Thinking that tends to focus on one solution to a problem.

cooperative learning   A set of instructional procedures that organizes students into groups in collaborative efforts to learn content or master skills.

creativity   The ability to create original and divergent products in the solution of some problem.

crisis   In Erikson's theory a time of particular vulnerability to a certain psychological challenge.

criterion referencing   The assignment of a grade or value to a test according to a predetermined standard.

critical thinking   The ability to accurately and efficiently gather, interpret, and evaluate information.

cues   Antecedent stimuli that prompt the learner to display desired behavior.

cultural deficit models   A view of cultural differences suggesting that the linguistic, social, or cultural backgrounds of minority children are the primary cause of poor academic performance or failure.

cultural difference models   A view of cultural differences which emphasizes the strengths of different cultures and looks for ways that instructional practice can recognize and build on those strengths.

cultural inversion   The tendency for involuntary minorities to regard certain forms of behavior, events, symbols, and meanings as inappropriate for them because these are characteristic of white Americans.

culturally responsive teaching   Teaching that acknowledges cultural diversity in classrooms and accommodates this diversity in instruction.

culture   The collective attitudes, values, beliefs, and ways of acting and interacting that characterizes a social group.

curiosity   A cognitive view of motivation that is based on the idea that students derive pleasure from activities with an optimal (intermediate) level of surprise, discrepancy, or incongruity—each of which induces arousal.

curriculum-based measurement   The assessment of special education students in specific areas of the curriculum that they will encounter in the regular classroom.

curriculum compacting   An approach to individualization that identifies mastered content, concentrates teaching on content not yet mastered, and uses the time saved for acceleration or enrichment.

deaf   An exceptionality in which hearing is impaired enough so that other channels such as lip reading or manual spelling are used to communicate.

declarative knowledge   Knowledge of facts, definitions, generalizations, and rules and the ability to verbalize this knowledge.

deficiency needs   The four lowest levels of Maslow's needs—survival, safety, belonging, and self-esteem; these must be met before higher needs can be focused upon.

definition   A description that includes the concept name, a superordinate concept, and the concept's characteristics.

desist   A teacher action designed to stop a student behavior.

development   Orderly, durable changes in a learner resulting from a combination of learning, experience, and maturation.

diagnostic test   A test designed to provide a detailed description of pupils' strengths and weaknesses in a particular skill area, such as reading or math.

dialect   A variation of Standard English that is distinct in vocabulary, grammar, or pronunciation.

direct instruction   A highly structured, teacher-centered, goal-oriented approach to teaching, characterized by teacher presentation, teacher modeling, and student practice with feedback.

discipline   The subset of management that focuses directly on teacher actions in reaction to student behavior that detracts from the order and safety of the environment or interferes with the opportunity to learn.

discovery learning   An instructional approach that provides students with data and then requires them to process this information into meaningful patterns or abstractions.

discrimination   The ability to give different responses to related but not identical stimuli; the process of making perceptual distinctions.

discussions   Interactive student-centered instructional approaches designed to stimulate thinking, challenge attitudes and beliefs, and develop interpersonal skills through student to student communication.

distracters   The incorrect alternatives on a test item, designed to seem plausible to students who don't fully understand the content being measured in the item.

divergent thinking   Thinking in which problem solvers consider solutions that are novel or alternate ways of conceptualizing or thinking about the original problem.

drawing analogies   An attempt to solve unfamiliar problems by comparing them with familiar ones that have already been solved.

dynamic assessment   An approach to evaluation which emphasizes measurement in realistic settings.

egocentrism   The developmentally-related inability to interpret an event from someone else's point of view.

elaboration   The process of increasing the number of associations between items of information in long-term memory, which in turn increases meaningfulness, retention, and retrieval.

elaborative questioning   The process of drawing inferences, citing examples, or identifying implications of the materials being studied.

elaborative rehearsal   The process of associating information the person wants to remember with information already stored in long-term memory.

emphasis   A signal alerting students to important information in a lesson; occurs through vocal or verbal behavior, or repetition.

encoding   The process of forming mental representations based on the critical features of a learning task.

English as a second language (ESL) programs   "Pull-out" programs designed to help students learn English as quickly as possible.

enrichment   An educational program that provides richer and more varied content through strategies that supplement or go beyond normal grade level work.

entity view of ability   The view that ability is fixed and cannot be altered with effort; can be characteristic of failure-avoiding students.

equilibration   The drive for order that involves the testing of patterns or structures against the real world.

equilibrium   An instinctive or innate need in people to find order, structure, and predictability in their existence.

essay items   Extended response items testing the ability to organize ideas, to make and defend arguments, or to express ideas through compositional writing.

essential management skills   The general management strategies effective managers use regardless of grade level or setting.

essential teaching skills   The teaching skills all teachers should display regardless of grade level, content area, or topic.

ethnicity   A student's ancestry or membership in a group in which members continue to identify themselves with the nation from which they or their ancestors came.

evaluation   Decisions made on the basis of measurements collected by teachers.

examples   Cases that illustrate a particular concept.

exceptionalities   Differences in a person that require special help and resources to help the learner reach his or her full potential.

expectancy × value theories   Theories of motivation suggesting that learners will be motivated to work on a task to the extent that they expect to succeed on the task and the degree to which they value achievement on the task.

expert   An individual who is highly skilled or knowledgeable in a given domain.

extinction   The gradual disappearance of a learned response when the conditioned stimulus occurs repeatedly in the absence of the unconditioned stimulus (classical conditioning); the gradual disappearance of a learned behavior when it isn't reinforced.

extrinsic motivation   Motivation that comes from outside the learner, such as reinforcement through grades or candy.

feedback   Information about the accuracy or appropriateness of a response or current behavior that can be used to improve future performance.

firmness   The viewing of students as capable of exercising responsibility and holding them accountable for their actions.

fixed-interval schedule   A schedule in which the learner is reinforced after a predictable length of time, such as every five minutes.

fixed-ratio schedule   A schedule in which the learner is reinforced after every third, or fifth, or some other predictable number of responses.

forgetting   The loss of, or inability to retrieve, information from memory.

formal measurement   Systematic measurement devices in which all students respond to the same items under the same conditions.

formal operational stage   Piaget's fourth state of development (approximately 11 years–adult), characterized by the ability to solve abstract and hypothetical problems and to think combinatorially.

formative evaluation   Measurements given strictly for the purpose of providing the teacher and students with instructional feedback; given, scored, and discussed but not included in any grading decision.

frequency distribution   A graphical means of summarizing test data by counting and displaying the number of people obtaining each score.

functional fixedness   The tendency to think of objects or ideas as having only one use or function.

general transfer   The ability to take knowledge previously learned and apply it to a broad range of unique situations.

generalization (behaviorism)   A process that occurs when a stimulus related to a conditioned stimulus elicits a conditioned response all by itself (classical conditioning); responses given to similar but not identical stimuli that occur as a result of reinforcement (operant conditioning).

generalization   In strategy instruction the spontaneous use of a cognitive strategy in a unique situation; in terms of content, abstractions that express relationships between concepts and which summarize large amounts of information.

generative knowledge   Meaningful knowledge that can be used to interpret new situations.

generativity   Erikson's stage of psychosocial development in middle adulthood, characterized by productivity, creativity, and a concern for the next generation and achieved through success on the job and a growing sense of social responsibility.

gifted and talented students   Students at the upper end of the ability continuum who need supplemental help to realize their full potential; includes not only students who do well on IQ tests (typically 130 and above) but also those who demonstrate or exhibit above-average talents in such diverse areas as math, creative writing, or music.

grade equivalent   The comparison of an individual's score on a standardized test with those of a particular age group.

Gronlund's instructional objectives   A popular approach to preparing objectives that include a general term, such as *know, understand,* or *apply,* followed by specific learning outcomes that operationally define what we mean when we say a learner "knows," "understands," or "applies,"

growth needs   The highest levels of needs, according to Maslow, including intellectual achievement (knowing and understanding), aesthetic appreciation (order, truth, and beauty), and self-actualization.

guided discovery   An instructional approach in which the teacher identifies a content goal, arranges the data or examples so that patterns can be found, and guides the search for patterns through questioning.

heuristics   A general, open-ended, approach to problem solving that is widely applicable to a broad range of problem types.

holophrases   One- and two-word utterances (e.g., "Cookie," "me go") that carry as much meaning for a child as complete sentences.

humanistic psychology   An approach to psychology that reacts against thinking about human behavior as a response to either the environment or internal instincts and instead examines the total person—intellectual,

emotional, and interpersonal—and how these factors affect learning and motivation.

"I-messages"   Verbal statements that address behavior rather than personality, describe the effects on the sender, and identify the feelings generated in the sender.

identity   Erikson's stage of psychosocial development in adolescence (approximately 12–18 years), characterized by the defining of a personal, social, sexual, and occupational identity resulting from success in school and experimentation with different roles.

identity crisis   A psychosocial crisis within Erikson's theory characterized by individuals' feelings of uncertainty about who they are.

ill-defined problem   A problem which has an ambiguous desired state and no generally agreed-on strategy for solving it.

inclusion   A comprehensive approach to educating students with exceptionalities that advocates a total, systematic, and coordinated web of services.

incremental view of ability   A pattern of setting challenging goals that allows people to improve their skills in some area, resulting in sustained, successful learning and feelings of competence and self-worth; a characteristic of people with a high need for achievement.

individualization   A form of instruction adapted to meet the specific learning needs of each student.

Individualized Education Program (IEP)   An individually prescribed instructional plan devised by teams of special education and regular teachers and parents to meet the specific needs of a student; typically specifies long- and short-term program objectives, services, or strategies to be used, schedule for program implementation, and criteria to be used in evaluating the program's success.

industry   Erikson's stage of psychosocial development in middle childhood (approximately 6–12 years), characterized by enjoyment of mastery and competence through success and mastery of content.

inert knowledge   Knowledge that exists in isolated pieces in long term memory that is incapable of being used to interpret other knowledge.

informal measurements   A teacher's observation of verbal responses or other classroom behaviors, e.g., noticing a student's puzzled look or seeing that a student isn't paying attention.

information processing   A cognitive theory that describes the ways new knowledge is entered, stored, and retrieved from memory.

information stores   Constructs in information-processing theory that are repositories for data after the data have entered a learner's information-processing system.

inhibition   A self-imposed restriction on one's behavior that is either strengthened or weakened through modeling.

initiative   Erikson's stage of psychosocial development in early childhood (approximately 3–6 years), characterized by an exploratory and investigative attitude resulting from meeting and accepting challenges.

instructional alignment   Congruence between objectives and learning activities.

integrity   Erikson's final stage of psychosocial development in old age, characterized by the acceptance of one's life and achieved by an understanding of a person's place in the life cycle.

intelligence   A general aptitude for learning characterized by the ability to learn, to deal with abstractions, and to solve problems.

intelligence test   A type of standardized test used to measure an individual's ability to learn, to deal with abstractions, and to solve problems.

interference   A concept that suggests that people forget information because something else they learned either before or after detracts from the learning.

intermittent reinforcement   A schedule that reinforces a behavior periodically rather than continually; it leads to slow rates of extinction.

internalization   The process of learners gaining control for their thoughts and actions.

interpersonal harmony stage   Kohlberg's third stage of moral development, characterized by the valuing of loyalty and living up to the expectations of others.

interval schedules   A schedule in which the learner is reinforced on the basis of the passage of certain amounts of time.

intimacy   Erikson's stage of psychosocial development in young adulthood, leading to openness to others and the development of meaningful relationships resulting from interaction with others.

intrinsic motivation   An inclination to learn based upon needs that exist within the learner, such as curiosity, the need to know, and feelings of competence or growth.

introductory focus   A method of initially attracting student attention to a lesson through unique, attractive, eye-catching, or discrepant events that promote a sense of arousal and appeal to learners' curiosity and sense of challenge.

involvement   The active participation of students in a learning activity.

irreversibility   The inability to mentally trace a line of reasoning or a process back to its beginning.

Jigsaw II   A form of cooperative learning in which individual group members become experts on subsections of a topic and teach that subsection to other group members.

LAD (language acquisition device)   A genetically driven set of language-processing capabilities that enables children to understand the rules governing others' speech and to use these in their own speech.

language disorder   A problem with the ability to understand language or to use language to express ideas; often connected to other impairments such as a hearing impairment, a learning disability, or mental retardation.

law and order stage   Kohlberg's fourth stage of moral development, characterized by valuing the ethics of order, doing one's duty, obeying the law, and maintaining an orderly society.

learned helplessness   A student attitude, based on past unsuccessful experiences, that no amount of effort can lead to success.

learning   From a *cognitive* perspective, a change in individuals' mental structures that gives them the capacity to demonstrate changes in behavior; from a *behaviorist* perspective, an enduring change in observable behavior that occurs as a result of experience.

learning disabilities (LD)   Disorders that hamper learning within a domain or context, usually reading, writing, and listening.

learning goals   Student goals that focus on the challenge and mastery of a task.

least restrictive environment (LRE)   An educational setting that is as normal as possible and still meets a learner's special academic, social, and physical needs.

lecture-recitations   An interactive instructional format in which the teacher presents information, monitors comprehension through questioning, and leads students to explore relationships through planned discussion.

levels of processing   A view of learning that suggests the more deeply information is processed, the more meaningful it becomes.

linear rational model of planning   A design for planning and instruction developed by Ralph Tyler that is divided into four sequential steps: (a) specify objectives, (b) select learning activities, (c) organize learning activities, and (d) specify evaluation procedures.

long-term memory   The permanent information store from which information can be retrieved for reference and use; has large capacity and indefinite duration.

Mager's behavioral objectives   An approach to stating goals that describes what the student will be doing when demonstrating his or her achievement; the three parts to these objectives are: (a) an observable behavior, (b) the conditions under which the behavior will occur, and (c) criteria for an acceptable performance.

mainstreaming   The practice of placing students with exceptionalities (or disabilities) in as realistic a setting as possible, in the mainstream of education (often the regular classroom), and giving them special help to succeed in that environment.

maintenance bilingual programs   Programs designed to help non-native English-speaking students become proficient in English while retaining and strengthening their native tongue.

maintenance rehearsal The process of repeating information over and over, either aloud or mentally, without altering its form.

market exchange stage Kohlberg's second stage of moral development, characterized by the valuing of the ethic of "What's in it for me?" and by obeying rules and exchanging favors when judged of benefit to the person.

matching format A test-item format in which students are asked to identify connections between columns of information (e.g., names and dates or authors and works).

maturation The biological changes seen in individuals as a result of the interaction of their genetic makeup with the environment.

mean The average score, obtained by adding all the scores and dividing by the number of scores.

meaningfulness A term that describes the number of connections or associations between one idea and other ideas in long-term memory.

means-ends analysis A problem-solving strategy in which the problem solver attempts to break down the problem into subgoals and works successively on each.

measurement The process of gathering information as part of the assessment process.

measures of central tendency Quantitative descriptions of how a group performed as a whole; includes the mean, the median, and the mode.

median The middle score in the distribution of a set of scores.

mental retardation An exceptionality characterized by significantly subaverage general intellectual functioning resulting in or associated with concurrent impairment in adaptive behavior, and manifested during the developmental period.

meta-attention Individuals' knowledge about their own attention and their ability to monitor and control it.

metacognition The awareness and monitoring of one's own thinking process.

metamemory Students' awareness of and ability to use and strategically monitor memory strategies.

minimum competency testing Evaluation in which progression from one grade to the next, graduation from school, or admission into advanced programs is determined by a predetermined passing score on a test.

mnemonic devices A memory strategy that aids retrieval by forming associations that don't exist naturally in the content.

mode The most frequent score in a set of scores.

model A representation that helps us describe and visualize what is often impossible to observe directly.

modeling Imitation of behaviors through observations; often used to teach attitudes, beliefs, and skills.

momentum The force and flow of a lesson.

monitoring The constant checking of students' verbal and nonverbal behavior for evidence of learning.

moral dilemma A hypothetical situation that requires a person to decide if an issue is "right" or "wrong" and to justify that decision in some way.

motivation The general process or force that energizes and directs behavior.

motivational control The inclination to set goals, evoke positive beliefs about one's skills and abilities, and adjust effort as learning progresses.

multiple-choice items Test items composed of two basic parts: (a) the stem, a question or an incomplete statement that identifies a question or problem, and (b) several alternatives (typically three, four, or five) that require students to choose the best one.

multiple trait scoring A scoring system that creates different criteria for different dimensions of a product.

nature view of intelligence A theoretical position asserting that intelligence is solely determined by genetics.

need The lower level of Maslow's hierarchy including survival, safety, belonging, and self-esteem.

negative reinforcement (NR) The strengthening of a behavior by eliminating or removing an undesirable or aversive consequence.

neutral stimuli Input from the environment that doesn't elicit any response.

nontransformation The developmentally linked inability of an individual to mentally record and rerverse the process of physical or mental operations changing from one state to another.

nonverbal behavior The tone of voice and body language through which unspoken messages are conveyed.

norm referencing The assignment of a grade or value to a score based on a comparison to other students.

normal distribution Distribution of test scores in which the mean, median, and mode are all the same score and, when charted, form a bell-shaped curve.

norming group People who are similar in age, grade level, and background and whose standardized test scores are used as a comparison with others taking the same test.

novice An individual who operates at a low conceptual and skill level in a domain.

nurture view of intelligence A theoretical position that emphasizes the influence of the environment on the development of intelligence.

object permanence The developmental ability which appears during the Sensorimotor Stage to represent objects in memory.

open-ended questions Teacher queries for which a variety of answers are acceptable; allow assessment and promote active involvement.

organization (classroom) The characteristics of having materials and demonstrations prepared in advance, starting on time, having well-established routines, and making transitions smoothly and quickly.

organization (cognitive development) An individual's innate need to structure experiences and information into coherent patterns and maintain equilibrium.

organized bodies of knowledge A logical cluster of interrelated topics; the combination of facts, concepts, and generalizations and the relationship among them.

overgeneralization The use of a term to refer to a broader class of objects than is appropriate, e.g., "Dad" for all men.

overlapping The essential management skill that describes the teacher's ability to attend to two incidents at the same time without focusing exclusively on either one.

partial hearing impairment A hearing condition in which the learner uses a hearing aid and hears well enough to be taught through auditory channels.

pedagogical content knowledge Teacher knowledge of effective ways to represent topics for learners plus an understanding of what makes topics difficult or easy to learn for students of different ages.

percentile A ranking that compares an individual's score with the scores of all the others who have taken the test.

percentile bands Standardized test score performance described in percentile ranges, rather than as precise percentages.

perception The process by which meaning or interpretation is attached to experiences.

performance assessments Authentic assessments that measure skill and understanding by directly measuring student performance in a natural setting.

performance goals Goals that focus on demonstrating high ability and avoiding any display of low ability (in contrast with learning goals).

personalization An instructional variable that makes lesson content more meaningful for students through the use of intellectually and/or emotionally familiar examples.

planning A process that includes the organization of content, the selection and sequencing of learning activities, student grouping, assignments, grading practices, and classroom management, as well as consideration of student motivation, emotional well-being, and social interaction.

portfolios Collections of work that are reviewed against preset criteria in order to evaluate a student or a program.

positive reinforcement Strengthening a behavior by giving the learner something valued positively or desired after the behavior.

potency A reinforcer's ability to strengthen behaviors.

precise terminology An aspect of communication that occurs when teachers define concepts clearly and eliminate vague terms from presentations and answers to students' questions.

Premack Principle The principle that a more frequent or more preferred activity can be used as a reinforcer for a less frequent or less preferred activity.

preoperational stage Piaget's second stage of development (approximately 2–7 years), characterized by the beginning use of symbolic thought and domination by perception.

presentation punishment The presentation of an undesirable consequence after a student demonstrates an undesirable behavior.

principles Relationships between concepts that are accepted as valid for all known cases; also called laws.

private speech Self-talk that guides thinking and action.

problem A situation which exists when you're in a state that differs from a desired goal or end state and there is some uncertainty about reaching the goal state.

procedural knowledge Knowledge of how to perform tasks.

procedural skills Cognitive operations that have a specific set of identifiable procedures, can be illustrated with a large and varied number of examples, and are developed through practice.

procedures The routines classes follow in their daily activities, such as how students pass in papers.

prompting Questioning or directing by the teacher following a partial or incorrect student response.

propositions The smallest bits of information a person can judge to be true or false; one of the building blocks of schemes in long term memory.

prototype A case that is a good example of a particular concept.

psychomotor domain The area of the curriculum dealing with objectives for physical development and coordination.

psychosocial theory A developmental theory that integrates principles of personal, psychological, cultural and social development.

punishment (behaviorism) A decrease in the frequency or duration of behavior caused by some stimulus.

punishment-obedience stage Kohlberg's first stage of moral development, characterized by determining good or bad through the consequences of an action.

range The distance between the top and bottom scores on a particular test.

rating scale A systematic means of evaluating statements or observations on an assessment form (e.g., 1 = agree; 2 = neutral; 3 = disagree).

ratio schedules A schedule of reinforcement based on a predetermined number of responses.

raw score The number of items an individual answers correctly on a test.

reciprocal teaching A teaching strategy specifically designed to help students learn to monitor their comprehension, combining self-questioning and summarizing, together with clarifying and predicting, into a coherent sequence.

reflection   The process of continually assessing one's performance through personal questioning and self-monitoring.

reflective teaching   An approach to teaching characterized by a thorough understanding of students, the way they learn, what motivates them, and continual introspection about the most efficient ways of organizing and implementing instruction.

reinforcer   A stimulus that increases the frequency or duration of a behavior.

reliability   The extent to which tests are consistent in repeated administrations.

removal punishment   The decreasing of a behavior through elimination of something desirable or the inability to get positive reinforcement.

resilience   A heightened likelihood of success in school and in other aspects of life despite environmental adversities.

response   The behavior or change that results from stimuli received from the environment.

response cost   The application of removal punishment by taking away reinforcers already given.

retrieval   The process of bringing back or accessing information from long-term memory.

review   A summary of previous work and a link between information previously learned and what is coming.

rules   Global standards for student behavior, such as "Remain silent when another person in talking."

satiation   The reinforcement of a behavior occurring so frequently that the reinforcer loses its potency.

scaffolding   Instructional assistance that allows the learner to progress through the zone of proximal development.

schemas   The cognitive structures in long term memory containing the knowledge, procedures, and relationships with which we attempt to understand and function in the world; sets of interconnected ideas, relationships, and procedures.

schemes   From a Piagetian perspective, the mental patterns or systems that describe the ways people think about the world.

script   An organized plan of action for a particular situation.

self-concept   The sum total of one's perceptions about one's academic, social, and physical self.

self-efficacy   One's perceptions of one's own ability to succeed on valued tasks.

self-esteem   People's evaluation of themselves derived by comparing their ideal and real selves.

self-regulation   A learner's conscious use of encoding strategies—activity, organization, elaboration, and mnemonics—and motivational control that occurs without direction from teachers.

sensorimotor stage   Piaget's first stage of development (approximately 0–2 years), characterized by the acquisition of goal-directed behavior and object permanence (the ability to represent objects in memory).

sensory focus   The use of stimuli—concrete objects, pictures, and models—to attract and maintain learners' attention.

sensory memory   The information store that briefly holds stimuli from the environment until they can be attended to and further processed.

seriation   The ordering of objects according to increasing or decreasing length, weight, volume, or some other dimension.

shaping   The process of reinforcing successive approximations of a desired behavior.

shared understanding   A common understanding of a task between students and the teacher.

social contract   Stage five of Kohlberg's theory of moral development in which individuals or groups agree upon principles of behavior and ethics in order for society to function effectively.

social cognitive theory   A cognitive theory of learning that examines the processes involved as people learn from observing others and gradually acquire control over their own behavior.

socioeconomic status (SES)   A measure of a family's relative position in a community, determined by a combination of parents' income, occupations, and levels of education.

special education   Instruction designed to meet the unique needs of students with exceptionalities.

specific transfer   The ability to solve problems or use examples to test concepts, principles, and generalizations in one setting that is very similar to the setting in which the original learning took place.

speech disorders   Expressive disorders that involve problems in the forming and sequencing of sounds, i.e., speaking.

STAD (Student Teams Achievement Division)   A model that implements cooperative learning by using a structured system of reinforcers to promote concept, skill, and fact learning.

standard deviation   A statistical measure of the spread of scores around the mean.

standard error of measurement   A range of scores within which an individual's true scores is likely to fall.

standard scores   Scores based on the standard deviation (e.g., T-score, z-score).

standardized tests   Tests given to large samples of students under uniform conditions and scored according to uniform procedures; an individual's score is compared to the scores of a norming group, similar in age or grade level, who have taken the test, and performance is reported in relation to that group.

stanine   A way of reporting standardized test scores that describes a range of scores, with stanine 5 in the center of the distribution and stanines 4, 3, and 2 each a band of scores one half a standard deviation in width extending below stanine 5, and stanines 6, 7, and 8 a half standard deviation in width extending above stanine 5.

stimuli   The sights, sounds, smells, and other external influences received by senses from the environment.

strategies   Plans for accomplishing learning goals.

student groupwork   An instructional strategy that has learners working together in groups small enough so that everyone can participate on assigned tasks.

study strategies   Cognitive strategies specifically applied to learner's comprehension and retention of content in written materials and teacher presentations.

summarization   A cognitive strategy that enhances comprehension and encoding by asking learners to prepare a concise statement of the essential meaning of a verbal or written passage.

summative evaluation   Tests, quizzes, homework, and other performance measures that are used to make grading decisions.

superordinate concept   A large class into which related concepts fit.

systematic observation   An assessment strategy for evaluating student performance (or student learning) that specifies criteria and evaluates learners in authentic tasks based on the criteria.

T-score   A standard score using a mean of 50 and a standard deviation equal to 10.

table of specifications   A matrix derived from a teacher's objectives that classifies topics measured on a test by cognitive level and topic.

task analysis   The behavioristically-based process of taking a skill or other form of content and breaking it down into its component parts.

task comprehension   Factor influencing motivation that emphasizes students' understanding both of what they're supposed to be learning and why they're learning it.

teacher effectiveness literature   A body of knowledge which describes patterns of teacher actions that are associated with high student achievement.

teaching efficacy   The belief that teachers and schools have an important positive effect on students.

test anxiety   A relatively stable, unpleasant reaction to tests and testing situations that influences test performance.

theory   A set of interrelated principles that summarizes and relates research findings.

tracking   The longitudinal separation by classes or curricula of students with different abilities.

transfer   The ability to learn something at one time and place and to apply it later in another setting.

transition signals   An instructional indicator that communicates that one idea is ending and another is beginning.

transitional bilingual programs   Programs for non-native English speakers that use the first language as a medium for instruction until students become proficient in English.

true-false format   A test-item format in which students have to judge statements as being correct or incorrect.

trust   Erikson's stage of psychosocial development in infancy (approximately 0–1 year), characterized by trust in the world developed through consistent and continuous love and support.

unconditioned response   An involuntary and emotional reaction induced by a particular situation or stimulus (e.g., the unconditioned stimulus).

unconditioned stimulus   Input that induces an involuntary response (e.g., a loud noise).

undergeneralization   The use of a word or concept too narrowly, such as "Kitty" used only for a child's cat but not for cats in general.

universal principles   The highest stage of Kohlberg's theory of moral development in which moral reasoning is based on abstract and general principles above society's rules.

unstructured discovery   Learning in a natural or an unplanned setting in which learners discover concepts or principles on their own.

validity   The degree to which a test measures what it is supposed to measure; also the appropriateness of the interpretations made from test scores and other evaluation results.

variable-interval schedule   A reinforcement schedule in which the amount of time between reinforcers is changed unpredictably.

vicarious learning   Occurs when people observe the consequences of another person's behavior and adjust their own behavior accordingly.

visual disability   Types of visual impairment that cannot be corrected by corrective lenses, surgery, or therapy and that interfere with learning in the regular classroom.

wait-time   A period of silence, both before and after a student responds to a question, that gives learners in a class time to think.

well-defined problem   A problem in which the goal is clear and the potential solution paths to the goal are known or can be easily accessed.

withitness   A teacher's awareness of what is going on in all parts of the classroom all the time and communication of this awareness to students both verbally and nonverbally.

working memory   An information store for the performance of mental operations, like mental arithmetic; also called the workbench of memory.

z-score   A standard score that indicates the number of standard deviation units below or above the mean a raw score is located.

zone of proximal development   In Vygotskyan learning theory the phase in learning in which a student can profit from assistance or help.

Name Index

Subject Index